Flutter

Apprentice

Fourth Edition

By Kevin D Moore, Vincent Ngo, Stef Patterson & Alejandro Ulate Fallas

AF813103

Flutter Apprentice

By Kevin David Moore, Vincent Ngo, Stef Patterson & Alejandro Ulate Fallas

Copyright ©2024 Kodeco Inc.

Notice of Rights

All rights reserved. No part of this book or corresponding materials (such as text, images, or source code) may be reproduced or distributed by any means without prior written permission of the copyright owner.

Notice of Liability

This book and all corresponding materials (such as source code) are provided on an "as is" basis, without warranty of any kind, express of implied, including but not limited to the warranties of merchantability, fitness for a particular purpose, and noninfringement. In no event shall the authors or copyright holders be liable for any claim, damages or other liability, whether in action of contract, tort or otherwise, arising from, out of or in connection with the software or the use of other dealing in the software.

Trademarks

All trademarks and registered trademarks appearing in this book are the property of their own respective owners.

ISBN: 978-1-950325-92-4

Table of Contents

Book License

By purchasing *Flutter Apprentice*, you have the following license:

- You are allowed to use and/or modify the source code in *Flutter Apprentice* in as many apps as you want, with no attribution required.
- You are allowed to use and/or modify all art, images and designs that are included in *Flutter Apprentice* in as many apps as you want, but must include this attribution line somewhere inside your app: “Artwork/images/designs: from *Flutter Apprentice*, available at www.kodeco.com”.
- The source code included in *Flutter Apprentice* is for your personal use only. You are NOT allowed to distribute or sell the source code in *Flutter Apprentice* without prior authorization.
- This book is for your personal use only. You are NOT allowed to reproduce or transmit any part of this book by any means, electronic or mechanical, including photocopying, recording, etc. without previous authorization. You may not sell digital versions of this book or distribute them to friends, coworkers or students without prior authorization. They need to purchase their own copies.

All materials provided with this book are provided on an “as is” basis, without warranty of any kind, express or implied, including but not limited to the warranties of merchantability, fitness for a particular purpose and noninfringement. In no event shall the authors or copyright holders be liable for any claim, damages or other liability, whether in an action of contract, tort or otherwise, arising from, out of or in connection with the software or the use or other dealings in the software.

All trademarks and registered trademarks appearing in this guide are the properties of their respective owners.

Before You Begin

This section tells you a few things you need to know before you get started, such as what you'll need for hardware and software, where to find the project files for this book, and more.

What You Need

To follow along with this book, you'll need the following:

- **Xcode 15.0.1 or later**. Xcode is iOS's main development tool, so you need it to build your Flutter app for iOS. You can download the latest version of Xcode from Apple's developer site here: apple.co/2asi58y or from the Mac App Store. Xcode 15.0.1 requires a Mac running **macOS Ventura (13) or later**.

> **Note**: You also have the option of using Linux or Windows, but you won't be able to install Xcode or build apps for iOS on those platforms.

- **Cocoapods 1.14.2 or later**. Cocoapods is a dependency manager Flutter uses to run code on iOS.
- **Flutter SDK 3.16.9 or later**. You can download the Flutter SDK from the official Flutter site at https://flutter.dev/docs/get-started/install/macos. Installing the Flutter SDK will also install the **Dart SDK**, which you need to compile the Dart code in your Flutter apps.

- **Android Studio 2023.1.1 or later**, available at https://developer.android.com/studio. This is the IDE in which you'll develop the sample code in this book. It also includes the Android SDK and the build system for running Flutter apps on Android.
- **Flutter Plugin for Android Studio 77.2.1 or later**, installed by going to Android Studio **Preferences** on macOS (or **Settings** on Windows/Linux) and choosing **Plugins**, then searching for "Flutter".

You have the option of using **Visual Studio Code** for your Flutter development environment instead of Android Studio. You'll still need to install Android Studio to have access to the Android SDK and an Android emulator. If you choose to use Visual Studio Code, follow the instructions on the official Flutter site at https://flutter.dev/docs/get-started/editor?tab=vscode to get set up.

Chapter 1, "Getting Started" explains more about Flutter history and architecture. You'll learn how to start using the Flutter SDK, then you'll see how to use Android Studio and Xcode to build and run Flutter apps.

Book Source Code & Forums

Book Source Code

The materials for this book are all available here:

- https://github.com/kodecocodes/flta-materials/archive/refs/heads/editions/4.0.zip

You can download the entire set of materials for the book from that page.

Forum

We've also set up an official forum for the book at https://forums.kodeco.com/c/books/flutter-apprentice/. This is a great place to ask questions about the book or to submit any errors you may find.

"To my wife and daughter who support me unconditionally. Thank you for the silly nights, profound conversations and unmeasurable love."

— *Alejandro Ulate Fallas*

"To my wife and family for letting me create and learn new things."

— *Kevin David Moore*

"To my loving parents and sister. Thank you for your patience, love, support and always being there for me."

— *Vincent Ngo*

"To Angela Yu for introducing me to Flutter. To Simon Lightfoot, the Flutter Whisperer, who never passes judgement when I need help. To my *Flutter Apprentice* team and the Flutteristas for all your support and encouragement. Most of all, thank you, Sean and Ryan, for your patience and love."

— *Stef Patterson*

About the Authors

Alejandro Ulate Fallas is an author of this book. He is a Mobile Developer based in Costa Rica and has been developing apps for over 6 years. He likes to learn new things and share it with others. In his spare time he enjoys handy, watching sports and spending time with his family.

Kevin David Moore is an author of this book. He is a Google Developer Expert in Flutter and has been developing Android apps for over 13 years and Flutter apps for over 3 years. He's written several articles, books and videos at Kodeco. He is a cat lover with three cats and he is working towards his black belt in taekwondo.

Vincent Ngo is an author of this book. A software developer by day at a growing startup, and an iOS/Flutter enthusiast by night, he believes that sharing knowledge is the best way to learn and grow as a techie. Vincent starts every morning with a Cà phê sữa đá (Vietnamese coffee) to fuel his day. He enjoys playing golf, meditating, and watching animated movies. You can find him on Twitter: https://twitter.com/vincentngo2.

Stef Patterson is an author and tech editor for this book. Stef is passionate about helping others learn, which includes mentoring, writing and editing documentation, data wrangling and coding by example. Throughout most of her career, she has worked as a senior SQL developer and analyst. In 2013, she started creating iOS apps using kodeco.com books and articles. Now, thanks to Flutter, she is creating natively compiled cross-platform apps. Stef loves movies, trivia nights, Sci-Fi and spending time with her husband, daughter and their dogs. You can find her on Mastodon at https://fluttercommunity.social/@GeekMeSpeakStef and Twitter at https://twitter.com/GeekMeSpeakStef.

About the Editors

Leanna Guzzi is the English language editor of this book. She is a Brit who now lives in America with her husband and cat. She loves winter, cheese and all things literature. When she isn't empowering young minds and convincing everyone to read, she is planning her next snowboarding or adventure holiday.

Shrihriday, one of the technical editors of this book, is also the founder of Codeaamy, an app development company. Recognized as a Google Developer Expert in Flutter and Dart, he is passionate about teaching and sharing his knowledge of Flutter. He has mentored many developers and frequently gives talks on Flutter and Dart, aiming to inspire and educate others in the developer community.

Cesare Rocchi is the final pass editor for this book. Cesare runs https://studiomagnolia.com, an interactive studio that creates compelling web and mobile applications. He blogs at https://www.upbeat.it. You can find him on Twitter at https://twitter.com/_funkyboy.

Acknowledgements

Content Development

We would like to thank **Tim Sneath** and **Chris Sells** who are former members of Google's Flutter team. Both provided key insights and constant encouragement during the gestation and development of this book.

We would also like to thank **Joe Howard** for his work as an FPE for the book in its early stages. Joe's path to software development began in the fields of computational physics and systems engineering. He started as a web developer and also has been a native mobile developer on iOS and Android since 2009. Joe has a passion for system and enterprise architecture including building robust, testable, maintainable, and scalable systems. He currently focuses on the full stack using web frameworks like React and Angular, Node.js microservices, GraphQL, and devops tools like Docker, Kubernetes, and Terraform. He lives in Boston and is a Senior Architect at CVS Health.

Finally, thanks to **Michael Katz** and **Vincenzo Guzzi** for writing previous versions of some chapters included in this book.

Introduction

Welcome to *Flutter Apprentice*!

Flutter is an incredible user interface (UI) toolkit that lets you build apps for iOS and Android — and even the web and desktop platforms like macOS, Windows and Linux — all from a single codebase.

Flutter has all the benefits of other cross-platform tools, especially because you're targeting multiple platforms from one codebase. Furthermore, it improves upon most cross-platform tools thanks to a super-fast rendering engine that makes your Flutter apps perform as native apps.

In addition, Flutter features are generally independent of native features, since you use Flutter's own type of UI elements, called widgets, to create your UI. And Flutter has the ability to work with native code, so you can integrate your Flutter app with native features when you need to.

If you're coming from a platform like iOS or Android, you'll find the Flutter development experience refreshing! Thanks to a feature called "hot reload", you rarely need to rebuild your apps as you develop them. A running app in a simulator or emulator will refresh with code changes automatically as you save your source files!

In this book, you'll see how to build full-featured Flutter apps, gain experience with a wide range of Flutter widgets and learn how to deploy your apps to mobile app stores.

How to Read This Book

In the first section of the book, you'll learn how to set up a Flutter development environment. Once that's done, you'll start building your first Flutter app.

The next two sections focus on UI development with Flutter widgets. You'll see just how impressive Flutter user interfaces can be.

The fourth section switches to building a new app. You'll use it to learn about using networking and databases with Flutter, as well as the all-important topic of state management.

The fifth section teaches you how to work with Firebase Cloud Firestore. In particular you'll learn how to add an instant messaging feature to the **Yummy** app.

The sixth section is about testing. You'll learn how to take advantage of unit and widget tests to make sure you app behaves as expected.

The seventh section shows you how to incorporate platform-specific assets into your app, then demonstrates how to deploy your apps to the mobile app stores.

Here's a breakdown of these seven main sections of the book:

Section I: Build Your First Flutter App

The chapters in this section introduce you to Flutter, get you up and running with a Flutter development environment and walk you through building your first Flutter app.

You'll learn about where Flutter came from and why it exists, understand the structure of Flutter projects and see how to create the UI of a Flutter app.

You'll also get your first introduction to the key component found in Flutter user interfaces: widgets!

Section II: Everything's a Widget

In this section, you'll start to build a full-featured recipe app named **Yummy**. You'll gain an understanding of the wide range of widgets available in Flutter and put them to use. Then you'll learn the theory of how widgets work behind the scenes.

Finally, you'll dive deeper into layout widgets, scrollable widgets and interactive widgets.

Section III: Navigating Between Screens

You'll continue working on the **Yummy** app in this section, learning about navigating between screens and working with deep links.

Topics you'll learn include Navigator 2.0 and Flutter Web.

Section IV: Networking, Persistence & State

Most apps interact with the network to retrieve data and then persist that data locally in some form of cache, such as a database. In this section, you'll build a new app that lets you search the Internet for recipes, bookmark recipes and save their ingredients into a shopping list.

You'll learn about making network requests, parsing the network JSON response and saving data in a SQLite database. You'll also get an introduction to using Dart streams.

Finally, this section will dive deeper into the important topic of app state, which determines where and how to refresh data in the UI as a user interacts with your app.

Section V: Working With Firebase Cloud Firestore

When it comes to storing data in the cloud you can build your own backend system or you can leverage an existing system, built exactly for that.

This section will explain how to use Firebase Cloud Firestore to implement a messaging feature into your app. You'll learn how to integrate Firebase into your project, how to set up authentication and how to make queries to populate your UI.

Section VI: Testing your Flutter app

Building an app is fun, but along the way you'll add features, tweak flows and fix bugs. How do you make sure that a set of changes doesn't introduce bugs or issues in a previous version of the app? Enter testing. Testing helps you mitigate the risk of introducing issues into an existing app and to prevent regressions.

In this section you'll learn about both unit and widget tests. You'll see how unit tests are a good fit to keep in check your business logic. Finally, you'll learn how to make use of widget tests to verify that your UI widgets are rendered as expected.

Section VII: Deployment

Building an app for your own devices is great; sharing your app with the world is even better!

In this section, you'll go over the steps and processes to release your apps to the iOS App Store and Google Play Store. You'll also see how to use platform-specific assets in your apps.

Section I: Build Your First Flutter App

The chapters in this section will introduce you to Flutter, get you up and running with a Flutter development environment and walk you through building your first Flutter app.

You'll learn about where Flutter came from and why it exists, understand the structure of Flutter projects, and see how to create the user interface of a Flutter app.

You'll also get your first introduction to the key component found in Flutter user interfaces: Widgets!

Chapter 1: Getting Started

By Michael Katz & Alejandro Ulate

Congratulations. By opening "The Flutter Apprentice", you've taken your first step toward becoming a Flutter master. This book will be your guide to learning the **Flutter UI Toolkit**, Google's platform for building apps for mobile, desktop and web from a single codebase.

The seven sections of this book will progressively teach you how to create an app using Flutter. You'll learn all about **widgets**, which are components that you compose to build your apps. You'll also learn about navigation and transitions, handling state and network management. Finally, you'll learn how to deploy the app to testers and users.

This book assumes you're familiar with development for a native mobile platform, such as iOS with Swift or Android with Kotlin... but you don't need to be an expert by any means. These chapters will show you how to build a Flutter app from scratch, so if you're completely new, you'll catch up just fine.

What is Flutter?

In the simplest terms, Flutter is a software development toolkit from Google for building cross-platform apps. Flutter apps consist of a series of packages, plugins and widgets — but that's not all. Flutter is a process, a philosophy and a community as well.

It's also the easiest way to get an app up and running on any one platform, let alone multiple. You can be more productive than you thought possible thanks to Flutter's declarative, widget-based UI structure, first-class support for reactive programming, cross platform abstractions and its virtual machine that allows for hot reloading of code changes.

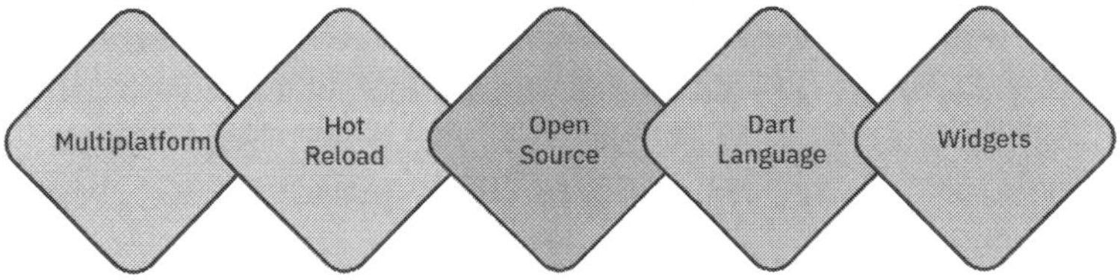

One thing Flutter is *not* is a language. Flutter uses **Dart** as its programming language. If you know Kotlin, Swift, Java or TypeScript, you'll find Dart familiar, since it's an object-oriented C-style language.

You can compile Dart to native code, which makes it fast. It also uses a virtual machine (VM) with a special feature: **hot reload**. This lets you update your code and see the changes live without redeploying it.

For years, programmers have been promised the ability to **write once and run anywhere**; Flutter may well be the best attempt yet at achieving that goal.

Seriously?

Yes, Flutter is that awesome. You *can* build a high-quality app that's performant and looks great, very quickly. This book will show you how.

In the first few chapters, you'll get your feet under you with the basic UI. By the end of the book, you'll be able to build apps that look great and perform well.

And it truly does work well with both desktop and web.

Other cross-platform toolkits have tried to abstract the underlying OS by adding a layer on top of the native UI layer. This leaves the developer with the lowest common set of features available — not to mention, degraded performance.

In contrast, Flutter's widgets exist parallel to native widgets due to its custom user interface rendering engine, Skia (https://skia.org). That means that the toolkit controls how the UI looks and behaves, which allows for consistent behavior between platforms. From a performance perspective, there's no penalty from additional layers of abstraction.

Who's Flutter for?

Flutter is for both the new or experienced developer who want to start an app with minimal overhead. Flutter is for someone looking to make an app that runs on multiple devices, either right away or in the future. It's for someone who prefers to build declarative UIs with the support of a large, open-source community.

Additionally, Flutter is for developers with experience on one platform who want to develop an app that works across many. This is doubly true if you're a web developer with deep JavaScript or TypeScript knowledge, but haven't gotten started on mobile or desktop yet. You can learn major platforms at once!

If you don't have an existing app, Flutter is a great way to develop something quickly to validate an idea or to build a full, multi-platform production app.

On the other hand, if you already have a great app on one platform with the native toolkits, then you should evaluate your ongoing maintenance costs to see if it makes sense to build out for the other platforms by using Flutter or the native toolkits.

Great Things About Flutter

Here's just a sample of some of the great things about using Flutter:

- Flutter is **open-source**. That means you can watch its evolution and know what's coming — and even try out new features in development. You can also create your own patches and packages or contribute code. And you can be involved in the community to help others or contribute to its future direction.
- Flutter uses the **Dart** programming language. Dart (https://dart.dev) is a modern, UI-focused language that's compiled to native ARM or x86 code or cross-compiled to JavaScript. It supports all the great language features people have come to like and expect, such as `async/await` for concurrency management and **type inference** for clean, type-safe code.
- One of the best features of Flutter is **hot reload**. Hot reload allows you to make updates to the code and the UI that rebuild the widget tree, then deliver them live to emulators and devices — without having to reload state or recompile your app.
- Sometimes, you make changes that affect too much of the widget tree or app state to hot reload easily. In those cases, you can use **hot restart**. Hot restart takes a little longer than hot reload because it loads the changes, restarts the app and resets the state, but it's still faster than a **full restart**, which recompiles and redeploys. You need to use a full restart when you make certain significant changes to the code, including anything changing state management.
- These restart features leverage Dart's VM to inject the updated code, so they're only available in debug mode and not in a production app.
- Other cross-platform toolkits produce apps with a stock look and feel — boring! Flutter is purposely attractive, using Google's **Material Design** out of the box. It's also easy to apply Cupertino widgets to get an iOS-like appearance. The UI is fully customizable, allowing you to make an app that looks right for your brand.
- Flutter comes with great animations and transitions, and you can build custom widgets as well. Because widgets are **composable**, you can be creative and flexible with the UI. For example, you can put videos behind a scroll view or put a toolbar on top of a canvas.
- The sheer number of widgets (https://docs.flutter.dev/ui/widgets) and the declarative syntax for building UIs lets you be extremely productive, building a rich app quickly with minimal overhead and boilerplate. Stateful widgets are bound to data and automatically update as the data model changes.

- If you've used SwiftUI or Jetpack Compose recently, you're already familiar with many of Flutter's concepts. But Flutter is even better — it has fewer limitations on the tools and you can build for multiple platforms at once.
- Flutter was designed with **accessibility** in mind, with out-of-the-box support for dynamic font sizes and screen readers and a ton of best practices around language, contrast and interaction methods.
- Platform integration is important for accessing libraries written in other languages or using platform-specific features that don't have a Flutter support package yet. Flutter supports C and C++ interoperability as well as **platform channels** for connecting to Kotlin and Java on Android and Swift or Objective-C on iOS.

Are You Convinced Yet?

If you're not yet convinced that there's a place for Flutter, check out the Flutter showcase (https://flutter.dev/showcase) that shows multiple apps built with Flutter.

There, you'll see the top companies using Flutter and how diverse the apps you can make with it are. These aren't limited to "JSON-in-a-table" apps, but also include media-rich dynamic and interactive apps.

These apps help you be more productive, better informed, communicate more easily and have more fun. Flutter's native performance and system integrations make it a better choice than a web or hybrid app for most mobile applications.

Popular apps from some of the world's biggest companies are built with Flutter. These include:

- Abbey Road Studios
- BMW
- eBay
- Google Pay
- Hamilton
- Tencent
- Toyota
- US Department of Veterans Affairs

Take a look at some recent examples:

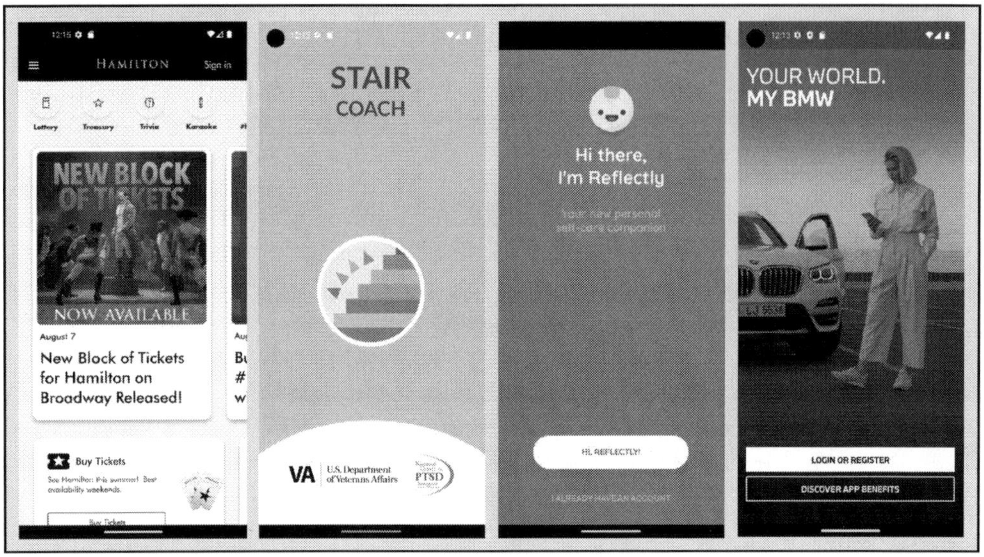

When Not to Use Flutter

Flutter isn't the best tool for every application. Here are some areas where Flutter is an evolving platform.

Games and Audio

Creating casual games with Flutter is out of the scope of this book, but Kodeco (https://www.kodeco.com/) does have Flutter game tutorials, including some 2D games built using the Flame Engine (https://flame-engine.org) that is written in Flutter. Flutter also has a casual games toolkit (https://flutter.dev/games) to help you get started.

For complex 2D and 3D games, you'd probably prefer to base your app on a cross-platform game engine technology like Unity or Unreal. They have more domain-specific features like physics, sprite and asset management, game state management, multiplayer support and so on.

Flutter doesn't have a sophisticated audio engine yet, so audio editing or mixing apps are at a disadvantage over those that are purpose-built for a specific platform.

Apps With Specific Native SDK Needs

Flutter supports many, but not all, native features. Fortunately, you can usually create bridges to platform-specific code. However, if the app is highly integrated with a device's features and platform SDKs, it might be worth writing the app using the platform-specific tools. Flutter also produces app binaries that are bigger in size than those built with platform frameworks.

Flutter might not be a practical choice if you are only interested in a single platform app and you have deep knowledge of that platform's tools and languages. For example, if you're working with a highly-customized iOS app based on CloudKit that uses all the native hardware, MLKit, StoreKit, extensions and so on, maintaining and taking advantage of those features will be easier using SwiftUI. Of course, the same goes for a heavily-biased Android app using Jetpack Compose.

Certain Platforms

Flutter doesn't support every platform. Platforms like watchOS, tvOS and certain iOS app extensions have specific needs that Flutter doesn't yet support.

In these instances, you'll have to build those components natively and add them to your Flutter-based app. Depending on how sophisticated the apps is, it might not be worth the hassle to write both native and Flutter code.

Flutter's History

Flutter comes from a tradition of trying to improve web performance. It's built on top of several open-source technologies developed at Google to bring native performance and modern programming to the web through Chrome.

The Flutter team chose the Dart language, which Google also developed, for its productivity enhancements. Its object-oriented type system and support for reactive and asynchronous programming give it clear advantages over JavaScript. Most importantly, Google built the Dart VM into the Chrome browser, allowing web apps written in Dart to run at native speeds.

Another piece of the puzzle is the inclusion of Skia as the graphics rendering layer. Skia is another Google-based open source project that powers the graphics on Android, Chrome browsers, Chrome OS and Firefox. It runs directly on the GPU using Vulkan on Android and Metal on iOS, making the graphics layer fast on mobile devices. Its API allows Flutter widgets to render quickly and consistently, regardless of the host platform.

Note: Flutter is migrating to a new rendering engine called Impeller that brings better performance and consistency. It provides the same benefits as Skia and improves upon them. For the most part, you won't have to interact directly with it, but it's important that you are aware of its existence since Impeller is the default rendering engine for all iOS apps developed with Flutter 3.10 and above.

You may also see warning message when running your apps, see the Impeller documentation (https://docs.flutter.dev/perf/impeller) for more details or to report any issues.

The Flutter Architecture

Flutter has a modular, layered architecture. This allows you to write your application logic once and have consistent behavior across platforms, even though the underlying engine code differs depending on the platform. The layered architecture also exposes different points for customization and overriding, as necessary.

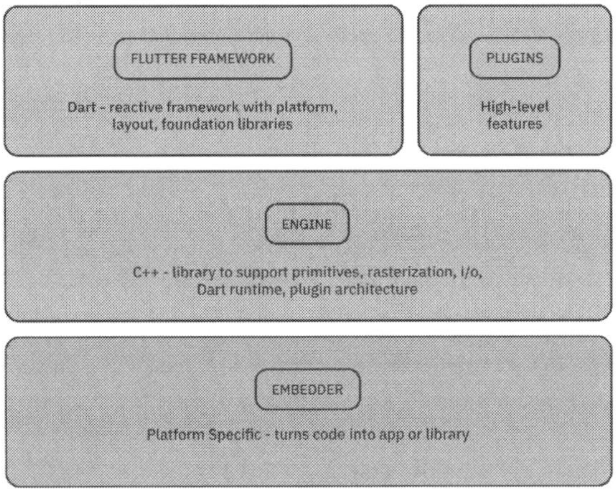

The Flutter architecture consists of three main layers:

1. The **Framework** layer is written in Dart and contains the high-level libraries that you'll use directly to build apps. This includes the UI theme, widgets, layout and animations, gestures and foundational building blocks. Alongside the main Flutter framework are **plugins**: high-level features like JSON serialization, geolocation, camera access, in-app payments and so on. This plugin-based architecture lets you include only the features your app needs.

2. The **Engine** layer contains the core C++ libraries that make up the primitives that support Flutter apps. The engine implements the low-level primitives of the Flutter API, such as I/O, graphics, text layout, accessibility, the plugin architecture and the Dart runtime. The engine is also responsible for rasterizing Flutter scenes for fast rendering onscreen.

3. The **Embedder** is different for each target platform and handles packaging the code as a stand-alone app or embedded module.

Each of the architecture layers is made up of other sublayers and modules, making them almost fractal. Of particular import to general app development is the makeup of the framework layer:

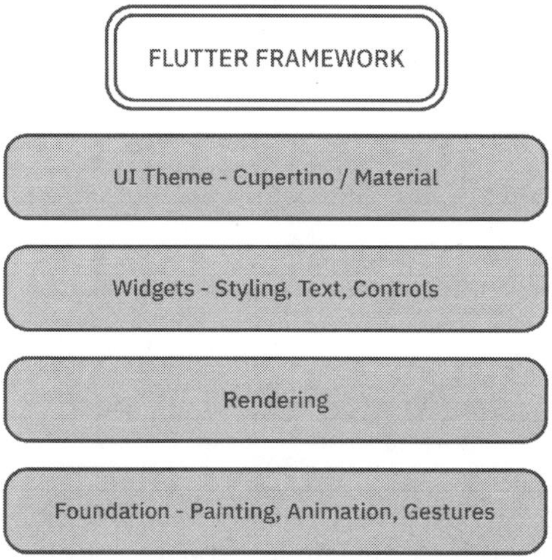

The Flutter framework consists of several sublayers:

- At the top is the **UI theme**, which uses either the Material (Android) or Cupertino (iOS) design language. This affects how the controls appear, allowing you to make your app look just like a native one.
- The **widget layer** is where you'll spend the bulk of your UI programming time. This is where you compose design and interactive elements to make up the app.
- Beneath the widgets layer is the **rendering layer**, which is the abstraction for building a layout.
- The **foundation layer** provides basic building blocks, like animations and gestures, that build up the higher layers.

What's Ahead

This book is divided into six sections:

- Section 1 is the **introduction**. You're here! In this section, you'll get an overview of Flutter, learn how to get started and make sure you have everything set up to develop great apps. You'll build a simple app to get a taste of the Dart language and Flutter SDKs.
- Section 2 is all about **widgets**, the building blocks you use to make your app.
- Section 3 covers **navigation** and **deep links**. If you think about widgets as making up screens, navigation ties them together to let the user accomplish various tasks within the app.
- Section 4 goes over **state** and **data**. You'll learn how to save data and work with local persistence and networking.
- Section 5 shows you how to build an instant messaging application using **Firebase Cloud Firestore**.
- Section 6 covers the importance of **testing** your Flutter apps. You'll learn how to challenge the quality of your apps with unit and widget tests.
- Section 7 takes you in a journey to add proper **accessibility** support to your apps and make it truly available for all users.

By the end of the book, you'll be able to take an idea, turn it into a great-looking multi-platform app and submit it for publication.

Getting Started

Now that you've decided Flutter is right for you, your next step is to get the tools necessary to build Flutter apps: the Flutter SDK and Dart compiler. You'll also need an IDE with a Flutter plugin along with the tools to build and deploy for the various platforms. The latter means Xcode for iOS and Android Studio for Android.

To start, visit https://flutter.dev/. This portal is the source of truth for any installation instructions or API changes that occur between this book's publication and the time you read it. If there are any contradictions, the information at **flutter.dev** supersedes.

What You Need

- A computer. You can develop Flutter apps on Windows, macOS, Linux or ChromeOS. However, Xcode only runs on macOS, making a Mac necessary to build and deploy apps for iOS.

> **Note**: Because of the Xcode limitation for macOS, this book uses the Flutter toolchain on Mac. You can follow along on any platform of your choice — just skip any iOS- or Mac-specific steps.

- The Flutter SDK.
- An editor, such as Android Studio or Visual Studio Code.
- At least one device. You can run in an iOS Simulator or Android emulator, but running Flutter apps on a physical device will give you the true user experience.
- Developer accounts (optional). To deploy to the Apple App Store or Google Play Store, you'll need a valid account on each.

Getting the Flutter SDK

The first step is to download the SDK. You can follow the steps on **flutter.dev** or jump right into Flutter's release page (https://docs.flutter.dev/release).

One thing to note is that Flutter organizes its SDK around **channels**, which are different development branches. New features or platform support will be available first on a **beta channel** for developers to try out. This is a great way to get early access to certain features like new platforms or native SDK support.

For this book and development in general, use the **stable channel**. That branch has been vetted and tested and has less chance of breaking. Follow the instructions to download the SDK (https://docs.flutter.dev/get-started). Installation is as simple as unarchiving and putting the **bin** folder in your path.

> **Note**: Because installation varies based on computer platform, this book will not walk through the details installation for all platforms. See Flutter documentation (https://docs.flutter.dev) for detailed installation instructions if you are using a different platform for app development.

Once you have Flutter installed, you'll have access to the Flutter command-line app, which is your starting point. To check you've set it up correctly, run the following command in a terminal:

```
flutter help
```

In response, you should see the main help instructions:

```
Manage your Flutter app development.

Common commands:

  flutter create <output directory>
    Create a new Flutter project in the specified directory.

  flutter run [options]
    Run your Flutter application on an attached device or in an
emulator.

Usage: flutter <command> [arguments]
...
```

These `flutter` subcommands are a gateway to all the tools that come with Flutter. You'll see project management tools, package management tools and tools to run and test your apps. You'll dive into many of these in this and future chapters.

Getting Everything Else

In addition to the Flutter SDKs, you'll need Java, the Android SDK, the iOS SDKs and an IDE with Flutter extensions. To make this process easier, Flutter includes the **Flutter Doctor**, which guides you through installing all the missing tools.

Just run:

```
flutter doctor
```

That checks for all the necessary components and provides the links or instructions to download ones you're missing.

Here's an example:

```
Doctor summary (to see all details, run flutter doctor -v):
[✓] Flutter (Channel stable, 3.13.4, on macOS 13.5.2 21G5037d
darwin-arm, locale en-US)
[✗] Android toolchain - develop for Android devices
    ✗ Flutter requires Android SDK 30 and the Android BuildTools
30.0.2
```

```
      To update using sdkmanager, run:
        "/Users/michael/Library/Android/sdk/tools/bin/
sdkmanager"
        "platforms;android-30" "build-tools;30.0.2"
      or visit https://flutter.dev/docs/get-started/install/
macos
      for detailed instructions.
[!] Xcode - develop for iOS and macOS (Xcode 14.3.1)
    ✗ CocoaPods not installed.
        CocoaPods is used to retrieve the iOS platform side's
plugin
        code that responds to your plugin usage on the Dart
side.
        Without CocoaPods, plugins will not work on iOS or
macOS.
        For more info, see https://flutter.dev/platform-plugins
      To install:
        sudo gem install cocoapods
[✗] Chrome - develop for the web (Cannot find Chrome executable
at
    /Applications/Google Chrome.app/Contents/MacOS/Google
Chrome)
    ! Cannot find Chrome. Try setting CHROME_EXECUTABLE to a
Chrome executable.
[!] Android Studio (not installed)

[☠] Connected device (the doctor check crashed)
    ✗ Due to an error, the doctor check did not complete. If the
error message below is not helpful, please let us know
      about this issue at https://github.com/flutter/flutter/
issues.
    ✗ Exception: Unable to run "adb", check your Android SDK
installation and ANDROID_HOME environment variable:
      /Users/michael/Library/Android/sdk/platform-tools/adb

! Doctor found issues in 4 categories.
```

In this example output, Flutter Doctor has identified a series of issues: mainly, no Java, an outdated Android toolchain and that CocoaPods, Android Studio and Google Chrome are missing.

The tool has helpfully suggested commands and links to get the missing dependencies. The tool also terminated before completing, which is common if it doesn't find major dependencies.

For your specific setup, follow the suggestions to install whatever you're missing. Then keep running `flutter doctor` until you get all green checkmarks. You'll likely have to run it more than a couple of times to clear all the issues.

> **Note**: If Flutter Doctor's suggestions don't work, you may have to manually install missing tools, like Java or Android Studio, by following the instructions on their respective websites. Just take it one step at a time. Setting up the development environment is the hardest part of working with Flutter.

Setting Up an IDE

The Flutter team officially supports three editors: Android Studio, Visual Studio Code and Emacs. However, there are many other editors that support the Dart language, work with the Flutter command line or have third-party Flutter plugins.

This book's examples use Android Studio, but the code and examples will all work in your editor of choice. Flutter Doctor will have you install this IDE anyway, to get all the Android tools, so using Android Studio keeps you from having to install additional editors. Additionally, Flutter Doctor will tell you to install the Android Studio **Flutter plugin**, which also triggers an install of the **Dart plugin** for Android Studio.

Once you go through all of the `flutter doctor` steps, you'll have everything you need to create Flutter apps in Android studio. If you see **New Flutter project** in the Android Studio welcome window, you're good to go.

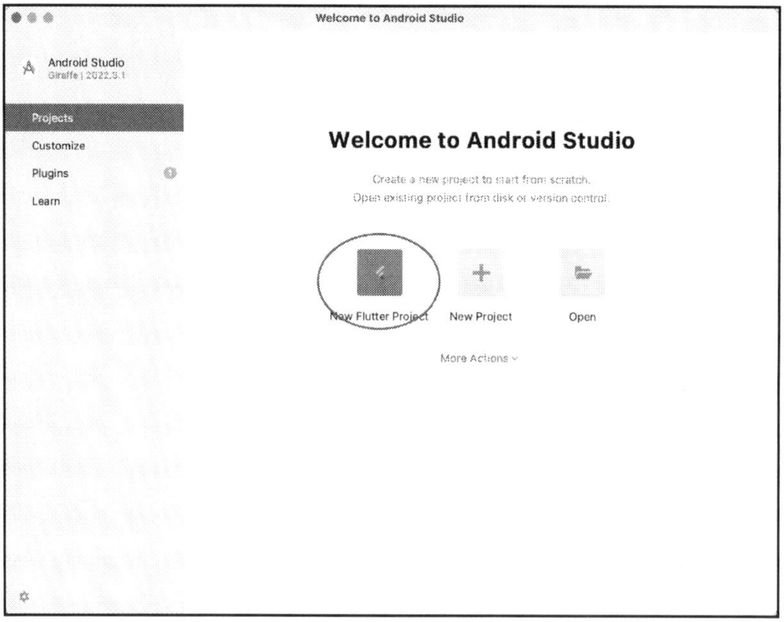

Trying It Out

Downloading all the components is the hardest part of getting a Flutter app up and running. Next, you'll try actually building an app.

There are two recommended ways to create a new project: with the IDE or through the `flutter` command-line tool in a terminal. In this chapter, you'll use the IDE shortcut and in the next chapter, you'll use the command line.

In Android Studio, click the **New Flutter Project** option. Leave the default app selected and click the **Next** button to continue to the next screen.

For this example, you can keep the default values or change them to something more convenient. Click the **Next** button to continue.

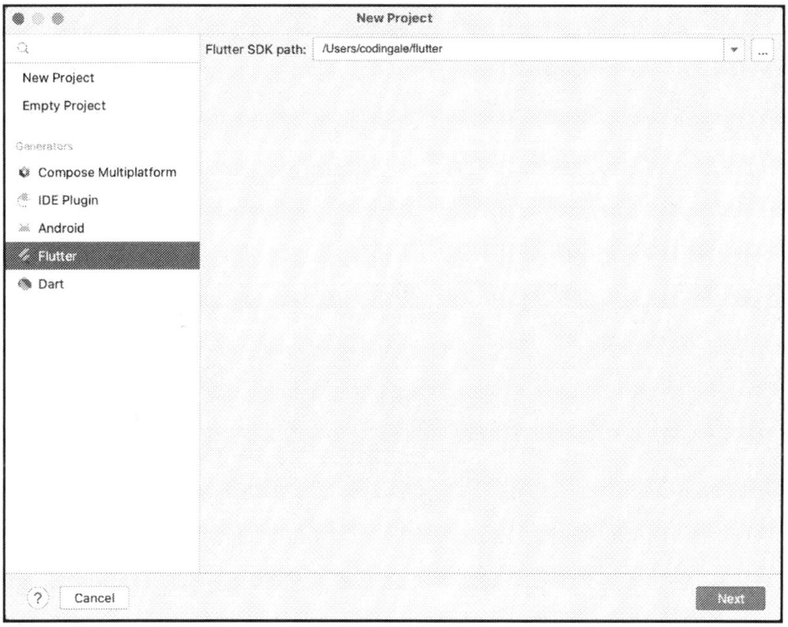

The options here let you include platform support or change the package name. You'll learn more about these options later. For now, click the **Finish** button.

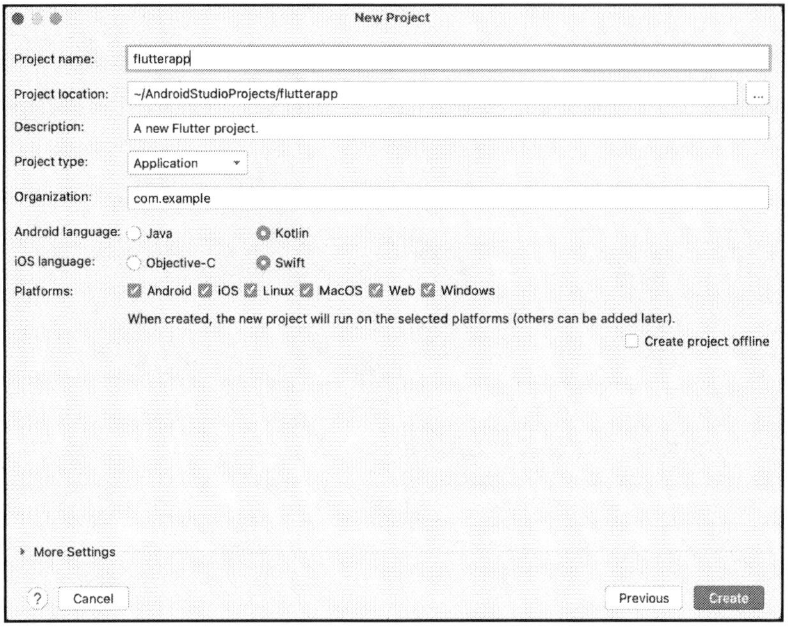

If you use Visual Studio Code, the process is similar. To create a new project, use **View ▸ Command Palette... ▸ Flutter: New Project**. After that, click through the project form that comes up.

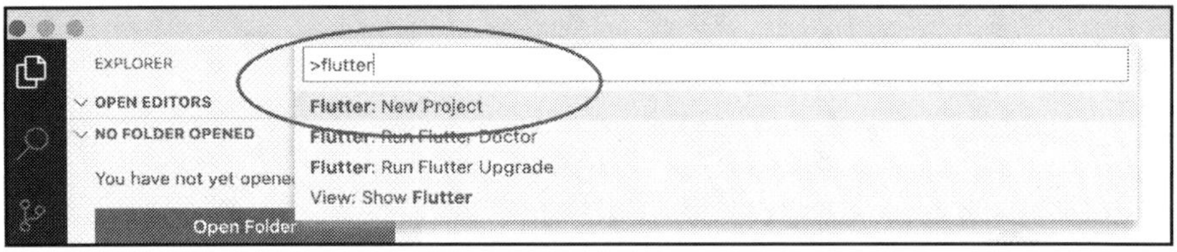

With either editor, you might see pop-ups or messages to download or update various tools and components. Follow the directions until you resolve the messages.

For example, this Android Studio banner shows: **'Pub get' has not been run**. Clicking **Get dependencies** resolves this.

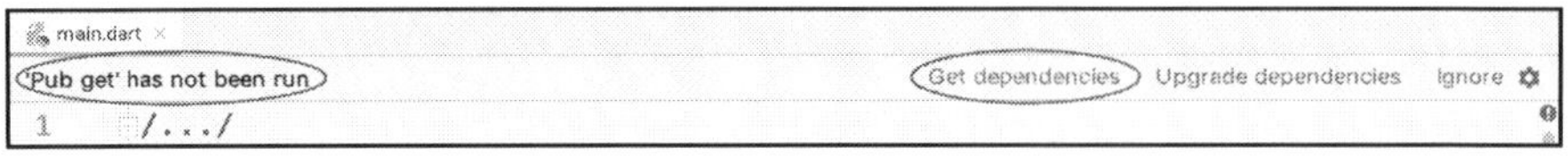

The Template Project

The default new project is the same in either editor. It's a simple Flutter demo. The demo app counts the number of times you tap a button.

To give it a try, select a connected device, an iOS simulator or an Android emulator.

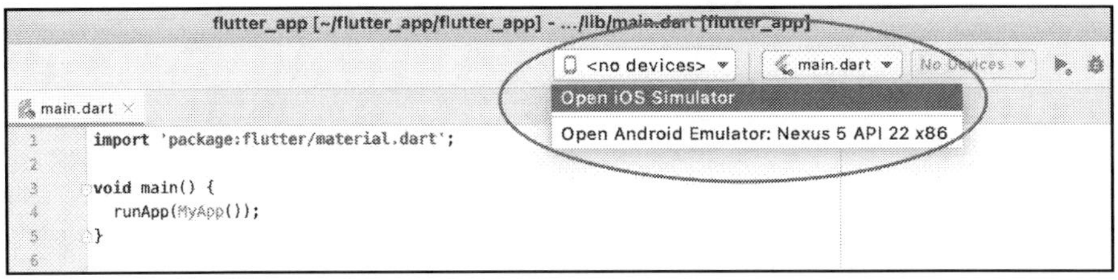

Launch the app by clicking the **Run** icon:

It might take a while to compile and launch the first time. When you're done, you'll see the following:

Congratulations, you've made your first Flutter app! Click the button and see the increment response update the label.

All the code for this app is in **lib/main.dart** in the default project. Feel free to take a look at it.

Throughout the rest of this book, you'll dive into Flutter apps, widgets, state, themes and many other concepts that will help you build beautiful apps.

Bonus: Try Hot Reload

You'll learn a lot more about hot reload in future chapters, but it's just too cool of a feature to not indulge in a little taste at this point. Before starting, adjust your IDE window so you can see both it and the simulator or emulator with your app running in it.

In **main.dart**, find the following `Text` widget:

```
Text(
  'You have pushed the button this many times:',
),
```

Next, change the string to: **'Thou hast pushed the button this many times:'** to give it a faux-medieval flair.

Here's the not-so-tricky part: Just save the file. Now, look at the running app and observe the change.

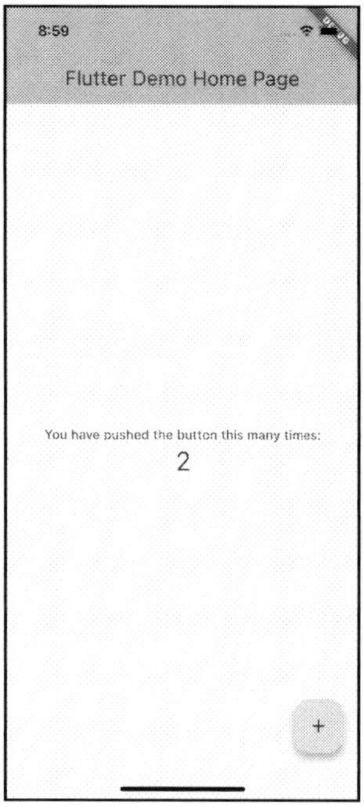

Et voila! Your changes reload without stopping the app and redeploying.

Sometimes, saving the file does not automatically trigger the hot reload. In that case, just press the **Hot Reload** icon, which looks like a lightning bolt, in the toolbar.

If you're trying out different simulators/emulators at the same time, you'll need to do hot reload on each **Run** tab.

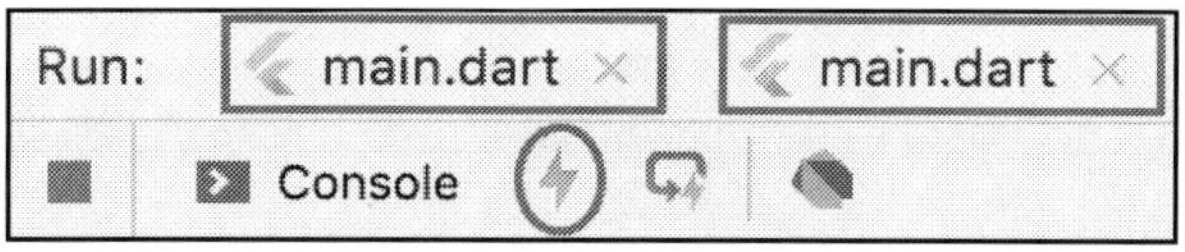

Key Points

- Flutter is a **software development toolkit** from Google for building cross-platform apps using the Dart programming language.
- With Flutter, you can build a **high-quality app** that's performant and looks great, very quickly.
- Flutter is for both **new** and **experienced developers** who want to start a mobile app with minimal overhead.
- Install the **Flutter SDK** and associated tools using instructions found at Flutter's documentation (https://flutter.dev).
- The `flutter doctor` command helps you install and update your Flutter tools.
- This book will use **Android Studio** as the IDE for Flutter development.

Where to Go From Here?

Your home for all things Flutter is flutter.dev (and dart.dev for the Dart language). If you get stuck at any of the installation steps, go there for updated instructions.

flutter.dev contains the official documentation and reference pages (https://flutter.dev/docs). These will be your source for complete and up-to-date information about the SDKs.

Also, there's the community around Flutter (https://flutter.dev/community), which has links to all the official Flutter communities on multiple social media platforms. In particular, check out Google Developers' Flutter YouTube channel (https://www.youtube.com/c/flutterdev/).

Finally, available on kodeco.com is Dart Apprentice: Fundamentals (https://www.kodeco.com/books/dart-apprentice-fundamentals), a companion book to learn more about Dart. For a quick start, check out this free Dart Basics article (https://www.kodeco.com/4482551-dart-basics) or the video course Programming in Dart: Fundamentals (https://www.kodeco.com/4921688-programming-in-dart-fundamentals).

Chapter 2: Hello, Flutter

By Michael Katz & Alejandro Ulate

Now that you've had a short introduction, you're ready to start your Flutter apprenticeship. Your first task is to build a basic app from scratch, giving you the chance to get the hang of the tools and the basic Flutter app structure. You'll customize the app and find out how to use a few popular widgets like `ListView` and `Slider` to update its UI in response to changes.

Creating a simple app will let you see just how quick and easy it is to build cross-platform apps with Flutter — and it will give you a quick win.

By the end of the chapter, you'll have built a lightweight recipe app. Since you're just starting to learn Flutter, your app will offer a hard-coded list of recipes and let you use a `Slider` to recalculate quantities based on the number of servings.

Here's what your finished app will look like:

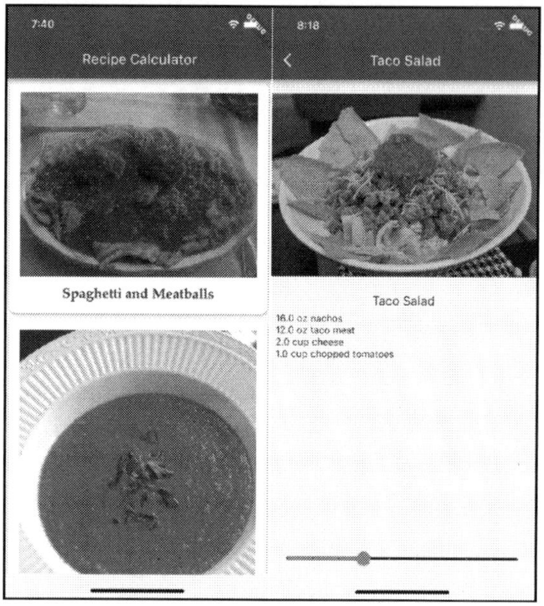

All you need to start this chapter is to have Flutter set up. If the `flutter doctor` results show no errors, you're ready to get started. Otherwise, go back to Chapter 1, "Getting Started", to set up your environment.

Creating a New App

There are two simple ways to start a new Flutter app. In the last chapter, you created a new app project through the IDE. Alternatively, you can create an app with the `flutter` command. You'll use the second option here.

Open a terminal window, then navigate to the location where you want to create a new folder for the project. For example, you can use this book's materials and go to **flta-materials/02-hello-flutter/projects/starter/**.

Creating a new project is straightforward. In the terminal, run:

```
flutter create recipes
```

This command creates a new app in a new folder, both named **recipes**. It has the demo app code, as you saw in the previous chapter, with support for running on iOS, Android, Linux, macOS, web and Windows.

Using your IDE, open the **recipes** folder as an existing project.

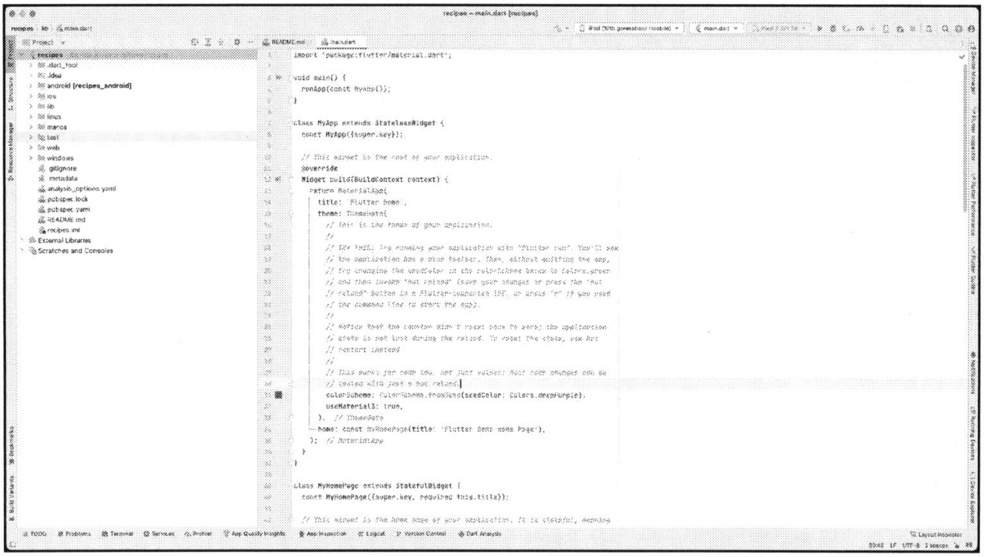

Build and run and you'll see the same demo app as in Chapter 1, "Getting Started".

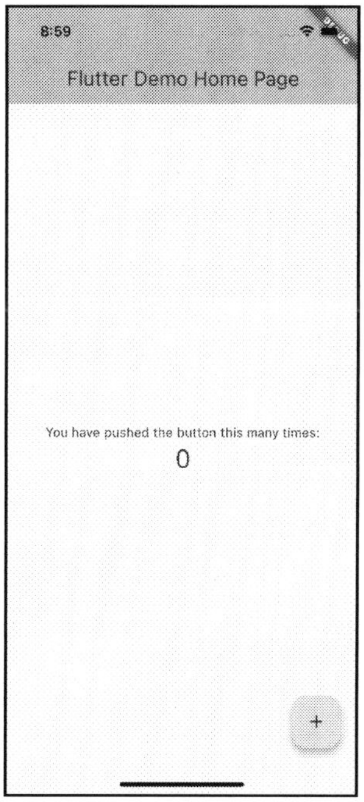

Tapping the + button increments the counter.

Making the App Yours

The ready-made app is a good place to start because the `flutter create` command puts all the boilerplate together for you to get up and running. But this is not *your* app. It's literally **MyApp**, as you can see near the top of **main.dart**:

```
class MyApp extends StatelessWidget {
```

This defines a new Dart `class` named `MyApp` which **extends** — or inherits from — `StatelessWidget`. In Flutter, almost everything that makes up the user interface is a **Widget**. A `StatelessWidget` doesn't change after you build it. You'll learn a lot more about widgets and states in the next section. For now, just think of `MyApp` as the container for the app.

Since you're building a recipe app, you don't want your main `class` to be named `MyApp` — you want it to be `RecipesApp`.

While you could change it manually in multiple places, you'll reduce the chance of a copy-and-paste error or typo by using the IDE's **rename** action instead. This lets you rename a symbol at its definition and all its callers at the same time.

In Android Studio, you can use the **Refactor ▸ Rename** menu item or by using the right-click menu.

Click on `MyApp` in `class MyApp...` and navigate to either refactor option.

In the popup, rename **MyApp** to **RecipesApp** and tap on the **Refactor** button.

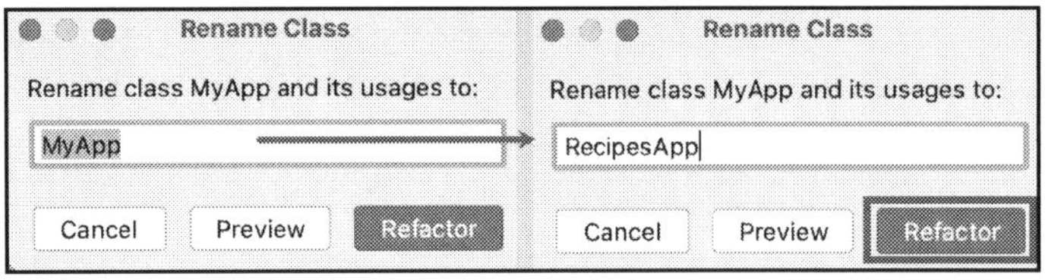

The result will look like this:

```
void main() {
  runApp(const RecipesApp());
}

class RecipesApp extends StatelessWidget {
  const RecipesApp({super.key});
```

`main()` is the entry point for the code when the app launches. `runApp()` tells Flutter which is the top-level widget for the app.

A hot reload won't include the code changes you just made. To run the new code you need to perform a **hot restart**.

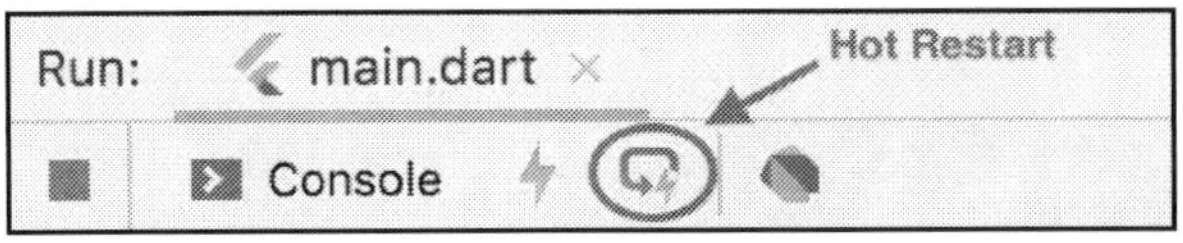

Note: As mentioned in Chapter 1, "Getting Started", when you save your changes, hot reload automatically runs and updates the UI. If this doesn't happen, check your IDE settings for Flutter to make sure it's enabled. If you don't want it to trigger it when you save changes you can run it manually. The shortcut for Android Studio is **Option-Command-**.

With hot reload you can quickly see the effect of code changes and the app state is preserved. For example, if the user was in a "logged in" state before the code changed, a hot reload will preserve such a state and you won't need to log in again to test your changes.

If you've made significant changes, like adding a new property to a state or changing `main()` like in the case above, then you need to hot restart, so that the new change is detected and included in the new build.

For even bigger changes, like adding dependencies or assets, you need to perform a full build and run.

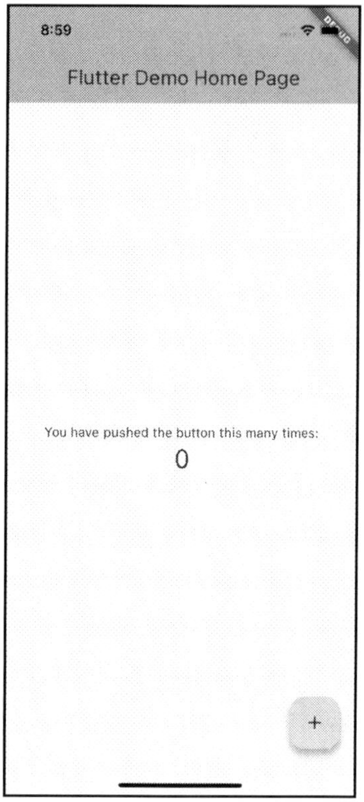

In this specific case you won't notice any change in the UI.

Styling Your App

To continue making this into a new app, you'll customize the appearance of your widgets next.

Replace `RecipesApp`'s `build()` with:

```
// 1
@override
Widget build(BuildContext context) {
  // 2
  final ThemeData theme = ThemeData();
  // 3
  return MaterialApp(
    // 4
    title: 'Recipe Calculator',
    // 5
    theme: theme.copyWith(
        colorScheme: ColorScheme.fromSeed(
          seedColor: Colors.greenAccent,
```

```
        ),
      ),
      // 6
      home: const MyHomePage(
        title: 'Recipe Calculator',
      ),
    );
  }
```

This code changes the appearance of the app:

1. A widget's `build()` method is the entry point for composing together other widgets to make a new widget. The `@override` annotation tells the Dart analyzer that this method is supposed to replace the default method from `StatelessWidget`.
2. A theme determines visual aspects like color. The default `ThemeData` will show the standard Material defaults.
3. `MaterialApp` uses Material Design and is the widget that will be included in `RecipesApp`.
4. The title of the app is a description that the device uses to identify the app. The UI won't display this.
5. By copying the theme and replacing the color scheme with a custom one you are changing the app's colors. Here, by using the special `fromSeed` constructor, you are generating shades and tones that `ThemeData` uses to style widgets following Material Design specifications.
6. This still uses the same `MyHomePage` widget as before, but now, you've updated the title and displayed it on the device.

When you relaunch the app now, you'll see the same widgets, but they have a more sophisticated style.

You've taken the first step towards making the app your own by customizing the `MaterialApp` body. You'll finish cleaning up the app in the next section.

Clearing the App

You've themed the app, but it's still displaying the counter demo. Clearing the screen is your next step. To start, replace the existing `_MyHomePageState` class with:

```
class _MyHomePageState extends State<MyHomePage> {
  @override
  Widget build(BuildContext context) {
    // 1
    return Scaffold(
      // 2
      appBar: AppBar(
        title: Text(widget.title),
      ),
      // 3
      body: SafeArea(
        // TODO: Replace child: Container()
        // 4
        child: Container(),
      ),
    );
  }

  // TODO: Add buildRecipeCard() here
}
```

A quick look at what this shows:

1. A `Scaffold` provides the high-level structure for a screen. In this case, you're using two properties.
2. `AppBar` gets a title property by using a `Text` widget that has a `title` passed in from `home: MyHomePage(title: 'Recipe Calculator')` in the previous step.
3. `body` has `SafeArea`, which keeps the app from getting too close to the operating system interfaces such as the notch or interactive areas like the Home Indicator at the bottom of some iOS screens.
4. `SafeArea` has a `child` widget, which is an empty `Container` widget.

> **Note:** Some widgets like `AppBar`, can also receive custom appearance properties. In the template project generated by Flutter's toolkit, `AppBar` has `backgroundColor` set to `inversePrimary` in `_MyHomePageState`. In this case, you've removed any custom appearance to `AppBar` which causes a change in it's coloring.

One hot reload later, and you're left with a clean app:

Building a Recipe List

An empty recipe app isn't very useful. The app should have a nice list of recipes for the user to scroll through. Before you can display these, however, you need the data to fill out the UI.

Adding a Data Model

You'll use `Recipe` as the main data structure for recipes in this app.

Create a new **Dart file** in the **lib** folder, named **recipe.dart**.

Add the following class to the file:

```
class Recipe {
  String label;
  String imageUrl;
  // TODO: Add servings and ingredients here

  Recipe(
    this.label,
    this.imageUrl,
  );
  // TODO: Add List<Recipe> here
}

// TODO: Add Ingredient class here
```

This is the start of a `Recipe` model with a label and an image.

You'll also need to supply some data for the app to display. In a full-featured app, you'd load this data either from a local database or a JSON-based API. For the sake of simplicity as you get started with Flutter, however, you'll use hard-coded data in this chapter.

Add the following property to `Recipe` by replacing `// TODO: Add List<Recipe> here` with:

```
static List<Recipe> samples = [
  Recipe(
    'Spaghetti and Meatballs',
    'assets/2126711929_ef763de2b3_w.jpg',
  ),
  Recipe(
    'Tomato Soup',
    'assets/27729023535_a57606c1be.jpg',
  ),
  Recipe(
    'Grilled Cheese',
    'assets/3187380632_5056654a19_b.jpg',
  ),
  Recipe(
    'Chocolate Chip Cookies',
    'assets/15992102771_b92f4cc00a_b.jpg',
  ),
```

```
    Recipe(
      'Taco Salad',
      'assets/8533381643_a31a99e8a6_c.jpg',
    ),
    Recipe(
      'Hawaiian Pizza',
      'assets/15452035777_294cefced5_c.jpg',
    ),
  ];
```

This is a hard-coded list of recipes. You'll add more detail later, but right now, it's just a list of names and images.

> **Note**: A `List` is an ordered collection of items; in some programming languages, it's called an array. `List` indexes start with 0.

You've created a `List` with images, but you don't have any images in your project yet. To add them, go to **Finder** and copy the **assets** folder from the top level of **02-hello-flutter** in the book materials of your project's folder structure. Then paste it into the project. When you're done, it should live at the same level as the **lib** folder. That way, the app will be able to find the images when you run it.

You'll notice that by copy-pasting in Finder, the folder and images automatically display in the Android Studio project list.

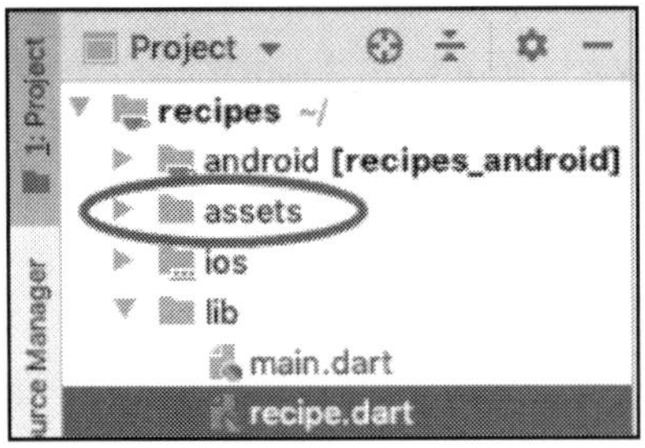

But just adding assets to the project doesn't display them in the app. To tell the app to include those assets, open **pubspec.yaml** in the **recipes** project root folder.

Under `# To add assets to your application...` add the following lines:

```
  assets:
    - assets/
```

These lines specify that **assets/** is an assets folder and must be included with the app. Make sure that the first line here is aligned with the `uses-material-design: true` line above it.

After modifying **pubspec.yaml** your IDE might show a notification to get the dependencies for your project again:

This happens because **pubspec.yaml** works as your app's manifest. So, when you change it, you also need to let Dart's VM that it changed and it needs to update all the bundled code. Keep an eye out since these type of changes require that you fully restart your app.

Displaying the List

With the data ready to go, your next step is to create a place for the data to go *to*.

Back in **main.dart**, you need to import the data file. Add the following to the top of the file, under the other import lines:

```
import 'recipe.dart';
```

Next, in `_MyHomePageState` find and replace `// TODO: Replace child: Container()` and the two lines beneath it with:

```
// 4
child: ListView.builder(
  // 5
  itemCount: Recipe.samples.length,
  // 6
  itemBuilder: (BuildContext context, int index) {
    // 7
    // TODO: Update to return Recipe card
    return Text(Recipe.samples[index].label);
  },
),
```

This code does the following:

4. Builds a list using `ListView`.
5. `itemCount` determines the number of rows the list has. In this case, `length` is the number of objects in the `Recipe.samples` list.

6. `itemBuilder` builds the widget tree for each row.

7. A `Text` widget displays the name of the recipe.

Perform a hot reload now and you'll see the following list:

Data is there, the next step is to display it in a prettier way. :]

Putting the List Into a Card

It's great that you're displaying real data now, but this is barely an app. To spice things up a notch, you need to add images to go along with the titles.

To do this, you'll use a `Card`. In Material Design, `Card`s define an area of the UI where you've laid out related information about a specific entity. For example, a `Card` in a music app might have labels for an album's title, artist and release date along with an image for the album cover and maybe a control for rating it with stars.

Your recipe `Card` will show the recipe's label and image. Its widget tree will have the following structure:

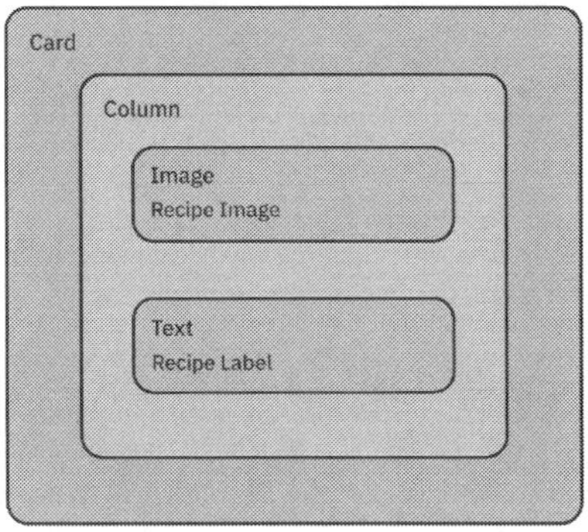

In **main.dart**, at the bottom of `_MyHomePageState` create a **custom widget** by replacing `// TODO: Add buildRecipeCard() here` with:

```
Widget buildRecipeCard(Recipe recipe) {
  // 1
  return Card(
    // 2
      child: Column(
        // 3
        children: <Widget>[
          // 4
          Image(image: AssetImage(recipe.imageUrl)),
          // 5
          Text(recipe.label),
        ],
      ),
  );
}
```

Here's how you define your new custom `Card` widget:

1. You return a `Card` from `buildRecipeCard()`.
2. The `Card`'s child property is a `Column`. A `Column` is a widget that defines a vertical layout.
3. The `Column` has two `children`.
4. The first child is an `Image` widget. `AssetImage` states that the image is fetched from the local **asset** bundle defined in **pubspec.yaml**.
5. A `Text` widget is the second child. It will contain the `recipe.label` value.

To use the card, go to `_MyHomePageState` and replace `// TODO: Update to return Recipe card` and the `return` line below it with this:

```
// TODO: Add GestureDetector
return buildRecipeCard(Recipe.samples[index]);
```

That instructs the `itemBuilder` to use the custom `Card` widget for each recipe in the `samples` list.

Hot restart the app to see the image and text cards.

Notice that `Card` doesn't default to a flat square at the bottom of the widget. Material Design provides a standard corner radius and drop shadow.

Looking At the Widget Tree

Now's a good time to think about the widget tree of the overall app. Do you remember that it started with `RecipesApp` from `main()`?

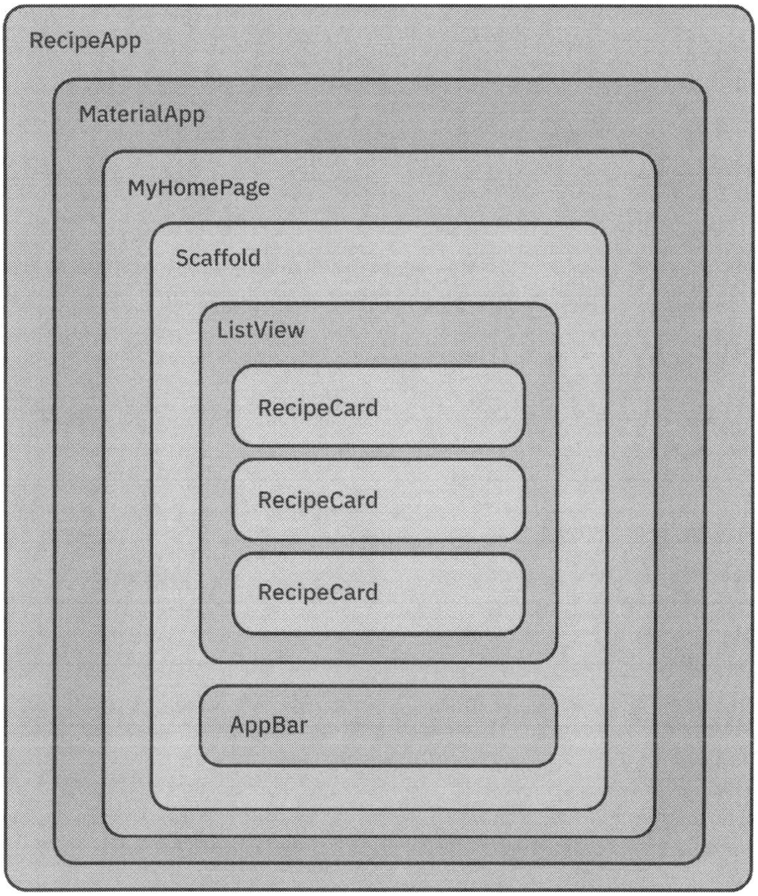

`RecipesApp` built a `MaterialApp`, which in turn used `MyHomePage` as its home. That builds a `Scaffold` with an `AppBar` and a `ListView`. You then updated the `ListView` builder to make a `Card` for each item.

Thinking about the widget tree helps explain the app as the layout gets more complicated and as you add interactivity. Fortunately, you don't have to hand-draw a diagram each time.

In Android Studio, open the **Flutter Inspector** from the **View ▸ Tool Windows ▸ Flutter Inspector** menu while your app is running. This opens a powerful UI debugging tool.

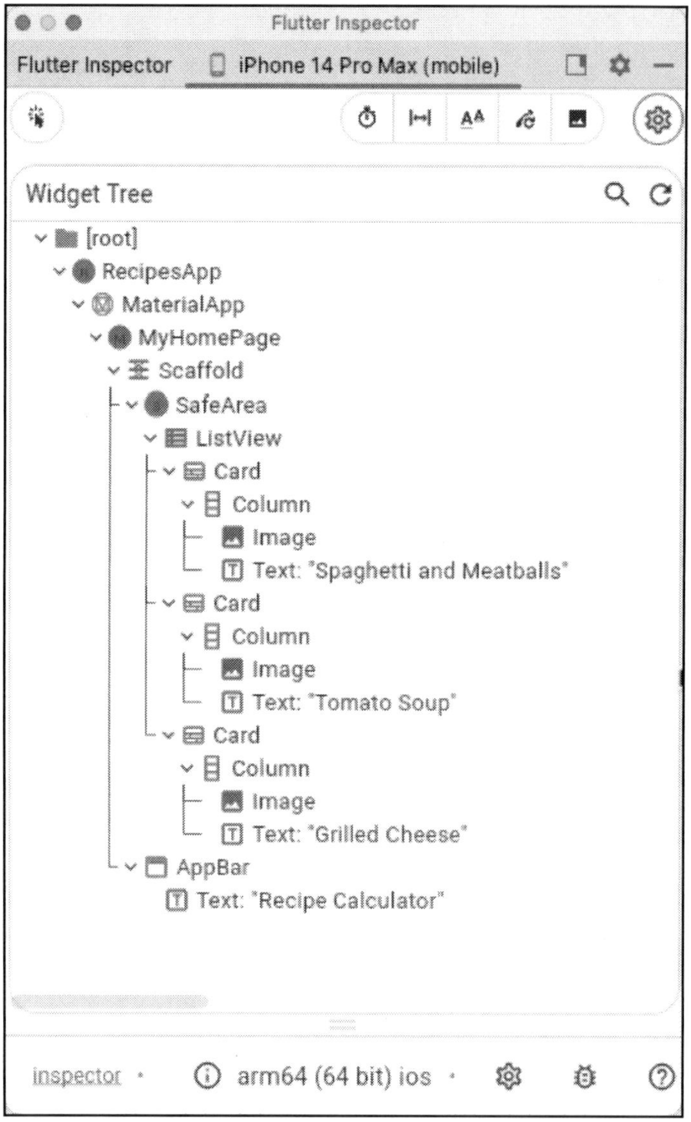

This view shows you all the widgets onscreen and how they are composed. As you scroll, you can refresh the tree. You might notice the number of cards change. That's because the `List` doesn't keep every item in memory at once to improve performance. You'll cover more about how that works in Chapter 4, "Understanding Widgets".

Making It Look Nice

The default cards look okay, but they're not as nice as they could be. With a few added extras, you can spiffy the card up. These include wrapping widgets in layout widgets like `Padding` or specifying additional styling parameters.

Get started by replacing `buildRecipeCard()` with:

```
Widget buildRecipeCard(Recipe recipe) {
  return Card(
    // 1
    elevation: 2.0,
    // 2
    shape: RoundedRectangleBorder(
      borderRadius: BorderRadius.circular(10.0)),
    // 3
    child: Padding(
      padding: const EdgeInsets.all(16.0),
      // 4
      child: Column(
        children: <Widget>[
          Image(image: AssetImage(recipe.imageUrl)),
          // 5
          const SizedBox(
            height: 14.0,
          ),
          // 6
          Text(
            recipe.label,
            style: const TextStyle(
              fontSize: 20.0,
              fontWeight: FontWeight.w700,
              fontFamily: 'Palatino',
            ),
          )
        ],
      ),
    ),
  );
}
```

This has a few updates to look at:

1. A card's `elevation` determines *how high off the screen* the card is, affecting its shadow.
2. `shape` handles the shape of the card. This code defines a rounded rectangle with a `10.0` corner radius.
3. `Padding` insets its child's contents by the specified `padding` value.

4. The padding child is still the same vertical `Column` with the image and text.
5. Between the image and text is a `SizedBox`. This is a blank view with a fixed size.
6. You can customize `Text` widgets with a `style` object. In this case, you've specified a `Palatino` font with a size of `20.0` and a bold weight of `w700`.

Hot reload and you'll see a more styled list.

You can play around with these values to get the list to look "just right" for you. With hot reload, it's easy to make changes and instantly see their effect on the running app.

Using the Widget inspector, you'll see the added `Padding` and `SizedBox` widgets. When you select a widget, such as the `SizedBox`, it shows you all its real-time properties in a separate pane, which includes the ones you set explicitly and those that were inherited or set by default.

Selecting a widget also highlights where it was defined in the source.

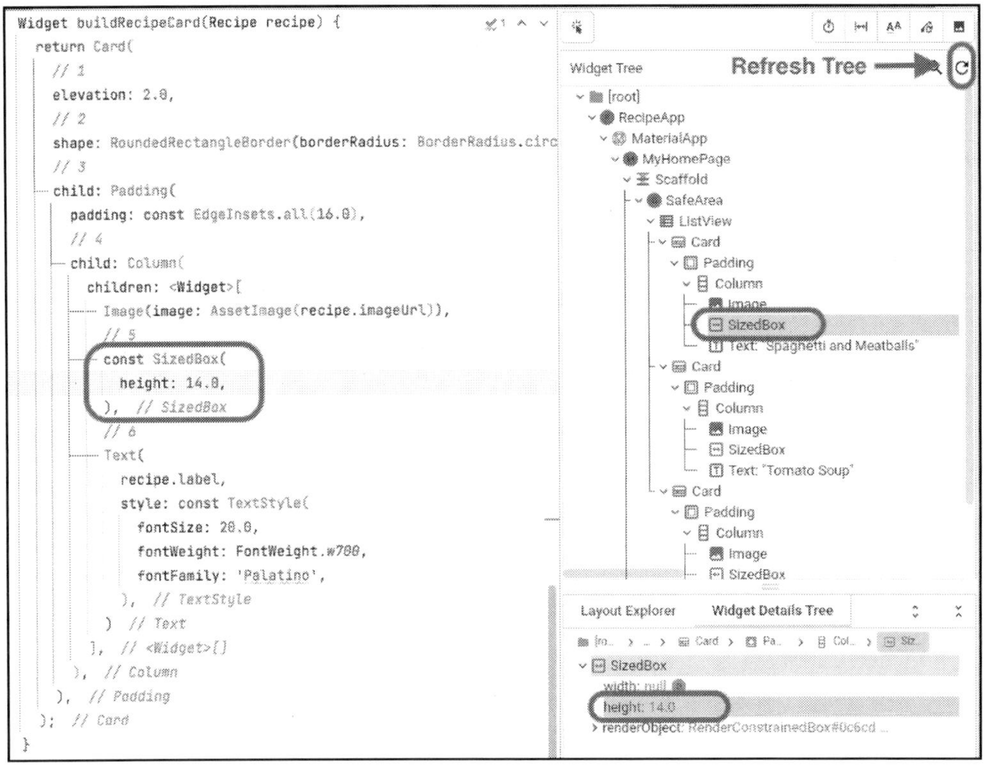

> **Note**: You may need to click the **Refresh Tree** button to reload the widget structure in the inspector. See Chapter 4, "Understanding Widgets" for more details.

Adding a Recipe Detail Page

You now have a pretty list, but the app isn't interactive yet. What would make it great is to show the user details about a recipe when they tap the card. You'll start implementing this by making the card react to a tap.

Making a Tap Response

Inside _MyHomePageState, locate `// TODO: Add GestureDetector` and replace the `return` statement beneath it with the following:

```
// 7
return GestureDetector(
  // 8
  onTap: () {
    // 9
    Navigator.push(
      context,
      MaterialPageRoute(
        builder: (context) {
          // 10
          // TODO: Replace return with return RecipeDetail()
          return Text('Detail page');
        },
      ),
    );
  },
  // 11
  child: buildRecipeCard(Recipe.samples[index]),
);
```

This introduces a few new widgets and concepts. Looking at the lines one at a time:

7. Introduces a `GestureDetector` widget, which, as the name implies, detects gestures.
8. Implements an `onTap()` function, which is the callback called when the widget is tapped.
9. The `Navigator` widget manages a stack of pages. Calling `push()` with a `MaterialPageRoute` will push a new Material page onto the stack. Section III, "Navigating Between Screens", will cover navigation in a lot more detail.
10. `builder` creates the destination page widget.
11. `GestureDetector`'s child widget defines the area where the gesture is active.

Hot reload the app and now each card is tappable. **Tap** a recipe and you'll see a black **Detail page**:

Creating an Actual Target Page

The resulting page is just a placeholder. Not only is it ugly, but because it doesn't have all the normal page trappings, the user is now stuck here, at least on iOS devices without a back button. But don't worry, you can fix that!

In **lib**, create a new **Dart file** named **recipe_detail.dart**.

Now, add this code to the file, and ignore the red squiggles for now:

```
import 'package:flutter/material.dart';
import 'recipe.dart';

class RecipeDetail extends StatefulWidget {
  final Recipe recipe;

  const RecipeDetail({
    Key? key,
```

```
    required this.recipe,
  }) : super(key: key);

  @override
  State<RecipeDetail> createState() {
    return _RecipeDetailState();
  }
}

// TODO: Add _RecipeDetailState here
```

This creates a new `StatefulWidget` which has an initializer that takes the `Recipe` details to display. This is a `StatefulWidget` because you'll add some interactive state to this page later.

You need `_RecipeDetailState` to build the widget, replace `// TODO: Add _RecipeDetailState here` with:

```
class _RecipeDetailState extends State<RecipeDetail> {
  // TODO: Add _sliderVal here

  @override
  Widget build(BuildContext context) {
    // 1
    return Scaffold(
      appBar: AppBar(
        title: Text(widget.recipe.label),
      ),
      // 2
      body: SafeArea(
        // 3
        child: Column(
          children: <Widget>[
            // 4
            SizedBox(
              height: 300,
              width: double.infinity,
              child: Image(
                image: AssetImage(widget.recipe.imageUrl),
              ),
            ),
            // 5
            const SizedBox(
              height: 4,
            ),
            // 6
            Text(
              widget.recipe.label,
              style: const TextStyle(fontSize: 18),
            ),
            // TODO: Add Expanded
```

```
            // TODO: Add Slider() here
          ],
        ),
      ),
    );
  }
}
```

The body of the widget is the same as you've already seen. Here are a few things to notice:

1. `Scaffold` defines the page's general structure.
2. In the `body`, there's a `SafeArea`, a `Column` with some `SizedBox` and `Text` children.
3. `SafeArea` keeps the app from getting too close to the operating system interfaces, such as the notch or the interactive area of most iPhones.
4. One new thing is the `SizedBox` around the `Image`, which defines resizable bounds for the image. Here, the `height` is fixed at 300 but the `width` will adjust to fit the aspect ratio. The unit of measurement in Flutter is **logical pixels**.
5. There is a spacer `SizedBox`.
6. The `Text` for the `label` has a `style` that's a little different than the main `Card`, to show you how much customizability is available.

Next, go back to **main.dart** and add the following line to the top of the file:

```
import 'recipe_detail.dart';
```

Then find `// TODO: Replace return with return RecipeDetail()` replace it and the existing `return` statement with:

```
return RecipeDetail(recipe: Recipe.samples[index]);
```

Perform a hot restart by choosing **Run ▸ Flutter Hot Restart** from the menu to set the app state back to the original list. Tapping a recipe card will now show the `RecipeDetail` page.

> **Note**: You need to use hot restart here because hot reload won't update the UI after you update the state.

Because you now have a `Scaffold` with an `appBar`, Flutter will automatically include a back button to return the user to the main list.

Adding Ingredients

To complete the detail page, you'll need to add additional details to the `Recipe` class. Before you can do that, you have to add an ingredient list to the recipes.

Open **recipe.dart** and replace `// TODO: Add Ingredient class here` with the following class:

```
class Ingredient {
  double quantity;
  String measure;
  String name;

  Ingredient(
    this.quantity,
    this.measure,
    this.name,
  );
}
```

This is a simple data container for an ingredient. It has a name, a unit of measure — like "cup" or "tablespoon" — and a quantity.

At the top of the `Recipe` class, replace `// TODO: Add servings and ingredients here` with the following, ignore any red squiggles:

```
int servings;
List<Ingredient> ingredients;
```

This adds properties to specify that `serving` is how many people the specified quantity feeds and `ingredients` is a simple list.

To use these new properties, go to your `samples` list inside the `Recipe` class and change the `Recipe` constructor from:

```
Recipe(
  this.label,
  this.imageUrl,
);
```

to:

```
Recipe(
  this.label,
  this.imageUrl,
  this.servings,
  this.ingredients,
);
```

You may see red squiggles under part of your code because the values for `servings` and `ingredients` have not been set. You'll fix that next.

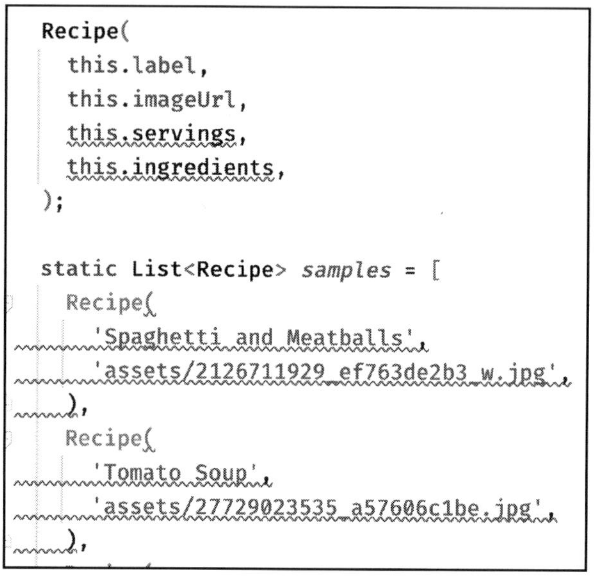

To include the new `servings` and `ingredients` properties, replace the existing `samples` definition with the following:

```
static List<Recipe> samples = [
  Recipe(
    'Spaghetti and Meatballs',
    'assets/2126711929_ef763de2b3_w.jpg',
    4,
    [
      Ingredient(1, 'box', 'Spaghetti',),
      Ingredient(4, '', 'Frozen Meatballs',),
      Ingredient(0.5, 'jar', 'sauce',),
    ],
  ),
  Recipe(
    'Tomato Soup',
    'assets/27729023535_a57606c1be.jpg',
    2,
    [
      Ingredient(1, 'can', 'Tomato Soup',),
    ],
  ),
  Recipe(
    'Grilled Cheese',
    'assets/3187380632_5056654a19_b.jpg',
    1,
    [
```

```
      Ingredient(2, 'slices', 'Cheese',),
      Ingredient(2, 'slices', 'Bread',),
    ],
  ),
  Recipe(
    'Chocolate Chip Cookies',
    'assets/15992102771_b92f4cc00a_b.jpg',
    24,
    [
      Ingredient(4, 'cups', 'flour',),
      Ingredient(2, 'cups', 'sugar',),
      Ingredient(0.5, 'cups', 'chocolate chips',),
    ],
  ),
  Recipe(
    'Taco Salad',
    'assets/8533381643_a31a99e8a6_c.jpg',
    1,
    [
      Ingredient(4, 'oz', 'nachos',),
      Ingredient(3, 'oz', 'taco meat',),
      Ingredient(0.5, 'cup', 'cheese',),
      Ingredient(0.25, 'cup', 'chopped tomatoes',),
    ],
  ),
  Recipe(
    'Hawaiian Pizza',
    'assets/15452035777_294cefced5_c.jpg',
    4,
    [
      Ingredient(1, 'item', 'pizza',),
      Ingredient(1, 'cup', 'pineapple',),
      Ingredient(8, 'oz', 'ham',),
    ],
  ),
];
```

That fills out an ingredient list for these items. Please don’t cook these at home, these are just examples. :]

Hot reload the app now. No changes will be visible, but it should build successfully.

Showing the Ingredients

A recipe doesn't do much good without the ingredients. Now, you're ready to add a widget to display them.

In **recipe_detail.dart**, replace `// TODO: Add Expanded` with:

```
// 7
Expanded(
  // 8
  child: ListView.builder(
    padding: const EdgeInsets.all(7.0),
    itemCount: widget.recipe.ingredients.length,
    itemBuilder: (BuildContext context, int index) {
      final ingredient = widget.recipe.ingredients[index];
      // 9
      // TODO: Add ingredient.quantity
      return Text(
          '${ingredient.quantity} ${ingredient.measure} $
```

```
{ingredient.name}');
    },
  ),
),
```

This code adds:

7. An `Expanded` widget, which expands to fill the space in a `Column`. This way, the ingredient list will take up the space not filled by the other widgets.
8. A `ListView`, with one row per ingredient.
9. A `Text` that uses **string interpolation** to populate a string with runtime values. You use the `${expression}` syntax inside the string literal to denote these.

Hot restart by choosing **Run ▸ Flutter Hot Restart** and navigate to a detail page to see the ingredients.

Nice job, the screen now shows the recipe name and the ingredients. Next, you'll add a feature to make it interactive.

Adding a Serving Slider

You're currently showing the ingredients for a suggested serving. Wouldn't it be great if you could change the desired quantity and have the amount of ingredients updated automatically?

You'll do this by adding a **Slider** widget to allow the user to adjust the number of servings.

First, create an instance variable to store the slider value. Still in **recipe_detail.dart** replace `// TODO: Add _sliderVal here` with:

```
int _sliderVal = 1;
```

Now find `// TODO: Add Slider() here` and replace it with the following:

```
Slider(
  // 10
  min: 1,
  max: 10,
  divisions: 9,
  // 11
  label: '${_sliderVal * widget.recipe.servings} servings',
  // 12
  value: _sliderVal.toDouble(),
  // 13
  onChanged: (newValue) {
    setState(() {
      _sliderVal = newValue.round();
    });
  },
  // 14
  activeColor: Colors.green,
  inactiveColor: Colors.black,
),
```

`Slider` presents a round thumb that can be dragged along a track to change a value. Here's how it works:

10. You use `min`, `max` and `divisions` to define how the slider moves. In this case, it moves between the values of 1 and 10, with ten discreet stops. That is, it can only have values of 1, 2, 3, 4, 5, 6, 7, 8, 9 or 10.
11. `label` updates as the `_sliderVal` changes and displays a scaled number of servings.
12. The slider works in `double` values, so this converts the `int` variable.

13. Conversely, when the slider changes, this uses `round()` to convert the `double` slider value to an `int`, then saves it in `_sliderVal`.

14. This sets the slider's colors to something more "on brand". The `activeColor` is the section between the minimum value and the thumb, and the `inactiveColor` represents the rest.

Hot reload the app, adjust the slider and see the value reflected in the indicator.

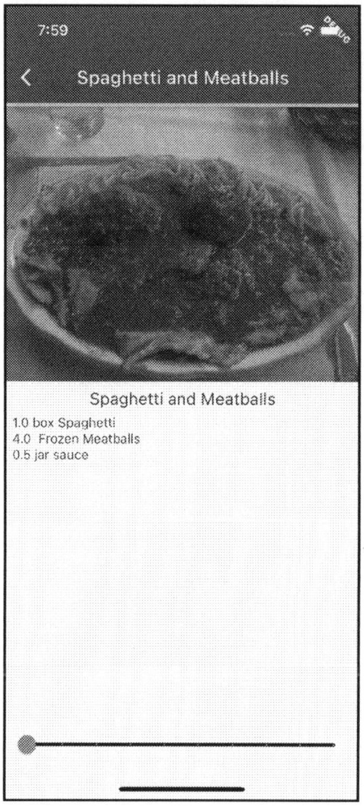

Updating the Recipe

It's great to see the changed value reflected in the slider, but right now, it doesn't affect the recipe itself.

To do that, you just have to change the `Expanded` ingredients `itemBuilder` return statement to include the current value of `_sliderVal` as a factor for each ingredient.

Replace `// TODO: Add ingredient.quantity` and the whole `return` statement beneath it with:

```
return Text('${ingredient.quantity * _sliderVal} '
            '${ingredient.measure} '
            '${ingredient.name}');
```

After a hot reload, you'll see that the recipe's ingredients change when you move the slider.

That's it! You've now built a cool, interactive Flutter app that works just the same on multiple devices.

In the next few sections, you'll continue to explore how widgets and state work. You'll also learn about important functionality like networking.

Key Points

- Build a new app with `flutter create`.
- Use widgets to compose a screen with controls and layout.
- Use widget parameters for styling.
- A `MaterialApp` widget specifies the app, and `Scaffold` specifies the high-level structure of a given screen.
- State allows for interactive widgets.
- When state changes, you usually need to hot restart the app instead of hot reload. In some cases, you may also need to rebuild and restart the app entirely.

Where to Go From Here?

Congratulations, you've written your first app!

To get a sense of all the widget options available, the documentation (https://api.flutter.dev/) should be your starting point. In particular, the Material library (https://api.flutter.dev/flutter/material/material-library.html) and Widgets catalog (https://docs.flutter.dev/development/ui/widgets) will cover most of what you can put on screen. Those pages list all the parameters, and often have in-browser interactive sections where you can experiment.

For more information about the Dart language, annotations, and its constructs, check out Dart Apprentice: Fundamentals (https://www.kodeco.com/books/dart-apprentice-fundamentals) and Dart Apprentice: Beyond the Basics (https://www.kodeco.com/books/dart-apprentice-beyond-the-basics).

Chapter 3, "Basic Widgets", is all about using widgets and Chapter 4, "Understanding Widgets", goes into more detail on the theory behind widgets. Future chapters will go into more depth about other concepts briefly introduced in this chapter.

Section II: Everything's a Widget

In this section you'll start to build a full-featured recipe app named **Yummy**. You'll gain an understanding of and use a wide range of widgets available in Flutter, and learn about the theory of how widgets work behind the scenes.

You'll then dive deeper into layout widgets, scrollable widgets and interactive widgets.

Chapter 3: Basic Widgets

By Vincent Ngo

Dive into the world of Flutter, where everything is a widget! This chapter unveils three fundamental widget categories essential for:

- Structure and navigation
- Displaying information
- Positioning widgets

By the end of the chapter, you'll construct a social food app called **Yummy**. You'll use various widgets to create three distinct tabs: **Category**, **Post**, and **Restaurant**.

Ready? Dive in by taking a look at the starter project.

Getting Started

Start by downloading this chapter's project from the book materials repo https://github.com/kodecocodes/flta-materials.

Locate the **projects** folder and open **starter**. Navigate to **pubspec.yaml** and tap **Pub get** to get all your flutter dependencies.

Run the app, and you'll see an app bar and a simple text:

lib/main.dart serves as the launchpad of any Flutter application. Open it to see:

```
import 'package:flutter/material.dart';

void main() {
  // 1
  runApp(const Yummy());
}

class Yummy extends StatelessWidget {
  // TODO: Setup default theme

  // 2
  const Yummy({super.key});

  // TODO: Add changeTheme above here

  @override
  Widget build(BuildContext context) {
    const appTitle = 'Yummy';

    // TODO: Setup default theme

    //3
    return MaterialApp(
      title: appTitle,
      //debugShowCheckedModeBanner: false, // Uncomment to
remove Debug banner

      // TODO: Add theme

      // TODO: Replace Scaffold with Home widget
      // 4
      home: Scaffold(
        appBar: AppBar(
          // TODO: Add action buttons
          elevation: 4.0,
          title: const Text(
            appTitle,
            style: TextStyle(fontSize: 24.0),
          ),
        ),
        body: const Center(
          child: Text(
            'You Hungry?😋',
            style: TextStyle(fontSize: 30.0),
          ),
        ),
      ),
    );
  }
}
```

Take a moment to explore what the code does:

1. **Widget Initialization**: Every journey with Flutter commences with a widget. The `runApp()` function initializes the app by accepting the root widget, in this case, an instance of `Yummy`.
2. Every widget must override the `build()` method.
3. The `Yummy` widget starts by composing a `MaterialApp` widget to give it a **Material Design** system look and feel. See https://material.io for more details.
4. **Scaffold** defines the app's visual structure, containing an `AppBar` and a body for starts.

Styling Your App

Flutter, being cross-platform, supports Android's Material Design and iOS's Cupertino design systems.

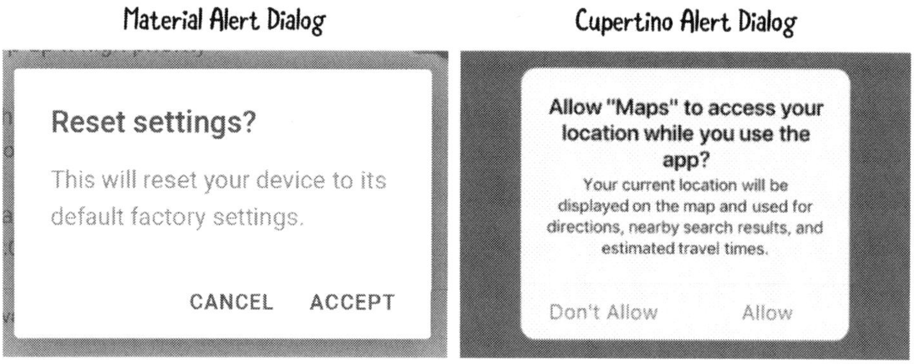

Android uses the **Material Design** system, which you'd import like this:

```
import 'package:flutter/material.dart';
```

iOS uses the **Cupertino** system. Here's how you'd import it:

```
import 'package:flutter/cupertino.dart';
```

Throughout this book, you'll learn to use the Material Design system. You'll find the look and feel quite customizable!

> **Note**: Switching between Material and Cupertino is beyond the scope of this book. For more information about what these packages offer in terms of UI components, check out:
>
> • Material UI Components: https://flutter.dev/docs/development/ui/widgets/material
>
> • Cupertino UI Components: https://flutter.dev/docs/development/ui/widgets/cupertino

Now that you've settled on a design, you'll set a theme for your app in the next section.

Defining a Theme Class

Spice up your app with a custom theme! With Material 3, theme management is streamlined, focusing on defining color variations.

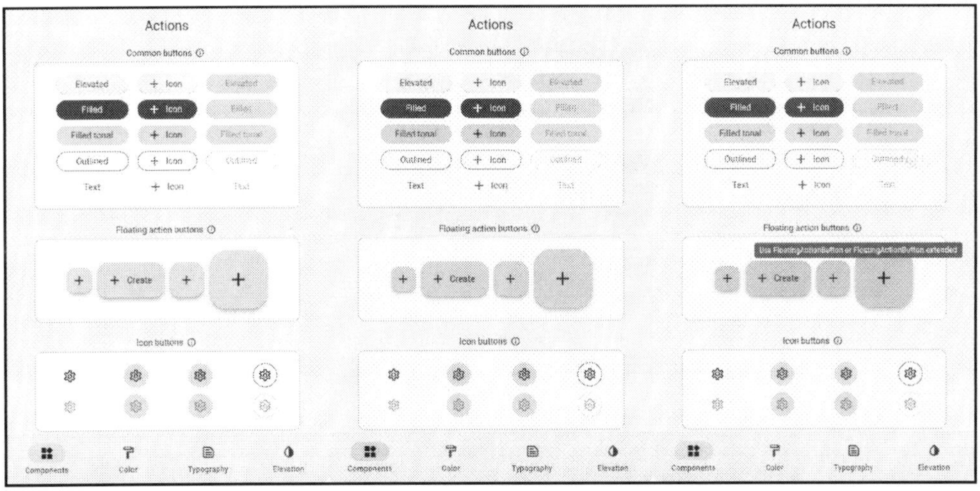

Open **lib/constants.dart** and examine the code included in your starter project:

```
import 'package:flutter/material.dart';

enum ColorSelection {
  // 1
  deepPurple('Deep Purple', Colors.deepPurple),
  purple('Purple', Colors.purple),
```

```
  indigo('Indigo', Colors.indigo),
  blue('Blue', Colors.blue),
  teal('Teal', Colors.teal),
  green('Green', Colors.green),
  yellow('Yellow', Colors.yellow),
  orange('Orange', Colors.orange),
  deepOrange('Deep Orange', Colors.deepOrange),
  pink('Pink', Colors.pink);

  // 2
  const ColorSelection(
    this.label,
    this.color,
  );

  final String label;
  final Color color;
}
```

`ColorSelection` enum enables users to select and customize the app's appearance with:

1. Structured color options. The name listed (e.g. Deep Purple) is what will be displayed.
2. Each has a `label` and a `color` object.

Now, you'll learn to apply the color themes to your app.

Applying the Theme

In **main.dart**, import your predefined color themes:

```
import 'constants.dart';
```

Locate `// TODO: Setup default theme` and replace it with the following code to establish your default theme mode and primary color, ignore the red squiggles:

```
ThemeMode themeMode = ThemeMode.light; // Manual theme toggle
ColorSelection colorSelected = ColorSelection.pink;
```

Next, locate the comment `// TODO: Add theme` and insert the subsequent code to apply your theme configurations:

```
themeMode: themeMode,
theme: ThemeData(
  colorSchemeSeed: colorSelected.color,
  useMaterial3: true,
```

```
    brightness: Brightness.light,
  ),
  darkTheme: ThemeData(
    colorSchemeSeed: colorSelected.color,
    useMaterial3: true,
    brightness: Brightness.dark,
  ),
```

This code snippet sets the global theme mode. It defines both light and dark themes utilizing the color you previously specified, ensuring a cohesive and adaptive visual appearance across your app.

Since the theme can change, you need to remove `const` from the following two locations:

```
runApp(const Yummy());

...

const Yummy({super.key});
```

Save your changes and perform a hot restart.

Locate `// Manual theme toggle` and change `light` to `dark` to observe theme variations. Make sure you do a hot restart.

The two themes look like this:

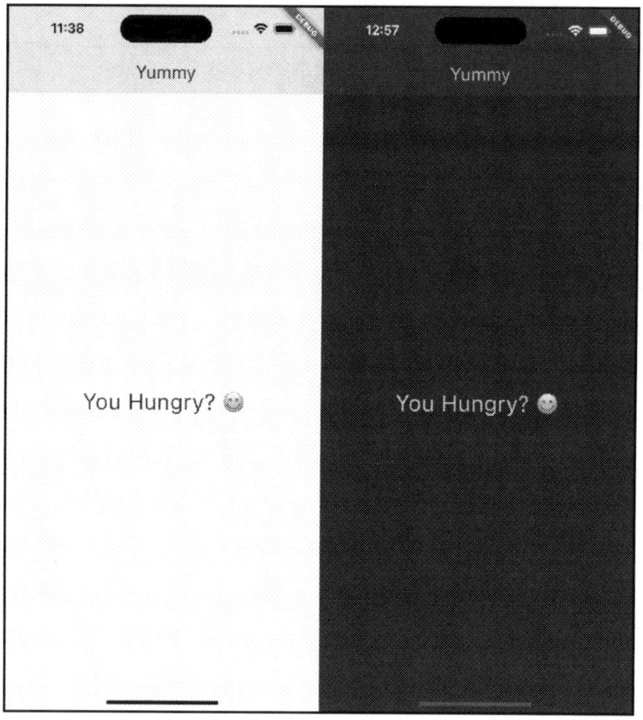

Next, you'll create a way to enable users to toggle between light and dark modes and select a custom color theme.

Switching Themes

To enable theme switching within your app, you need to manage state by converting the `Yummy` widget to a `StatefulWidget`. The good news is that instead of converting manually, you can just use a right-click menu shortcut to do it automatically.

Right-click the class name `Yummy`. Then click **Show Context Actions** from the menu that pops up:

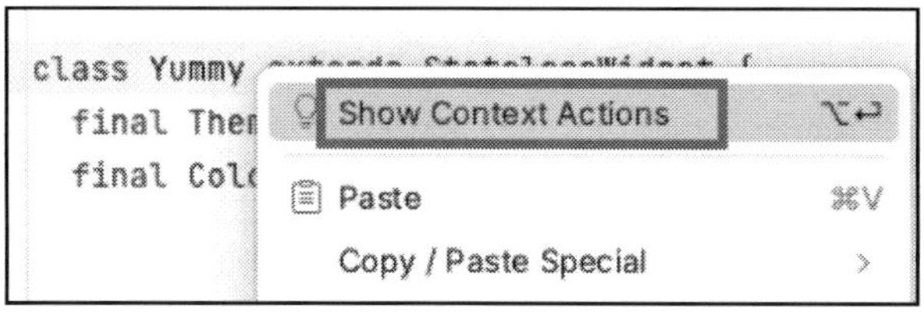

Select **Convert to StatefulWidget**.

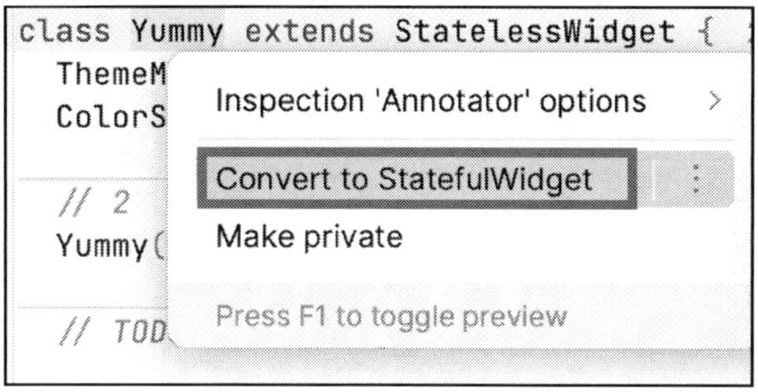

There are now two classes:

```
class Yummy extends StatefulWidget {
  ...

  @override
  State<Yummy> createState() => _YummyState_();
}

class _YummyState extends State<Yummy> {
  ...
  @override
  Widget build(BuildContext context) {
    ...
  }
```

A couple of things to notice in the code above:

- The refactor converted Yummy from a `StatelessWidget` into a `StatefulWidget`. It added a `createState()` implementation.
- The refactor also created the `_YummyState` state class. It stores mutable data that can change over the lifetime of the widget.

Don't you love it when there's an automatic way to save time? Next, you're going to implement the theme state changes.

Implementing Theme State Changes

Within `_YummyState` class, locate `// TODO: Add changeTheme above here` and replace it with the following functions:

```
void changeThemeMode(bool useLightMode) {
  setState(() {
    // 1
    themeMode = useLightMode
      ? ThemeMode.light //
      : ThemeMode.dark;
  });
}

void changeColor(int value) {
  setState(() {
    // 2
    colorSelected = ColorSelection.values[value];
  });
}
```

Here's how the code works:

1. Update theme mode based on user selection.
2. Update theme color based on user selection.

Calling these functions will update the theme or color of your app.

Now, you need to create custom buttons to update the theme.

Creating Custom Buttons to Switch Color and Mode

Now it's time to create two buttons that will allow your users to:

- Switch between light and dark mode.
- Select the color theme of the entire app.

Creating a Theme Button

You'll create a button to toggle between light and dark mode. In **lib** directory, create a new folder called **components** and create a new file called **theme_button.dart** in that directory, add the following code to it:

```
import 'package:flutter/material.dart';

class ThemeButton extends StatelessWidget {
  // 1
  const ThemeButton({
    Key? key,
    required this.changeThemeMode,
  }) : super(key: key);

  // 2
  final Function changeThemeMode;

  @override
  Widget build(BuildContext context) {
    // 3
    final isBright = Theme.of(context).brightness ==
Brightness.light;
    // 4
    return IconButton(
      icon: isBright
          ? const Icon(Icons.dark_mode_outlined) //
          : const Icon(Icons.light_mode_outlined),
      // 5
      onPressed: () => changeThemeMode(!isBright),
    );
  }
}
```

Take a moment to go over the code:

1. The `ThemeButton` widget is initialized with a constructor requiring a function `changeThemeMode` parameter.
2. `changeThemeMode` is a callback function passed as a parameter to be called when the user presses the button. This function notifies the parent widget about the brightness change, enabling it to adjust the theme accordingly.
3. `isBright` is a Boolean that checks whether the current theme brightness is light.

4. An `IconButton` widget that will display light or dark mode icon based on the `isBright` Boolean.

5. `IconButton`, when pressed, toggles the theme brightness by invoking `changeThemeMode`.

Next, you'll create a button for users to select their favorite color to apply the entire app theme.

Creating the Color Button

In **lib/components** directory, create a new file called **color_button.dart** and add the following code to it:

```
import 'package:flutter/material.dart';
import '../constants.dart';

class ColorButton extends StatelessWidget {
  // 1
  const ColorButton({
    super.key,
    required this.changeColor,
    required this.colorSelected,
  });

  // 2
  final void Function(int) changeColor;
  final ColorSelection colorSelected;

  @override
  Widget build(BuildContext context) {
    // 3
    return PopupMenuButton(
      icon: Icon(
        Icons.opacity_outlined,
        color: Theme.of(context).colorScheme.onSurfaceVariant,
      ),
      // 4
      shape: RoundedRectangleBorder(
        borderRadius: BorderRadius.circular(10),
      ),
      // 5
      itemBuilder: (context) {
        // 6
        return List.generate(
          ColorSelection.values.length,
          (index) {
            final currentColor = ColorSelection.values[index];
            // 7
            return PopupMenuItem(
```

```
              value: index,
              enabled: currentColor != colorSelected,
              child: Wrap(
                children: [
                  Padding(
                    padding: const EdgeInsets.only(left: 10),
                    child: Icon(
                      Icons.opacity_outlined,
                      color: currentColor.color,
                    ),
                  ),
                  Padding(
                    padding: const EdgeInsets.only(left: 20),
                    child: Text(currentColor.label),
                  ),],),);},);},
      // 8
      onSelected: changeColor,
    );
  }
}
```

Take a moment to go over the code:

1. Initializes `ColorButton` with the required callback and color.
2. Property `changeColor` is a callback to handle the color selection, and `colorSelected` is the currently selected color.
3. Creates a button that displays a menu.
4. Applies rounded corners to the popup menu.
5. Generates the menu items.
6. Creates a list of color options from `ColorSelection`.
7. Configures each menu item with an icon and text.
8. Calls `changeColor` when an item is selected.

Now that you've created the buttons, it's time to add them to your app.

Adding Action Buttons to the App Bar

In **main.dart** add the following imports:

```
import 'components/theme_button.dart';
import 'components/color_button.dart';
```

Next, locate `// TODO: Add action buttons` and replace it with the following code:

```
actions: [
  ThemeButton(
    changeThemeMode: changeThemeMode,
  ),
  ColorButton(
    changeColor: changeColor,
    colorSelected: colorSelected,
  ),
],
```

With a hot restart, you should see the two new buttons on the top right. Try to switch between light and dark mode and change the color theme.

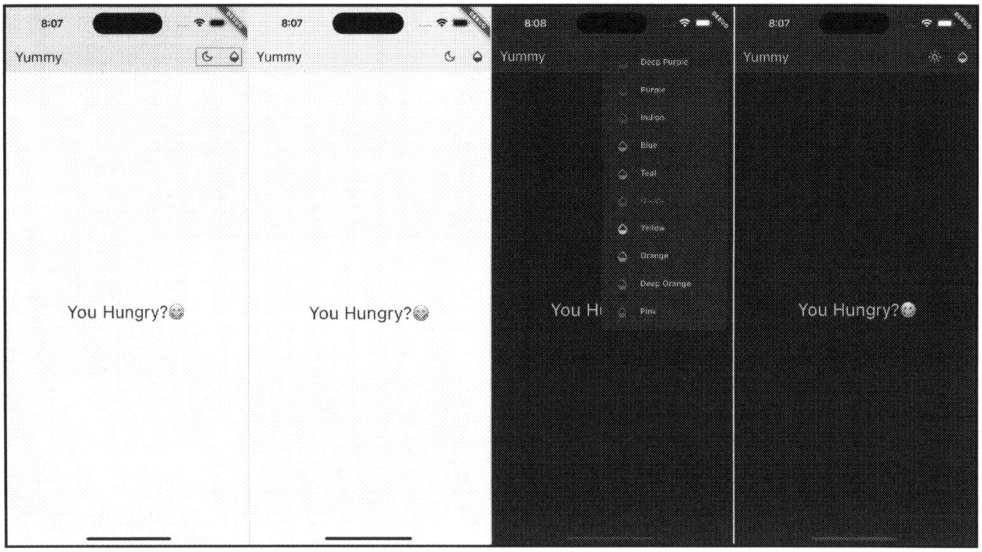

Next, you'll learn about an important aspect of building an app — understanding which app structure to use.

Understanding App Structure and Navigation

Establishing your app's structure from the beginning is important for the user experience. Applying the right navigation structure makes it easy for your users to navigate the information in your app.

Yummy uses the `Scaffold` widget for its starting app structure. `Scaffold` is one of the most commonly used Material widgets in Flutter. Next, you'll learn how to implement it in your app.

Using Scaffold

The `Scaffold` widget implements all your basic visual layout structure needs. It's composed of the following parts:

- AppBar
- BottomSheet
- BottomNavigationBar
- Drawer
- FloatingActionButton
- SnackBar

`Scaffold` has a lot of functionality out of the box!

The following diagram represents some of the previously mentioned items as well as showing left and right nav options:

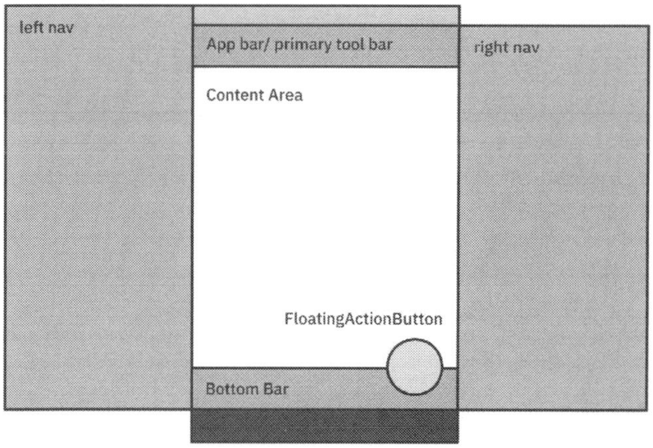

For more information, check out Flutter's documentation on **Material Components widgets**, including app structure and navigation: https://flutter.dev/docs/development/ui/widgets/material

Now, it's time to add more functionality.

Setting Up the Home Widget

As you build large-scale apps, you'll start to compose a staircase of widgets. Widgets composed of other widgets can get really long and messy. It's a good idea to break your widgets into separate files for readability.

To avoid making your code overly complicated, you'll create the first of these separate files now.

Your next step is to move code out of **main.dart** into a new `StatefulWidget` named `Home`. In the **lib** directory, create a new file called **home.dart** and add the following:

```
import 'package:flutter/material.dart';
import 'components/theme_button.dart';
import 'components/color_button.dart';
import 'constants.dart';

class Home extends StatefulWidget {
  const Home({
    super.key,
    required this.changeTheme,
    required this.changeColor,
    required this.colorSelected,
  });

  final void Function(bool useLightMode) changeTheme;
  final void Function(int value) changeColor;
  final ColorSelection colorSelected;

  @override
  State<Home> createState() => _HomeState();
}

class _HomeState extends State<Home> {
  // TODO: Track current tab

  // TODO: Define tab bar destinations

  @override
  Widget build(BuildContext context) {
    // TODO: Define pages

    return Scaffold(
      appBar: AppBar(
        elevation: 4.0,
        backgroundColor:
Theme.of(context).colorScheme.background,
        actions: [
          ThemeButton(
            changeThemeMode: widget.changeTheme,
          ),
```

```
          ColorButton(
            changeColor: widget.changeColor,
            colorSelected: widget.colorSelected,
          ),
        ],
      ),
      // TODO: Switch between pages
      body: Padding(
        padding: const EdgeInsets.all(16.0),
        child: Text(
            'You Hungry?😋',
            style: Theme.of(context).textTheme.displayLarge,
          ),
      ),
      // TODO: Add bottom navigation bar
    );
  }
}
```

You simply copied the **main.dart** `Scaffold` into a new widget in **home.dart**.

> **Note**: Remember if you see your widget tree starting to get too big, it's a good idea to break it apart into separate widgets.

Go back to **main.dart** to update it so it can use the new `Home` widget. At the top, add the following import statement:

```
import 'home.dart';
```

Next, locate `TODO: Apply Home widget` and replace it and the whole `home: Scaffold(...),` with the following:

```
home: Home(
  changeTheme: changeThemeMode,
  changeColor: changeColor,
  colorSelected: colorSelected,
),
```

Finally, remove the following imports in **main.dart**:

```
import 'components/theme_button.dart';
import 'components/color_button.dart';
```

These aren't used anymore. With that done, you'll move on to addressing `Scaffold`'s bottom navigation.

Adding a BottomNavigationBar

Open **home.dart**, locate `// TODO: Track current tab` and replace it with the following:

```
int tab = 0;
```

`tab` property will be used to keep track of the current tab the user is on.

Your next step is to define a list of tabs the user can navigate between. Locate `// TODO: Define tab bar destinations` and replace it with the following code:

```
List<NavigationDestination> appBarDestinations = const [
  NavigationDestination(
    icon: Icon(Icons.credit_card),
    label: 'Category',
    selectedIcon: Icon(Icons.credit_card),
  ),
  NavigationDestination(
    icon: Icon(Icons.credit_card),
    label: 'Post',
    selectedIcon: Icon(Icons.credit_card),
  ),
  NavigationDestination(
    icon: Icon(Icons.credit_card),
    label: 'Restaurant',
    selectedIcon: Icon(Icons.credit_card),
  ),
];
```

You'll have a total of three tabs where you'll create three distinct card widgets.

Finally, locate the comment `// TODO: Add bottom navigation bar` and replace it with the following:

```
// 1
bottomNavigationBar: NavigationBar(
  // 2
  selectedIndex: tab,
  // 3
  onDestinationSelected: (index) {
    setState(() {
      tab = index;
    });
  },
  // 4
  destinations: appBarDestinations,
),
```

Here's how the code works:

1. Assigns `NavigationBar` to `bottomNavigationBar`.
2. Sets the active `tab` using `selectedIndex`.
3. Updates the active tab on user selection.
4. Defines the list of tabs with `appBarDestinations`.

With that complete, your app should look like this:

Now that you've set up the bottom navigation bar, you need to implement the navigation between pages.

Navigating Between Pages

To navigate between pages, you first need to define the list of pages the user may potentially navigate to. Still in **home.dart**, locate the comment `// TODO: Define pages` and replace it with the following:

```
final pages = [
  // TODO: Replace with Category Card
  Container(color: Colors.red),
  // TODO: Replace with Post Card
```

```
    Container(color: Colors.green),
    // TODO: Replace with Restaurant Landscape Card
    Container(color: Colors.blue)
  ];
```

This contains a list of containers with different colors. You'll replace each one with a unique card soon.

Next, locate the comment `// TODO: Switch between pages` and replace it and all the `body: Padding(...)` code with the following:

```
  body: IndexedStack(
    index: tab,
    children: pages,
  ),
```

`IndexedStack` stacks and displays one widget from pages based on the tab index, preserving the state of all widgets in the stack.

After restarting, your app will look different for each tab item, like this:

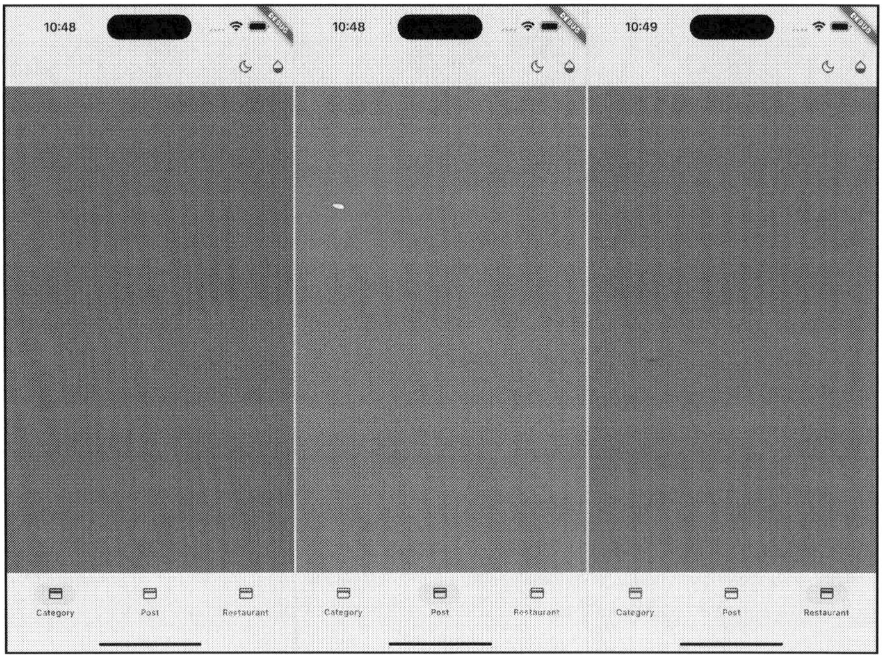

Now that you've set up your tab navigation, it's time to create beautiful cards!

Creating Custom Cards

In this section, you'll compose three cards by combining a mixture of display and layout widgets.

> **Note**: To help construct these cards, the **models** folder already contains models and mock data for each model to use to display in your custom widgets. Have a look at **food_category.dart**, **post.dart**, and **restaurant.dart** to learn more!

Display widgets handle what the user sees onscreen. Examples of display widgets include:

- Text
- Image
- Button

Layout widgets help with the arrangement of widgets. Examples of layout widgets include:

- Container
- Padding
- Stack
- Column
- SizedBox
- Row

> **Note**: Flutter has a plethora of layout widgets to choose from, but this chapter only covers the most common. For more examples, check out https://flutter.dev/docs/development/ui/widgets/layout.

Composing Category Card

The first card you'll compose looks like this:

`CategoryCard` is composed of the following widgets:

- `Card`: A material design container that holds content and actions about a single subject.
- `Column`: Vertically arranges its widget children, here, a `StackandListTile`.
- `ListTile`: A widget that contains title and subtitle text.

In the **lib/components** directory, create a new file called **category_card.dart** and add the following code to it:

```
import 'package:flutter/material.dart';
import '../models/food_category.dart';

class CategoryCard extends StatelessWidget {
  // 1
  final FoodCategory category;

  const CategoryCard({
    super.key,
    required this.category,
  });

  @override
  Widget build(BuildContext context) {
    // TODO: Get text theme
```

```
    // TODO: Replace with Card widget
    return Container(); // 2
  }
}
```

Here you set up the basic structure for the `CategoryCard` widget.

1. It simply takes in a `FoodCategory` object, which you'll use later to display data in your UI.
2. Returns an empty `Container`.

Next, open **home.dart** and add the following import:

```
import 'components/category_card.dart';
import 'models/food_category.dart';
```

Locate `// TODO: Replace with Category Card` and replace the first container with the following:

```
// 1
Center(
  // 2
  child: ConstrainedBox(
    constraints: const BoxConstraints(maxWidth: 300),
    // 3
    child: CategoryCard(category: categories[0]),),),
```

Take a moment to go over how `CategoryCard` is laid out on the page.

1. `Center` widget ensures the card widget is centered on the screen.
2. Applies a maximum width of 300 pixels to the card widget.
3. Set `CategoryCard` widget as the child, and pass the first mock category to be displayed.

You've now set up `CategoryCard`. Hot restart and the app will currently look like this:

It's a little bland, isn't it? For your next step, you'll spice it up with an image.

Constructing the Widget

Switch to **category_card.dart**. Locate `// TODO: Get text theme` and replace it with the following:

```
final textTheme = Theme.of(context)
    .textTheme
    .apply(displayColor:
Theme.of(context).colorScheme.onSurface);
```

Here, you get the text theme, which you'll later use to apply to text widgets.

Next, locate `// TODO: Replace with Card widget` and replace it and the code below with the following:

```
// 1
return Card(
  // 2
```

```
    child: Column(
      mainAxisSize: MainAxisSize.min,
      children: [
        // TODO: Add Stack Widget
        // TODO: Add ListTile widget
      ],
    ),
  );
```

You replace the `Container` widget with a `Card` widget, and within the card, you use a `Column` widget to vertically arrange the child widgets.

Adding Stacked Elements to the Card

Adding the first widget to the column. Locate `// TODO: Add Stack Widget` and replace it with the following:

```
Stack(
  children: [
    // 1
    ClipRRect(
      borderRadius: const BorderRadius.vertical(
        top: Radius.circular(8.0)),
      child: Image.asset(category.imageUrl),
    ),
    // 2
    Positioned(
      left: 16.0,
      top: 16.0,
      child: Text(
        'Yummy',
        style: textTheme.headlineLarge,
      ),
    ),
    // 3
    Positioned(
      bottom: 16.0,
      right: 16.0,
      child: RotatedBox(
        quarterTurns: 1,
        child: Text(
          'Smoothies',
          style: textTheme.headlineLarge,
        ),
      ),
    ),
  ],
),
```

Recall that the `Stack` widget allows you to overlay widgets on top of each other.

Here's what's overlayed in the stack:

1. Add a `ClipRRect` widget, which clips the image with rounded corners at the top.
2. Position the text "Yummy" on the top-left.
3. Rotate the text "Smoothies" 90 degrees and place it at the bottom-right.

After a hot restart, the `CategoryCard` now look like this:

Adding a Footer to the Card

Adding the second widget to the column. Locate `// TODO: Add ListTile widget` and replace it with the following:

```
ListTile(
  // 1
  title: Text(
```

```
        category.name,
        style: textTheme.titleSmall,),
    // 2
    subtitle: Text(
        '${category.numberOfRestaurants} places',
        style: textTheme.bodySmall,),),
```

Take a moment to go over the code:

1. Display the category name with a smaller title style.
2. Display the number of restaurants in a small body text style

After these updates, the final `CategoryCard` looks like this:

Great, you finished the first card! It's time to move on to the next!

> **Tip**: Leverage Material 3's typography text theme for consistent text styles across your app, avoiding hardcoded font sizes and colors.

Composing Post Card

It's time to start composing the next card, the post card. Here's how it will look by the time you're done:

`PostCard` is composed of the following widgets:

- `Card`: Provides a material design card that can hold related pieces of information or content.
- `Padding`: Adds a uniform padding of 16.0 pixels around the content inside it to provide some spacing.

This structure ensures a clean, organized layout where the user's avatar is displayed alongside their post content, with the post comment and timestamp neatly presented below it.

In the **lib/components** directory, create a new file called **post_card.dart**. Add the following code:

```
import 'package:flutter/material.dart';
import '../models/post.dart';

class PostCard extends StatelessWidget {
  final Post post;

  const PostCard({
    super.key,
    required this.post,
  });

  @override
  Widget build(BuildContext context) {
    final textTheme = Theme.of(context)
        .textTheme
        .apply(
          displayColor: Theme.of(context).colorScheme.onSurface,
        );

    return Card(
      child: Padding(
        padding: const EdgeInsets.all(16.0),
```

```
          child: Row(
            crossAxisAlignment: CrossAxisAlignment.start,
            children: [
              // TODO: Add CircleAvatar
              // TODO: Add spacing
              // TODO: Add Expanded Widget
            ],
          ),
        ),
      );
    }
  }
```

Here, you set up the basic structure for the `PostCard` widget. It simply takes in a `Post` object, which you'll use later to display data in your UI.

Next, open **home.dart** and add the following import:

```
import 'components/post_card.dart';
import 'models/post.dart';
```

Locate `// TODO: Replace with Post Card` and replace the container beneath it with the following:

```
Center(child: Padding(
  padding: const EdgeInsets.all(16.0),
  child: PostCard(post: posts[0]),
),),
```

Then, perform a hot restart.

Tap the **Post** tab bar item. Your app should look like this:

Adding the Child Widgets

Here's how PostCard's layout will look after you've added the Row's children widgets:

In **post_card.dart** locate `// TODO: Add CircleAvatar`, and replace it with the following:

```
CircleAvatar(
  radius: 25,
  backgroundImage: AssetImage(post.profileImageUrl),
),
```

`CircleAvatar` is often used to display a profile image or user's avatar in a circular shape.

Next, locate `// TODO: Add spacing` and replace it with the following:

```
const SizedBox(
  width: 16.0,
),
```

Add 16-pixel padding between the two widgets.

Finally, locate `// TODO: Add Expanded Widget` and replace it with the following:

```
// 1
Expanded(
  // 2
  child: Column(
    mainAxisSize: MainAxisSize.min,
    crossAxisAlignment: CrossAxisAlignment.start,
    children: [
      // 3
      Text(
        post.comment,
        maxLines: 2,
        overflow: TextOverflow.ellipsis,
        style: textTheme.titleMedium),
      Text(
        '${post.timestamp} mins ago',
        style: textTheme.bodySmall,
      ),],),),
```

Here's what you've added:

1. `Expanded` widget makes the child occupy all available space.
2. `Column` widget vertically stacks children. `MainAxisSize.min` aligns them to occupy minimum space. `CrossAxisAlignment.start` horizontally aligns the child widgets to the left side.
3. Display two `Text` widgets, the post contents followed by the post's timestamp.

After a hot restart, your `PostCard` widget should look like this:

And that's all you need to do for the post card. Next, you'll move on to the final one.

Composing Restaurant Landscape Card

`RestaurantLandscapeCard` is the last card you'll create for this chapter. This card lets the user explore popular restaurant trends and order food.

The following widgets compose `RestaurantLandscapeCard`:

- `Card`: A material design card that contains related pieces of information.
- `Column`: Arranges its children widgets in a vertical line.
- `ClipRRect`: Clips its child with a rounded rectangle border.
- `AspectRatio`: Constrains the child's aspect ratio.
- `Image`: Displays the restaurant's image, covering the available space.
- `ListTile`: A widget that contains title and subtitle text.

In the **lib/components** directory, create a new file called **restaurant_landscape_card.dart**. Add the following code:

```
import 'package:flutter/material.dart';

import '../models/restaurant.dart';

class RestaurantLandscapeCard extends StatelessWidget {
  final Restaurant restaurant;

  const RestaurantLandscapeCard({
    super.key,
    required this.restaurant,
  });

  @override
  Widget build(BuildContext context) {
    final textTheme = Theme.of(context)
        .textTheme
        .apply(
          displayColor: Theme.of(context)
          .colorScheme
          .onSurface);
    return Card(
      child: Column(
        mainAxisSize: MainAxisSize.min,
        children: [
          // TODO: Add Image
          // TODO: Add ListTile
        ],),),);}}
```

Here, you set up the basic structure for the `RestaurantLandscapeCard` widget. It simply takes in an instance of `Restaurant`, which you'll use later to display data in your UI.

Next, open **home.dart** and add the following import:

```
import 'components/restaurant_landscape_card.dart';
import 'models/restaurant.dart';
```

Locate `// TODO: Replace with Restaurant Landscape Card` and replace the container beneath it with the following:

```
// 1
Center(
  //2
  child: ConstrainedBox(
    constraints: const BoxConstraints(maxWidth: 400),
    // 3
    child: RestaurantLandscapeCard(
      restaurant: restaurants[0],),),),
```

Take a moment to go over how `RestaurantLandscapeCard` is laid out on the page:

1. `Center` widget ensures the card widget is centered on the screen.
2. Applies a maximum width of 400 pixels to the card widget.
3. Set `RestaurantLandscapeCard` widget as the child, and pass the first mock restaurant to be displayed.

Now you've set up `RestaurantLandscapeCard`, perform a hot restart. Tap the **Restaurant** tab bar item.

Your app should look like this:

Composing Restaurant’s Child Widgets

Open **restaurant_landscape_card.dart**, locate `// TODO: Add Image` and replace it with the following:

```
ClipRRect(
  // 1
  borderRadius:
      const BorderRadius.vertical(top: Radius.circular(8.0),),
  // 2
  child: AspectRatio(
      aspectRatio: 2,
      child: Image.asset(restaurant.imageUrl, fit:
BoxFit.cover,),),),
```

Here is how the image is formed:

1. `borderRadius` rounds the top corners with an 8.0 unit radius.
2. `AspectRatio` displays an image with a 2:1 width-to-height ratio. The image scales to fit its container.

Next, locate `// TODO: Add ListTile` and replace it with the following:

```
ListTile(
  // 1
  title: Text(restaurant.name, style: textTheme.titleSmall,),
  // 2
  subtitle: Text(restaurant.attributes,
      maxLines: 1, style: textTheme.bodySmall,),
  // 3
  onTap: () {
    // ignore: avoid_print
    print('Tap on ${restaurant.name}');
  },),
```

The code represents a `ListTile` in Flutter:

1. `title` shows the restaurant's name with a specific style.
2. `subtitle` displays the restaurant's attributes, truncated if more than one line.
3. `onTap` prints the restaurant's name to the console when tapped.

Save your changes and hot restart. Now, your card looks like this:

Now that `Yummy` is a `StatefulWidget` you can add back the `const` declarations. Open **main.dart** and change:

```
runApp(Yummy());
```

to

```
runApp(const Yummy());
```

Then change:

```
Yummy({super.key});
```

to

```
const Yummy({super.key});
```

When you finish your app, there is one last step - remove the **Debug** label.

Still in **main.dart** find `// Uncomment to remove Debug banner` and remove the `//` at the beginning of the line. Hot restart your app, and the banner is gone.

You did it! You've finished this chapter. Along the way, you've applied three different categories of widgets. You learned how to use structural widgets to organize different screens, and you created three custom cards and applied different widget layouts to each.

Well done!

Key Points

- Three main categories of widgets are: structure and navigation, displaying information, and positioning widgets.
- There are two main visual design systems available in Flutter, **Material** and **Cupertino**. They help you build apps that look native on Android and iOS, respectively.
- Using the **Material** theme, you can build quite varied user interface elements to give your app a custom look and feel.
- It's generally a good idea to establish a common theme object for your app, giving you a single source of truth for your app's style.
- The **Scaffold** widget implements all your basic visual layout structure needs.
- The **Container** widget can be used to group other widgets together.
- The **Stack** widget layers child widgets on top of each other.

Where to Go From Here?

There's a wealth of Material Design widgets to play with, not to mention other types of widgets — too many to cover in a single chapter.

Fortunately, the Flutter team created a Widget UI component library that shows how each widget works! Check it out here: https://gallery.flutter.dev/

In this chapter, you got started right off with using widgets to build a nice user interface. In the next chapter, you'll dive into the theory of widgets to help you better understand how to use them.

Chapter 4: Understanding Widgets

By Vincent Ngo

You may have heard that everything in Flutter is a widget. While that might not be absolutely true, most of the time when you're building apps, you only see the top layer: **widgets**. In this chapter, you'll dive into widget theory. You'll explore:

- Widgets
- Widget rendering
- Flutter Inspector
- Types of widgets
- Widget lifecycle

It's time to jump in!

> **Note**: This chapter is mostly theoretical. You'll make just a few code changes to the project near the end of the chapter.

What Is a Widget?

A **widget** is a building block for your user interface. Using widgets is like combining Legos. Like Legos, you can mix and match widgets to create something amazing.

Flutter's declarative nature makes it super easy to build a UI with widgets. A widget is a blueprint for displaying the **state** of your app.

UI = f (state)

Screen Build

You can think of widgets as a function of UI. Given a state, the `build()` method of a widget constructs the widget UI.

Unboxing CategoryCard

In the previous chapter, you created three cards. Now, you'll look at the widgets that compose `CategoryCard` in more detail:

Do you remember which widgets you used to build this card?

Recall that the card consists of the following:

- **Card widget**: A material design container that wraps the content.
- **Column widget**: Organizes content vertically, with a Stack for images and texts and a ListTile for category details.
- **Stack widget**: Overlays multiple widgets, used here to layer the image with two pieces of text.
- **ClipRRect widget**: Provides rounded corners for the image.
- **Image widget**: Loads the image.
- **Positioned widget**: Positions "Yummy" and "Smoothies" texts over the image.

- **Text widget**: Displays text from category details and static labels.
- **RotatedBox widget**: Rotates the text by 90°.
- **ListTile widget**: Displays the category's name and number of associated restaurants.

Widget Trees

Every widget contains a `build()` method. In this method, you create a UI composition by nesting widgets within other widgets. This forms a tree-like data structure. Each widget can contain other widgets, commonly called **children**. Below is a visualization of `CategoryCard`'s widget tree:

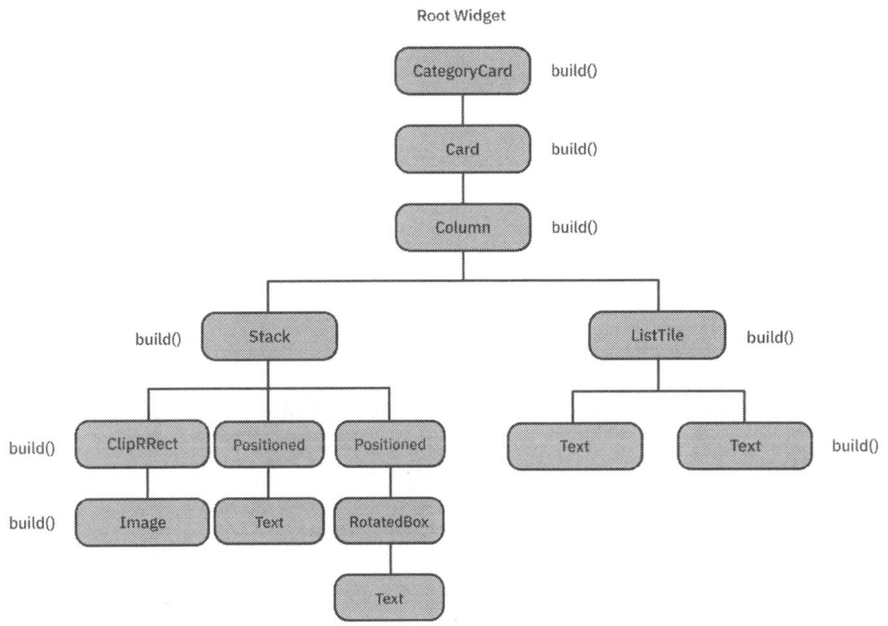

The widget tree provides a blueprint that describes how you want to lay out your UI. The framework traverses the nodes in the tree and calls each `build()` method to compose your entire UI.

Rendering Widgets

In Chapter 1, "Getting Started," you learned that Flutter's architecture contains three layers:

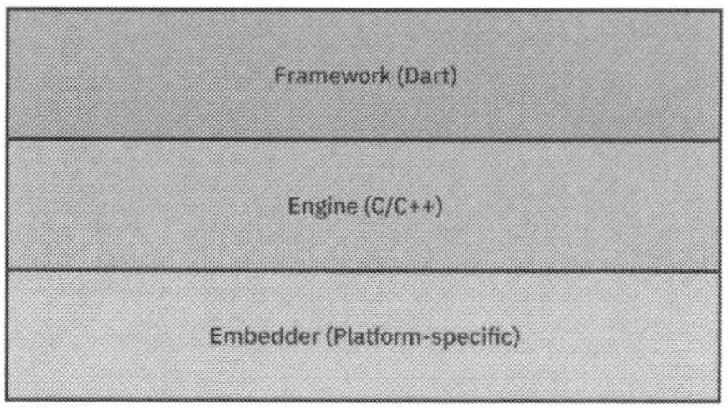

In this chapter, you'll focus on the **framework layer**. You can break this layer into four parts:

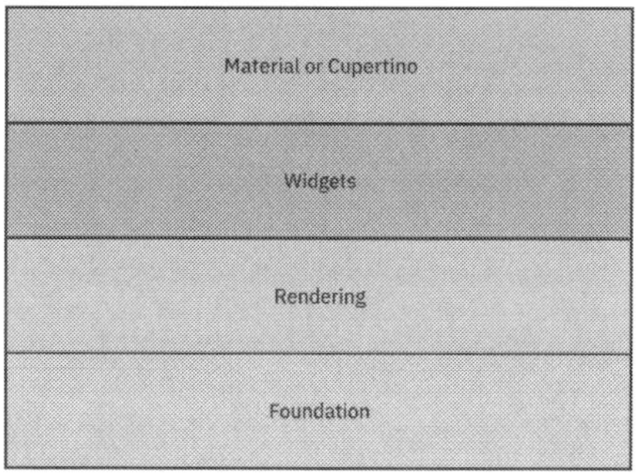

- **Material** and **Cupertino** are UI control libraries built on top of the widget layer. They make your UI look and feel like Android and iOS apps, respectively.
- The **Widgets** layer is a composition abstraction on widgets. It contains all the primitive classes needed to create UI controls. Check out the official documentation here: https://api.flutter.dev/flutter/widgets/widgets-library.html.
- The **Rendering** layer is a layout abstraction that draws and handles the widget's layout. Imagine having to recompute every widget's coordinates and frames manually. Yuck!
- **Foundation**, also known as the **dart:ui** layer, contains core libraries that handle animation, painting and gestures.

Three Trees

Flutter's framework actually manages not one, but three trees in parallel:

- Widget Tree
- Element Tree
- RenderObject Tree

Here's how a single widget works under the hood:

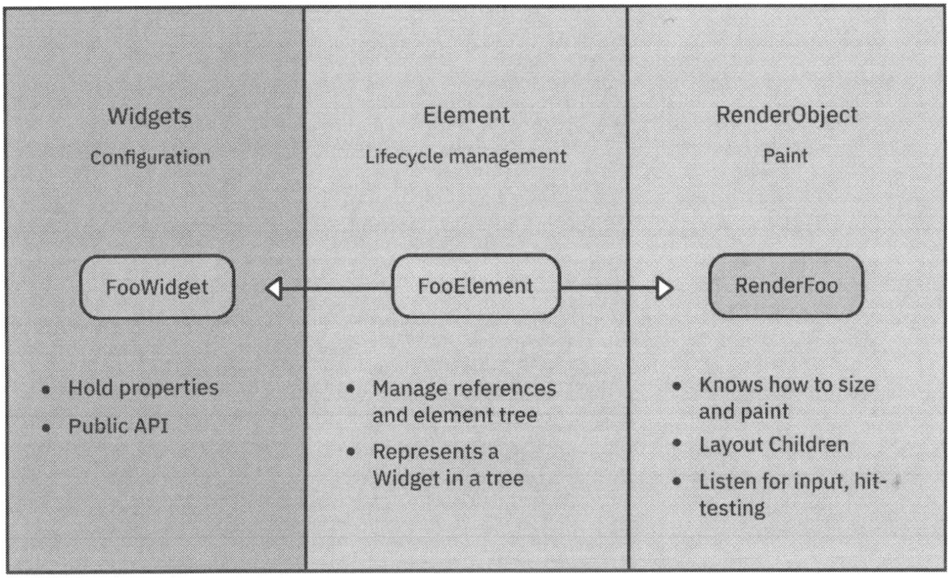

- **Widget**: The public API or blueprint for the framework. Developers usually just deal with this layer.
- **Element**: Manages a widget and a widget's render object. For every widget instance in the tree, there is a corresponding element.
- **RenderObject**: Responsible for drawing and laying out a specific widget instance. Also handles user interactions, like hit-testing and gestures.

Types of Elements

There are two types of elements:

- **ComponentElement**: A type of element composed of other elements. This corresponds to composing widgets inside other widgets.
- **RenderObjectElement**: A type of element that holds a render object.

You can think of **ComponentElement** as a group of elements and **RenderObjectElement** as a single element. Remember that each element contains a render object to perform widget painting, layout and hit testing.

Example Trees for CategoryCard

The image below shows an example of the three trees for the `CategoryCard` widget:

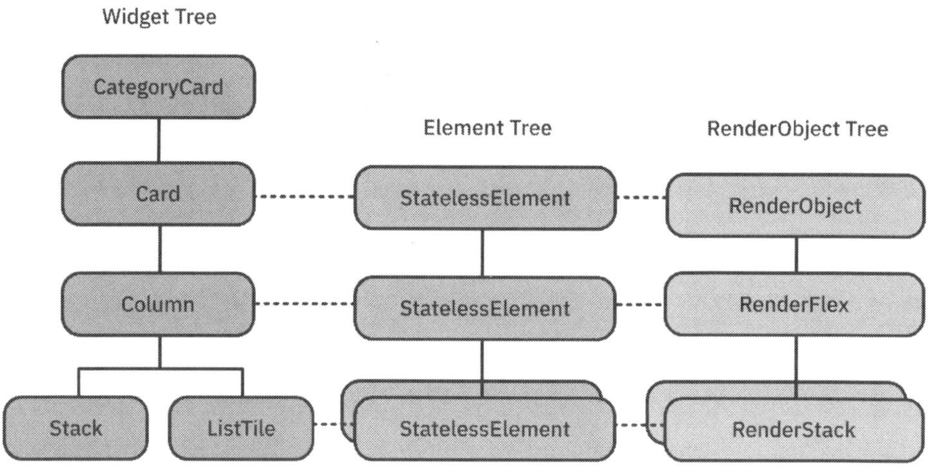

As you saw in previous chapters, Flutter starts to build your app by calling `runApp()`. Every widget's `build()` method then composes a subtree of widgets. Flutter creates a corresponding **element** for each widget in the widget tree.

The element tree manages each widget instance and associates a render object to tell the framework how to render a particular widget.

> **Note**: For more details on Flutter widget rendering, check out the Flutter team's talk they gave in China on how to render widgets: https://youtu.be/996ZgFRENMs.

Getting Started

Open the **starter** project in Android Studio, run `flutter pub get` if necessary, and then run the app. You'll see the **Yummy** app from the previous chapter:

Next, open **DevTools** by tapping the **blue Dart** icon, as shown below:

DevTools will open in your browser.

Note: It works best with the Google Chrome web browser. Click the ⚙ icon to switch between dark and light mode.

Select a widget on the left to see its layout on the right.

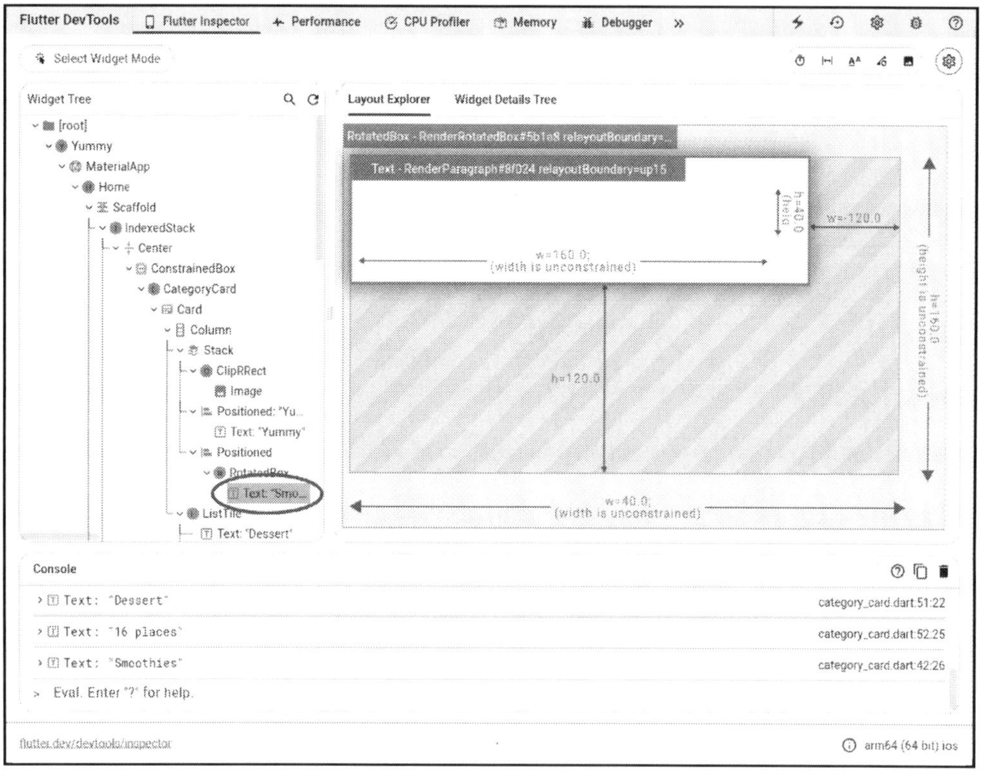

DevTools Overview

DevTools provides all kinds of awesome tools to help you debug your Flutter app. These include:

- **Flutter Inspector**: Used to explore and debug the widget tree.
- **Performance**: Allows you to analyze Flutter frame charts, timeline events and CPU profiler.
- **CPU Profiler**: Allows you to record and profile your Flutter app session.
- **Memory**: Shows how objects in Dart are allocated, which helps find memory leaks.
- **Debugger**: Supports breakpoints and variable inspection on the call stack. Also allows you to step through code right within DevTools.
- **Network**: Allows you to inspect HTTP, HTTPS and web socket traffic within your Flutter app.
- **Logging**: Displays events fired on the Dart runtime and app-level log events.
- **App Size**: Helps you analyze your total app size.

There are many different tools to play with, but in this chapter, you'll only look at the **Flutter Inspector**. For information about how the other tools work, check out:https://flutter.dev/docs/development/tools/devtools/overview.

Flutter Inspector

The Flutter Inspector has four key benefits. It helps you:

- Visualize your widget tree.
- Inspect the properties of a specific widget in the tree.
- Experiment with different layout configurations using the **Layout Explorer**.
- Enable slow animation to show how your transitions look.

Flutter Inspector tools

Here are some of the important tools to use with the Flutter Inspector.

- **Select Widget Mode**: When enabled, this allows you to tap a particular widget on a device or simulator to inspect its properties.

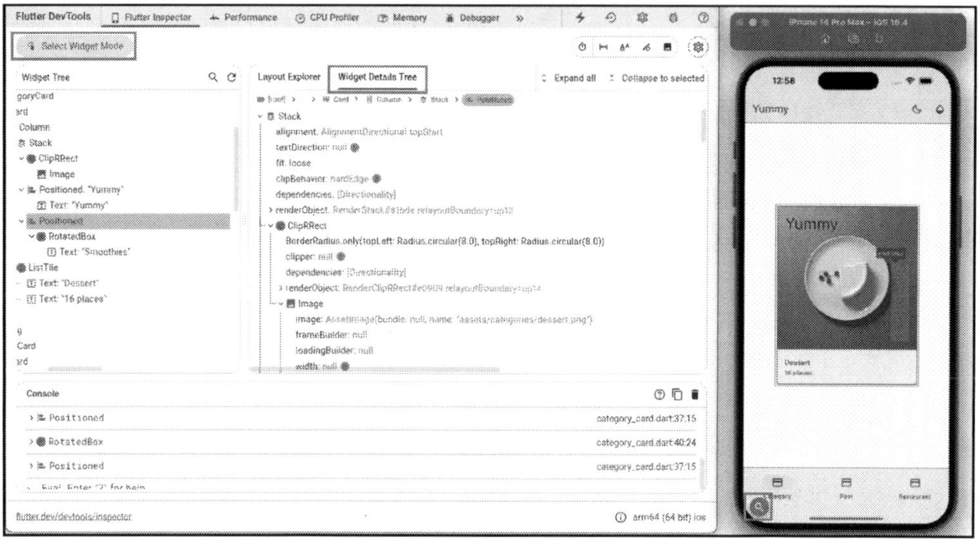

Clicking any element in the widget tree also highlights the widget on the device and jumps to the exact line of code. How cool is that!

- **Refresh Tree**: Simply reloads the current widget's info.

Depending on if your browser is expanded or collapsed, you'll see one of the following toolsets.

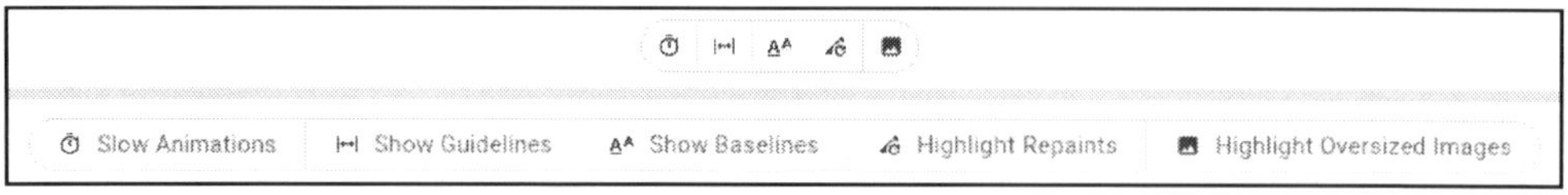

Look at each tool to see how it can help you identify issues.

- **Slow Animation**: Slows down the animation so you can visually inspect the UI transitions.

- **Show Guidelines**: Shows visual debugging hints. That allows you to check your widgets' borders, paddings and alignment.

Here's a screenshot of how guidelines look on a device:

- **Show Baselines**: When enabled, this tells `RenderBox` to paint a line under each text's baseline.

Here, you can see the green line under the baseline of each `Text` widget:

- **Highlight Repaints**: Adds a random border to a widget every time Flutter repaints it. This is useful if you want to find unnecessary repaints.

If you feel bored, you can spice things up by enabling disco mode, as shown below:

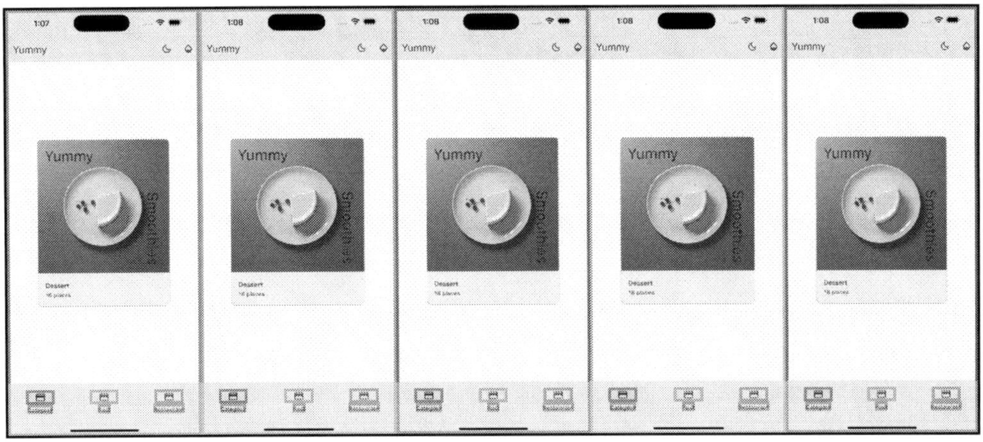

- **Highlight Oversized Images**: Tells you which images in your app are oversized.

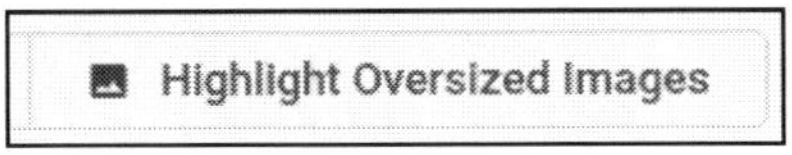

If an image is oversized, it'll invert the image's colors and flip it upside down. As shown below:

Inspecting the Widget Tree

In the emulator, select the first tab, then click **Refresh Tree** in the DevTools. Finally, select `CategoryCard` and click **Widget Details Tree** tab, as shown below:

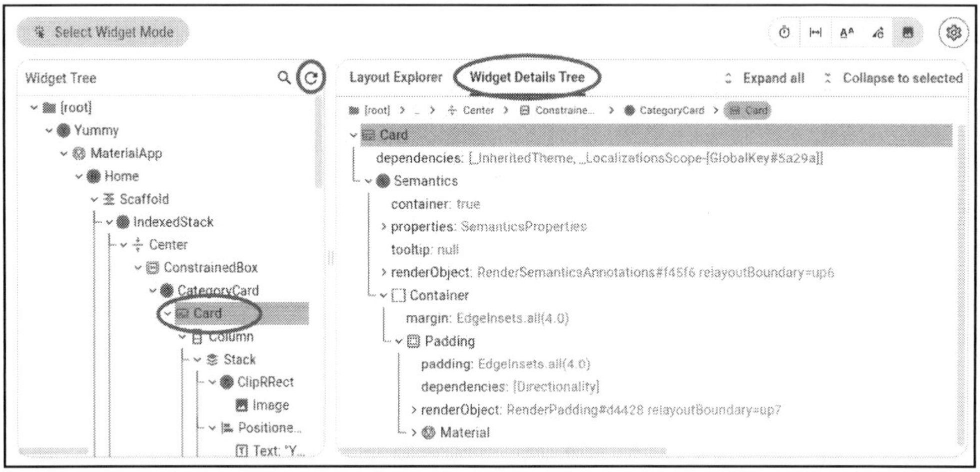

Note that:

- In the left panel, there's a portion of the Flutter widget tree under investigation, starting from the root.
- When you tap a specific widget in the tree, you can inspect its sub-tree, as shown in the **Widget Details Tree** tab on the right panel.
- The Details Tree represents the element tree and displays all the important properties that make up the widget. Notice that it references **renderObject**.

The **Details Tree** is a great way for you to inspect and experiment with how a specific widget property works.

Click a `Text` widget, and you'll see all the properties you can configure:

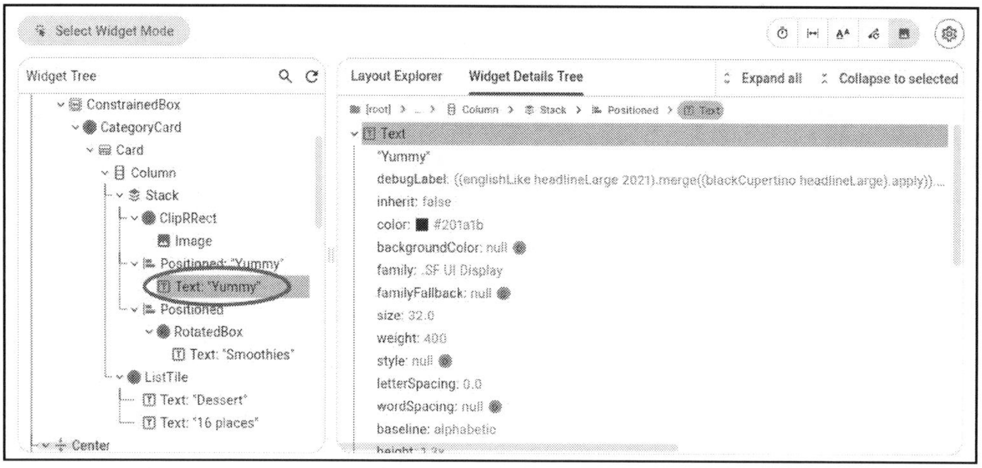

How useful is this? You can examine all the properties, and if something doesn't make sense, you can pull up the Flutter widget documentation to read more about that property!

Inspecting Like a Pro

Besides checking the properties in **Details Tree**, you can evaluate your widgets in two other ways:

- Hover over any widget, and it'll show a pop-up with all the properties.
- Click on a widget to print the widget's object, properties and state in the console.

As shown below:

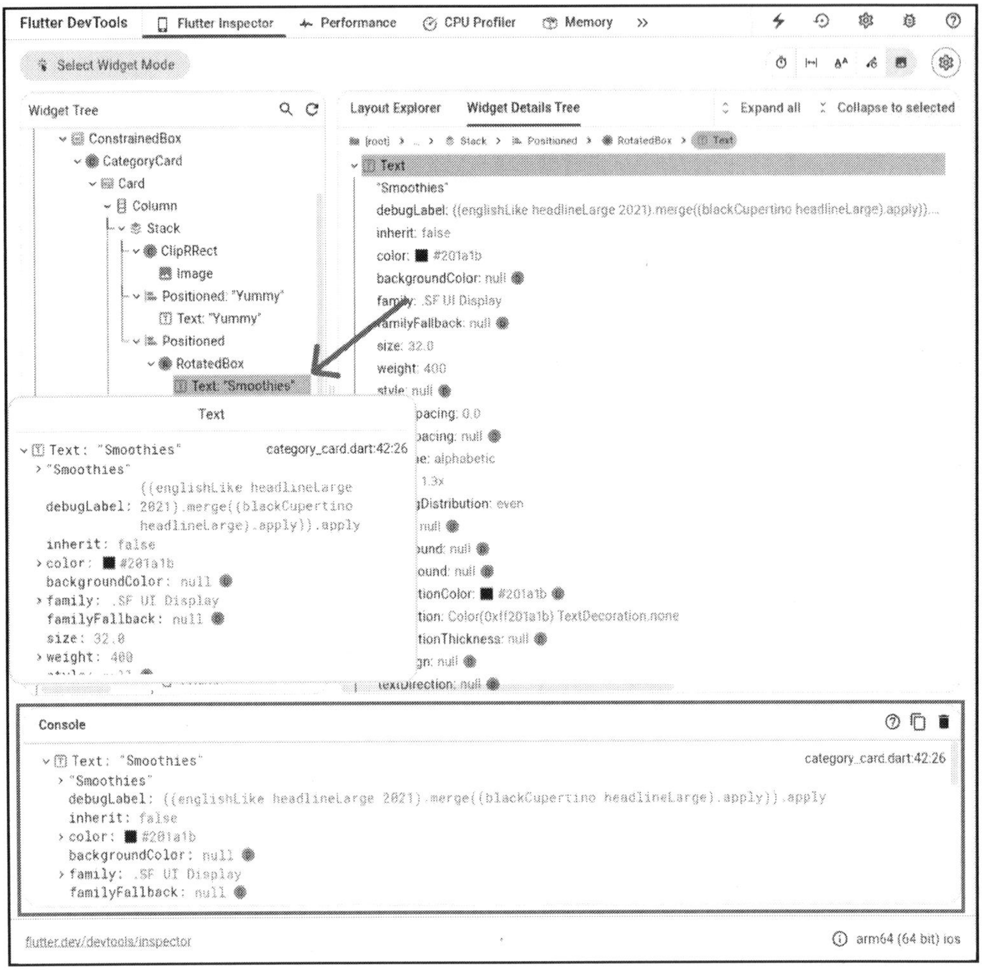

Layout Explorer

Next, click the **Layout Explorer** tab, as shown below:

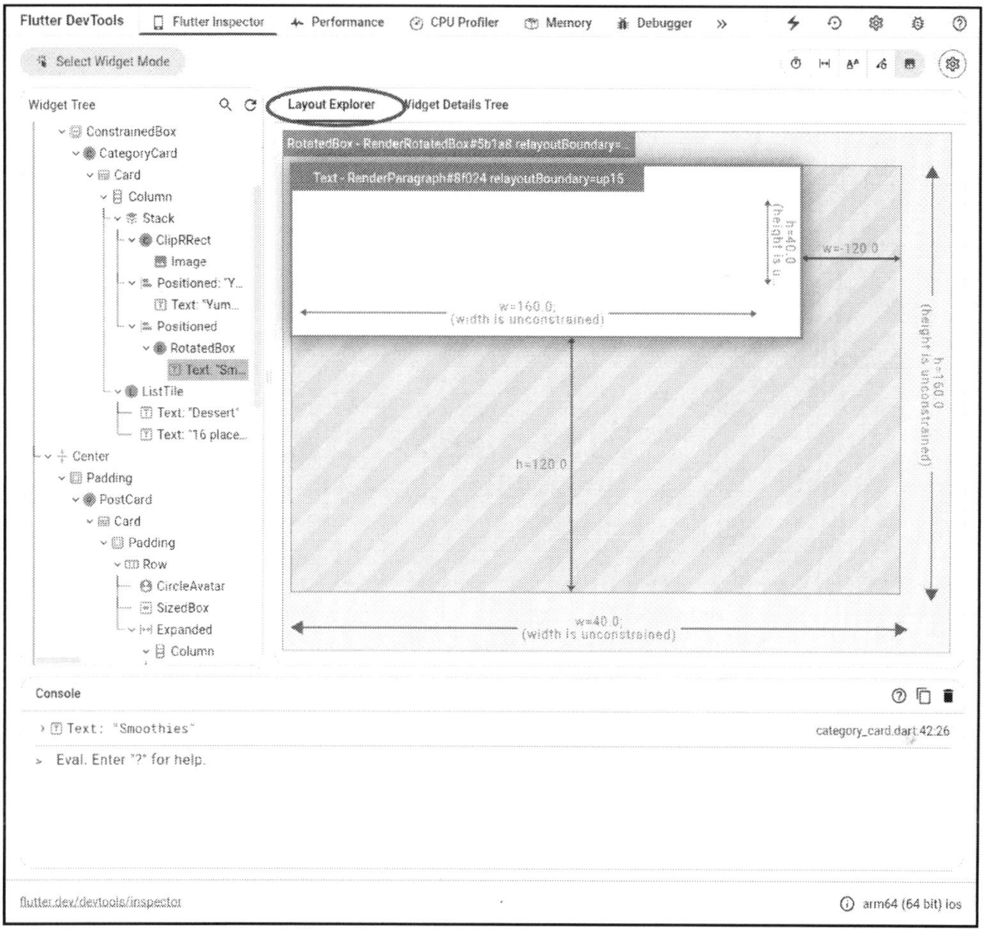

You can use the Layout Explorer to visualize how your `Text` widget is laid out within the `Stack`.

Next, follow these instructions:

1. Make sure your device is running, and DevTools is open in your browser.
2. Click **Post** in the bottom navigation bar.
3. Click the **Refresh Tree** button.
4. Select the **Row** element in the tree.
5. Click **Layout Explorer**.

You'll see the following:

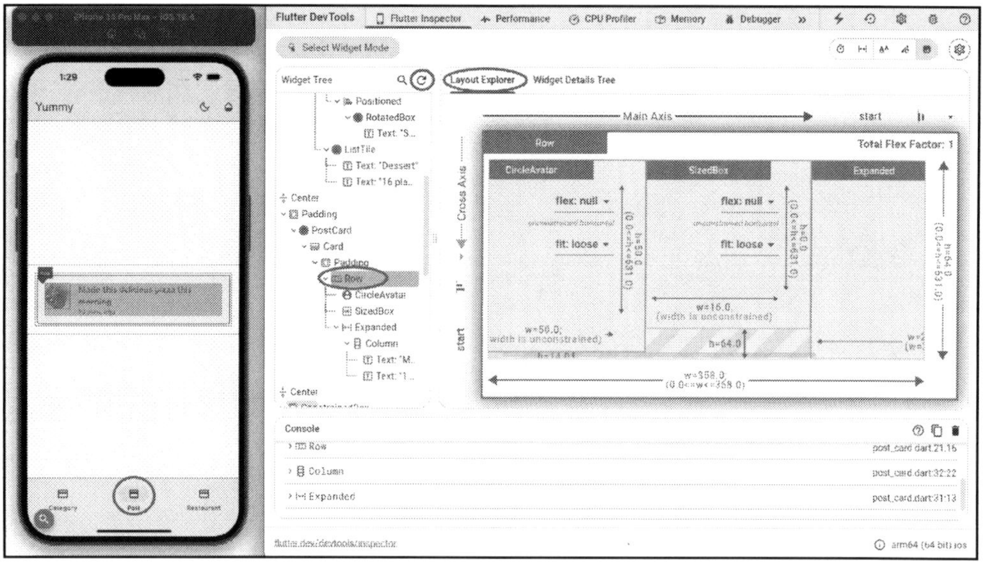

The Layout Explorer is handy for modifying flex widget layouts in real-time.

The explorer supports modifying:

- `mainAxisAlignment`
- `crossAxisAlignment`
- `flex`
- `fit`

Click **start** within the **Cross Axis** and change the value to **stretch**. Notice that the `PostCard` widget stretches the entire screen:

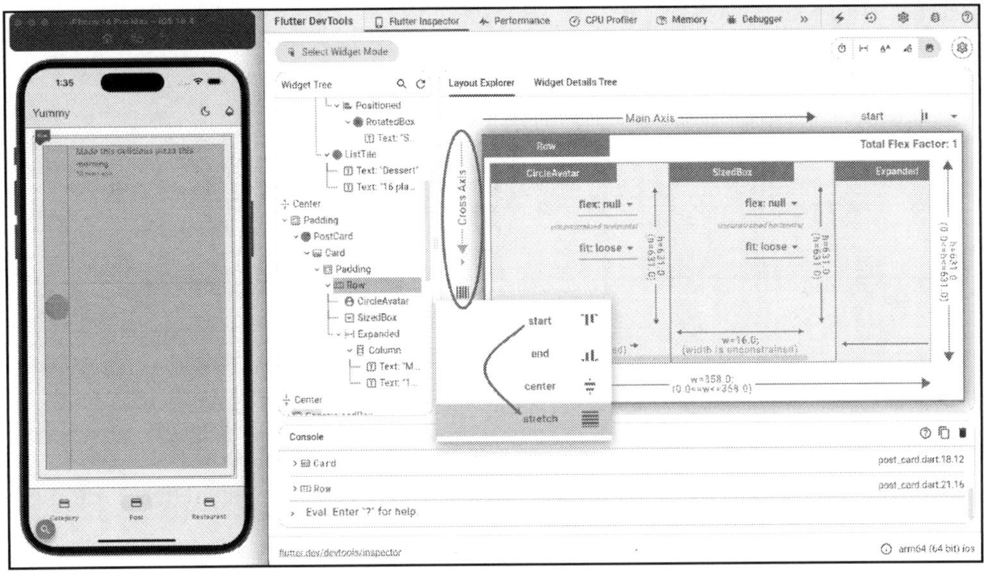

This is useful when you need to inspect and tweak layouts at runtime.

Feel free to experiment and play around with the Layout Explorer. You can create simple column or row widgets to mess around with the layout axis.

You now have all the tools you need to debug widgets! In the next section, you'll learn about the types of widgets and when to use them.

Learning the Types of Widgets

There are three major types of widgets: **Stateless**, **Stateful** and **Inherited**. All widgets are immutable, but some have a state attached to them using their element. You'll learn more about the differences between these next.

Stateless Widgets

The state or properties of a stateless widget can't be altered once it's built. When your properties don't need to change over time, it's generally a good idea to start with a stateless widget.

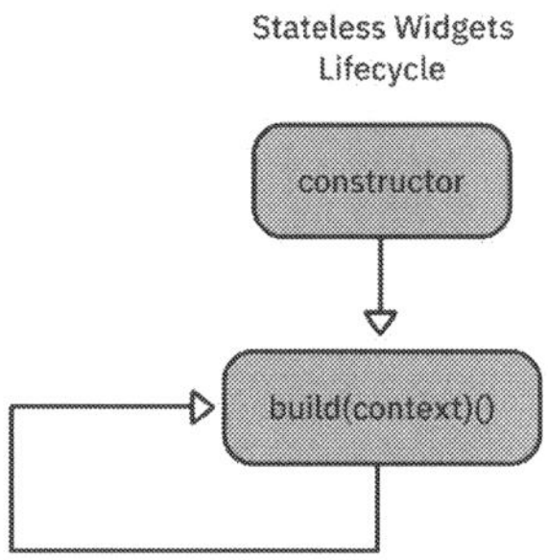

The lifecycle of a stateless widget starts with a constructor, which you can pass parameters to, and a `build()` method, which you override. The visual description of the widget is determined by the `build()` method.

The following events trigger this kind of widget to update:

- The widget is inserted into the widget tree for the first time.
- The state of a dependency or inherited widget — ancestor nodes — changes.

Stateful Widgets

Stateful widgets preserve state, which is useful when parts of your UI need to change dynamically.

For example, one good time to use a stateful widget is when a user taps a **Favorite** button to toggle a simple Boolean value on and off.

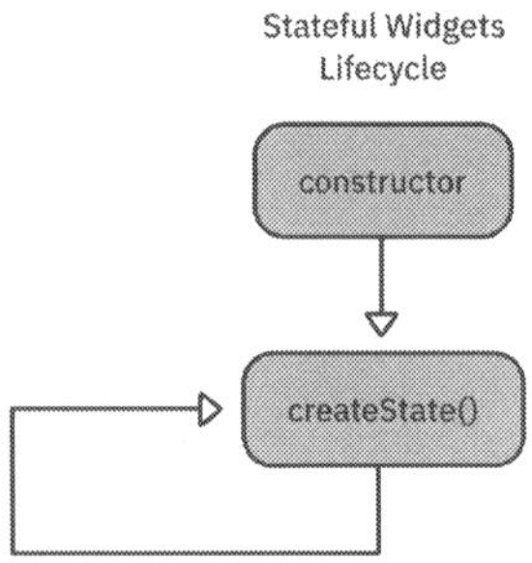

Stateful widgets store their mutable state in a separate `State` class. That's why every stateful widget must override and implement `createState()`.

Next, take a look at the stateful widget's lifecycle.

State Object Lifecycle

Every widget's `build()` method takes a `BuildContext` as an argument. The build context tells you where you are in the tree of widgets. You can access the **element** for any widget through the `BuildContext`. Later, you'll see why the build context is important, especially for accessing state information from parent widgets.

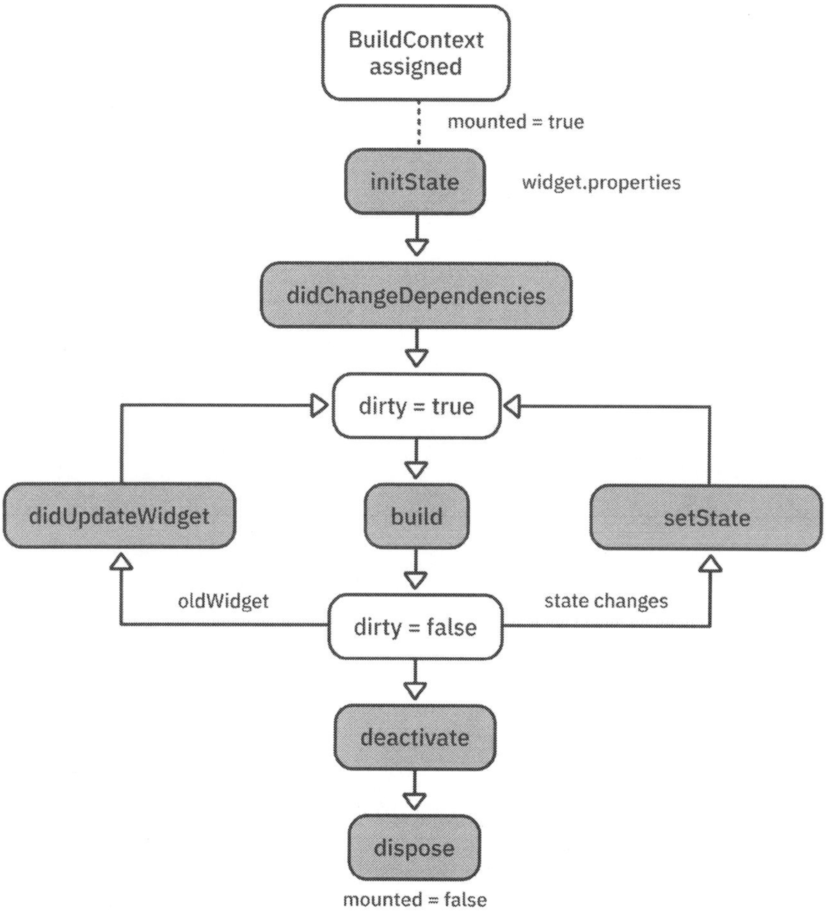

Now, take a closer look at the lifecycle:

1. When you assign the build context to the widget, an internal flag, `mounted`, is set to `true`. This lets the framework know that this widget is currently on the widget tree.

2. `initState()` is the first method called after a widget is created. This is similar to `onCreate()` in Android or `viewDidLoad()` in iOS.

3. The first time the framework builds a widget, it calls `didChangeDependencies()` after `initState()`. It might call `didChangeDependencies()` again if your state object depends on an **inherited widget** that has changed. There's more on inherited widgets below.

4. Finally, the framework calls `build()` after `didChangeDependencies()`. This function is the most important for developers because it's called every time a widget needs rendering. Every widget in the tree triggers a `build()` method recursively, so this operation has to be very fast.

> **Note**: You should always perform heavy computational functions asynchronously and store their results as part of the state for later use with the `build()` function.
>
> `build()` should never do anything that's computationally demanding. This is similar to how you think of the iOS or Android main thread. For example, you should never make a network call that stalls the UI rendering.

5. The framework calls `didUpdateWidget(_)` when a parent widget makes a change or needs to redraw the UI. When that happens, you'll get the `oldWidget` instance as a parameter so you can compare it with your current widget and do any additional logic.

6. Whenever you want to modify the state in your widget, you call `setState()`. The framework then marks the widget as `dirty` and triggers a `build()` again.

> **Note**: Asynchronous code should always check if the `mounted` property is true before calling `setstate()`, because the widget may no longer be part of the widget tree.

7. When you remove the object from the tree, the framework calls `deactivate()`. In some cases, the framework can reinsert the state object into another part of the tree.

8. The framework calls `dispose()` when you permanently remove the object and its state from the tree. This method is very important because you'll need it to handle memory cleanup, such as unsubscribing streams and disposing of animations or controllers.

The rule of thumb for `dispose()` is to check any properties you define in your state and make sure you've disposed of them properly.

Adding Stateful Widgets

Wouldn't it be great if your users could save their list of favorite restaurants to gain quick access to reorder again? You'll add a heart button to `RestaurantLandscapeCard` for users to save a restaurant.

`RestaurantLandscapeCard` is currently a `StatelessWidget`, which means the widget can't manage state dynamically. To fix this, you'll change this card into a `StatefulWidget`.

Open **restaurant_landscape_card.dart** and right-click `RestaurantLandscapeCard`. Then click **Show Context Actions** from the menu that pops up:

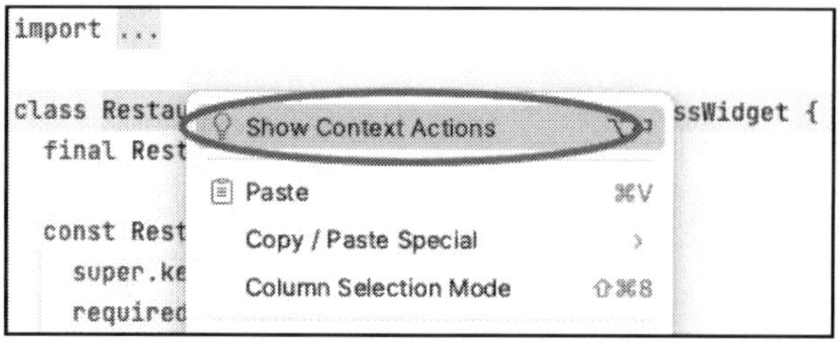

Select **Convert to StatefulWidget**. Instead of converting manually, you can just use this menu shortcut to do it automatically:

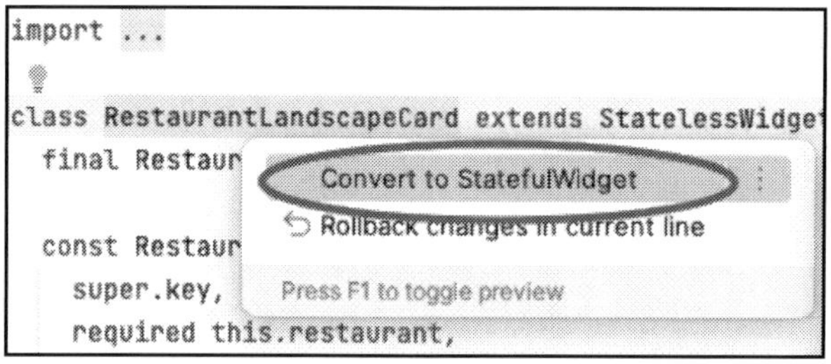

There are now two classes:

```
class RestaurantLandscapeCard extends StatefulWidget {
  ...

  @override
  State<RestaurantLandscapeCard> createState() =>
    _RestaurantLandscapeCardState();
}

class _RestaurantLandscapeCardState extends
State<RestaurantLandscapeCard> {
  // TODO: Add _isFavorited property
  @override
  Widget build(BuildContext context) {
    ...
  }
```

A couple of things to notice in the code above:

- The refactor converted `RestaurantLandscapeCard` from a `StatelessWidget` into a `StatefulWidget`. It added a `createState()` implementation.
- The refactor also created the `_RestaurantLandscapeCardState` state class. It stores mutable data that can change over the lifetime of the widget.

Implementing Favorites

In `_RestaurantLandscapeCardState`, find `// TODO: Add _isFavorited property` and replace it with the following property:

```
bool _isFavorited = false;
```

Now that you've created a new state, you need to manage it. Locate the comment `// TODO: Convert to a stack` and replace it and the whole `child` property below it with the following:

```
// 1
child: Stack(
  fit: StackFit.expand,
  children: [
    // 2
    Image.asset(
      widget.restaurant.imageUrl,
      fit: BoxFit.cover,
    ),
    // 3
    Positioned(
      top: 4.0,
      right: 4.0,
      child: IconButton(
        // 4
        icon: Icon(_isFavorited
            ? Icons.favorite  //
            : Icons.favorite_border,
          ),
        iconSize: 30.0,
        color: Colors.red[400],
        // 5
        onPressed: () {
          setState(() {
            _isFavorited = !_isFavorited;
          });
        },
      ),
    ),
  ],
)
```

Here's how the code works:

1. `Stack` widget overlays multiple elements. Here, it's used to layer a favorite button over a restaurant's image, ensuring you utilize the full space.
2. The restaurant's image is displayed, with a scaling set to fill the entire container.
3. The `IconButton` is positioned at the top-right corner of the image, serving as the favorite action.
4. The icon displayed depends on the `_isFavorited` status. A filled heart represents a favorite, while an outlined heart indicates otherwise.
5. Tapping the favorite button toggles the `_isFavorited` state, effectively switching between the two heart icons. This is done via a call to `setState()`.

Save the change to trigger a hot reload, and on the **Restaurant** card, see the heart button. Toggle the heart button on and off when you tap it, as shown below:

Examining the Widget Tree

Now that you've turned `RestaurantLandscapeCard` into a stateful widget, your next step is to look at how the element tree manages state changes.

Recall that the framework will construct the widget tree and, for every widget instance, create an element object. The element, in this case, is a `StatefulElement`, and it manages the state object, as shown on the next page.

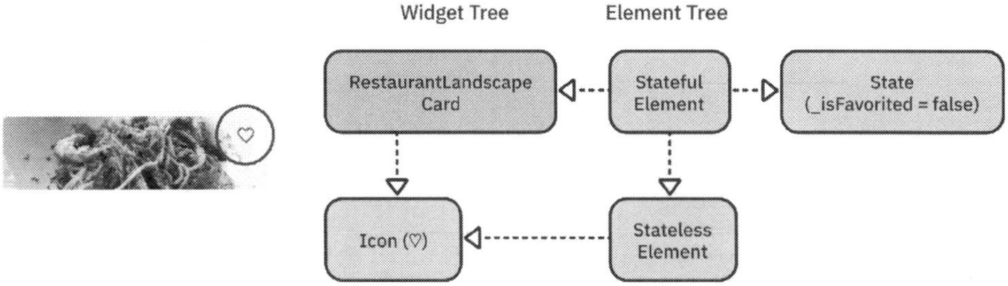

When the user taps the heart button, `setState()` runs and toggles `_isFavorited` to true. Internally, the state object marks this element as **dirty**. That triggers a call to `build()`.

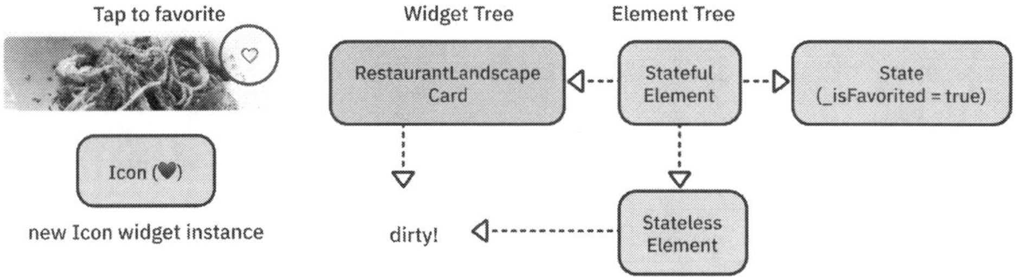

This is where the element object shows its strength. It removes the old widget and replaces it with a new instance of `Icon` that contains the filled heart icon.

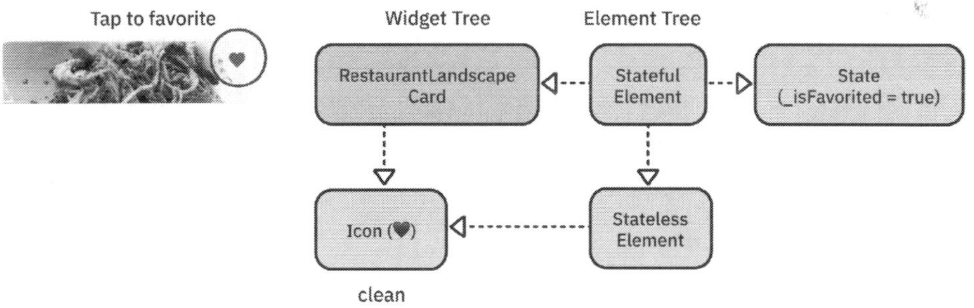

Rather than reconstructing the whole tree, the framework only updates the widgets that need to be changed. It walks down the tree hierarchy and checks for what's changed. It reuses everything else.

Now, what happens when you need to access data from some other widget, located elsewhere in the hierarchy? You use inherited widgets.

Inherited Widgets

Inherited widgets let you access state information from the parent elements in the tree hierarchy. Imagine you have a piece of data way up in the widget tree that you want to access. One solution is to pass the data down as a parameter on each nested widget — but that quickly becomes annoying and cumbersome.

Wouldn't it be great if there was a centralized way to access such data?

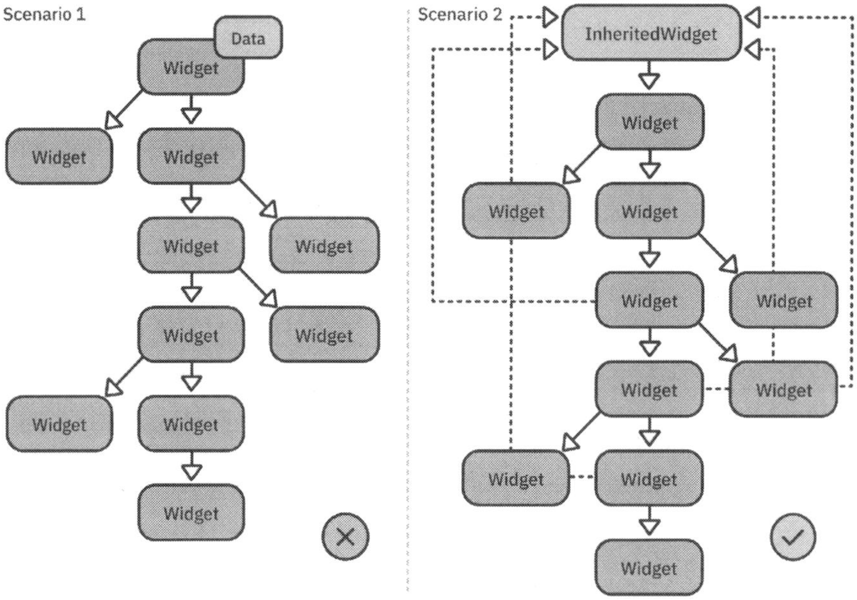

That's where inherited widgets come in! By adopting an inherited widget in your tree, you can reference the data from any of its descendants. This is known as **lifting state up**.

For example, you use an inherited widget when:

- Accessing a `Theme` object to change the UI's appearance.
- Calling an API service object to fetch data from the web.
- Subscribing to streams to update the UI according to the data received.

Inherited widgets are an advanced topic. You'll learn more about them in Section 4, "Networking, Persistence and State", which covers state management and the **Riverpod** package — a framework built on top of `InheritedWidget`.

Key Points

- Flutter maintains three trees in parallel: the **Widget**, **Element** and **RenderObject** trees.
- A Flutter app is performant because it maintains its structure and only updates the widgets that need redrawing.
- The **Flutter Inspector** is a useful tool to debug, experiment with and inspect a widget tree.
- You should always start by creating `StatelessWidgets` and only use `StatefulWidgets` when you need to manage and maintain the state of your widget.
- Inherited widgets are a good solution to access state from the top of the tree.

Where to Go From Here?

If you want to learn more theory about how widgets work, check out the following links:

- Detailed architectural overview of Flutter and widgets:https://flutter.dev/docs/resources/architectural-overview.
- The Flutter team created a YouTube series explaining widgets under the hood:https://www.youtube.com/playlist?list=PLjxrf2q8roU2HdJQDjJzOeO6J3FoFLWr2.
- The Flutter team gave a talk in China on how to render widgets:https://youtu.be/996ZgFRENMs.

In the next chapter, you'll get back to more practical concerns and see how to create scrollable widgets.

Chapter 5: Scrollable Widgets

By Vincent Ngo

Building scrollable content is an essential part of UI development. There's only so much information a user can process at a time, let alone fit on an entire screen in the palm of your hand!

In this chapter, you'll learn everything you need to know about scrollable widgets. In particular, you'll learn:

- How to use `ListView`.
- How to nest scroll views.

You'll continue to build the **Yummy** app by adding **HomeScreen**, a new view that enables users to explore different restaurants, food categories, and view friends' posts.

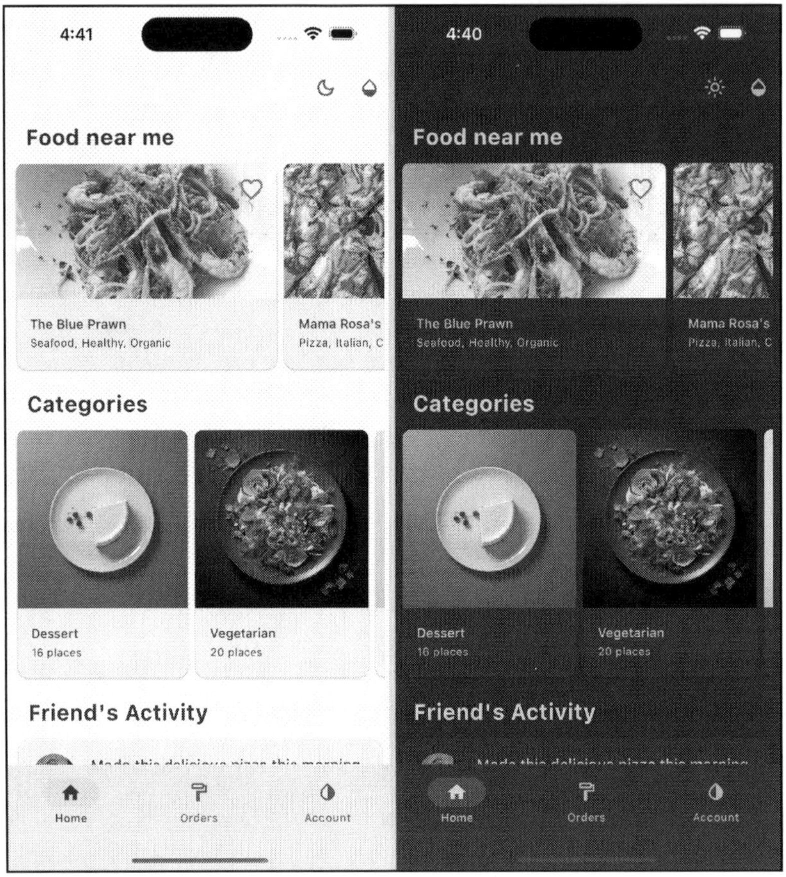

By the end of this chapter, you'll be a scrollable widget wizard!

Getting Started

Open the starter project in Android Studio, then run `flutter pub get` if necessary and run the app.

You'll see a placeholder for each tab as shown below:

Project Files

There are new files in this starter project to help you out. Before you learn how to create scrollable widgets, take a look at them.

Assets Folder

The **assets** directory contains all the images that you'll use to build your app.

Sample Images

- **categories**: Contains images for food categories.
- **food**: Contains sample food items from a restaurant menu.
- **profile_pics**: Contains Kodeco team member pictures.
- **restaurants**: Contains restaurant hero images.

New Classes

In the **lib** directory, you'll also notice the new **api** folder, as shown below:

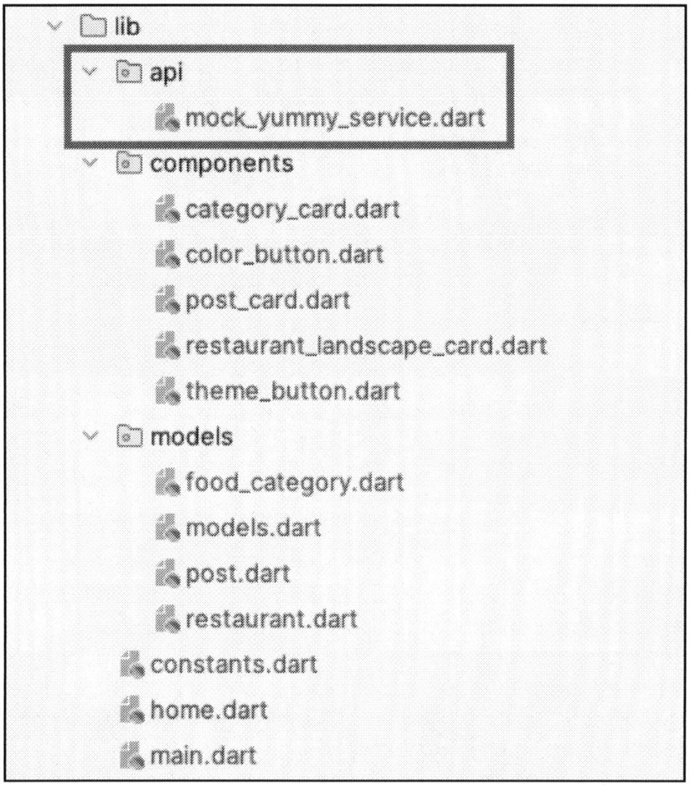

API Folder

The **api** folder contains a mock service class.

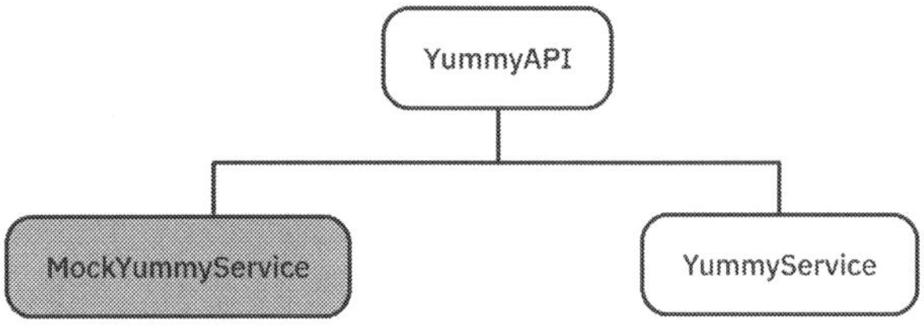

`MockYummyService` is a service class that mocks a server response. It has `async` functions that wait to load mock data defined in each model class, `FoodCategory`, `Post`, and `Restaurant`.

> **Pro tip**: Sometimes your back-end service is not ready to consume. Creating a mock service is a flexible way to build your UI.

In this chapter, you'll use two API calls:

- **getExploreData()**: Returns `ExploreData`. Internally, it makes a batch request and returns three lists: restaurants, food categories, and friend posts.

> **Note**: Unfamiliar with how `async` works in Dart? Check out Chapter 12, "Futures" in Dart Apprentice: Beyond the Basics (https://www.kodeco.com/books/dart-apprentice-beyond-the-basics/v1.0/chapters/12-futures) or read this article to learn more:https://dart.dev/codelabs/async-await.

Now that you have a mock service, you can focus on displaying the data with scrollable widgets!

Introducing ListView

ListView is a very popular Flutter component. It's a linear scrollable widget that arranges its children linearly and supports horizontal and vertical scrolling.

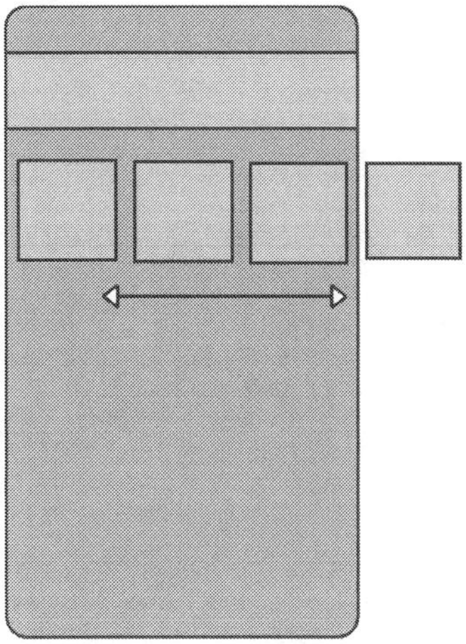

> **Fun fact**: `Column` and `Row` widgets are like `ListView` but without the scroll view.

Introducing Constructors

A `ListView` has four constructors:

- The default constructor takes an explicit list of widgets called `children`. That will construct every single child in the list, even the ones that aren't visible. You should use this if you have a small number of children.
- `ListView.builder()` takes in an `IndexedWidgetBuilder` and builds the list on demand. It will only construct the children that are visible onscreen. You should use this if you need to display a large or infinite number of items.
- `ListView.separated()` takes **two** `IndexedWidgetBuilders`: `itemBuilder` and `seperatorBuilder`. This is useful if you want to place a separator widget between your items.
- `ListView.custom()` gives you more fine-grain control over your child items.

> **Note**: For more details about ListView constructors, check out the official documentation: https://api.flutter.dev/flutter/widgets/ListView-class.html

Next, you'll learn how to use the first three constructors!

Setting Up the Explore Screen

The first screen you'll create is the `ExploreScreen`. It contains three sections:

- **RestaurantSection**: A horizontal scroll view that lets you pan through different restaurants.
- **CategorySection**: A horizontal scroll view that pans through different categories.
- **PostSection**: A vertical scroll view that shows what your friends are up to.

In the **lib** folder, create a new directory called **screens**.

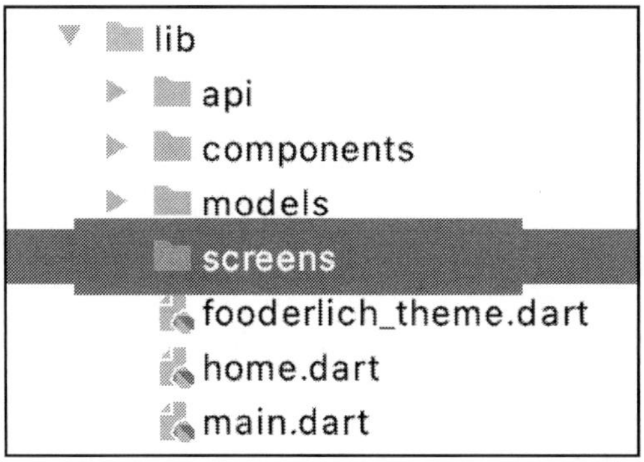

Within the new **screens** directory, create a new file called **explore_page.dart** and add the following code:

```
import 'package:flutter/material.dart';
import '../api/mock_yummy_service.dart';

class ExplorePage extends StatelessWidget {
  // 1
  final mockService = MockYummyService();

  ExplorePage({super.key});

  @override
  Widget build(BuildContext context) {
    // TODO: Add Listview Future Builder
    // 2
    return const Center(
        child: Text('Explore Page Setup',
        style: TextStyle(fontSize: 32.0),),);
  }
}
```

Here's how the code works:

1. Create a `MockYummyService`, to mock server responses.
2. Display a placeholder text. You'll replace this later.

Leave **explore_page.dart** open; you'll soon be making some changes.

Updating the Navigation Pages

In **lib/home.dart**, locate `// TODO: Replace with ExplorePage` and replace `Center` below it with the following:

```
ExplorePage(),
```

This will display the newly created `ExplorePage` in the first tab.

Make sure the new `ExploreScreen` has been imported. If your IDE didn't add it automatically, add this import:

```
import 'screens/explore_page.dart';
```

Hot restart the app. It will look like this:

You'll replace the `Containers` later in this chapter.

Creating a FutureBuilder

How do you display your UI with an asynchronous task?

`MockYummyService` contains asynchronous functions that return a `Future` object. `FutureBuilder` comes in handy here, as it helps you determine the state of a `Future`. For example, it tells you whether data is still loading or the fetch operation has finished.

In **explore_page.dart**, replace the whole `return` statement below `// TODO: Add Listview Future Builder` with the following code:

```
// 1
  return FutureBuilder(
    // 2
    future: mockService.getExploreData(),
    // 3
    builder: (context, AsyncSnapshot<ExploreData> snapshot) {
      // 4
      if (snapshot.connectionState == ConnectionState.done) {
        // 5
        final restaurants = snapshot.data?.restaurants ?? [];
        final categories = snapshot.data?.categories ?? [];
        final posts = snapshot.data?.friendPosts ?? [];
        // TODO: Replace this with Restaurant Section
        return const Center(
          child: SizedBox(
            child: Text('Show RestaurantSection'),
          ),
        );
      } else {
        // 6
        return const Center(
          child: CircularProgressIndicator(),
        );
      }
    },
  );
```

Here's what the code does:

1. `FutureBuilder` is a widget that works with asynchronous operations, allowing you to build UI based on the latest snapshot of a `Future`.

2. `FutureBuilder` takes in a **future**. You're using `getExploreData()` to fetch data, which returns an instance of `ExploreData`.

3. `builder()` is a function that decides what the UI should look like based on the current state of the `Future`. This is provided by the `snapshot`.

4. If `snapshot.connectionState` is `done`, it means the data is available to consume.
5. Extract the data from `snapshot.data`, providing default values if the data is null. For now, the widgets return a placeholder, you will replace it with actual content later.
6. If the data is not ready to consume, show a loading spinner.

> **Note**: For more information, check out Flutter's `FutureBuilder` documentation: https://api.flutter.dev/flutter/widgets/FutureBuilder-class.html.

Perform a hot reload. You'll see the loading spinner first. After the future completes, it shows the placeholder text.

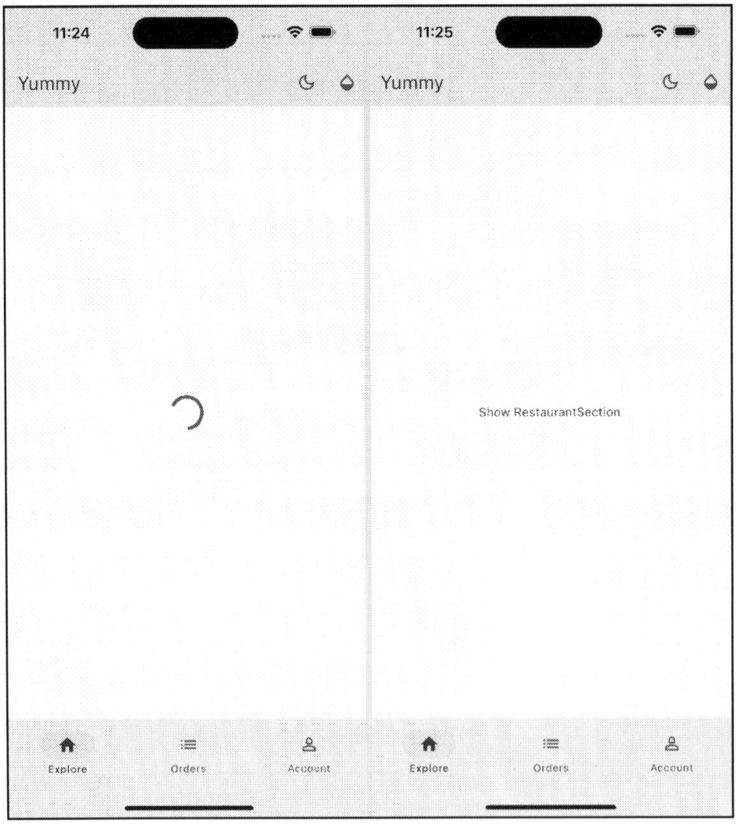

Now that you've set up the loading UI, it's time to build the actual list view!

Building Restaurant Section

The first scrollable component you'll build is `RestaurantSection`. This is the top section of the `ExplorePage`. It will be a horizontal list view.

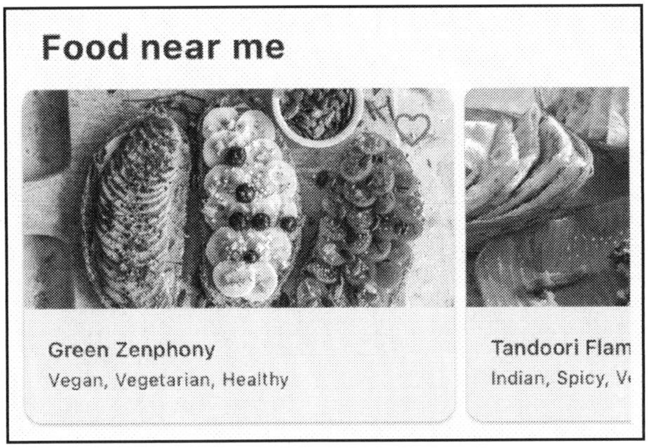

In **lib/components**, create a new file called **restaurant_section.dart**. Add the following code:

```
import 'package:flutter/material.dart';

// 1
import '../components/restaurant_landscape_card.dart';
import '../models/restaurant.dart';

class RestaurantSection extends StatelessWidget {
  // 2
  final List<Restaurant> restaurants;

  const RestaurantSection({
    super.key,
    required this.restaurants,
  });

  @override
  Widget build(BuildContext context) {
    // 3
    return Padding(
      padding: const EdgeInsets.all(8.0),
      // 4
      child: Column(
        crossAxisAlignment: CrossAxisAlignment.start,
        children: [
          const Padding(
            padding: EdgeInsets.only(left: 16.0, bottom: 8.0),
            // 5
```

```
              child: Text(
                'Food near me',
                style: TextStyle(
                  fontSize: 24,
                  fontWeight: FontWeight.bold,
                ),
              ),
            ),
            // TODO: Add Restaurant List View
            // 6
            Container(
              height: 400,
              // TODO: Add ListView Here
              color: Colors.grey,
            ),
          ],
        ),
      );
    }
  }
```

Here's how the code works:

1. Import restaurant card component and model.
2. `RestaurantSection` is a `StatelessWidget` that requires a list of restaurants.
3. Within `build()`, start by applying some padding.
4. Add a `Column` to place widgets in a vertical layout.
5. In the column, add a `Text`. This is the header for the "Food near me" section.
6. Add a `Container`, 400 pixels tall, and set the background color to `grey`. This container is a placeholder for your `ListView` of restaurants.

Adding the Restaurant Section

Open **explore_page.dart** and add the following `import`:

```
import '../components/restaurant_section.dart';
```

This means you don't have to call additional imports when you use the new component.

Replace `// TODO: Replace this with Restaurant Section` and the `return` statement below with the following:

```
// TODO: Wrap in a ListView
return RestaurantSection(restaurants: restaurants);
```

If your app is still running, it will now look like this:

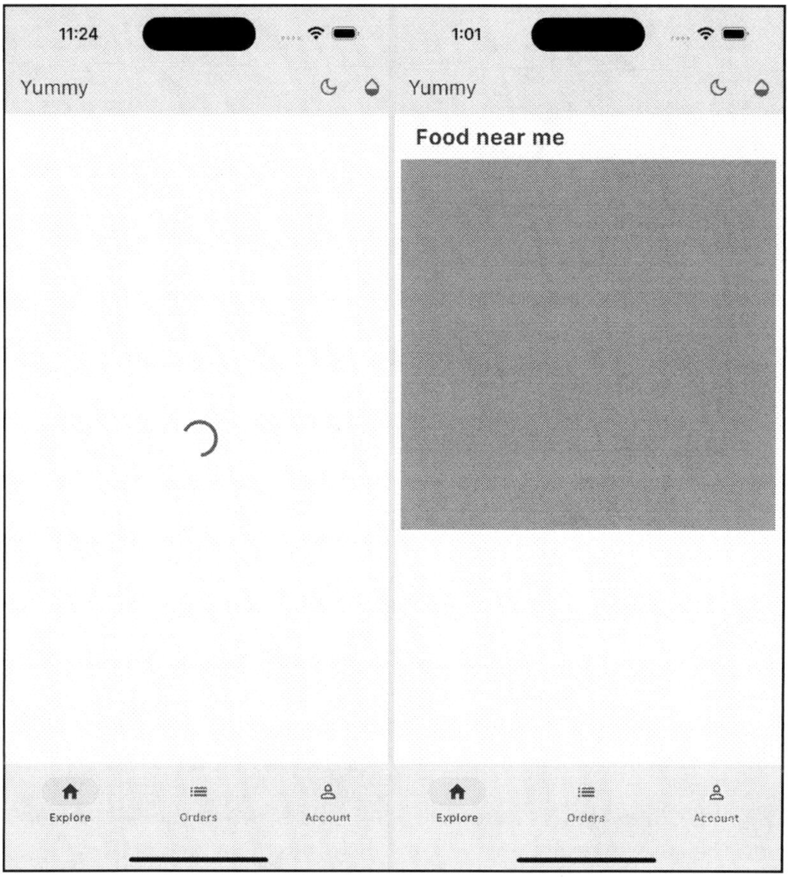

Now it's finally time to add the `ListView`.

In **restaurant_section.dart**, replace `// TODO: Add Restaurant List View` and the `Container` beneath it with the following:

```
// 1
SizedBox(
  height: 230,
  // 2
  child: ListView.builder(
    // 3
    scrollDirection: Axis.horizontal,
    // 4
```

```
      itemCount: restaurants.length,
      // 5
      itemBuilder: (context, index) {
        // 6
        return SizedBox(
          width: 300,
          // 7
          child: RestaurantLandscapeCard(
            restaurant: restaurants[index],
          ),
        );
      },
    ),
  ),
```

Here's how the code works:

1. The `ListView` will have a fixed height of `230` pixels. It acts as a container to constraint the height of the child.
2. `ListView.builder` widget dynamically creates a list of items based on the provided data.
3. Configure the items in the `ListView` to scroll horizontally.
4. Set the `itemCount` to be the length of `restaurants` list. This determines how many items the list should render.
5. `itemBuilder` is a function that returns a widget for a given index of the list. It's invoked for each item in the `restaurant` list.
6. Set a fixed width of `300` pixels for every restaurant card.
7. Create a `RestaurantLandscapeCard` widget and pass in the `restaurant` object based on the current `index`.

Add the following `import`:

```
import 'restaurant_landscape_card.dart';
```

Save the changes to trigger a hot restart and Yummy will now look like this; don't forget, you can switch between light and dark mode:

You can scroll through the list of delicious restaurants. Finally!

Next, you'll continue to add two new sections to `ExplorePage`.

Nested ListViews

There are two approaches to adding the category and post sections: the `Column` approach and the nested `ListView` approach. You'll take a look at each of them now.

Column Approach

You could put the list views in a `Column`, that arranges items in a vertical layout. So that makes sense right?

The diagram shows two **rectangular boundaries** that represent two scrollable areas.

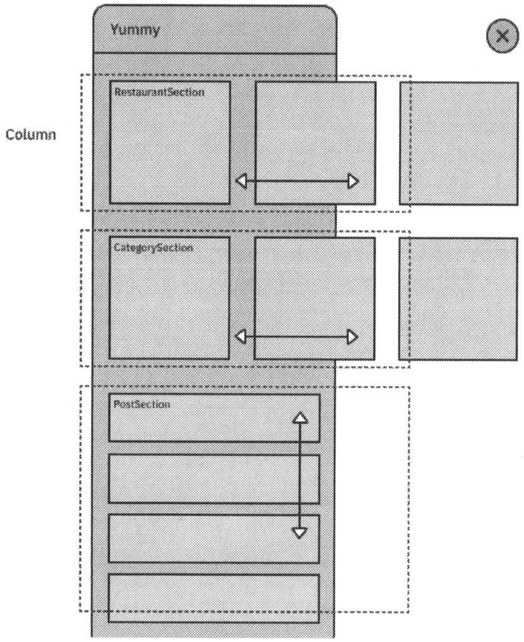

The pros and cons of this approach are:

- `RestaurantSection` and `CategorySection` are OK because the scroll direction is horizontal. All the cards also fit on the screen and everything looks great!
- `PostSection` scrolls in the vertical direction, but it only has a small scroll area. So as a user, you can't see many of your friend's posts at once.

This approach has a bad user experience because the content area is too small! The `Cards` already take up most of the screen. How much room will there be for the vertical scroll area on small devices?

Nested ListView Approach

In the second approach, you nest multiple list views in a parent list view.

The diagram shows one big **rectangular boundary**.

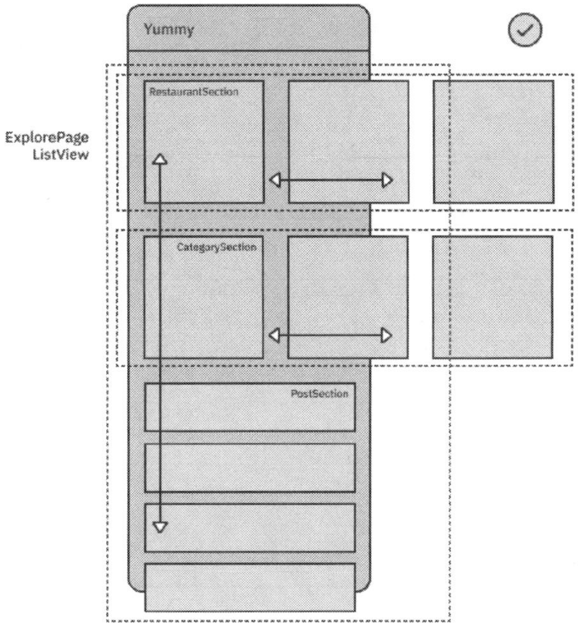

`ExplorePage` holds the parent `ListView`. Since there are only three children `ListViews`, you can use the default constructor, which returns an explicit list of children.

The benefits of this approach are:

1. The scroll area is a lot bigger, using 70–80% of the screen.
2. You can view more of your friends' posts.
3. You can continue to scroll `RestaurantSection` or `CategorySection` in the horizontal direction.
4. When you scroll upward, Flutter listens to the scroll event of the parent `ListView`. So it will scroll both `RestaurantSection`, `CategorySection` and `PostSection` upwards, giving you more room to view all the content!

Nested `ListView` sounds like a better approach, doesn't it?

Adding a Nested ListView

First, go back to **explore_page.dart** locate the comment `// TODO: Wrap in a ListView` and replace it and `return RestaurantSection` widget with the following:

```
// 1
return ListView(
  // 2
  shrinkWrap: true,
  // 3
  scrollDirection: Axis.vertical,
  // 4
  children: [
    RestaurantSection(restaurants: restaurants),
    // TODO: Add CategorySection
    Container(
      height: 300,
      color: Colors.green,
    ),
    // TODO: Add PostSection
    Container(
      height: 300,
      color: Colors.orange,
    ),
  ],
);
```

Here's how the code works:

1. Initialize a scrollable list of widgets.
2. `shrinkWrap` sizes the `ListView` based on its children's height.
3. The list scrolls vertically.
4. The list contains three child list view widgets. You will replace the two placeholder containers later.

Your app now looks like this, try scrolling up and down:

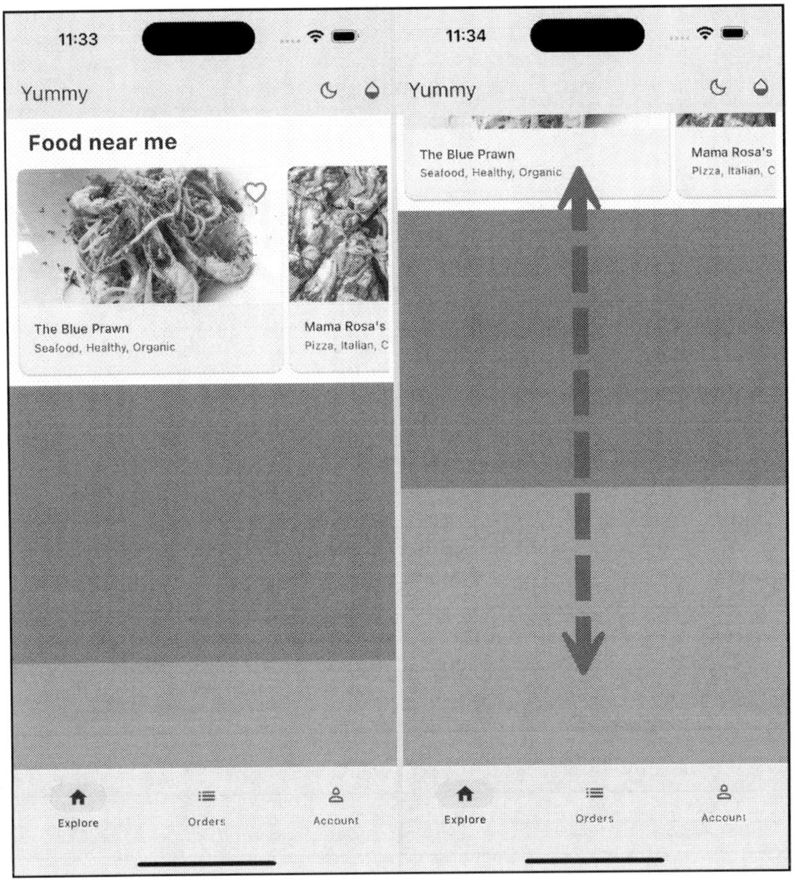

Notice that you can still scroll the `Cards` horizontally. When you scroll up and down, you'll notice the entire area scrolls!

Now that you have the desired scroll behavior, it's time to build the `CategorySection`.

Building Category Section

The second scrollable component you'll build is `CategorySection`. Users will be able to scroll through a list of food categories horizontally.

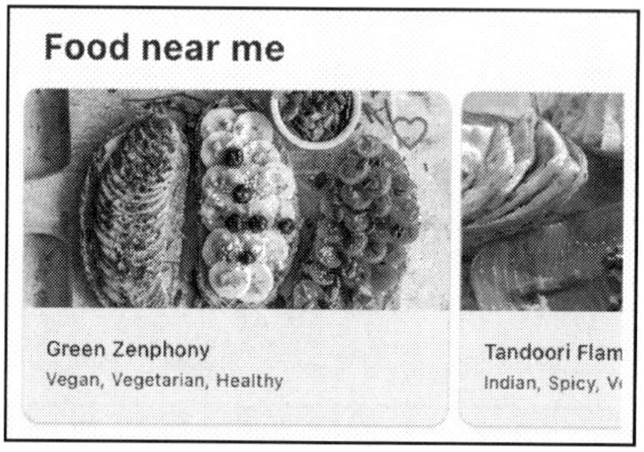

In **lib/components**, create a new file called **category_section.dart**. Add the following code:

```
import 'package:flutter/material.dart';
import '../models/food_category.dart';
import 'category_card.dart';

// 1
class CategorySection extends StatelessWidget {
  final List<FoodCategory> categories;
  const CategorySection({super.key, required this.categories});

  @override
  Widget build(BuildContext context) {
    // 2
    return Padding(
      padding: const EdgeInsets.all(8.0),
      // 3
      child: Column(
        crossAxisAlignment: CrossAxisAlignment.start,
        children: [
          // 4
          const Padding(
            padding: EdgeInsets.only(left: 16.0, bottom: 8.0),
            child: Text(
              'Categories',
              style: TextStyle(
                fontSize: 24,
                fontWeight: FontWeight.bold,
              ),
            ),
          ),
          // 5
```

```
          SizedBox(
            height: 275,
            child: ListView.builder(
              scrollDirection: Axis.horizontal,
              itemCount: categories.length,
              itemBuilder: (context, index) {
                // 6
                return SizedBox(
                  width: 200,
                  child: CategoryCard(
                    category: categories[index],
                  ),
                );
              },
            ),
          ),
        ],
      ),
    );
  }
}
```

Here's how the code works:

1. `CategorySection` is a `StatelessWidget` and requires a list of categories. The purpose of this widget is to display a list of various food categories.
2. The entire widget is wrapped by `Padding` widget to ensure *8.0* pixel space all around.
3. The `Column` widget is used to arrange child widgets vertically.
4. At the top of the column there is a title that displays "Categories".
5. After the title there is a horizontally-scrolling `ListView.builder` which displays a list of `CategoryCard` widgets, each with a height of 200 pixels.

Now that you have created your category section, it's time to add it to the list view.

Adding Category Section

Returning to **explore_page.dart**, locate `// TODO: Add CategorySection` and replace it and the `Container` below it with the following:

```
CategorySection(categories: categories),
```

Add the following import at the top:

```
import '../components/category_section.dart';
```

Your app now looks like this:

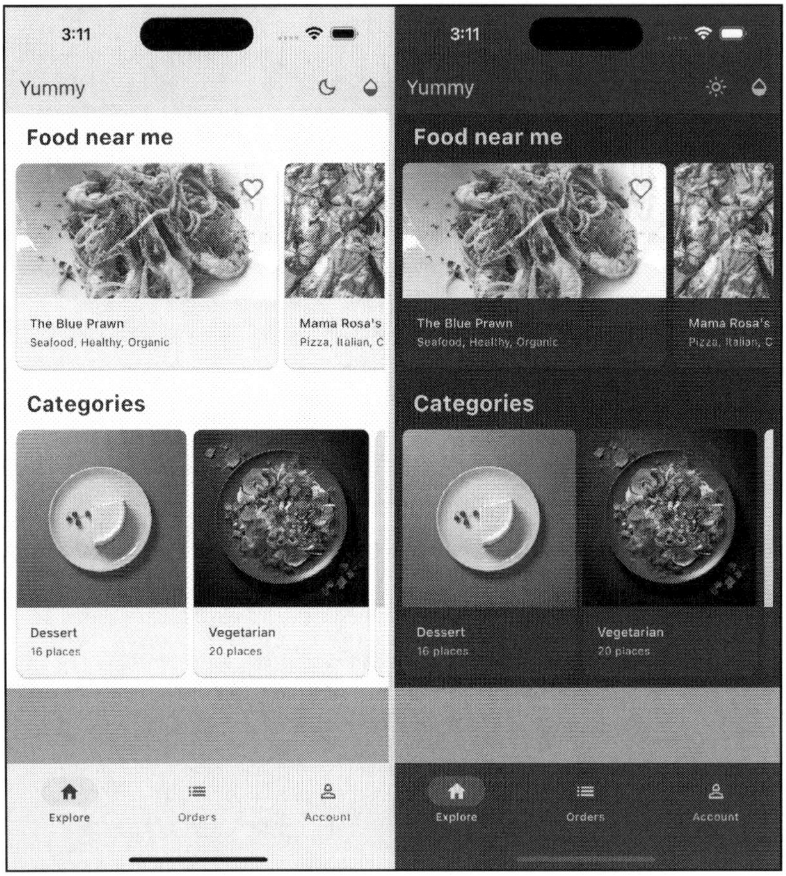

Next, you'll replace the orange placeholder container with a `PostSection`.

Building the Post Section

The third scrollable component you'll build is `PostSection`. Users will be able to scroll through a list of friend posts vertically.

In **lib/components**, create a new file called **post_section.dart**. Add the following code, ignoring any red squiggles:

```
import 'package:flutter/material.dart';
import '../models/post.dart';

// 1
class PostSection extends StatelessWidget {
  final List<Post> posts;
  const PostSection({
    super.key,
    required this.posts,
  });

  @override
  Widget build(BuildContext context) {
    // 2
    return Padding(
      padding: const EdgeInsets.all(8.0),
      // 3
      child: Column(
        crossAxisAlignment: CrossAxisAlignment.start,
        children: [
          const Padding(
            padding: EdgeInsets.only(left: 16.0, bottom: 8.0),
            // 4
            child: Text(
              'Friend\'s Activity',
              style: TextStyle(
                fontSize: 24,
```

```
                    fontWeight: FontWeight.bold,
                  ),
                ),
              ),
              // 5
              // TODO: Add Post List View
            ],
          ),
        );
      }
    }
```

Here's how the code works:

1. `PostSection` is a stateless widget and requires a list of `Posts`.
2. Apply overall padding of 8.0 pixels.
3. Create a `Column` to position the `Text` followed by the posts in a vertical layout.
4. Create the `Text` widget header.
5. Use a placeholder comment to add the list of posts.

Next, locate the comment `// TODO: Add Post List View` and replace it with the following code:

```
// 1
ListView.separated(
  // 2
  primary: false,
  // 3
  shrinkWrap: true,
  // 4
  scrollDirection: Axis.vertical,
  // 5
  physics: const NeverScrollableScrollPhysics(),
  itemCount: posts.length,
  // 6
  itemBuilder: (context, index) {
    return PostCard(post: posts[index]);
  },
  separatorBuilder: (context, index) {
    // 7
    return const SizedBox(height: 16);
  },
),
```

Here's how you defined the new `ListView`:

1. Create `ListView.separated` with two `IndexWidgetBuilder` callbacks.
2. Since you're nesting two list views, it's a good idea to set `primary` to **false**. That lets Flutter know that this isn't the primary scroll view.
3. Set `shrinkWrap` to `true` to create a **fixed-length** scrollable list of items. This gives it a fixed height. If this were **false**, you'd get an unbounded height error.
4. Make this list view vertically scrollable.
5. Set the scrolling physics to `NeverScrollableScrollPhysics`. Even though you set `primary` to false, it's also a good idea to disable the scrolling for this list view. That will propagate up to the parent list view.
6. For every item in the list, create a `Post` widget.
7. For every item, also create a `SizedBox` to space each item by 16 pixels.

> **Note**: There are several different types of scroll physics you can play with:
>
> - `AlwaysScrollableScrollPhysics`
> - `BouncingScrollPhysics`
> - `ClampingScrollPhysics`
> - `FixedExtentScrollPhysics`
> - `NeverScrollableScrollPhysics`
> - `PageScrollPhysicsRange`
> - `MaintainingScrollPhysics`
>
> Find more details at https://api.flutter.dev/flutter/widgets/ScrollPhysics-class.html.

If it didn't automatically happen, add the following import at the top:

```
import 'post_card.dart';
```

The squiggles should be gone now. Next, you'll add the code to show your friends' posts.

Adding Post Section

Go back to **explore_page.dart** and find `// TODO: Add PostSection` and replace it and `Container` with the following:

```
PostSection(posts: posts),
```

If it's not there, add the following import:

```
import '../components/post_section.dart';
```

Restart or hot reload the app. The final **Explore** page should look like the following in light mode:

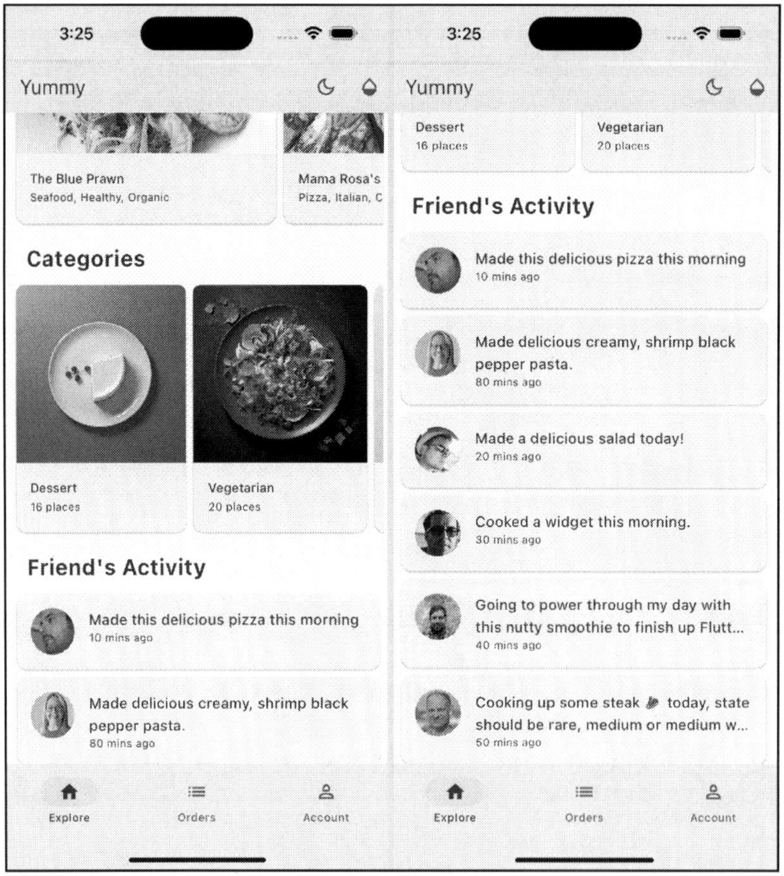

Here's what it looks like in dark mode:

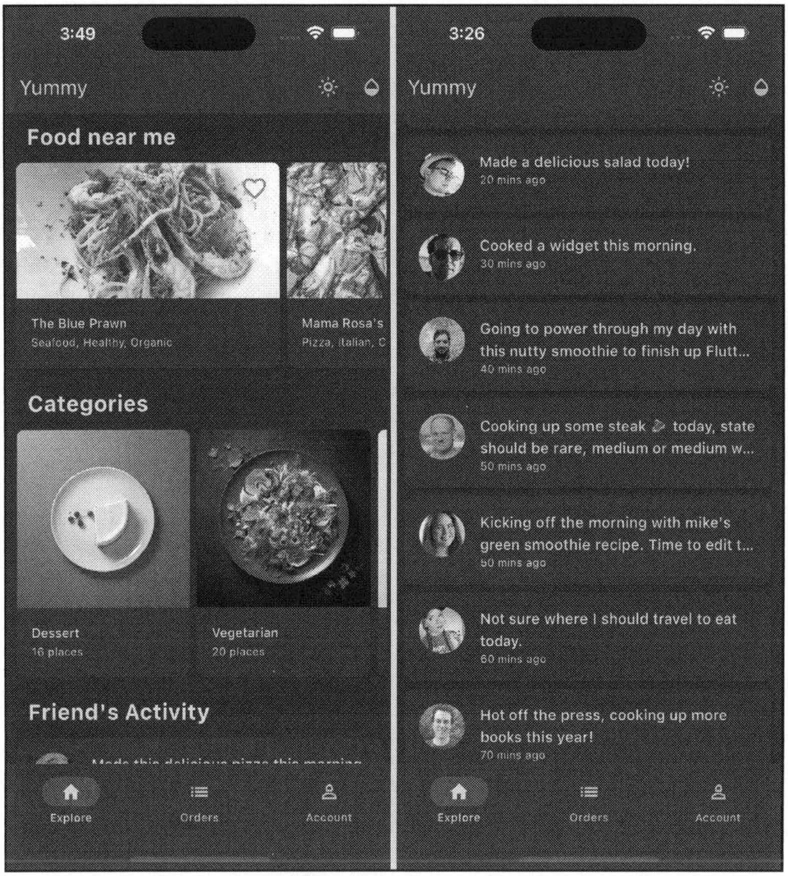

Aren't nested scroll views a neat technique? :]

And that's it, you're done. Congratulations!

Other Scrollable Widgets

There are many more scrollable widgets for various use cases. Here are some not covered in this chapter:

- **CustomScrollView**: A widget that creates custom scroll effects using slivers. Ever wonder how to collapse your navigation header on scroll? Use `CustomScrollView` for more fine-grain control over your scrollable area!

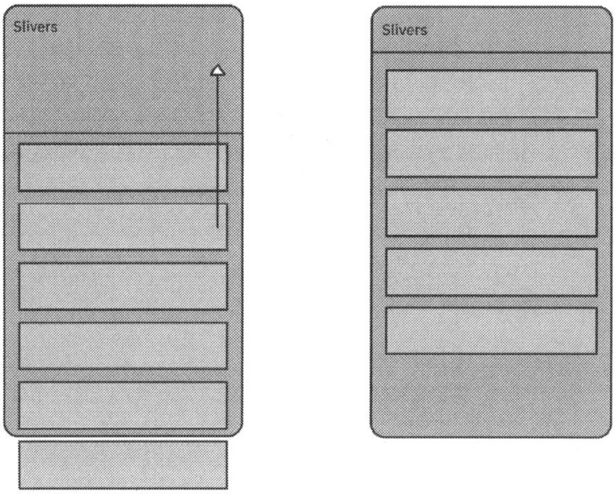

- **PageView**: A scrollable widget that scrolls page by page, making it perfect for an onboarding flow. It also supports a vertical scroll direction.

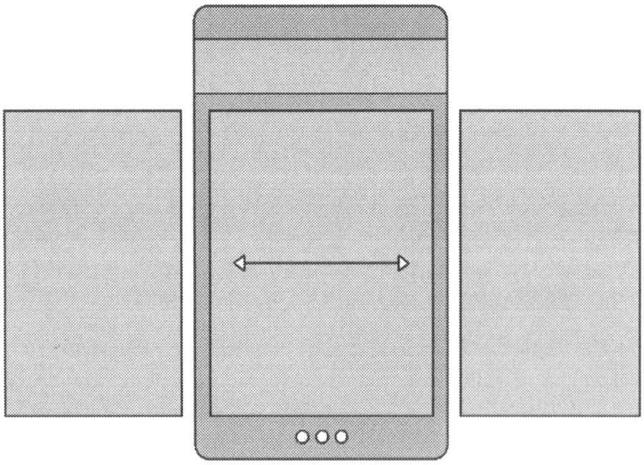

- **StaggeredGridView**: A grid view package that supports columns and rows of varying sizes. If you need to support dynamic height and custom layouts, this is the most popular package.

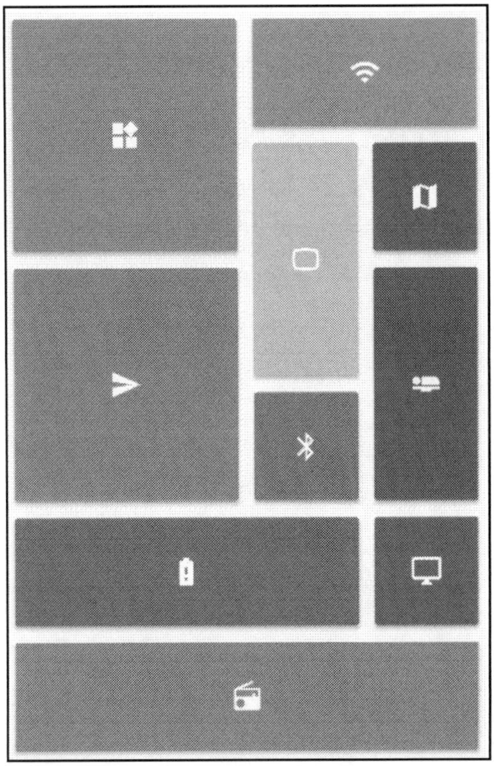

Key Points

- **ListView** and **GridView** support both horizontal and vertical scroll directions.
- The **primary** property lets Flutter know which scroll view is the primary scroll view.
- **physics** in a scroll view lets you change the user scroll interaction.
- Especially in a **nested list view**, remember to set `shrinkWrap` to **true** so you can give the scroll view a fixed height for all the items in the list.
- Use a **FutureBuilder** to wait for an asynchronous task to complete.
- You can nest scrollable widgets. For example, you can place a grid view within a list view. Unleash your wildest imagination!

Where to Go From Here?

At this point, you've learned how to create `ListViews`. They are much easier to use than iOS's `UITableView` and Android's `RecyclerView`, right? Building scrollable widgets is an important skill you should master!

Flutter makes it easy to build and use such scrollable widgets. It offers the flexibility to scroll in any direction and the power to nest scrollable widgets. With the skills you've learned, you can build cool scroll interactions.

You're ready to look like a pro in front of your friends :]

For more examples check out the Flutter Gallery at https://gallery.flutter.dev/#/, which showcases some great examples to test out.

In the next chapter, you'll take a look at some more interactive widgets.

Chapter 6: Advanced Scrollable Widgets

By Vincent Ngo

You've got the hang of scrollable widgets, but there's so much more to explore. Don't limit your app to just mobile screens—Flutter excels at adapting to various devices, from phones to tablets, desktops and the web. With Flutter, create an app that's not only mobile-friendly but effortlessly scales to any screen size. Embrace versatility and go universal.

In this chapter, you'll delve deeper into the world of scrollable widgets. You'll learn how to:

- Create custom scroll effects with the `Sliver` widget.
- Make your UI responsive with the `GridView` widget.

You'll continue to build out your food app, **Yummy**, by introducing a new feature: the **RestaurantPage**. Here, users can tap on a restaurant to explore everything from today's menu to a gallery of enticing dishes, all displayed responsively.

> **Heads up**: Grab a snack! The sight of food pictures might just work up an appetite

Here is what the mobile view looks like:

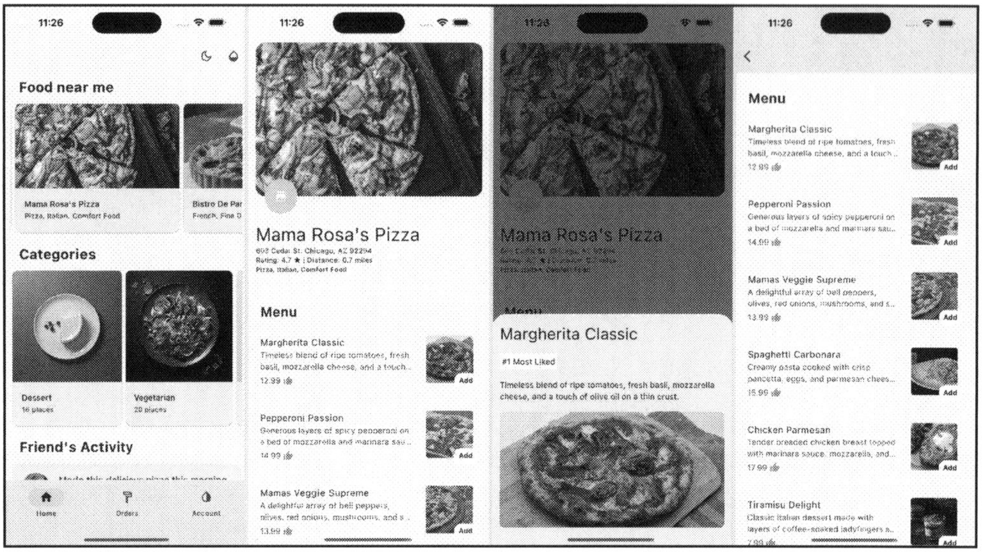

And here's the experience reimagined for the web:

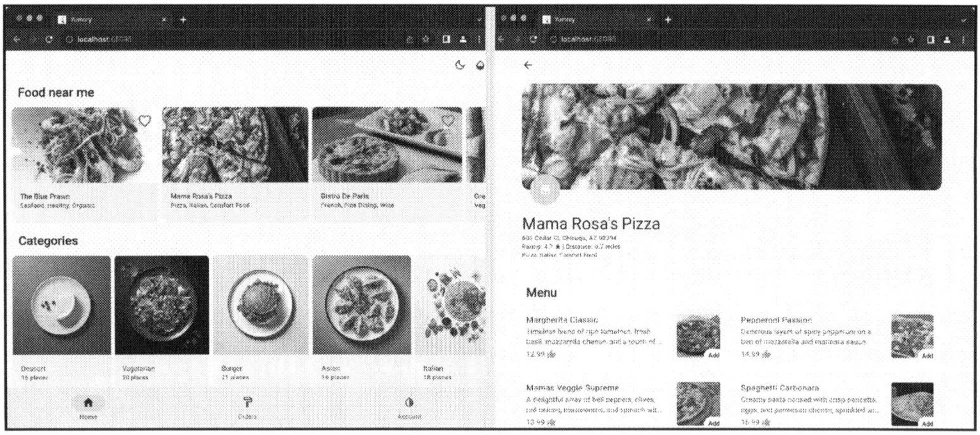

In a bit your app will look and function beautifully on any device, providing a seamless and responsive experience from mobile devices to the web.

Getting Started

Open the starter project in Android Studio, then run `flutter pub get` if necessary and run the app.

You'll see the explore page as shown below:

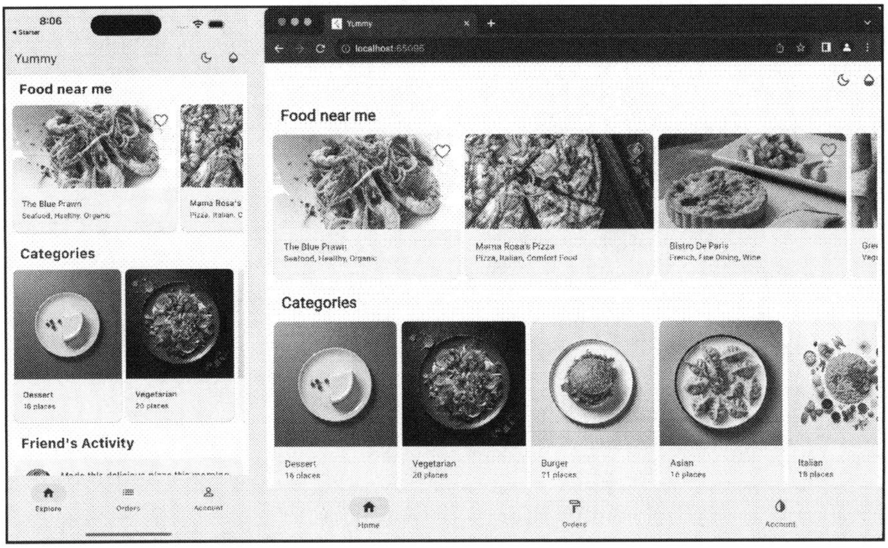

> **Note** In this chapter you'll be running the app on mobile and web to test and develop responsive a UI. In Android Studio you can run multiple devices by clicking the drop-down menu as shown below:

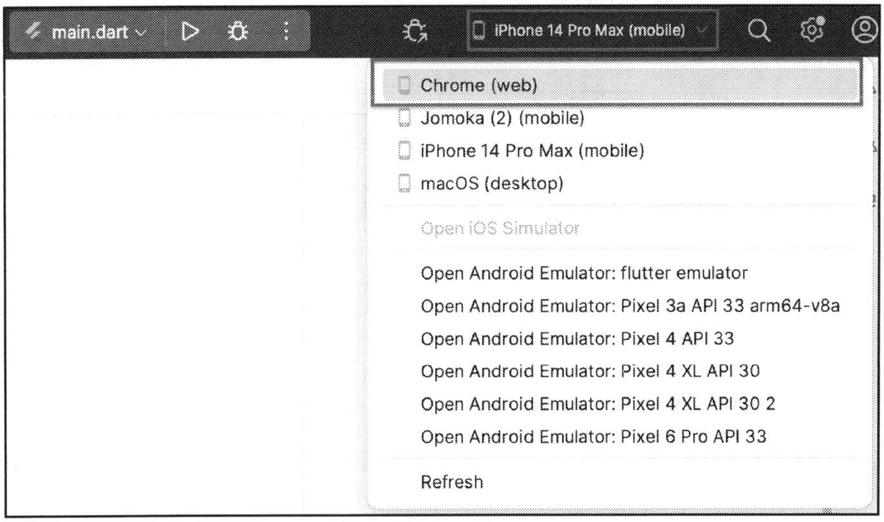

New Files in the Project

There are new files in this starter project to help you out. Before you start take a look at them.

Open the new **lib/components/restaurant_item.dart** file. You'll find the class `RestaurantItem`.

This widget is designed to showcase individual menu items in a restaurant's menu.

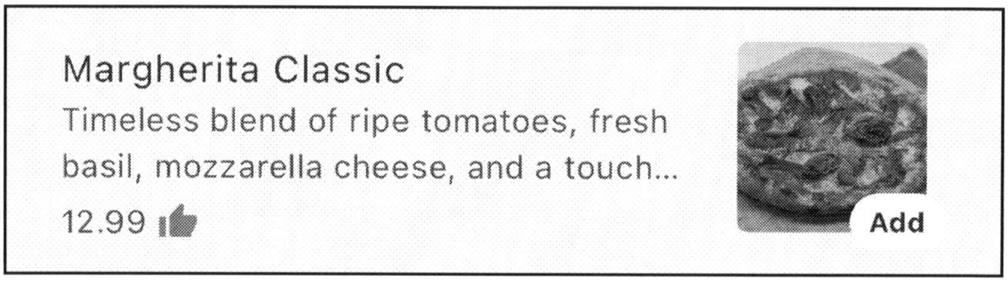

Here's a breakdown of its components:

- Title
- Description
- Price
- Popularity indicator
- Image
- **Add** button, to add an item to the cart

Introducing Slivers

Slivers in Flutter are a fundamental part of creating custom scroll effects in a scrollable area. They are a family of widgets that provide various ways to lay out a list of children in a scrolling view.

Unlike more straightforward widgets like `ListView` or `GridView`, slivers give developers fine-grained control over scroll behavior, animation, and the geometry of scrolling elements, making them the building blocks for complex scrollable areas.

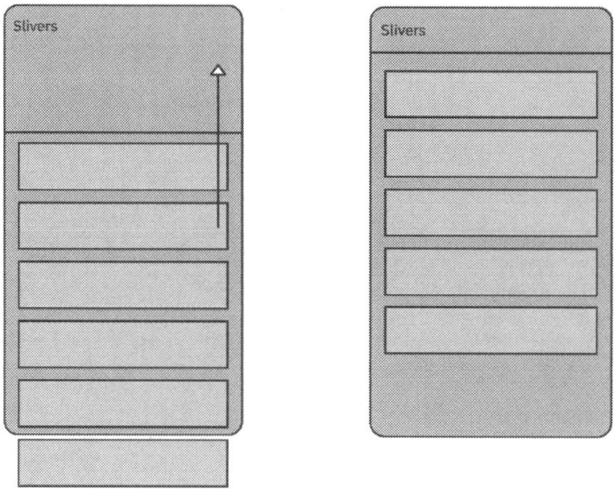

Types of Slivers

Slivers operate within the `CustomScrollView` widget, which allows them to combine different scrolling behaviors in a single scroll view.

- `SliverList` and `SliverGrid` are the sliver equivalents of `ListView` and `GridView`, respectively. They allow you to lay out items linearly or in a grid pattern.
- `SliverAppBar` is a highly flexible app bar that can expand, collapse, float, and snap as you scroll.
- `SliverToBoxAdapter` allows you to place a single non-sliver widget within a `CustomScrollView`.
- `SliverFillRemaining` and `SliverFillViewport` let you size children based on the remaining space in the viewport, creating dynamic effects as you scroll.

> **Note**: For a deeper dive into how you can leverage slivers to create various scrolling effects, you can review Flutter's documentation (https://docs.flutter.dev/ui/layout/scrolling/slivers).

Ready to explore the world of slivers? Let's get scrolling!

Building the Restaurant Page

First you need to set up the `RestaurantPage`. When users click on a restaurant in the **Food Near Me** section of your app it will direct them to this page that displays the restaurant's menu.

In **lib/screens**, create a new file called **restaurant_page.dart**. Add the following code:

```
// 1
import 'package:flutter/material.dart';
import '../models/restaurant.dart';

// 2
class RestaurantPage extends StatefulWidget {
  final Restaurant restaurant;

  // 3
  const RestaurantPage({
    super.key,
    required this.restaurant,
  });

  @override
  State<RestaurantPage> createState() => _RestaurantPageState();
}

// 4
class _RestaurantPageState extends State<RestaurantPage> {
  // TODO: Add Desktop Threshold
  // TODO: Add Constraint Properties
  // TODO: Calculate Constrained Width
  // TODO: Add Calculate Column Count

  // TODO: Build Custom Scroll View
  // TODO: Build Sliver App Bar
  // TODO: Build Info Section
  // TODO: Build Grid Item
  // TODO: Build Section Title
  // TODO: Build Grid View
  // TODO: Build Grid View Section

  // TODO: Replace build method
  @override
  Widget build(BuildContext context) {
    // 5
    return Scaffold(
      body: Center(
        // TODO: Replace with Custom Scroll View
        child: Text(
```

```
          'Restaurant Page',
          style: TextStyle(fontSize: 16.0),),
      ),
    );
  }
}
```

Here's how the code works:

1. Import necessary packages and classes.
2. Define a new class `RestaurantPage` as a `StatefulWidget` so we can have a mutable state.
3. `RestaurantPage` takes in a `restaurant` object which contains data such as restaurant info and menu to display on the page.
4. `_RestaurantPageState` is a class that holds the state for `RestaurantPage`.
5. The `build()` method currently returns a temporary placeholder text that displays `Restaurant Page`. This is where you'll add the new elements of this view.

Navigating to a Restaurant Page

Let's first implement a way to display a single restaurant.

Open **lib/components/restaurant_landscape_card.dart**.

Locate `// TODO: Push Restaurant Page` and replace it with the following code:

```
// 1
Navigator.push(
  // 2
  context,
  // 3
  MaterialPageRoute(
    // 4
    builder: (context) =>
      RestaurantPage(restaurant: widget.restaurant,
    )
  ),
);
```

When the user taps on a restaurant it navigates to its `RestaurantPage`. Here's how the code works:

1. `Navigator.push` starts the navigation to a new screen.
2. `context` tells Flutter where the navigation starts from within the widget tree.
3. `MaterialPageRoute` is used to create a route with a standard transition animation.
4. Navigate to `RestaurantPage` and pass in the current restaurant object to be displayed.

Add the following import:

```
import '../screens/restaurant_page.dart';
```

Perform a hot reload. In the **Foods Near Me** section tap on a restaurant and you should see the new `RestaurantPage` as shown below:

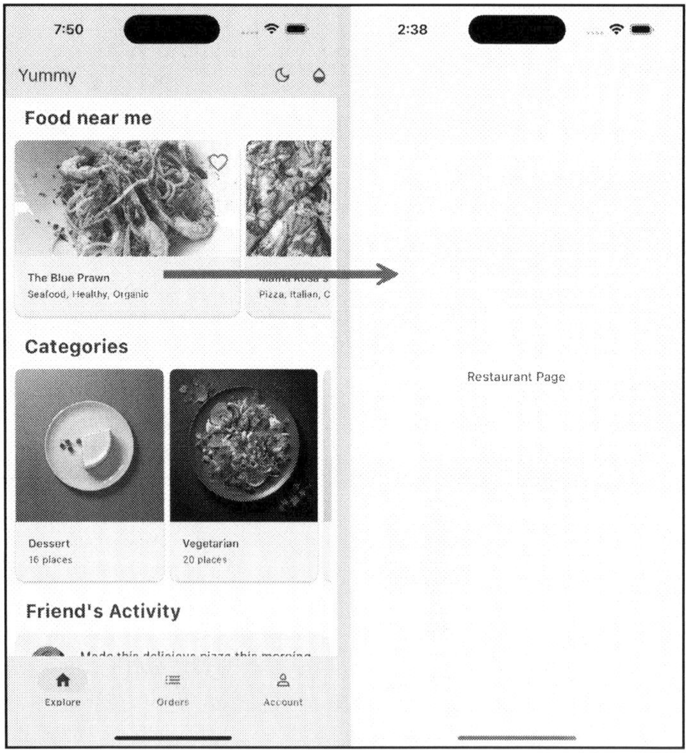

Now that your page is set up you're now ready to construct your sliver.

Building a Sliver for the Restaurant Page

Return to **lib/screens/restaurant_page.dart**, replace `// TODO: Build Custom Scroll View` with the following:

```
CustomScrollView _buildCustomScrollView() {
  return CustomScrollView(
    slivers: [
      // TODO: Add Sliver App Bar
      SliverToBoxAdapter(
          child: Container(
              height: 200.0,
              color: Colors.red,),),
      // TODO: Add Restaurant Info Section
      SliverToBoxAdapter(
          child: Container(
              height: 300.0,
              color: Colors.green,),),
      // TODO: Add Menu Item Grid View Section
      SliverFillRemaining(
          child: Container(
              color: Colors.blue,),),
    ],
  );
}
```

This function returns a `CustomScrollView`, a versatile widget that coordinates a variety of sliver widgets to create a multifaceted scrolling interface. Initially, this scroll view is populated with placeholder slivers:

- `SliverToBoxAdapter` is a handy widget that adapts a standard, non-sliver widget for use within a sliver list.
- `SliverFillRemaining` sizes its children to occupy the available remaining space in the viewport, perfect for expanding content areas.

These placeholders will be replaced later with the actual content for the app's scrolling layout.

In the same file, locate the comment `// TODO: Replace with Custom Scroll View` and replace it and `child` with the following:

```
child: _buildCustomScrollView(),
```

Perform a hot reload, and you should see the following screen(s):

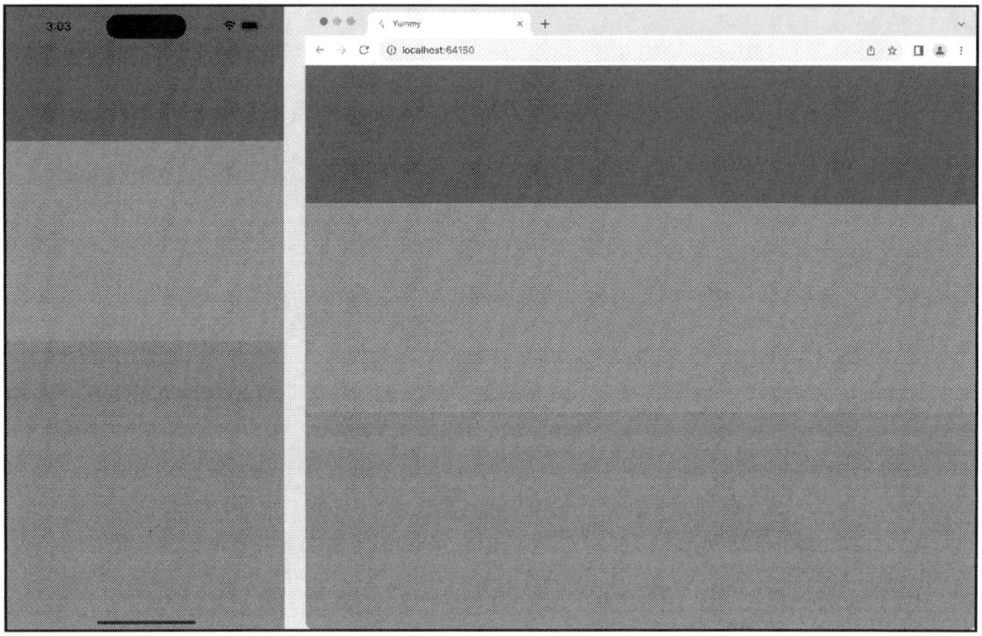

Next, you'll create a `SliverAppBar` that remains pinned to the top of a scrollable area.

Building a Sliver App Bar

A `SliverAppBar` expands to reveal a large image of a restaurant with a circular icon overlayed at the bottom left. As the user scrolls up, the app bar will remain at the top, and shrink the regular app bar size.

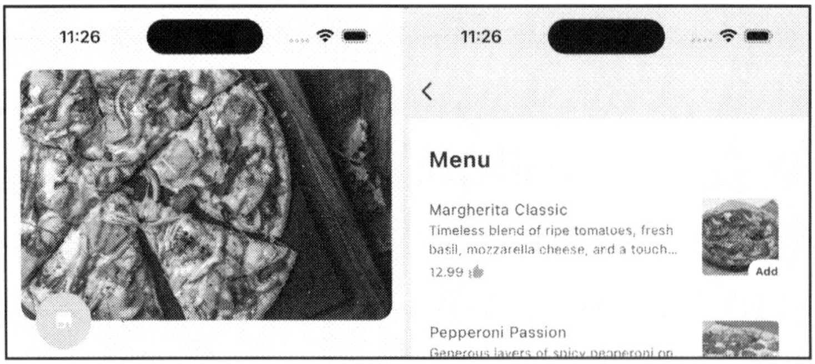

Locate `// TODO: Build Sliver App Bar` and replace it with the following code:

```
SliverAppBar _buildSliverAppBar() {
  // 1
  return SliverAppBar(
    // 2
    pinned: true,
    // 3
    expandedHeight: 300.0,
    // 4
    flexibleSpace: FlexibleSpaceBar(
      // 5
      background: Center(
        // 6
        child: Padding(
          padding: const EdgeInsets.only(
            left: 16.0,
            right: 16.0,
            top: 64.0,
          ),
          // 7
          child: Stack(
            children: [
              // 8
              Container(
                margin: const EdgeInsets.only(bottom: 30.0),
                decoration: BoxDecoration(
                  color: Colors.grey,
                  borderRadius: BorderRadius.circular(16.0),
                  // 9
                  image: DecorationImage(
                    image:
AssetImage(widget.restaurant.imageUrl),
                    fit: BoxFit.cover,),),
                  ),
              // 10
              const Positioned(
                bottom:0.0,
                left: 16.0,
                child: CircleAvatar(
                  radius: 30,
                  child: Icon(Icons.store, color:
Colors.white,),
                ),
              ),
            ],
          ),
        ),
      ),
    ),
  );
}
```

Here's how the code works:

1. The function returns a `SliverAppBar` widget that creates a collapsible app bar.
2. Keep the app bar pinned at the top of the view.
3. Specify `expandedHeight` of **300.0** pixels for maximum height when fully expanded.
4. Use a `FlexibleSpaceBar` for the collapsible part of the app bar.
5. Within the `FlexibleSpaceBar`, set a background widget.
6. Apply some padding to create internal spacing for the background.
7. Arrange elements using a `Stack`.
8. Create a `Container` for the backdrop with styling.
9. Show the restaurant image as a background using `DecorationImage`.
10. Place a circular icon at the bottom left using `Positioned` widget.

Integrate the Sliver App Bar

Now add the app bar to your custom scroll view. Locate `// TODO: Add Sliver App Bar` and replace it and `SliverToBoxAdapter` with the following:

```
_buildSliverAppBar(),
```

Perform a hot reload. Tap on a restaurant, and you should see the app bar as shown below:

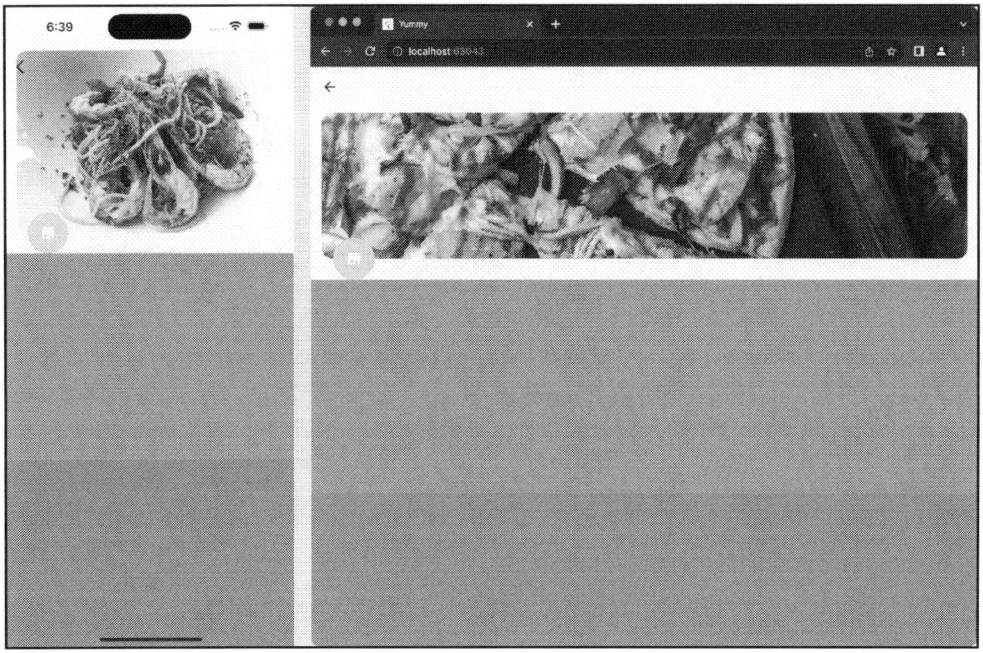

When you look at a restaurant knowing its details is helpful, but you don't have that. No worries, you'll add the info section next.

Building the Restaurant Info Section

After adding a sliver containing the restaurant's information such as the name, address, rating, distance and attributes your app bar will look like this:

Locate the comment `// TODO: Build Info Section` and replace it with the following code:

```
// 1
SliverToBoxAdapter _buildInfoSection() {
  // 2
  final textTheme = Theme.of(context).textTheme;
  // 3
  final restaurant = widget.restaurant;
  // 4
  return SliverToBoxAdapter(
    // 5
    child: Padding(
      padding: const EdgeInsets.all(16.0),
      // 6
      child: Column(
        crossAxisAlignment: CrossAxisAlignment.start,
        children: [
          // 7
          Text(restaurant.name, style:
textTheme.headlineLarge,),
          Text(restaurant.address, style: textTheme.bodySmall,),
          Text(
            restaurant.getRatingAndDistance(),
```

```
            style: textTheme.bodySmall,),
          Text(restaurant.attributes, style:
textTheme.labelSmall,),
        ],
      ),
    ),
  );
}
```

Here's how the code works:

1. Create `_buildInfoSection()` to construct a UI section for the restaurant's details.
2. Retrieve the application's text styles for consistent theming.
3. Access the restaurant's data passed to the widget.
4. Create a `SliverToBoxAdapter` to enable a column of text widgets in a sliver-based layout.
5. Apply padding around the column for spacing.
6. Create a column and align text elements to the start of the column.
7. Display the restaurant's name, address, rating, and attributes with styled text widgets.

Replace `// TODO: Add Restaurant Info Section` and `SliverToBoxAdapter` beneath it with:

```
_buildInfoSection(),
```

Perform a hot reload. Tap on a restaurant, and you should see the app bar as shown below:

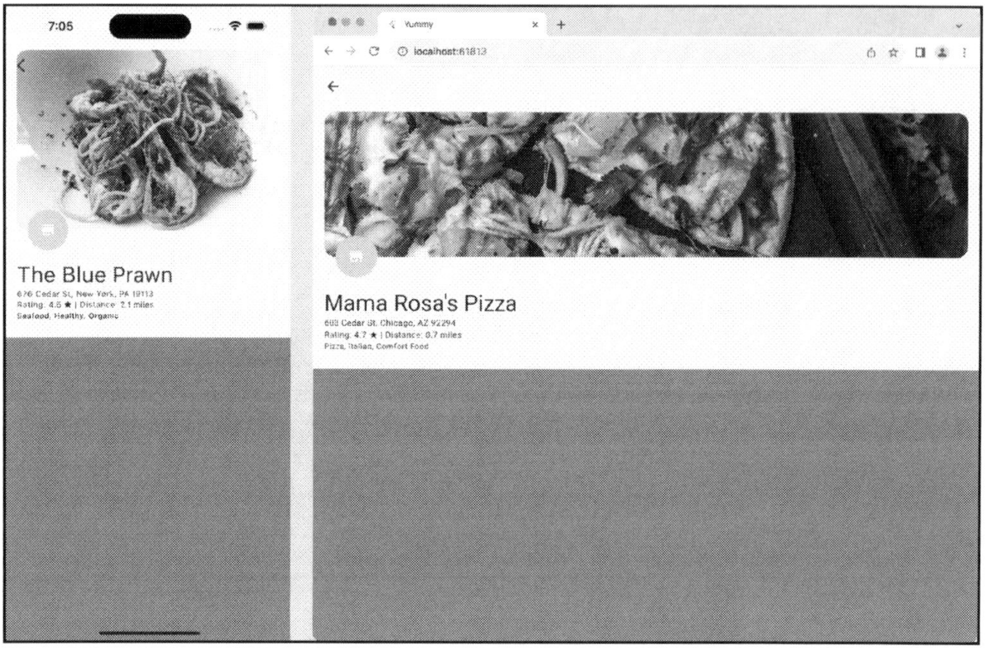

Next, you'll use a grid view to display the collection of menu items for a restaurant. Before you do that, take a moment to get acquainted with the `GridView` widget.

Introducing GridView

`GridView` is a 2D array of scrollable widgets. Similar to its linear counterpart, the `ListView`, it supports both horizontal and vertical scrolling, but it arranges its children in a grid format, which is perfect for displaying multiple items in a clean, organized layout.

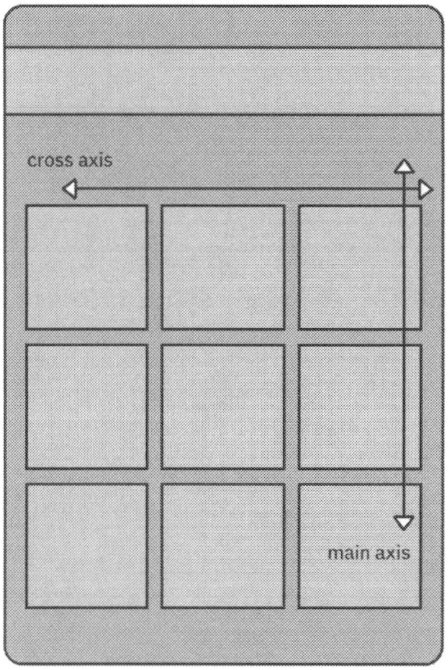

Getting used to `GridView` is easy. Like `ListView` it inherits from `ScrollView`, so their constructors are very similar.

- The default `GridView.count()` constructor is great for creating a grid with a fixed number of tiles in the cross-axis. You would use this if you know the number of columns or rows you want upfront.
- `GridView.builder()` works similarly to `ListView.builder()` by lazily constructing items as they're scrolled into the viewport, ideal for displaying a large or indeterminate number of items.
- `GridView.custom()` offers the highest level of customization, letting you use a custom `SliverGridDelegate` for precise control over how your grid is laid out.
- `GridView.extent()` allows you to specify the maximum extent of the tiles in the cross-axis, and it will determine the number of tiles in each row or column dynamically based on the available space.

GridView Key Parameters

Here are some parameters you should pay attention to:

- **crossAxisSpacing**: The spacing between each child in the cross-axis.
- **mainAxisSpacing**: The spacing between each child on the main axis.
- **crossAxisCount**: The number of children in the cross-axis. You can also think of this as the number of columns you want in a grid.
- **shrinkWrap**. Controls the fixed scroll area size.
- **physics**: Controls how the scroll view responds to user input.
- **primary**: Helps Flutter determine which scroll view is the primary one.
- **scrollDirection**: Controls the axis along which the view will scroll.

> **Note** `GridView` has a plethora of parameters to experiment and play with. Check out Greg Perry's article to learn more: https://medium.com/@greg.perry/decode-gridview-9b123553e604.

Understanding the Cross and Main Axis

What's the difference between the **main** and **cross** axis? Remember that `Columns` and `Rows` are like `ListViews`, but without a scroll view.

The main axis always corresponds to the scroll direction!

If your scroll direction is horizontal, you can think of this as a `Row`. The main axis represents the horizontal direction, as shown below:

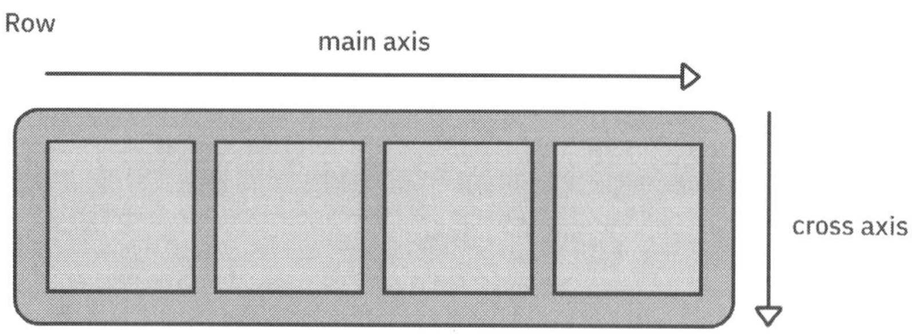

If your scroll direction is vertical, you can think of it as a `Column`. The main axis represents the vertical direction, as shown below:

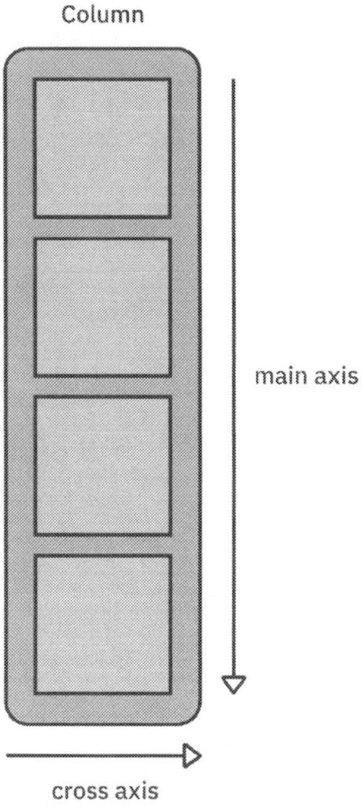

Understanding Grid Delegates

Grid delegates help you figure out the spacing and the number of columns to use to lay out the children in a `GridView`.

Aside from customizing your grid delegates, Flutter provides two delegates you can use out of the box:

- `SliverGridDelegateWithFixedCrossAxisCount`
- `SliverGridDelegateWithMaxCrossAxisExtent`

The first creates a layout that has a fixed number of tiles along the cross-axis. The second creates a layout with tiles that have a maximum cross-axis extent.

Building the Grid View Section

You'll use the `GridView` widget to display a collection of items on a restaurant's menu. `GridView` is a great widget to make your app responsive on different screens.

For example, depending on the screen width, you could have the grid view display one or two columns to show more information and leverage the real estate of a bigger screen, as shown below:

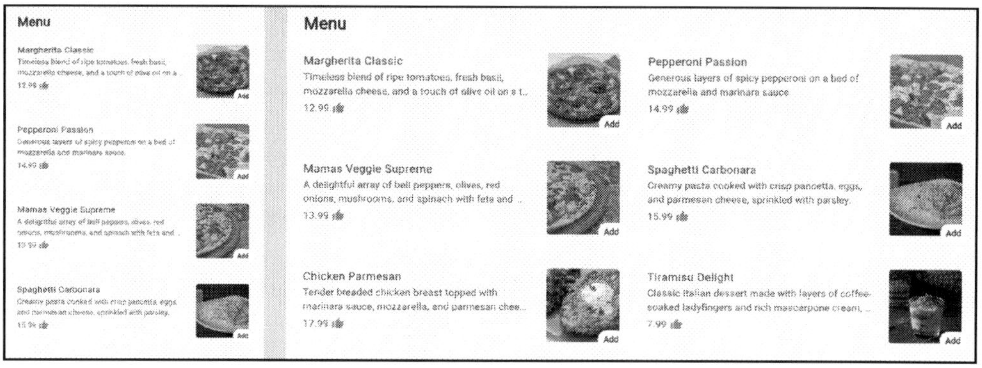

Building the Grid Item

Still within **restaurant_page.dart** locate `// TODO: Build Grid Item` and replace it with the following:

```
Widget _buildGridItem(int index) {
  final item = widget.restaurant.items[index];
  return InkWell(
    onTap: () {
      // Present Bottom Sheet in the future.
    },
    child: RestaurantItem(item: item),
  );
}
```

This function takes an index and uses it to access a specific item from the restaurant's menu. It then creates a `RestaurantItem` widget for that menu item. By wrapping the widget in an `InkWell`, we lay the groundwork for interactive functionality, such as opening a detail view in a bottom sheet upon tapping, which will be implemented in the next chapter.

Add this `import` at the top of the file:

```
import '../components/restaurant_item.dart';
```

Building the Section Title

Next, locate `// TODO: Build Section Title` and replace it with the following:

```
Widget _sectionTitle(String title) {
  return Padding(
    padding: const EdgeInsets.all(8.0),
    child: Text(
      title,
      style: const TextStyle(
        fontSize: 24,
        fontWeight: FontWeight.bold,),
    ),
  );
}
```

Here you simply create a `Text` with some custom padding.

Building the Grid View

Replace `// TODO: Build Grid View` with the following:

```
// 1
GridView _buildGridView(int columns) {
  // 2
  return GridView.builder(
    padding: const EdgeInsets.all(0),
    // 3
    gridDelegate: SliverGridDelegateWithFixedCrossAxisCount(
      mainAxisSpacing: 16,
      crossAxisSpacing: 16,
      childAspectRatio: 3.5,
      crossAxisCount: columns,
    ),
    // 4
    itemBuilder: (context, index) => _buildGridItem(index),
    // 5
    itemCount: widget.restaurant.items.length,
    // 6
    shrinkWrap: true,
    // 7
    physics: const NeverScrollableScrollPhysics(),
  );
}
```

Here's how the code works:

1. The function `_buildGridView()` accepts the number of columns as a parameter. This is used to determine the number of columns to display on different devices.
2. `GridView.builder()` is used for efficient, on-demand building of grid items.
3. Set up `SliverGridDelegateWithFixedCrossAxisCount` to define the grid's column count and spacing.
4. Each grid item is built via `_buildGridItem()`, called within the `itemBuilder` callback.
5. Set the number of items to display in the grid.
6. The `shrinkWrap` property is enabled, allowing the `GridView` to size itself according to its children vertically.
7. Set the physics to `NeverScrollableScrollPhysics`, to prevent scrolling within the grid itself.

Now that you've created your grid view, it is time to wrap it in a sliver.

Building the Grid View Sliver Section

Find `// TODO: Add Desktop Threshold` and replace it with the following:

```
static const desktopThreshold = 700;
```

This constant is used to determine whether to adapt the restaurant menu layout to big or small screens.

You need to calculate the number of columns depending on the screen's width. Replace `// TODO: Calculate Column Count` with:

```
int calculateColumnCount(double screenWidth) {
  return screenWidth > desktopThreshold ? 2 : 1;
}
```

Depending on the screen width the function will either return 2 or 1.

Find `// TODO: Build Grid View Section` and replace it with the following code:

```
// 1
SliverToBoxAdapter _buildGridViewSection(String title) {
  // 2
  final columns =
calculateColumnCount(MediaQuery.of(context).size.width);
  // 3
  return SliverToBoxAdapter(
    // 4
    child: Container(
      padding: const EdgeInsets.all(16.0),
      // 5
      child: Column(
        crossAxisAlignment: CrossAxisAlignment.start,
        children: [
          // 6
          _sectionTitle(title),
          // 7
          _buildGridView(columns),
        ],
      ),
    ),
  );
}
```

Here's how the code works:

1. Create a section with a title and grid view.
2. Calculate the number of columns based on the screen's width.
3. Build a `SliverToBoxAdapter` to embed a non-sliver widget.
4. Initialize a container for content with some padding.
5. Set up a vertical layout with a `Column` widget.
6. Add a section title using a custom method.
7. Add a grid view with the specified number of columns.

Finally, locate `// TODO: Add Menu Item Grid View Section` and replace it and the sliver placeholder widget with the following:

```
_buildGridViewSection('Menu'),
```

Perform a hot reload, tap on a restaurant, and you should see the following on mobile or web:

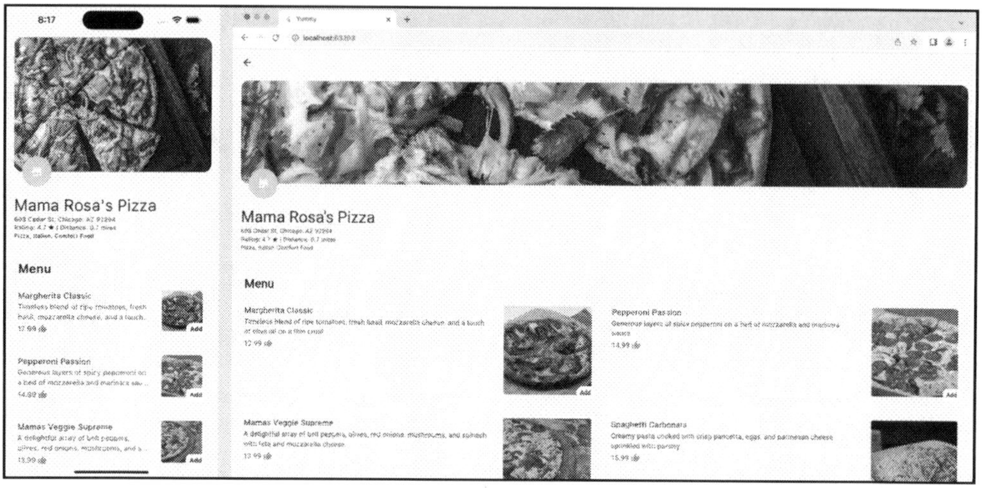

When building for multiple platforms, it's important to make sure that your app looks great on each platform. A web app has more screen real estate than a mobile app, so it's important to make sure that the menu is responsive and adapts to the screen size. That's what you'll do in the next section.

Implementing a Responsive Menu

Crafting a responsive restaurant menu for web applications is a pivotal task that strikes a balance between optimal use of screen real estate, readability, and visual appeal.

When transitioning from mobile to web views, it's crucial to consider how the menu's layout adapts to larger screens. Let's explore two primary strategies:

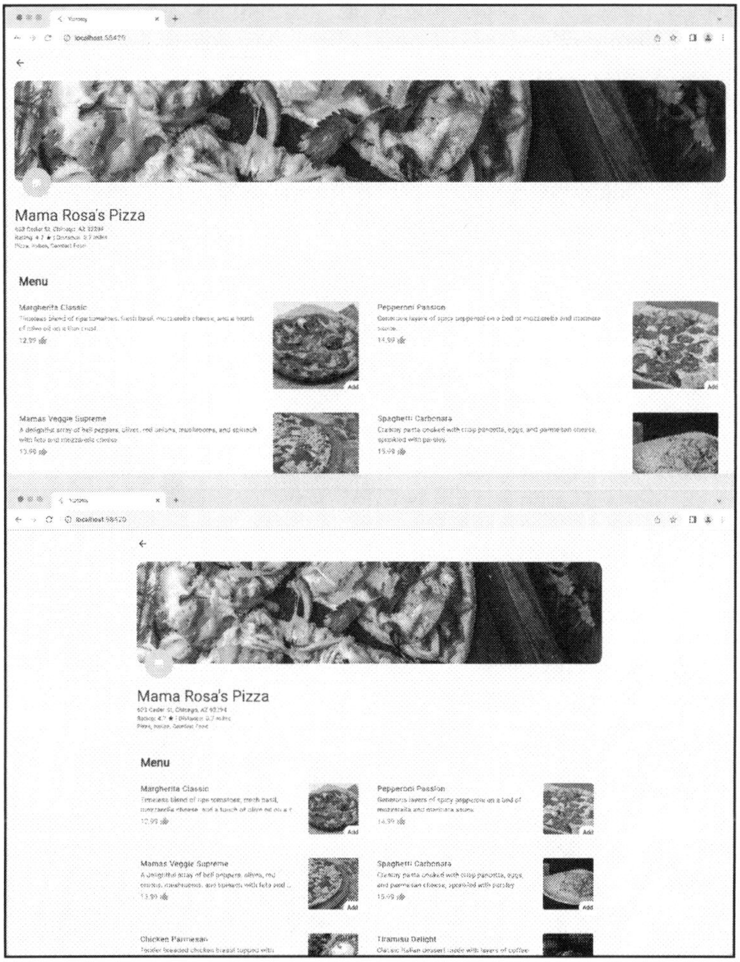

- **Option 1: Full-Screen Stretch** - This approach extends the menu across the full width of the screen. While it maximizes space, it can also make the menu appear too large. The vastness can overwhelm users, presenting too much information at once and detracting from the ability to focus on individual items.
- **Option 2: Fixed Width** - The alternative is to constrain the menu within a fixed-width container. This design is more aligned with standard web browsing expectations. It offers a structured layout with ample white space around the menu, which enhances visual appeal and improves content legibility.

Implementing Responsive Design

Next, you'll delve into the technical implementation to achieve a responsive and visually pleasant menu for web users.

Still in **restaurant_page.dart**, locate the comment `// TODO: Add Constraint Properties` and replace it with the following:

```
static const double largeScreenPercentage = 0.9;
static const double maxWidth = 1000;
```

These constants represent the maximum allowable width and the percentage of screen width the menu should occupy on larger screens.

Next, locate the comment `// TODO: Calculate Constrained Width` and replace it with the following:

```
double _calculateConstrainedWidth(double screenWidth) {
  return (screenWidth > desktopThreshold
          ? screenWidth * largeScreenPercentage //
          : screenWidth)
      .clamp(0.0, maxWidth);
}
```

This function ensures that on larger screens the menu width is proportional to the screen size, up to a maximum width.

Now find `// TODO: Replace build method` and replace it and the entire `build()` method with the following:

```
@override
Widget build(BuildContext context) {
  final screenWidth = MediaQuery.of(context).size.width;
  final constrainedWidth =
_calculateConstrainedWidth(screenWidth);

  return Scaffold(
    body: Center(
      child: SizedBox(
        width: constrainedWidth,
        child: _buildCustomScrollView(),
      ),
    ),
  );
}
```

With these changes, your restaurant menu will dynamically adapt to both mobile and web screen sizes. The result is a seamless user experience across devices.

Perform a hot reload, build, run your app and look at the restaurant menu on both mobile and web.

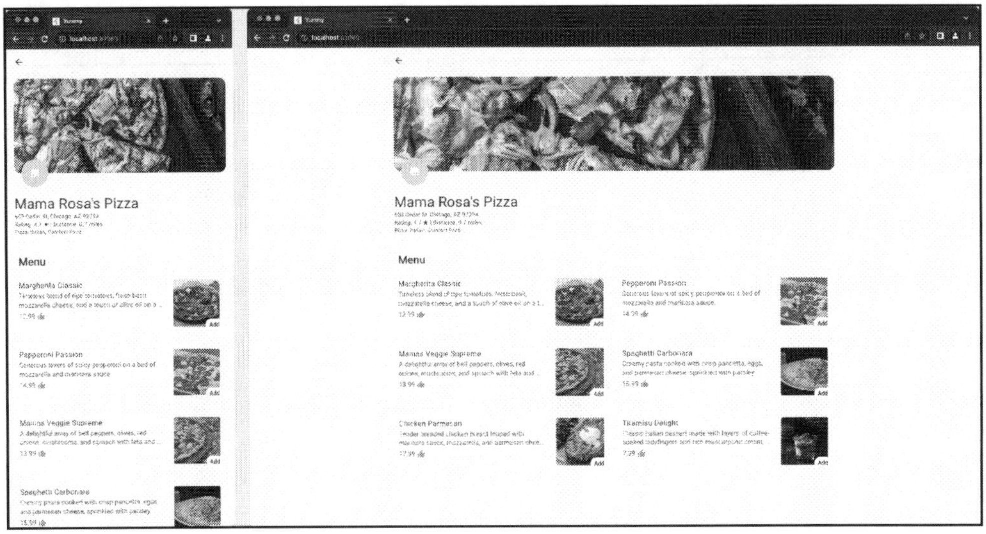

Try resizing your web browser window. You'll observe how elegantly your restaurant menu adapts to various screen sizes – a testament to responsive design in action!

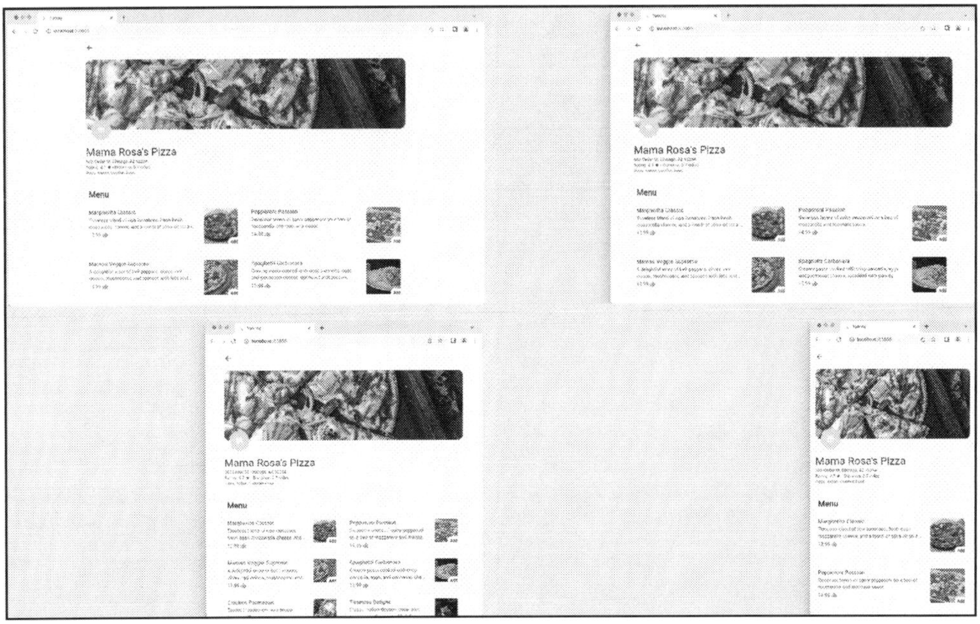

And there you have it – a responsive, visually appealing, and user-friendly restaurant menu for your Flutter application!

Key Points

- **Slivers** allow building intricate scrolling layouts with `CustomScrollView` and various sliver widgets.
- With **GridView** you can create grid layouts with customizable columns and spacing.
- **SliverToBoxAdapter** enables the integration of non-sliver widgets into sliver lists.
- Manage scroll behavior and direction with properties like **physics**.
- Embed grid views within sliver lists for complex scrollable structures.
- Use **MediaQuery** to create responsive grid layouts with **GridView**, adjusting the number of columns based on the screen size.

Where to Go From Here?

Now that you've a grasp of slivers and grid views in Flutter, you can create complex and custom scrollable layouts that look good and perform well on a wide range of devices. Slivers enable you to make scrollable areas in your app that look and behave exactly how you want.

In the next chapter, you'll take a look at some more interactive widgets.

Chapter 7: Interactive Widgets

By Vincent Ngo

In the previous chapter, you learned how to capture lots of data with scrollable widgets. But how do you make your app more engaging? How do you collect input and feedback from your users?

In this chapter, you'll explore interactive widgets. In particular, you'll learn to create:

- Bottom Sheets widgets
- Gesture-based widgets
- Time and date picker widgets
- Input and selection widgets
- Dismissable widgets

You'll continue to work on **Yummy**, building a more immersive experience. Users will be able to view menu items in detail, adjust quantities, manage and track order status.

You'll start by enhancing the way users can view and select menu items for their cart.

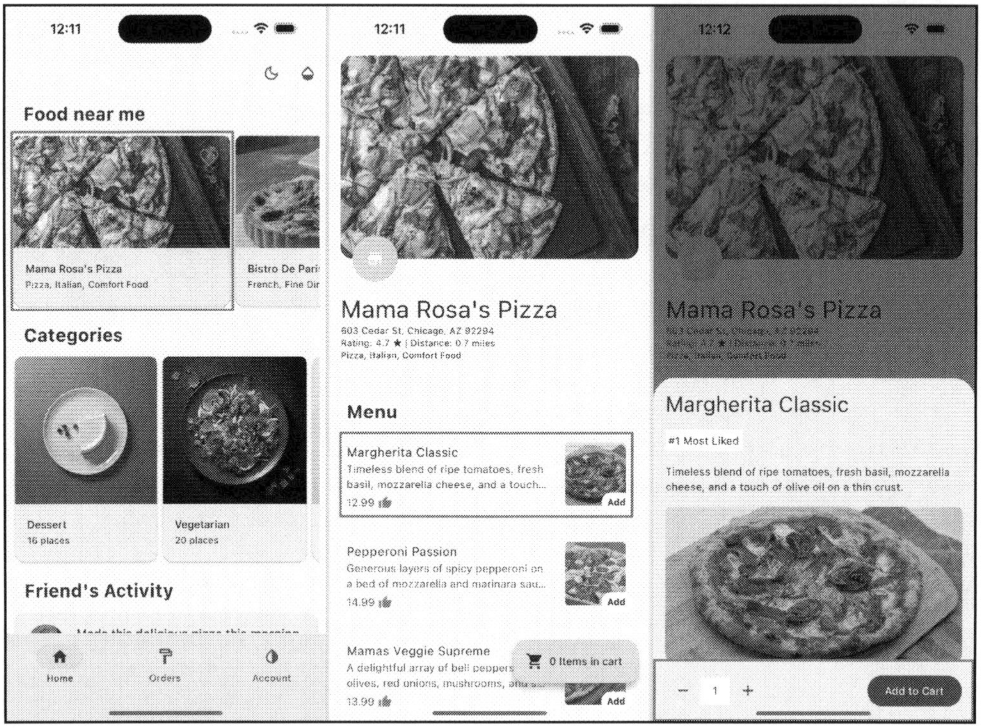

Next, you'll implement features for managing order details, including options for delivery or pickup and setting preferences for the date and time. Users will also be able to review their order summary and edit it before submission. Once an order is placed, they can track it in the **Orders** tab.

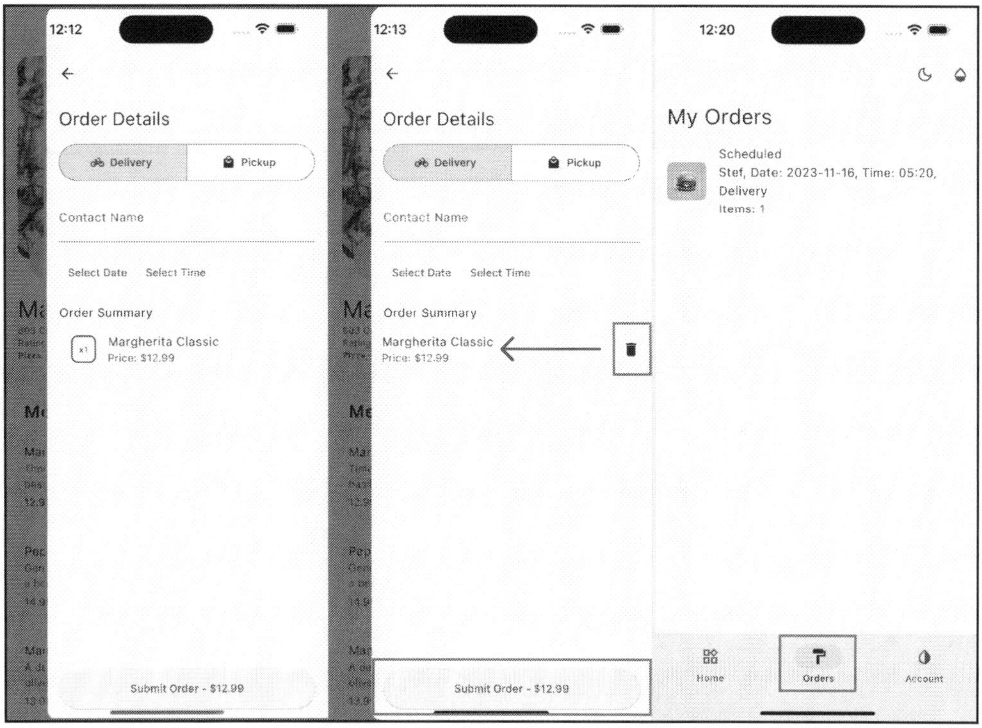

Additionally, you'll ensure your app remains responsive in web mode, providing a seamless experience across different devices.

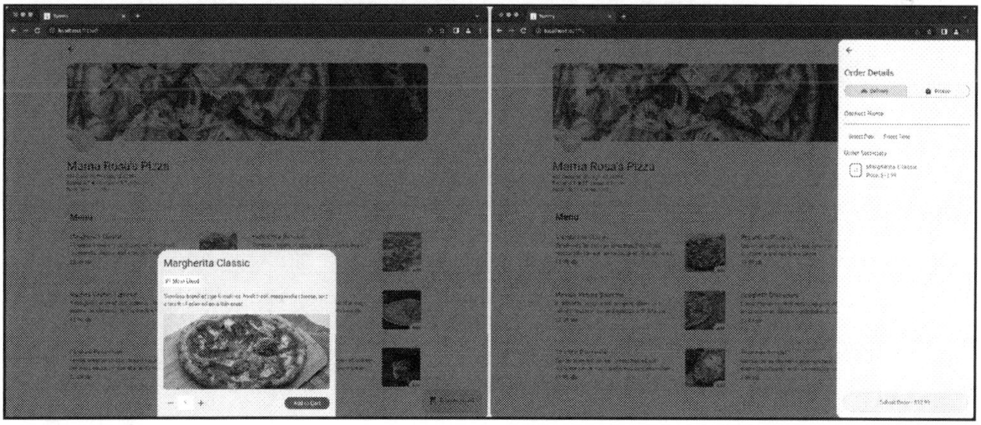

It's time to get started.

Getting Started

Open the starter project in Android Studio and run `flutter pub get`, if necessary. Then, run the app. You'll see the following:

New Project Files

There are new files in this starter project to help you out. Before you learn how to utilize interactive widgets, take a look at them.

New Packages

In **pubspec.yaml** under `dependencies`, there are two new packages:

- **uuid**: Generates unique keys for each menu item. This helps you know which item to add, update or remove.
- **intl**: Provides internationalization and localization utilities. You'll use this to format dates.

Don't forget to always run `flutter pub get` after updating **pubspec.yaml** entries.

New Files in the Models Folder

For your convenience two manager classes have been provided to manage state in your app:

- **CartManager**: Manages the user's shopping cart. For example number of items in the cart, functions to update the cart, the total cost, delivery or self-pickup and pickup.
- **OrdersManager**: Manages all the orders the user has submitted.

Starting from **main.dart** you will notice the manager objects are initialized and passed all the way down to **restaurant_page.dart**. Feel free to dive into the code to see how these objects are passed down the widget tree.

With all these new additions you are now ready to start.

Presenting Item Details

Before you display a specific menu item, you'll need a way to present its widget.

Building a Bottom Sheet

Within **lib/screens/restaurant_page.dart** locate the comment `// TODO: Show Bottom Sheet` and replace it with the following:

```
// 1
void _showBottomSheet(Item item) {
  // 2
  showModalBottomSheet<void>(
    // 3
    isScrollControlled: true,
```

```
      // 4
      context: context,
      // 5
      constraints: const BoxConstraints(maxWidth: 480),
      // 6
      // TODO: Replace with Item Details Widget
      builder: (context) => Container(
        color: Colors.red,
        height: 400,
      ),
    );
  }
```

Here's how it works:

1. Define a function `_showBottomSheet()` that accepts the selected menu item to display in the bottom sheet.
2. When invoked, create a modal bottom sheet that slides up from the bottom.
3. `isScrollControlled` is `true`, to allow the bottom sheet to have dynamic height.
4. Pass in the current context to display the bottom sheet.
5. Constraint the bottom sheet to have a max width of 480. This is to support responsive UI on mobile or desktop.
6. `builder()` returns the details to display, but for now it's just a placeholder container.

Next, you'll present the bottom sheet.

Presenting the Bottom Sheet

Within the same file, find and replace `// TODO: Replace _buildGridItem()` and the whole `_buildGridItem()` function beneath it with the following:

```
  Widget _buildGridItem(int index) {
    final item = widget.restaurant.items[index];
    return InkWell(
      onTap: () => _showBottomSheet(item),
      child: RestaurantItem(item: item),
    );
  }
```

When the user taps on a menu item you'll present the item details in a bottom sheet as shown below:

Leave **restaurant_page.dart** open, you'll be coming back to it.

Building Item Details

When you tap on a specific menu item it shows a bottom sheet to focus on that specific item. Showing the title, popularity, description and enlarged image of the item.

Within the **lib/components** directory, create a new file called **item_details.dart** and add the following code:

```
import 'package:flutter/material.dart';
import '../models/cart_manager.dart';
import '../models/restaurant.dart';

class ItemDetails extends StatefulWidget {
  final Item item;
  final CartManager cartManager;
  final void Function() quantityUpdated;
```

```
  // 1
  const ItemDetails({
    super.key,
    required this.item,
    required this.cartManager,
    required this.quantityUpdated,
  });

  @override
  State<ItemDetails> createState() => _ItemDetailsState();
}

class _ItemDetailsState extends State<ItemDetails> {
  @override
  Widget build(BuildContext context) {
    // 2
    final textTheme = Theme.of(context)
        .textTheme
        .apply(displayColor:
Theme.of(context).colorScheme.onSurface);
    // 3
    final colorTheme = Theme.of(context).colorScheme;

    // 4
    return Padding(
      padding: const EdgeInsets.all(16.0),
      // 5
      child: Wrap(
        children: [
          // 6
          Column(
            crossAxisAlignment: CrossAxisAlignment.start,
            children: [
              Text(
                widget.item.name,
                style: textTheme.headlineMedium,
              ),
              // TODO: Add Liked Badge
              Text(widget.item.description),
              // TODO: Add Item Image
              // TODO: Add Cart Control
            ],
          ),
        ],
      ),
    );
  }

  // TODO: Create Most Liked Badge
  // TODO: Create Item Image
  // TODO: Create Cart Control

}
```

Here's how the code works:

1. The `ItemDetails` widget takes in the selected item and a cart manager to manage cart operations. `quantityUpdated` is a callback that notifies the parent widget that the user updated the quantity.
2. Retrieve the `textTheme` and ensure the text color matches the surface color of the color scheme.
3. Retrieve the `colorTheme`, this ensures the app has a consistent color theme across all widgets in your app.
4. Add uniform padding of **16.0** all around.
5. The `Wrap` widget organizes children in horizontal or vertical runs, adjusting the layout based on space.
6. `Column` widget aligns child widgets vertically.

Leave **item_details.dart** open.

You'll next replace all the TODOs and add the components to the item details widget.

Showing Item Details

Return to **restaurant_page.dart** and locate the comment `// TODO: Replace with Item Details Widget` and replace it and the builder function with the following:

```
builder: (context) =>
ItemDetails(
  item: item,
  cartManager: widget.cartManager,
  quantityUpdated: () {
    setState(() {});
  },
),
```

When the bottom sheet is presented, it initializes the `ItemDetails` widget. When the `quantityUpdated()` callback is invoked, you call `setState()` to trigger a new render of the widget.

Next, add the following import at the top:

```
import '../components/item_details.dart';
```

Close and open the bottom sheet, it should now look like this:

Now you are ready to add more widgets!

Creating a Most Liked Badge

Back in **item_details.dart**, locate the comment `// TODO: Create Most Liked Badge` and replace it with the following:

```
// 1
Widget _mostLikedBadge(ColorScheme colorTheme) {
  // 2
  return Align(
    // 3
    alignment: Alignment.centerLeft,
    // 4
    child: Container(
        padding: const EdgeInsets.all(4.0),
        color: colorTheme.onPrimary,
        // 5
        child: const Text('#1 Most Liked'),
      ),
  );
}
```

Here's how the code works:

1. Define a method `_mostLikedBadge()`, which takes in a `ColorScheme`. This method will create a badge to indicate whether an item is most liked.
2. The `Align` widget is used to align the badge within the parent widget.
3. Align the widget center-left.
4. A `Container` is used to apply padding and color.
5. A `Text` widget is used to display the content of the badge. In this case, it reads **#1 Most Liked**.

Next, locate the comment `// TODO: Add Liked Badge` and replace it with the following:

```
const SizedBox(height: 16.0),
_mostLikedBadge(colorTheme),
const SizedBox(height: 16.0),
```

Here you add **16.0** padding between the liked badge.

The details view now looks like this:

Showing an Item Image

Locate the comment `// TODO: Create Item Image` and replace it with the following:

```
// 1
Widget _itemImage(String imageUrl) {
  // 2
  return Container(
    height: 200,
    decoration: BoxDecoration(
      borderRadius: BorderRadius.circular(8.0),
      // 3
      image: DecorationImage(
        image: NetworkImage(imageUrl),
        fit: BoxFit.cover,
      ),
    ),
  );
}
```

Here's how it works:

1. `_itemImage()` takes in an `imageUrl`.
2. Apply a container to style the image, adding a fixed height and rounded corners.
3. Set the background image.

Now, replace `// TODO: Add Item Image` with:

```
const SizedBox(height: 16.0),
_itemImage(widget.item.imageUrl),
const SizedBox(height: 16.0),
```

Here is what the details view looks like now:

Creating a Widget to Control the Cart

For the final piece of the item details view you'll create a cart control component to update the quantity.

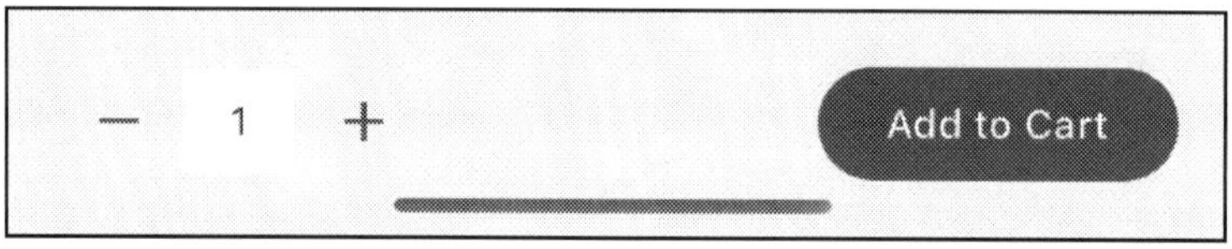

Within the **lib/components** directory, create a new file called **cart_control.dart** and add the following code:

```
import 'package:flutter/material.dart';

// 1
class CartControl extends StatefulWidget {
  // 2
  final void Function(int) addToCart;

  const CartControl({
    required this.addToCart,
    super.key,
```

```
  });

  // 3
  @override
  State<CartControl> createState() => _CartControlState();
}

// 4
class _CartControlState extends State<CartControl> {
  // 5
  int _cartNumber = 1;

  @override
  Widget build(BuildContext context) {
    // 6
    final colorScheme = Theme.of(context).colorScheme;
    // 7
    return Row(
      // 8
      mainAxisAlignment: MainAxisAlignment.spaceBetween,
      // 9
      children: [
        // TODO: Add Cart Control Components
        Container(
          color: Colors.red,
          height: 44.0,
        ),
      ],
    );
  }

  // TODO: Build Minus Button
  // TODO: Build Cart Number
  // TODO: Build Plus Button
  // TODO: Build Add Cart Button
}
```

Here's how it works:

1. Define a stateful widget called `CartControl`.
2. Define an `addToCart()` callback function, which returns an integer to specify the number of items in the cart.
3. Link this widget to its state `_CartControlState()`.
4. Define the `CartControl` state class.
5. `_cartNumber` is a private state variable used to keep track of the quantity of items to be added to the cart. The default value is **1**.

6. Within the `build()` method, retrieve the color scheme for consistency.
7. Return a `Row` widget to layout children horizontally.
8. Use `MainAxisAlignment.spaceBetween` to space the children evenly.
9. Add a placeholder container which will eventually be replaced by cart control components.

Time to add the components!

Creating the Minus Button

First you'll create the minus button.

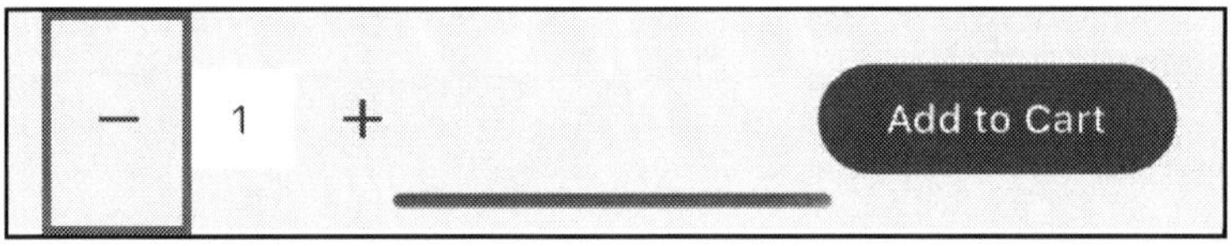

Still in **cart_control.dart**, locate the comment `// TODO: Build Minus Button` and replace it with the following:

```
// 1
Widget _buildMinusButton() {
  // 2
  return IconButton(
    icon: const Icon(Icons.remove),
    // 3
    onPressed: () {
      setState(() {
        // 4
        if (_cartNumber > 1) {
          _cartNumber--;
        }
      });
    },
    // 5
    tooltip: 'Decrease Cart Count',
  );
}
```

Here's how the code works:

1. Create a button to decrease the number of items in the cart.
2. Initialize an `IconButton` with the `remove` symbol that renders like a minus sign.
3. Configure the `onPressed()` callback to trigger a `setState()` to update the UI

4. Decrements `_cartNumber` by 1 if it's greater than 1 preventing it from going below 1.

5. Provides a tooltip for accessibility and user guidance.

Creating Cart Number Container

Next, you'll add the container to display the quantity.

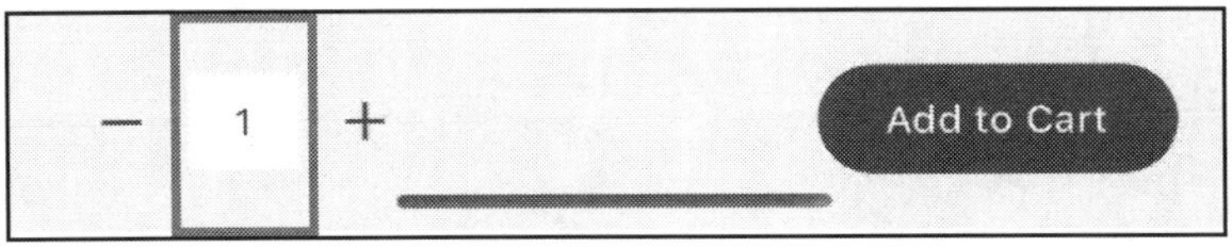

Locate the comment `// TODO: Build Cart Number` and replace it with the following:

```
// 1
Widget _buildCartNumberContainer(ColorScheme colorScheme) {
  // 2
    return Container(
      padding: const EdgeInsets.symmetric(horizontal: 16.0,
vertical: 8.0),
      color: colorScheme.onPrimary,
      // 3
      child: Text(_cartNumber.toString()),
    );
}
```

Here's how the code works:

1. The method takes a `ColorScheme` to style the widget.

2. It returns a container with spacing and alignment.

3. Displays the cart number as a text.

Creating the Plus Button

The next step is to add the plus button.

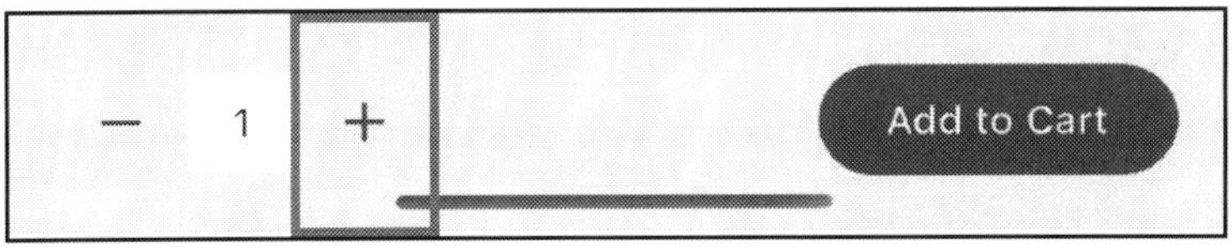

Locate the comment `// TODO: Build Plus Button` and replace it with the following:

```
Widget _buildPlusButton() {
  return IconButton(
    icon: const Icon(Icons.add),
    onPressed: () {
      setState(() {
        _cartNumber++;
      });
    },
    tooltip: 'Increase Cart Count',
  );
}
```

Similar to the minus button you increment the `_cartNumber` variable.

Creating the Add to Cart Button

The final component you'll add is the **Add to Cart** button.

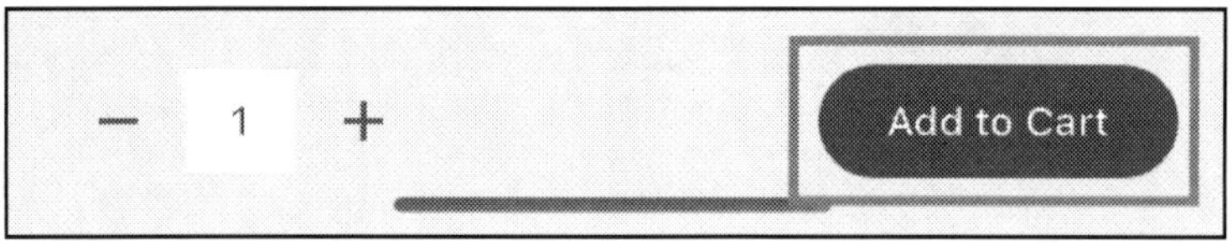

Replace `// TODO: Build Add Cart Button` with:

```
Widget _buildAddCartButton() {
  // 1
  return FilledButton(
    // 2
    onPressed: () {
      widget.addToCart(_cartNumber);
    },
    // 3
    child: const Text('Add to Cart'),
  );
}
```

Here's how the code works:

1. Initialize a `FilledButton` which is a button that fills the button's background.
2. When the user presses the button, trigger the `addToCart()` callback and pass the number of items the user selected.
3. The button displays the text **Add to Cart**.

Showing the Cart Control Components

Now that you've built all the components, it's time to put them to use.

Replace `// TODO: Add Cart Control Components` and the `Container` beneath it with the following:

```
_buildMinusButton(),
_buildCartNumberContainer(colorScheme),
_buildPlusButton(),
const Spacer(),
_buildAddCartButton(),
```

The `Spacer` widget is used to create space between the surrounding widgets.

Using the Cart Control

You'll now add the cart control to the item details view.

Go back to **item_details.dart**, find `// TODO: Create Cart Control` and replace it with:

```
// 1
Widget _addToCartControl(Item item) {
  // 2
  return CartControl(
    // 3
    addToCart: (number) {
      const uuid = Uuid();
      final uniqueId = uuid.v4();
      final cartItem = CartItem(
          id: uniqueId,
          name: item.name,
          price: item.price,
          quantity: number,
        );
      // 4
      setState(() {
        widget.cartManager.addItem(cartItem);
        // 5
        widget.quantityUpdated();
      });
      // 6
      Navigator.pop(context);
    },
  );
}
```

Here's how it works:

1. `_addToCartControl()` takes in the selected `Item` object.
2. It returns a `CartControl` widget.
3. The `addToCart()` callback function will return the item quantity and create a new `CartItem`. A `CartItem` requires a uniquely generated id, item name, price and the quantity selected.
4. Update the state by adding the new cart item managed by `CartManager`.
5. Invoke the callback to notify the parent widget that the quantity has been updated.
6. Close the bottom sheet.

> **Note**: Ensure that `setState()` is the most appropriate way to manage state in this context. If your app scales, you might need a more robust state management solution. For more advanced state management techniques check out Chapter 13, "Managing State".

Add the following imports:

```
import 'package:uuid/uuid.dart';
import 'cart_control.dart';
```

If you're wondering why the cart control isn't displaying, stop worrying you're adding it next.

Applying the Cart Control

Locate the comment `// TODO: Add Cart Control` and replace it with the following:

```
_addToCartControl(widget.item),
```

After hot reload runs, your bottom sheet should look like this:

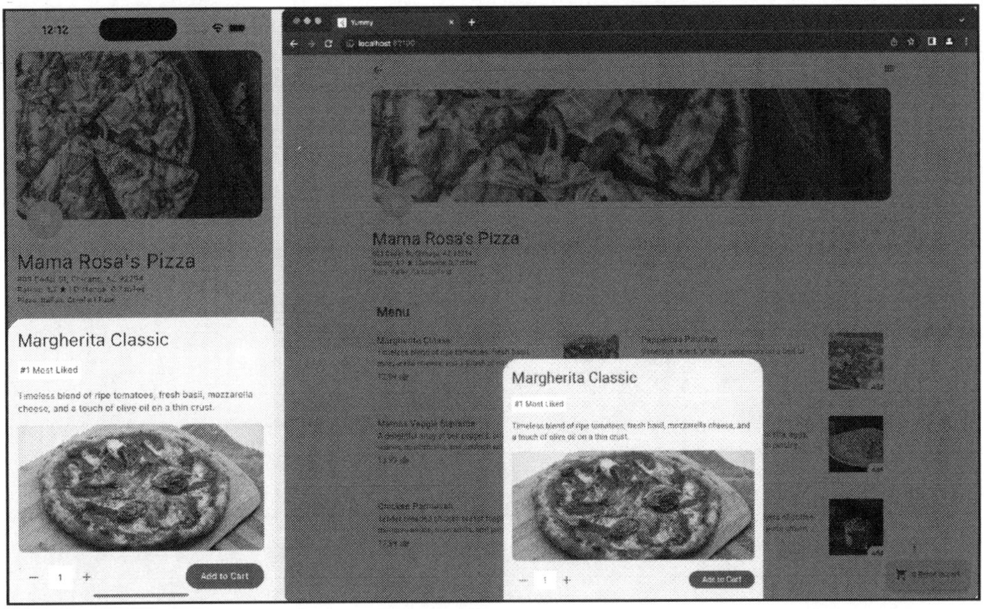

Now the user can add items to their cart!

You still need to create a way to manage the cart and allow users to submit the order. Don't worry, that's next!

Building the Checkout Page

In this next section, you'll learn about how to create drawers and leverage input widgets to capture data.

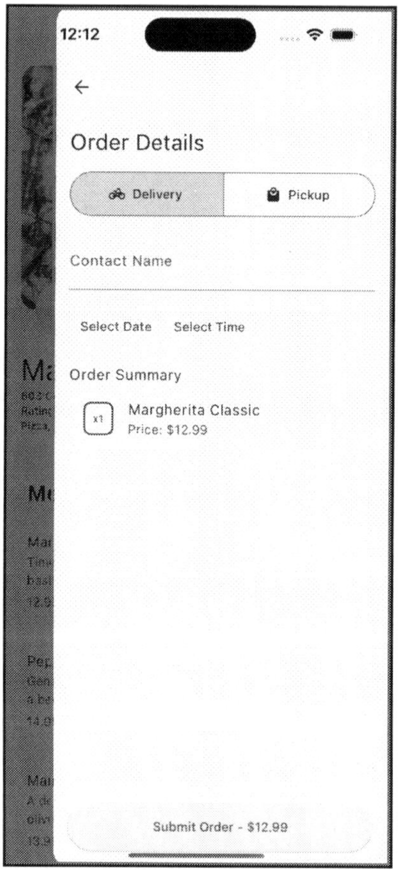

The user will be able to do the following:

- Select whether the order is delivered or picked up
- Name of the recipient
- Select date and time
- Manage the cart items
- Submit their order

Adding a Drawer

Drawers are commonly used for secondary navigation options.

In **restaurant_page.dart**, locate `// TODO: Define Drawer Max Width` and replace it with:

```
static const double drawerWidth = 375.0;
```

Here you define a constant variable to determine the max width of the drawer.

Replace `// TODO: Create Drawer` with the following:

```
Widget _buildEndDrawer() {
  return SizedBox(
    width: drawerWidth,
    // TODO: Replace with Checkout Page
    child: Container(color: Colors.red),
  );
}
```

The `_buildEndDrawer()` function creates a simple drawer with a specific width and a placeholder red container.

Next, to apply the drawer locate the comment: `// TODO: Apply Drawer` and replace it with the following:

```
endDrawer: _buildEndDrawer(),
```

The scaffold widget is a top-level widget used in Flutter to implement the basic visual layout structure of an app. It includes the `endDrawer` property to define a drawer that slides in from the right.

Now you need a way to open such a drawer.

Adding a Floating Action Button

You'll use a floating action button when clicked on to present the drawer.

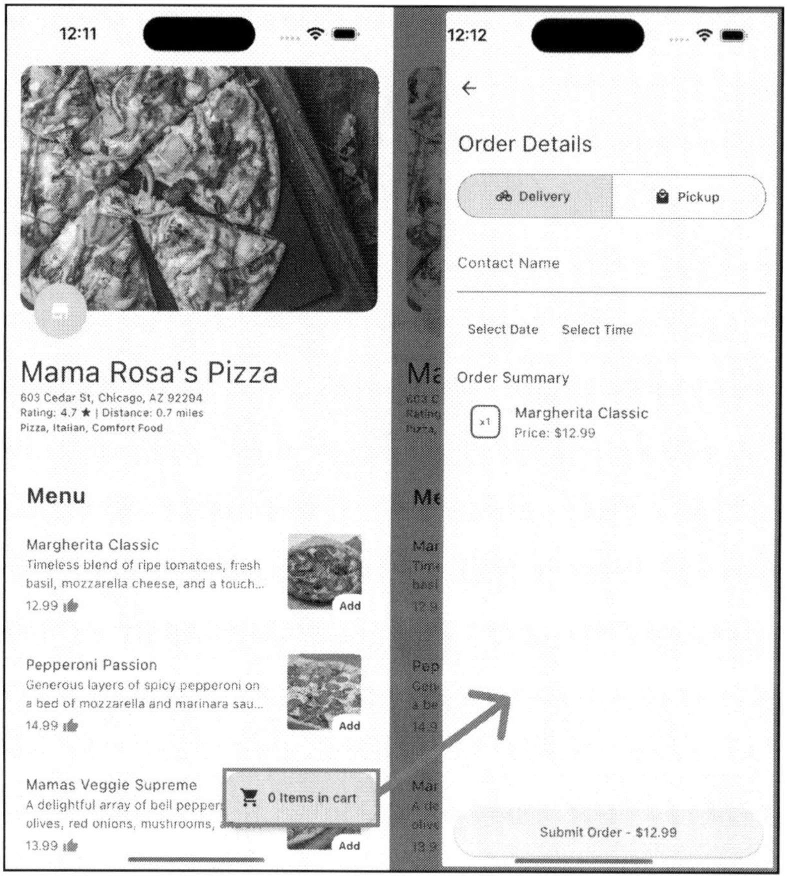

Opening the Drawer

Locate the comment `// TODO: Define Scaffold Key` and replace it with the following:

```
final GlobalKey<ScaffoldState> scaffoldKey =
GlobalKey<ScaffoldState>();
```

Having a `GlobalKey` for your `Scaffold` allows you to control the scaffold from anywhere in your code. This is particularly useful for opening drawers, snack bars, or any other action that requires a reference to the `ScaffoldState`.

Next, locate `// TODO: Add Scaffold Key` and replace it with:

```
key: scaffoldKey,
```

Find and replace `// TODO: Open Drawer` with the following function:

```
void openDrawer() {
  scaffoldKey.currentState!.openEndDrawer();
}
```

When `openDrawer()` is invoked, it will try to access the scaffold's current state and open the drawer. The `!` operator asserts that the current state is not null.

Add a Floating Action Button

Now you need to create the floating action button to open the drawer.

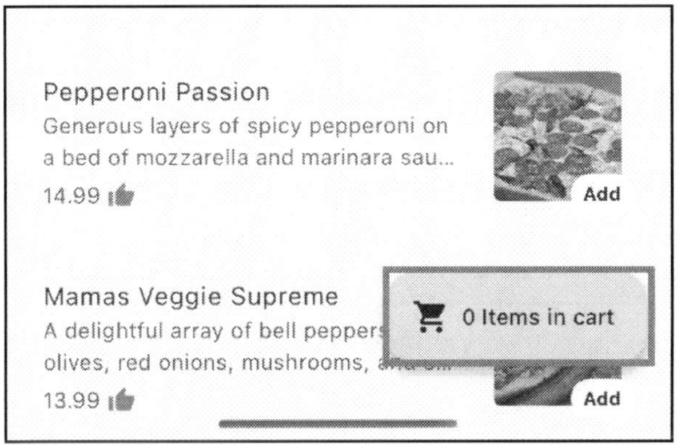

Locate the comment `// TODO: Create Floating Action Button` and replace it with the following:

```
// 1
Widget _buildFloatingActionButton() {
  // 2
  return FloatingActionButton.extended(
    // 3
    onPressed: openDrawer,
    // 4
    tooltip: 'Cart',
    // 5
    icon: const Icon(Icons.shopping_cart),
    // 6
    label: Text('${widget.cartManager.items.length} Items in
cart'),
  );
}
```

Here's how the code works:

1. The function returns a `FloatingActionButton` widget.
2. Instantiate a `FloatingActionButton.extended`, which allows the button to have both an icon and a label.
3. When the button is pressed, `openDrawer()` is invoked.
4. Show a tooltip for accessibility.
5. Set the button's icon.
6. The label displays the number of items in the cart.

Find and replace `// TODO: Apply Floating Action Button` with this code:

```
floatingActionButton: _buildFloatingActionButton(),
```

Here you set the floating action button within the scaffold widget.

Perform a hot reload. Click a restaurant and press the floating cart button, you'll see the red drawer shown below:

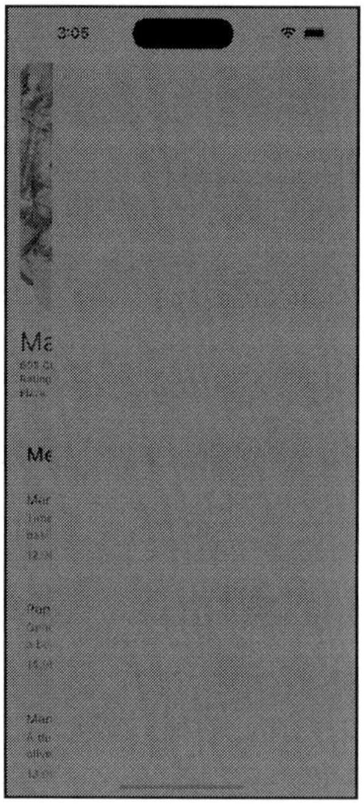

Now you are ready to start to build your checkout page!

Creating the Checkout Page

Within the **lib/screens** directory, create a new file called **checkout_page.dart** and add the following code:

```
// 1
import 'package:flutter/material.dart';
import '../models/cart_manager.dart';
import '../models/order_manager.dart';

class CheckoutPage extends StatefulWidget {
  // 2
  final CartManager cartManager;
  // 3
  final Function() didUpdate;
  // 4
  final Function(Order) onSubmit;

  const CheckoutPage(
      {super.key,
      required this.cartManager,
      required this.didUpdate,
      required this.onSubmit,
    });

  @override
  State<CheckoutPage> createState() => _CheckoutPageState();
}

class _CheckoutPageState extends State<CheckoutPage> {
  // 5
  // TODO: Add State Properties
  // TODO: Configure Date Format
  // TODO: Configure Time of Day
  // TODO: Set Selected Segment
  // TODO: Build Segmented Control
  // TODO: Build Name Textfield
  // TODO: Select Date Picker
  // TODO: Select Time Picker
  // TODO: Build Order Summary
  // TODO: Build Submit Order Button

  @override
  Widget build(BuildContext context) {
    // 6
    final textTheme = Theme.of(context)
        .textTheme
        .apply(displayColor:
Theme.of(context).colorScheme.onSurface);

    // 7
```

```
    return Scaffold(
      // 8
      appBar: AppBar(
        leading: IconButton(
          icon: const Icon(Icons.arrow_back),
          onPressed: () => Navigator.of(context).pop(),
        ),
      ),
      // 9
      body: Padding(
        padding: const EdgeInsets.all(16.0),
        child: Column(
          crossAxisAlignment: CrossAxisAlignment.stretch,
          children: [
            Text(
              'Order Details',
              style: textTheme.headlineSmall,
            ),
            // TODO: Add Segmented Control
            // TODO: Add Name Textfield
            // TODO: Add Date and Time Picker
            // TODO: Add Order Summary
            // TODO: Add Submit Order Button
          ],
        ),
      ),
    );
  }
}
```

Here's how the checkout page is initialized:

1. Import necessary `material` library and manager models.
2. `CheckoutPage` is a stateful widget that requires `CartManager` to manage and update cart items.
3. Declare a `didUpdate()` callback to notify when something changes in the cart.
4. Create an `onSubmit()` callback to notify that the user tapped on the submit button.
5. Spread some TODO comments to add all the interactive widgets to your checkout page.
6. Retrieve the current text theme and apply the color theme to be consistent throughout the app.

7. Create a `Scaffold` widget that sets the app bar and body.
8. `AppBar` displays a back button that dismisses the drawer when clicked.
9. The `body` sets up padding and uses a `Column` widget to layout child widgets vertically.

Using the Checkout Page

Back in **restaurant_page.dart** locate the comment `// TODO: Replace with Checkout Page` and replace it and the `child` beneath it with the following:

```
// 1
child: Drawer(
  // 2
  child: CheckoutPage(
    // 3
    cartManager: widget.cartManager,
    // 4
    didUpdate: () {
      setState(() {});
    },
    // 5
    onSubmit: (order) {
      widget.ordersManager.addOrder(order);
      Navigator.popUntil(context, (route) => route.isFirst);
    },
  ),
),
```

Here's how the code works:

1. Initialize the `Drawer` widget that slides from the side of the screen.
2. Use `CheckoutPage` as the primary content of the drawer.
3. Pass in `cartManager` to manage and display cart items.
4. Configure the `didUpdate()` callback to refresh the state of the parent widget.
5. Set `onSubmit()` so that, when the user taps on the submit button, it adds a new order and closes the drawer.

Add the following import:

```
import 'checkout_page.dart';
```

Open and close the drawer, you should now see the following:

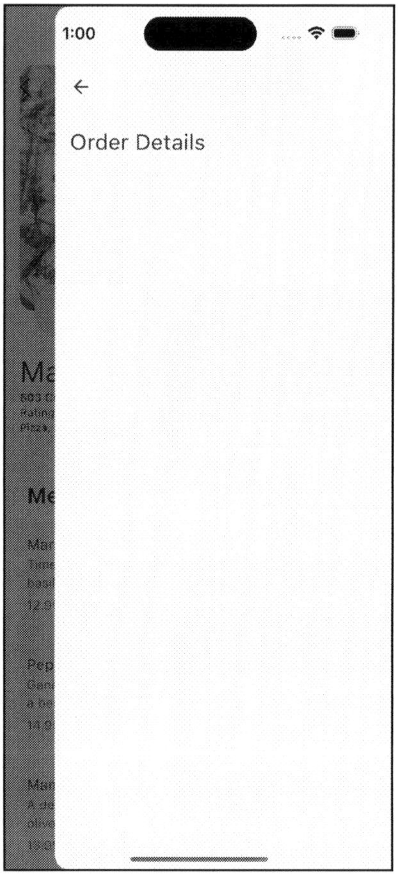

Now you're ready to add all the input widgets!

Adding Checkout State Properties

Back in **checkout_page.dart**, locate `// TODO: Add State Properties` and replace it with the following:

```
// 1
final Map<int, Widget> myTabs = const <int, Widget>{
  0: Text('Delivery'),
  1: Text('Self Pick-Up'),
};
// 2
Set<int> selectedSegment = {0};
// 3
TimeOfDay? selectedTime;
```

```
// 4
DateTime? selectedDate;
// 5
final DateTime _firstDate = DateTime(DateTime.now().year - 2);
final DateTime _lastDate = DateTime(DateTime.now().year + 1);
// 6
final TextEditingController _nameController =
TextEditingController();
```

Here is what each property is used for:

1. Declare a mapping from integer to delivery type.
2. Determines whether the user selected *Delivery* or *Self Pick-Up*.
3. `selectedTime` stores the selected time.
4. `selectedDate` stores the selected date.
5. `_firstDate` and `_lastDate` determines the date range the user can select from.
6. `_nameController` refers to the text field used to enter the customer's name.

Adding a Segmented Control

The first widget you will build is a segmented control. This is a way for users to toggle between food delivery or pick-up.

Replace the comment `// TODO: Set Selected Segment` with:

```
void onSegmentSelected(Set<int> segmentIndex) {
  setState(() {
    selectedSegment = segmentIndex;
  });
}
```

This function updates the user's order type.

Next locate `// TODO: Build Segmented Control` and replace it with the following:

```
Widget _buildOrderSegmentedType() {
  // 1
  return SegmentedButton(
    // 2
    showSelectedIcon: false,
    // 3
    segments: const [
      ButtonSegment(
          value: 0,
```

```
          label: Text('Delivery'),
          icon: Icon(Icons.pedal_bike),
        ),
      ButtonSegment(
          value: 1,
          label: Text('Pickup'),
          icon: Icon(Icons.local_mall),
        ),
    ],
    // 4
    selected: selectedSegment,
    // 5
    onSelectionChanged: onSegmentSelected,
  );
}
```

Here's how the code works:

1. Returns a `SegmentedButton` widget.
2. Hide the icons in the segmented button.
3. Define two button segments for the user to choose. **Delivery** or **Pickup**
4. Set the selected segment.
5. When a user makes a choice update the selected segment.

Find `// TODO: Add Segmented Control` and replace it with:

```
const SizedBox(height: 16.0),
_buildOrderSegmentedType(),
```

You should now see the segmented control in the drawer:

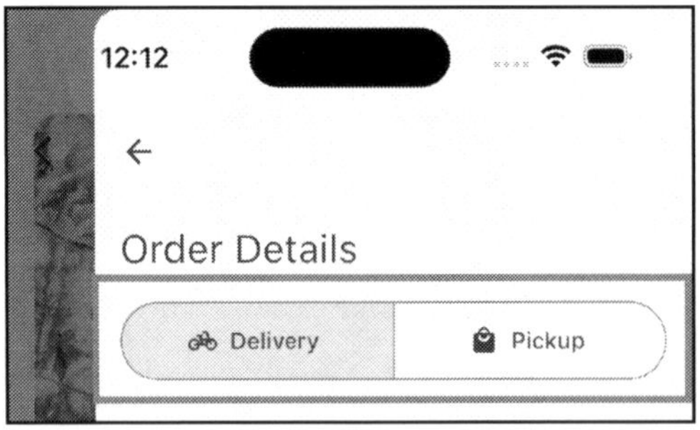

Adding a Textfield to Enter the Customer Name

You'll now need a way to gather the customer's name. This will help the restaurant or the delivery team to know how to address the recipient.

Replace `// TODO: Build Name Textfield` with:

```
Widget _buildTextField() {
  // 1
  return TextField(
    // 2
    controller: _nameController,
    // 3
    decoration: const InputDecoration(
      labelText: 'Contact Name',
    ),
  );
}
```

Here's how the code works:

1. The function returns a `TextField` widget.
2. `Textfield` uses the controller to manage the text being edited. It allows you to read the current value of the text field, update it, or listen for changes.
3. Add a placeholder text, to give the user some context about what to type.

Next, to apply the text field, locate the comment `// TODO: Add Name Textfield` and replace it with the following:

```
const SizedBox(height: 16.0),
_buildTextField(),
```

You'll now see the text field in the drawer:

Onwards with date and time!

Creating a Date Picker

Now you'll need a way for the user to select the date to pick up or have the food delivered.

Locate the comment `// TODO: Configure Date Format` and replace it with the following:

```
// 1
String formatDate(DateTime? dateTime) {
  // 2
  if (dateTime == null) {
    return 'Select Date';
  }
  // 3
  final formatter = DateFormat('yyyy-MM-dd');
  return formatter.format(dateTime);
}
```

This function determines what text the date button should read. Here's how the code works:

1. The function takes an optional `DateTime` as a parameter.
2. If the `dateTime` is null, return the text **Select Date**, to ask the user to select a date.
3. If a `dateTime` exists, return the formatted date.

Add the following import:

```
import 'package:intl/intl.dart';
```

Here you've added the `intl` package, which provides internationalization helpers needed by `DateFormat`.

Next locate the comment `// TODO: Select Date Picker` and replace it with the following:

```
// 1
void _selectDate(BuildContext context) async {
  // 2
  final picked = await showDatePicker(
    // 3
    context: context,
    // 4
    initialDate: selectedDate ?? DateTime.now(),
    // 5
    firstDate: _firstDate,
    lastDate: _lastDate,
  );
  // 6
  if (picked != null && picked != selectedDate) {
    setState(() {
      selectedDate = picked;
    });
  }
}
```

Here's how the date picker works:

1. `_selectDate()` is an asynchronous function that takes `BuildContext` as a parameter.
2. `showDatePicker()` opens the date picker dialog. The function waits for the user to pick or cancel the date picker and stores it in the `picked` property.
3. You pass in the context to display the dialog.
4. `initialDate` sets the selected date or defaults to the current date.
5. Define the date range the user can pick from.
6. If the picked date is not null and is different from the currently selected date, update the `selectedDate` and trigger a rebuild of the widget to reflect the new selection.

Next you'll also need a way to select the time.

Creating a Time Picker

Here's how your time picker will look like.

Find `// TODO: Configure Time of Day` and replace it with the following:

```
// 1
String formatTimeOfDay(TimeOfDay? timeOfDay) {
  // 2
  if (timeOfDay == null) {
    return 'Select Time';
  }
  // 3
  final hour = timeOfDay.hour.toString().padLeft(2, '0');
  final minute = timeOfDay.minute.toString().padLeft(2, '0');
  return '$hour:$minute';
}
```

1. This function takes in `TimeOfDay` as a parameter.
2. If the `timeOfDay` is null, return **Select Time** to indicate to the user to select a time.
3. Otherwise, return the formatted time.

Next, locate `// TODO: Select Time Picker` and replace it with this code:

```
// 1
void _selectTime(BuildContext context) async {
  // 2
  final picked = await showTimePicker(
    // 3
    context: context,
```

```
      // 4
      initialEntryMode: TimePickerEntryMode.input,
      // 5
      initialTime: selectedTime ?? TimeOfDay.now(),
      // 6
      builder: (context, child) {
        return MediaQuery(
          data: MediaQuery.of(context).copyWith(
            alwaysUse24HourFormat: true,
          ),
          child: child!,
        );
      },
    );
    // 7
    if (picked != null && picked != selectedTime) {
      setState(() {
        selectedTime = picked;
      });
    }
  }
```

Here's how the time picker works:

1. `_selectTime()` is an asynchronous function that takes `BuildContext` as a parameter.
2. `showTimePicker()` opens the time picker dialog. The function waits for the user to pick or cancel the time picker and stores it in the `picked` property.
3. You still pass in the context to display the dialog.
4. `initialEntryMode` sets the mode to enter the time. `input` mode allows the user to enter values via the keyboard.
5. Set the `initialTime` to the `selectedTime`, if null, default to the current time.
6. The `builder()` function builds the time picker. `MediaQuery` forces it to always show the 24-hour time format, regardless of the device's default setting.
7. If the picked time is not null and is different from the currently selected time, update the `selectedTime` and trigger a rebuild of the widget to reflect the new selection.

Now that you have all your widgets ready, it's time to show them in the drawer.

Showing the Date and Time Pickers

Replace `// TODO: Add Date and Time Picker` with:

```
// 1
const SizedBox(height: 16.0),
// 2
Row(
  children: [
    TextButton(
      // 3
      child: Text(formatDate(selectedDate)),
      // 4
      onPressed: () => _selectDate(context),
    ),
    TextButton(
      // 5
      child: Text(formatTimeOfDay(selectedTime)),
      // 6
      onPressed: () => _selectTime(context),
    ),
  ],
),
// 7
const SizedBox(height: 16.0),
```

Here's how the code works:

1. Add a **16.0** vertical space from the widget on top.
2. Use a `Row` to display the two buttons horizontally.
3. The first text button displays **Select Date** or the currently selected date.
4. Tapping the button presents the date picker.
5. The second text button displays **Select Time** or the currently selected time.
6. Tapping the button presents the time picker.
7. Add **16.0** vertical spacing between the widget below.

Now, perform a hot reload.

Select a restaurant and tap the **Items in cart** button.

You should see **Select Date** and **Select Time** buttons. Tap each of them to open the pickers and select a date and a time.

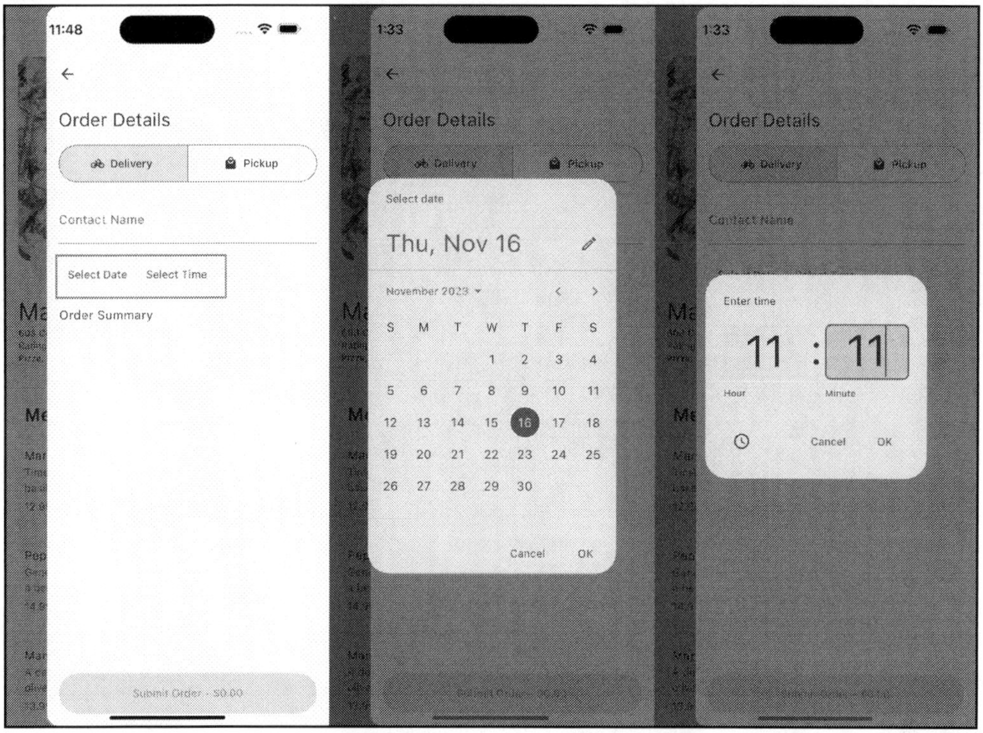

But wait, where's the order? Don't worry, you'll do that next.

Creating Order Summary

Now you'll create a way to display the list of items the user selected.

Locate the comment `// TODO: Build Order Summary` and replace it with the following:

```
// 1
Widget _buildOrderSummary(BuildContext context) {
  // 2
```

```
  final colorTheme = Theme.of(context).colorScheme;

  // 3
  return Expanded(
    // 4
    child: ListView.builder(
      // 5
      itemCount: widget.cartManager.items.length,
      itemBuilder: (context, index) {
        // 6
        final item = widget.cartManager.itemAt(index);
        // 7
        // TODO: Wrap in a Dismissible Widget
        return ListTile(
          leading: Container(
            padding: const EdgeInsets.all(8.0),
            decoration: BoxDecoration(
              borderRadius: const BorderRadius.all(
                Radius.circular(8.0)),
              border: Border.all(
                color: colorTheme.primary,
                width: 2.0,
              ),
            ),
            child: ClipRRect(
              borderRadius: const BorderRadius.all(
                Radius.circular(8.0)),
              child: Text('x${item.quantity}'),
            ),
          ),
          title: Text(item.name),
          subtitle: Text('Price: \$${item.price}'),
        );
      },
    ),
  );
}
```

Here's how the code works:

1. `_buildOrderSummary()` takes `BuildContext` as a parameter.
2. Retrieve the color theme for consistency throughout your app.
3. Return an `Expanded` widget that allows `ListView` to use all available space in its parent widget.
4. Use `ListView.builder()` to create a scrollable list of items.

5. Set item count.
6. Build each item by retrieving the menu item for a given index.
7. Construct a `ListTile` to display the menu item selected, display the quantity and the total price for each item.

To add order summary and a title, replace `// TODO: Add Order Summary` with:

```
const Text('Order Summary'),
_buildOrderSummary(context),
```

Hot reload and you'll see the order summary.

But what if the user wants to remove an item from the order? You'll add that next.

Deleting an Item From an Order

The user will swipe left to remove a menu item.

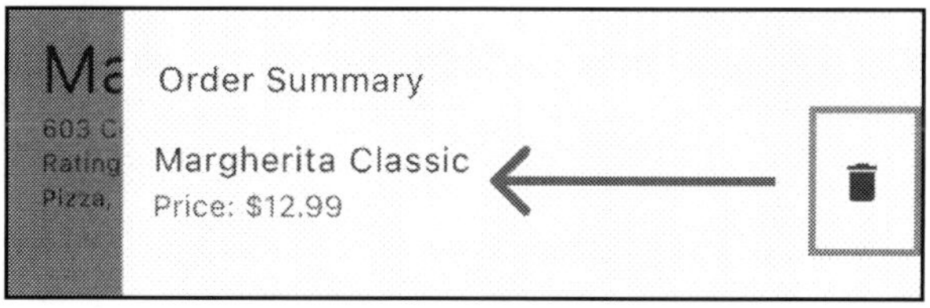

Find `// TODO: Wrap in a Dismissible Widget`. Right-click `ListTile` widget on the line below and select **Show Context Actions** as shown below:

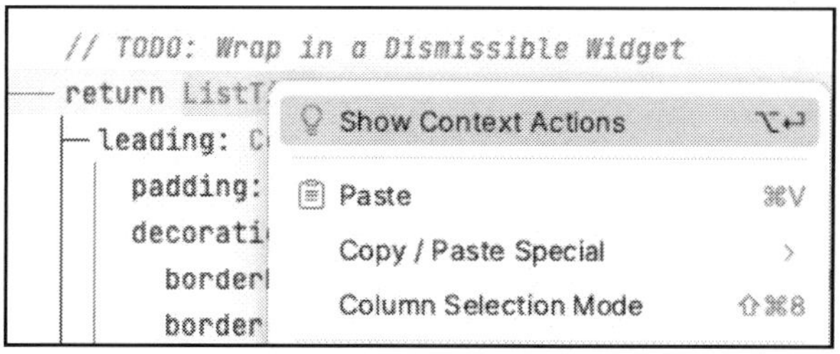

Next, select **Wrap with widget** as shown below:

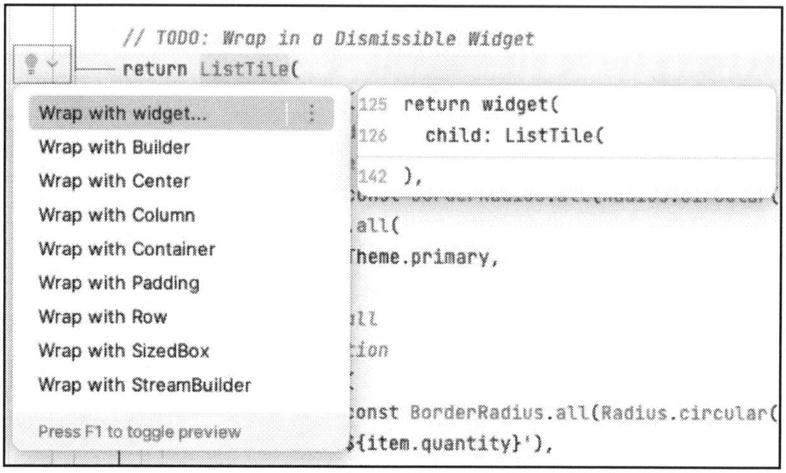

Rename `widget` to `Dismissible` and add the following properties to the widget just above the `child`:

```
// 1
key: Key(item.id),
// 2
direction: DismissDirection.endToStart,
// 3
background: Container(),
// 4
secondaryBackground: const SizedBox(
  child: Row(
    mainAxisAlignment: MainAxisAlignment.end,
    children: [
      Icon(Icons.delete),
    ],
  ),
),
// 5
onDismissed: (direction) {
  setState(() {
    widget.cartManager.removeItem(item.id);
  });
  // 6
  widget.didUpdate();
},
```

Here's how the code works:

1. `Key` is used to uniquely identify each dismissible item in the list.
2. Configure the dismiss `direction` swiping from right to left.
3. Set an empty background container.
4. Set a secondary background and show a delete (trash) icon aligned to the right end.
5. When `onDismissed()` is triggered, call `setState()` to remove the item from the cart.
6. Invoke `didUpdate()` to notify the parent to refresh the UI or perform other actions.

You have added all the interactive widgets to collect an order.

Now you need a submit button to process the order!

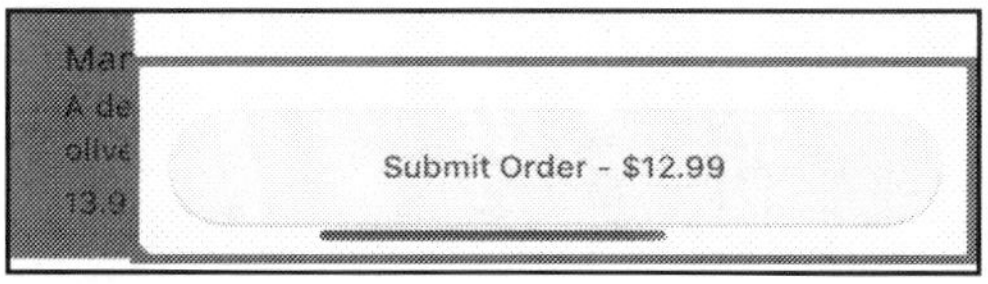

Locate the comment `// TODO: Build Submit Order Button` and replace it with the following:

```
Widget _buildSubmitButton() {
  // 1
  return ElevatedButton(
    // 2
    onPressed: widget.cartManager.isEmpty
        ? null
        // 3
        : () {
            final selectedSegment = this.selectedSegment;
            final selectedTime = this.selectedTime;
            final selectedDate = this.selectedDate;
            final name = _nameController.text;
            final items = widget.cartManager.items;
            // 4
            final order = Order(
              selectedSegment: selectedSegment,
              selectedTime: selectedTime,
              selectedDate: selectedDate,
              name: name,
              items: items,
            );
```

```
              // 5
              widget.cartManager.resetCart();
              // 6
              widget.onSubmit(order);
            },
      child: Padding(
        padding: const EdgeInsets.all(16.0),
        // 7
        child: Text(
          '''Submit Order - \$$
{widget.cartManager.totalCost.toStringAsFixed(2)}'''),
      ),
    );
}
```

Here's how the code works:

1. The function returns an `ElevatedButton` widget.
2. When the cart is empty, `onPressed()` disables the button by setting it to `null`.
3. If the cart is not empty, `onPressed()` retrieves all the user data such as selected order type, time, date, name and list of items.
4. Create an order object.
5. Reset the cart.
6. Submit the order.
7. Show the total cost of the order.

To apply the button, locate `// TODO: Add Submit Order Button` and replace it with the following:

```
_buildSubmitButton(),
```

Perform a hot reload if needed and try to add items to your cart. You'll see the **Submit Order** button enabled or disabled based on the number of items in the cart.

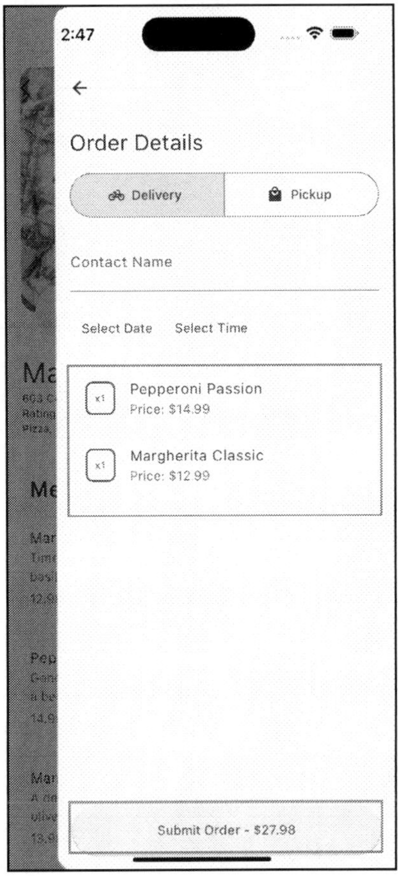

Now that you created a way to capture the order data, why not add a page to display the list of orders submitted? That's up next.

Building the Orders Page

When someone places an order they likely want to see the list of orders they've placed. When you're done with this section the **Orders** tab will look like this:

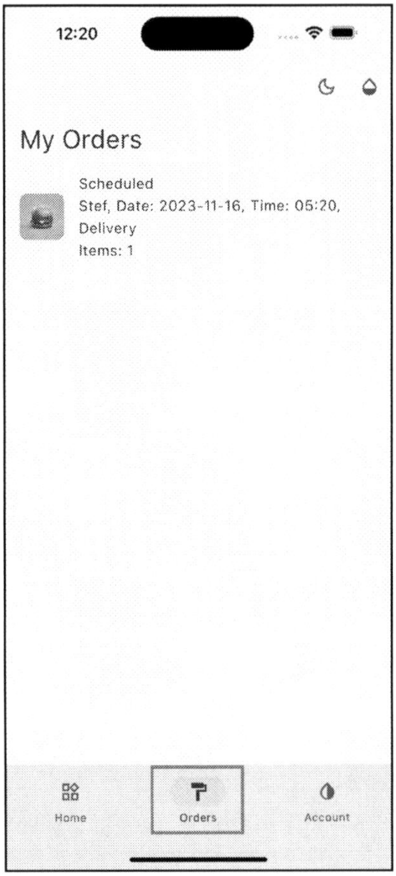

Within the **lib/screens** directory, create a new file called **myorders_page.dart** and add the following code:

```
import 'package:flutter/material.dart';
import '../models/order_manager.dart';

class MyOrdersPage extends StatelessWidget {
  final OrderManager orderManager;

  // 1
  const MyOrdersPage({
    super.key,
    required this.orderManager,
```

```
  });

  @override
  Widget build(BuildContext context) {
    final textTheme = Theme.of(context)
      .textTheme
      .apply(displayColor:
Theme.of(context).colorScheme.onSurface);
    // 2
    return Scaffold(
      appBar: AppBar(
        centerTitle: false,
        title: Text('My Orders', style:
textTheme.headlineMedium),
      ),
      // 3
      body: ListView.builder(
        // 4
        itemCount: orderManager.totalOrders,
        itemBuilder: (context, index) {
          // 5
          return OrderTile(order: orderManager.orders[index]);
        },
      ),
    );
  }
}

// 6
class OrderTile extends StatelessWidget {
  final Order order;

  const OrderTile({super.key, required this.order});

  @override
  Widget build(BuildContext context) {
    final textTheme = Theme.of(context)
      .textTheme
      .apply(displayColor:
Theme.of(context).colorScheme.onSurface);

    // 7
    return ListTile(
      leading: ClipRRect(
        borderRadius: BorderRadius.circular(8.0),
        // 8
        child: Image.asset(
          'assets/food/burger.webp',
          width: 50.0,
          height: 50.0,
          fit: BoxFit.cover,
        ),
      ),
```

```
        // 9
        title: Column(
          crossAxisAlignment: CrossAxisAlignment.start,
          children: [
            // 10
            Text(
              'Scheduled',
              style: textTheme.bodyLarge,
            ),
            // 11
            Text(order.getFormattedOrderInfo()),
            // 12
            Text('Items: ${order.items.length}'),
          ],
        ),
      );
    }
  }
```

The `MyOrdersPage` widget is pretty standard:

1. It takes an `orderManager` as a parameter. This is used to retrieve the list of orders.
2. It defines a `Scaffold` that has an `AppBar`
3. Displays a `ListView` in the body.
4. Sets the list view count.
5. For each order, it creates an `OrderTile` widget and passes the current order's index.
6. It defines an `OrderTile` widget to display the order.
7. A tile wraps a `ListTile`.
8. The `ListTile` leading widget is an image with rounded corners.
9. The title displays a `Column` to align the order details vertically.

Next you'll add the `MyOrdersPage` to your **Orders** tab.

Showing the Orders Page

Open **home.dart** and locate `// TODO: Replace with Order Page` and replace it and the `Center` code beneath it with the following:

```
MyOrdersPage(orderManager: widget.ordersManager),
```

Add the following import:

```
import 'screens/myorders_page.dart';
```

Now add items to the cart and submit the order.

Tap on the **Orders** tab, you should see the list of orders submitted!

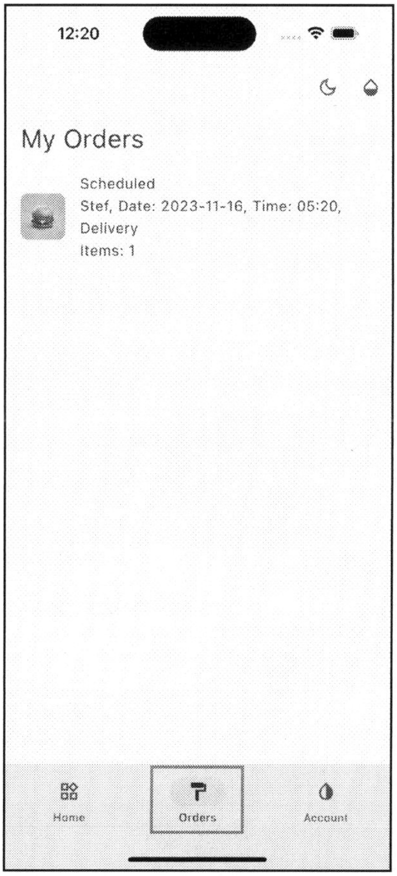

Your app now lets your users look at menus and order items for either delivery or pick up. Congratulations!

Key Points

- You can pass data around with callbacks
- You can use callbacks also to pass data one level up.
- Manager objects help you manage functions and state changes in one place.
- `TextEditingController` is used to listen for changes in a `TextField` widget.
- Split your widgets by screen to keep your code modular and organized.
- Gesture widgets recognize and determine the type of touch event. They provide callbacks to react to events like `onTap()` or `onDrag()`.
- You can use dismissible widgets to swipe away items in a list.

Where to Go From here?

There are many ways to engage and collect data from your users. You've learned to pass data around using callbacks. You learned to create different input widgets. You also learned to apply touch events to navigate to parts of your app.

That's a lot, but you've only scratched the surface! There's a plethora of widgets out there. You can explore other packages at https://pub.dev, a place where you can find the most popular widgets created by the Flutter community!

In the next section, you'll dive into navigation.

Section III: Navigating Between Screens

You'll continue working on the Yummy app in this section, learning about navigating between screens and working with deep links.

Topics you'll learn include Navigator 2.0, **go_router** and Flutter Web.

Chapter 8: Routes & Navigation

By Vincent Ngo

Navigation, or how users switch between screens, is an important concept to master. Good navigation keeps your app organized and helps users find their way around without getting frustrated.

In the previous chapter, you got a taste of navigation where users tapped on a restaurant to view its menu items as shown below:

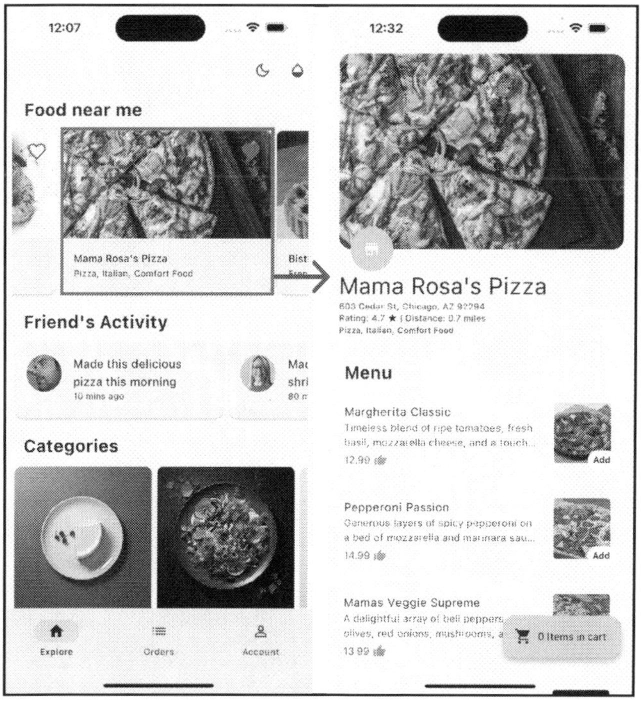

But this uses the imperative style of navigation, known as **Navigator 1.0**. In this chapter, you'll learn to navigate between screens the **declarative** way.

You'll cover the following topics:

- Overview of `Navigator` 1.0.
- Overview of `Router API`.
- How to use **go_router** to handle **routes** and **navigation**.

By the end of this chapter, you'll have everything you need to navigate to different screens!

> **Note**: If you'd like to skip straight to the code, jump to **Getting Started**. If you'd like to learn the theory first, read on!

Introducing Navigation

If you come from an iOS background, you might be familiar with **UINavigationController** from UIKit, or **NavigationStack** from SwiftUI.

In Android, you use **Jetpack Navigation** to manage various fragments.

In Flutter, you use a **Navigator** widget to manage your screens or pages. Think of screens and pages as **routes**.

> **Note**: This chapter uses these terms interchangeably because they all mean the same thing.

A **stack** is a data structure that manages pages. You insert the elements **last-in, first-out** (LIFO), and only the element at the top of the stack is visible to the user.

For example, when a user views a list of restaurants, tapping a restaurant **pushes** `RestaurantPage` to the top of the stack. Once the user finishes making changes, you **pop** it off the stack.

Here's a top-level and a side-level view of the navigation stack:

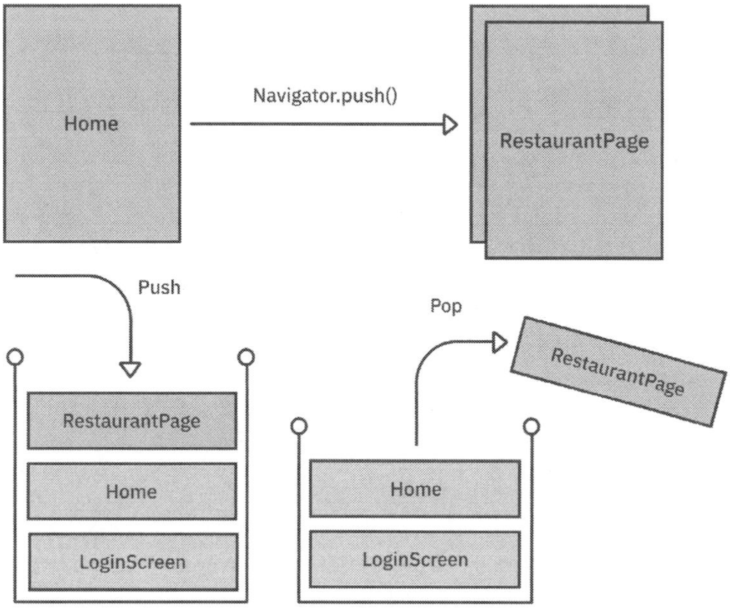

Now, it's time for a quick overview of Navigator 1.0.

Navigator 1.0 Overview

Before Flutter 1.22, you could only shift between screens by issuing direct commands like "show this now" or "remove the current screen and go back to the previous one". Navigator 1.0 provides a simple set of APIs to navigate between screens. The most common ones are:

- `push()`: **Adds** a new route on the stack.
- `pop()`: **Removes** a route from the stack.

So, how do you add a navigator to your app?

Most Flutter apps start with `WidgetsApp` as the root widget.

> **Note**: So far, you've used `MaterialApp`, which extends `WidgetsApp`.

`WidgetsApp` wraps many other common widgets that your app requires. Among these wrapped widgets there's a top-level `Navigator` to manage the pages you **push** and **pop**.

Pushing and Popping Routes

To show the user another screen, you need to push a `Route` onto the `Navigator` stack using `Navigator.push(context)`. Here's an example:

```
bool result = await Navigator.push<bool>(
  context,
  MaterialPageRoute<bool>(
    builder: (BuildContext context) =>RestaurantPage(
      restaurant: restaurants[index],
      cartManager: cartManager,
      ordersManager: orderManager,
    )
  ),
);
```

Here, `MaterialPageRoute` returns an instance of your new screen widget. `Navigator` returns the result of the push whenever the screen pops off the stack.

Here's how you pop a route off the stack:

```
Navigator.pop(context);
```

This seems easy enough. So why not just use Navigator 1.0? Well, it has a few disadvantages.

Navigator 1.0's Disadvantages

The imperative API may seem natural and easy to use, but, in practice, it's hard to manage and scale.

There's no good way to manage your pages without keeping a mental map of where you push and pop a screen.

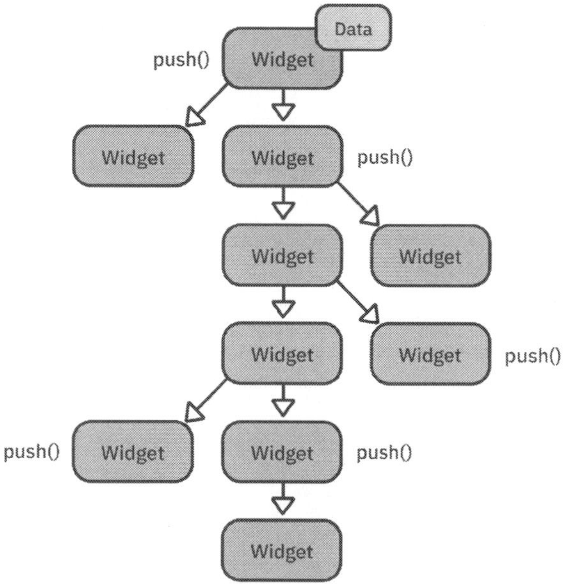

Imagine a new developer joining your team. Where do they even start? They'd surely be confused.

Moreover, Navigator 1.0 doesn't expose the route stack to developers. It's difficult to handle complicated cases, like adding and removing a screen **between pages**.

For example, in Yummy, you only want to show the Onboarding screen if the user hasn't completed the onboarding yet. Handling that with Navigator 1.0 is complicated.

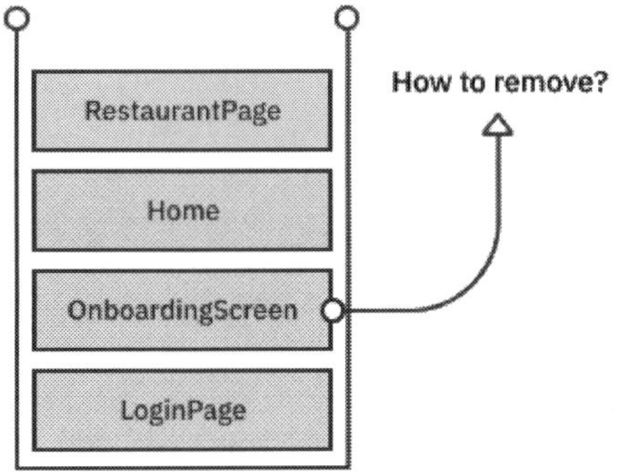

Another disadvantage is that Navigator 1.0 doesn't update the web **URL** path. When you go to a new page, you only see the base URL, like this: **www.localhost:8000/#/**. Additionally, the web browser's forward and backward buttons may not work as expected.

Finally, the **Back** button on Android devices might not work with Navigator 1.0 when you have nested navigators or add Flutter to your host Android app.

Wouldn't it be great to have a declarative API that solves most of these pain points? That's why **Router API** was designed!

> To learn more about Navigator 1.0, check out the Flutter documentation (https://flutter.dev/docs/cookbook/navigation).

Router API Overview

Flutter 1.22 introduced the **Router API**, a new declarative API that lets you control your navigation stack completely. Also known as Navigator 2.0, the Router API aims to feel more Flutter-like while solving the pain points of Navigator 1.0.

Its main goals include:

- **Exposing the navigator's page stack**: You can now **manipulate** and manage your page routes. More power, more control!
- **Backward compatibility with imperative API**: You can use imperative and declarative styles in the same app.
- **Handling operating system events**: It works better with events like the Android and Web system's **Back button**.
- **Managing nested navigators**: It gives you control over which navigator has **priority**.
- **Managing navigation state**: You can **parse routes** and handle **web URLs** and **deep linking**.

Here are the new abstractions that make up Router's declarative API:

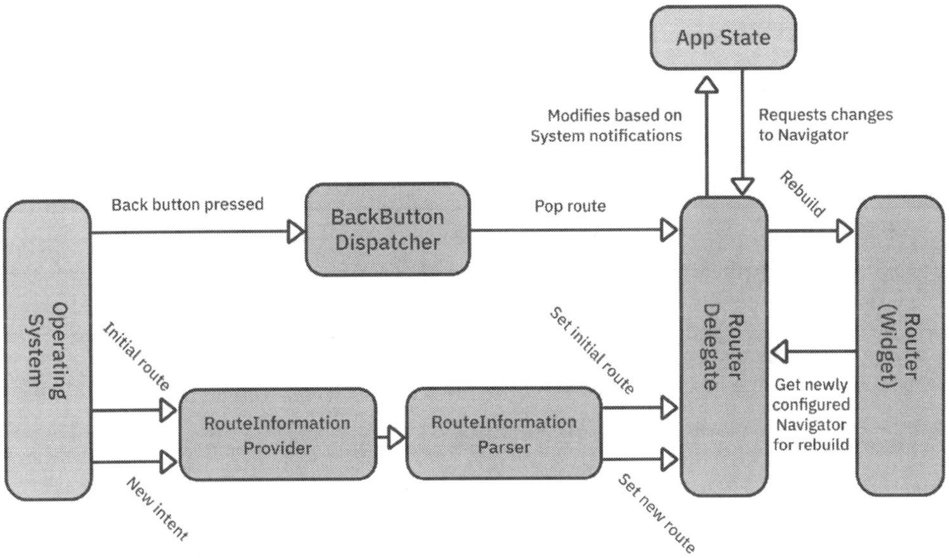

The new API includes the following key components:

- **Page**: An abstract class that describes the **configuration** for a route.
- **Router**: Handles configuring the list of **pages** the Navigator displays.
- **RouterDelegate**: Defines how the router **listens** for changes to the app state to rebuild the navigator's configuration.
- **RouteInformationProvider**: Provides `RouteInformation` to the router. Route information contains the **location info** and **state** objects to configure your app.
- **RouteInformationParser**: Parses route information into a **user-defined** data type.
- **BackButtonDispatcher**: Reports presses on the platform system's Back button to the router.
- **TransitionDelegate**: Decides how pages transition into and out of the screen.

> **Note**: This chapter will leverage a routing package, **go_router**, to make the Router API easier to use.
>
> If you want to know how to use the vanilla version of the Router API, check out Edition 2.0 (https://www.kodeco.com/books/flutter-apprentice/v2.0/) of this book.

Navigation and Unidirectional Data Flow

As discussed with Navigator 1.0, the imperative API is very basic. It forces you to place `push()` and `pop()` functions all over your widget hierarchy which couples all your widgets! To present another screen, you must place callbacks up the widget hierarchy.

With the new declarative API, you can manage your navigation state **unidirectionally**. The widgets are **state-driven**, as shown below:

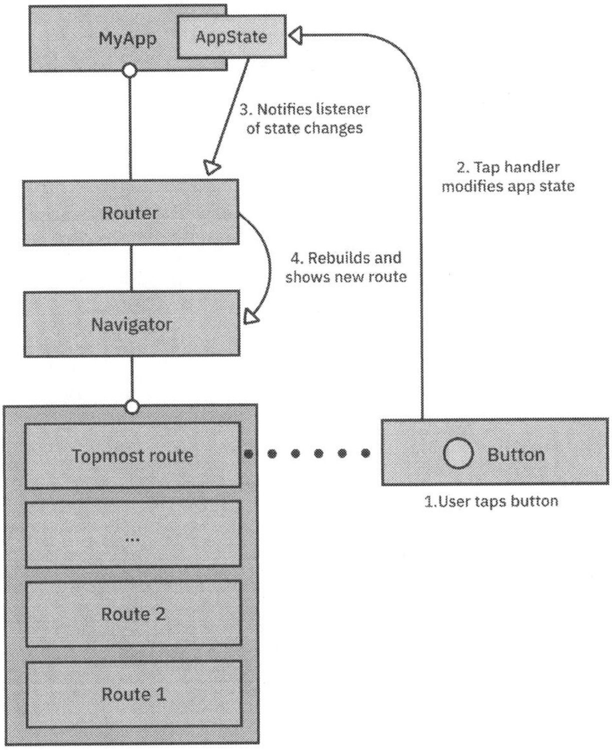

Here's how it works:

1. A user **taps** a button.
2. The button handler tells the **app state** to update.
3. The router is a **listener** of the state, so it receives a **notification** when the state changes.
4. Based on the new state changes, the router **reconfigures** the list of pages for the navigator.
5. The navigator detects if there's a new page in the list and handles the **transitions** to show the page.

That's it! Instead of having to build a mental mind map of how every screen presents and dismisses, the state drives which pages appear.

Is Declarative Always Better Than Imperative?

You don't have to migrate or convert your existing code to use the new API if you have an existing project.

Here are some tips to help you decide which is more beneficial for you:

- **For medium to large apps**: Consider using a **declarative API** and a router widget when managing a lot of your navigation state.
- **For small apps**: The **imperative API** is suitable for rapid prototyping or creating a small app for demos. Sometimes push and pop are all you need!

Next, you'll get some hands-on experience with declarative navigation.

> **Note**: To learn more about Navigator 1.0, check:
>
> • Flutter's Dev Cookbook Tutorials (https://flutter.dev/docs/cookbook/navigation)
>
> • Flutter Navigation: Getting Started (https://www.kodeco.com/4562634-flutter-navigation-getting-started)

Getting Started

Open the **starter** project in Android Studio. Run `flutter pub get` and then run the app.

> **Note**: It's better to start with the starter project rather than continuing with the project from the last chapter because it contains some changes specific to this chapter.

You'll see that **Yummy** only shows the **Login** screen. Of course, it also supports responsive UI on different devices!

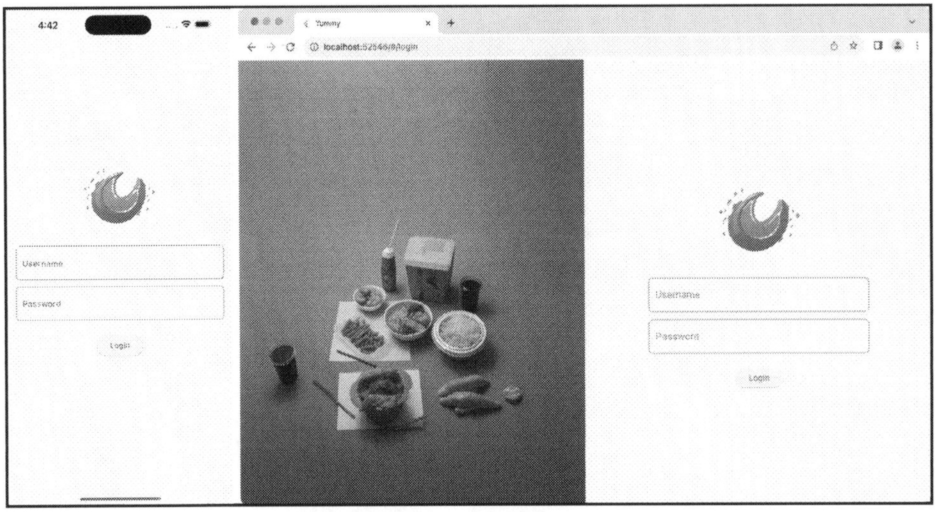

Don't worry. You'll connect all the screens soon. You'll build a simple flow that features a **login screen** and an **onboarding** widget before showing the existing tab-based app you've made so far. But first, take a look at some changes to the project files.

Changes to the Project Files

Before you dive into navigation, there are new files in this starter project to help you out.

What's New in the Screens Folder

There are new changes in **lib/** and **lib/screens/**:

- **home.dart**: Now includes a **Profile** button at the top-right for the user to view their profile.
- **screens.dart**: A **barrel** file that groups all the screens into a single import.
- **login_page.dart**: Lets the user log in.
- **account_page.dart**: Lets users check their **profile**, update settings and log out.

Later, you'll use these to construct your authentication UI flow.

What's New in the Models Folder

There are three new model objects in **lib/models/**.

- **models.dart**: A barrel file that groups all the models into a single import.
- **auth.dart**: Manages user **authentication** state, whether they are login in or out.
- **user.dart**: Describes a single **user** and includes information like the user's role, profile picture, full name and app settings.

What's New in the Components Folder

There is one change in **lib/components/**.

- **components.dart**: A barrel file that groups all the components into a single import.

New Packages

There are three new packages in **pubspec.yaml**:

```
url_launcher: ^6.2.1
go_router: ^13.0.1
shared_preferences: ^2.2.2
```

Here's what they do:

- **url_launcher**: A cross-platform library to help launch a **URL**.
- **go_router**: A package built to reduce the complexity of the Router API. It helps developers easily implement **declarative navigation**.
- **shared_preferences**: Wraps platform-specific **persistent storage** for simple data. `AppCache` uses this package to store the login state.

Now that you know what's changed, it's time for a quick overview of the UI flow you'll build in this chapter.

Looking Over the UI Flow

Here are the first two screens you show the user:

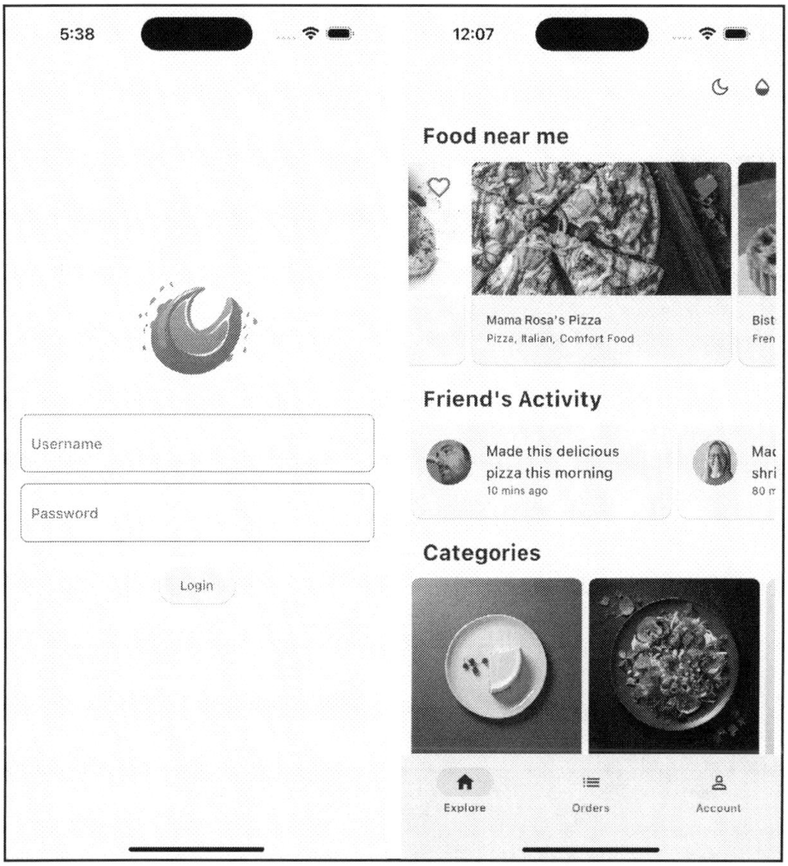

1. When the user launches the app, he must log in by entering their **username** and **password**, then tap **Login**.
2. Once the user logs in, the user goes to the app's **Home**. They can now start using the app.

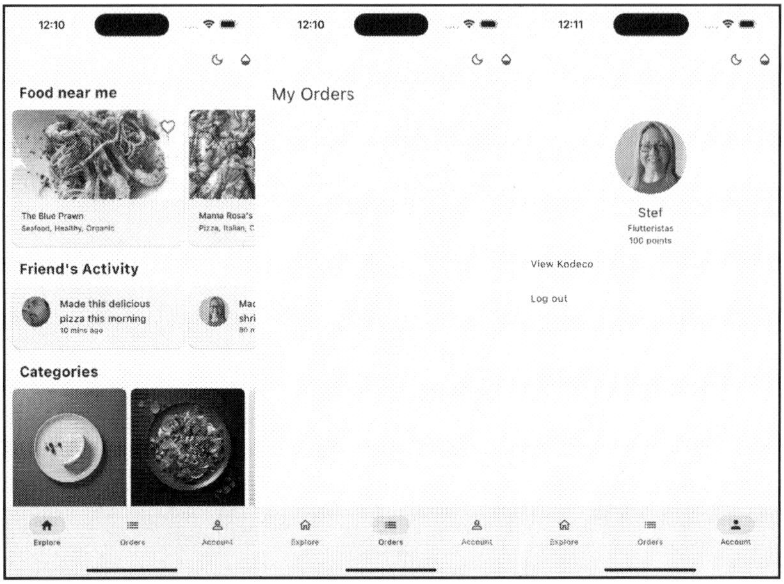

The app presents the user with three tabs with these options:

1. **Home**: View restaurants, friend posts, and food categories.
2. **Orders**: Track all orders submitted.
3. **Account**: View the user's profile and logout.

Next, the user can **tap** on a restaurant to view the menu to order food. They can **select** items to add to their cart and **submit** an order.

Once the order is submitted, the user is redirected to **Orders** tab:

On the **Account** screen, they can:

- View their profile and see how many points they've earned.
- Visit the Kodeco website.
- Log out of the app.

Below you'll see an example:

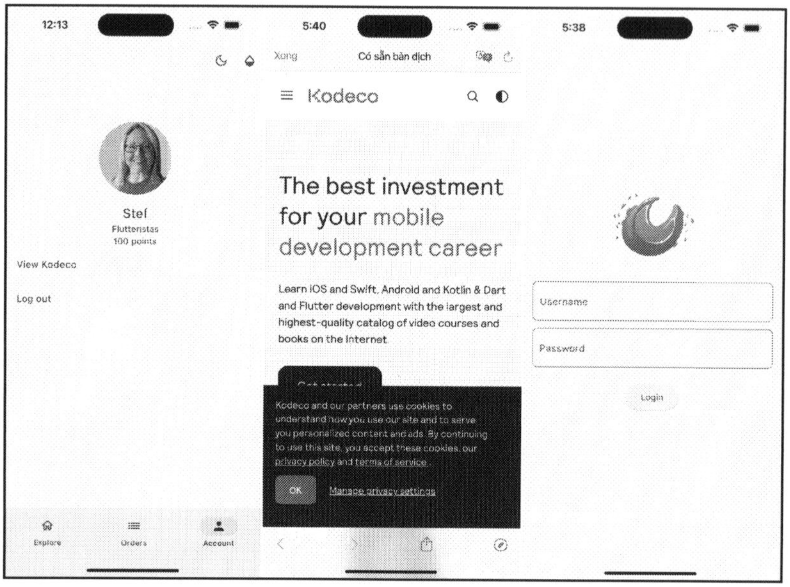

Your app is going to be awesome when it's finished. Now it's time to learn about **go_router**!

Introducing go_router

The **Router API** gives you more abstractions and control over your navigation stack. However, the API's complexity and usability hindered a bit the developer experience.

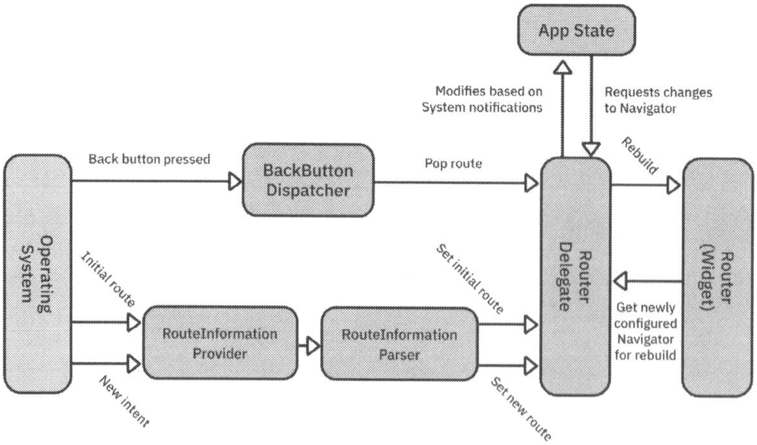

For example, you must create your RouterDelegate, bundle your app state logic with your navigator and configure when to show each route.

To support the web platform or handle **deep links**, you must implement RouteInformationParser to parse route information.

Eventually, developers and even Google realized the same thing: creating these components wasn't straightforward. As a result, developers wrote other routing packages to make the process easier.

> **Interesting Read**: Google's Flutter team came out with a research paper evaluating different routing packages. You can check it out here (https://github.com/flutter/uxr/blob/master/nav2-usability/Flutter%20routing%20packages%20usability%20research%20report.pdf).

Of the many packages available, you'll focus on GoRouter. Such a package, created by Chris Sells, is now fully maintained by the Flutter team. GoRouter aims to make it easier for developers to handle routing, letting them focus on building the best app they can.

In this chapter you'll focus on how to:

- Create routes.
- Handle errors.
- Redirect to another route.

Time to code!

Creating the go_router

Within **main.dart**, add the following import:

```
import 'package:go_router/go_router.dart';
```

Next locate the comment // TODO: Initialize GoRouter and replace it with the following:

```
// 1
late final _router = GoRouter(
  // 2
```

```
    initialLocation: '/login',
    // TODO: Add App Redirect
    // 3
    routes: [
      // TODO: Add Login Route
      // TODO: Add Home Route
    ],
    // TODO: Add Error Handler
  );
```

Here's how it works:

1. **Initializes** an instance of `GoRouter`, a declarative router for Flutter.
2. Sets the **initial route** that the app will navigate to. When the user opens the app they will navigate to the login page.
3. `routes` contains a list of possible routes for the application. Each route will typically be defined with a path, builder or redirect function.

There are other configurations you can set such as **app redirect**, and **error handling**. For example, if the user is logged in it should redirect to home, or if the user enters a wrong path it should show an error or a **404 page**.

> **Note** on `late final` in **Router Declaration**: The `late final` keyword is used for the router to defer its **initialization** until necessary, such as waiting for user authentication. It ensures the router is **non-nullable** and remains constant once initialized, aligning with the needs of dependent states or objects in the app.

Using Your Router

Next, locate `// TODO: Replace with Router`. Replace it and the entire `return MaterialApp();` code with:

```
// 1
return MaterialApp.router(
  debugShowCheckedModeBanner: false,
  // 2
  routerConfig: _router,
  // TODO: Add Custom Scroll Behavior
  title: 'Yummy',
  scrollBehavior: CustomScrollBehavior(),
  themeMode: themeMode,
  theme: ThemeData(
    colorSchemeSeed: colorSelected.color,
    useMaterial3: true,
    brightness: Brightness.light,
  ),
  darkTheme: ThemeData(
    colorSchemeSeed: colorSelected.color,
    useMaterial3: true,
    brightness: Brightness.dark,
  ),
);
```

Here's how it works:

1. `MaterialApp.router`. This constructor is used for apps with a navigator that uses a declarative routing approach. It takes a **router configuration** rather than a set of routes.

2. `routeConfig` reads `_router` to know about navigation properties. This will help the `MaterialApp` to set up the essential parts of a router. Under the hood, it will configure `routerDelegate`, `routeInformationParser`, and `routeInformationProvider`.

Your router is all set!

Adding Screens

With all the infrastructure in place, it's time to define which screen to display according to the route. But first, check out the current situation.

Build and run on iOS. You'll notice an error screen exception:

If the route isn't found, GoRouter provides a **Page Not Found** screen by default. That's because you haven't defined any routes yet!

Setting Up Your Error Handler

You can tweak `GoRouter` to show a custom error page. It's common for users to enter the wrong URL path, especially with web apps. Web apps usually show a **404** error screen.

Next locate `// TODO: Add Error Handler` and replace it with:

```
errorPageBuilder: (context, state) {
  return MaterialPage(
    key: state.pageKey,
    child: Scaffold(
      body: Center(
        child: Text(
          state.error.toString(),
        ),
      ),
    ),
  );
},
```

Here you simply show your error page and the error exception.

Trigger a hot restart. Your custom error page now displays.

Next, you'll start working on your login page.

Adding the Login Route

You'll start by displaying the **Login** screen.

Locate `// TODO: Add Login Route` and replace it with:

```
GoRoute(
  // 1
  path: '/login',
  // 2
  builder: (context, state) =>
    // 3
    LoginPage(
      // 4
      onLogIn: (Credentials credentials) async {
        // 5
        _auth
          .signIn(credentials.username, credentials.password)
          // 6
          .then((_) => context.go('/${YummyTab.home.value}'));
    })),
```

Here's how you define a route:

1. The route is set to `/login`. When the URL or path matches `/login` go to the login route.
2. The `builder()` function creates the widget to display when the user hits a route.
3. The function returns a `Login` widget.
4. The `Login` widget takes a callback named `onLogIn` which returns the user credentials.
5. Use the credentials to log in.
6. If the login is successful, navigate to the path `/0`, which is the first tab.

Trigger a hot restart. You'll see the Login Page:

You just added your first route!

Adding the Home Route

Once you log in, you need to navigate to the home route. Locate the comment `// TODO: Add Home Route` and replace it with the following:

```
// 1
GoRoute(
  path: '/:tab',
  builder: (context, state) {
    // 2
  return Home(
    //3
    auth: _auth,
    //4
    cartManager: _cartManager,
    //5
    ordersManager: _orderManager,
    //6
    changeTheme: changeThemeMode,
    //7
    changeColor: changeColor,
    //8
    colorSelected: colorSelected,
    //9
    tab: int.tryParse(state.pathParameters['tab'] ?? '') ?? 0);
```

```
    },
    // 10
    routes: [
    // TODO: Add Restaurant Route
  ]),
```

Here's how it works:

1. The route is set to `/`. When the URL or path matches `/` go to the home route. `:tab` is a path parameter used to switch between different tabs.
2. The builder function returns a `Home` widget.
3. Pass `auth` for handling authentication
4. Use `cartManager` to manage the items that the user added to the cart.
5. Use `ordersManager` to manage all the orders submitted.
6. Set a callback to handle user changes from light to dark mode.
7. Set a callback to handle user app color theme changes.
8. Pass the currently selected color theme.
9. Set the current tab, default to **0** if the path parameter is absent or not an integer.

Perform a hot reload if needed, click the **Login** button and now you'll land on **Home**.

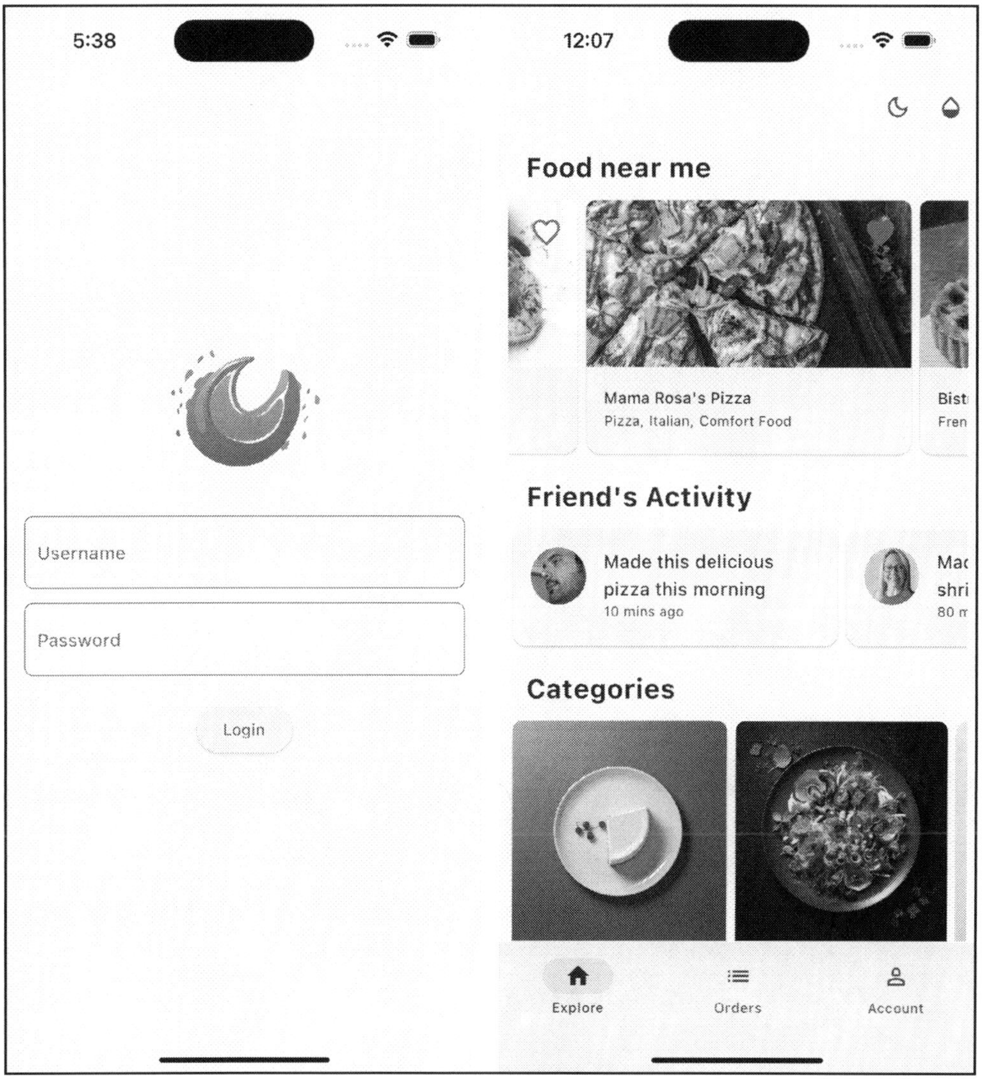

Navigate to the Current Tab

Try clicking on the tab bar items and notice that nothing works. You'll now add a way to navigate between tabs.

In **lib/home.dart** locate `// TODO: Navigate to specific tab` and replace it with the following:

```
context.go('/$index');
```

Don't forget to import `go_router`:

```
import 'package:go_router/go_router.dart';
```

Now you can navigate to different tabs.

Hot reload again and notice that the app goes back to the login screen. Wouldn't it be great when the user opens **Yummy** app again to go straight to the home page if the user is already logged in?

Handling Redirects

You redirect when you want your app to go to a different location. `GoRouter` lets you do this with its `redirect` handler.

Most apps require some type of login authentication flow, and redirect is perfect for this situation. For example, some of these scenarios may happen to your app:

- The user logs out of the app.
- The user tries to go to a restricted page that requires them to log in.
- The user's session token expires. In this case, they're automatically logged out.

It would be nice to redirect the user back to the login screen in all these cases. Open **lib/main.dart** and locate the comment `// TODO: Add Redirect Handler` and replace it with:

```
// 1
Future<String?> _appRedirect(
  BuildContext context, GoRouterState state) async {
  // 2
  final loggedIn = await _auth.loggedIn;
  // 3
  final isOnLoginPage = state.matchedLocation == '/login';

  // 4
  // Go to /login if the user is not signed in
  if (!loggedIn) {
    return '/login';
  }
  // 5
  // Go to root if the user is already signed in
  else if (loggedIn && isOnLoginPage) {
    return '/${YummyTab.home.value}';
  }
```

```
    // 6
    // no redirect
    return null;
  }
```

Here's how it works:

1. _appRedirect() is an asynchronous function that returns a future, optional string. It takes in a build context and the go router state.
2. Get the login status.
3. Check if the user is currently on the login page.
4. If the user is not logged in yet, redirect to the login page.
5. If the user is logged in and is on the login page, redirect to the home page.
6. Don't redirect if no condition is met.

Next to apply the handler, locate `// TODO: Add App Redirect` and replace it with:

```
redirect: _appRedirect,
```

Hot reload and you will notice that the app now goes to the home page directly.

Adding the Restaurant Route

When the user taps on a restaurant on the **Explore** page, the app navigates to a subroute. Locate `// TODO: Add Restaurant Route` and replace it with:

```
GoRoute(
  // 1
  path: 'restaurant/:id',
  builder: (context, state) {
    // 2
    final id =
        int.tryParse(state.pathParameters['id'] ?? '') ?? 0;
    // 3
    final restaurant = restaurants[id];
    // 4
    return RestaurantPage(
      restaurant: restaurant,
      cartManager: _cartManager,
      ordersManager: _orderManager,
    );
  }),
```

Here's how it works:

1. The route is defined with the path `restaurant/:id`. The `:id` part is a path parameter, which allows for dynamic routing based on the restaurant's ID.
2. Within the `builder()` function, you extract the `id` from `pathParameters`.
3. Get the restaurant based on the `id``.
4. Return the `RestaurantPage` widget with the specific restaurant, cart and order manager.

Now that you have set up the restaurant route, you need to navigate to it.

Navigate to the Restaurant Page

Open **lib/components/restaurant_section.dart**, locate the comment `// TODO: Navigate to Restaurant` and replace it with the following:

```
context.go('/${YummyTab.home.value}/restaurant/$
{restaurants[index].id}');
```

Don't forget to add the necessary imports:

```
import 'package:go_router/go_router.dart';
import '../constants.dart';
```

From the home page, based on the selected restaurant, navigate to the specific restaurant with the specific restaurant id.

> **Note**: There are two ways to navigate to different routes:
>
> 1.) `context.go(path)`
>
> 2.) `context.goNamed(name)`
>
> You should use `goNamed()` instead of `go()` as it's **error-prone**, and the actual URI format can change over time.
>
> `goNamed()` performs a **case-insensitive** lookup by using the name parameter you set with each route. It also helps you pass query parameters to your route.

Navigate to the Order Page

Once a user adds items to the cart and submits an order, it would be nice to navigate to the orders tab, so that customers can review the order.

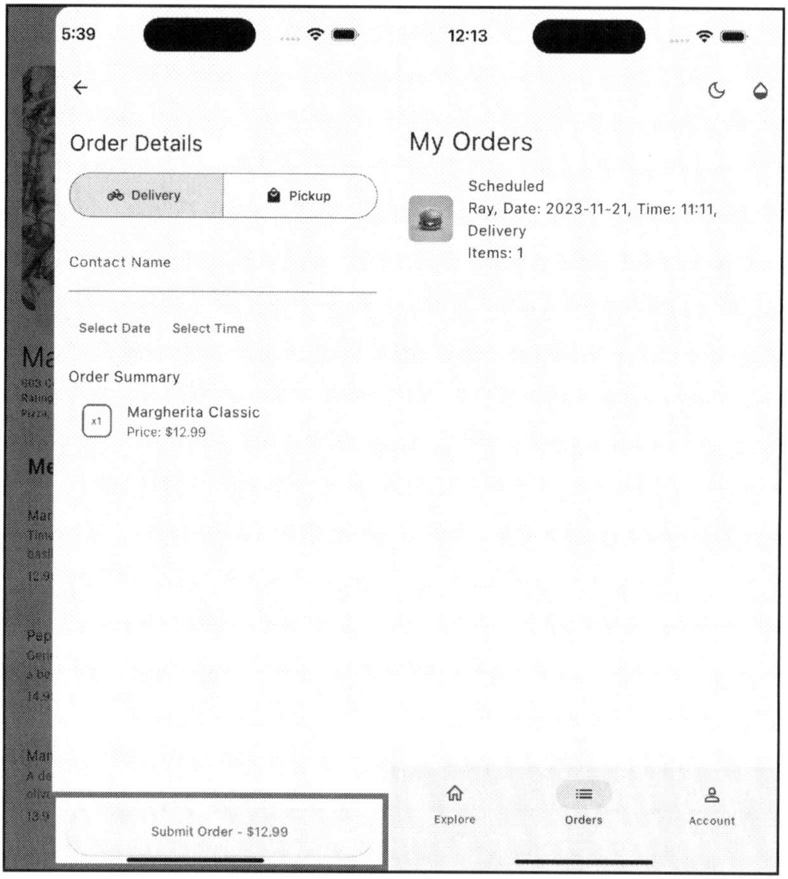

Open **restaurant_page.dart** and add the following imports:

```
import 'package:go_router/go_router.dart';
import '../constants.dart';
```

Next locate `// TODO: Navigate to Orders Page` and replace it with:

```
context.pop();
context.go('/${YummyTab.orders.value}');
```

Now, when the user taps on the **Submit order** button, the app navigates to the **Orders** tab.

Handle Log Out

Lastly you'll work on the logout functionality.

Open **home.dart**, locate the `// TODO: Logout and go to login` and replace it with the following:

```
widget.auth.signOut().then((value) => context.go('/login'));
```

Here you call `signOut()`, which resets the entire app state and redirects you back to the **Login** screen.

Save your changes. Now, tap the **Log out** button on the **Account** screen. You'll notice it goes back to the **Login** screen, as shown below:

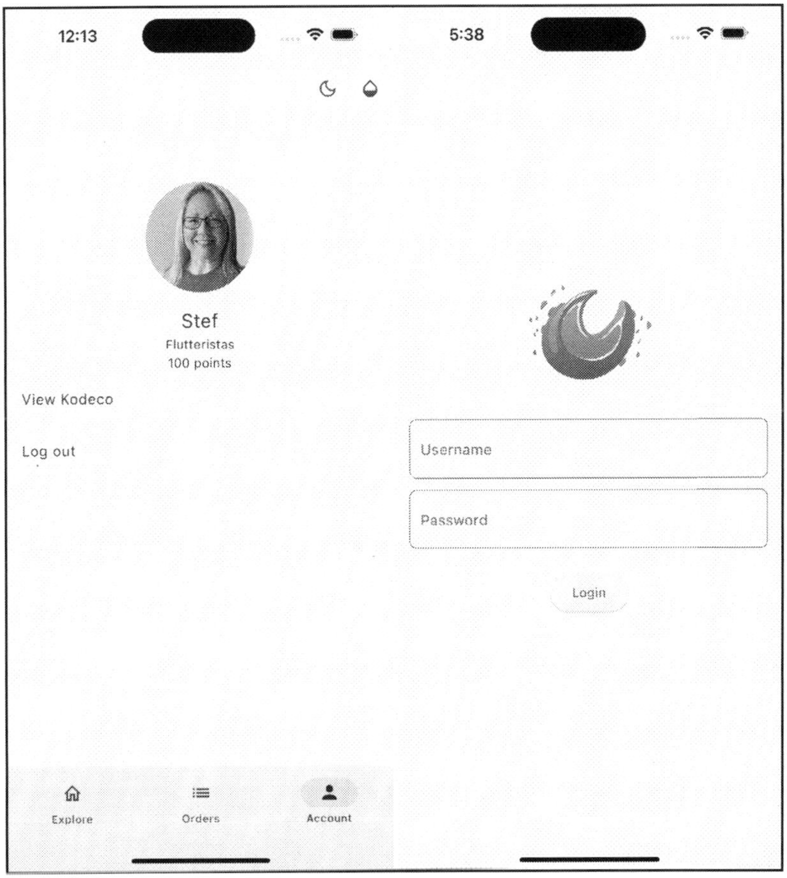

Congratulations, you've now completed the entire **UI navigation flow**.

Key Points

- **Navigator 1.0** is useful for quick and simple prototypes, presenting alerts and dialogs.
- **Router API** is useful when you need more control when managing the **navigation stack**.
- `GoRouter` is a wrapper around the **Router API** that makes it easier for developers to build navigation logic.
- With `GoRouter`, you navigate to other routes using `goNamed()` instead of `go()`.
- Use a **router widget** to listen to navigation state changes and configure your navigator's list of pages.
- If you need to navigate to another page after some state change, handle that with the `redirect()` handler.
- You can customize the error page by implementing the `errorPageBuilder`.

Where to Go From Here?

You've now learned how to navigate between screens the **declarative** way. Instead of calling `push()` and `pop()` in different widgets, you use multiple managers to manage your state.

You also learned how to create a `GoRouter` widget, which encapsulates and configures all the routes for a navigator. Now, you can easily manage your navigation flow in a single router object!

To learn about navigation in Flutter, here are some recommendations:

- To understand the motivation behind Navigator 2.0, check out the design document (https://docs.google.com/document/d/1Q0jx0l4-xymph9O6zLaOY4d_f7YFpNWX_eGbzYxr9wY/edit).
- Watch this presentation by Chun-Heng Tai (https://youtu.be/xFFQKvcad3s?t=3158), who contributed to the new declarative API.
- In this video, Simon Lightfoot walks you through a Navigator 2.0 example (https://www.youtube.com/watch?v=Y6kh5UonEZ0).

- Flutter Navigation 2.0 by Dominik Roszkowski goes through the differences between Navigator 1.0 and 2.0, including a video example (https://youtu.be/JmfYeF4gUu0?t=9728).
- For in-depth knowledge about `Navigator`, check out Flutter's documentation (https://api.flutter.dev/flutter/widgets/Navigator-class.html).
- Finally, here's the GoRouter documentation (https://pub.dev/documentation/go_router/latest/).

Other Libraries to Check Out

`GoRouter` is just one of the many libraries trying to make the Router API easier to use. Check them out here:

- Beamer (https://pub.dev/packages/beamer)
- Flow Builder (https://pub.dev/packages/flow_builder)
- Fluro (https://pub.dev/packages/fluro)
- Vrouter (https://pub.dev/packages/vrouter)
- Auto Route (https://pub.dev/packages/auto_route)

There are so many more things you can do with Router API. In the next chapter, you'll look at supporting web URLs and deep linking!

Chapter 9: Deep Links & Web URLs

By Vincent Ngo

Sometimes, opening your app and working through the navigation to get to a screen is just too much trouble for the user. Redirecting to a specific part of your app is a powerful marketing tool for user engagement. For example, generating a special QR code for a promotion that users can scan to visit that specific product in your app is a cool and effective way to build interest in the product.

In the last chapter, you learned how to use `GoRouter` to move between screens, navigating your app in a declarative way. Now you'll learn how to **deep link** to screens in your app and explore web URLs on the web.

Take a look at how **Yummy** looks in the Chrome web browser:

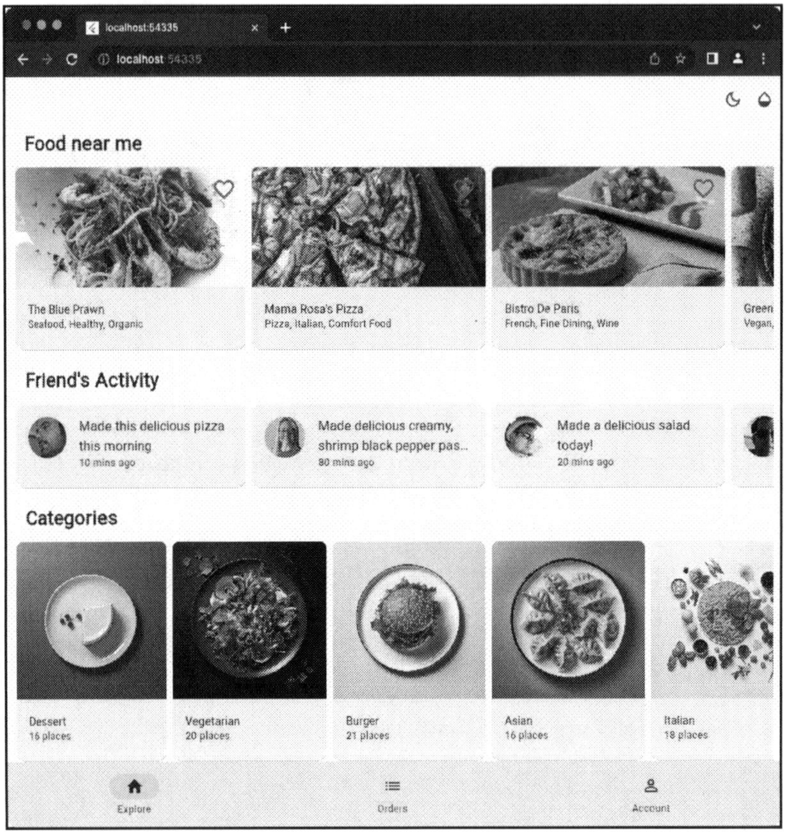

By the end of this chapter, you'll:

- Have a better understanding of the **router API**.
- Know how to support **deep linking** on iOS and Android.
- Explore the Yummy app on the **web**.

You'll learn how to **direct** users to any screen of your choice.

> **Note**: You'll need to install the Chrome web browser to view Yummy on the web. If you don't have Chrome, you can get it here (https://www.google.com/chrome/). The Flutter web project can run on other browsers, but this chapter only covers testing and development with Chrome.

Understanding Deep Links

A **deep link** is a URL that navigates to a **specific destination** in your mobile app. Think of deep links like a URL address you enter into a web browser to go to a specific page of a website rather than the home page.

Deep links help with **user engagement** and **business marketing**. For example, if you're running a sale, you can direct the user to a specific product page in your app instead of making them search for it.

Just imagine, your app **Yummy** is a user-friendly food app that allows customers to quickly scan a QR code at restaurants, instantly access menus and seamlessly deep-link to detailed restaurant pages in for an enhanced dining experience.

With deep linking, Yummy is more automated. It brings the user directly to the restaurant page making it easier to view the menu.Without deep linking, the process is more manual. The user has to launch the app, navigate to the **Explore** tab find the correct restaurant, or search the restaurant name, and finally get to the restaurant page to view the menu. That takes three steps instead of one and likely some head-scratching, too!

Types of Deep Links

There are three types of deep links:

- **URI schemes**: An app's own URI scheme. **yummy://kodeco.com/home** is an example of Yummy's URI scheme. This form of deep link only works if the user has **installed** your app.
- **iOS Universal Links**: In the root of your web domain, you place a file that points to a specific **app ID** to say whether to **open** your app or to direct the user to the **App Store**. You must register that specific app ID with Apple to handle links from that domain.
- **Android App Links**: Like iOS Universal Links, Android App Links take users to a link's specific content directly in your app. They leverage **HTTP URLs** and are associated with a website. For users that don't have your app installed, these links go directly to the content of your **website**.

In this chapter, you'll only look at **URI Schemes**. For more information on how to set up iOS Universal Links and Android App Links, check out these tutorials:

- Universal Links: Make the Connection (https://www.kodeco.com/6080-universal-links-make-the-connection)
- Deep Links in Android: Getting Started (https://www.kodeco.com/18330247-deep-links-in-android-getting-started)

Getting Started

> **Note**: We recommend you use the starter project for this chapter rather than continuing with the project from the last chapter.

Open the starter project in Android Studio and run `flutter pub get`. Then, run the app on iOS or Android.

You'll see that **Yummy** shows the **Login** screen.

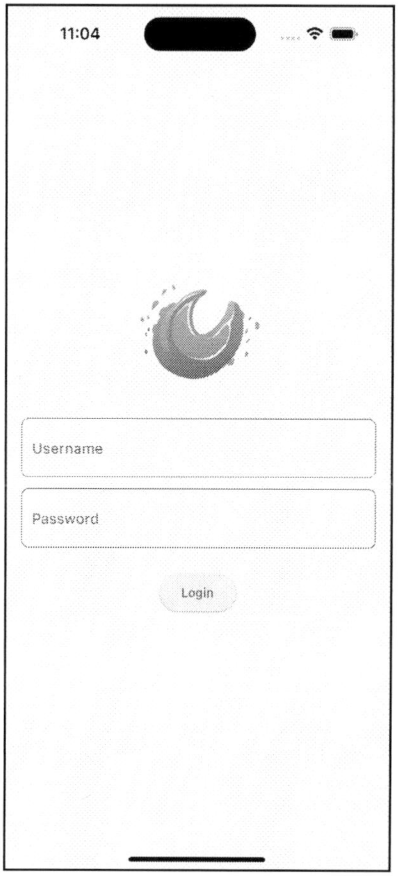

Soon, you'll be able to redirect users to different parts of the app. But first, take a moment to review what's changed in the starter project since the last chapter.

Project Files

Before diving in, you need to be aware of some new files.

New Flutter Web Project

The starter project includes a pre-built Flutter web project.

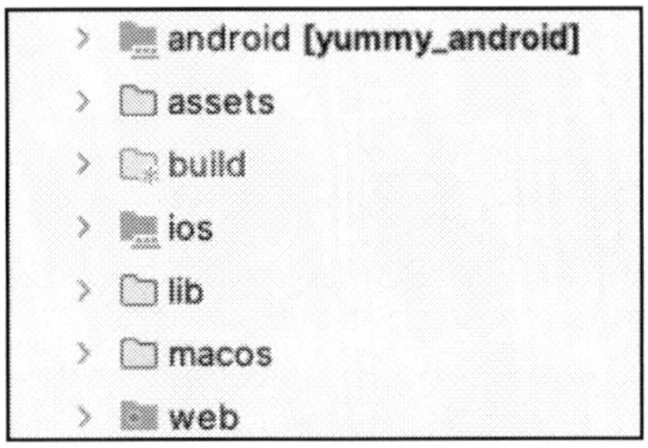

> **Note**: To speed things up, the web project is pre-built in your starter project. To learn how to create a Flutter web app, check out the Flutter documentation (https://flutter.dev/docs/get-started/web#add-web-support-to-an-existing-app).

Setting Up Deep Links

To enable deep linking on iOS and Android, you must add metadata tags on the respective platforms. These tags have already been added to the starter project.

Setting Up Deep Links on iOS

Open **ios/Runner/Info.plist**. You'll see some new key-value pairs, which enable deep linking for iOS:

```
...
<key>FlutterDeepLinkingEnabled</key>
<true/>
<key>CFBundleURLTypes</key>
<array>
  <dict>
  <key>CFBundleTypeRole</key>
  <string>Editor</string>
  <key>CFBundleURLName</key>
  <string>kodeco.com</string>
  <key>CFBundleURLSchemes</key>
```

```
  <array>
  <string>yummy</string>
  </array>
  </dict>
</array>
...
```

CFBundleURLName is a **unique URL** that distinguishes your app from others that use the same scheme. yummy is the URL scheme you'll use later.

Setting Up Deep Links on Android

Open **android/app/src/main/AndroidManifest.xml**. Here you'll also find two new definitions in the <data> tag:

```
...
<!-- Deep linking -->
<meta-data android:name="flutter_deeplinking_enabled"
android:value="true" />
<intent-filter>
<action android:name="android.intent.action.VIEW" />
<category android:name="android.intent.category.DEFAULT" />
<category android:name="android.intent.category.BROWSABLE" />
<data
  android:scheme="yummy"
  android:host="kodeco.com" />
</intent-filter>
...
```

Like in iOS, you set the same values for scheme and host.

When you create a deep link for Yummy, the custom URL scheme looks like this:

```
yummy://kodeco.com/<path>
```

Now, take a quick look at the URL paths you'll create.

Overview of Yummy Paths

Yummy has many screens you can deep link to. Here are all the possible paths you can direct your users to the following.

Path: /

The app initializes and checks the app cache to see if the user is logged in.

- **/login**: Redirects to the **Login** screen if the user isn't logged in yet.

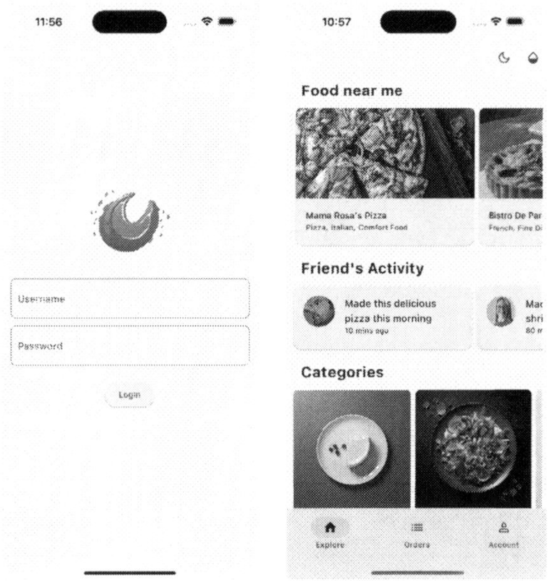

yummy://kodeco.com/login yummy://kodeco.com/

Path: /:tab

Once the user logs in, they're redirected to `/:tab`. It contains one parameter, `tab`, which directs to a **tab index**. The screenshots below show that the tab index is `0`, `1` or `2`, respectively.

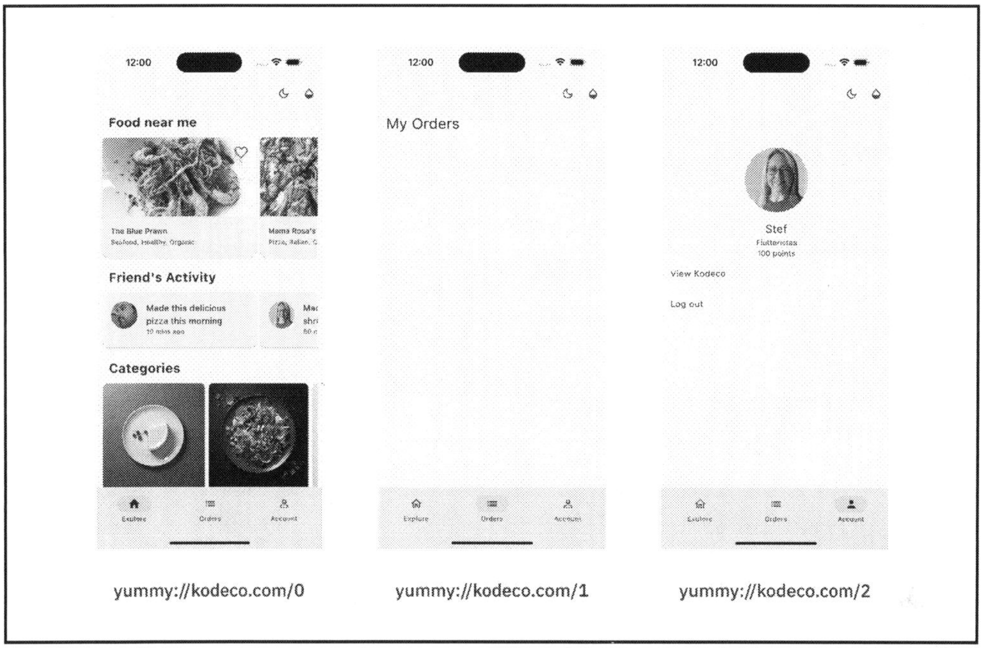

Path: /restaurant/:id

The restaurant page is a **sub route** of the **Explore** page. You can present a restaurant from any tab.

`/restaurant/:id` contains one parameter, `id`.

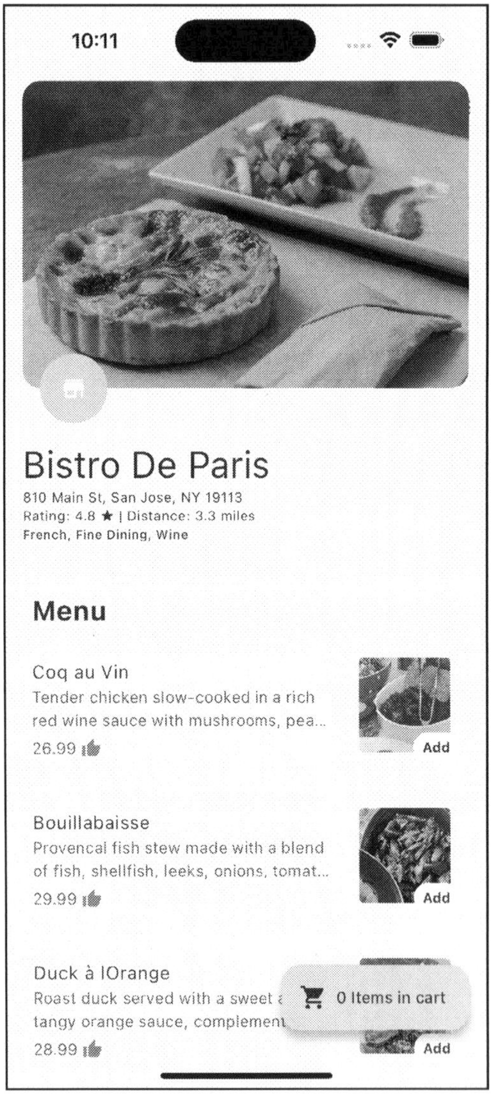

Note: Keep in mind that these URL paths work similarly for mobile and web apps.

When you deep link on **mobile**, you'll use the following URI scheme:

```
yummy://kodeco.com/<path>
```

On the **web**, the URI scheme is like any web browser URL:

```
http://localhost:60738/#/<path>
```

Before exploring deep links, take a moment for a quick Router API recap.

Router API Recap

In the last chapter, you learned how to use `GoRouter` to set up routes and navigate to screens. `GoRouter` conveniently manages the Router API for you. How amazing is that? :]

However, it's still good to understand how routing works behind the scenes. Here's a diagram of what makes up the Router API:

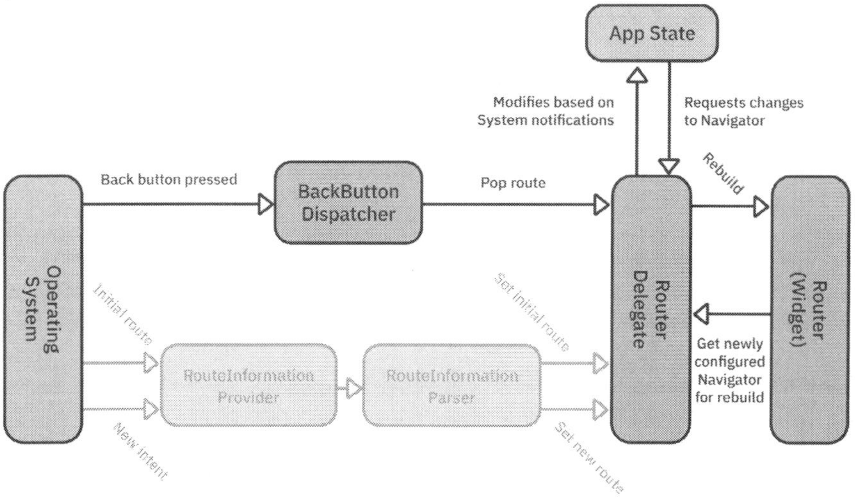

- **Router** is a widget that extends `RouterDelegate`. The router ensures that the messages get to the `RouterDelegate`.
- **Navigator** defines a stack of `MaterialPages` in a declarative way. It also handles any `onPopPage()` event.
- **BackButtonDispatcher** handles platform-specific system **back button presses**. It listens to requests by the OS and tells the router delegate to pop a route.

Next, you'll look at **RouteInformationProvider** and **RouteInformationParser**.

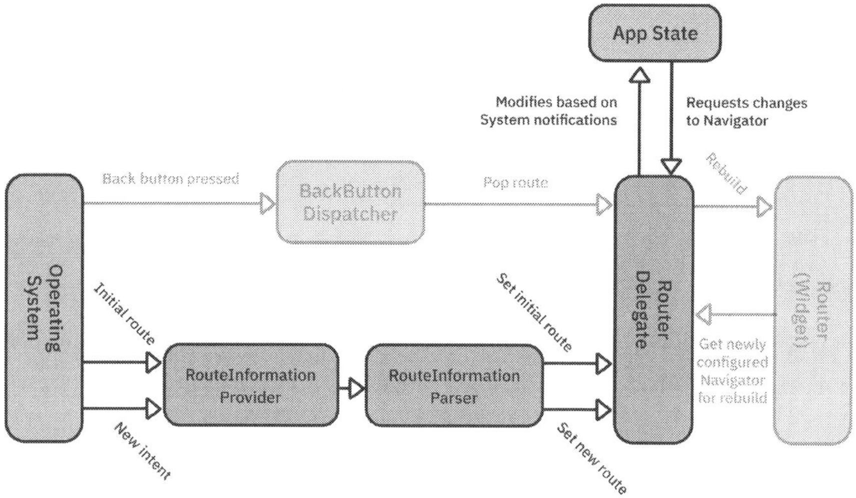

- **RouteInformationProvider**: Provides the route information to the router. It informs the router about the **initial route** and notifies **new intents.**
- **RouteInformationParser**: Gets the route string from `RouteInformationProvider`, then parses the URL string to a generic **user-defined** data type. This data type is a navigation configuration.

> **Note**: `GoRouter` implements its own `RouteInformationParser` called **GoRouteInformationParser**. Based on the `routeInformation`, it tries to search for a route match based on the route's location. Check out the code in this GitHub repository (https://github.com/flutter/packages/blob/main/packages/go_router/lib/src/parser.dart).

Since `GoRouter` provides and manages all of these components, it's a good idea to jump straight into `GoRouter`'s implementation to learn more and see how they configure things.

Enough theory. It's time to get started!

Testing Deep Links

Next, you'll test how deep linking works on iOS, Android and the web.

Testing Deep Links on iOS

In Android Studio, select an iOS device and press **Run**:

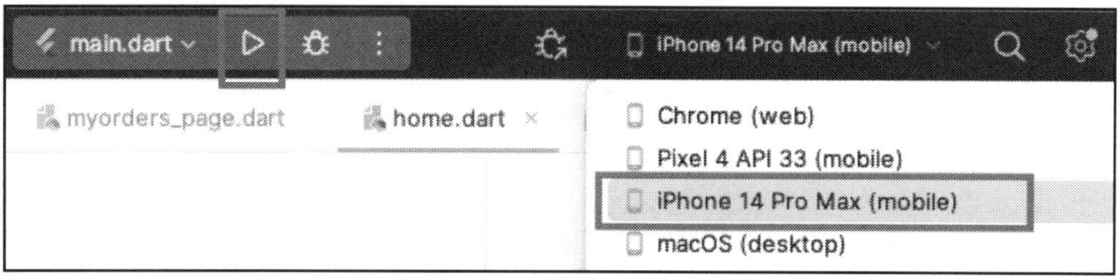

Once the simulator is running, log in as shown below:

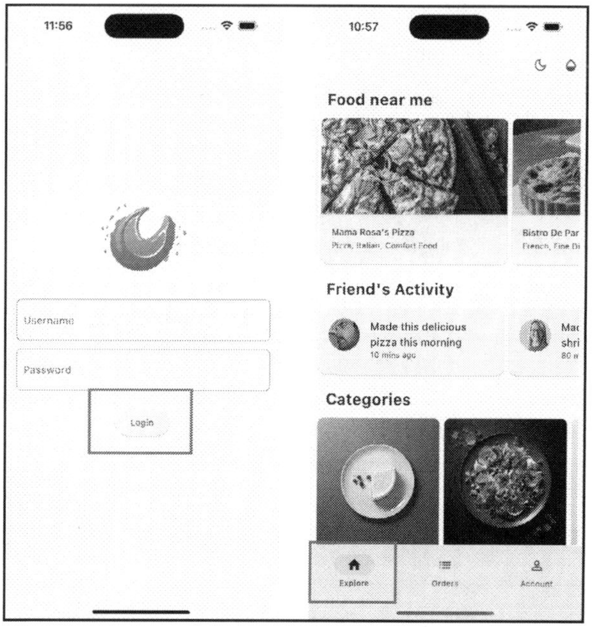

Deep Linking to the Orders Page

Enter the following in your terminal:

```
xcrun simctl openurl booted 'yummy://kodeco.com/1'
```

> **Note**: You have to be logged into the app. Otherwise, it will just show the **Login** page. Note that the first time you run this command the simulator might show a popup. If so, allow it to proceed.

In the simulator, this automatically switches to the second tab, as shown below:

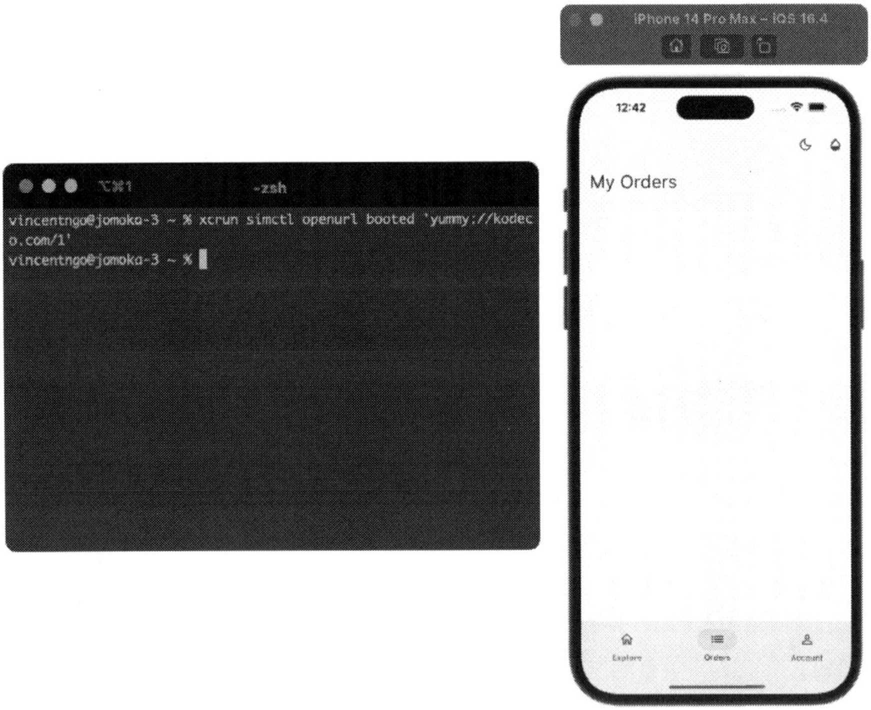

Deep Linking to the Account Page

Next, run the following command:

```
xcrun simctl openurl booted 'yummy://kodeco.com/2'
```

This command directs to the **Account** page:

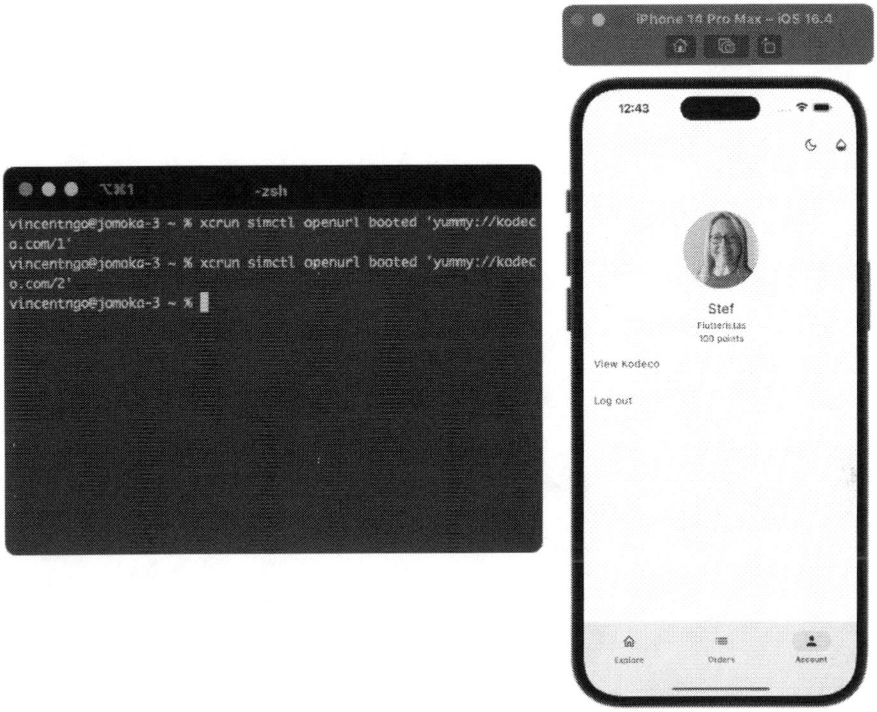

Deep Linking to the Home Page

Next, run the following command:

```
xcrun simctl openurl booted 'yummy://kodeco.com/0'
```

This command directs to the home page, named **Explore**:

Deep Linking to a Specific Restaurant

Next, run the following command:

```
xcrun simctl openurl booted 'yummy:/0/restaurant/2'
```

Observe that the route is structured as `/:tab/restaurant/:id`. Here, the restaurant page acts as a **subroute** under the home route. To navigate to a specific restaurant, you need to identify the **active tab**, followed by the restaurant's **unique ID**. This hierarchical routing ensures precise and context-aware navigation within the app.

The restaurant page will now show:

Following this pattern, you can build paths to any location in your app!

Resetting the Cache in the iOS Simulator

Recall that `AppStateManager` checks with `AppCache` to see whether the user is logged in. If you want to reset the cache to see the **Login** screen again, you have two options:

1. Go to the **Account** view and tap **Log out** to invalidate the app cache.

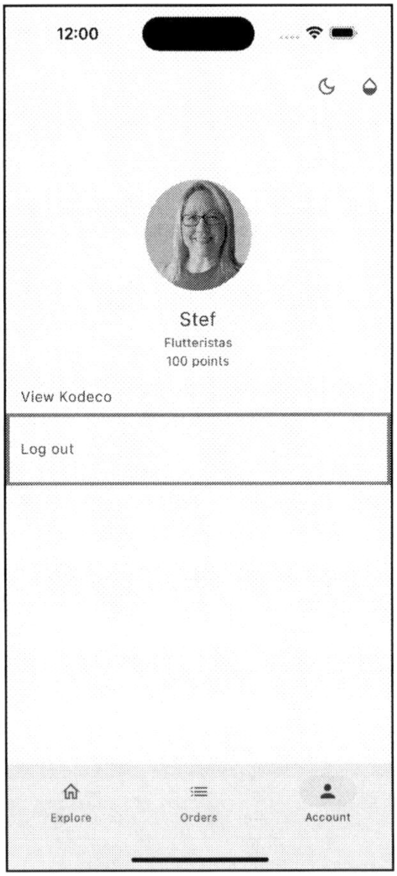

2. In the iOS simulator menu, you can select **Erase All Content and Settings...** to clear the cache.

Note: This will delete any other apps you have on the simulator.

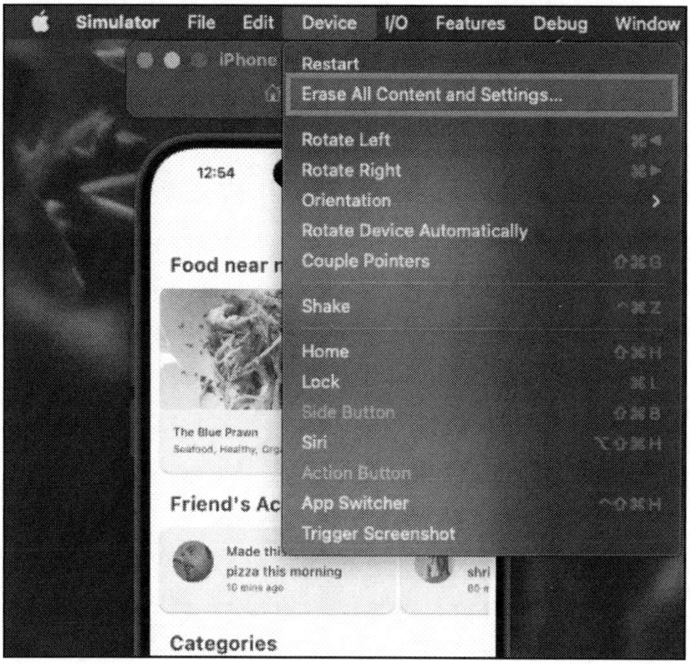

Testing Deep Links on Android

Stop running on iOS. In **Android Studio**, select an Android emulator or device and click the **Run** button:

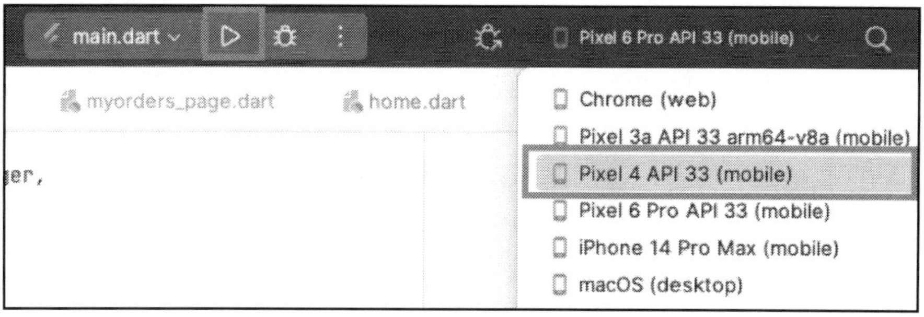

Once the emulator or device is running, log in:

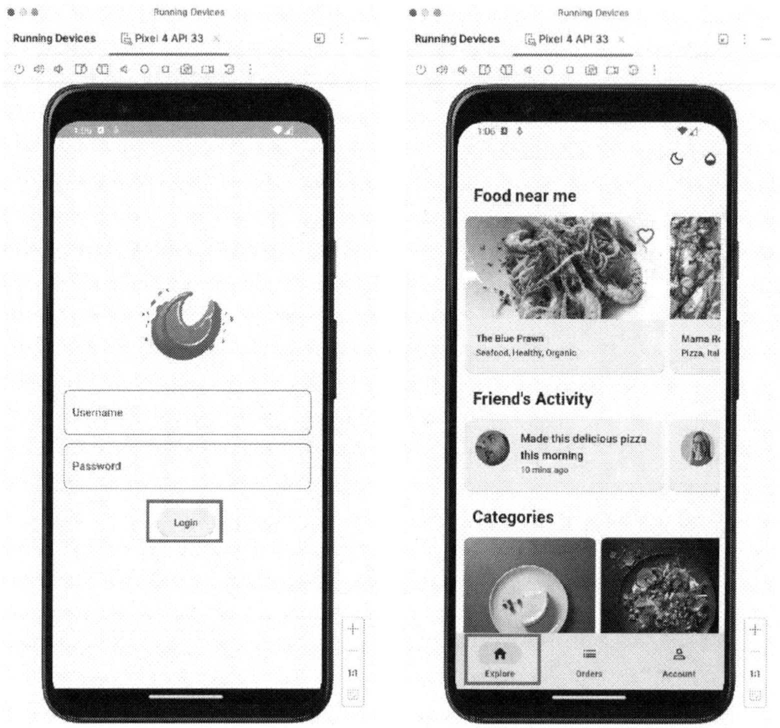

Deep Linking to the Orders Page

Enter the following in your terminal:

```
~/Library/Android/sdk/platform-tools/adb shell am start -a
android.intent.action.VIEW \
    -c android.intent.category.BROWSABLE \
    -d 'yummy://kodeco.com/1'
```

> **Note**: If you receive a message in Terminal like: `Warning: Activity not started, intent has been delivered to currently running top-most instance`, ignore it. It just means that the app is already running.
>
> The entire path is listed to ensure that you can still execute this command if you don't have `adb` in your $PATH. The \ at each line's end formats the script nicely across multiple lines.

This command directs to the second tab of Yummy, that is **Orders**:

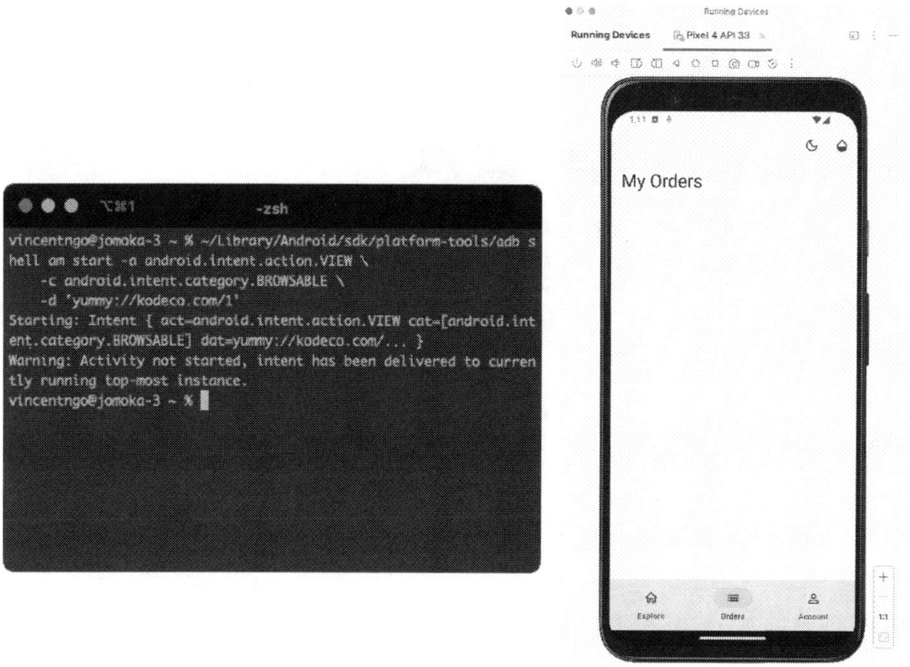

Deep Linking to the Account Page

Next, run the following command:

```
~/Library/Android/sdk/platform-tools/adb shell am start -a
android.intent.action.VIEW \
    -c android.intent.category.BROWSABLE \
    -d 'yummy://kodeco.com/2'
```

This command navigates to the **Account** screen:

Deep Linking to Restaurant Page

Next, run the following:

```
~/Library/Android/sdk/platform-tools/adb shell am start -a
android.intent.action.VIEW \
    -c android.intent.category.BROWSABLE \
    -d 'yummy://kodeco.com/2/restaurant/1'
```

The selected restaurant page appears, as shown below:

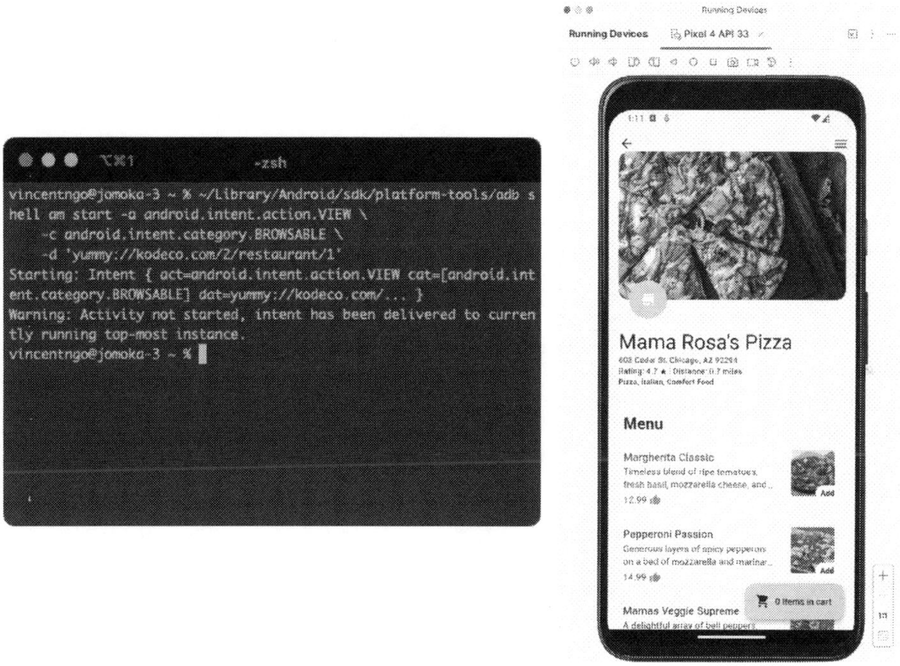

Resetting the Cache in Android

If you need to reset your emulator cache:

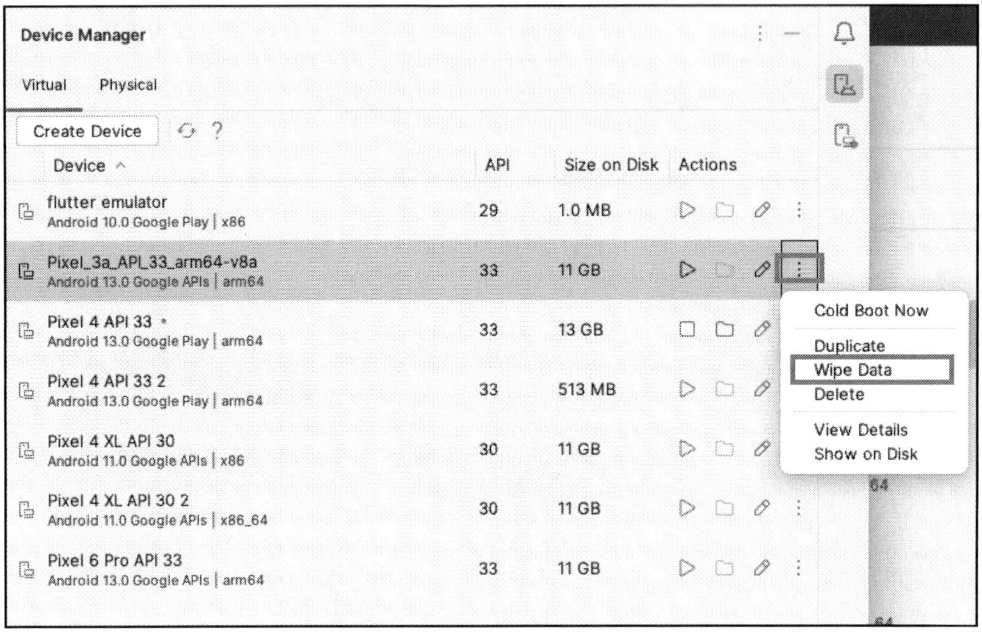

In **Android Studio** go to **Tools/Device Manager** and you'll see your list of virtual devices. Click the 3 dotted action bar and select **Wipe Data**

Now, it's time to test how Yummy handles URLs on the web.

Running the Web App

Stop running on Android. In Android Studio, select **Chrome (web)** and click **Run**:

> **Note**: Your data won't persist between app launches because Flutter web runs the equivalent of incognito mode (https://support.google.com/chrome/answer/95464) during development.
>
> If you build and release your Flutter web app, it'll work as expected. For more information on how to build for release, check the Flutter documentation (https://flutter.dev/docs/deployment/web#building-the-app-for-release).

Go through the Yummy UI flow, and you'll see that the web browser's address bar changes:

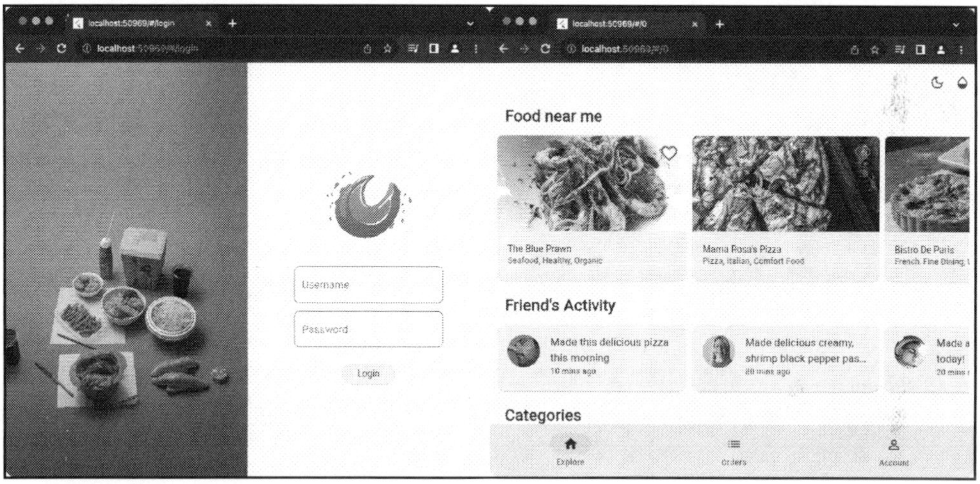

If you change the `tab` query parameter's value to **0**, **1** or **2**, the app automatically switches to that tab.

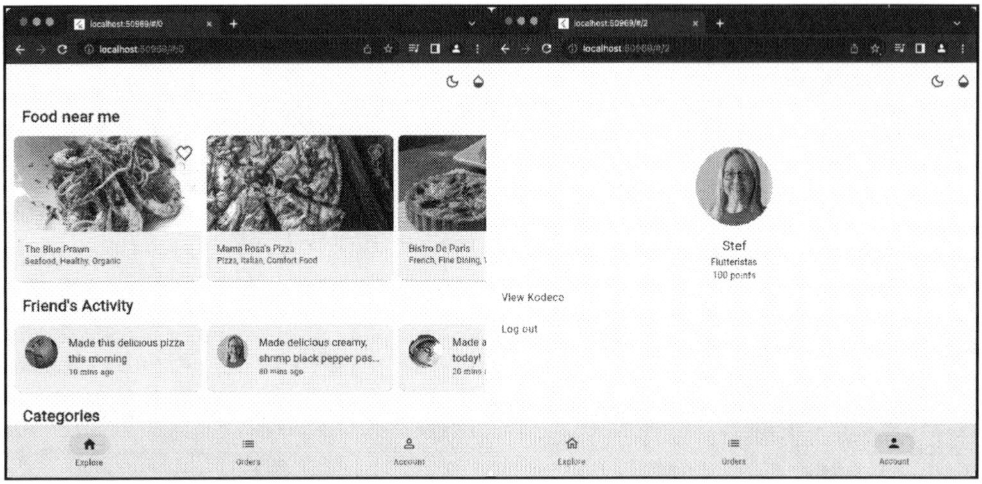

Next on the **Explore** tab, tap on a restaurant

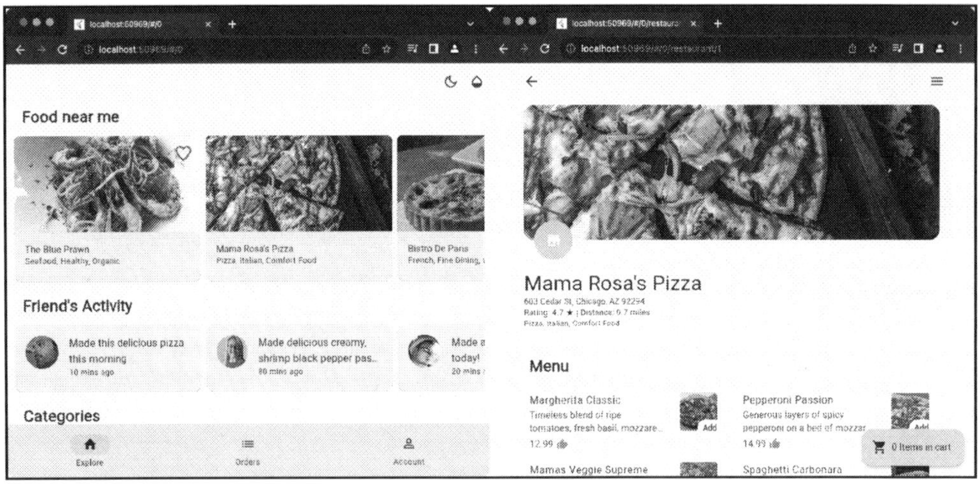

Notice that the app stores the entire browser history. Pretty cool!

Tap the **Back** and **Forward** buttons and the app restores that state! How cool is that? You can also **long-press** the **Back** button to jump to a specific state in the browser history.

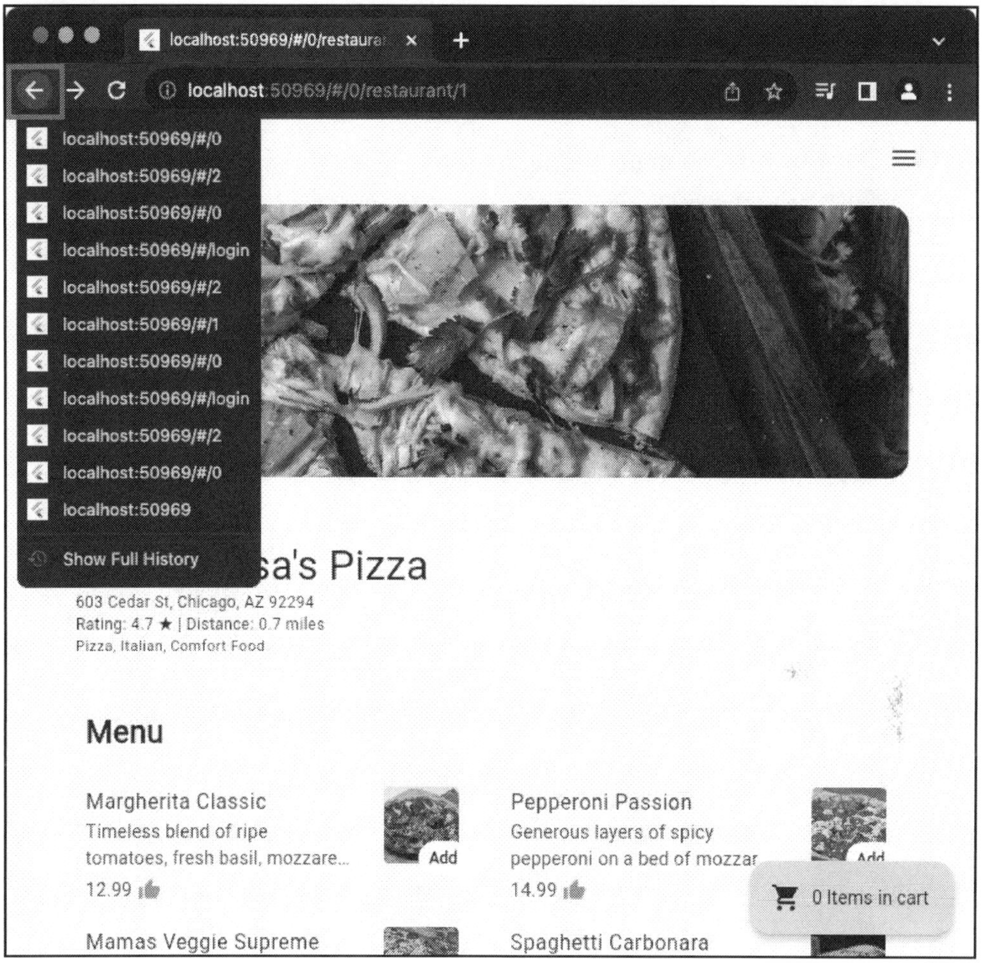

Congratulations on learning how to work with deep links in your Flutter app!

Key Points

- The app notifies `RouteInformationProvider` when there's a new route to navigate to.
- The provider passes the route information to `RouteInformationParser` to parse the URL string.
- The parser converts the route information state to and from a URL string.
- `GoRouter` converts route information state to and from a `RouteMatchList`.
- `GoRouter` supports deep linking and web browser address bar paths out of the box.
- In development mode, the Flutter web app doesn't persist data between app launches. The web app generated in release mode will work on other browsers.

Where to Go From Here?

Flutter renders web apps in two different ways. Explore how that works in the Flutter documentation on web renderers (https://flutter.dev/docs/development/tools/web-renderers).

For more examples of various navigation use-cases with `GoRouter`, check out these examples (https://github.com/flutter/packages/tree/main/packages/go_router/example).

In this chapter, you continued to learn how the Router API works behind the scenes and explore how to test and perform deep links on iOS, Android and the Web.

Deep linking helps bring users to specific destinations within your app, building better user engagement!

Flutter's ability to support routes and navigation for multiple platforms isn't just powerful; it's magical.

Section IV: Networking, Persistence & State

Most apps interact with the network to retrieve data and then persist that data locally in some form of cache, such as a database. In this section, you'll build a new app that lets you search the Internet for recipes, bookmark recipes, and save their ingredients into a shopping list.

You'll learn about making network requests, parsing the network JSON response, and saving data in a SQLite database. You'll also get an introduction to using Dart streams.

Finally, this section will also dive deeper into the important topic of app state, which determines where and how your user interface stores and refreshes data in the user interface as a user interacts with your app.

Chapter 10: Handling Shared Preferences

By Kevin David Moore

Picture this: You're browsing recipes and find one you like. You're in a hurry and want to bookmark it to check it later. Can you build a Flutter app that does that? You sure can! Read on to find out how.

In this chapter, your goal is to learn how to use the **shared_preferences** plugin to save important pieces of information to your device.

You'll start with a new project showing two tabs at the bottom of the screen for two views: Recipes and Groceries.

The first screen is where you'll search for recipes you want to prepare. Once you find a recipe you like, just bookmark it, and the app will add the recipe to your **Bookmarks** page. It will also add all the ingredients you need to your shopping list. You'll use a web API to search for recipes and store the ones you bookmark in a local database.

The completed app will look something like this:

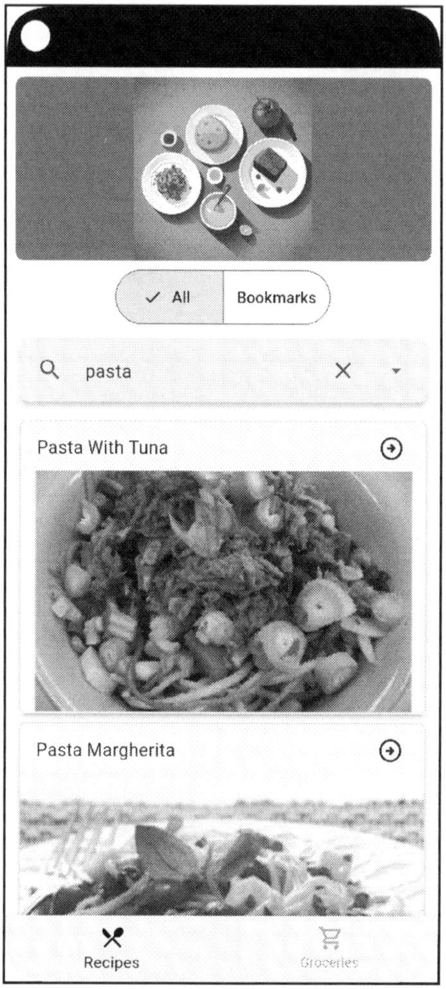

This shows the **Recipes** tab with the results you get when searching for **Pasta**. It's as easy as typing in the search text field and tapping the **Search** icon. The app stores your search term history in the combo box to the right of the text field.

When you tap a card, you'll see something like this:

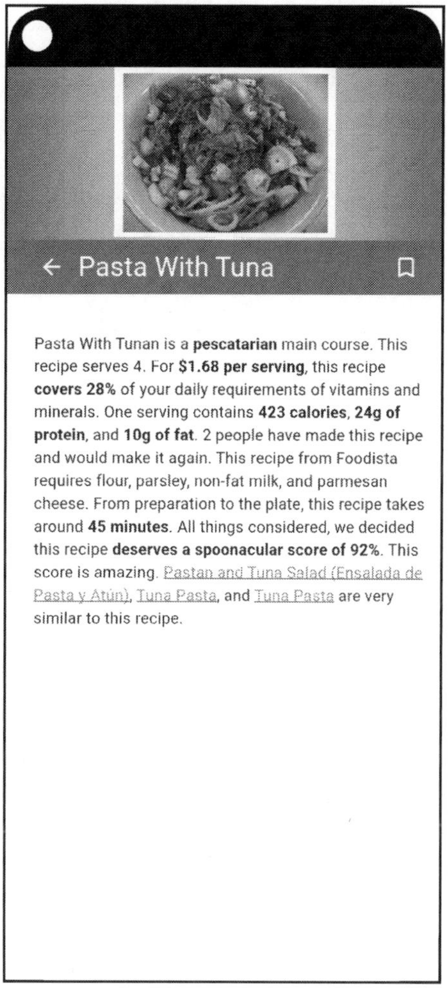

To save a recipe, just tap the **Bookmark** button. When you tap on the **Bookmarks** selector, you'll see that the recipe has been saved:

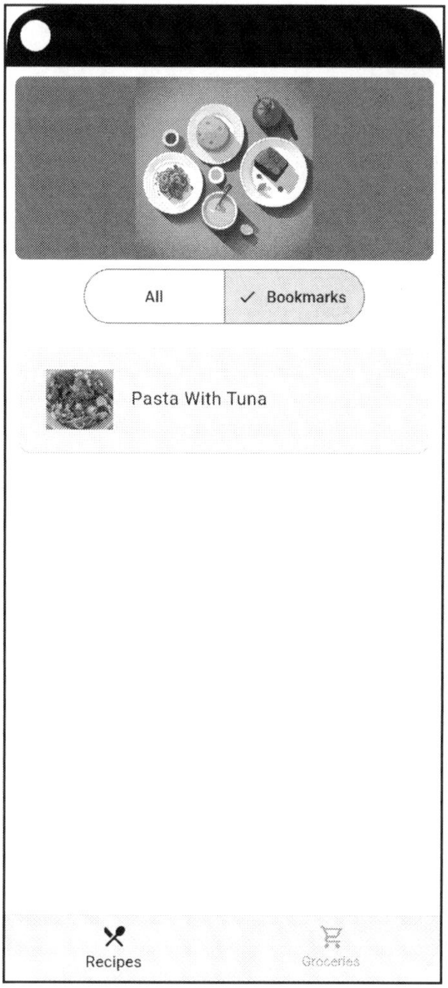

If you don't want the recipe anymore, swipe left or right, and you'll see a delete button that allows you to remove it from the list of bookmarked recipes.

The **Groceries** tab shows the ingredients you need to make the recipes you've bookmarked.

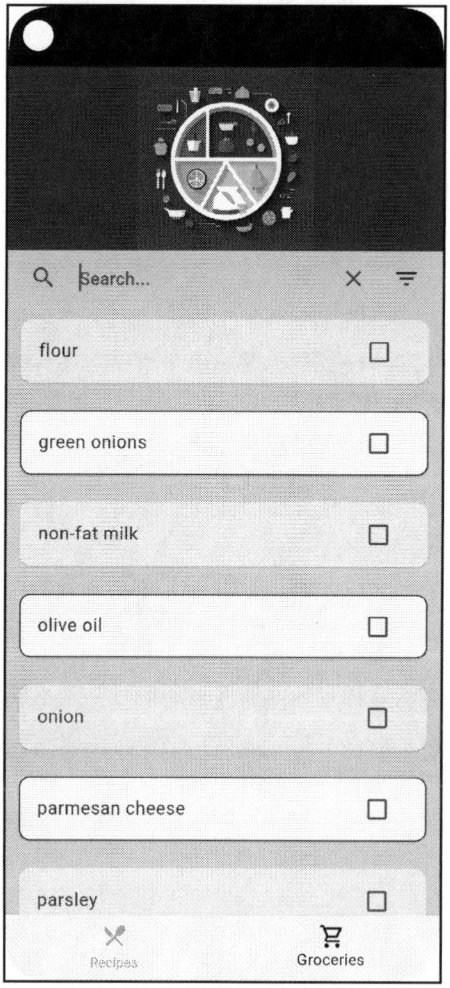

You'll build this app over the next few chapters. In this chapter, you'll use shared_preferences to save simple data like the selected tab and also to cache the searched items in the Recipes tab.

By the end of the chapter, you'll know:

- What shared preferences are.
- How to use the shared_preferences plugin to save and retrieve objects.

Note: Feel free to explore the entire app. There is a lot there to explore and learn that isn't covered in the book. Copy any code you like for your projects.

Now that you know what your goal is, it's time to jump in!

Getting Started

Open the **starter** project for this chapter in Android Studio. Open the **pubspec.yaml** file and click `pub get`, then run the app.

Notice the two tabs at the bottom — each will show a different screen when you tap it. Only the **Recipes** screen currently shows any UI. It looks like this:

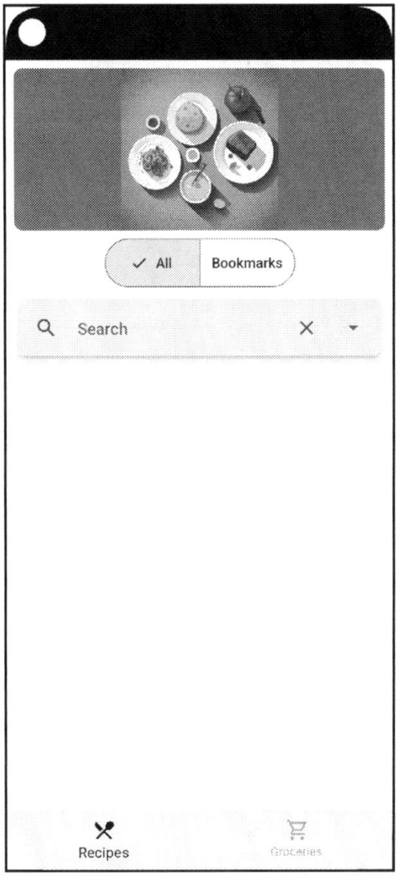

App Libraries

The starter project includes quite a few libraries in **pubspec.yaml**:

```
dependencies:
  ...
  auto_size_text:
  flutter_adaptive_scaffold:
  desktop_window:
  path:
  cached_network_image:
  flutter_slidable:
  platform:
  freezed_annotation:
  flutter_svg:
  ....
  flutter_riverpod:
```

Here's what they help you do:

- **auto_size_text**: Useful library for ensuring text fits in the given space.
- **flutter_adaptive_scaffold**: Library changing your UI based on changing sizes. Useful for the desktop, web and folding phones.
- **desktop_window**: Library for the desktop app for setting the window size.
- **path**: Library for handling files.
- **cached_network_image**: Download and cache the images you'll use in the app.
- **flutter_slidable**: Build a widget that lets the user slide a card left and right to perform different actions, like deleting a saved recipe.
- **platform**: For accessing platform-specific information.
- **freezed_annotation**: Part of the freezed library. Generates useful JSON and related utility functions.
- **flutter_svg**: Load SVG images without the need to use a program to convert them to vector files.
- **flutter_riverpod**: State management library. You'll learn more about this library in Chapter 13, "Managing State".

Now that you've looked at the libraries take a moment to think about how you save data before you begin coding your app.

Saving Data

There are three primary ways to save data to your device:

1. Write formatted data, like JSON, to a file.
2. Use a library or plugin to write simple data to a shared location.
3. Use a SQLite database.

Writing data to a file is simple, but it requires you to handle reading and writing data in the correct format and order.

You can also use a library or plugin to write simple data to a shared location managed by the platform, like iOS and Android. This is what you'll do in this chapter.

You can save the information to a local database for more complex data. You'll learn more about that in **Chapter 15, "Saving Data Locally"**.

Saving Small Bits of Data

Why would you save small bits of data? Well, there are many reasons to do this. For example, you could save the user ID when the user has logged in — or if the user has logged in at all. You could also save the onboarding state or data the user has bookmarked to consult later.

Note that this simple data saved to a shared location is lost when the user uninstalls the app.

The shared_preferences Plugin

shared_preferences is a Flutter plugin that allows you to save data in a key-value format so you can easily retrieve it later. Behind the scenes, it uses the aptly named **SharedPreferences** on Android and the similar **UserDefaults** on iOS.

For this app, you'll learn to use the plugin by saving the search terms the user entered and the tab currently selected.

One of the great things about this plugin is that it doesn't require any setup or configuration. Just create an instance of the plugin, and you're ready to fetch and save data.

> **Note**: The shared_preferences plugin gives you a quick way to persist and retrieve data, but it only supports saving simple properties like strings, numbers, and Boolean values.
>
> In later chapters, you'll learn about alternatives you can use when you want to save complex data.
>
> Be aware that shared_preferences is not a good fit to store sensitive data. To store passwords or access tokens, check out the Android Keystore for Android and Keychain Services for iOS, or consider using the **flutter_secure_storage** plugin.

To use shared_preferences, you first need to add it as a dependency. Open **pubspec.yaml** and underneath the `flutter_svg` library, add the following:

```
shared_preferences: ^2.2.0
```

Make sure you indent it the same as the other libraries.

Now, click the **Pub Get** button to get the shared_preferences library.

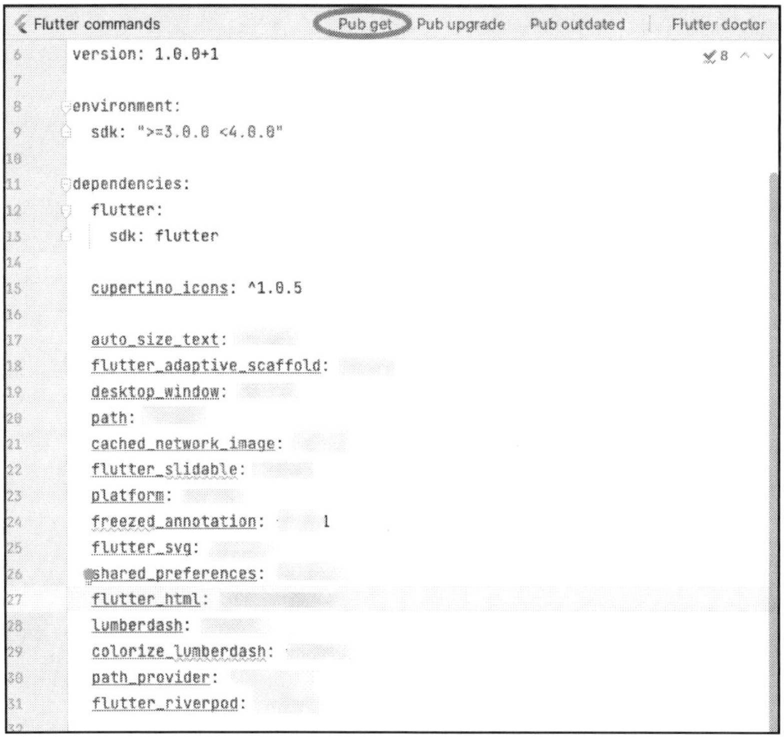

You can also run pub get from the command line:

```
flutter pub get
```

How Does it Work?

The shared_preferences library uses the system's API's to store data into a file. These are small bits of information like integers, strings or Booleans. It has three main sets of function calls:

1. `setXXX`: Set methods save the data of that specific data type.
2. `getXXX`: Get methods retrieve the data of that specific data type.
3. `clear()`: This method deletes all saved data.
4. `remove()`: This method removes a specific value.

All of these methods except the `clear()` method use a **key** to access an item. By giving the library a unique key, you can store, retrieve and delete specific items. Here's an example:

```
final CURRENT_USER_KEY = 'CURRENT_USER_KEY';
final sharedPrefs = await SharedPreferences.getInstance();
sharedPrefs.setString(CURRENT_USER_KEY, '1011442433');
...
sharedPrefs.remove(CURRENT_USER_KEY);
```

In this example, you get an instance of the shared preference library and then set a string using that key. Later on, you remove that item if the user logged out, for example.

There are several other interesting methods:

1. `containsKey()`: Returns true if the key exists.
2. `getBool()`, `getDouble()`, `getInt()`: Methods to retrieve specific types.
3. `setBool()`, `setDouble()`, `setInt()`: Methods to store specific types.

There aren't a lot of methods, but it's a very useful library.

You're now ready to store data. You'll start by saving the **searches** the user makes so they can easily select them again in the future.

Running Code in the Background

To understand the code you'll be adding next, you need to know a bit about running code in the **background**.

Most modern UI toolkits have a **main thread** that runs the UI code. Any code that takes a long time needs to run on a different thread or process so it doesn't block the UI. Dart uses a technique similar to *JavaScript* to achieve this. The language includes these two keywords:

- `async`
- `await`

`async` marks a method or code section as **asynchronous**. You then use the `await` keyword inside that method to wait until an asynchronous process finishes in the background.

Saving UI States

You'll use **shared_preferences** to save a list of saved searches in this section. Later, you'll also save the tab that the user has selected so the app always opens to that tab.

You'll start by preparing your search to store that information.

Adding Shared Preferences as a Provider

This app uses the **Riverpod** library to provide resources to other parts of the app. Chapter 13, "Managing State" covers **Riverpod** in more detail. For now, you want to create an instance of the `SharedPreferences` library on startup and provide it to other parts of the app. To do so, open up **lib/providers.dart** and import shared preferences library:

```
import 'package:shared_preferences/shared_preferences.dart';
```

Then replace `// TODO Add Shared Pref Provider` with the following:

```
final sharedPrefProvider = Provider<SharedPreferences>((ref) {
  throw UnimplementedError();
});
```

This creates a **Riverpod Provider** for our shared preference. Notice how we throw a `UnimplementedError`. This is because you'll provide it in the **main.dart** file.

Open up **main.dart**. Add the shared preferences library and providers import:

```
import 'package:shared_preferences/shared_preferences.dart';
import 'providers.dart';
```

Find `// TODO Add Shared Preferences`. Replace this and the line below it with the following:

```
// 1
final sharedPrefs = await SharedPreferences.getInstance();
// 2
runApp(ProviderScope(overrides: [
  // 3
  sharedPrefProvider.overrideWithValue(sharedPrefs),
], child: const MyApp()));
```

Here's what that code's doing:

1. Create an instance of the **SharedPreferences** library. Notice the `await` keyword. This will wait until the instance is created.
2. **Riverpod** requires a `ProviderScope` above the app where you'll provide providers. These allow you to make functionalities like shared_preferences available to other parts of the app.
3. Override the `sharedPrefProvider` value with the shared pref you just created.

Because the main function has the `async` keyword, you can `await` getting an instance of `SharedPreferences`. By using `overrideWithValue()`, you replace the `unimplemented exception` with a real value. `ProviderScope` will be discussed more in Chapter 13, "Managing State" but is required for **Riverpod** to run.

Next, you'll add an entry to the search list.

Adding an Entry

First, you'll change the UI so that when the user presses the search icon, the app will add the search entry to the search list.

Open **lib/ui/recipes/recipe_list.dart**, locate `// TODO: Add imports` and replace it with:

```
import '../../providers.dart';
```

That imports the provider's file.

Next, you'll give each search term a unique key. Find `// TODO Add Search Index Key` and replace it with the following:

```
static const String prefSearchKey = 'previousSearches';
```

All preferences need to use a unique key. Here, you're simply defining a constant for the **preference search key**.

Saving Previous Searches

Still in **recipe_list.dart**, replace `// TODO Save Current Index` with:

```
// 1
final prefs = ref.read(sharedPrefProvider);
// 2
prefs.setStringList(prefSearchKey, previousSearches);
```

1. **ref.read** extracts the preferences from the provider you set up previously.

2. Saves the list of previous searches using the `prefSearchKey` key.

The `setStringList` method is a nice way to save a list of strings. Next, replace `// TODO: TODO Get Current Index` with the following:

```
// 1
final prefs = ref.read(sharedPrefProvider);
// 2
if (prefs.containsKey(prefSearchKey)) {
  // 3
  final searches = prefs.getStringList(prefSearchKey);
  // 4
  if (searches != null) {
    previousSearches = searches;
  } else {
    previousSearches = <String>[];
  }
}
```

Here, you:

1. Extract the preferences object.

2. Check if the **preference** for your saved list already exists.

3. Get the list of **previous searches**.

4. If the list is not `null`, set the previous searches, otherwise initialize an empty list.

This method is called when the **recipe list** starts loading any previous searches.

Showing the Previous Searches

To perform a search, you first need to clear any of your variables and save the new search value. Take a look at `startSearch()`:

```
void startSearch(String value) {
  //1
  if (value.isEmpty) {
    return;
  }
  // 2
  setState(() {
    // 3
    currentSearchList.clear();
    currentCount = 0;
    currentEndPosition = pageCount;
    currentStartPosition = 0;
    hasMore = true;
    value = value.trim();

    // 4
    if (!previousSearches.contains(value)) {
      // 5
      previousSearches.add(value);
      // 6
      savePreviousSearches();
    }
  });
}
```

In this method, you:

1. Checks the input value to make sure it's not empty.
2. Tell the system to update the widgets by calling `setState()`.
3. Clear the current search list and reset the `currentCount`, `currentStartPosition` and `currentEndPosition`.
4. Check to ensure the **search text** hasn't already been added to the previous search list.
5. Add the **search item** to the previous search list.
6. Save the new list of previous searches.

You used a text field with a drop-down menu to show the list of previous text searches. That's a row with a `TextField` and a `CustomDropDownMenuItem`. The menu item shows the search term and an icon on the right. It will look something like this:

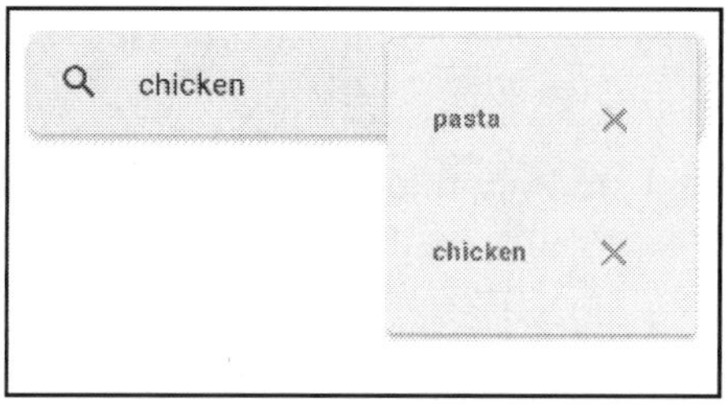

Tapping the **X** will delete the corresponding entry from the list.

Testing the App

It's time to test the app. You'll see something like this:

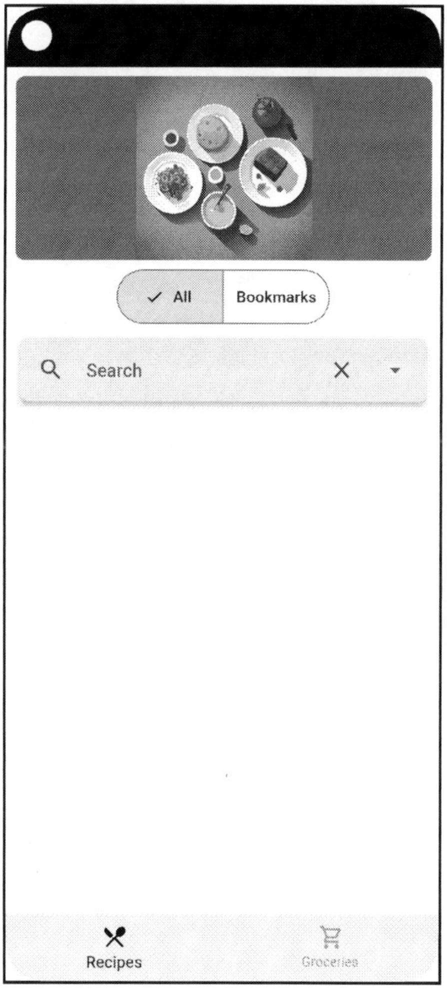

The arrow button displays a menu when tapped and calls the method `onSelected()` when the user selects a menu item.

Enter a food item like **pasta** and you hit the search button. Then make sure that the app adds your search entry to the drop-down list.

Don't worry about errors — that happens when no data exists. Your app should look like this when you tap the drop-down arrow:

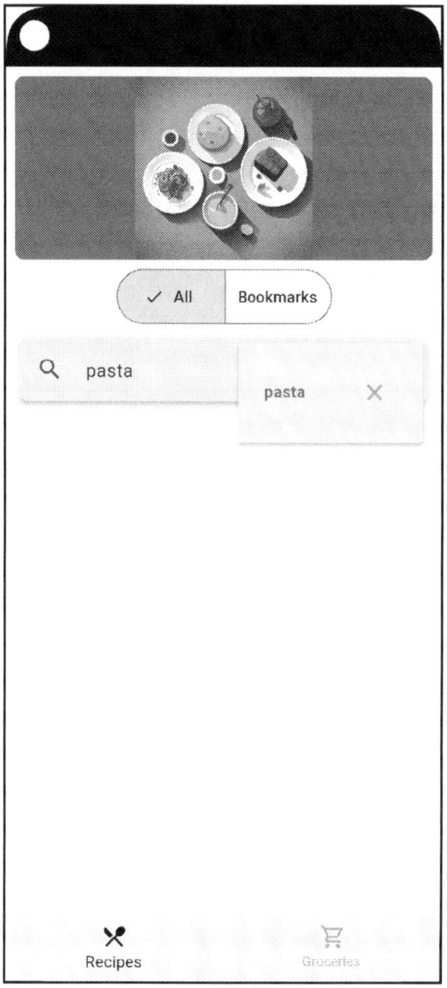

Now, stop the app by clicking the red stop button.

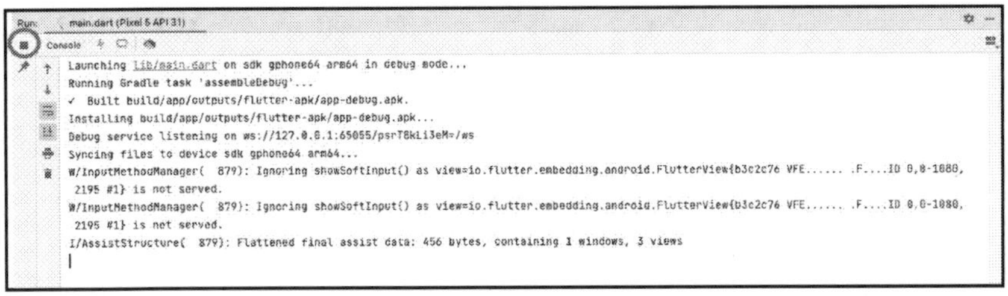

Run the app again and tap the drop-down button. The pasta entry is there. It's time to celebrate. :]

The next step is to use the same approach to save the selected tab.

> **Note**: If you're testing this on the web, you may notice that the drop-down menus are empty. This is because Android Studio will use random port numbers for the web, and this will cause different values to be shown. To fix this, you need to start the web with the same port number each time. You can do that by adding the `--web-port` launch parameter.

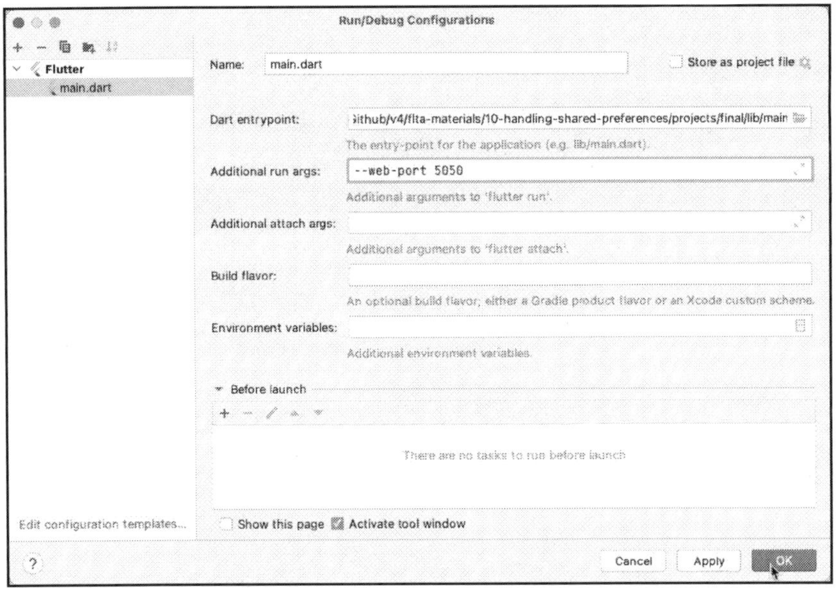

> This will ensure you'll see the same list each time.

Saving the Selected Tab

In this section, you'll use shared_preferences to save the current UI tab that the user has navigated to.

Open **lib/ui/main_screen.dart** and add the following import:

```
import '../providers.dart';
```

Next, replace `// TODO Add Index Key` with:

```
static const String prefSelectedIndexKey = 'selectedIndex';
```

You'll use this constant for the selected index **preference key**.

Next, add this in the `saveCurrentIndex()` method by replacing `// TODO Save Current Index` with this:

```
final prefs = ref.read(sharedPrefProvider);
prefs.setInt(prefSelectedIndexKey, _selectedIndex);
```

Here, you:

1. **ref.read** extracts the shared preferences as usual.
2. Save the **selected index** as an integer.

Now, find and replace `// TODO Get Current Index` with this:

```
  // 1
final prefs = ref.read(sharedPrefProvider);
  // 2
if (prefs.containsKey(prefSelectedIndexKey)) {
    // 3
  setState(() {
    final index = prefs.getInt(prefSelectedIndexKey);
    if (index != null) {
      _selectedIndex = index;
    }
  });
}
```

With this code, you:

1. Get the shared preferences reference.
2. Check if a **preference** for your current index already exists.

3. Get the **current index** and update the state accordingly.

Now, *hot reload* the app and select either the **first** or the **second** tab.

Go to the **Groceries** tab and quit the app. Run it again to make sure the app uses the **saved index** to go to the Groceries tab when it starts.

At this point, your app should show a list of **previously searched** items and also take you to the last selected tab when you start the app again. Here's what it will look like:

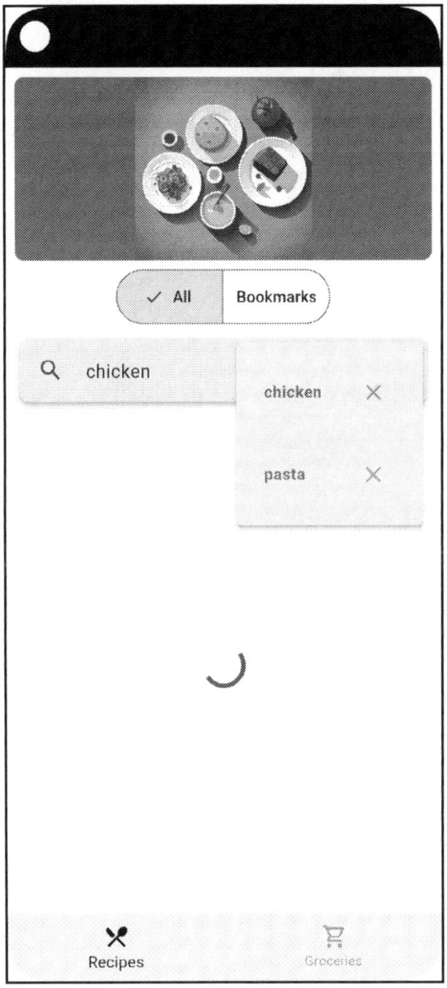

Congratulations! You've saved the state for both the **current tab** and any **previous searches** the user made.

Key Points

- There are multiple ways to save data in an app: to **files**, in **shared preferences** and to a **SQLite** database.
- Shared preferences are best used to store simple, **key-value pairs** of primitive types like `strings`, `numbers` and `Booleans`.
- An example of when to use **shared preferences** is to save the tab a user is viewing, so the next time the user starts the app, they're brought to the same tab.
- The `async`/`await` keyword pair lets you run **asynchronous** code off the main UI thread and then wait for the response. An example is getting an instance of `SharedPreferences`.
- The shared_preferences plugin shouldn't be used to hold sensitive data. Instead, consider using the **flutter_secure_storage** plugin.

Where to Go From Here?

In this chapter, you learned how to persist simple data types in your app using the shared_preferences plugin.

If you want to learn more about Android **SharedPreferences**, go to https://developer.android.com/reference/kotlin/android/content/SharedPreferences?hl=en.

For iOS, check **UserDefaults** https://developer.apple.com/documentation/foundation/userdefaults.

In the next chapter, you'll continue building the same app and learn how to serialize JSON in preparation for getting data from the internet. See you there!

Chapter 11: Serialization With JSON

By Kevin David Moore

In this chapter, you'll learn how to **serialize** JSON data into model classes. A **model class** represents **data structure** and defines **attributes** and **operations** for a particular object. An example is a recipe model class, which usually has a title, an ingredient list and steps to cook it.

You'll continue with the previous project, which is the starter project for this chapter. You'll add a class that models a recipe, and its properties. Then, you'll integrate that class into the existing project.

By the end of this chapter, you'll know:

- How to **serialize JSON** into model classes.
- How to use Dart tools to automate the generation of model classes from JSON.

What is JSON?

JSON, which stands for **JavaScript Object Notation**, is an **open-standard** format used on the web and in mobile clients. It's the most widely used format for **Representational State Transfer** (REST)-based APIs that servers provide (https://en.wikipedia.org/wiki/Representational_state_transfer). If you talk to a server that has a **REST API**, it will most likely return data in a **JSON format**. An example of a JSON response looks something like this:

```
{
  "results": [
    {
      "id": 296687,
      "title": "Chicken",
      "image": "https://spoonacular.com/recipeImages/
296687-312x231.jpeg",
      "imageType": "jpeg"
    },
    ...
    ]
  }
```

That's an example recipe response containing a list of results with four fields inside an object.

While it's possible to treat the JSON as just a long string and try to **parse** out the data, it's much easier to use a package that already knows how to do that. Flutter has a built-in package for **decoding** JSON, but in this chapter, you'll use the **json_serializable** and **json_annotation** packages to help make the process easier.

> **Note**: **JSON parsing** is the process of converting a JSON object in **String format** to a **Dart object** that can be used inside a program.

Flutter's built-in **dart:convert** package contains methods like `json.decode()` and `json.encode()`, which converts a JSON string to a `Map<String, dynamic>` and back. While this is a step ahead of manually parsing JSON, you'd still have to write extra code that takes that map and puts the values into a new class.

The **json_serializable** package is useful because it can generate model classes for you according to the annotations you provide via **json_annotation**. Before taking a look at **automated serialization**, you need to see how to manually serialize JSON.

Writing the Code Yourself

So, how do you go about writing code to serialize JSON yourself? Typical model classes have `toJson()` and `fromJson()` methods. The `toJson()` method helps to convert objects into JSON strings, and the `fromJson()` method helps to parse a JSON string into an object so you can use it inside the program.

In the next section, you learn how to use **automated serialization**. For now, you don't need to type this into your project, but you need to understand the methods to convert the JSON above to a model class.

First, you'd create a `Recipe` model class:

```
class Recipe {
  final String uri;
  final String label;

  Recipe({this.uri, this.label});
}
```

Then you'd add a `toJson()` factory method and a `fromJson()` method:

```
factory Recipe.fromJson(Map<String, dynamic> json) {
  return Recipe(json['uri'] as String, json['label'] as String);
}

Map<String, dynamic> toJson() {
  return <String, dynamic>{ 'uri': uri, 'label': label}
}
```

In `fromJson()`, you grab data from the JSON map variable named `json` and convert it to arguments you pass to the `Recipe` constructor. In `toJson()`, you construct a map using the JSON field names.

While it doesn't take much effort to do that by hand for two fields, what if you had multiple model classes, each with, say, five fields, or more? What if you renamed one of the fields? Would you remember to rename all of the occurrences of that field?

The more model classes you have, the more complicated it becomes to maintain the code behind them. Fear not, that's where automated code generation comes to the rescue.

Automating JSON Serialization

In this chapter, you'll use two packages: **json_annotation** and **json_serializable** from Google.

You use the first to add annotations to model classes so that **json_serializable** can generate **helper classes** to convert a JSON `string` to a model and back.

To do that, you mark a class with the `@JsonSerializable()` annotation so the **builder package** can generate code for you. Each field in the class should either have the same name as the field in the JSON string, or use the `@JsonKey()` annotation to give it a different name.

Most builder packages work by generating a **.part** file. That will be a file that's automatically created for you. All you need to do is add a few factory methods, which will call the generated code.

> **Note**: The **freezed** package is also used in the project and uses the **json_serializable** package to generate serialization code. You could just use the freezed package by itself if you wanted to, as it has additional functionality.

Adding Dependencies for JSON Serialization and Deserialization

Continue with your current project, or open the **starter** project in the **projects** folder. Add the following package to **pubspec.yaml** in the Flutter `dependencies` section underneath and make sure it's aligned with `flutter_riverpod`:

```
json_annotation: ^4.8.1
```

In the `dev_dependencies` section replace `# TODO: Add new dev_dependencies` with the following:

```
json_serializable: ^6.7.1
```

Make sure these are all indented correctly. `build_runner`, which is already included, is the package that helps generate the code.

Finally, click the **Pub get** button you should see at the top of the file, or run `flutter pub get` in the terminal. You're now ready to generate **model classes**.

Generating Model Classes From JSON

The JSON that you're trying to serialize looks something like this:

```
{
  "results": [
    {
      "id": 296687,
      "title": "Chicken",
      "image": "https://spoonacular.com/recipeImages/
296687-312x231.jpeg",
      "imageType": "jpeg"
    },
    {
      "id": 379523,
      "title": "Chicken",
      "image": "https://spoonacular.com/recipeImages/
379523-312x231.jpeg",
      "imageType": "jpeg"
    },
    ...
  ],
  "offset": 0,
  "number": 10,
  "totalResults": 51412
}
```

- The `results` list is a list of recipe objects.
- Each recipe has an `id`, `title`, `image` and `imageType`.
- `offset` is the **starting position** for the search. 0 means start at the beginning, while a value of 10 would start at the 10th element. This is useful for paging long lists.
- `number` is the total number of results returned in this list.
- `totalResults` is the total results available for this search query.

Your next step is to generate the **classes** that model that data.

Creating Model Classes

Start by opening **lib/network/spoonacular_model.dart** and add the following import at the top:

```
import 'package:json_annotation/json_annotation.dart';
```

```
import '../data/models/models.dart';

part 'spoonacular_model.g.dart';
```

The `json_annotation` library lets you mark a class as **serializable**. The file **spoonacular_model.g.dart** doesn't exist yet, you'll generate it in a later step.

Next, replace `// TODO: Add SpoonacularResults class` with a class named `SpoonacularResults` with a `@JsonSerializable()` annotation:

```
@JsonSerializable()
class SpoonacularResults {
  // TODO: Add Fields
  // TODO: Add Constructor
  // TODO: Add fromJson
  // TODO: Add toJson
}

// TODO: Add SpoonacularResult
```

That marks the `SpoonacularResults` class as serializable so the **json_serializable** package can generate the corresponding **.g.dart** file.

Command-Click on `JsonSerializable`, scroll down, and you'll see its definition:

```
...

/// Creates a new [JsonSerializable] instance.
const JsonSerializable({
  @Deprecated('Has no effect') bool? nullable,
  this.anyMap,
  this.checked,
  this.constructor,
  this.createFieldMap,
  this.createFactory,
  this.createToJson,
  this.disallowUnrecognizedKeys,
  this.explicitToJson,
  this.fieldRename,
  this.ignoreUnannotated,
  this.includeIfNull,
  this.converters,
  this.genericArgumentFactories,
  this.createPerFieldToJson,
});

...
```

For example, you can make the class `nullable` and add extra checks for **validating** JSON properly. Close the **json_serialization.dart** source file after reviewing it.

Converting to and From JSON

Now, you need to add JSON conversion methods within the `SpoonacularResults` class. Return to **spoonacular_model.dart** and replace `// TODO: Add Fields` with:

```
List<SpoonacularResult> results;
int offset;
int number;
int totalResults;
```

This is the list of results, offset, number and total results. The `SpoonacularResult` class doesn't exist yet. Next, replace `// TODO: Add Constructor` with:

```
SpoonacularResults({
  required this.results,
  required this.offset,
  required this.number,
  required this.totalResults,
});
```

The `required` annotation says that these fields are mandatory when creating a new instance.

Next, replace `// TODO: Add fromJson` with:

```
factory SpoonacularResults.fromJson(Map<String, dynamic> json)
=>
    _$SpoonacularResultsFromJson(json);
```

The above method converts the JSON string to a `SpoonacularResults` object.

Note that the method to the right of the arrow operator doesn't exist yet and will be present in `spoonacular_model.g.dart` after generating the code, so ignore any red squiggles. They'll be created later by running the **build_runner** command.

Also note that this is a `factory` method. That's because you need a class-level method when creating the instance.

> **Note**: To know more about factory methods check Chapter 9 in the Dart Apprentice: Fundamentals Book (https://www.kodeco.com/books/dart-apprentice-fundamentals/v1.0/chapters/9-constructors#b8d9168fc0febd62f39468aa2163ed3dc1155760373beaad55df1175605bda58).

Now, replace `// TODO: Add toJson` with the following:

```
Map<String, dynamic> toJson() =>
_$SpoonacularResultsToJson(this);
```

The above method connects `SpoonacularResultsToJson` to the `toJson()` method.The `_$SpoonacularResultsToJson` method will be created for you. This method will return a map and is useful for saving its data.

Then, find `// TODO: Add SpoonacularResult`, and replace it with the following new class, continuing to ignore the red squiggles:

```
// 1
@JsonSerializable()
class SpoonacularResult {
  // 2
  int id;
  String title;
  String image;
  String imageType;

  // 3
  SpoonacularResult({
    required this.id,
    required this.title,
    required this.image,
    required this.imageType,
  });

  // 4
  factory SpoonacularResult.fromJson(Map<String, dynamic> json)
=>
      _$SpoonacularResultFromJson(json);


  Map<String, dynamic> toJson() =>
_$SpoonacularResultToJson(this);
}
```

Here's what this code does:

1. Marks the class `JsonSerializable`.
2. Defines several fields: `id`, `title`, `image` and `imageType`.
3. Defines a `constructor` that accepts these fields.
4. Adds the methods for JSON serialization.

Now, uncomment the rest of the code in **lib/network/spoonacular_model.dart**. This will add two new classes, `SpoonacularRecipe` and `ExtendedIngredient` plus some conversion methods. This is to save time, as the detailed recipe information from **Spoonacular** is quite extensive.

For your next step, you'll generate the code to automatically parse the recipes' JSON.

Generating the code for JSON Serialization and Deserialization

Open the terminal in Android Studio by clicking the `Terminal` panel in the lower left, or by selecting **View ▸ Tool Windows ▸ Terminal**, and type:

```
dart run build_runner build
```

The expected output will look something like this:

```
[INFO] Generating build script completed, took 155ms
[INFO] Precompiling build script... completed, took 3.3s
[INFO] Building new asset graph completed, took 372ms
[INFO] Checking for unexpected pre-existing outputs. completed,
took 15.0s
[INFO] Generating SDK summary completed, took 2.3s
[INFO] Running build completed, took 11.8s
[INFO] Caching finalized dependency graph completed, took 44ms
[INFO] Succeeded after 11.8s with 11 outputs (82 actions)
→
```

> **Note**: If you have problems running the command, ensure you've installed Flutter on your computer and you have a path set up to point to it. See Flutter installation documentation for more details, https://docs.flutter.dev/get-started/install.

You may encounter a problem that looks like this:

```
[INFO] Found 6 declared outputs which already exist on disk.
This is likely because the`.dart_tool/build` folder was deleted,
or you are submitting generated files to your source repository.
Delete these files?
1 - Delete
2 - Cancel build
3 - List conflicts
1
```

Choose 1 to delete the files.

This command creates the **spoonacular_model.g.dart** file, which has all the generated code in the **network** folder. If you don't see the file, right-click on the network folder and choose **Reload from disk**.

If you still don't see it, restart Android Studio, so it recognizes the presence of the newly generated file when it starts up.

If you want the program to run every time you make a change to your file, you can use the `watch` command like this:

```
dart run build_runner watch
```

The command will continue to run and watch for changes to files. To stop the process, you can press Ctrl-C. Now, open **spoonacular_model.g.dart**. Here's the first generated method:

```
// GENERATED CODE - DO NOT MODIFY BY HAND

part of 'spoonacular_model.dart';
// 1
SpoonacularResults _$SpoonacularResultsFromJson(Map<String,
dynamic> json) =>
    SpoonacularResults(
      // 2
      results: (json['results'] as List<dynamic>)
          .map((e) => SpoonacularResult.fromJson(e as
Map<String, dynamic>))
          .toList(),
      // 3
      offset: json['offset'] as int,
      // 4
      number: json['number'] as int,
      // 5
      totalResults: json['totalResults'] as int,
    );
```

Notice that it takes a map of `<String, dynamic>`, which is typical of JSON data in Flutter. The key is the string, and the value will either be a primitive, a list or another map. The method:

1. Returns a new `SpoonacularResults` class.
2. Maps each element of the `results` list to an instance of `SpoonacularResult`.
3. Maps the `offset` key to a `offset` field.

4. Maps the `number` integer to the `number` field.
5. Maps the `totalResults` integer to the `totalResults` field.

You could've written this code yourself, but it can get a bit tedious and is error-prone. Having a tool generate the code for you saves a lot of time and effort. Look through the rest of the file to see how the generated code converts the JSON data to all the other model classes.

Hot restart the app to make sure it still compiles and works as before. You won't see any changes in the UI, but the code is now set up to parse recipe data.

Testing the Generated JSON Code

Now that you can parse model objects from JSON, you'll read one of the JSON files included in the starter project and show one card to make sure you can use the generated code.

Open **ui/recipes/recipe_list.dart** and add the following imports at the top:

```
import 'dart:convert';
import '../../network/spoonacular_model.dart';
import 'package:flutter/services.dart';
```

In `fetchData()`, replace `// TODO: Load Recipes` with:

```
// 1
final jsonString = await rootBundle.loadString('assets/
recipes1.json');
// 2
final spoonacularResults =
    SpoonacularResults.fromJson(jsonDecode(jsonString));
// 3
final recipes = spoonacularResultsToRecipe(spoonacularResults);
// 4
final apiQueryResults = QueryResult(
    offset: spoonacularResults.offset,
    number: spoonacularResults.number,
    totalResults: spoonacularResults.totalResults,
    recipes: recipes);
// 5
currentResponse = Future.value(Success(apiQueryResults));
```

This is what that code does:

1. `rootBundle` is from the services page and allows you to load data from the **assets** directory.
2. **Decode** the JSON string and convert it to a `SpoonacularResults` class.
3. Convert that result into a list of recipes.
4. Create a new query result that contains the results. This is the class that will be used in Chapter 12, "Networking in Flutter".
5. Return a `Success` response.

Perform a hot reload, run a search and the app will show some chicken recipe cards:

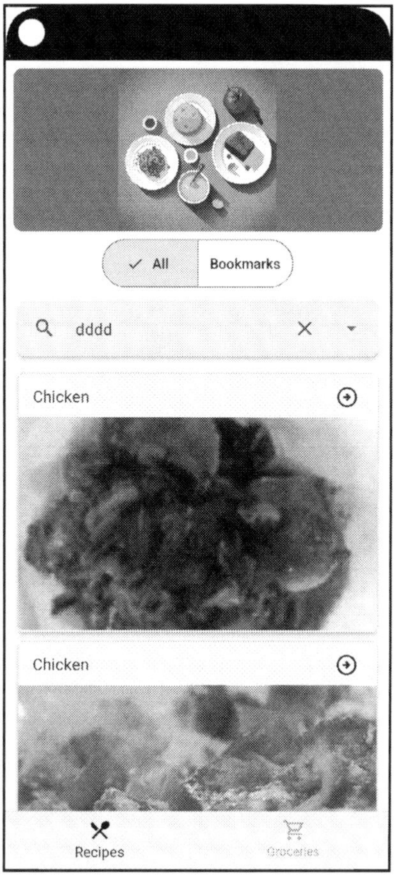

Mock Service

Now that you've manually loaded a sample JSON file, it's time to implement the **Mock Service**. This service class will randomly load one of two recipe files: One for **chicken** and one for **pasta**.

While in **recipe_list.dart**, comment out the code you just entered and uncomment this code:

```
final recipeService = ref.watch(serviceProvider);
currentResponse = recipeService.queryRecipes(
    searchTextController.text.trim(), currentStartPosition,
pageCount);
```

Open **mock_service/mock_service.dart** and add the following imports:

```
import 'dart:convert';
import 'package:flutter/services.dart';
import '../network/spoonacular_model.dart';
```

Uncomment the code in `loadRecipes()` This will randomly load recipes either from **recipes1.json** or **recipes2.json** in the **assets** folder. Next, open **main.dart** and add the following import:

```
import 'mock_service/mock_service.dart';
```

Then replace `// TODO: Create Mock service` with:

```
final service = await MockService.create();
```

Finally replace `// TODO: Inject mock service` with:

```
serviceProvider.overrideWithValue(service),
```

This will inject this service via the **Riverpod** library. You'll read more about that library in Chapter 13, "Managing State". Do a hot restart *not* reload. Type anything in the search field and press enter, or click the search icon. You should see a list of chicken or pasta recipes.

Now that the data model classes work as expected, you're ready to load recipes from the web. Fasten your seat belt. :]

Key Points

- JSON is an open-standard format used on the web and in mobile clients, especially with REST APIs.
- In mobile apps, JSON code is usually parsed into the model objects that your app will work with.
- You can write JSON parsing code yourself, but it's usually easier to let a JSON package generate the parsing code for you.
- **json_annotation** and **json_serializable** are packages that will let you generate the parsing code.

Where to Go From Here?

In this chapter, you've learned how to create models that you can parse from JSON and then use when you fetch JSON data from the network. If you want to learn more about json_serializable, go to https://pub.dev/packages/json_serializable.

In the next chapter, you'll build on what you've done so far and learn about loading recipes from the internet.

Chapter 12: Networking in Flutter

By Kevin David Moore

Loading data from the network to show it in a UI is a very common task for apps. In the previous chapter, you learned how to serialize JSON data. Now, you'll continue the project to learn about retrieving JSON data from the network.

> **Note**: You can also start fresh by opening this chapter's **starter** project. If you choose to do this, remember to click the **pub get** button or execute `flutter pub get` from Terminal.

By the end of this chapter, you'll know how to:

- Sign up for a recipe **API service**.
- Trigger a search for **recipes by name**.
- Convert data returned by the API to **model classes**.
- **Display recipes** in the current UI.

Without further ado, it's time to get started!

Signing Up With the Recipe API

For your remote content, you'll use the **Spoonacular Food API**. Open this link in your browser: https://spoonacular.com/food-api.

Click the **Start Now** button in the top right to create an account.

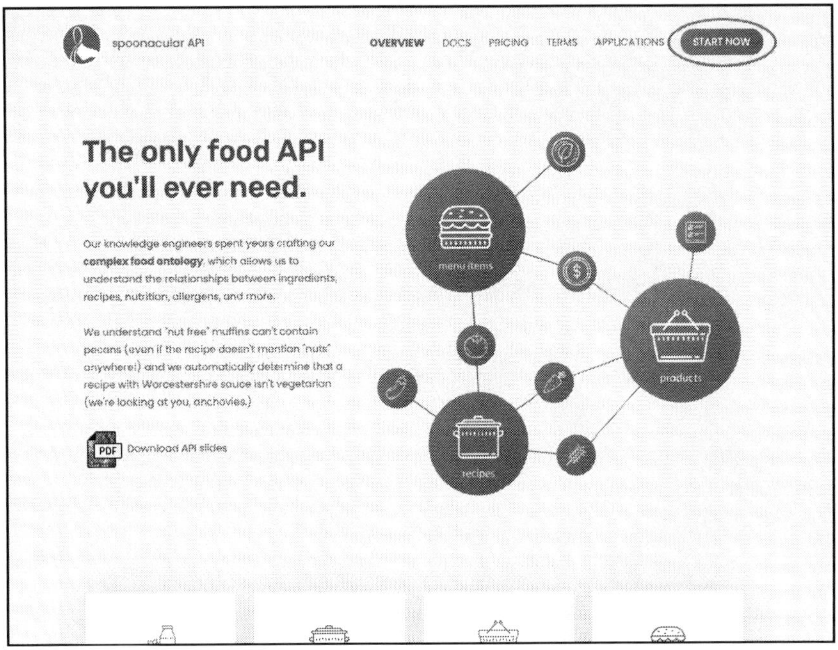

Fill in an email and password, then click the checkbox and sign up. Go through the steps to finish the process. You can choose the free tier.

Click **Sign Up**, and you should see this:

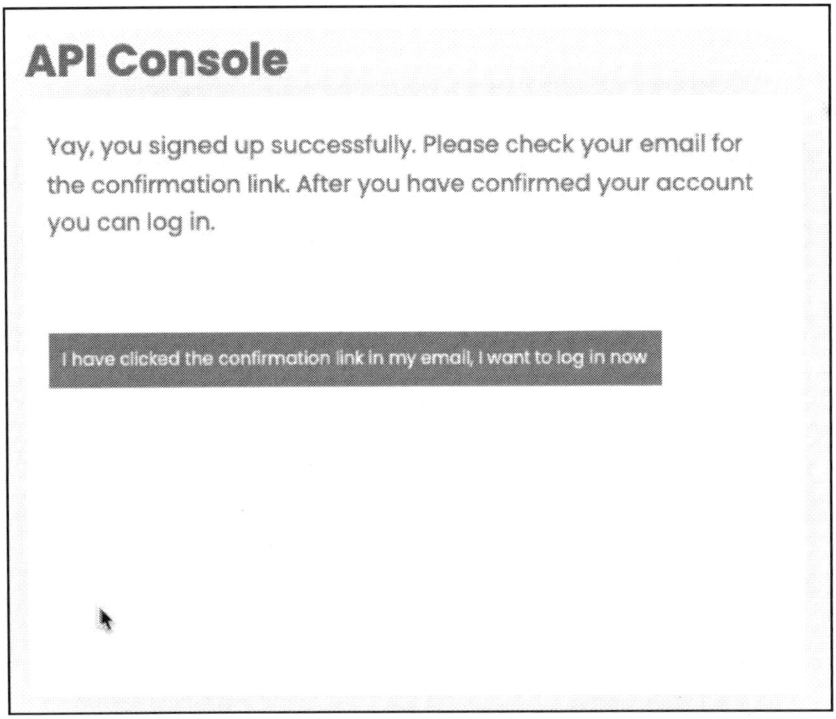

Once you've confirmed your email, visit https://spoonacular.com/food-api/console and log in.

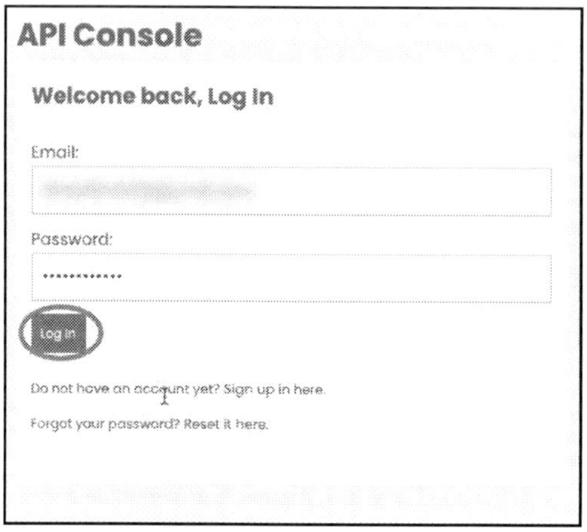

You should see your Console. Once you start making requests, you'll see the graph fill up.

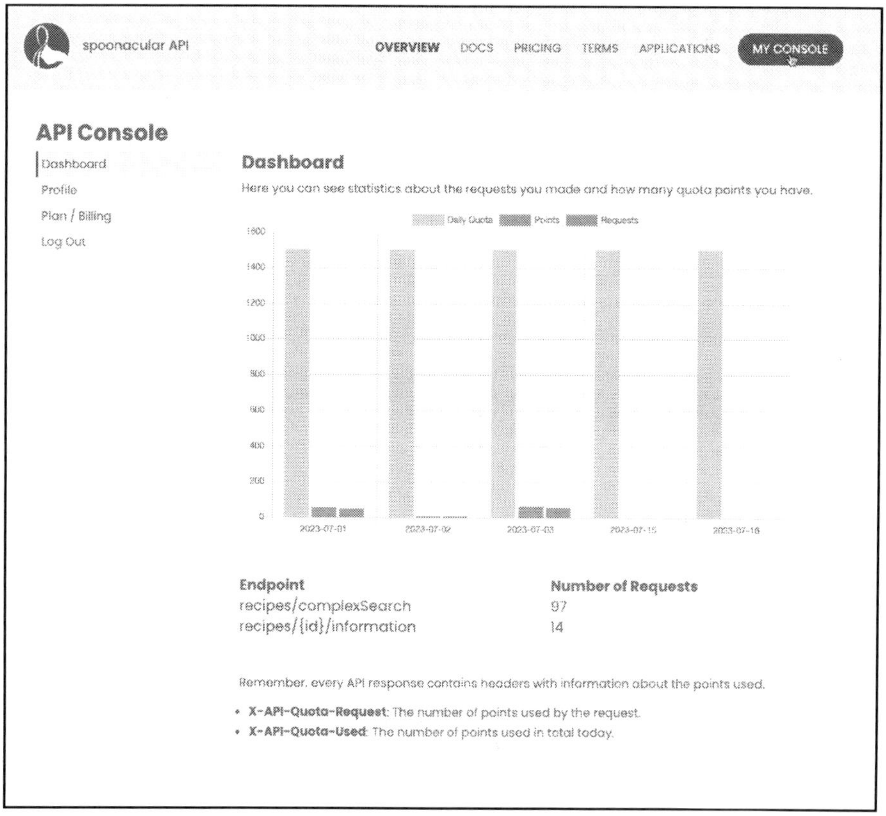

Now go to **docs** and click **Full Documentation**:

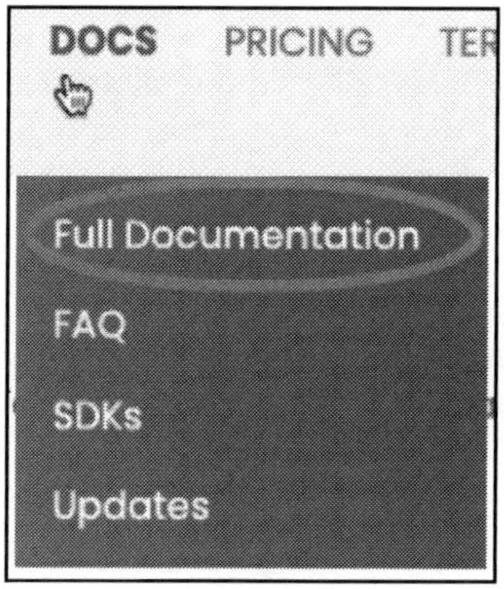

Here, you can see the docs for searching for recipes:

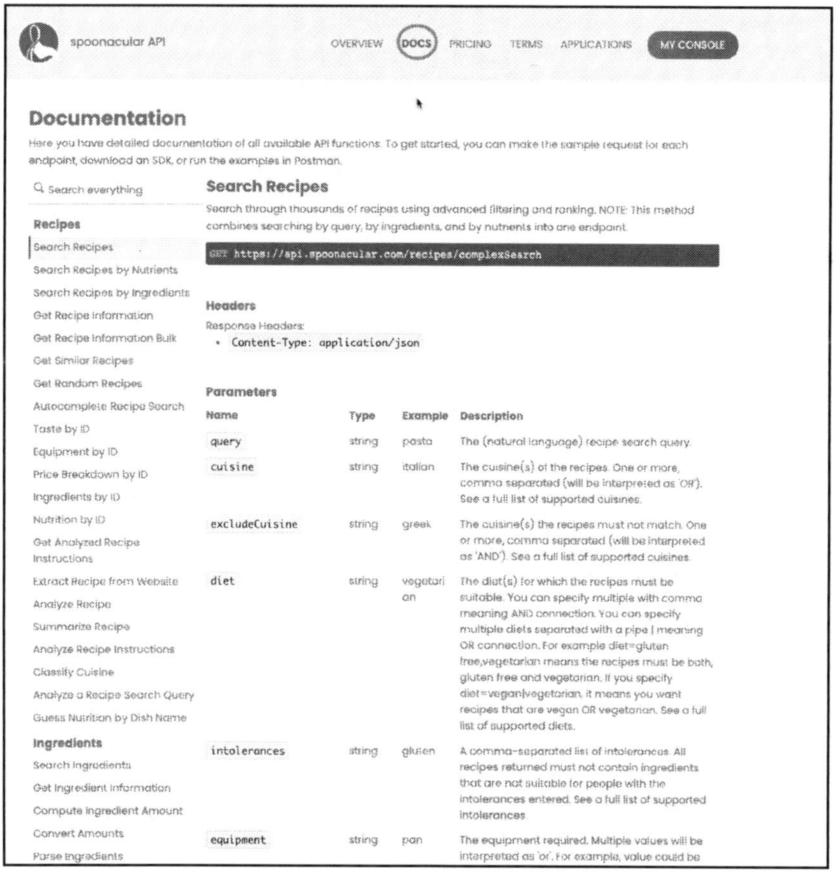

If you scroll down, you can see a lot of fields returned. We're not interested in most of these fields.

You'll see a complete API URL and a list of the parameters available for the `GET` request you'll make.

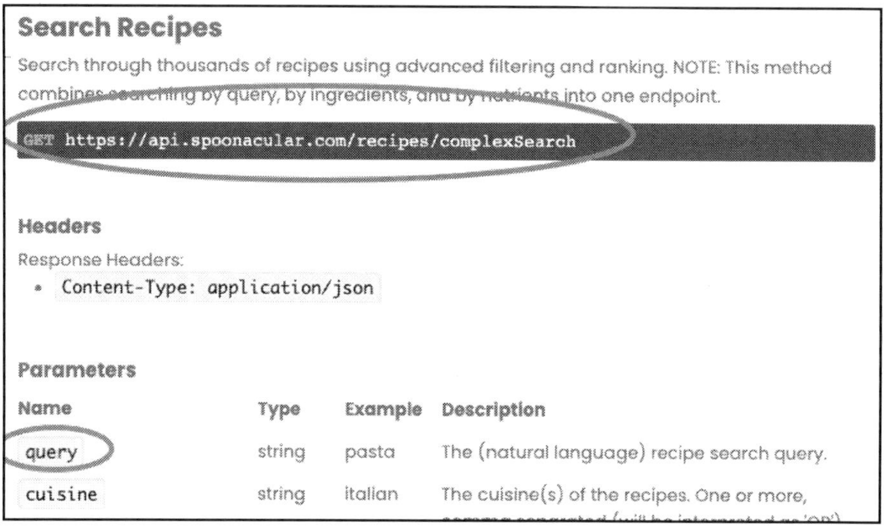

There's much more API information on this page than you'll need for your app, so you might want to bookmark it for the future.

Click **My Console**, then the **Profile** section and you'll end up on this link https://spoonacular.com/food-api/console#Profile:

Click **Show/Hide API key**. Copy the API Key and save it in a secure place.

For your next step, you'll use your newly created API key to fetch recipes via HTTP requests.

> **Note**: The free developer version of the API is rate-limited. If you use the API a lot, you'll probably receive some JSON responses with errors and emails warning you about the limit.

Preparing the Pubspec File

Open either your project or the chapter's **starter** project. To use the **http** package for this app, you need to add it to **pubspec.yaml**, so open that file and add the following after the **json_annotation** package:

```
http: ^1.1.0
```

Click the **Pub get** button to install the package, or run `flutter pub get` from the **Terminal**.

Using the HTTP package

The package contains only a few files and methods that you'll use in this chapter. The REST protocol has methods such as:

- **GET**: Gets the data.
- **POST**: Posts/sends new data.
- **PUT**: Updates data.
- **DELETE**: Deletes data.

You'll use `GET`, specifically the function `get()` in the http package, to retrieve recipe data from the API. This function uses the API's URL and a list of optional headers to retrieve data from the API service. In this case, you'll send all the information via **query parameters**.

Connecting to the Recipe Service

To fetch data from the recipe API, you'll create a **Dart class** to manage the connection. Such a class file will contain your API Key and URL.

In the Project sidebar, right-click **lib/network**, create a new Dart file and name it **spoonacular_service.dart**. After the file opens, import the HTTP package along with the required files:

```
import 'dart:convert';
import 'dart:developer';
import 'package:http/http.dart' as http;

import '../data/models/recipe.dart';
import '../mock_service/mock_service.dart';
import 'model_response.dart';
import 'query_result.dart';
import 'service_interface.dart';
import 'spoonacular_model.dart';
```

> **Note**: Here, we import the http package as `http` so that we can append `http` to the `get()` method and prevent any naming conflicts or confusion.

Now, add the constants that you'll use when calling the APIs:

```
const String apiKey = '<Add Your Key Here>';
const String apiUrl = 'https://api.spoonacular.com/';
```

Copy the **API key** from your Spoonacular account and replace the existing `apiKey` string with your value.

The `apiUrl` constant holds the base URL for the Spoonacular search API from the recipe API documentation. You'll append the path to this URL to get the data you want.

Still in **spoonacular_service.dart**, add the following class and method to get the data from the API:

```
class SpoonacularService implements ServiceInterface {
  // 1
  Future getData(String url) async {
    // 2
    final response = await http.get(Uri.parse(url));
    // 3
```

```
    if (response.statusCode == 200) {
      // 4
      return response.body;
    } else {
      // 5
      log(response.statusCode.toString());
    }
  }
  // TODO: Add getRecipes
}
```

Here's a breakdown of what's going on:

1. `getData()` returns a value in `Future`, with an upper case "F", because it takes some time to get the data from the Server. An API's returned data type is determined in the future, lower case "f". `async` signifies this method performs an asynchronous operation.
2. `response` has to wait until the HTTP gets the data from the server. The `await` keyword tells the function to wait. `Response` and `get()` are from the HTTP package. `get()` fetches data from the provided `url`.
3. A `statusCode` of **200** means the request was successful.
4. You `return` the results embedded in `response.body`.
5. Otherwise, print the `statusCode` to the console if you have an error.

> **Note**: To learn more about `Future` and `async` operations, check out chapters 11 and 12 of **Dart Apprentice: Beyond the Basics** book https://www.kodeco.com/books/dart-apprentice-beyond-the-basics.

Now, replace `// TODO: Add getRecipes` with:

```
// 1
@override
Future<Result<Recipe>> queryRecipe(String recipeId) {
  // TODO: implement queryRecipe
  throw UnimplementedError();
}

// 2
@override
Future<RecipeResponse> queryRecipes(
    String query, int offset, int number) async {
  // 3
```

```
    final recipeData = await getData(
        '${apiUrl}recipes/complexSearch?
apiKey=$apiKey&query=$query&offset=$offset&number=$number');
    // 4
    final spoonacularResults =
        SpoonacularResults.fromJson(jsonDecode(recipeData));
    // 5
    final recipes =
spoonacularResultsToRecipe(spoonacularResults);
    // 6
    final apiQueryResults = QueryResult(
        offset: spoonacularResults.offset,
        number: spoonacularResults.number,
        totalResults: spoonacularResults.totalResults,
        recipes: recipes);
    // 7
    return Success(apiQueryResults);
  }
```

In this code, you:

1. Override an unimplemented method for querying a specific recipe. That will be implemented later.
2. Create a new method, `queryRecipes()`, with the parameters `query`, `offset` and `number`. These help you get specific pages from the complete query. `offset` starts at 0, and `number` is calculated by adding the `offset` index to your page size. You use a return type of `Future<RecipeResponse>` for this method because the response will be a `RecipeResponse` in the future when it finishes. `async` signals that this method runs asynchronously.
3. `final` creates a non-changing variable. You use `await` to tell the app to wait until `getData()` returns its result. Look closely at `getData()` and note that you're creating the API URL with the variables passed in.
4. Convert the **JSON string** to a `SpoonacularResults` class with the help of `fromJson` method.
5. Convert the `SpoonacularResults` class object into a list of recipes.
6. Create a `QueryResult` object with those results.
7. Return a Success with the query results.

> **Note**: This method doesn't handle errors.

Now that you've written the service, it's time to update the UI code to use it.

Updating the User Interface

Open **main.dart** and add the following:

```
import 'network/spoonacular_service.dart';
```

Then, after the `sharedPrefProvider` override, replace:

```
final service = await MockService.create();
```

with:

```
final service = SpoonacularService();
```

This creates a new instance of `SpoonacularService`. This will be the start of using real data taken from the internet instead of mock data.

Now remove the import of `mock_service.dart`, as it's not needed anymore.

Retrieving Recipe Data

Great, it's time to try out the app!

Run the app, type **Chicken** in the text field, and tap the **Search** icon. While the app gets data from the API, you'll see the circular progress bar.

After the app receives the data, you'll see a list of images with different types of chicken recipes.

Well done! You've updated your app to receive real data from the internet. Try different search queries and go and show your friends what you've created. :]

> **Note**: If you make too many queries, you could get an error from the Spoonacular site. That's because the free account limits your number of calls.

The http package is easy to use to handle network calls, but it's also pretty basic. Let's explore Chopper, a library that simplifies the creation of code that manages HTTP calls.

Why Chopper?

Chopper is a library that streamlines the process of writing code that performs HTTP requests. For example:

- It generates code to simplify the development of networking code.
- It allows you to organize that code modularly, making it easier to change.

> **Note**: If you come from the Android side of mobile development, you're probably familiar with the **Retrofit** library, which is similar. If you have an iOS background, **AlamoFire** is a very similar library.

Preparing to use Chopper

To use Chopper, you need to add the package to **pubspec.yaml**. To log network calls, you also need the **logging** package, which is already included in the project.

Open **pubspec.yaml** and add the following after the HTTP package:

```
chopper: ^6.1.4
```

You also need **chopper_generator**, which is a package that generates the boilerplate code for you in the form of a part file. In the **dev_dependencies** section, after **json_serializable**, add the following:

```
chopper_generator: ^6.0.3
```

Next, either click **Pub get** or run `flutter pub get` in Terminal to get the new packages.

Now that the new packages are ready to be used... fasten your seat belt! :]

Handling Recipe Results

In this scenario, creating a generic response class that holds either a successful response or an error is good practice. While these classes aren't required, they make it easier to deal with the responses that the server returns.

Take a look inside the **lib/network** folder and open **model_response.dart**.

```
// 1
sealed class Result<T> {
}

// 2
class Success<T> extends Result<T> {
  final T value;

  Success(this.value);
}

// 3
class Error<T> extends Result<T> {
  final Exception exception;

  Error(this.exception);
}
```

Here's what that does:

1. Defines a `sealed class`. It's a simple blueprint for a result with a generic type `T`.
2. The `Success` class extends `Result` and holds a value when the response is successful. This could hold JSON data or a de-serialized class.
3. The `Error` class extends `Result` and holds an exception. This will model errors that occur during an HTTP call, like using the wrong credentials or trying to fetch data without authorization.

> **Note**: The sealed modifier prevents a class from being extended or implemented outside its own library. Sealed classes are implicitly abstract. To refresh your knowledge of classes in Dart, check out our **Dart Apprentice: Fundamentals** book https://www.kodeco.com/books/dart-apprentice-fundamentals/.

You'll use these classes to model the data fetched via HTTP using Chopper. Now that Chopper has been added, you need to update the definition of the result types defined in **lib/network/service_interface.dart**. In that file, add the Chooper import:

```
import 'package:chopper/chopper.dart';
```

Then replace:

```
typedef RecipeResponse = Result<QueryResult>;
typedef RecipeDetailsResponse = Result<Recipe>;
```

with:

```
typedef RecipeResponse = Response<Result<QueryResult>>;
typedef RecipeDetailsResponse = Response<Result<Recipe>>;
```

Instead of returning a `Result` directly, you'll return a `Response` that contains a `Result`. This is because Chopper will handle the conversion of the response to a `Result` for you.

This will mess up the existing `MockService` class as now you have passed `Response` instead of `QueryResult`. Open up **mock_service.dart** and add the following imports:

```
import 'package:http/http.dart' as http;
import 'package:chopper/chopper.dart';
```

In the `queryRecipes` methods, wrap each `Success` call with a `Response`. Like this:

```
return Future.value(
        Response(
          http.Response(
            'Dummy',
            200,
            request: null,
          ),
          Success<QueryResult>(_currentRecipes1),
        ),
      );
```

Do this three times. Make sure you keep the correct values. Also, modify `queryRecipe()` like this:

```
  return Future.value(
      Response(
        http.Response(
          'Dummy',
          200,
          request: null,
        ),
        Success<Recipe>(recipeDetails),
      ),
    );
```

It's time to integrate the code that Chopper will generate into the existing service.

Preparing the Recipe Service

Open **spoonacular_service.dart**.

Replace the existing imports with the following:

```
import 'package:chopper/chopper.dart';

import 'model_response.dart';
import 'query_result.dart';
import 'service_interface.dart';
import '../data/models/models.dart';

part 'spoonacular_service.chopper.dart';
```

The **.chopper** file doesn't exist yet, but you'll generate it soon. Change the definition of the class to look like this:

```
// 1
@ChopperApi()
// 2
abstract class SpoonacularService extends ChopperService
    implements ServiceInterface {
```

1. `@ChopperApi()` tells the Chopper generator to build a file. This generated file will have the same name as this file but with **.chopper** added to it. In this case, it will be **spoonacular_service.chopper.dart**. Such a file will hold the boilerplate code.

2. Define an abstract class. Chopper will create the real class that extends the `ChopperService` and implements the `ServiceInterface`.

Now remove the `getData()` method. It's now time to set up Chopper!

Setting Up the Chopper Client

Your next step is to update the queries needed to implement the service. Replace the definitions of `queryRecipes()` and `queryRecipe()` with:

```
/// Get the details of a specific recipe
@override
@Get(path: 'recipes/{id}/information?includeNutrition=false')
Future<RecipeDetailsResponse> queryRecipe(
  @Path('id') String id,
);

/// Get a list of recipes that match the query string
```

```
@override
@Get(path: 'recipes/complexSearch')
Future<RecipeResponse> queryRecipes(
  @Query('query') String query,
  @Query('offset') int offset,
  @Query('number') int number,
);

// TODO: Add create Service
```

The first method returns the details of a specific recipe. The second method returns a list of recipes:

- `@Get` is an annotation that tells the generator this is a GET request.
- `path` is the path to the API call. Chopper will append this path to the base URL, which you've defined as the `apiUrl` constant in `SpoonacularService` class.
- In the first method, you're using a path parameter to get the details of the specific recipe by passing a recipe ID as a dynamic parameter. In the second method, you're using a path to get a list of recipes.
- There are other HTTP methods you can use, such as `@Post`, `@Put` and `@Delete`, but you won't use them in this chapter.
- `@Query` is a query parameter used to define the query name in the URL that's created for this API call. In the second method, you're using `@Query` to get the `query`, `offset` and `number` of recipes.
- These methods return a `Future` response.

Note that you have defined a generic interface to make network calls so far. No actual code performs tasks like adding the API key to the `request` or transforming the `response` into data objects. This is a job for converters and interceptors.

Converting Request and Response

To use the returned API data, you need a converter to transform `requests` and `responses`. To attach a converter to a Chopper client, you need an **interceptor**. You can think of an interceptor as a function that runs every time you send a `request` or receive a `response`. It's a sort of hook to which you can attach functionalities, like converting or decorating data, before passing such data along.

Right-click **lib/network**, create a new file named **spoonacular_converter.dart** and add the following imports:

```
import 'dart:convert';
import 'package:chopper/chopper.dart';
import 'model_response.dart';
import 'query_result.dart';
import 'spoonacular_model.dart';
```

This adds the built-in Dart convert package, which transforms data **to** and **from** JSON, plus the Chopper package and your model files.

Next, create `SpoonacularConverter` by adding the following:

```
// 1
class SpoonacularConverter implements Converter {
  // 2
  @override
  Request convertRequest(Request request) {
    // 3
    final req = applyHeader(
      request,
      contentTypeKey,
      jsonHeaders,
      override: false,
    );

    // 4
    return encodeJson(req);
  }

  // TODO encode JSON

  // TODO Decode Json

  // TODO Convert Response to Model
}
```

Here's what you're doing with this code:

1. Create `SpoonacularConverter` class to implement the Chopper `Converter` abstract class.
2. Override `convertRequest()`, which takes in a request and returns a new request.
3. Add a header to the request that says you have a request type of `application/json` using `jsonHeaders`. These constants are part of Chopper.
4. Call `encodeJson()` to convert the request to a JSON-encoded one, as required by the server API.

The remaining code consists of placeholders, which you'll include in the next section.

Encoding and Decoding JSON

To make it easy to expand your app in the future, you'll separate encoding and decoding. This gives you flexibility if you need to use them separately later.

Whenever you make network calls, you want to ensure that you encode the request before you send it and decode the response string into your **model classes**, which you'll use to display data in the UI.

Encoding JSON

To encode the request in JSON format, replace `// TODO encode JSON` with the following:

```
Request encodeJson(Request request) {
  // 1
  final contentType = request.headers[contentTypeKey];
  // 2
  if (contentType != null && contentType.contains(jsonHeaders))
{
    // 3
    return request.copyWith(body: json.encode(request.body));
  }
  return request;
}
```

In this code, you:

1. Get the content type from the request headers.
2. Check if `contentType` is not `null` and `contentType` is of type `application/json`.
3. Return a copy of the `request` with a JSON-encoded body.

Essentially, this method takes a `Request` instance and returns an encoded copy ready to be sent to the server. What about decoding? Well, I'm glad you asked. :]

Decoding JSON

Now, it's time to add the functionality to decode JSON. A server response is usually a `String`, so you'll have to parse the JSON string and transform it into the corresponding model class.

Replace `// TODO Decode Json` with:

```
Response<BodyType> decodeJson<BodyType, InnerType>(Response
response) {
    final contentType = response.headers[contentTypeKey];
    var body = response.body;
    // 1
    if (contentType != null &&
contentType.contains(jsonHeaders)) {
      body = utf8.decode(response.bodyBytes);
    }
    try {
      // 2
      final mapData = json.decode(body) as Map<String, dynamic>;

      // 3
      // This is the list of recipes
      if (mapData.keys.contains('totalResults')) {
        // 4
        final spoonacularResults =
SpoonacularResults.fromJson(mapData);
        // 5
        final recipes =
spoonacularResultsToRecipe(spoonacularResults);
        // 6
        final apiQueryResults = QueryResult(
            offset: spoonacularResults.offset,
            number: spoonacularResults.number,
            totalResults: spoonacularResults.totalResults,
            recipes: recipes);
        // 7
        return response.copyWith<BodyType>(
          body: Success(apiQueryResults) as BodyType,
        );
      } else {
        // This is the recipe details
        // 8
        final spoonacularRecipe =
SpoonacularRecipe.fromJson(mapData);
        // 9
        final recipe =
spoonacularRecipeToRecipe(spoonacularRecipe);
        // 10
        return response.copyWith<BodyType>(
          body: Success(recipe) as BodyType,
```

```
        );
      }
    } catch (e) {
      // 11
      chopperLogger.warning(e);
      final error = Error<InnerType>(Exception(e.toString()));
      return Response(response.base, null,
          error: error);
    }
}
```

There's a lot to think about here. To break it down, you:

1. Check if the `contentType` is not null and check if `contentType` contains the `jsonHeaders`. Later you decode the `response` and save to body.
2. Use JSON decoding to convert that string into a map representation.
3. Check if the call has the "totalResults" text. This means it's from the `queryRecipes` call.
4. Convert the JSON to a `SpoonacularResults` instance using `fromJson()`.
5. Convert `SpoonacularResults` to a list of recipes.
6. Create a `QueryResult` with the recipes.
7. Return a copy of `Response` with `Success` result.
8. Convert the map to a detailed `SpoonacularRecipe`.
9. Convert the `spoonacularRecipe` to the recipe.
10. Return a copy of `Response` with `Success` that wraps the result.
11. If you get any kind of error, wrap the `response` with a generic instance of `Error`.

You still have to override one more method: `convertResponse()`. This method changes the given response to the one you want.

Replace the existing `// TODO Convert Response to Model` with the following:

```
@override
Response<BodyType> convertResponse<BodyType, InnerType>(Response
response) {
  // 1
  return decodeJson<BodyType, InnerType>(response);
}
```

1. This returns the decoded JSON response by calling `decodeJson()`, which you defined earlier.

Now, it's time to use the converter in the appropriate spots and to add some interceptors.

Using Interceptors

As mentioned earlier, interceptors can intercept either the request, the response or both. In a request interceptor, you can add headers or handle authentication. In a response interceptor, you can manipulate a response and transform it into another type, as you'll see shortly. You'll start with decorating the request.

Automatically Including Your API Key

To request any recipes, the API needs your `api_key`. Instead of adding this field manually to each query, you can use an interceptor to add this to each call.

Open **spoonacular_service.dart** and add the following method *outside* of the `SpoonacularService` class definition:

```
Request _addQuery(Request req) {
  // 1
  final params = Map<String, dynamic>.from(req.parameters);
  // 2
  params['apiKey'] = apiKey;
  // 3
  return req.copyWith(parameters: params);
}
```

This is a request interceptor that adds the API key to the query parameters. Here's what the code does:

1. Creates a `Map`, which contains key-value pairs from the existing `Request` parameters.
2. Adds the `apiKey` parameter to the map.
3. Returns a new copy of the `Request` with the parameters contained in the map.

The benefit of this method is that once you hook it up, all your calls will use it. While you only have one call for now, if you add more, they'll include those parameters automatically. Also, if you want to add a new parameter to every call, you'll change only this method.

I hope you're starting to see the advantages of Chopper. :]

You have interceptors to decorate `requests`, and you have a converter to transform `responses` into model classes. Next, you'll put them to use!

Wiring Up Interceptors and Converters

It's time to create an instance of the service that will fetch recipes.

Still in **spoonacular_service.dart**, add the following import, and make sure it's placed *before* the `part` statement:

```
import 'spoonacular_converter.dart';
```

Then locate `// TODO: Add create Service` and replace it with the following code. Don't worry about the red squiggles; they're warning you that the boilerplate code is missing because you haven't generated it yet.

```
static SpoonacularService create() {
  // 1
  final client = ChopperClient(
    // 2
    baseUrl: Uri.parse(apiUrl),
    // 3
    interceptors: [_addQuery, HttpLoggingInterceptor()],
    // 4
    converter: SpoonacularConverter(),
    // 5
    errorConverter: const JsonConverter(),
    // 6
    services: [
      _$SpoonacularService(),
    ],
  );
  // 7
  return _$SpoonacularService(client);
}
```

In this code, you:

1. Create a `ChopperClient` instance.
2. Pass in a base URL using the `apiUrl` constant.
3. Pass in two interceptors. `_addQuery()` adds your API key to the query. `HttpLoggingInterceptor` is part of Chopper and logs all calls. While you're developing, it's handy to see traffic between the app and the server.

4. Set the `converter` as an instance of `SpoonacularConverter`.
5. Use the built-in `JsonConverter` to decode any errors.
6. Define the services created when you run the generator script.
7. Return an instance of the generated service.

It's all set, you're ready to generate the boilerplate code!

Generating the Chopper File

Your next step is to generate **spoonacular_service.chopper.dart**, which works with the `part` keyword. Remember from Chapter 11, "Serialization With JSON", `part` will include the specified file and make it part of one big file.

> **Note**: It might seem weird to import a file before it's been created, but the generator script will fail if it doesn't know what file to create.

Now, open **Terminal** in Android Studio. By default, it'll be in your project folder.

Execute the following:

```
dart run build_runner build --delete-conflicting-outputs
```

> **Note**: Using `--delete-conflicting-outputs` will delete all generated files before generating new ones.

While it's executing, you'll see something like this:

```
Terminal:  Local  +
→ starter git:(master) ✗ flutter pub run build_runner build --delete-conflicting-outputs
[INFO] Generating build script...
[INFO] Generating build script completed, took 354ms

[WARNING] Deleted previous snapshot due to missing asset graph.
[INFO] Creating build script snapshot......
[INFO] Creating build script snapshot... completed, took 11.8s

[INFO] Initializing inputs
[INFO] Building new asset graph...
[INFO] Building new asset graph completed, took 622ms

[INFO] Checking for unexpected pre-existing outputs....
[INFO] Deleting 1 declared outputs which already existed on disk.
[INFO] Checking for unexpected pre-existing outputs. completed, took 3ms

[INFO] Running build...
[INFO] Generating SDK summary...
[INFO] 3.8s elapsed, 0/12 actions completed.
[INFO] Generating SDK summary completed, took 3.8s

[INFO] 5.0s elapsed, 0/12 actions completed.
[INFO] 6.0s elapsed, 2/12 actions completed.
[INFO] 7.1s elapsed, 2/12 actions completed.
[INFO] 8.1s elapsed, 2/12 actions completed.
[INFO] 10.5s elapsed, 2/12 actions completed.
[INFO] 11.5s elapsed, 2/12 actions completed.
[INFO] 16.3s elapsed, 4/12 actions completed.
[INFO] 17.3s elapsed, 7/12 actions completed.
[INFO] Running build completed, took 17.8s

[INFO] Caching finalized dependency graph...
[INFO] Caching finalized dependency graph completed, took 41ms

[INFO] Succeeded after 17.9s with 3 outputs (39 actions)

→ starter git:(master) ✗
```

Once it finishes, you'll see the new **spoonacular_service.chopper.dart** in **lib/network**. You may need to refresh the **network** folder before it appears.

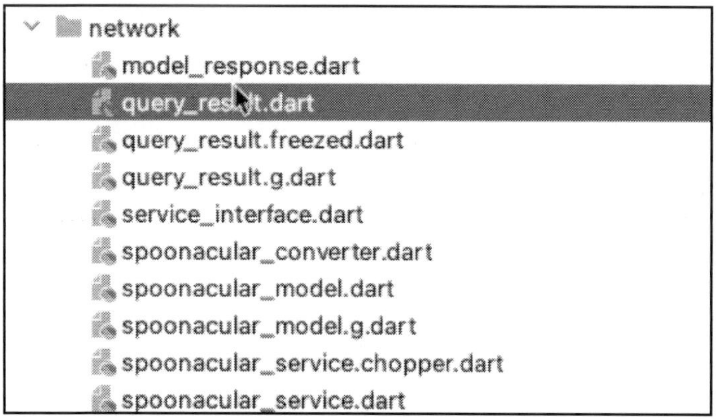

> **Note**: In case you don't see the file or Android Studio doesn't detect its presence, right-click on the network folder and select "Reload from disk".

Open it and check it out. The first thing you'll see is a comment stating not to modify the file by hand. Looking farther down, you'll see a class called `_$SpoonacularService`. Below that, you'll notice that `queryRecipes()` has been overridden to build the parameters and the request. It uses the client to send the request.

It may not seem like much, but as you add different calls with different paths and parameters, you'll start to appreciate the help of a code generator like the one included in Chopper.

Now that you've changed `SpoonacularService` to use Chopper, it's time to put on the finishing touches.

Using the Chopper Client

Open **main.dart** and after `sharedPrefs`, replace:

```
final service = SpoonacularService();
```

with:

```
final service = SpoonacularService.create();
```

This method will create a new instance of the service with the Chopper client.

Updating the UI

Now open **lib/ui/recipe_details.dart**. In `loadRecipe()`, replace:

```
final result = response;
if (result is Success<Recipe>) {
  final body = result.value;
  recipeDetail = body;
  if (mounted) {
    setState(() {});
  }
} else {
  logMessage('Problems getting Recipe $result');
}
```

with:

```
final result = response.body;
if (result is Success<Recipe>) {
```

```
    final body = result.value;
    recipeDetail = body;
    if (mounted) {
      setState(() {});
    }
  } else  {
    logMessage('Problems getting Recipe $result');
  }
```

This will retrieve the recipe detail.

In `readRecipe()`, replace:

```
  final result = snapshot.data;
  if (result is Success<Recipe>) {
    final body = result.value;
    recipeDetail = body;
  }
```

with:

```
  final result = snapshot.data?.body;
  if (result is Success<Recipe>) {
    final body = result.value;
    recipeDetail = body;
  }
```

Open **recipe_list.dart** and add:

```
  import 'dart:collection';
```

In `_buildRecipeLoader()`, replace:

```
  final result = snapshot.data;
  // Hit an error
  if (result is Error) {
    const errorMessage = 'Problems getting data';
    return const SliverFillRemaining(
      child: Center(
        child: Text(
          errorMessage,
          textAlign: TextAlign.center,
          style: TextStyle(fontSize: 18.0),
        ),
      ),
    );
  }
```

with:

```
if (false == snapshot.data?.isSuccessful) {
  var errorMessage = 'Problems getting data';
  if (snapshot.data?.error != null &&
      snapshot.data?.error is LinkedHashMap) {
    final map = snapshot.data?.error as LinkedHashMap;
    errorMessage = map['message'];
  }
  return SliverFillRemaining(
    child: Center(
      child: Text(
        errorMessage,
        textAlign: TextAlign.center,
        style: const TextStyle(fontSize: 18.0),
      ),
    ),
  );
}
final result = snapshot.data?.body;
if (result == null || result is Error) {
  inErrorState = true;
  return _buildRecipeList(context, currentSearchList);
}
```

This uses the new response type that wraps the result of an API call.

Now, replace the existing `fetchData()` with:

```
Future<RecipeResponse> fetchData() async {
  if (!newDataRequired && currentResponse != null) {
    return currentResponse!;
  }
  newDataRequired = false;
  final recipeService = ref.watch(serviceProvider);
  currentResponse = recipeService.queryRecipes(
      searchTextController.text.trim(), currentStartPosition,
pageCount);
  return currentResponse!;
}
```

This will use the services `queryRecipes()` instead of the older HTTP call.

Stop the app, run it again and choose the search value **chicken** from the drop-down button. Verify that you see the recipes displayed in the UI.

Now, look in the **Run** window of **Android Studio**, where you'll see lots of `[log] INFO` messages related to your network calls. This is a great way to see how your requests and responses look and figure out what's causing problems.

You made it! You can now use Chopper to make calls to the server API and retrieve recipes.

Key Points

- The **http** package is a simple-to-use set of methods for retrieving data from the internet.
- The built-in `json.decode()` transforms JSON strings into a map of objects that you can use in your code.
- The Chopper package provides easy ways to retrieve data from the internet.
- You can add headers to each network request.
- Interceptors can intercept both requests and responses and change those values.
- Converters can modify requests and responses.

Where to Go From Here?

You've learned how to retrieve data from the internet and parse it into data models. If you want to learn more about the HTTP package and get the latest version, go to https://pub.dev/packages/http.

If you want to learn more about the Chopper package, go to https://pub.dev/packages/chopper. For more info on the Logging library, visit https://pub.dev/packages/logging.

In the next chapter, you'll learn about the important topic of state management.

Chapter 13: Managing State

By Kevin David Moore

The main job of a UI is to represent **state**. Imagine, for example, you're loading a list of recipes from the network. While the recipes are loading, you show a spinning widget. When the data loads, you swap the spinner with the list of loaded recipes. In this case, you move from a **loading** to a **loaded** state. Handling such state changes manually, without following a specific pattern, quickly leads to code that's difficult to understand, update and maintain. One solution is to adopt a pattern that programmatically establishes how to track changes and broadcast details about states to the rest of your app. This is called **state management**.

To learn about state management and see how it works for yourself, you'll continue working with the previous project.

> **Note**: You can also start fresh by opening this chapter's **starter** project. If you choose to do this, remember to click the **Get dependencies** button or execute `flutter pub get` from Terminal. You'll also need to add your API Key to **lib/network/spoonacular_service.dart**.

By the end of the chapter, you'll know:

- Why you need state management.
- How to implement state management using **Riverpod**.

- How to save the current list of bookmarks and ingredients.
- What a repository is.
- Different ways to manage state.

Architecture

When you write apps and the amount of code gets larger and larger over time, you learn to appreciate the importance of separating code into manageable pieces. When files contain more than one **class** or when **classes** combine multiple functionalities, it's harder to fix bugs and add new features.

One way to handle this is to follow **Clean Architecture** principles by organizing your project so it's easy to change and understand. You do this by separating your code into directories and classes, each handling just *one* task. You also use interfaces to define contracts that different classes can implement, allowing you to easily swap in different classes or reuse classes in other apps.

You should design your app with some or all of the components below:

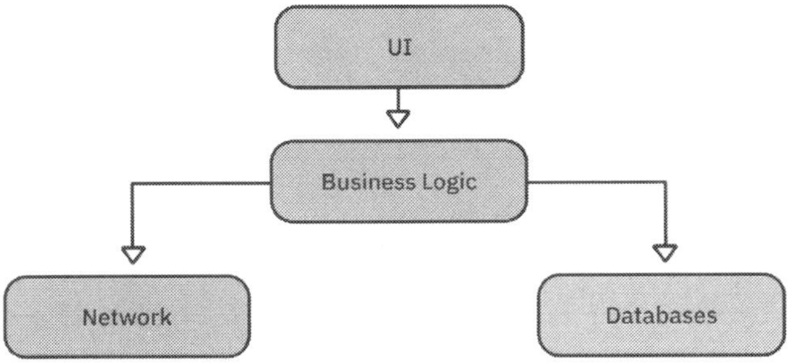

Notice that the **UI** is separate from the **business logic**. It's easy to start an app and put your database and business logic into your UI code — but what happens when you need to change your app's behavior and that behavior is spread throughout your UI code? That makes it difficult to change and causes duplicate code you might forget to update.

Communicating between these layers is important as well. How does one layer talk to the other? The easy way is just to create those classes when you need them. However, this results in multiple instances of the same class, which causes problems coordinating calls.

For example, what if two classes each have their own **database handler class** and make conflicting calls to the database? Both Android and iOS use **Dependency Injection** or **DI** to create instances in one place and inject them into other classes that need them. This chapter will cover the **Riverpod** package for DI and state management.

> **Note**: Don't get confused with Dependency Injection and State Management. They are two different things. Dependency Injection is a way to inject or provide the dependencies needed inside the app, and State Management is a way to manage the app's state.

Ultimately, the business logic layer should decide how to react to the user's actions and delegate tasks like **retrieving** and **saving data** to other classes.

Why You Need State Management

First, what do the terms **state** and **state management** mean? State is when a widget is active and stores its data in memory. The Flutter framework handles some state, but as mentioned earlier, Flutter is declarative. That means it rebuilds the UI from memory when the state or data changes or when another part of your app uses it.

State management is, as the name implies, how you manage the state of your widgets and app.

There are two types of state to consider - **ephemeral state**, also known as **local state**, which is limited to the widget, and **app state**, also known as **global state**.

- Use ephemeral state when no other component in the widget tree needs to access a widget's data. Examples include whether a `TabBarView` tab is selected or `FloatingActionButton` is pressed.
- Use app state to manage the entire state of the app and when other parts of your app need to access some state data. One example is an image that changes over time, like an icon for the current weather. Another example is information that the user selects on one screen, which should then display on another screen, like when the user adds an item to a shopping cart.

Next, you'll learn more about the different types of state and how they apply to your recipe app.

Widget State

In Chapter 4, "Understanding Widgets", you saw the difference between **stateless** and **stateful widgets**. A stateless widget is drawn with the same state it had when it was created. A stateful widget preserves its state and uses it to (re)draw itself when there's any change in the widget's state.

Your current **Recipes** screen has a card with the list of previous searches and a `GridView` with a list of recipes:

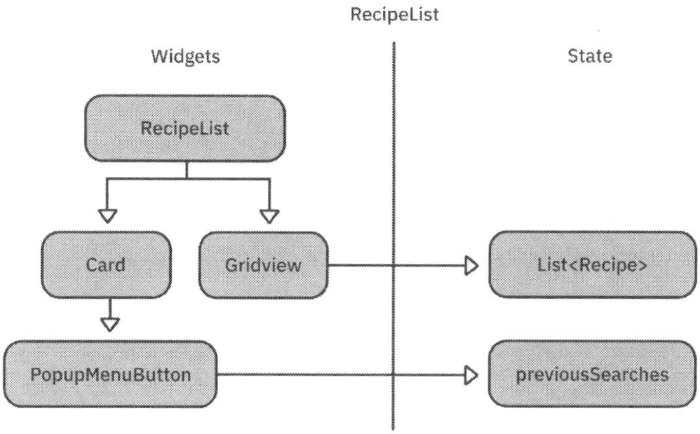

The left side shows some of the `RecipeList` widgets, while the right side shows the state objects that store the information each widget uses. An element tree stores both the widgets themselves and the states of all the stateful widgets in `RecipeList`:

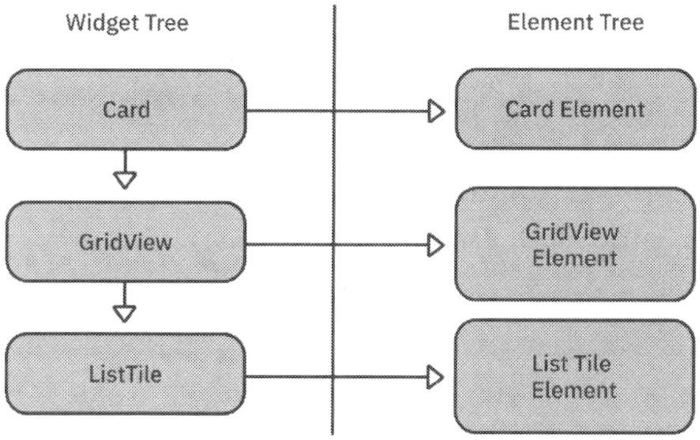

If the state of a widget updates, the state object also updates, and the widget is redrawn with that updated state.

Application State

In Flutter, a `StatefulWidget` can hold state. Its children can access it, and even pass (pieces of) it to other screens. However, that complicates your code, and you have to remember to pass data objects down the tree. Wouldn't it be great if child widgets could easily access their parent data without having to pass in that data?

There are several different ways to achieve that, both with **built-in widgets** and with **third-party packages**. You'll look at built-in widgets first.

Managing State in Your App

The Recipes Finder app needs to save four things: the **currently selected screen**, the list to show in the **Recipes** screen, the user's **bookmarks** and the **ingredients**. In this chapter, you'll use state management to save this information so other screens can use it.

These methods are still relevant for sharing data between screens. Here's a general idea of how your classes will look:

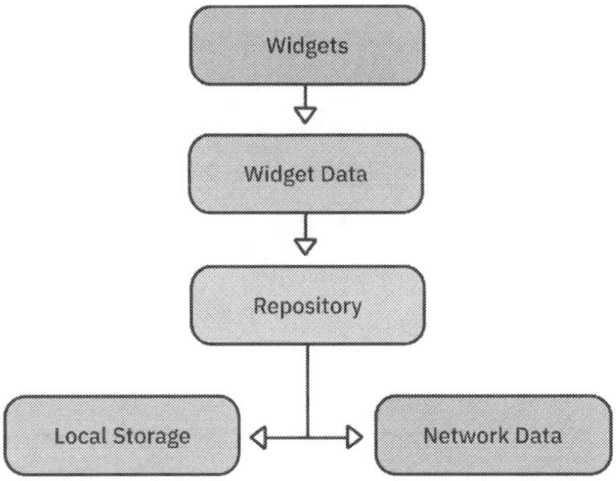

Stateful Widgets

`StatefulWidget` is one of the most basic ways of saving state. The `RecipeList` widget, for example, saves several fields for later usage, including the current search list and the start and end positions of search results for pagination.

When you create a `StatefulWidget`, the `createState()` method gets called, which creates and stores the state internally in Flutter. The parent needs to rebuild the widget when there's a change in the state of the widget.

You use `initstate()` to initialize the widget in its starting state. You use it for one-time work, like initializing text controllers. Then, you use `setState()` to set the new changed state, triggering a rebuild of the widget.

For example, in Chapter 10, "Handling Shared Preferences", you used `setState()` to set the selected tab. This tells the system to rebuild the UI to select a page. `StatefulWidget` is great for maintaining an internal state, but not for a state outside the widget.

One way to achieve an architecture that allows sharing state between widgets is to adopt **InheritedWidget**.

InheritedWidget

`InheritedWidget` is a built-in class allowing child widgets to access its data. It's the basis for a lot of other state management widgets. If you create a class that extends `InheritedWidget` and gives it some data, any child widget can access it by calling `context.dependOnInheritedWidgetOfExactType<class>()`.

Wow, that's quite a mouthful! As shown below, `<class>` represents the name of the class extending `InheritedWidget`.

```
class RecipeWidget extends InheritedWidget {
  final Recipe recipe;
  RecipeWidget(Key? key, required this.recipe, required Widget
child}) :
      super(key: key, child: child);

  @override
  bool updateShouldNotify(RecipeWidget oldWidget) => recipe !=
oldWidget.recipe;

  static RecipeWidget of(BuildContext context) =>
context.dependOnInheritedWidgetOfExactType<RecipeWidget>()!;

}
```

You can then extract data from that widget. Since that's such a long method name to call, the convention is to create an `of()` method.

Then a child widget, like the text field that displays the recipe title, can just use:

```
RecipeWidget recipeWidget = RecipeWidget.of(context);
print(recipeWidget.recipe.label);
```

> **Note**: `updateShouldNotify()` compares two recipes, which requires `Recipe` to implement `equals`. Otherwise, you need to compare each field.

An advantage of using `InheritedWidget` is it's a built-in widget so you don't need to worry about using external packages.

A disadvantage of using `InheritedWidget` is that the value of a recipe can't change unless you rebuild the whole widget tree because `InheritedWidget` is immutable. So, if you want to change the displayed recipe title, you'll have to rebuild the whole `RecipeWidget`.

Provider

Remi Rousselet designed **Provider** to build state management functionalities on top of `InheritedWidget`.

Google even includes details about it in their state management docs https://flutter.dev/docs/development/data-and-backend/state-mgmt/simple#providerof.

RiverPod

Provider's author, Remi Rousselet, wrote Riverpod to address some of Provider's weaknesses. In fact, Riverpod is an anagram of Provider! Rousselet wanted to solve the following problems:

1. Easily **access state** from anywhere.
2. Allow the **combination of states**.
3. Enable **override providers** for testing.

You'll use RiverPod to implement state management in your app.

Keypoints of Riverpod

Before you start using Riverpod, you need to understand some of its key points.

- **ProviderScope**: A provider scope is a widget that provides a **scope** for providers. The `AppWidget` must be wrapped in ProviderScope to use Riverpod.
- **Provider**: A provider is a class that provides a value to other classes. It's the most basic class in Riverpod. There are many types of providers. You'll see them later.
- **Consumer**: A consumer is a widget that listens to changes in a provider and rebuilds itself when the value changes. There are two types of consumers: **Consumer** and **ConsumerWidget.** You'll see examples later.
- **Ref**: A ref is a reference to a provider. You use it to access other providers. You can obtain a **ref** from providers and ConsumerWidgets.

Types of Providers

There are several different types of providers:

- **Provider**: Returns any **value.** Useful as DI.
- **StateProvider**: Returns any **type** and provides a way to modify it's **state**.
- **FutureProvider**: Returns a **Future**.
- **StreamProvider**: Returns a **Stream**.
- **StateNotifierProvider**: Returns a subclass of **StateProvider** and provides a way to modify its state through an interface.
- **NotifierProvider**: Listen to and expose a **Notifier**.
- **AsyncNotifierProvider**: Listen to and expose an **Asyncotifier**, AsyncNotifier is a Notifier that can be asynchronously initialized.
- **ChangeNotifierProvider**: Returns a **ChangeNotifier**. This is for migrating from the old ChangeNotifier.

> **Note**: **ChangeNotifierProvider** is a mutable provider, and its use is discouraged. It's only for transitioning from provider to Riverpod. It's advisable to use **NotifierProvider** instead.

Provider

`Provider` is the most basic class that provides a value to other classes. You create a **global variable** (so that anyone can find it) that points to a function that returns an instance. You create a provider like this:

```
final myProvider = Provider((ref) {
  return MyValue();
});
```

The variable `myProvider` is final and doesn't change. It provides a function that will create the state. You can also use the `ref` variable to access other providers. You can also provide multiple providers that return the same type.

StateProvider

`StateProvider` is a simplified version of `StateNotifierProvider`. It allows you to modify simple variables. This includes strings, Booleans, numbers or lists of items. You can also use classes. A simple example looks like this:

```
class Item {
  Item({required this.name, required this.title});

  final String name;
  final String title;
}

final itemProvider = StateProvider<Item>((ref) => Item(name:
'Item1', title: 'Title1'));
```

The variable `itemProvider` is final and doesn't change. You use this variable to access the state of the value provided by the provider and can change the value as follows:

```
ref.read(itemProvider.notifier).state = Item(name: 'Item2',
title: 'Title2');
```

There is also the `update()` method:

```
ref.read(itemProvider.notifier).update((state) => Item(name:
'Item2', title: 'Title2'));
```

FutureProvider

`FutureProvider` works like other providers but for asynchronous code and returns a `Future`. They are generally used in place of `FutureBuilder`.

```
final itemProvider = FutureProvider<Item>((ref) async {
  return someLongRunningFunction();
});
```

A `Future` is handy when a value is not readily available but will be in the future. Examples include calls that request data from the internet or asynchronously read data from a database. You can use `FutureProvider` like this:

```
AsyncValue<Item> futureItem = ref.watch(itemProvider);
  return futureItem.when(
    loading: () => const CircularProgressIndicator(),
    error: (err, stack) => Text('Error: $err'),
    data: (item) {
      return Text(item.name);
    },
  );
```

StreamProvider

You'll learn about **streams** in detail in the next chapter. For now, you just need to know that Riverpod also has a provider specifically for streams and works the same way as `FutureProvider`. `StreamProviders` are handy when data comes in via streams and values change over time, like, for example, when you're monitoring the connectivity of a device.

StateNotifierProvider

`StateNotifierProvider` is used to listen to changes in `StateNotifier`. A simple example looks like this:

```
class ItemNotifier extends StateNotifier<Item> {
  ItemNotifier() : super(Item(name: 'Item1', title: 'Title1'));

  void updateItem(Item item) {
    state = item;
  }
}

final itemProvider = StateNotifierProvider<ItemNotifier,
Item>((ref) => ItemNotifier());
```

Here the constructor of `ItemNotifier` sets the initial state for an `Item`.To change the value of the provider, you use its `updateItem()` method as follows:

```
ref.read(itemProvider.notifier).updateItem(Item(name: 'Item2',
title: 'Title2'));
```

NotifierProvider and AsyncNotifierProvider

`NotifierProvider` is used to listen to and expose a Notifier. `AsyncNotifierProvider` is a Notifier that you can asynchronously initialize. You generally use it to expose the state, which can change over time after reacting to custom events, like button taps and data changes.

```
class ItemNotifier extends Notifier<Item> {
  @override
  Item build(){
    return Item(name: 'Item1', title: 'Title1');
  }

  void updateItem(Item item) {
    state = item;
  }
}

final itemNotifierProvider = NotifierProvider<ItemNotifier,
Item>(() => ItemNotifier());
```

The `build()` function returns the initial state of the `Item` and is called when the provider is first accessed.

To change the value of the provider, you use again its `updateItem()` method:

```
ref.read(itemNotifierProvider.notifier).updateItem(Item(name:
'Item2', title: 'Title2'));
```

Adopting Riverpod in the Recipe Finder App

You're now ready to start working on your recipe project. If you're following along with your app from the previous chapters, open it and keep using it with this chapter. If not, just locate this chapter's **projects** folder and open **starter** in Android Studio.

> **Note**: If you use the starter app, don't forget to add your `apiKey` in **network/spoonacular_service.dart**.

Overview of Existing Providers

Open up **providers.dart**. It should look like this:

```
// 1
final sharedPrefProvider = Provider<SharedPreferences>((ref) {
  throw UnimplementedError();
});

// 2
final repositoryProvider =
ChangeNotifierProvider<MemoryRepository>((ref) {
  return MemoryRepository();
});

// 3
final serviceProvider = Provider<ServiceInterface>((ref) {
  throw UnimplementedError();
});
```

This code:

1. Defines a provider for **Shared preferences**. Note that it throws an `UnimplementedError`. Explanation below.
2. Defines a `ChangeNotifierProvider` for the`MemoryRepository`.
3. Defines a provider for `ServiceInterface`. This will allow you to substitute any `ServiceInterface` class.

Now open **main.dart** and look at the following:

```
// 1
final sharedPrefs = await SharedPreferences.getInstance();
// 2
final service = SpoonacularService.create();
// 3
runApp(ProviderScope(overrides: [
  sharedPrefProvider.overrideWithValue(sharedPrefs),
  serviceProvider.overrideWithValue(service),
], child: const MyApp()));
```

1. Get an **instance** of the `SharedPreferences` library.
2. Create a `SpoonacularService`.
3. **Override** the definitions above with these newly created instances.

Since getting a shared preference instance is an asynchronous call, we do this in the main method that uses the async keyword.

Updating Repositories

Inside the **data/repositories** directory are two repository files: **repository.dart** contains the abstract definition of a repository, and **memory_repository.dart** defines a memory-based repository. This repository will hold your **recipes** and **ingredients** while running. Once the app closes, the data goes away. In Chapter 15, "Saving Data Locally", you'll learn how to store such data locally.

Updating the Memory Repository

Open up **data/repositories/memory_repository.dart**. Notice that it currently uses `ChangeNotifier, which isn't recommended when using **Riverpod**. You'll convert this class to the Riverpod **Notifier** class.

To be a **Notifier** - a class has to have an object that notifies others about the change. This class will be **CurrentRecipeData**. This will contain the current **recipes** and **ingredients** list. Create a new file in **data/models** called **current_recipe_data.dart**.

Add the following:

```
import 'package:freezed_annotation/freezed_annotation.dart';
import 'models.dart';
part 'current_recipe_data.freezed.dart';

@freezed
class CurrentRecipeData with _$CurrentRecipeData {
  const factory CurrentRecipeData({
    @Default(<Recipe>[]) List<Recipe> currentRecipes,
    @Default(<Ingredient>[]) List<Ingredient>
currentIngredients,
  }) = _CurrentRecipeData;
}
```

This uses the Freezed package to create a few helper methods like `copyWith()`. The `@Default` annotation helps assign the default value to the variables. From a terminal run:

```
dart run build_runner build
```

This will create the **current_recipe_data.freezed.dart** file.

Back in **memory_repository.dart**, replace the import of **foundation.dart** with:

```
import 'package:flutter_riverpod/flutter_riverpod.dart';
import '../models/current_recipe_data.dart';
```

Then change the class definition to:

```
class MemoryRepository extends Notifier<CurrentRecipeData>
    implements Repository {
```

On the next line, add the following method. This will initialize the notifier and set the initial state of `CurrentRecipeData`.

```
@override
CurrentRecipeData build() {
  const currentRecipeData = CurrentRecipeData();
  return currentRecipeData;
}
```

Now, remove all of the calls to `notifyListeners()` methods, as they'll be throwing compilation errors. Next, remove the declaration of `_currentRecipes` and `_currentIngredients` fields. Since those two fields are in `CurrentRecipeData` and we have a state of `currentRecipeData`, you'll just use that.

Substitute all the occurrences of `_currentRecipes` with `state.currentRecipes`.

For example, `findAllRecipes()` should turn into this:

```
@override
List<Recipe> findAllRecipes() {
  return state.currentRecipes;
}
```

Similarly, change all occurrences of `_currentIngredients` with `state.currentIngredients`.

> **Note**: **State** is a getter that returns the current state of the **notifier** and you can access the current state. You can also update the state of the notifier by assigning **new state**. You don't need to call `notifyListeners()` as it's done automatically.

If you need help, look at the file in the final project. Hint - find and replace works great!

Since `CurrentRecipeData` is immutable, meaning you can't modify it, you'll have to create new instances instead of modifying the lists. Where are the lists modified, you may wonder? In the methods that insert and delete recipes and ingredients. Find `// TODO: Update insertRecipe()` and replace the line below it with:

```
if(state.currentRecipes.contains(recipe)) {
  return 0;
}
state = state.copyWith(currentRecipes: [...state.currentRecipes,
recipe]);
```

First, you check if the recipe is already on the list. If it is, you return 0. If not, you assign the current state with a new instance of state of `CurrentRecipeData` by copying the existing one (`copyWith()` comes from Freezed) with the current list of recipes and a new one. Notice that using `[]` makes a new list.

Now replace the line below `// TODO: Update insertIngredients()` with:

```
state = state.copyWith(currentIngredients:
[...state.currentIngredients,
  ...ingredients]);
```

This does something similar but adds two lists together. Next, replace `// TODO: Update deleteRecipe()` and the subsequent line with the following:

```
final updatedList = [...state.currentRecipes];
updatedList.remove(recipe);
state = state.copyWith(currentRecipes: updatedList);
```

This creates a new list using the **spread operator**: `...`, which unfolds the list of items.Now replace the whole body of `deleteIngredient()` with:

```
final updatedList = [...state.currentIngredients];
updatedList.remove(ingredient);
state = state.copyWith(currentIngredients: updatedList);
```

Then substitute the whole body of `deleteIngredients()` with:

```
final updatedList = [...state.currentIngredients];
updatedList.removeWhere((ingredient) =>
ingredients.contains(ingredient));
state = state.copyWith(currentIngredients: updatedList);
```

And finally, change the body of `deleteRecipeIngredients()` as follows:

```
final updatedList = [...state.currentIngredients];
updatedList.removeWhere((ingredient) => ingredient.recipeId ==
recipeId);
state = state.copyWith(currentIngredients: updatedList);
```

Now that `MemoryRepository` has changed, open **lib/providers.dart** to adopt NotifierProvider.Add the following import:

```
import 'data/models/current_recipe_data.dart';
```

and then change `repositoryProvider` to:

```
final repositoryProvider =
    NotifierProvider<MemoryRepository, CurrentRecipeData>(() {
  return MemoryRepository();
});
```

Rerun your app to make sure it compiles successfully.

It's now time to use the new **repositoryProvider** in the UI.

Using the Repository for Recipes

You'll implement code to add a recipe to the **Bookmarks** screen and ingredients to the **Groceries** screen. First, open **ui/recipes/recipe_details.dart**.

Displaying the Recipes' Details

You need to show the recipe's image, label and calories on the **Details** page. The repository already stores all of your currently bookmarked recipes.

> **Note**: If your **recipe_details.dart** file does not have the // TODO comments, take a look at the starter project.

Find `// TODO: Add Repository` and replace it with:

```
final repository = ref.read(repositoryProvider.notifier);
```

This reads the `repositoryProvider` as a **class instance** so that you can use it to access the **functions** you defined in the repository. You'll use it to add the bookmark.

Next, replace `// TODO: Insert Recipe` with:

```
repository.insertRecipe(recipeDetail!);
```

This adds the recipe to your repository's list of recipes. To delete the recipe, replace: `// TODO: Delete Recipe` with:

```
repository.deleteRecipe(recipeDetail!);
```

This just removes it from the memory repository's list of recipes.

Now, hot reload the app. Enter **chicken** in the search box and tap the magnifying glass to perform the search. You'll see something like this:

Select a recipe to go to the details page:

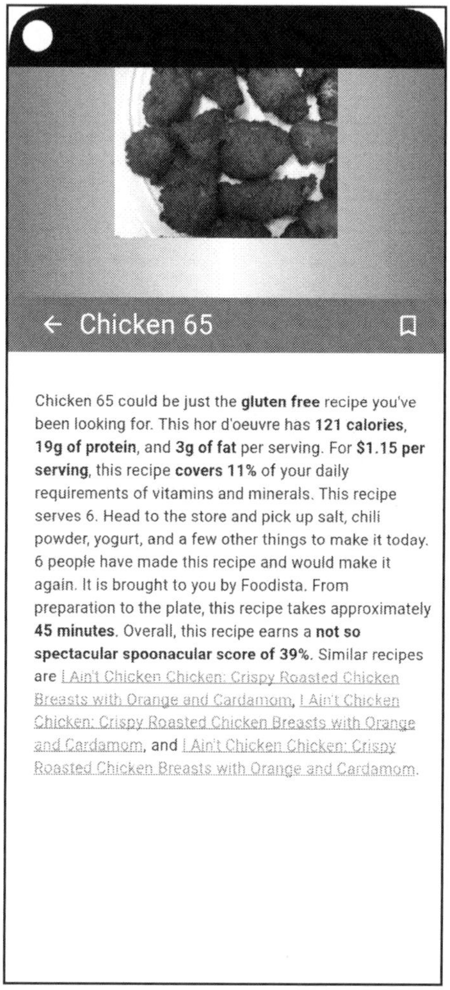

Tap the **Bookmark** button and the details page will disappear.

Now, select the **Bookmarks** tab. At this point, you'll see a blank screen — you haven't implemented it yet.

Showing bookmarked recipes in the **Bookmarks** tab is your next step.

Implementing the Bookmarks Screen

Open **ui/bookmarks/bookmarks.dart** and add the following imports:

```
import '../../providers.dart';
import '../recipes/recipe_details.dart';
```

This includes the Riverpod providers to retrieve the repository as well as the `RecipeDetails` class.

Find `// TODO: Add Repository` and add:

```
final repository = ref.watch(repositoryProvider);
recipes = repository.currentRecipes;
```

This watches the repository for changes and updates the widget. It also gets the current list of recipes from the repository.

On the **Bookmarks** page, the user can delete a bookmarked recipe by swiping left or right and selecting the delete icon. To implement this, find and replace `// TODO: Add Delete Recipe` at the bottom of the class with:

```
  void deleteRecipe(Recipe recipe) {
    ref.read(repositoryProvider.notifier).deleteRecipe(recipe);
  }
```

In this code, you use: `ref.read` to get the repository and then call `deleteRecipe()` on it.

Go back up in the file and replace the two instances of `// TODO Add Delete` with:

```
deleteRecipe(recipe);
```

This will call the method you just created and pass the recipe to delete. Replace `// TODO: Add Push to Recipe Details Page` with:

```
Navigator.push(context, MaterialPageRoute(
  builder: (context) {
    return RecipeDetails(
        recipe: recipe.copyWith(bookmarked: true));
  },
));
```

This will take the user to the **recipe details** page with a copy of the recipe and `bookmarked` set to true.

If you left your app running while making all of the above changes, hot reload the app.

If you stopped your app or did a hot restart instead of a hot reload, then return to the **Recipes** tab and bookmark a recipe.

Select the **Bookmarks** tab, and you should see the recipe you bookmarked. Something like this:

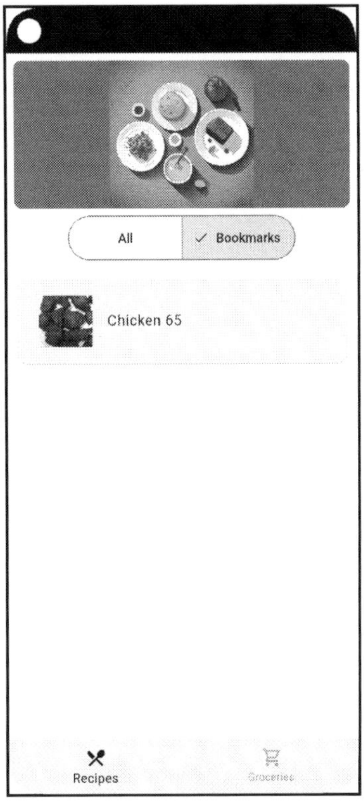

You're almost done, but if you go to the **Groceries** tab, you'll see that the view is currently blank. Your next step is to add the functionality to show the ingredients of bookmarked recipes.

Implementing the Groceries Screen

Open **ui/groceries/groceries.dart** and add the following:

```
import '../../providers.dart';
```

Here, you import your providers.

Find `// TODO: Add Repository 1` and replace with:

```
final repository = ref.watch(repositoryProvider);
currentIngredients = repository.currentIngredients;
```

Find `// TODO: Add Repository 2` and replace with:

```
final repository = ref.watch(repositoryProvider);
currentIngredients = repository.currentIngredients;
```

Hot reload and make sure you still have one bookmark saved.

Now, go to the **Groceries** tab to see the ingredients of the recipe you bookmarked. You'll see something like this:

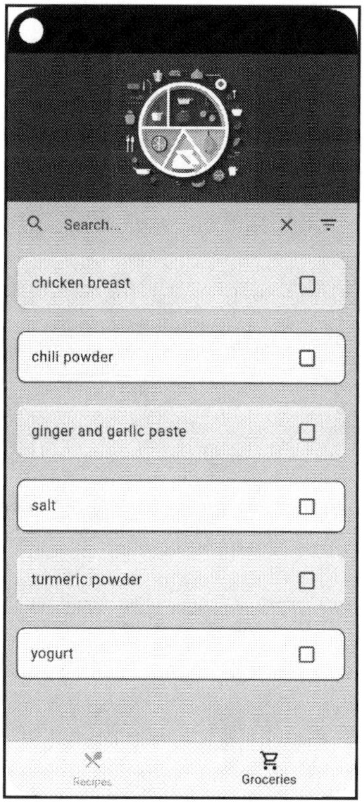

Congratulations, you made it! You now have an app where you can monitor state changes and get notifications across different screens, thanks to the infrastructure of Riverpod.

Implementing the Main Screen State

The main screen also has a state, and that is the currently selected bottom navigation item. This state will use the `StateProvider` class from Riverpod.

In the **ui** directory, create a new file named **main_screen_state.dart**. Add the following:

```
import 'package:flutter_riverpod/flutter_riverpod.dart';
import 'package:freezed_annotation/freezed_annotation.dart';

part 'main_screen_state.freezed.dart';

// 1
@freezed
class MainScreenState with _$MainScreenState {
  const factory MainScreenState({
    @Default(0) int selectedIndex,
  }) = _MainScreenState;
}

// 2
class MainScreenStateProvider extends
StateNotifier<MainScreenState> {
  MainScreenStateProvider() : super(const MainScreenState());

  // 3
  void updateSelectedIndex(int index) {
    state = MainScreenState(selectedIndex: index);
  }
}
```

1. `MainScreenState` just holds the currently selected index.
2. `MainScreenStateProvider` is a provider for that state.
3. One method (`updateSelectedIndex`) is provided to update the index. It creates a new state.

This uses the Freezed package to create a few helper methods. From a terminal run:

```
dart run build_runner build
```

Now add this provider to **providers.dart**:

```
import 'ui/main_screen_state.dart';

final bottomNavigationProvider =
    StateNotifierProvider<MainScreenStateProvider,
MainScreenState>((ref) {
  return MainScreenStateProvider();
});
```

Open up **main_screen.dart** and remove `int _selectedIndex = 0;`. Inside of `saveCurrentIndex()` replace the last line with:

```
final bottomNavigation = ref.read(bottomNavigationProvider);
prefs.setInt(prefSelectedIndexKey,
bottomNavigation.selectedIndex);
```

Find `// TODO: Update getCurrentIndex()` and replace the line below it with:

```
ref
    .read(bottomNavigationProvider.notifier)
    .updateSelectedIndex(index);
```

Change the line below `// TODO: Update _onItemTapped()` with:

```
ref.read(bottomNavigationProvider.notifier).updateSelectedIndex(
index);
```

Then find `// TODO: Update largeLayout() 1` and replace the line below it with:

```
selectedIndex:
    ref.watch(bottomNavigationProvider).selectedIndex,
```

Finally find `// TODO: Update largeLayout() 2` and replace the subsequent line with:

```
index: ref.watch(bottomNavigationProvider).selectedIndex,
```

The next step is to update `getRailNavigations()`. First, replace the line below `// TODO: Update getRailNavigations() 1` with:

```
ref.watch(bottomNavigationProvider).selectedIndex == 0
    ? selectedColor
    : Colors.black,
```

And then change the line after `// TODO: Update getRailNavigations() 2` with:

```
ref.watch(bottomNavigationProvider).selectedIndex == 0
    ? selectedColor
    : Colors.black,
```

Now find `// TODO: Update mobileLayout()` and change the line below it to:

```
index: ref.watch(bottomNavigationProvider).selectedIndex,
```

In `createBottomNavigationBar()` , find `// TODO: Add index` and replace it with:

```
final bottomNavigationIndex =
    ref.read(bottomNavigationProvider).selectedIndex;
```

Finally, change all of the remaining instances of `_selectedIndex` to:

```
bottomNavigationIndex
```

Now it's time to get rid of the calls to `setState()`. Update `_onItemTapped()` so it looks like this:

```
void _onItemTapped(int index) {

ref.read(bottomNavigationProvider.notifier).updateSelectedIndex(
index);
  saveCurrentIndex();
}
```

and change `getCurrentIndex()` as follows:

```
void getCurrentIndex() async {
  final prefs = ref.read(sharedPrefProvider);
  if (prefs.containsKey(prefSelectedIndexKey)) {
    final index = prefs.getInt(prefSelectedIndexKey);
    if (index != null) {

ref.read(bottomNavigationProvider.notifier).updateSelectedIndex(
index);
    }
  }
}
```

Finally, make sure that `getCurrentIndex()` is called after the build method. To achieve that, change the last line of `initState()` like this.

```
Future.microtask(() async {
  getCurrentIndex();
});
```

Stop and restart the app and verify that you can add and delete bookmarks. Check also that the **Groceries** tab shows the ingredients of the bookmarked recipes.

Congrats! Now you know how to manage state across different screens of your app using Riverpod. And that's just the beginning!

Is Riverpod the only option for state management? No. Here's a quick tour of alternative libraries.

Other State Management Libraries

There are other packages that help with state management and provide even more flexibility when managing state in your app. While Riverpod features classes for widgets lower in the widget tree, other packages provide more generic state management solutions for the whole app, often enabling a unidirectional data flow architecture.

Such libraries include **Redux**, **BLoC** and **MobX**. Here's a quick overview of each.

Redux

If you come from web or React development, you might be familiar with Redux, which uses concepts such as actions, reducers, views and stores. The flow looks like this:

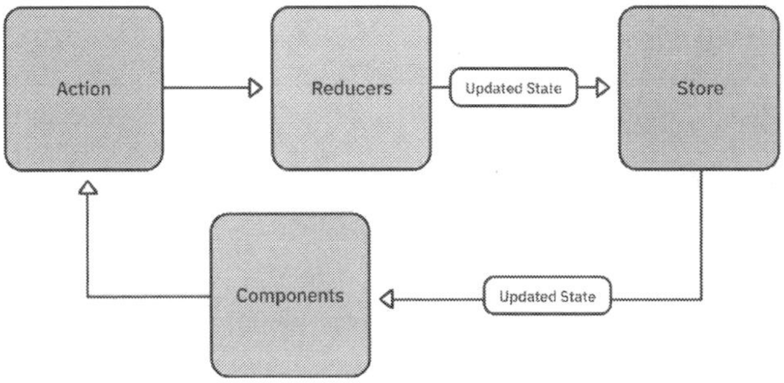

Actions, like clicks on the UI or events from network operations, are sent to reducers, which turn them into a state. That state is saved in a store, which notifies listeners, like views and components, about changes.

The nice thing about the Redux architecture is that a view can simply send actions and wait for updates from the store.

You need two packages to use Redux in Flutter: **redux** and **flutter_redux**.

For React developers migrating to Flutter, an advantage of Redux is that it's already familiar. It might take a bit to learn if you aren't familiar with it.

BLoC

BLoC stands for **B**usiness **Lo**gic **C**omponent. It's designed to separate UI code from the data layer and business logic, helping you create reusable code that's easy to test. Think of it as a stream of events; some widgets submit events, and others respond to them. BLoC sits in the middle and directs the conversation, leveraging the power of streams.

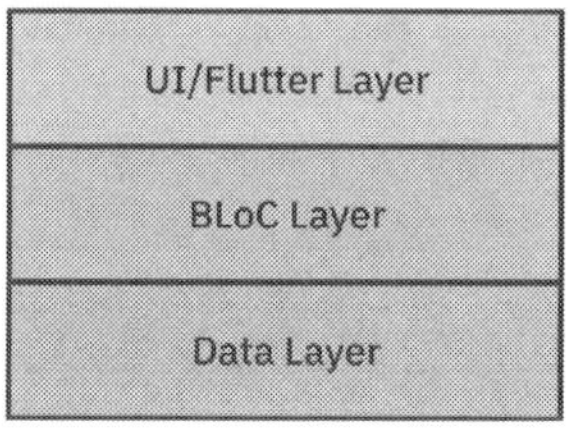

It's quite popular in the Flutter Community and very well documented.

MobX

MobX comes to Dart from the web world. It uses the following concepts:

- **Observables**: Hold the state.
- **Actions**: Mutate the state.
- **Reactions**: React to the change in observables.

MobX has annotations that help you write your code and simplify it.

One advantage is that MobX allows you to wrap any data in an observable. It's relatively easy to learn and requires smaller generated code files than BLoC.

Key Points

- State management is key to Flutter development.
- Riverpod is a great package that helps with state management.
- Other packages for handling application state include Redux, Bloc, and MobX.
- Repositories are a pattern for providing data.
- You can switch between repositories by providing an interface for the repository. For example, you can switch between real and mocked repositories.
- Mock services are a way to provide dummy data.

Where to Go From Here?

If you want to learn more about:

- State management, go to https://flutter.dev/docs/development/data-and-backend/state-mgmt/intro.
- Flutter Redux go to https://pub.dev/packages/flutter_redux.
- Bloc, go to https://bloclibrary.dev/#/.
- MobX, go to https://github.com/mobxjs/mobx.dart.
- Riverpod, go to https://riverpod.dev/.
- Clean Architecture, go to https://pusher.com/tutorials/clean-architecture-introduction.

In the next chapter, you'll learn all about **streams** that handle data that can be sent and received continuously. See you there!

Chapter 14: Working With Streams

By Kevin David Moore

Imagine yourself sitting by a creek, having a wonderful time. While watching the water flow, you see a piece of wood or a leaf floating down the stream and decide to take it out of the water. You could even have someone upstream purposely float things down the creek for you to grab.

You can imagine Dart **streams** in a similar way: as data flowing down a creek, waiting for someone to grab it. That's what a stream does in Dart — it sends data events for a listener to grab.

With Dart streams, you can send one data event at a time while other parts of your app listen for those events. Such events can be collections, maps or any other type of data you've created.

Streams can send errors in addition to data; you can also stop the stream if you need to.

In this chapter, you'll update Recipe Finder to use streams in two different locations. You'll use one for **bookmarks** to let the user mark favorite recipes and automatically update the UI to display them. You'll also use one to update your **ingredient** and **grocery** lists.

But before you jump into the code, you'll learn more about how streams work.

Types of Streams

Streams are part of Dart, and Flutter inherits them. There are two types of streams in Flutter: **single subscription streams** and **broadcast streams**.

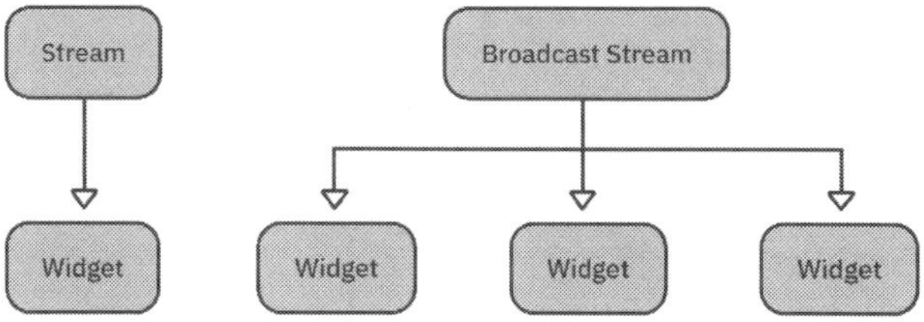

Single subscription streams are the default. They work well when you're only using a particular stream on one screen.

A single subscription stream can only be listened to once. It doesn't start generating events until it has a **listener**, and it stops sending events when the listener stops listening, even if the source of events could still provide more data.

Single subscription streams are useful for downloading a file or for any single-use operation. For example, a widget can subscribe to a stream to receive updates about a value, like the progress of a download, and update its UI accordingly.

If you need multiple parts of your app to access the same stream, use a **broadcast stream**, instead.

A broadcast stream allows any number of listeners. It fires when its events are ready, whether there are listeners or not.

To create a broadcast stream, you simply call `asBroadcastStream()` on an existing single subscription stream.

```
final broadcastStream = singleStream.asBroadcastStream();
```

You can differentiate a broadcast stream from a single subscription stream by inspecting its Boolean property `isBroadcast`.

In Flutter, some key classes are built on top of `Stream` that simplify programming with streams.

The following diagram shows the main classes used with streams:

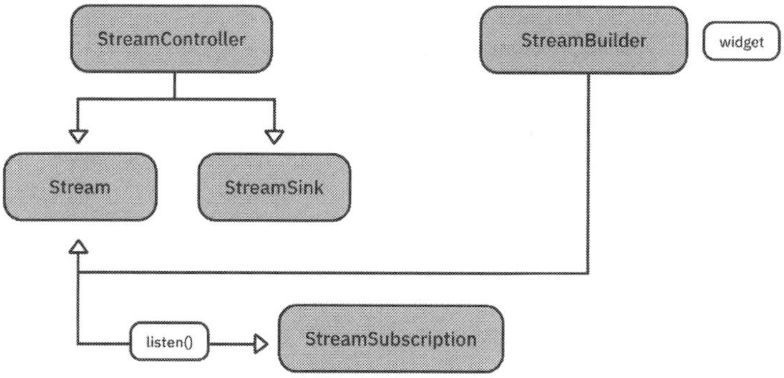

Next, you'll take a deeper look at each one.

StreamController and Sink

When you create a stream, you usually use `StreamController`, which holds both the stream and `StreamSink`.

A sink is a destination for data. When you want to add data to a stream, you'll add it to the **sink**. Since the `StreamController` owns the sink, it listens for data on the sink and sends the data to its stream listeners.

Here's an example that uses `StreamController`:

```
final _recipeStreamController =
StreamController<List<Recipe>>();
final _stream = _recipeStreamController.stream;
```

To add data to a stream, you add it to its sink:

```
_recipeStreamController.sink.add(_recipesList);
```

This uses the sink field of the controller to "place" a list of recipes on the stream. That data will be sent to any current listeners.

When you're done with the stream, make sure you close it, like this:

```
_recipeStreamController.close();
```

StreamSubscription

Using `listen()` on a stream returns a `StreamSubscription`. You can use this subscription class to cancel the stream when you're done, like this:

```
StreamSubscription subscription = stream.listen((value) {
    print('Value from controller: $value');
});
...
...
// You are done with the subscription
subscription.cancel();
```

Sometimes, it's helpful to have an automated mechanism to avoid managing subscriptions manually. That's where `StreamBuilder` comes in.

StreamBuilder

`StreamBuilder` is handy when you want to use a stream. It takes two parameters: a stream and a builder. As you receive data from the stream, the builder takes care of building or updating the UI.

Here's an example:

```
final repository = ref.watch(repositoryProvider);
return StreamBuilder<List<Recipe>>(
  stream: repository.recipesStream(),
  builder: (context, AsyncSnapshot<List<Recipe>> snapshot) {
    // extract recipes from snapshot and build the view
  }
)
...
```

`StreamBuilder` is handy because you don't need to use a subscription directly, and it unsubscribes from the stream automatically when the widget is destroyed.

> **Note**: Riverpod has a **StreamProvider**, which you can use to provide a stream to a widget. You can learn more about it at https://riverpod.dev/docs/providers/stream_provider.

Now that you understand how streams work, you'll convert your existing project to use them.

Adding Streams to Recipe Finder

You're now ready to start working on your recipe project. If you're following along with your app from the previous chapters, open it and keep using it with this chapter. If not, just locate the **projects** folder for this chapter and open **starter** in Android Studio.

> **Note**: If you use the starter app, don't forget to add your `apiKey` in **network/spoonacular_service.dart**.

To convert your project to use streams, you need to change `MemoryRepository` to add two new methods that return one stream for **recipes** and another for **ingredients**. Instead of just returning a list of static recipes, you'll use streams to modify that list and refresh the UI to display the change.

This is what the flow of the app looks like:

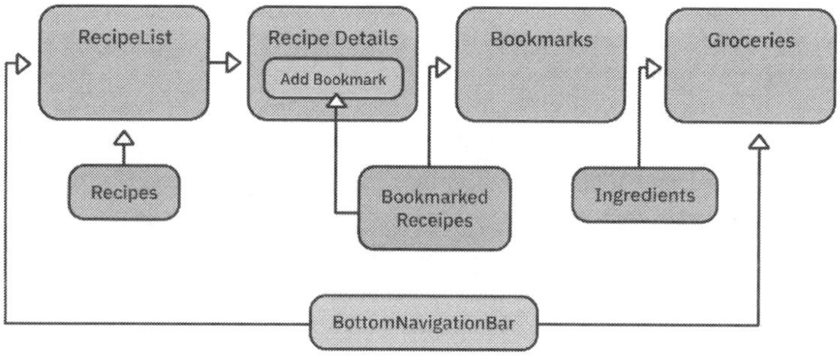

Here, you can see that the **Recipes** screen has a list of recipes. Bookmarking a recipe adds it to the bookmarked recipe list and updates both the bookmarks and the groceries screens.

You'll start by converting your repository code to return `Streams` and `Futures`.

Adding Futures and Streams to the Repository

Open **data/repositories/repository.dart** and change all of the return types to return a `Future`, except for the `init` and `close` methods. For example, change the existing `findAllRecipes()` to:

```
Future<List<Recipe>> findAllRecipes();
```

Do this for all the methods except `init()` and `close()`.

Your final class should look like this:

```
Future<List<Recipe>> findAllRecipes();

Future<Recipe> findRecipeById(int id);

Future<List<Ingredient>> findAllIngredients();

Future<List<Ingredient>> findRecipeIngredients(int recipeId);

Future<int> insertRecipe(Recipe recipe);

Future<List<int>> insertIngredients(List<Ingredient>
ingredients);

Future<void> deleteRecipe(Recipe recipe);

Future<void> deleteIngredient(Ingredient ingredient);

Future<void> deleteIngredients(List<Ingredient> ingredients);

Future<void> deleteRecipeIngredients(int recipeId);

Future init();

void close();
```

These updates allow you to have methods that work asynchronously to process data from a database or the network.

Next, add two new `Streams` after `findAllRecipes()`:

```
// 1
Stream<List<Recipe>> watchAllRecipes();
// 2
Stream<List<Ingredient>> watchAllIngredients();
```

Here's what this code does:

1. `watchAllRecipes()` listens for any changes to the list of recipes. For example, if the user does a new search, it updates the list of recipes and notifies listeners accordingly.
2. `watchAllIngredients()` listens for changes in the list of ingredients displayed on the **Groceries** screen.

You've now changed the interface, so you need to update the memory repository.

Cleaning Up the Repository Code

Before updating the code to use `streams` and `futures`, there are some minor housekeeping updates.

Open **data/repositories/memory_repository.dart** and notice there are some red squiggles. We'll address them step by step in a bit.

First, import the Dart **async** library:

```
import 'dart:async';
```

Next, add these new properties within the class:

```
//1
late Stream<List<Recipe>> _recipeStream;
late Stream<List<Ingredient>> _ingredientStream;
// 2
final StreamController _recipeStreamController =
    StreamController<List<Recipe>>();
final StreamController _ingredientStreamController =
    StreamController<List<Ingredient>>();
```

Here's what's going on:

1. `_recipeStream` and `_ingredientStream` are private fields for the streams. These will be captured the first time a stream is requested, which prevents new streams from being created for each call.
2. Creates `StreamControllers` for recipes and ingredients.

Next, add a constructor:

```
MemoryRepository() {
  // 1
  _recipeStream =
```

```
  _recipeStreamController.stream.asBroadcastStream(
      // 2
      onListen: (subscription) {
        // 3
        // This is to send the current recipes to new subscriber
        _recipeStreamController.sink.add(state.currentRecipes);
      },
    ) as Stream<List<Recipe>>;
    _ingredientStream =
  _ingredientStreamController.stream.asBroadcastStream(
      onListen: (subscription) {
        // This is to send the current ingredients to new
  subscriber

  _ingredientStreamController.sink.add(state.currentIngredients);
      },
    ) as Stream<List<Ingredient>>;
  }
```

This will initialize the streams.

1. Create a broadcast stream so that multiple listeners are available.
2. Add an `onListen` method to listen for new subscriptions.
3. Send the existing recipes to the new listener.

Here, you create a broadcast stream, which you need for multiple listeners, and then update the listener with the current list of recipes when they subscribe.

And now, add these new methods after `findAllRecipes()`:

```
// 3
@override
Stream<List<Recipe>> watchAllRecipes() {
  return _recipeStream;
}

// 4
@override
Stream<List<Ingredient>> watchAllIngredients() {
   return _ingredientStream;
}
```

The above functions are self-explanatory, `watchAllRecipes()` returns the stream of recipes as `_recipeStream` and `watchAllIngredients()` returns the stream of ingredients as `_ingredientStream`.

Updating the Existing Repository

`MemoryRepository` is full of red squiggles. That's because all the methods use the old signatures, and everything's now based on `Futures`.

Still in **data/repositories/memory_repository.dart**, replace the existing `findAllRecipes()` with this:

```
@override
// 1
Future<List<Recipe>> findAllRecipes() {
  // 2
  return Future.value(state.currentRecipes);
}
```

These updates:

1. Change the method to return a `Future`.
2. Wrap the return value with a `Future.value()`.

There are a few more updates you need to make before moving on to the next section.

First, in `init()` remove the `null` from the `return` statement so it looks like this:

```
@override
Future init() {
  return Future.value();
}
```

For this repository, there is no initialization needed, so just an empty future is returned. Then, update `close()` so it closes the streams.

```
@override
void close() {
  _recipeStreamController.close();
  _ingredientStreamController.close();
}
```

When dealing with `streams` and their controllers, you need to make sure you close them when you are finished. Closing them in the close method makes sure those streams are closed. In the next section, you'll update the remaining methods to return **futures** and add data to the **stream** using `StreamController`.

Sending Recipes Over the Stream

As you learned earlier, `StreamController`'s `sink` property adds data to streams. Since this happens in the future, you need to change the return type to `Future` and then update the methods to add data to the stream.

> **Note**: Make sure you add `@override` above each method.

To start, change `insertRecipe()` to:

```
@override
// 1
Future<int> insertRecipe(Recipe recipe) {
  if (state.currentRecipes.contains(recipe)) {
    return Future.value(0);
  }
  // 2
  state = state.copyWith(currentRecipes:
[...state.currentRecipes, recipe]);
  // 3
  _recipeStreamController.sink.add(state.currentRecipes);
  // 4
  final ingredients = <Ingredient>[];
  for (final ingredient in recipe.ingredients) {
    ingredients.add(ingredient.copyWith(recipeId: recipe.id));
  }
  insertIngredients(ingredients);
  // 5
  return Future.value(0);
}
```

Here's what you've updated:

1. Update the method's return type to `Future<int>`.
2. Update the state by adding the new recipe to the existing list.
3. Add the list to the recipe `sink`. You might wonder why you call `add()` with the same list instead of adding a single ingredient or recipe. The reason is that the stream expects a list, not a single value. Doing it this way replaces the previous list with the updated one.

4. Update all of the ingredients with the **recipe ID** and then insert the ingredients.
5. Return a `Future` value. You'll learn how to return the ID of the new item in a later chapter.

This replaces the previous list with the new list and notifies any stream listeners that the data has changed.

Now that you know how to convert the first method, it's time to convert the rest of the methods as an exercise. Don't worry, you can do it! :]

Exercise

Convert the remaining methods like you did with `insertRecipe()`. You'll need to do the following:

1. Update `MemoryRepository` methods to return a `Future` that matches the new `Repository` interface methods.
2. For all methods that change a watched item, add a call to add the item to the `sink`.
3. Remove all the calls to `notifyListeners()`. Hint - not all methods have this statement.
4. Wrap the return values in `Futures`.
5. Add `@override` before each method.

What do you think the return will look like for a method that returns a `Future<void>`? Got it? There might be a future for you yet.

```
return Future.value();
```

If you get stuck, check out **memory_repository.dart** in this chapter's **challenge** folder — but first, give it your best shot!

After you complete the exercise, `MemoryRepository` shouldn't have any more red squiggles — but you still have a few more tweaks to make before you can run your new, stream-powered app.

> **Note**: It's very important that you add recipes to the `_recipeStreamController.sink` method for recipes and `_ingredientStreamController.sink` for ingredients. Check the **challenge** project to ensure you did this correctly. You'll need to do the same for the delete methods as well.

Switching Between Services

In an earlier chapter, you used a `MockService` to provide local data that never changes, but you also have access to `SpoonacularService`.

An easy way to do that is with an interface, or, as it's known in Dart, an **abstract class**. Remember that an interface or abstract class is just a contract that implementing classes will provide the given methods.

It'll look like this:

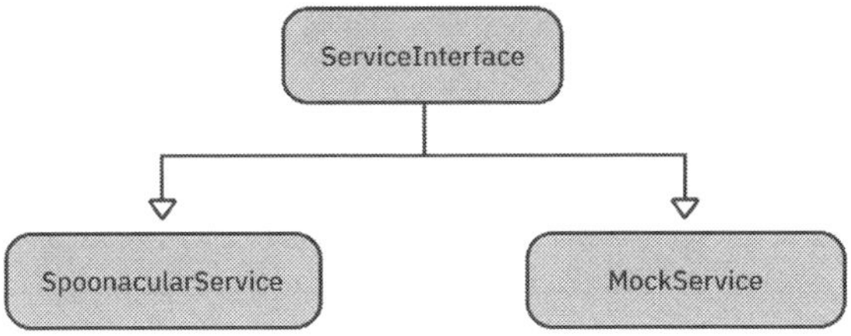

Go to the **network** folder and open **service_interface.dart**.

Here's what it looks like:

```
abstract class ServiceInterface {
  /// Query recipes with the given query string
  /// offset is the starting point
  /// number is the number of items
  Future<RecipeResponse> queryRecipes(
    String query,
    int offset,
    int number,
  );

  /// Get the details of a specific recipe
  Future<Response<Result<Recipe>>> queryRecipe(
    String id,
  );
}
```

This defines a class with two methods. One named `queryRecipes()`, for a list of recipes and `queryRecipe` for just a single recipe.

It has the same parameters and return values as `SpoonacularService` and `MockService`. Having each service implement this interface allows you to change the **providers** to provide this interface instead of a specific class.

You're now ready to integrate the new code based on streams. Fasten your seat belt! :]

Adding Streams to Bookmarks

The **Bookmarks** page uses `Consumer`, but you want to change it to a stream so it can react when a user bookmarks a recipe. To do this, you need to replace the reference to `MemoryRepository` with `Repository` and use a `StreamBuilder` widget.

Start by opening **ui/bookmarks/bookmarks.dart**. Replace `// TODO: Add Recipe Stream` with:

```
late Stream<List<Recipe>> recipeStream;
```

Next, replace `// TODO: Add initState` with:

```
@override
void initState() {
  super.initState();
  final repository = ref.read(repositoryProvider.notifier);
  recipeStream = repository.watchAllRecipes();
}
```

This will initialize the recipe stream.

Replace `// TODO: Replace with Stream` and the two subsequent lines with:

```
// 1
return StreamBuilder<List<Recipe>>(
  // 2
  stream: recipeStream,
  // 3
  builder: (context, AsyncSnapshot<List<Recipe>> snapshot) {
    // 4
    if (snapshot.connectionState == ConnectionState.active) {
      // 5
      recipes = snapshot.data ?? [];
    }
```

Don't worry about the red squiggles for now. This code:

1. Uses `StreamBuilder`, which uses a `List<Recipe>` stream type.
2. Uses the new `recipeStream` to return a stream of recipes for the builder to use.
3. Uses the builder callback to receive your **snapshot**.
4. Checks the state of the connection. When the state is active, you have data.

At the bottom of the method, find `// TODO: Add closing brackets` and replace it with:

```
  },
);
```

At this point, you've achieved one of your two goals: you've changed the **Recipes** screen to use streams. Next, you'll do the same for the **Groceries** tab.

Adding Streams to Groceries

To add streams to the grocery list, you'll need to watch the ingredient stream.

Open **ui/groceries/groceries.dart**.

Find the `initState()` method and replace `// TODO: Add Ingredient Stream` with:

```
final repository = ref.read(repositoryProvider.notifier);
final ingredientStream = repository.watchAllIngredients();
ingredientStream.listen(
  (ingredients) {
    setState(() {
      currentIngredients = ingredients;
    });
  },
);
```

In the `buildIngredientList()` method, remove:

```
final repository = ref.watch(repositoryProvider);
currentIngredients = repository.currentIngredients;
```

This is no longer needed as the stream is listened to above.

Finally, modify startSearch() as follows:

```
void startSearch(String searchString) {
  searching = searchString.isNotEmpty;
  searchIngredients = currentIngredients
      .where((element) => true ==
element.name?.contains(searchString))
      .toList();
  setState(() {});
}
```

Stop and restart your app. Make sure it works as before. Your main screen will look something like this after a search:

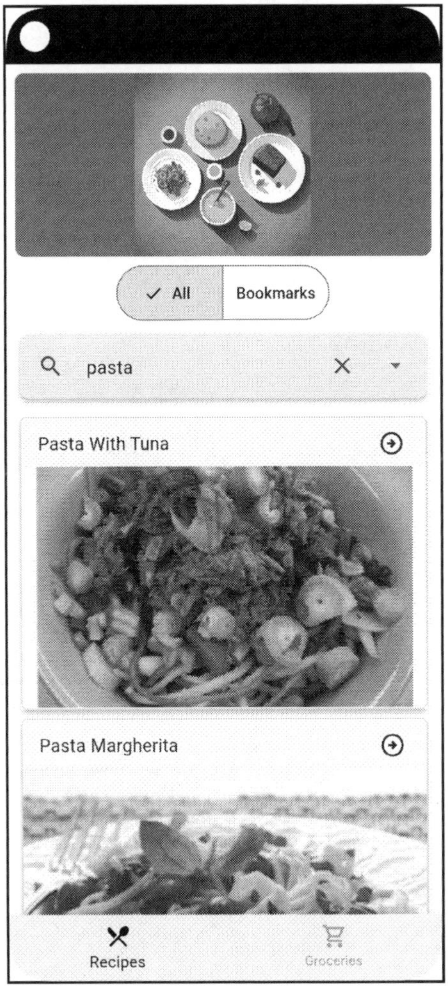

Tap a recipe. The **Details** page will look like this:

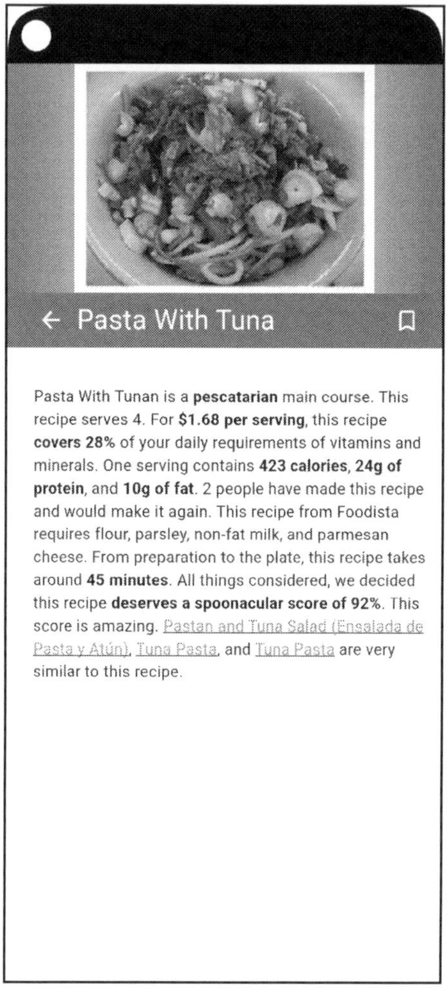

Next, tap the **Bookmark** button to return to the **Recipes** screen, then tap on the **Bookmarks** switch to see the recipe you just added:

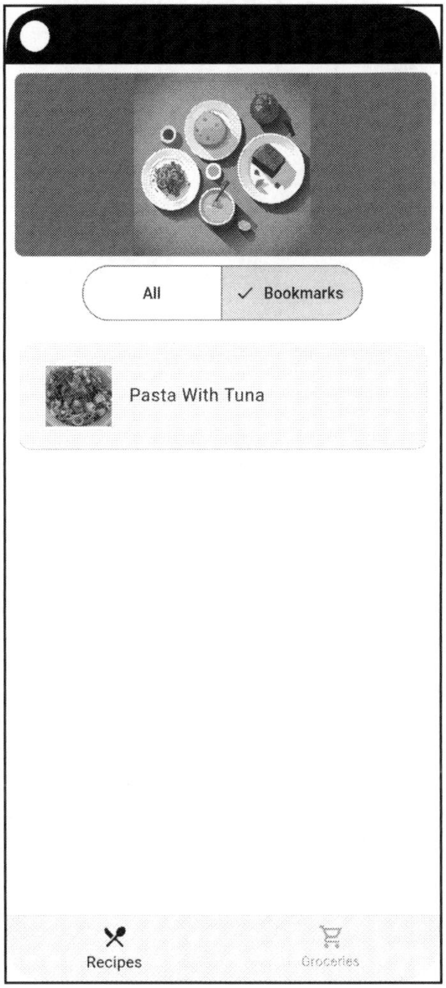

Finally, go to the **Groceries** tab and make sure the recipe ingredients are all showing.

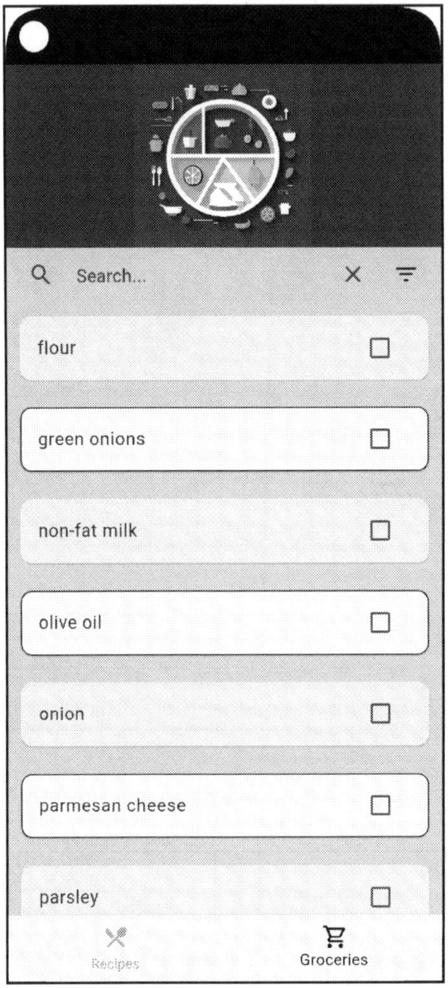

Congratulations! You're now using streams to control the flow of data. If any of the screens change, the other screens will know about that change and will update the screen.

You're also using the `Repository` interface, so you can go back and forth between a memory class and a different class in the future.

Key Points

- Streams are a way to asynchronously send data to other parts of your app.
- You usually create streams by using `StreamController`.
- Use `StreamBuilder` to add a stream to your UI.
- Abstract classes, or interfaces, are a great way to abstract functionality.

Where to Go From Here?

In this chapter, you learned how to use streams. If you want to learn more about the topic, visit the Dart documentation at https://dart.dev/tutorials/language/streams.

In the next chapter, you'll learn about databases and how to persist your data locally.

Chapter 15: Saving Data Locally

By Kevin David Moore

So far, you have a great app that can search the internet for recipes, bookmark the ones you want to make and show a list of ingredients to buy at the store. But what happens if you close the app, go to the store and try to look up your ingredients? They're gone! As you might have guessed, having an in-memory repository means that the data doesn't persist after your app closes.

One of the best ways to persist data is with a **database**. Android, iOS, macOS, Windows and the web provide the **SQLite** database system access. This allows you to **insert**, **read**, **update** and **remove** structured data that are persisted on disk.

In this chapter, you'll learn about using the **Drift** and **sqlbrite** packages.

By the end of the chapter, you'll know:

- How to **insert**, **fetch** and **remove recipes** or **ingredients**.
- How to use the **sqlbrite** library and receive updates via streams.
- How to leverage the features of the **Drift** library when working with databases.

Databases

Databases have been around for a long time, but being able to put a full-blown database on a phone is pretty amazing.

What *is* a database? Think of it like a file cabinet containing folders with sheets of paper. A database has tables, file folders that store data, and sheets of paper.

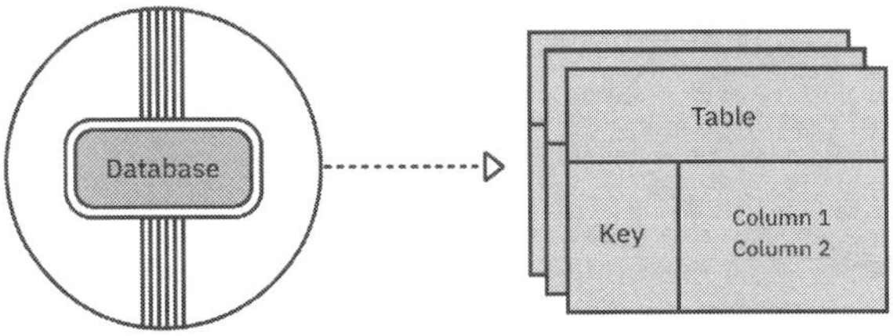

Database tables have columns defining data, which are then stored in rows. One of the most popular database management languages is **Structured Query Language**, commonly known as **SQL**.

You use SQL commands to get the data in and out of the database.

Using SQL

The SQLite database system on Android and iOS is an embedded engine that runs in the same process as the app. SQLite is lightweight, taking up less than **500 KB** on most systems.

When SQLite creates a database, it stores it in one file inside the app. These files are **cross-platform**, meaning you can pull a file off a phone and read it on a regular computer.

Unlike a database server, SQLite needs no server configuration or server process.

While SQLite is small and runs fast, it still requires some knowledge of the SQL language and how to create databases, tables and execute SQL commands.

Writing Queries

One of the most important parts of SQL is writing a **query**. A query is a **question** or **inquiry** about a data set. To make a query, use the SELECT command followed by any columns you want the database to return, then the table name. For example:

```
// 1
SELECT name, address FROM Customers;
// 2
SELECT * FROM Customers;
// 3
SELECT name, address FROM Customers WHERE name LIKE 'A%';
```

Here's what's happening in the code above:

1. Returns the name and address columns from the CUSTOMERS table.
2. Using *, returns all columns from the specified table.
3. Uses WHERE to filter the returned data. In this case, it only returns data where NAME starts with A.

Adding Data

You can add data using the INSERT statement:

```
INSERT INTO Customers (NAME, ADDRESS) VALUES (value1, value2);
```

While you don't have to list all the columns, if you want to add all the values, the values must be in the order you used to define the columns. It's best practice to list the column names whenever you insert data. That makes it easier to update your values list if, say, you add a column in the middle.

Deleting Data

To delete data, use the DELETE statement:

```
DELETE FROM Customers WHERE id = 1;
```

If you don't use the WHERE clause, you'll delete all the data from the table. Here, you delete the customer whose id equals 1. You can use broader conditions, of course. For example, you might delete all the customers with a given city.

Updating Data

You use `UPDATE` to update your data. You won't need this command for this app, but for reference, the syntax is:

```
UPDATE customers
SET
  phone = '555-12345',
WHERE id = 1;
```

This updates the customer's phone number whose `id` equals 1.

sqlbrite

The sqlbrite library is a reactive stream wrapper around sqflite. It allows you to set up streams so you can receive events when there's a change in your database. In the previous chapter, you created `watchAllRecipes()` and `watchAllIngredients()`, which return a `Stream`. To create these streams from a database, sqlbrite uses a similar approach.

Adding a Database to Recipe Finder

If you're following along with your app, open it and keep using it with this chapter. If not, locate this chapter's **projects** folder and open the **starter** folder.

> **Note**: If you use the starter app, don't forget to add your **apiKey** in **network/spoonacular_service.dart**.

Your app manages two types of data: **recipes** and **ingredients**, which you'll model according to this diagram:

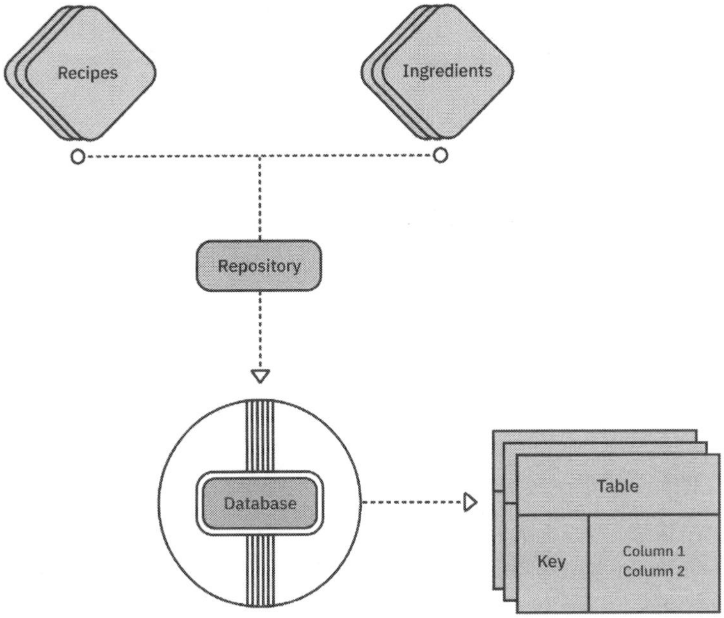

In this chapter, you'll use the **Drift** package. You'll then swap the memory repository for the new database repository.

Adding Libraries

Open **pubspec.yaml** and add the following packages after the **flutter_riverpod** package:

```
synchronized: ^3.1.0
sqlbrite: ^2.6.0
sqlite3_flutter_libs: ^0.5.18
web_ffi: ^0.7.2
sqlite3: ^2.1.0
```

These packages provide the following:

1. **synchronized**: Helps implement **lock mechanisms** to prevent concurrent access.
2. **sqlbrite**: Reactive wrapper around sqflite that receives changes happening in the database via streams.

3. **sqlite3_flutter_libs**: Native sqlite3 libraries for mobile.
4. **web_ffi**: `web_ffi` is a drop-in solution for using `dart:ffi` on the web. Used for Flutter web databases.
5. **sqlite3**: Provides **Dart bindings** to SQLite via dart:ffi

Run **Pub Get** or `flutter pub get`.

Now, you're ready to create your first database.

Using the Drift Library

Drift is a package that's intentionally similar to Android's **Room** library.

You don't need to write SQL code and the setup is a lot easier. You'll write specific **Dart classes**, and Drift will take care of the necessary **translations** to and from SQL code.

You need one file for dealing with the database and one for the repository. To start, add Drift to **pubspec.yaml**, after `sqlite3`:

```
  drift: ^2.13.1
```

Next, add the **Drift generator**, which will write code for you, in the `dev_dependencies` section after `chopper_generator`:

```
  drift_dev: ^2.13.2
```

Finally, run any of the following:

- `flutter pub get` from Terminal
- **Pub get** from the IDE window
- **Tools ▸ Flutter ▸ Flutter Pub Get**

Database Classes

For your next step, you need to create a set of classes that will describe and create the **database**, **tables** and **Data Access Objects** (DAOs). Below is a diagram showing how your database will look.

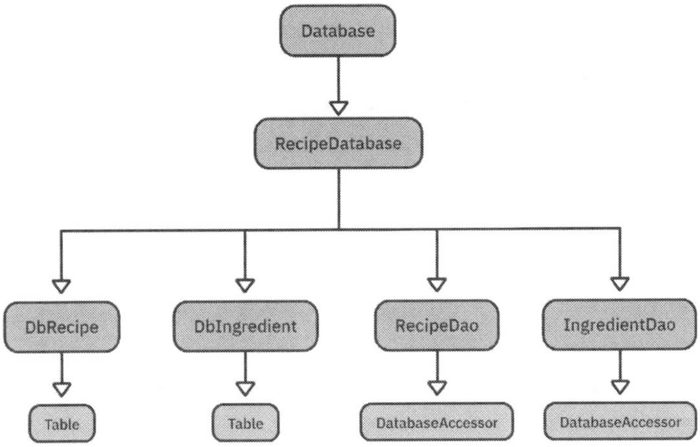

`Database`, `Table` and `DatabaseAccessor` are from Drift. You'll create the other classes.

> **Note**: A **DAO** (Data Access Object) is a class that's in charge of accessing data from the database. You use it to separate your business logic code, e.g., the one that fetches the ingredients of a recipe, from the details of the persistence layer, which is SQLite in this case. A DAO can be a class, an interface or an abstract class. In this chapter, you'll implement DAOs using classes.

Open the following files in the **data/database** directory and uncomment the code:

1. **unsupported.dart**
2. **native.dart**
3. **web.dart**

These files will be used below.

Inside **database**, create a file called **recipe_db.dart**. This file will define the database for recipes and ingredients. Add the following imports:

```
import 'package:drift/drift.dart';
import 'connection.dart' as impl;
import '../models/models.dart';
```

This will add **Drift** and your models. `connection.dart` allows the code to create a connection based on whether the app is running on mobile, desktop or the web.

Now, add a `part` statement and some TODOs:

```
part 'recipe_db.g.dart';

// TODO: Add DbRecipe table definition here

// TODO: Add DbIngredient table definition here

// TODO: Add @DriftDatabase() and RecipeDatabase() here

// TODO: Add RecipeDao here

// TODO: Add IngredientDao

// TODO: Add dbRecipeToModelRecipe here

// TODO: Add recipeToInsertableDbRecipe here

// TODO: Add dbIngredientToIngredient and
ingredientToInsertableDbIngredient here
```

Remember that the `part` statement is a way to combine one file into another to form a whole file. The **Drift generator** will create this file for you later when you run the `build_runner` command. Until then, it'll display a red squiggle.

Creating Recipe and Ingredient Tables

To create a table in Drift, you need to create a class that extends `Table`. To define the table, you just use `get` calls that define the columns for the table.

Still in **recipe_db.dart**, replace `// TODO: Add DbRecipe table definition here` with the following:

```
// 1
class DbRecipe extends Table {
  // 2
  IntColumn get id => integer().autoIncrement()();
```

```
  // 3
  TextColumn get label => text()();

  // 4
  TextColumn get image => text()();

  // 5
  TextColumn get description => text()();

  // 6
  BoolColumn get bookmarked  => boolean()();
}
```

Here's what you do in this code:

1. Create a class named `DbRecipe` that extends `Table`.
2. Create a column named `id` with type as an integer. `autoIncrement()` automatically creates and **increments** the IDs for you.
3. Create a **label** column made up of text.
4. Create an **image** column for storing the URL of the image.
5. Create a **description** text column.
6. Create a **bookmarked** column of type Boolean.

This definition is a bit unusual. You first define the column type with type classes that handle different types:

- **IntColumn**: Integers.
- **BoolColumn**: Booleans.
- **TextColumn**: Text.
- **DateTimeColumn**: Dates.
- **RealColumn**: Doubles.
- **BlobColumn**: Arbitrary blobs of data.

It also uses a "double" method call, where each call returns a builder. For example, to create `IntColumn`, you need to make a final call with the extra `()` to create it.

Defining the Ingredient Table

Now, find and replace `// TODO: Add DbIngredient table definition here` with the following:

```
class DbIngredient extends Table {
  IntColumn get id => integer().autoIncrement()();

  IntColumn get recipeId => integer()();

  TextColumn get name => text()();

  RealColumn get amount => real()();

}
```

Now, for the fun part.

Creating the Database Class

Drift uses **annotations**. The first one you need is `@DriftDatabase`. This specifies the **tables** and **Data Access Objects** (DAO) to use.

Still in **recipe_db.dart**, add this class with the annotation by replacing `// TODO: Add @DriftDatabase and RecipeDatabase() here` with the following:

```
// 1
@DriftDatabase(
  tables: [
    DbRecipe,
    DbIngredient,
  ],
  daos: [
    RecipeDao,
    IngredientDao,
  ]
)
// 2
class RecipeDatabase extends _$RecipeDatabase {
  // 3
  RecipeDatabase() : super(impl.connect());

  // 4
  @override
  int get schemaVersion => 1;
}
```

Here's what the above code does:

1. Describe the **tables**, which you defined above, and **DAOs** this database will use. You'll create the DAOs in a bit.
2. Extend `_$RecipeDatabase`, which the Drift generator will create. This doesn't exist yet, but the `part` import at the top will include it.
3. To support the **web platform**, one of the imports is `connection.dart`. This file will import either the **native** or **web files** so you get the proper database initialization.
4. Set the database or schema version to `1`. Increment this when your database changes.

There's still a bit more to do. You need to create DAOs, which are classes that are specific to a table and allow you to **call methods** to access that table.

Creating the DAO Classes

Your first step is to create the `RecipeDao` class. You'll see more red squiggles, just ignore them for now. With **recipe_db.dart** still open, replace `// TODO: Add RecipeDao here` with the following:

```
// 1
@DriftAccessor(tables: [DbRecipe])
// 2
class RecipeDao extends DatabaseAccessor<RecipeDatabase> with
_$RecipeDaoMixin {
  // 3
  final RecipeDatabase db;

  RecipeDao(this.db) : super(db);

  // 4
  Future<List<DbRecipeData>> findAllRecipes() =>
select(dbRecipe).get();

  // 5
  Stream<List<Recipe>> watchAllRecipes() {
    // TODO: Add watchAllRecipes code here
  }

  // 6
  Future<List<DbRecipeData>> findRecipeById(int id) =>
      (select(dbRecipe)..where((tbl) =>
tbl.id.equals(id))).get();
```

```
  // 7
  Future<int> insertRecipe(Insertable<DbRecipeData> recipe) =>
      into(dbRecipe).insert(recipe);

  // 8
  Future deleteRecipe(int id) => Future.value(
      (delete(dbRecipe)..where((tbl) =>
tbl.id.equals(id))).go());
}
```

Here's what's going on there:

1. `@DriftAccessor` annotation that specifies the following class is a **DAO class** for the `DbRecipe` table.
2. Create the DAO class that extends the Drift `DatabaseAccessor` with the mixin, `_$RecipeDaoMixin`. This mixin will be created for you.
3. Create a field to hold an **instance** of your **database**.
4. Use a simple `select()` query to **find** all recipes.
5. Define `watchAllRecipes()`, but skip the implementation for now.
6. Define a more complex query that uses `where` to **fetch** recipes by **ID**.
7. Use `into()` and `insert()` to **add** a new recipe.
8. Use `delete()` and `where()` to **delete** a specific recipe.

Drift can be a bit more complex to set up in some ways, but it's easy to use. Most of these calls are one-liners and quite easy to read.

Let's break down the find method:

```
(select(dbRecipe)..where((tbl) => tbl.id.equals(id))).get();
```

1. **select** takes a **table name**.
2. Use the `..` to **cascade** a `where` function.
3. This takes a **variable name** `tbl`. This can be any name.
4. It returns all **rows** whose IDs match the one in the table.
5. Call the `get` method to **execute** the query.

Inserting data is pretty simple. Just specify the **table** and **pass** in the class. Notice that you're not passing the model recipe, you're passing `Insertable`, which is an interface that Drift requires. When you generate the `part` file, you'll see a new class, `DbRecipeData`, which implements this interface. Let's break this down:

```
into(dbRecipe).insert(recipe)
```

1. This method will **insert** a record into the recipe table.
2. Execute the insert command with the given recipe.

Deleting requires the **table** and a `where`. This function just returns `true` for those rows you want to delete. Instead of `get()`, you use `go()`.

Now, replace `// TODO: Add IngredientDao` with the following. Again, ignoring the red squiggles. They'll go away when all the new classes are in place.

```
// 1
@DriftAccessor(tables: [DbIngredient])
// 2
class IngredientDao extends DatabaseAccessor<RecipeDatabase>
    with _$IngredientDaoMixin {
  final RecipeDatabase db;

  IngredientDao(this.db) : super(db);

  Future<List<DbIngredientData>> findAllIngredients() =>
      select(dbIngredient).get();

  // 3
  Stream<List<DbIngredientData>> watchAllIngredients() =>
      select(dbIngredient).watch();

  // 4
  Future<List<DbIngredientData>> findRecipeIngredients(int id)
=>
      (select(dbIngredient)..where((tbl) =>
tbl.recipeId.equals(id))).get();

  // 5
  Future<int> insertIngredient(Insertable<DbIngredientData>
ingredient) =>
      into(dbIngredient).insert(ingredient);

  // 6
  Future deleteIngredient(int id) =>
      Future.value((delete(dbIngredient)..where((tbl) =>
          tbl.id.equals(id))).go());
}
```

Here's what's going on above:

1. Similar to `RecipeDao`, you specify that this class is a DAO for `DbIngredient`.
2. Extend `DatabaseAccessor` with `_$IngredientDaoMixin`.
3. Call `watch()` to create a **stream**.
4. Use `where()` to **select** all ingredients that match the **recipe ID**.
5. Use `into()` and `insert()` to **add** a new ingredient.
6. Use `delete()` plus `where()` to **delete** a specific ingredient.

Now it's time to generate the part file.

Generating the Part File

Now, you need to create the Drift part file. In Terminal, run:

```
dart run build_runner build --delete-conflicting-outputs
```

This generates **recipe_db.g.dart**.

> **Note**: `--delete-conflicting-outputs` deletes previously generated files and then rebuilds them.

After the file has been generated, open **recipe_db.g.dart** and take a look. It's a very large file. It generated several classes, saving you a lot of work!

> **Note**: If Android Studio doesn't detect the presence of the newly generated **recipe_db.g.dart** file, right-click the lib folder and select **Reload from Disk**.

Now that you've defined these tables, you need to create methods that convert your database classes to your regular model classes and back.

Converting Your Drift Recipes

At the end of **recipe_db.dart**, replace `// TODO: Add dbRecipeToModelRecipe here` with:

```
// Conversion Methods
Recipe dbRecipeToModelRecipe(
    DbRecipeData recipe, List<Ingredient> ingredients) {
  return Recipe(
    id: recipe.id,
    label: recipe.label,
    image: recipe.image,
    description: recipe.description,
    bookmarked: recipe.bookmarked,
    ingredients: ingredients,
  );
}
```

This converts a **Drift recipe** to a **model recipe**.

The next method converts `Recipe` to a **class** that you can insert into a **Drift database**. Replace `// TODO: Add recipeToInsertableDbRecipe here` with this:

```
Insertable<DbRecipeData> recipeToInsertableDbRecipe(Recipe
recipe) {
  return DbRecipeCompanion.insert(
    id: Value.ofNullable(recipe.id),
    label: recipe.label ?? '',
    image: recipe.image ?? '',
    description: recipe.description ?? '',
    bookmarked: recipe.bookmarked,
  );
}
```

`Insertable` is an **interface** for objects that can be inserted into the database or updated. Use the generated `DbRecipeCompanion.insert()` to create that class.

Creating Classes for Ingredients

Next, you'll do the same for the **ingredients models**. Replace `// TODO: Add dbIngredientToIngredient and ingredientToInsertableDbIngredient here` with the following:

```
Ingredient dbIngredientToIngredient(DbIngredientData ingredient)
{
  return Ingredient(
    id: ingredient.id,
    recipeId: ingredient.recipeId,
    name: ingredient.name,
```

```
    amount: ingredient.amount,
  );
}

DbIngredientCompanion ingredientToInsertableDbIngredient(
    Ingredient ingredient) {
  return DbIngredientCompanion.insert(
    recipeId: ingredient.recipeId ?? 0,
    name: ingredient.name ?? '',
    amount: ingredient.amount ?? 0,
  );
}
```

These methods convert a Drift ingredient into an instance of `Ingredient` and vice versa.

Updating watchAllRecipes()

Now that you've written the conversion methods, you can update `watchAllRecipes()`.

You'll notice most of the red squiggles in **data/database/recipe_db.dart** are now gone. But there's one left.

> **Note**: If you're having problems, run `flutter clean` and `flutter pub get` in case your IDE isn't up to date with the newly generated files.
>
> If you're still having problems, try deleting `pubspec.lock`, then run `flutter clean`, and `flutter pub get`.

Locate `// TODO: Add watchAllRecipes code here` and replace it with:

```
// 1
return select(dbRecipe)
  // 2
  .watch()
  // 3
  .map((rows) {
    final recipes = <Recipe>[];
    // 4
    for (final row in rows) {
      // 5
      final recipe = dbRecipeToModelRecipe(row, <Ingredient>[]);
      // 6
      if (!recipes.contains(recipe)) {
          recipes.add(recipe);
      }
```

```
      }
      return recipes;
    },
  );
```

Here's the step-by-step:

1. Use `select()` to start a **query**.
2. Create a **stream**.
3. Map each list of **rows**.
4. For each row, execute the code below.
5. Convert the **recipe row** to a **regular recipe** with an **empty ingredient list**.
6. Add the **recipe** to your **recipes list**.

This creates a stream of recipes.

No more red squiggles. :]

Run the app to make sure everything works correctly. You can run it on Android, iOS, macOs, the web or Windows. On the web, it should look something like:

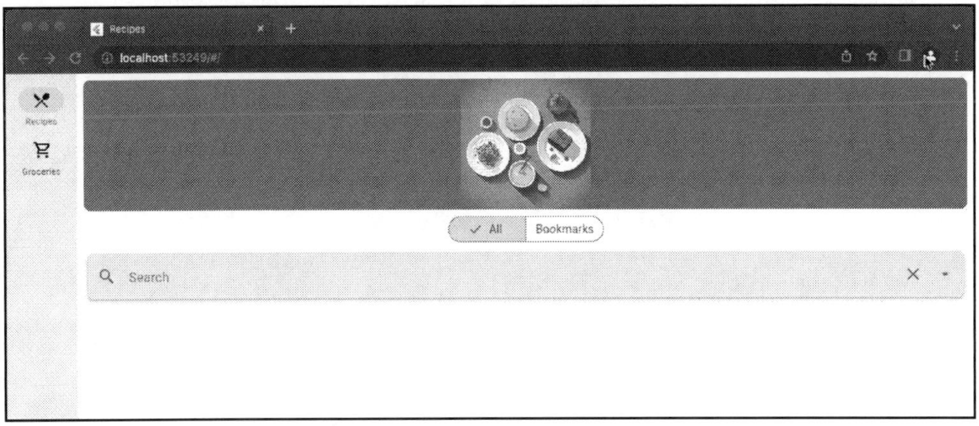

Creating the Drift Repository

Now that you have the Drift database code written, you need to write a **repository** to handle it. You'll create a class named `DBRepository` that implements `Repository`:

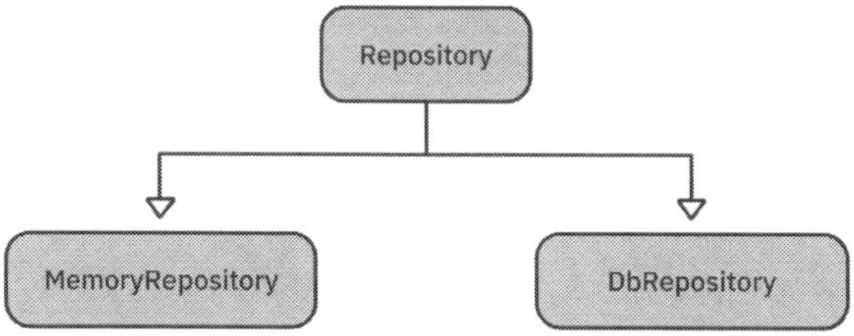

In the **repositories** directory, create a new file named **db_repository.dart**. Add the following imports:

```
import 'dart:async';
import 'package:flutter_riverpod/flutter_riverpod.dart';
import '../database/recipe_db.dart';
import '../models/current_recipe_data.dart';
import '../models/models.dart';
import '../repositories/repository.dart';
```

This imports your models, the repository interface and your newly-created **recipe_db.dart**.

Next, create `DBRepository` and some fields:

```
class DBRepository extends Notifier<CurrentRecipeData>
implements Repository {
  // 1
  late RecipeDatabase recipeDatabase;
  // 2
  late RecipeDao _recipeDao;
  // 3
  late IngredientDao _ingredientDao;
  // 4
  Stream<List<Ingredient>>? ingredientStream;
  // 5
  Stream<List<Recipe>>? recipeStream;

  @override
  CurrentRecipeData build() {
    const currentRecipeData = CurrentRecipeData();
    return currentRecipeData;
  }

  // TODO: Add findAllRecipes()
```

```
  // TODO: Add watchAllRecipes()
  // TODO: Add watchAllIngredients()
  // TODO: Add findRecipeById()
  // TODO: Add findAllIngredients()
  // TODO: Add findRecipeIngredients()
  // TODO: Add insertRecipe()
  // TODO: Add insertIngredients()
  // TODO: Add Delete methods

  @override
  Future init() async {
    // 6
    recipeDatabase = RecipeDatabase();
    // 7
    _recipeDao = recipeDatabase.recipeDao;
    _ingredientDao = recipeDatabase.ingredientDao;
  }

  @override
  void close() {
    // 8
    recipeDatabase.close();
  }
}
```

Here's what's happening in the code above:

1. Stores an instance of the Drift `RecipeDatabase`.
2. Stores a private `RecipeDao` to handle **recipes**.
3. Stores a private `IngredientDao` that handles **ingredients**.
4. Stores a **stream** that watches **ingredients**.
5. Stores a **stream** that watches **recipes**.
6. Creates your **database**.
7. Gets **instances** of your **DAOs**.
8. Closes the database.

Implementing the Repository

As you did in past chapters, you'll now add all the missing methods following the `TODO:` indications.Replace `// TODO: Add findAllRecipes()` with:

```
@override
Future<List<Recipe>> findAllRecipes() {
```

```
    // 1
    return _recipeDao.findAllRecipes()
      // 2
      .then<List<Recipe>>(
      (List<DbRecipeData> dbRecipes) async {
        final recipes = <Recipe>[];
        // 3
        for (final dbRecipe in dbRecipes) {
          // 4
          final ingredients = await
  findRecipeIngredients(dbRecipe.id);
          // 5
          final recipe = dbRecipeToModelRecipe(dbRecipe,
  ingredients);
          recipes.add(recipe);
        }
        return recipes;
      },
    );
  }
```

The code above does the following:

1. Uses `RecipeDao` to find all recipes.
2. Takes the **list** of `DbRecipeData` items, executing `then` after `findAllRecipes()` finishes.
3. For each recipe:
4. Gets a list of **ingredients** for the given **recipe ID**.
5. Converts the Drift recipe to a model recipe, then adds the recipe to the list.

The next step is simple. Find `// TODO: Add watchAllRecipes()` and substitute it with:

```
  @override
  Stream<List<Recipe>> watchAllRecipes() {
    recipeStream ??= _recipeDao.watchAllRecipes();
    return recipeStream!;
  }
```

This just calls the same method name on the recipe DAO class, then saves an instance so you don't create multiple streams.

Next, replace `// TODO: Add watchAllIngredients()` with:

```
  @override
  Stream<List<Ingredient>> watchAllIngredients() {
```

```
    if (ingredientStream == null) {
      // 1
      final stream = _ingredientDao.watchAllIngredients();
      // 2
      ingredientStream = stream.map((dbIngredients) {
        final ingredients = <Ingredient>[];
        // 3
        for (final dbIngredient in dbIngredients) {
          ingredients.add(dbIngredientToIngredient(dbIngredient));
        }
        return ingredients;
      },);
    }
    return ingredientStream!;
  }
```

This:

1. Gets a **stream** of **ingredients**.
2. Maps each ingredient in the stream to a stream of **model** ingredients
3. Converts each ingredient in the **list** to a **model ingredient**.

Finding Recipes and Ingredients

The find methods are a bit easier, but they still need to convert each database class to a model class.

Replace `// TODO: Add findRecipeById()` with:

```
@override
Future<Recipe> findRecipeById(int id) async {
    // 1
    final ingredients = await findRecipeIngredients(id);
    // 2
    return _recipeDao.findRecipeById(id).then((listOfRecipes) =>
        dbRecipeToModelRecipe(listOfRecipes.first,
ingredients));
}
```

1. Find all of the ingredients for the given recipe.
2. Since `findRecipeById()` returns a list, just take the first one and convert it.

Look for `// TODO: Add findAllIngredients()` and replace it with:

```
@override
Future<List<Ingredient>> findAllIngredients() {
```

```
    return
  _ingredientDao.findAllIngredients().then<List<Ingredient>>(
      (List<DbIngredientData> dbIngredients) {
        final ingredients = <Ingredient>[];
        for (final ingredient in dbIngredients) {
          ingredients.add(dbIngredientToIngredient(ingredient));
        }
        return ingredients;
      },
    );
  }
```

This method is almost like `watchAllIngredients()`, except it doesn't use a stream.

Finding all the ingredients for a recipe is similar. Replace `// TODO: Add findRecipeIngredients()` with:

```
@override
Future<List<Ingredient>> findRecipeIngredients(int recipeId) {
  return _ingredientDao.findRecipeIngredients(recipeId).then(
    (listOfIngredients) {
      final ingredients = <Ingredient>[];
      for (final ingredient in listOfIngredients) {
        ingredients.add(dbIngredientToIngredient(ingredient));
      }
      return ingredients;
    },
  );
}
```

This method finds all the **ingredients** associated with a **single recipe**.Now it's time to look at inserting recipes.

Inserting Recipes and Ingredients

To insert a recipe, you first insert the recipe itself and then insert all its ingredients. Replace `// TODO: Add insertRecipe()` with:

```
@override
Future<int> insertRecipe(Recipe recipe) {
  // 1
  if (state.currentRecipes.contains(recipe)) {
    return Future.value(0);
  }
  return Future(
    () async {
      // 2
      state =
          state.copyWith(currentRecipes:
```

```
[...state.currentRecipes, recipe]);
      // 3
      final id =
      await _recipeDao.insertRecipe(
        recipeToInsertableDbRecipe(recipe),
      );
      final ingredients = <Ingredient>[];
      for (final ingredient in recipe.ingredients) {
        // 4
        ingredients.add(ingredient.copyWith(recipeId: id));
      }
      // 5
      insertIngredients(ingredients);
      return id;
    },
  );
}
```

Here you:

1. Check to see if the recipe already exists.
2. Update the **state** with the **new recipe**.
3. Use the recipe **DAO** to insert a converted model recipe.
4. Add a **copy** of the **ingredient** with the **recipe ID** for each ingredient.
5. Insert all the ingredients. You'll define these next.

Now, it's finally time to add methods to insert ingredients. Replace `// TODO: Add insertIngredients()` with:

```
@override
Future<List<int>> insertIngredients(List<Ingredient>
ingredients) {
  return Future(
    () {
      // 1
      if (ingredients.isEmpty) {
        return <int>[];
      }
      final resultIds = <int>[];
      for (final ingredient in ingredients) {
        // 2
        final dbIngredient =
            ingredientToInsertableDbIngredient(ingredient);
        // 3
        _ingredientDao
            .insertIngredient(dbIngredient)
            .then((int id) => resultIds.add(id));
```

```
      }
      // 4
      state = state.copyWith(
        currentIngredients:
[...state.currentIngredients, ...ingredients]);

      return resultIds;
    },
  );
}
```

This code:

1. Checks to make sure you have at least one ingredient.
2. Converts the ingredient.
3. Inserts the ingredient into the **database** and adds a new ID to the list.
4. Update the state with the new **ingredients**.

Now, it's time to add code to delete recipes and ingredients.

Methods for Deleting Recipes and Ingredients

Deleting is much easier. You need to call the DAO methods. Replace `// TODO: Add Delete methods` with:

```
@override
Future<void> deleteRecipe(Recipe recipe) {
  if (recipe.id != null) {
    // 1
    final updatedList = [...state.currentRecipes];
    updatedList.remove(recipe);
    state = state.copyWith(currentRecipes: updatedList);
    // 2
    _recipeDao.deleteRecipe(recipe.id!);
    deleteRecipeIngredients(recipe.id!);
  }
  return Future.value();
}

@override
Future<void> deleteIngredient(Ingredient ingredient) {
  if (ingredient.id != null) {
    // 3
    return _ingredientDao.deleteIngredient(ingredient.id!);
  } else {
    return Future.value();
  }
```

```
}

@override
Future<void> deleteIngredients(List<Ingredient> ingredients) {
  for (final ingredient in ingredients) {
    if (ingredient.id != null) {
      _ingredientDao.deleteIngredient(ingredient.id!);
    }
  }
  return Future.value();
}

@override
Future<void> deleteRecipeIngredients(int recipeId) async {
  // 4
  final ingredients = await findRecipeIngredients(recipeId);
  // 5
  return deleteIngredients(ingredients);
}
```

The last method is the only one that's different. In the code above, you:

1. Delete the recipe from our state list.
2. Use the RecipeDao to delete the **recipe**.
3. Use the IngredientDao to delete the **ingredient**.
4. Find all ingredients for the given **recipe ID**.
5. Delete the **list** of ingredients.

Phew! The hard work is over.

Replacing the Repository

Now, you just have to replace your **memory repository** with your shiny new **db repository**.

Open **providers.dart**. Add the import:

```
import 'data/repositories/db_repository.dart';
```

and remove the `memory_repository.dart` import.

Change the `repositoryProvider` from:

```
final repositoryProvider =
    NotifierProvider<MemoryRepository, CurrentRecipeData>(() {
  return MemoryRepository();
});
```

to:

```
final repositoryProvider =
    NotifierProvider<DBRepository, CurrentRecipeData>(() {
      throw UnimplementedError();
});
```

Open **main.dart**. Add the import:

```
import 'data/repositories/db_repository.dart';
```

Delete the import statement: `import 'data/memory_repository.dart';` if present.

Add this after the `sharedPrefs`:

```
final repository = DBRepository();
await repository.init();
```

Then, add the repository to the overrides:

```
repositoryProvider.overrideWith(() { return repository; }),
```

Running the App

Stop the running app, build and run. Try performing searches, adding bookmarks, checking the groceries and deleting bookmarks. It will work just the same as with `MemoryRepository`, with the added value that bookmarks are persisted across application runs. Try running on Mac, Windows or the web.

Congratulations! Now, your app is using all the power provided by **Drift** to store data in a local database!

Key Points

- Databases **persist** data **locally** to the device.
- Data stored in databases are available after the **app restarts**.
- The **Drift** package is more powerful, easier to set up and you interact with the database via Dart classes that have clear responsibilities.

Where to Go From Here?

To learn about:

- **Databases and SQLite**, go to https://flutter.dev/docs/cookbook/persistence/sqlite.
- **Drift**, go to https://pub.dev/packages/drift.
- **sqlbrite** go to https://pub.dev/packages/sqlbrite.
- **The database that started it all**, go to https://www.sqlite.org/index.html.

In the next section, you'll learn about Firebase and how to use Firestore Database.

Section V: Working With Firebase Cloud Firestore

In this section you will learn how to create and use a Firebase Cloud Firestore. You will learn how to use it to add and retrieve data. Then you will learn about authentication and how to secure your data.

Chapter 16: Firebase Cloud Firestore

By Vincenzo Guzzi, Kevin David Moore & Stef Patterson

When you want to store information for many people, you can't realistically store it on one person's phone. It has to be stored in the cloud. You *could* hire a team of developers to design and implement a backend system that connects to a database via a set of APIs. But, this could take months. Wouldn't it be great if you could just connect to an existing system?

This is where **Firebase Cloud Firestore** comes in. You no longer need to write complicated apps that use thousands of lines of async tasks and threaded processes to simulate reactiveness. With Cloud Firestore, you'll be up and running in no time.

In this chapter, you'll add an instant messaging feature to the **Yummy** app.

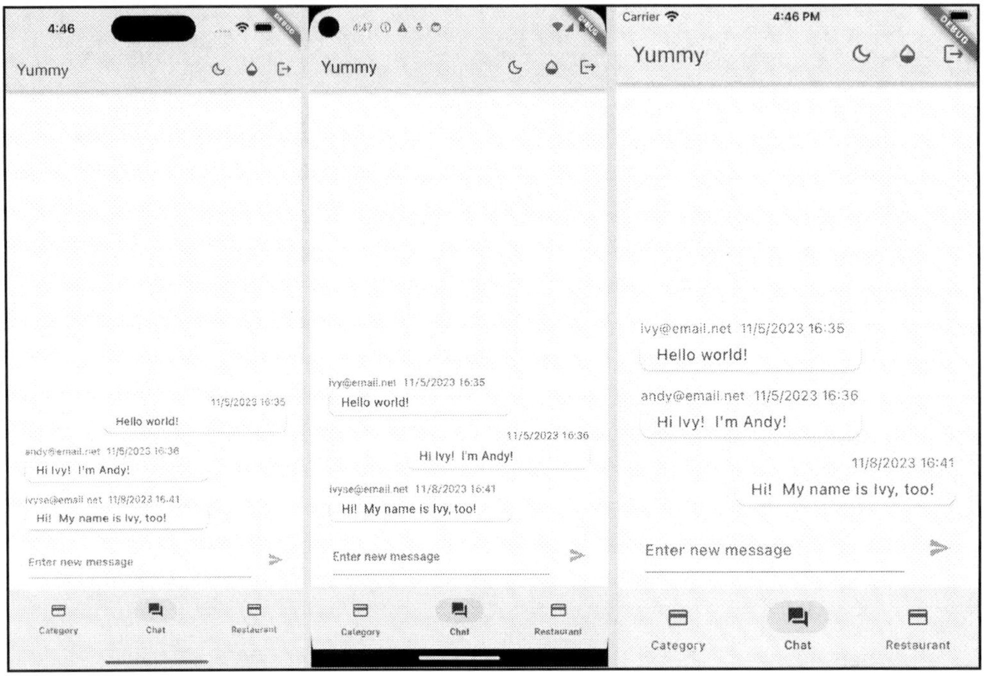

While adding this feature, you'll learn:

- About **Cloud Firestore** and when to use it.
- The steps required to set up a **Firebase project** with the **Cloud Firestore**.
- How to set up user **authentication**.
- How to connect to, **query** and **populate** the **Cloud Firestore**.
- How to use the **Cloud Firestore** to build your own **instant messaging app**.

Getting Started

First, open the **starter** project from this chapter's **project materials** and run `flutter pub get`.

Next, **build** and **run** your project. You'll see the Yummy app's **Chat** tab.

Right now, your app doesn't do much, but when you're done, you'll know how to use **Cloud Firestore** to send and receive messages.

What is Cloud Firestore?

Google has two **NoSQL document databases** within the Firebase suite of tools: **Realtime Database** and **Cloud Firestore**. But what's the difference?

Google created **Firestore** to enable large-scale software with deeply layered data. You can query data and receive it separately, creating a truly elastic environment that copes well as your data set grows.

Realtime Database, though still a document-driven NoSQL database, returns data in **JSON** format. When you query a tree of JSON data, it includes all of its child nodes. To keep your transactions light and nimble, you have to keep your **data hierarchy** as flat as possible.

Both of these solutions are great and have similarities. They each have a free plan, and after you've reached your limit, you can pay-as-you-go. In both solutions, you don't have to deploy and maintain your own servers, and each has live updates.

There are some differences, and it's important to know when to use one and not the other. Here are some key areas for each database:

Firebase Cloud Firestore

- Has a free plan but charges per transaction and, to a lesser extent, for storage used past the limit.
- It's easy to scale.
- Stores data in **document collections**.
- Can handle complex, deeply layered data sets and relations.
- Supports indexed queries with compound sorting and filtering.
- Available for mobile and web, including offline support.

Firebase Realtime Database

- Also has a free plan, but charges for storage used, not for queries made, past the limit.
- Extremely low latency.
- Data is stored in a single **JSON tree**.
- Easy to store simple data using JSON.
- You can either sort or filter on a query, but not both.
- Supports Apple and Android apps, including offline support. Doesn't support offline web clients.

In this chapter, you'll be using **Cloud Firestore**.

Note: To see a full comparison, see Google's Choose a Database: Cloud Firestore or Realtime Database (https://firebase.google.com/docs/database/rtdb-vs-firestore). Google has a lot of other database options (https://cloud.google.com/products/databases) beyond NoSQL databases.

Setting Up a Firebase Project

Before you can use any of Google's Cloud services, you have to create a project on the **Firebase Console**.

Note: You'll create your **free tier** Cloud Firestore database later.

First, go to https://console.firebase.google.com and click **Create a project**.

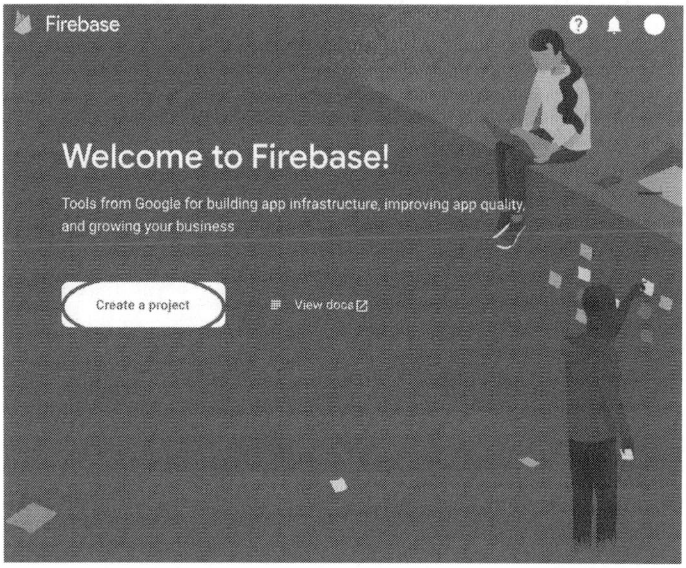

Name your project **KodecoChat**, and click **Continue**. If you've never created a Firebase project, you'll be prompted to read and accept the Firebase terms, shown below on the left.

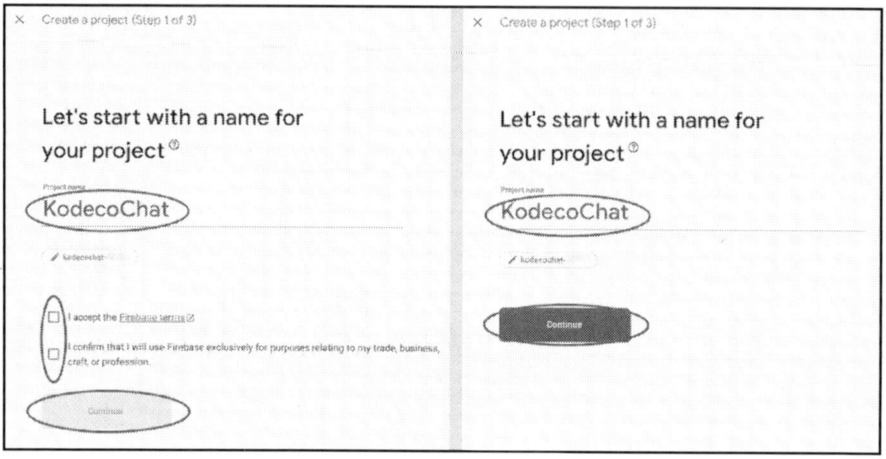

Disable **Google Analytics** since you don't need it for this chapter, and click **Create project**.

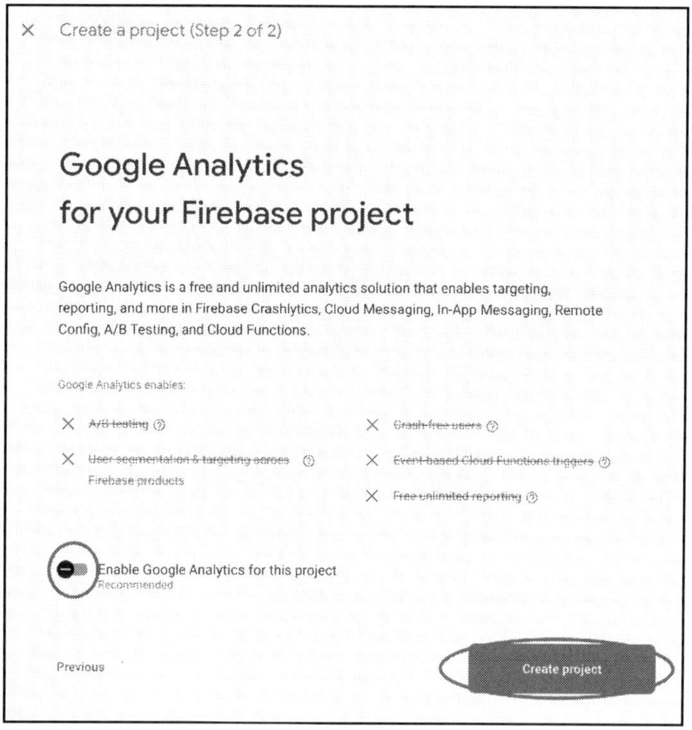

Give Google a minute to create your project.

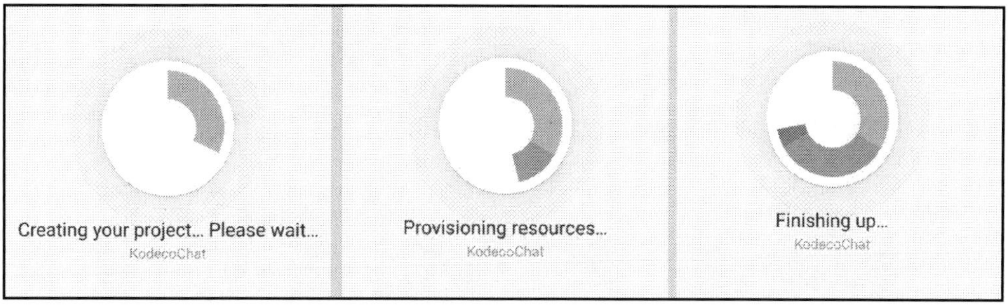

When your project's ready, click **Continue**.

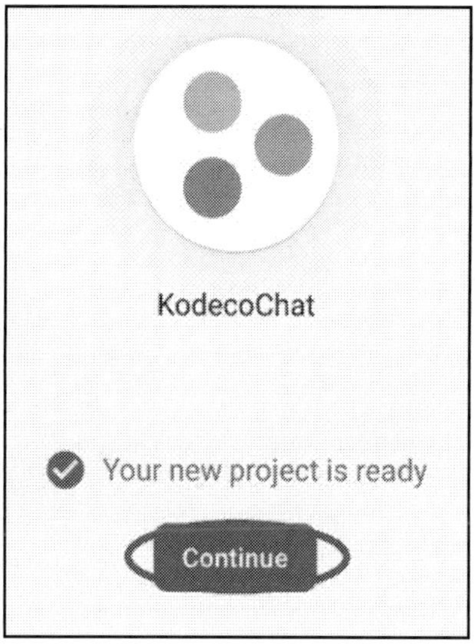

You should be returned to the Project Overview page.

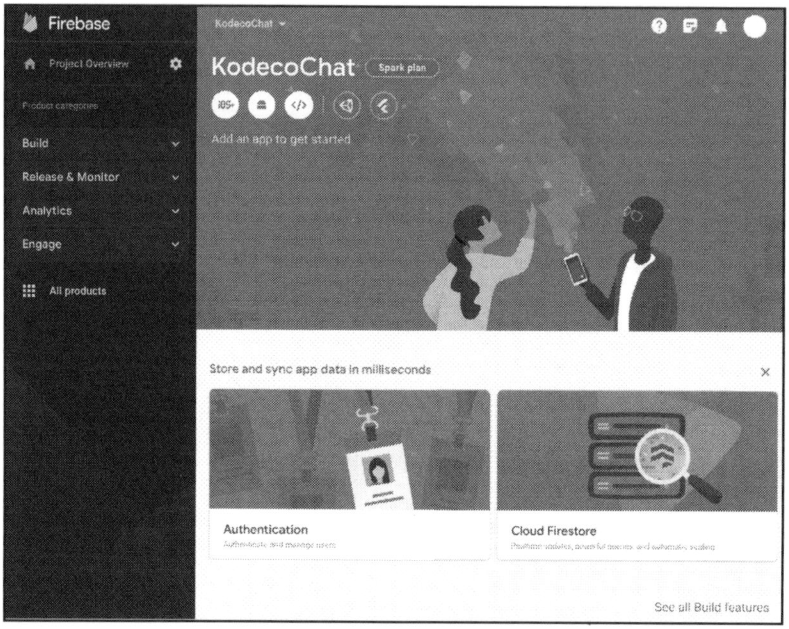

Before you can add Firebase to your app, you need to have **Firebase Command Line Interface (CLI)** installed. You can skip the next section if you have it already installed. Leave your Firebase Project Overview open.

Installing Firebase CLI

What is Firebase CLI? It's a Firebase management toolkit that enables running commands from **command-line**. Installation varies depending on your platform and preferred installation option — **standalone binary** or **Node Package Manager** (npm) that uses Node.js.

Google has great Firebase CLI reference (https://firebase.google.com/docs/cli) documentation that will walk you through installation based on your computer's operating system.

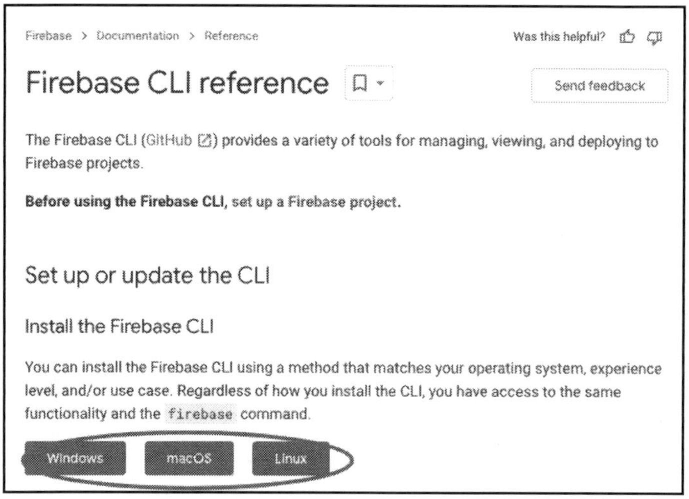

Once you've installed Firebase CLI, come back to continue adding Firebase to your app.

Using the Firebase CLI to Log In

To use Firebase from your IDE, you need to log in and select your project. Open **Terminal** and execute the following:

```
firebase login
```

This will ask you to allow Firebase to collect usage and error-reporting information.

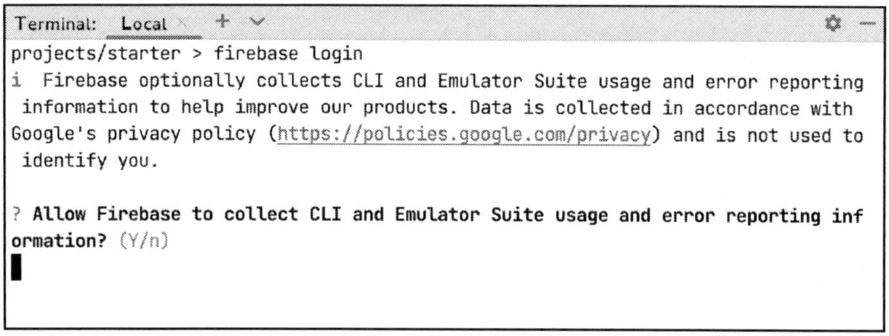

If you don't want to allow sharing, type n and press enter. Otherwise, press enter or accept — the default is Y.

Your browser should automatically open the Google login screen. Log in to the account you used to create your Firebase project.

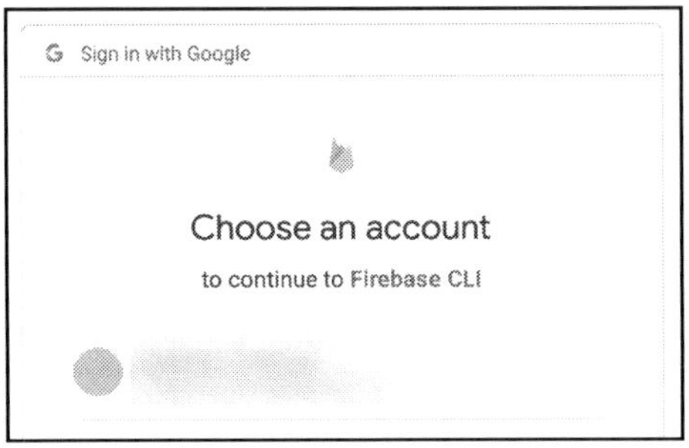

After logging in, a consent message is displayed. Read the details, and assuming you agree, click **Allow**.

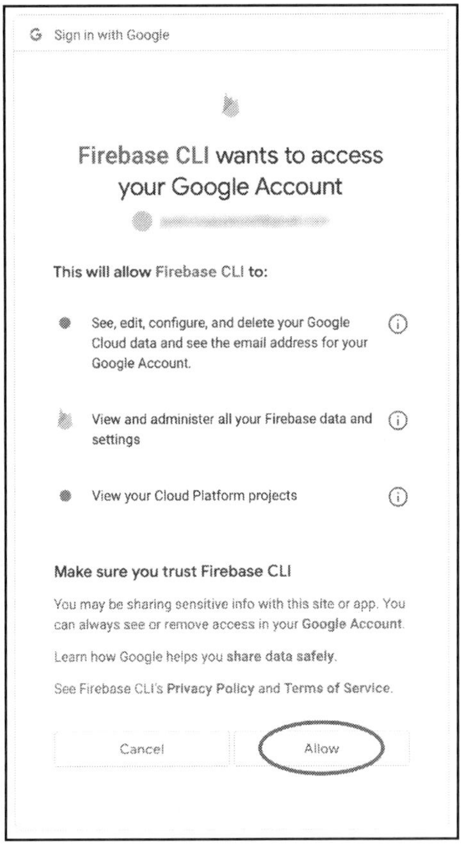

A login confirmation message is displayed. Close the tab/window.

Return to your **Flutter IDE**. In Terminal, you'll see a success message.

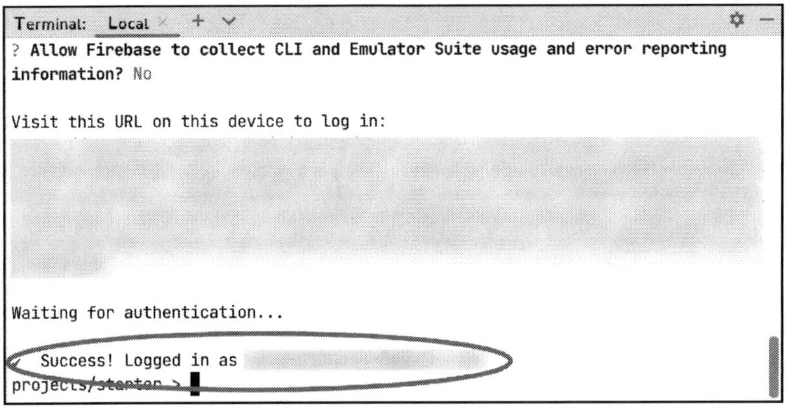

Well done! You are all set. Now it's time to add Firebase to your app.

Adding Firebase

The Firebase team has made things a lot easier for Flutter developers. You used to have to set up iOS, Android, and web apps separately. Now, you can add a Flutter app, and Firebase will do all the work for you.

Return to your **Firebase Console** in the browser. Tap the **Flutter logo** to add your app.

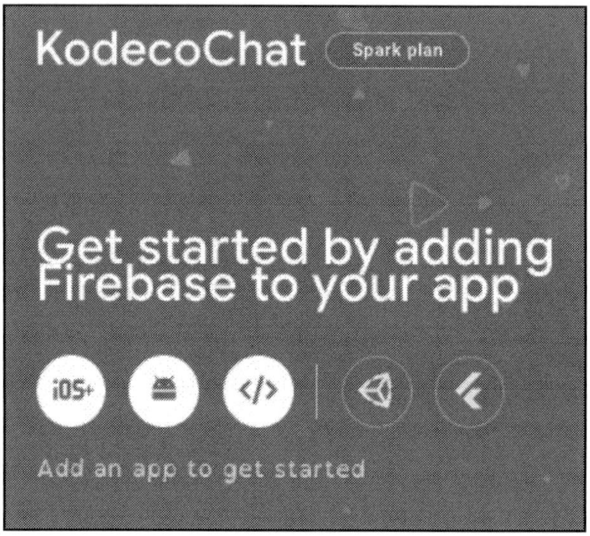

Tap **Next** since the Firebase CLI is ready to use and you already have a Flutter project.

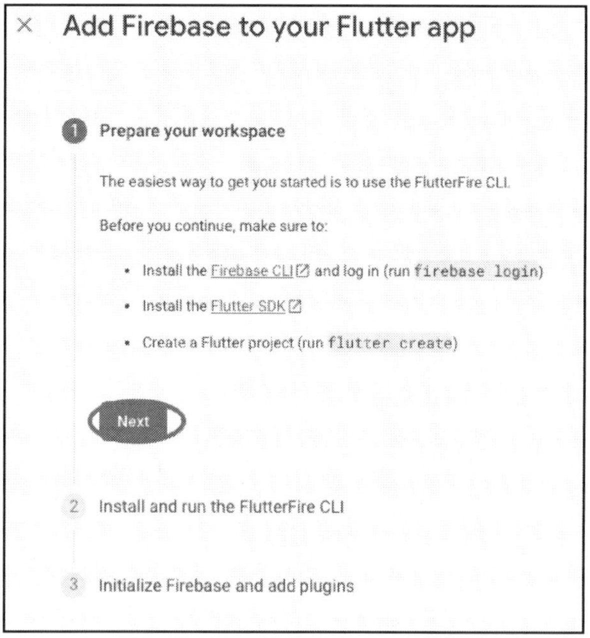

As you can see, the next step includes **command-line statements**.

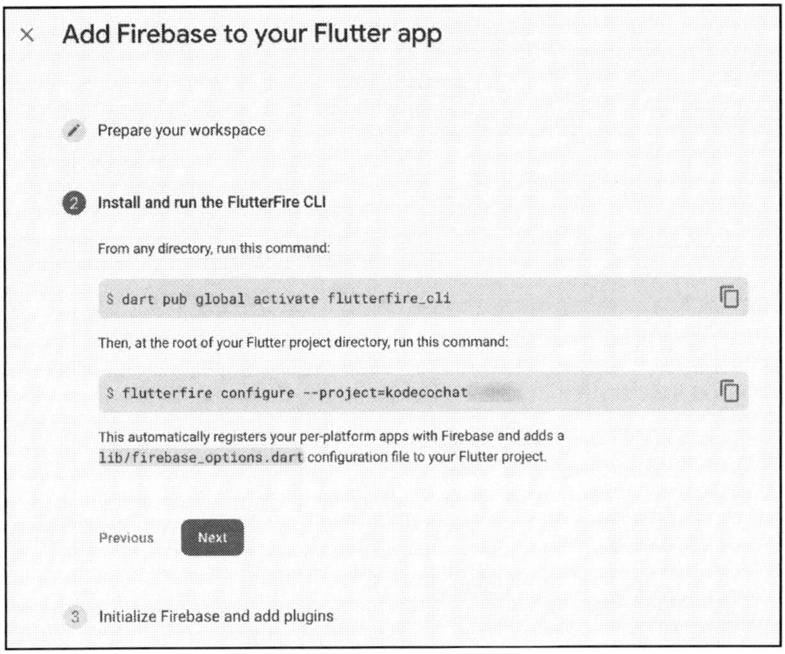

Don't close your browser. Return to your Flutter IDE, and in **Terminal**, execute the following:

```
dart pub global activate flutterfire_cli
```

`dart pub global` gives you command-line access to the specified package from anywhere. You've just activated `flutterfire_cli`.

Make sure you're at the root level of your **Flutter project** and run this, substituting the XXXXX for what your Firebase project reads.

```
flutterfire configure --project=kodecochat-XXXXX
```

Flutterfire connects to **Firebase** and lets you choose which platforms you wish to configure.

```
projects/starter > flutterfire configure --project=kodecochat-
i Found   Firebase projects. Selecting project kodecochat-
? Which platforms should your configuration support (use arrow keys & space to select)?
>
✔ android
✔ ios
✔ macos
✔ web
```

Use your **arrow keys** and **spacebar** if you wish to deselect a platform and press **Enter**. Wait a few minutes while your Firebase project is configured.

If there's an update needed, as shown below, press **Enter**.

```
✔ Which platforms should your configuration support (use arrow keys & space to select)? · android, ios, macos, web
i Firebase android app com.kodeco.kodeco_chat is not registered on Firebase project kodecochat-     .
i Registered a new Firebase android app on Firebase project kodecochat-     .
i Firebase ios app com.kodeco.kodecoChat is not registered on Firebase project kodecochat-     .
i Registered a new Firebase ios app on Firebase project kodecochat-     .
i Firebase macos app com.kodeco.kodecoChat.RunnerTests is not registered on Firebase project kodecochat-     .
i Registered a new Firebase macos app on Firebase project kodecochat-     .
i Firebase web app kodeco_chat (web) is not registered on Firebase project kodecochat-     .
i Registered a new Firebase web app on Firebase project kodecochat-     .
? The files android/build.gradle & android/app/build.gradle will be updated to apply Firebase configuration and gradle
 build plugins. Do you want to continue? (y/n) › yes
```

A message is displayed when the configuration is complete. It lists the Dart file it created as well as the Firebase App ID for each platform you selected.

```
Firebase configuration file lib/firebase_options.dart generated successfully
with the following Firebase apps:

Platform  Firebase App Id
web       1:          :web:
android   1:          :android:
ios       1:          :ios:
macos     1:          :ios:

Learn more about using this file and next steps from the documentation:
 > https://firebase.google.com/docs/flutter/setup
projects/starter >
```

Open **lib/firebase_options.dart**.

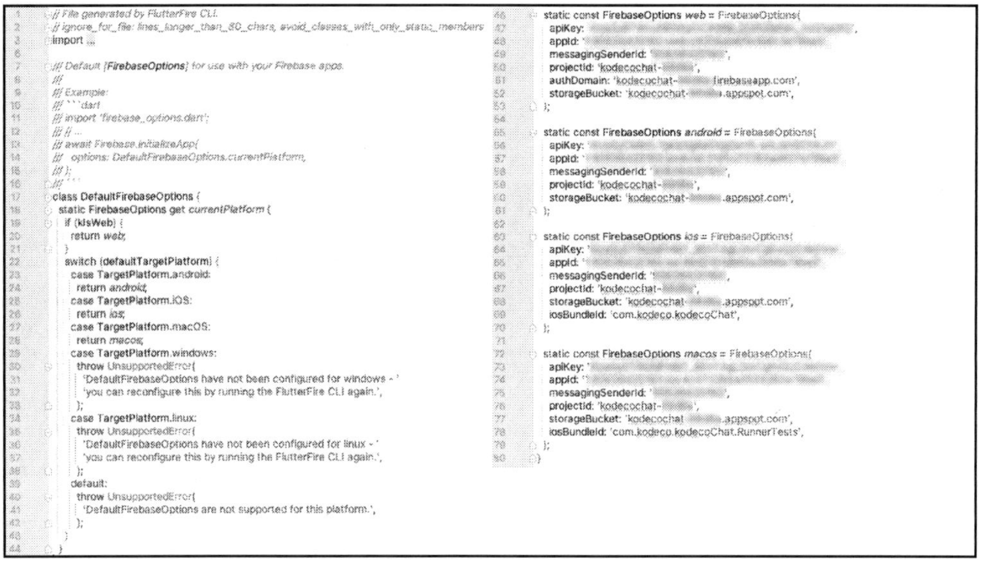

As you can see, Flutterfire CLI added all the code, including the new **App ID** details. Don't edit this file, and ignore the red squiggles.

Close **firebase_options.dart** and return to your browser and the Firebase Console. Click **Next**.

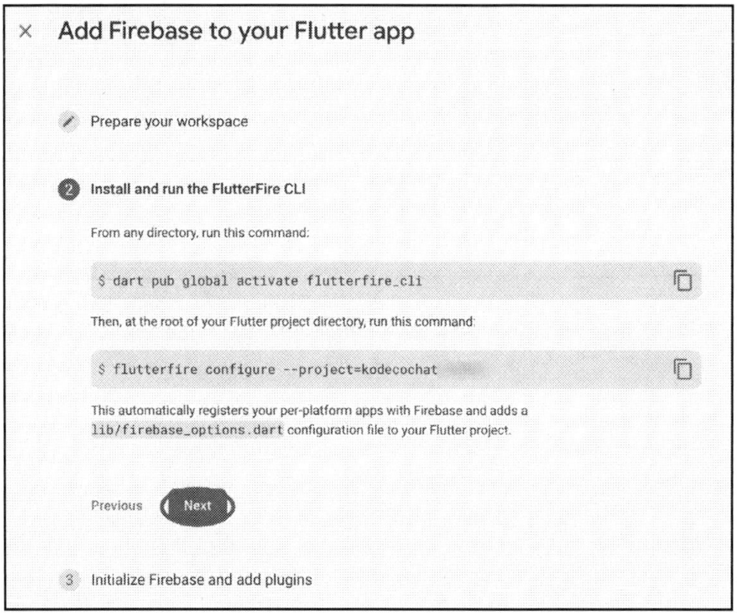

Next, Google displays the code used for initializing your app, but you won't be doing that step yet.

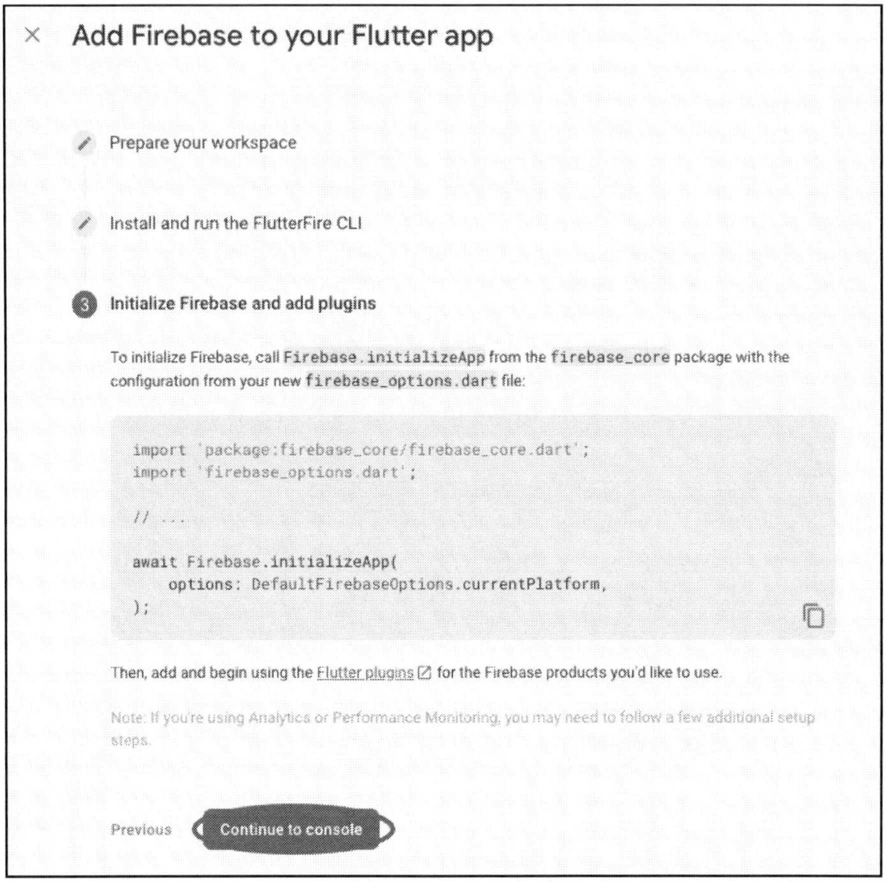

Click **Continue to console**. You'll see that Firebase now has your Flutter apps listed. Refresh your browser if you don't see them.

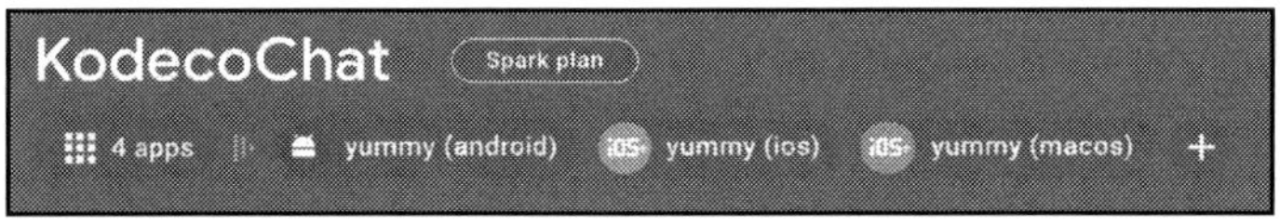

Tap the **X apps** button, where **X** is the number of platforms you chose when doing the **Flutterfire Initialization**, to see the automatically set up apps.

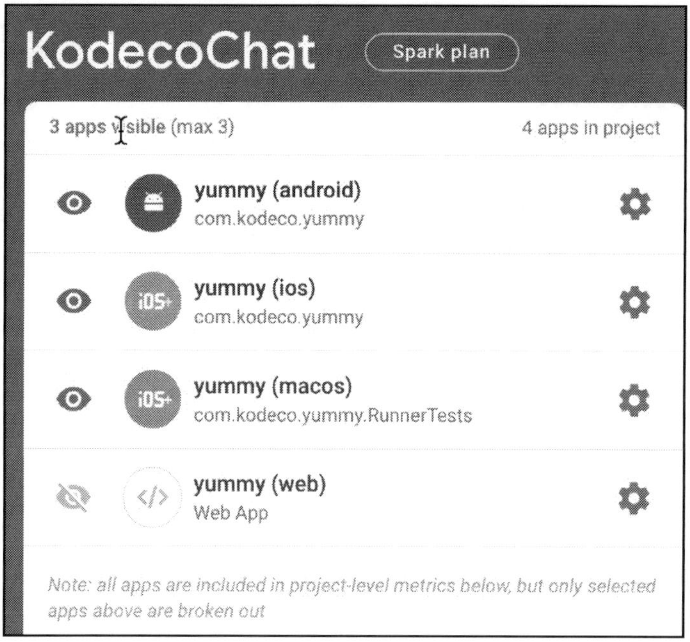

Awesome! Flutterfire has set up your Firebase project and has added code to your Flutter app. Now it's time to add functionality to **Yummy**.

Open **pubspec.yaml** and after `flutter_riverpod` add the following, aligning each of these with `flutter_riverpod`:

```
  firebase_auth: ^4.14.1
  firebase_core: ^2.23.0
  cloud_firestore: ^4.13.2
```

Run `flutter pub get` or click **Pub get**.

Open **main.dart** and look at the top of `main()`. You'll notice `WidgetsFlutterBinding.ensureInitialized()`. Whenever you're working with Firebase you need to have this to ensure there's a **platform channel** to the device's native code for Firebase initialization.

Replace `// TODO: Add Firebase App Initialization` with the following, ignoring any red squiggles:

```
await Firebase.initializeApp(
  options: DefaultFirebaseOptions.currentPlatform,
);
```

Next, replace `// TODO: Add Firebase core and options imports` with:

```
import 'package:firebase_core/firebase_core.dart';
import 'firebase_options.dart';
```

`initializeApp()` initializes a **Firebase instance** and should be run before using any Flutterfire packages.

> **Note**: If you receive an error message about **multidex**, this is because the Firebase package is so big. You need to **enable** multidex.
>
> From **Terminal**, run `flutter run --debug`, and when prompted, choose your Android device.
>
> When asked if you want to enable multidex support, enter `y` and press **Enter**. Your app will continue to run.
>
> When you're ready to continue with the chapter, return to **Terminal** and enter `q` to stop your app.
>
> For additional details, see the Flutter docs on enabling multidex support (https://docs.flutter.dev/deployment/android#enabling-multidex-support).

> **Note**: While your app will run on macOS, there are currently known macOS issues (https://github.com/firebase/flutterfire/labels/platform%3A%20macos) when using FlutterFire and Cloud Firestore. Depending on the situation, your app will run, but warnings will be printed.
>
> Check the FlutterFire GitHub repo for issues (https://github.com/firebase/flutterfire/issues). Some known issues are `trackingID` is deprecated (https://github.com/firebase/flutterfire/issues/11751) and Cloud Firestore Xcode build times can take several minutes to render (https://github.com/firebase/flutterfire/issues/2751).

Run your app, and you'll see that the UI hasn't changed.

When using the chat feature, users want to keep their messages separate from other people's. This means your app needs a way to keep track of each user and their messages. To do this, you need to add authentication to your app.

Adding Authentication

Firebase enables you to add user authentication without having to write and maintain your own **server-side code**. This can save you a lot of time and effort.

Firebase also gives you access to several different providers. For Yummy, you're going to use email and password.

The `FirebaseAuth` class allows you to:

- Create a new user.
- Sign in a user.
- Sign out a user.
- Get data from that user.

Setting up Firebase Authentication

Return to the **Firebase console** in the browser. Click the **Authentication** card.

The next couple of steps can vary depending on if you've used Firebase before or not.

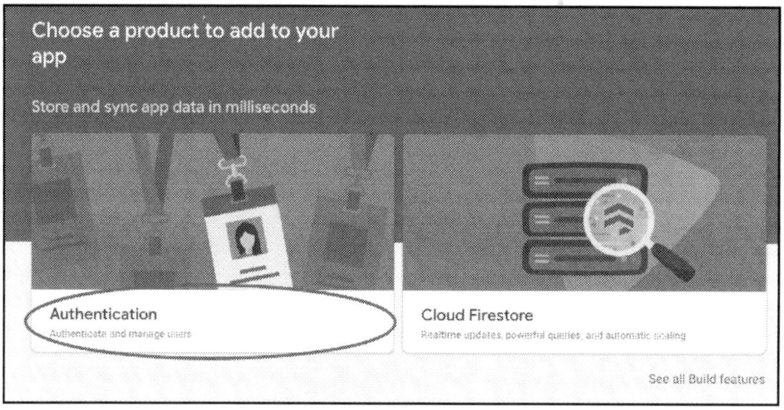

If prompted with another Authentication screen, click **Get started**. If not, go to the next step.

Next, if you see the **Set up sign-in method** button, click it. Otherwise, go to the next step.

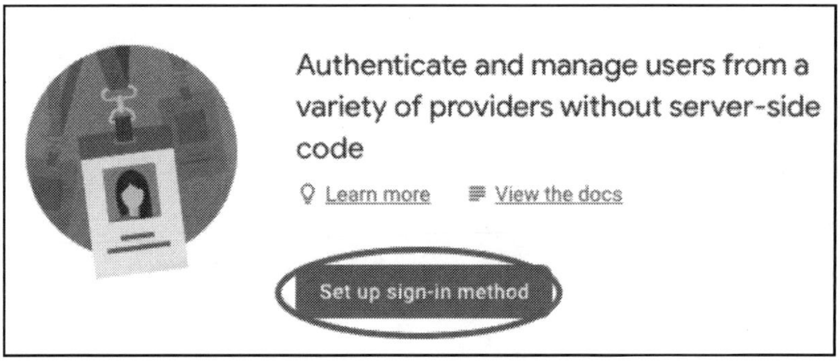

When you see the **Authentication** section, click **Add new provider**.

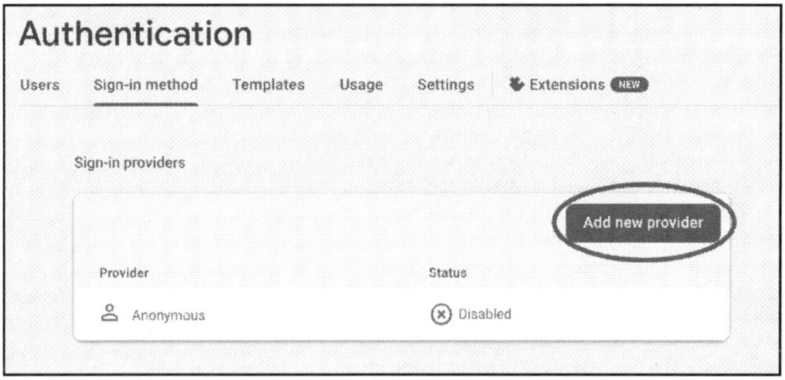

As mentioned before, you're going to be using **Email/Password** for Yummy, but before you proceed, take a look at all the different authentication options available.

When you're ready, under **Native providers**, choose **Email/Password**.

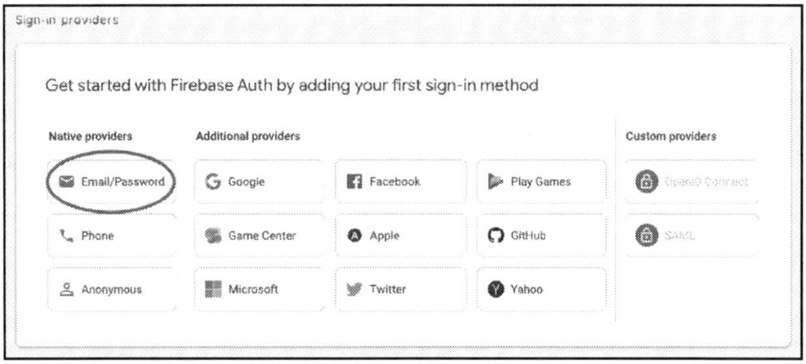

Click the Email/Password **Enable** switch, leaving the email link disabled and click **Save**.

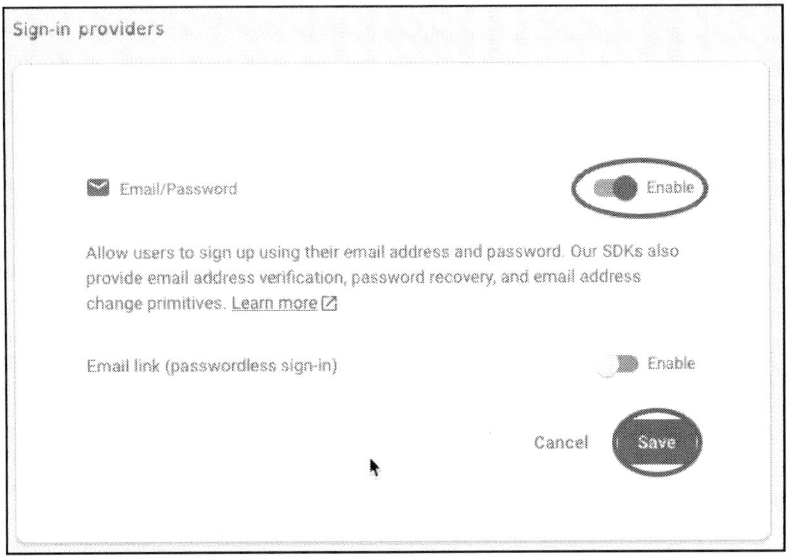

You've now enabled authentication. It's time to talk about how Firebase stores data.

Understanding Firestore Data Storage

Cloud Firestore stores data in **Documents** that are like **JSON** dictionaries in **key/value pairs**. These pairs are called **fields**. Documents can also contain nested **subcollections** and **arrays**.

Fields can have several different types:

- String
- Number
- Boolean
- Map
- Array

- Null
- Timestamp
- Geopoint
- Reference to another document

This is a very basic document example:

```
{
  "name": "Jane Doe",
  "department": 250,
  "occupation": "Flutter Developer"
}
```

This document has three fields: **name**, **department** and **occupation**. There are two `string` fields and one `number`.

A collection of documents is called... wait for it... **Collections**. Collections can only store **1 MB Documents**.

```
[
  {
    "name": "Jane Doe",
    "department": 250,
    "occupation": "Flutter Developer"
  },
  {
    "name": "John Doe",
    "department": 500,
    "occupation": "Flutter Developer"
  }
]
```

This collection contains two documents.

You can use **Firestore's console** to manually enter data and see the data appear almost immediately in your app. If you enter data in your app, you'll see it appear on the web and other apps just as fast.

Now that you know about collections, are you ready to create your app's database? Thought so. :]

Creating Cloud Firestore Database

Return to the Firebase Project Overview page.

Tap **Cloud Firestore**. If you don't see it tap **See all Build features**.

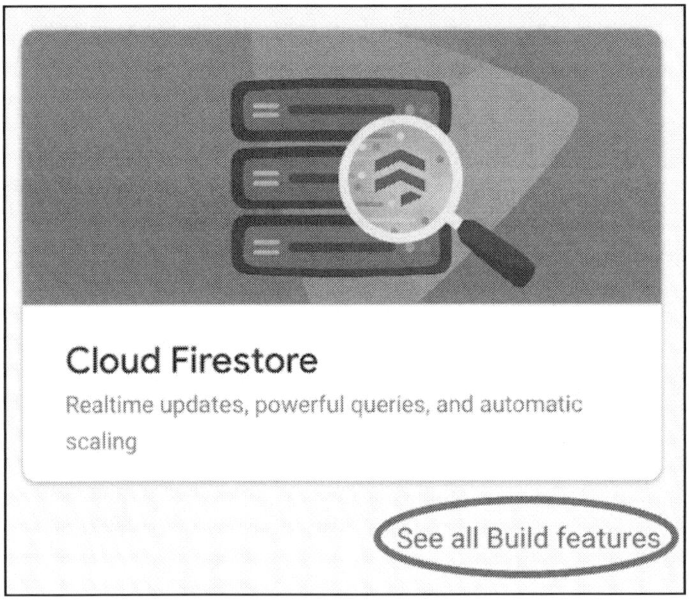

Select **Create Database**.

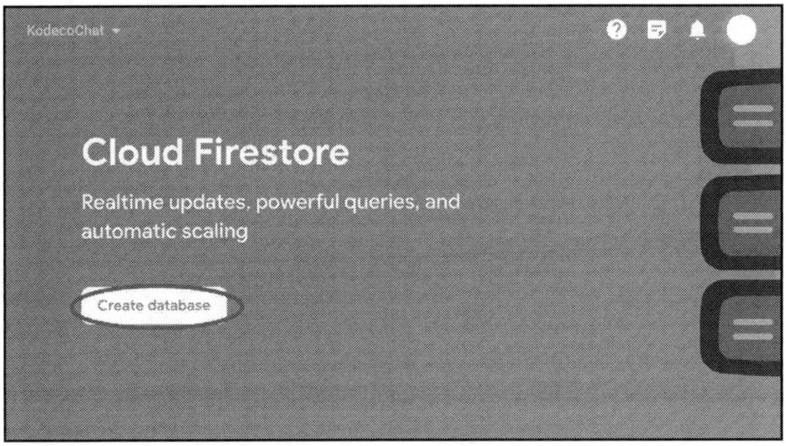

Next, select your region for your **Location** and then click **Next**:

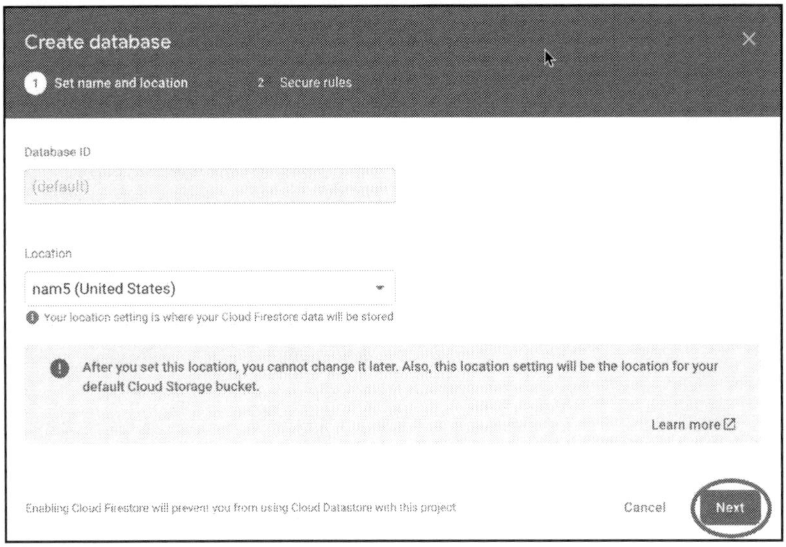

Select **Start in test mode** and click **Enable**.

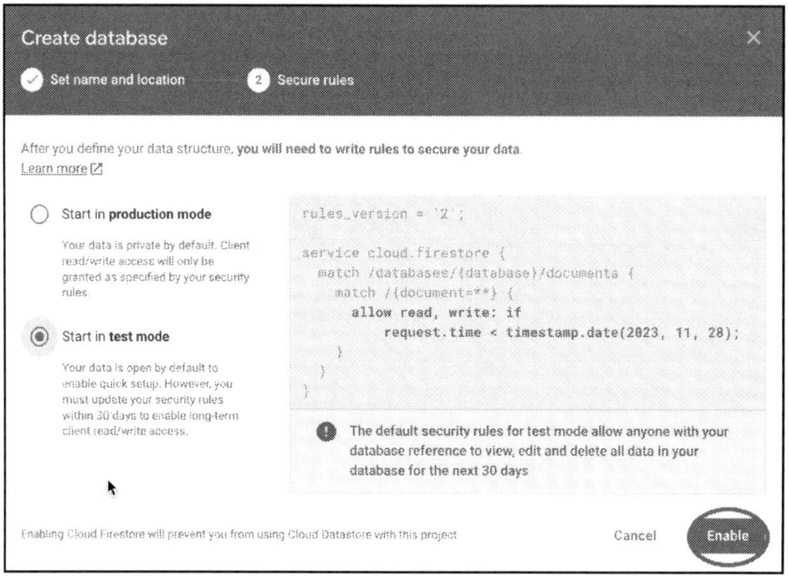

This ensures you can read and write data easily while developing your app.

You'll see steps displayed while your database is being created. It can go fast, so don't be worried if you don't see the same text.

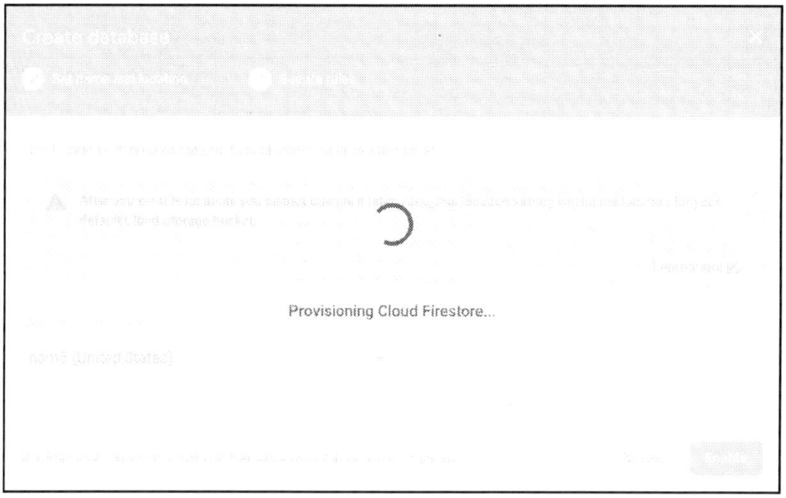

After your database has been created, you'll be redirected to your database console.

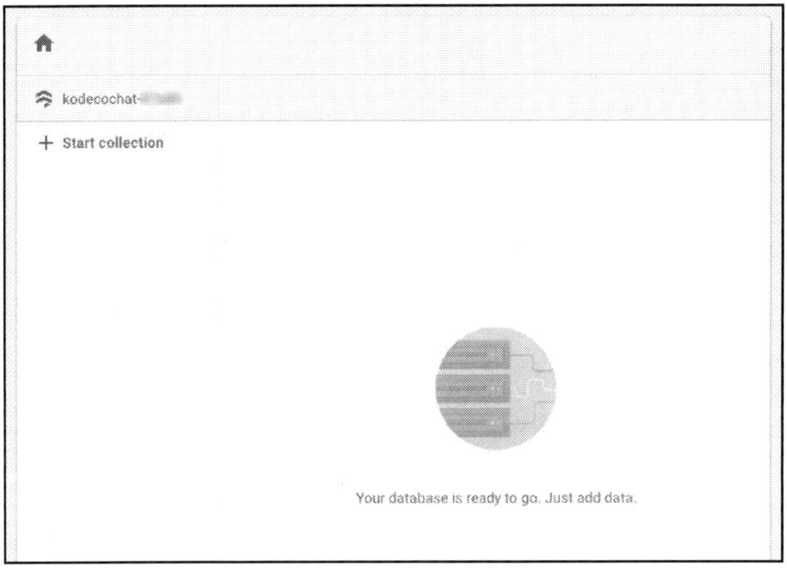

You can come back to the **Data** page later to see your app data in real time.

By default, Firestore is set up so that anyone can write to your database if they have the connection details. You don't want that, do you? Next, you'll set up database security and rules for limiting access.

Firebase Security Rules

Firebase database security consists of rules that limit who can read and/or write to specific paths. The rules consist of a **JSON** string in the **Rules** tab.

When you set up the database, you used the test ruleset. You need to lock down the database so that only those who have logged into your app can read and write messages.

From the Cloud Firestore Database screen, select the **Rules** tab.

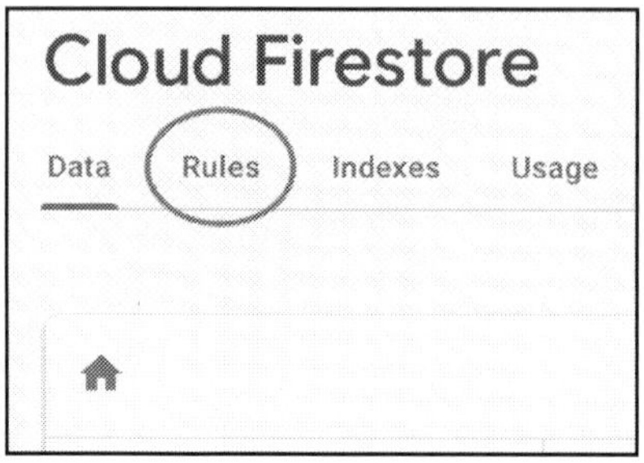

Replace the current rules with:

```
// 1
rules_version = '2';
service cloud.firestore {
  match /databases/{database}/documents {
    match /{document=**} {
      // 2
      allow read, write: if request.auth != null;
    }
  }
}
```

1. Rules version 2 changed **recursive** wildcard behavior and is required when using **collections**. For more details, see the Cloud Firestore Security documentation (https://firebase.google.com/docs/firestore/security/get-started)

2. `auth` is a special variable and contains the current user information. By checking to make sure that it's not `null`, you ensure a user is logged in.

When you're ready, click **Publish** to save the changes.

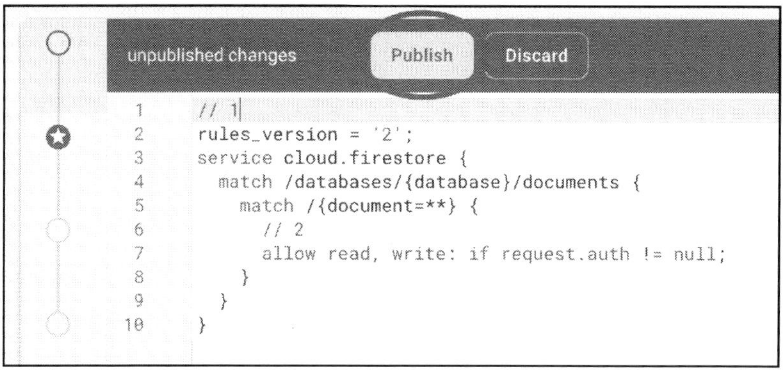

Now that your database is set up and security is in place, it's time to connect your app to your new Firebase project.

Modeling Data

Data modeling is an important part of your app development process. By creating a **data model**, you can ensure that the data is organized and stored in a way that is efficient, scalable and secure. To keep your data models separate from your UI, you'll use the **lib/models** folder to store your **data models** and **data access objects** (DAO).

Creating User Data Access Object (DAO)

In **lib/models**, create a new file named **user_dao.dart** and add the following:

```
import 'dart:developer';
import 'package:firebase_auth/firebase_auth.dart';
import 'package:flutter/material.dart';

// 1
class UserDao extends ChangeNotifier {
  String errorMsg = 'An error has occurred.';

  // 2
  final auth = FirebaseAuth.instance;

  // TODO: Add helper methods
}
```

Here are a few things to highlight in the code above:

1. The `UserDao` class extends `ChangeNotifier` so you can notify any listeners whenever a user has logged in or logged out.
2. The `auth` variable is used to hold on to an instance of `FirebaseAuth`.

Next, replace `// TODO: Add helper methods` with:

```
// 1
bool isLoggedIn() {
  return auth.currentUser != null;
}
// 2
String? userId() {
  return auth.currentUser?.uid;
}
//3
String? email() {
  return auth.currentUser?.email;
}

// TODO: Add signup
```

In this code, you:

1. Return `true` if the user is logged in. If the current user is `null`, they're logged out.
2. Return the **ID** of the **current user**, which could be `null`.
3. Return the **email** of the **current user**.

Signing Up

The first task for a user is to create an account. Replace `// TODO: Add signup` with:

```
// 1
Future<String?> signup(String email, String password) async {
  try {
    // 2
    await auth.createUserWithEmailAndPassword(
      email: email,
      password: password,
    );
    // 3
    notifyListeners();
    return null;
  } on FirebaseAuthException catch (e) {
    // 4
      if (email.isEmpty) {
        errorMsg = 'Email is blank.';
      } else if (password.isEmpty) {
        errorMsg = 'Password is blank.';
      } else if (e.code == 'weak-password') {
        errorMsg = 'The password provided is too weak.';
      } else if (e.code == 'email-already-in-use') {
        errorMsg = 'The account already exists for that email.';
      }
    return errorMsg;
  } catch (e) {
    // 5
    log(e.toString());
    return e.toString();
  }
}

// TODO: Add login
```

Here you:

1. Pass in the email and password the user entered. For a real app, you'll need to make sure those `Strings` meet your requirements. Return an error message if needed.
2. Call the Firebase method, which creates a new account with email and password.
3. Notify all listeners so they can then check when a user is logged in.
4. Handle some common errors.
5. Catch any other type of exception.

Logging In

Once a user has created an account, they can log in. Replace `// TODO: Add login` with:

```
// 1
Future<String?> login(String email, String password) async {
  try {
    // 2
    await auth.signInWithEmailAndPassword(
      email: email,
      password: password,
    );
    // 3
    notifyListeners();
    return null;
  } on FirebaseAuthException catch (e) {
    // 4
    if (email.isEmpty) {
      errorMsg = 'Email is blank.';
    } else if (password.isEmpty) {
      errorMsg = 'Password is blank.';
    } else if (e.code == 'invalid-email') {
      errorMsg = 'Invalid email.';
    } else if (e.code == 'INVALID_LOGIN_CREDENTIALS') {
      errorMsg = 'Invalid credentials.';
    } else if (e.code == 'user-not-found') {
      errorMsg = 'No user found for that email.';
    } else if (e.code == 'wrong-password') {
      errorMsg = 'Wrong password provided for that user.';
    }
    return errorMsg;
  } catch (e) {
    // 5
    log(e.toString());
    return e.toString();
```

```
  }
}

// TODO: Add logout
```

Here, you:

1. Pass in the email and password the user entered. Return an error message if needed.
2. Call the Firebase method to log in to their account.
3. Notify all listeners.
4. Handle some common errors.
5. Catch any other type of exception.

Logging Out

The final feature is **log out**. Replace `// TODO: Add logout` with:

```
void logout() async {
  await auth.signOut();
  notifyListeners();
}
```

Now that all the logic is in place, you'll build the UI to log in.

Adopting Riverpod

As you saw in Chapter 13, "Managing State", **Riverpod** is a great package for providing classes to its children. Your screens need access to these DAO classes. To do that, you'll create two providers: one for **user data** and the other for **messages**.

Create a new file, **providers.dart**, in the **lib** directory and add the following:

```
import 'package:flutter_riverpod/flutter_riverpod.dart';

import 'models/user_dao.dart';

// 1
final userDaoProvider = ChangeNotifierProvider<UserDao>((ref) {
  return UserDao();
});
```

```
// TODO: Add messageDaoProvider

// TODO: Add messageListProvider
```

1. `UserDao` extends `ChangeNotifier`; use `ChangeNotifierProvider` to provide an instance of `UserDao`.

Next, you'll create a login screen.

Creating the Login Screen

To use your app, a user needs to log in. To do that, they need to create an account. You'll create a dual-use login screen that will allow a user to either log in or sign up for a new account.

In the **components** folder, create a new file called **login.dart**. Add the following, ignoring the red squiggles for now:

```
import 'package:flutter/material.dart';
import 'package:flutter_riverpod/flutter_riverpod.dart';
import '../providers.dart';

class Login extends ConsumerStatefulWidget {
  const Login({
    super.key,
  });

  @override
  ConsumerState createState() => _LoginState();
}

class _LoginState extends ConsumerState<Login> {
  // 1
  final _emailController = TextEditingController();
  // 2
  final _passwordController = TextEditingController();
  // 3
  final GlobalKey<FormState> _formKey = GlobalKey<FormState>();

  @override
  void dispose() {
    // 4
    _emailController.dispose();
    _passwordController.dispose();
    super.dispose();
  }

// TODO: Add build
```

Here, you:

1. Create a **text controller** for the **email** field.
2. Create a **text controller** for the **password** field.
3. Create a **key** needed for a **form**.
4. Dispose of the **editing controllers**.

Now, you'll add the UI. Still ignoring the red squiggles, replace `// TODO: Add build` with:

```
@override
Widget build(BuildContext context) {
  // 1
  final userDao = ref.watch(userDaoProvider);
  return Scaffold(
     body: Padding(
      padding: const EdgeInsets.all(32.0),
      // 2
      child: Form(
        key: _formKey,

        // TODO: Add Column & Email
```

In this code, you:

1. Use the Riverpod's **ref** to watch the changes that take place in `UserDao`.
2. Create the `Form` with the **global key**.

Next, you'll create a column with four rows for **email field**, **password field**, **login button**, and a **signup button**.

Replace `// TODO: Add Column & Email` with:

```
child: Column(
  children: [
    Padding(
        padding: const EdgeInsets.symmetric(vertical: 10.0),
        // 1
        child: TextFormField(
          decoration: const InputDecoration(
            border: UnderlineInputBorder(),
            hintText: 'Email Address',
          ),
          autofocus: false,
          // 2
          keyboardType: TextInputType.emailAddress,
```

```
            // 3
            textCapitalization: TextCapitalization.none,
            autocorrect: false,
            // 4
            controller: _emailController,
            // 5
            validator: (String? value) {
              if (value == null || value.isEmpty) {
                return 'Email Required';
              }
              return null;
            },
          ),
      ),
      // TODO: Add Password
```

Here, you:

1. Create the field for the email address.
2. Use an email address keyboard type.
3. Turn off auto-correction and capitalization.
4. Set the editing controller.
5. Define a validator to check for empty strings. You can use regular expressions or any other type of validation if you like.

Next, add the password field. Replace `// TODO: Add Password` with:

```
Padding(
    padding: const EdgeInsets.symmetric(vertical: 10.0),
    child: TextFormField(
      decoration: const InputDecoration(
        border: UnderlineInputBorder(),
        hintText: 'Password',
      ),
      autofocus: false,
      obscureText: true,
      keyboardType: TextInputType.visiblePassword,
      textCapitalization: TextCapitalization.none,
      autocorrect: false,
      controller: _passwordController,
      validator: (String? value) {
        if (value == null || value.isEmpty) {
          return 'Password Required';
        }
        return null;
      },
    ),
```

```
    ),
    const Spacer(),
  // TODO: Add Buttons
```

This is almost the same as the email field except for the added password field.

Now replace `// TODO: Add Buttons` with:

```
    SizedBox(
      width: double.infinity,
      child: ElevatedButton(
        // 1
        onPressed: () async {
          if (_formKey.currentState!.validate()) {
            final errorMessage = await userDao.login(
              _emailController.text,
              _passwordController.text,
            );
            // 2
            if (errorMessage != null) {
              if (!mounted) return;
              ScaffoldMessenger.of(context).showSnackBar(
                SnackBar(
                  content: Text(errorMessage),
                  duration: const Duration(milliseconds: 700),
                ),
              );
            }
          }
        },
        child: const Text('Login'),
      ),
    ),
    Padding(
      padding: const EdgeInsets.symmetric(vertical: 10.0),
      child: SizedBox(
        width: double.infinity,
        child: ElevatedButton(
          // 3
          onPressed: () async {
            if (_formKey.currentState!.validate()) {
              final errorMessage = await userDao.signup(
                _emailController.text,
                _passwordController.text,
              );
              if (errorMessage != null) {
                if (!mounted) return;
                ScaffoldMessenger.of(context).showSnackBar(
                  SnackBar(
                    content: Text(errorMessage),
                    duration: const Duration(milliseconds: 700),
                  ),
```

```
                );
              }
            }
          },
          child: const Text('Sign Up'),
        ),
      ),
    ),
  // TODO: Add parentheses
```

Here, you:

1. Set the first button to call the `login()` method and show any error messages.
2. If there's an error message, first check to see if the state object is "mounted" (still showing), then show a **snackbar**.
3. Set the second button to call the `signup()` method and show any error messages.

Now, replace `// TODO: Add parentheses` with:

```
              ],
            ),
          ),
        ),
      );
    }
  }
```

Reformat the code to clean things up. You now have a screen that accepts an email address and password, and can log in or sign up a user.

Open **home.dart**, and in the build method, replace `// TODO: Add userDaoProvider` with the following, ignoring the red squiggles:

```
final userDao = ref.watch(userDaoProvider);
```

Using the `watch` method, any time the user state changes, you'll either show the login screen or the message screen.

find `// TODO: Add Login` and replace the below code with:

```
Center(
  child: userDao.isLoggedIn()
      ? const MessageList()
      : const Login(),
),
```

If the user is logged in, then `MessageList` is shown. Otherwise `Login` is shown.

Add the following imports at the top:

```
import '../components/login.dart';
import 'providers.dart';
```

Stop and restart your app. You should then see the new login screen. Enter an email and a password. Remember the password :).

> **Note**: Use at least six characters for the password.

Click **Login**.

An error is displayed because the user hasn't signed up yet. Try again, but this time click **Sign up**.

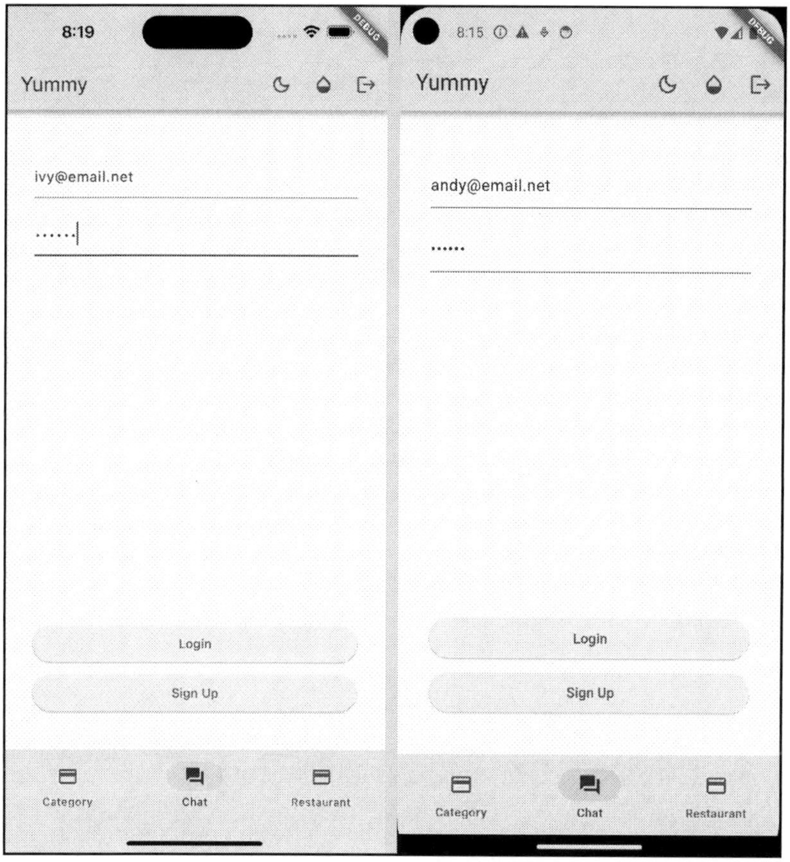

Back in your browser, check the Firebase **Authentication** panel on the **Users** tab. You should see the added email address(es):

The user can log in, but how do they log out? Next, you'll add a **logout button**.

Adding a Logout Button

Still in **home.dart**, replace `// TODO: Replace with logout button` with:

```
IconButton(
  onPressed: () {
    userDao.logout();
  },
  icon: const Icon(Icons.logout),
),
```

This will add the logout icon to `AppBar` and call `logout()` on the instance of `UserDao`.

Hot reload the app, and you'll see the **Messages** screen. Then click the **Logout** button:

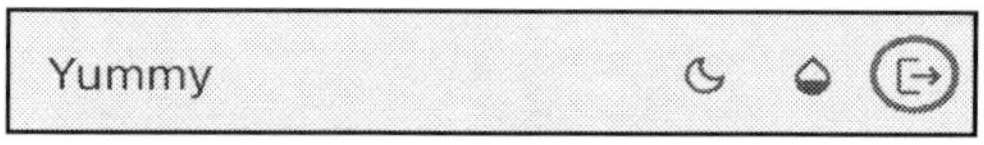

This will take you back to the login screen. Enter your email and password, and this time, click **Login**. You'll be logged back in.

It's time to display the messages list in the correct order and with the correct user details.

Adding Message Data Model

Create a new file in the **lib/components** directory called **message.dart**. Then, add the following class with `date`, `email`, `text` and `reference` properties:

```
import 'package:cloud_firestore/cloud_firestore.dart';

class Message {
  Message({
    required this.date,
    required this.email,
    required this.text,
    this.reference,
  });

  final DateTime date;
  final String email;
  final String text;

  DocumentReference? reference;
```

```
    // TODO: Add JSON converters
  }
```

You also need a way to transform your `Message` model from JSON since that's how it's stored in your Cloud Firestore. Replace `// TODO: Add JSON converters` with:

```
// 1
factory Message.fromJson(Map<dynamic, dynamic> json) => Message(
      date: (json['date'] as Timestamp).toDate(),
      email: json['email'] as String,
      text: json['text'] as String,
    );

// 2
Map<String, dynamic> toJson() => <String, dynamic>{
      'date': date,
      'email': email,
      'text': text,
    };

// TODO: Add fromSnapshot
```

1. This transforms the **JSON** received from Cloud Firestore into a `Message`.
2. This does the opposite — transforms the `Message` into **JSON** for saving.

Replace `// TODO: Add fromSnapshot` with:

```
factory Message.fromSnapshot(DocumentSnapshot snapshot) {
  // 1
  final message = Message.fromJson(
    snapshot.data() as Map<String, dynamic>,
  );
  // 2
  message.reference = snapshot.reference;
  return message;
}
```

1. This takes a **Firestore snapshot** and converts it to a message using `fromJson()`.
2. Sets the `reference` property.

Next, you'll set up the message DAO.

Adding Message DAO

Create a new file in **lib/models** called **message_dao.dart**. This is your DAO for your messages.

Add the following:

```
import 'package:cloud_firestore/cloud_firestore.dart';
import '../components/message.dart';
import 'user_dao.dart';

class MessageDao {
  MessageDao(this.userDao);

  final UserDao userDao;

  // 1
  final CollectionReference collection =
      FirebaseFirestore.instance.collection('messages');

  // TODO: Add saveMessage
}
```

This code:

1. Gets an instance of `FirebaseFirestore` and then gets the root of the messages collection by calling `collection()`.

Now, you need `MessageDao` to perform two functions: **saving** and **retrieving**.

Replace `// TODO: Add saveMessage` with:

```
void sendMessage(String text) {
  // 1
  final message = Message(
    date: DateTime.now(),
    email: userDao.email()!,
    text: text,
  );
  // 3
  collection.add(message.toJson()); // 2
}

// TODO: Add getMessageStream
```

This function:

1. Creates a `Message` object using the current `DateTime`, the users `email` and their message as text.
2. `toJson()` converts the message to a **JSON** string.
3. `add()` Adds the string to the **collection**. This updates the database immediately.

For the retrieval method, you only need to expose a `Stream<QuerySnapshot>`, which interacts directly with your `DatabaseReference`.

Replace `// TODO: Add getMessageStream` with:

```
Stream<List<Message>> getMessageStream() {
  return collection
    .orderBy('date', descending: true)
    .snapshots()
    .map((snapshot) {
      return [...snapshot.docs.map(Message.fromSnapshot)];
    });
}
```

This returns a stream of data at the root level, ordering the collection by the `date` in descending order.

Now you have your **message DAO**. As the name states, the data access object helps you access whatever data you have stored at the given Cloud Firestore reference. It will also let you store new data as you send messages.

Open **lib/providers.dart**, and, again ignoring red squiggles, replace `// TODO: Add messageDaoProvider` with the following:

```
final messageDaoProvider = Provider<MessageDao>((ref) {
  return MessageDao(ref.watch(userDaoProvider));
});
```

This returns `MessageDao`. Now, all you have to do is build your UI.

Replace `// TODO: Add messageListProvider` with the following:

```
final messageListProvider = StreamProvider<List<Message>>((ref)
{
  final messageDao = ref.watch(messageDaoProvider);
  return messageDao.getMessageStream();
});
```

Here you've used `StreamProvider` to get a stream of messages from the `MessageDao`.

Add the following to the top.

```
import 'components/message.dart';
import 'models/message_dao.dart';
```

Next, you'll use these providers to build your message list UI.

Creating New Messages

Open **components/message_list.dart**. Replace `// TODO: Replace _sendMessage` and the line beneath it with your new send message code:

```
void _sendMessage() {
  if (_messageController.text.isNotEmpty) {
    // 1
    final messageDao = ref.read(messageDaoProvider);
    // 2
    messageDao.sendMessage(_messageController.text.trim());
    _messageController.clear();
  }
}
```

Here you're using:

1. `ref.read()` to use the `MessageDao`
2. `trim()` to then send the message to remove leading and trailing blanks.

Add your new providers import at the top of the file:

```
import '../providers.dart';
```

Stop the app and re-run it on one device. You'll see the same screen as you did before. Type your first message and click the → button.

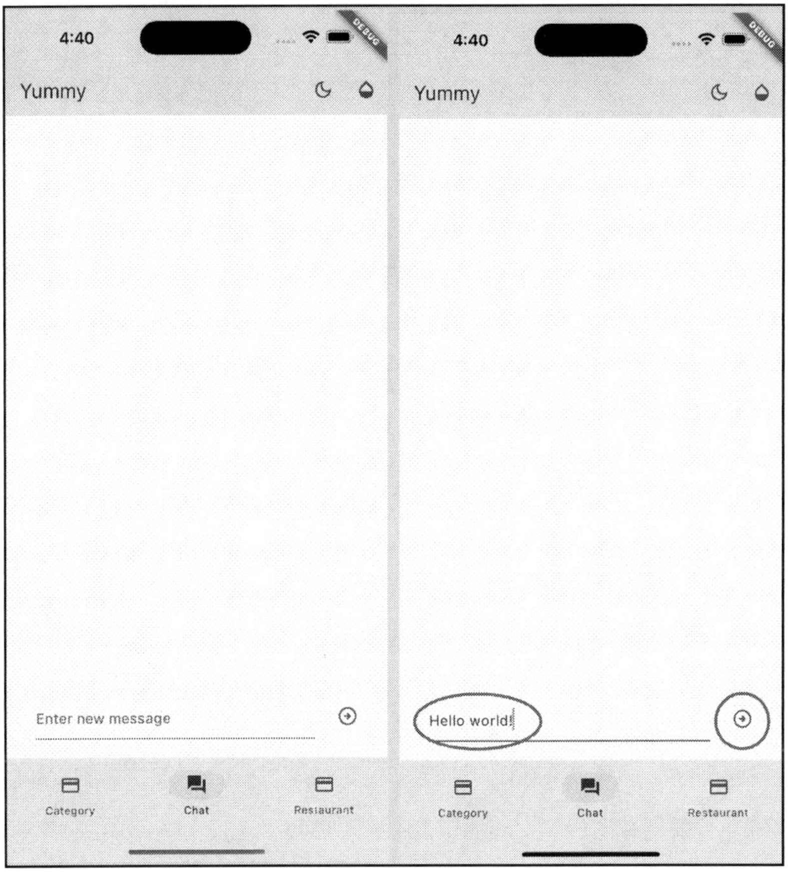

Now, go back to your **Firebase Console** and open your project's **Cloud Firestore**. You'll see your message as an entry:

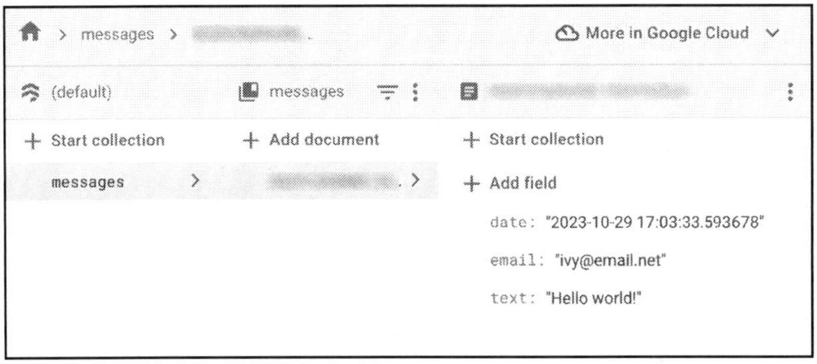

Great job! You've implemented a **remote database** and added an entry with very little code.

> **Note**: All of the blurred random letters will be different for each person.

Try adding a few more messages. You can even watch your **Cloud Firestore** as you enter each message to see them appear in real time.

Now, it's time to display those messages.

Reactively Displaying Messages

Now that you have a stream of messages, you want to display them.

Open **lib/components/message_widget.dart**.

Find `// TODO: Replace MessageWidget` and replace the `MessageWidget` with the below code, ignoring those pesky red squiggles:

```
const MessageWidget(
  this.message, {
    super.key,
  });

final Message message;
```

Here, you've added a `message` object to the `MessageWidget` constructor.

Find `// TODO: Add userDao and myMessage` and replace it with:

```
// 1
final userDao = ref.watch(userDaoProvider);
//2
final myMessage = message.email == userDao.email();
```

This code:

1. Uses `ref.watch()` to listen to the changes in `UserDao`.
2. Checks if the message's email is the same as the user's email.

At the top of the file, add the following import:

```
import 'package:intl/intl.dart';
import '../providers.dart';
import 'message.dart';
```

Display the message text by replacing `// TODO: Replace Text`, and the line under it with:

```
Text(
  message.text,
  style: theme.textTheme.bodyLarge!,
),
```

Find `// TODO: Remove const`, and remove the `const` from the `child` beneath it.

Next, you need to add a **row** to display the messages as they come in. Locate `// TODO: Add Row for message` and replace it with:

```
Row(
    // TODO: Add mainAxisAlignment
    children: [
      // Display email of others not ones sent from device
      !myMessage
        ? Text(
            message.email,
            style: TextStyle(
              color: theme.colorScheme.secondary,
            ),
          )
          // If message is sent from the device display nothing
        : const Text(''),
      // Display date and time message was sent
      Text(
        '  ${DateFormat.yMd().format(message.date)} '
        '${DateFormat.Hm().format(message.date)}',
        style: TextStyle(
          color: theme.colorScheme.secondary,
        ),
      ),
    ],
),
```

Here, you're displaying the message sender's email address if it's not from the device and the date and time it was sent.

To prevent the messages from taking up the whole width of the device. Find `// TODO: Add crossAxisAlignment` and replace it with the following:

```
crossAxisAlignment: myMessage //
  ? CrossAxisAlignment.end
  : CrossAxisAlignment.start,
```

If the message is from the device, then the **speech bubble** will be on the **right**. Otherwise, it's on the left.

Right now, the messages would align in the middle of the screen. Find and replace `// TODO: ADD alignment` in `FractionallySizedBox`.

```
alignment: myMessage //
  ? Alignment.topRight
  : Alignment.topLeft,
```

To have the email and date/time aligned with their speech bubble, replace `// TODO: Add mainAxisAlignment` with:

```
mainAxisAlignment: myMessage //
  ? MainAxisAlignment.end
  : MainAxisAlignment.start,
```

If the message is from the device, then it'll be on the right. Otherwise, it's on the left.

Since `MessageDao` has a `getMessageStream()` method that returns a stream, you'll use a `StreamBuilder` to display messages.

Back in **message_list.dart**, find `// TODO: Add Message List` and replace it and the whole `Expanded` widget with the following:

```
Expanded(
  // 1
  child: Consumer(
    builder: (BuildContext context, WidgetRef ref, Widget?
child) {
      final data = ref.watch(messageListProvider);
      return data.when(
        loading: () => const Center(
          child: LinearProgressIndicator(),
        ),
        data: (List<Message> messages) => ListView(
        controller: _scrollController,
        reverse: true,
        // 2
        children: [
          for (final message in messages) //
            Padding(
              padding:
                const EdgeInsets.fromLTRB(24.0, 12.0, 24.0,
4.0),
              child: MessageWidget(message),
            ),
          ],
        ),
        error: (error, stackTrace) {
          return Center(child: Text('$error'));
        },
      );
    },
  ),
),
```

Here you:

1. Create a **new message** from the given **snapshot**.
2. Pass the **message info** to the **MessageWidget**.

Add the following imports:

```
import 'message.dart';
import 'message_widget.dart';
```

Trigger a hot reload, and you'll see your messages in a list.

Load your app on multiple devices or simulators and watch as you communicate in real time and see the messages appear on them simultaneously.

Magic!

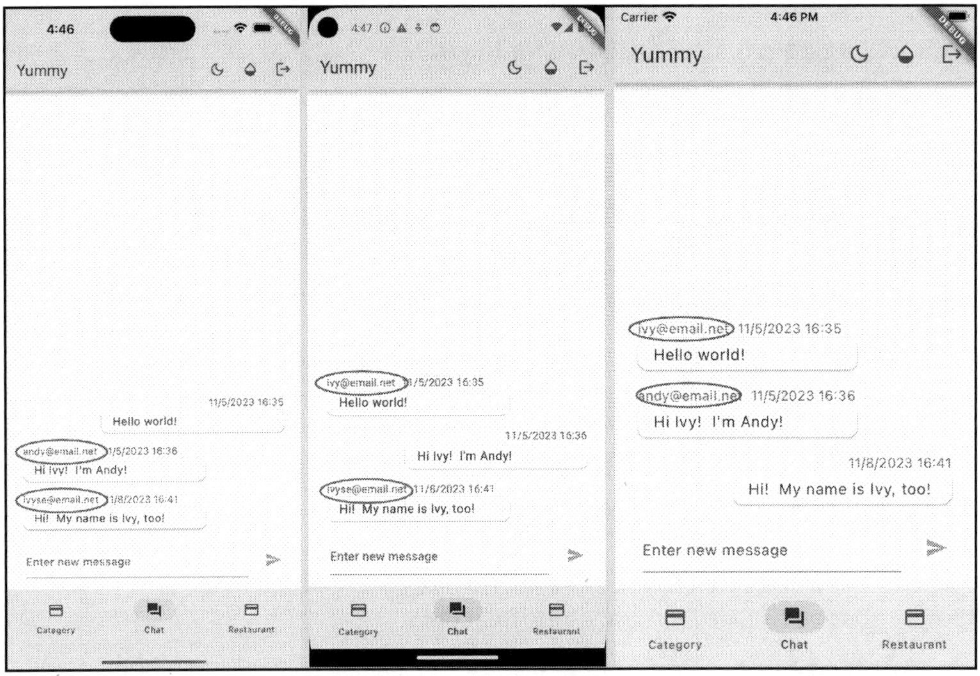

Notice how the messages are labeled with the email of the user who sent them, except on the device that sent the message. In that case, only the time is shown.

You now have a fully working chat app that can be used by multiple people. Great job!

Key Points

- **Cloud Firestore** is a good solution for **low-latency** database storage.
- **FlutterFire** provides an easy way to use **Firebase** packages.
- Firebase provides serverless **authentication** and security through **Rules**.
- Creating data access object (**DAO**) files helps to put Firebase functionalities in one place.
- Use Firestore to store and retrieve data in real time.
- You can choose many different types of authentication, from email to other services.

Where to Go From Here?

There are plenty of other Cloud Firestore features that can supercharge your app and give it enterprise-grade features. These include:

- **Offline capabilities**: Keep your data in sync even when offline. here: https://firebase.google.com/docs/firestore/manage-data/enable-offline.
- **Database Rules**: Make your database more secure, here: https://firebase.google.com/docs/database/security.
- **More sign-up methods**: Use similar features to Google and Apple sign-in.

There are plenty of other great Firebase products you can integrate with. Check out the rest of the Firebase API here: https://firebase.flutter.dev/docs/overview/#next-steps.

Section VI: Testing Your Flutter App

Building an app is a great adventure; checking that it works as expected makes it even better!

In this section you'll learn about the importance of testing your code and the different types of tests that you can implement. Specifically, you'll learn about unit and widget tests, their differences and how to adopt them in your app.

Chapter 17: Introduction to Testing

Alejandro Ulate

In this chapter, you'll revisit work on the Recipe Finder app from previous chapters. While doing so, you'll learn:

- About the importance of testing your code.
- The types of tests you can carry out in a Flutter project.
- How to perform **unit testing**.
- Good practices while testing.
- **Mocking** dependencies when necessary.

Improving Code Quality With Tests

Ensuring the quality of your Flutter project is essential for its success, that's where **testing** comes in. It'll help you identify defects, errors or issues within your project and increase your confidence in your code.

With testing, you can ensure that your project functions as expected, meets the specified requirements and delivers a reliable and high-quality user experience. Here are a few reasons why you should consider adding tests in all your projects:

1. **Error Identification**: Testing helps identify and locate software errors, defects or bugs. These errors can be simple syntax mistakes or more complex logic issues. Identifying and fixing these issues is important to prevent them from causing problems for your end-users.

2. **Risk Mitigation**: It helps manage and reduce project risks by detecting issues early in the development process. That way, developers can address them quickly, minimizing the potential impact on project timelines, budgets and customer satisfaction.

3. **Requirement Verification**: Testing also verifies that the software meets the specified requirements and aligns with the project's goals. It ensures that the software does what it's supposed to do and doesn't introduce unexpected behavior.

4. **Continuous Improvement**: Testing isn't a one-time activity. It's an ongoing process. It allows you to gather feedback, make improvements and release updates that enhance the software's performance, reliability and security.

5. **Regression Prevention**: As your app evolves and you add new features, there's a risk of introducing new defects while fixing existing ones. Testing, especially regression testing, helps prevent these regressions by ensuring that changes don't break existing functionality.

6. **Security and Compliance**: Testing is essential for identifying security vulnerabilities and ensuring compliance with industry standards and regulations. It helps protect sensitive data, user privacy and the overall integrity of the software.

7. **Cost-Efficiency**: Early detection and resolution of defects through testing are typically more cost-effective than addressing issues that arise after the software is in production. Testing reduces the expenses associated with fixing bugs in the later stages of development.

8. **Confidence and Trust**: Thorough testing increases confidence in both the development team and end-users. It demonstrates a commitment to quality and reliability.

In summary, testing ensures that your Flutter project is high quality, meets user expectations and is free from defects.

Learning About Tests

There are three main kinds of tests: **unit tests**, **widget tests** and **integration tests**. Each one has a different utility and effort related to them.

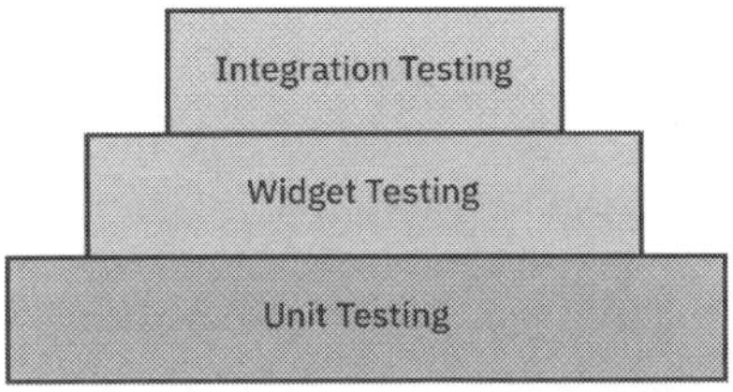

- **Unit Tests**: Focus on testing individual **functions**, **classes** or **methods** in isolation. They're a great place to validate your business logic.
- **Widget Tests**: Used to test widgets in isolation. They verify that a widget looks and behaves as expected. They're excellent for testing the visual components of your app.
- **Integration Tests**: Evaluate a complete app or a large part of it. They're useful to verify that all the widgets and services they're testing work together as expected. Integration tests run on real devices or an OS emulator, such as an iOS Simulator or Android Emulator.

You can think of these types of tests as a pyramid in which the base is unit testing. This is because having your business logic working as expected is key to your project and business's goals.

A well tested app should have a good balance between the different types of tests. However, it's important to note that the effort required to write and the confidence in each type of test is different.

	Unit	Widget	Integration
Confidence	Low	Higher	Highest
Maintenance cost	Low	Higher	Highest
Dependencies	Few	More	Most
Execution speed	Quick	Quick	Slow

The above table is a **CMDE** table. CMDE stands for Confidence, Maintenance cost, Dependencies, and Execution speed.

- **Confidence**: How confident you can be that the test is actually testing what you want it to.
- **Maintenance cost**: How much effort it takes to maintain the test.
- **Dependencies**: How many dependencies the test has.
- **Execution speed**: How fast the test runs.

Now that you've taken a closer look at testing, it's time to dive back into code.

Open **pubspec.yml** and add the following package to your `dev_dependencies` declaration:

```
test: ^1.24.3
```

This package contains most of the utilities needed for testing your app.

Create a new directory in the **root** of the project called **test**. Test files should generally reside inside a folder located at the root of your Flutter application or package.

A good way to organize your tests is to make your file structure in **test** match the one in your **lib** folder.

Now, add your first unit test by adding a new file called **ingredient_test.dart** in the same folder structure as **lib**. Your test file should be located at **test/data/models/ingredient_test.dart**.

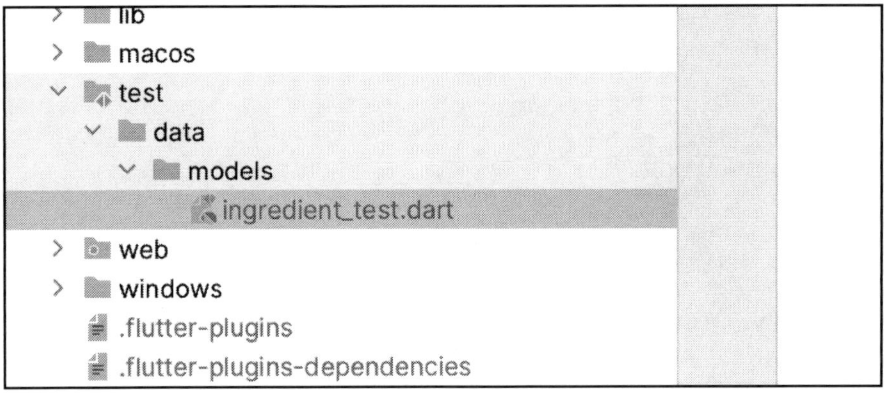

Test files should always end with **_test.dart**, this is the convention used by the **test runner** when searching for tests.

Run your tests by running the CLI command below:

```
flutter test test/data/models/ingredient_test.dart
```

You should see an error like this:

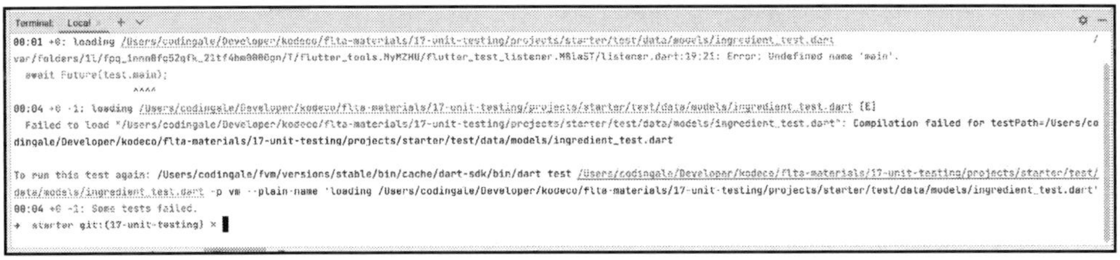

This happens because the test runner needs a `main()` function to run the tests in the file. The test runner is a **Dart program** itself and needs to know where to start.

Fix that by adding a `main` function like the code below:

```
void main() {
}
```

Run your tests again. You should see the following:

```
→  starter git:(17-unit-testing) × flutter test test/data/models/ingredient_test.dart

No tests ran.
No tests were found.
```

Now that `main()` exists, the test runner can successfully try to run the tests in the file. However, there are no tests yet.

Adding Unit Tests

Now that you've created a new test file, it's time to add some tests.

As previously stated, unit tests are a great place to test your business logic. That's why you'll start by testing `Ingredient`.

Testing the Ingredient Class

Add the following imports at the top of **ingredient_test.dart** to import the model and testing libraries:

```
import 'package:recipes/data/models/ingredient.dart';
import 'package:test/test.dart';
```

Then, add the following code inside `main`:

```
// 1.
group('Ingredient', () {
  // 2.
  test('can instantiate', () {
  });
});
```

Here's a quick rundown of the code above:

1. `group()`: is a helper function that allows you to group tests. You can set the group's name via a parameter, and all the tasks within the function will group together when you run the tests.
2. `test()`: is another helper function from the `test` package. It receives two parameters: the description of the test and a function that actually performs the test.

There are multiple ways to organize your test, but an easy one to remember is the **AAA** system: **Arrange**, **Act**, **Assert**.

The basic idea is that you first declare your test requirements, perform the desired action, and verify that the output matches the desired result.

Here's how it looks in practice. Paste the following code inside `test`:

```
// Arrange
late Ingredient ingredient;

// Act
ingredient = const Ingredient();

// Assert
expect(ingredient, isNotNull);
```

- In **Arrange**, you've declared your requirements for the test. In this case, it's about testing that you can instantiate the class.
- In **Act**, you've instantiated the class, which is the functionality to test.
- In **Assert**, you've verified that you instantiated the object correctly, and it's no longer null.

Run your tests using the Android Studio this time by clicking "**Run**" like in the screenshot below.

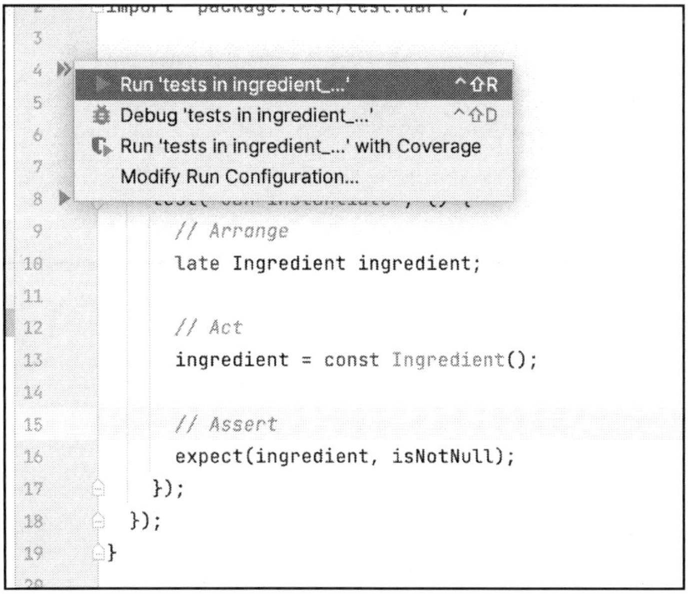

Make sure to enable **Show Passed** to display the tests that are succeeding:

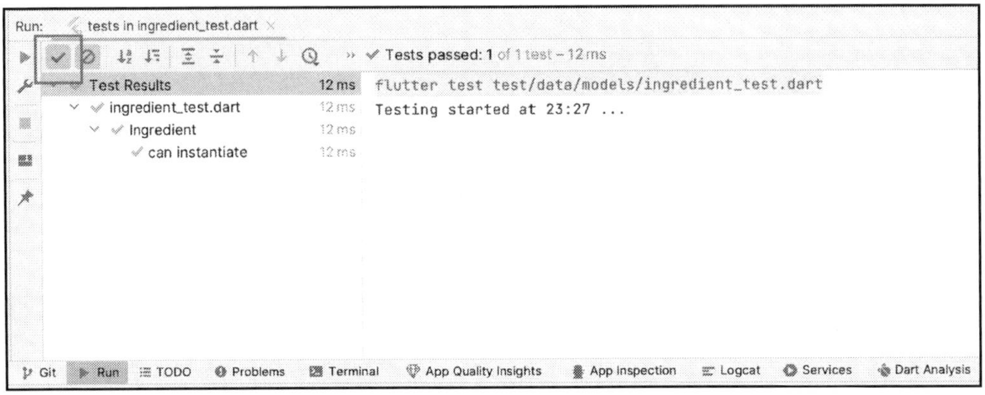

Now, there are a few more behaviors that you can test here. You could verify that the default parameters are correct when instantiated. You could also test that creating an `Ingredient` with parameters works as expected, and you could test that you can create `Ingredients` from **JSON** maps.

Copy the following code and add it at the bottom of `group`, after the previous test:

```
test('can set default properties', () {
  // Arrange
  late Ingredient ingredient;

  // Act
  ingredient = const Ingredient();

  // Assert
  expect(ingredient.id, isNull);
  expect(ingredient.recipeId, isNull);
  expect(ingredient.name, isNull);
  expect(ingredient.amount, isNull);
});
```

expect is a helper function from the `test` package that allows you to verify that a certain condition is met. It receives two parameters: the actual value and the expected value. If the condition is met, the test passes. Otherwise, it fails.

This test ensures that when you create a new `Ingredient`, all parameters have the correct default value, which in this case is `null`.

Add another test by placing the following code inside `group`:

```
test('can receive parameters', () {
  // Arrange
  late Ingredient ingredient;
```

```
    const id = 123;
    const recipeId = 54321;
    const name = 'Parmesan Cheese';
    const amount = 1.0;

    // Act
    ingredient = const Ingredient(
      id: id,
      recipeId: recipeId,
      name: name,
      amount: amount,
    );

    // Assert
    expect(ingredient.id, equals(id));
    expect(ingredient.recipeId, equals(recipeId));
    expect(ingredient.name, equals(name));
    expect(ingredient.amount, equals(amount));
  });
```

The code above verifies that when `Ingredient` is created with parameters, said parameters are assigned to the right properties of the class.

Finally, test if you can create `Ingredients` from **JSON** maps with the following test:

```
  test('can instantiate from JSON', () {
    late Ingredient ingredient;
    // 1.
    final jsonMap = <String, dynamic>{
      'id': 123,
      'recipeId': 54321,
      'name': 'Parmesan Cheese',
      'weight': 50.0,
      'amount': 1,
    };
    const id = 123;
    const recipeId = 54321;
    const name = 'Parmesan Cheese';
    const amount = 1.0;

    // 2.
    ingredient = Ingredient.fromJson(jsonMap);

    expect(ingredient.id, equals(id));
    expect(ingredient.recipeId, equals(recipeId));
    expect(ingredient.name, equals(name));
    expect(ingredient.amount, equals(amount));
  });
```

Run your tests again. They should all pass.

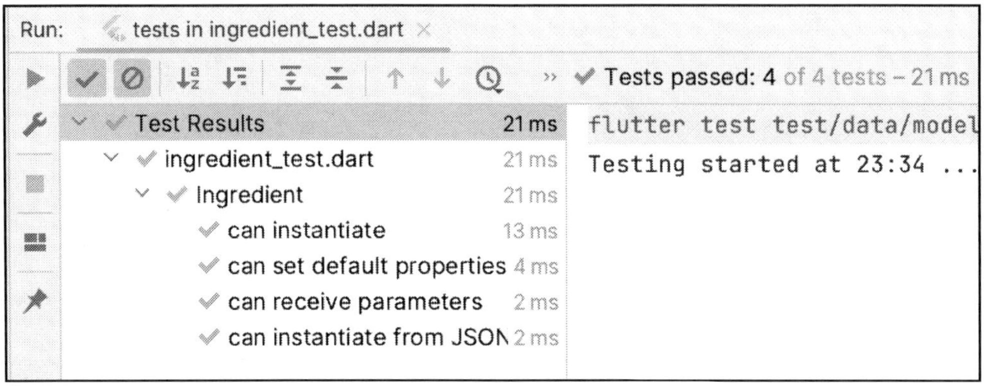

Good job! You've added your first tests to the project, and `Ingredient` is now fully tested and production-ready!

Testing Recipe Class

Now it's time to do the same for `Recipe`.

Create a new file at **test/data/models/recipe_test.dart** and add the following code inside:

```
import 'package:recipes/data/models/models.dart';
import 'package:test/test.dart';

void main() {
  group('Recipe', () {
    test('can instantiate', () {
      // Arrange
      late Recipe recipe;

      // Act
      recipe = const Recipe();

      // Assert
      expect(recipe, isNotNull);
    });
  });
}
```

This first test is essentially the same one you did for `Ingredient`. Which ensures it can be instantiated with the default values in the constructor.

Run your tests and check the results.

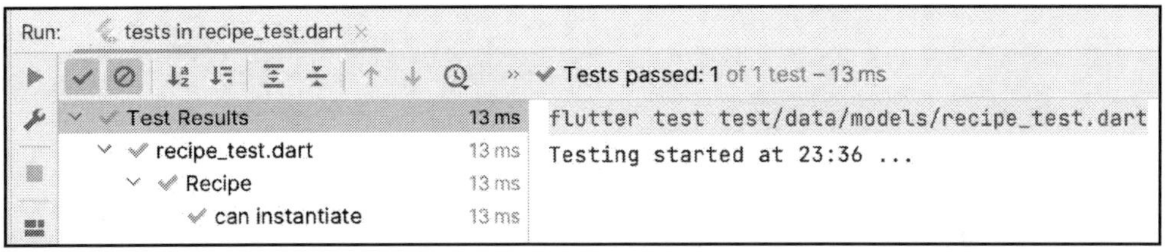

If you remember, `Recipe` is a class that's a bit more complex since it has a list of `Ingredients`. This means that `Recipe` is partially dependent on the behavior of `Ingredient`.

This scenario is fairly common when developing software. Testing these sorts of relations between classes enables the developers to catch possible errors when modifying the code.

This will be your next test. Copy the following code and paste it at the end of `group()`:

```
test('can receive parameters', () {
  late Recipe recipe;
  const id = 123;
  const label = 'Pasta with Garlic, Scallions, Cauliflower &
Breadcrumbs';
  const image = 'https://spoonacular.com/recipeImages/
716429-556x370.jpg';
  const description =
      'Pasta with Garlic, Scallions, Cauliflower & Breadcrumbs
might be a good recipe to expand your main course repertoire.
One portion of this dish contains approximately <b>19g of
protein </b>,  <b>20g of fat </b>, and a total of  <b>584
calories </b>. For  <b>\$1.63 per serving </b>, this recipe
<b>covers 23% </b> of your daily requirements of vitamins and
minerals. This recipe serves 2. It is brought to you by
fullbellysisters.blogspot.com. 209 people were glad they tried
this recipe. A mixture of scallions, salt and pepper, white
wine, and a handful of other ingredients are all it takes to
make this recipe so scrumptious. From preparation to the plate,
this recipe takes approximately  <b>45 minutes </b>. All things
considered, we decided this recipe  <b>deserves a spoonacular
score of 83% </b>. This score is awesome. If you like this
recipe, take a look at these similar recipes: <a href="https://
spoonacular.com/recipes/cauliflower-gratin-with-garlic-
breadcrumbs-318375">Cauliflower Gratin with Garlic Breadcrumbs</
a>, < href="https://spoonacular.com/recipes/pasta-with-
cauliflower-sausage-breadcrumbs-30437">Pasta With Cauliflower,
Sausage, & Breadcrumbs</a>, and <a href="https://
spoonacular.com/recipes/pasta-with-roasted-cauliflower-parsley-
and-breadcrumbs-30738">Pasta With Roasted Cauliflower, Parsley,
```

```
  And Breadcrumbs</a>.';
    const bookmarked = true;
    // 1.
    const ingredients = [
      Ingredient(
        id: 1123,
        recipeId: 123,
        name: 'Pasta',
        amount: 1.0,
      ),
      Ingredient(
        id: 1124,
        recipeId: 123,
        name: 'Garlic',
        amount: 1.0,
      ),
      Ingredient(
        id: 1125,
        recipeId: 123,
        name: 'Breadcrumbs',
        amount: 5.0,
      ),
    ];

    // 2.
    recipe = const Recipe(
      id: id,
      label: label,
      image: image,
      description: description,
      bookmarked: bookmarked,
      ingredients: ingredients,
    );

    // Assert
    expect(recipe.id, equals(id));
    expect(recipe.label, equals(label));
    expect(recipe.image, equals(image));
    expect(recipe.description, equals(description));
    expect(recipe.bookmarked, equals(bookmarked));
    // 3.
    expect(recipe.ingredients, equals(ingredients));
  });
```

Here's what that code does:

1. Defines the list of `Ingredient` objects for your recipe. If `Ingredient` fails instantiation, then it would fail while creating this list. This would mean that the test failed, and you could catch this error before merging failing code.

2. Creates a new `Recipe` object with the predefined parameters. This includes your `Ingredient` list.

3. Verifies that the ingredients in your recipe actually match the predefined ingredients you arranged earlier.

Run your tests again and check the result.

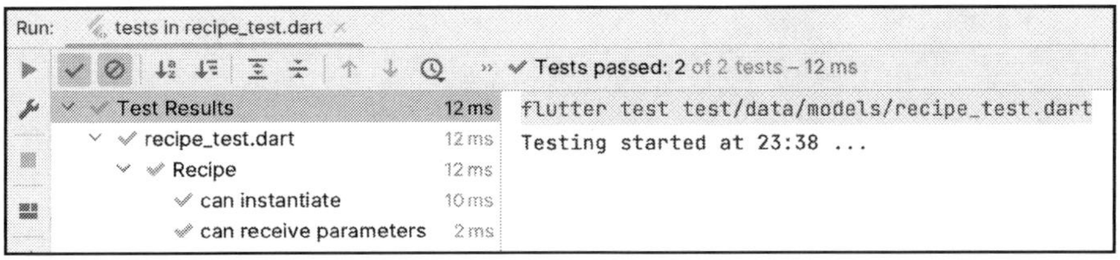

Great! You've tested `Recipe`. Now, your business logic models are covered by tests, and you can detect bugs early while developing.

Understanding Mocks

If you've ever done testing before, you might be familiar with the term **mocking**. But if you aren't, you'll understand the basics after this chapter.

Think of mocking like magic in the world of testing! Imagine you have a friendly wizard who can create look-alike or "mock" versions of things you need for your tests. These mock objects are like stunt doubles for real components such as databases, web services or other pieces of code.

Real components might be too slow, expensive or just too big to set up for testing. In those cases, you can use your magical mock skills to avoid needing them and make your tests more reliable.

Here are a few other reasons why you'd want to mock:

1. **Testing in Isolation**: When creating unit tests, it's important to isolate the unit of code under test from "external dependencies". This ensures that you're testing in isolation and not the behavior of other components. Mocking allows you to replace real dependencies with simulated objects that behave as you want.

2. **Predictable Behavior**: Mocking allows you to define the behavior of dependencies in a controlled manner. You can specify how mock objects should respond to method calls, ensuring that the test focuses on the specific scenario you want to evaluate. This predictability helps in reproducing different test cases and edge conditions.

3. **Speed and Efficiency**: Real dependencies, such as databases, APIs or external services, can be slow or have limited availability during testing. Mocks are typically lightweight and readily available, allowing tests to execute quickly and efficiently without external dependencies.
4. **Fault Injection**: Mocking enables you to simulate error conditions or exceptional situations that are hard to create with real dependencies. You can force a mock to throw exceptions, return unexpected values or simulate network errors, allowing you to test how your code handles such situations.
5. **Development Speed**: During **test-driven development** (TDD), mocking dependencies allow you to write tests for code that depends on components that have not been fully implemented yet. You can create mock objects to define expected interactions and design tests before implementing the actual dependencies.

In the context of Flutter and Dart, mocking dependencies is widely used in unit testing, particularly when testing the logic of your code. Mocking packages like `mockito` provide developers with the ability to create mocks for classes and dependencies, making it easier to write focused and isolated unit tests.

Wizard! It's time you use the magical mocking skills you've read about. Open **pubspec.yml** and add the following package to your `dev_dependencies` declaration:

```
mockito: ^5.4.2
```

Run your tests and ensure that every test is passing.

Now, add a new test file, **test/data/repositories/db_repository_test.dart** and paste in the following code:

```
import 'package:recipes/data/repositories/db_repository.dart';
import 'package:test/test.dart';

void main() {
  group('DBRepository', () {
    test('can instantiate', () {
      // Arrange
      late DBRepository dbRepository;

      // Act
      dbRepository = DBRepository();

      // Assert
      expect(dbRepository, isNotNull);
      expect(dbRepository.recipeDatabase, isNotNull);
    });
```

```
  });
}
```

Run your tests and check the results below.

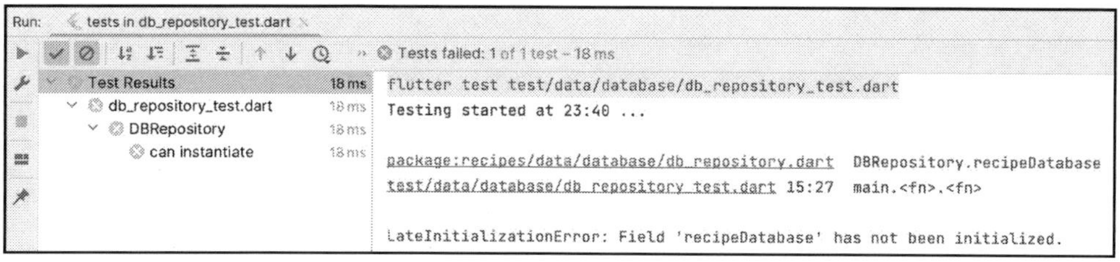

Ka-boom! Your tests just failed! But why is that? Keep on reading to find out the answer and recover your powers!

Making Your Code Testable

`DBRepository` has a hidden dependency that is not exposed in the constructor of the class. This makes it crash when you try to access `recipeDatabase`, and it's not initialized. To top it all, this property is key for other class variables and functions to work as expected.

`recipeDatabase` is assigned a value when calling `init()`, which isn't called in your test. At a simple glance, this doesn't look like that big of a deal, right? Should you just call `init` in the test to fix the issues? Well, the correct answer is *kind of*.

Consider the following scenario - A new team member is onboarded to work on the same app you're working on. What happens if they try to use `DBRepository` in a different part of your app? They might not be aware that calling any other method before `init` will result in a crash.

So, what should you do? One solution is to have your code speak for itself by making the dependencies of `DBRepository` explicit in the constructor.

Open **lib/data/repositories/db_repository.dart** and add the following constructor to the class:

```
DBRepository({RecipeDatabase? recipeDatabase})
    : recipeDatabase = recipeDatabase ?? RecipeDatabase();
```

Then, change `init` to the following:

```
@override
Future init() async {
  _recipeDao = recipeDatabase.recipeDao;
  _ingredientDao = recipeDatabase.ingredientDao;
}
```

This makes the dependencies of `DBRepository` a bit clearer. It maintains the behavior, allowing you to run the app without problems. It also makes your code testable since you can now mock the dependencies and not require a fully functional `RecipeDatabase` implementation to test `DBRepository`.

Now, run **db_repository_test.dart** again. The result should match the image below:

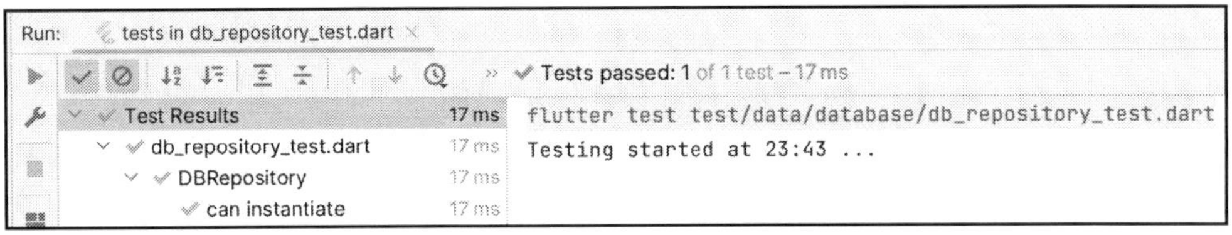

Great, the tests are passing again!

When dependencies aren't clear, errors can easily creep into your code, and a small modification can quickly turn into a headache. Unit testing can help you identify such scenarios in your code and fix them early in the development of your Flutter app.

Mocking With Mockito

You've already read that it's important to isolate the code under test from external dependencies when creating unit tests. In this case, having a fully functional `RecipeDatabase` might not be what you want in the tests for `DBRepository`. So, it's time to take out your magic wand and use some mocking spells.

`mockito` is a great toolbox to generate mocks without having to do too much work. This enables you to write focused and isolated tests without sacrificing time. To get started, still in **db_repository_test.dart**, add the following import to the test file:

```
import 'package:mockito/annotations.dart';
import 'package:mockito/mockito.dart';
import 'package:recipes/data/database/recipe_db.dart';
import 'package:recipes/data/models/ingredient.dart';
```

`mockito.dart` includes all mocking functions that you'll need to test. On the other hand, `annotations.dart` imports a couple of neat annotations for generating mocks via build runner.

Next, before the declaration of `main`, paste the following code:

```
@GenerateNiceMocks([
  MockSpec<RecipeDatabase>(),
  MockSpec<RecipeDao>(),
  MockSpec<IngredientDao>(),
])
```

This will tell mockito to generate mocks for all the classes listed in the parameter.

In the terminal, navigate to the **root** of your project and run `dart run build_runner build --delete-conflicting-outputs` to generate the mocked classes. After running it, a new file named **test/data/repositories/db_repository_test.mocks.dart** will show up. It'll contain the mocks you requested above.

Import the generated file at the top of **test/data/repositories/db_repository_test.dart**:

```
import 'db_repository_test.mocks.dart';
```

Now, add the following code at the start of `main()`:

```
// 1.
final mockDb = MockRecipeDatabase();
final mockIngredientDao = MockIngredientDao();
final mockRecipeDao = MockRecipeDao();

// 2.
final randomIngredients = [
  const Ingredient(
    id: 1123,
    recipeId: 123,
    name: 'Pasta',
    amount: 1.0,
  ),
  const Ingredient(
    id: 1124,
    recipeId: 123,
    name: 'Garlic',
    amount: 1.0,
  ),
  const Ingredient(
    id: 1125,
    recipeId: 123,
```

```
      name: 'Breadcrumbs',
      amount: 5.0,
    ),
  ];

  // 3.
  when(mockDb.ingredientDao).thenReturn(mockIngredientDao);
  when(mockDb.recipeDao).thenReturn(mockRecipeDao);
```

1. `MockRecipeDatabase`, `MockIngredientDao` and `MockRecipeDao` are generated by `mockito` using the build runner. These classes have the same variables and method signatures as the real implementations, with the exception that they can be controlled.
2. You're preparing a list of random ingredients that'll be used later in your tests.
3. `when` is a special function provided by `mockito` that allows you to control how a mock should behave. It indicates that whenever you try to access `mockDb.ingredientDao` or `mockDb.recipeDao`, the mocked version should be used.

Then, modify the test for instantiation so that when you create a `DBRepository`, you pass `mockDb` as the parameter like so:

```
  dbRepository = DBRepository(
    recipeDatabase: mockDb,
  );
```

This ensures that your test uses the mocked version of `RecipeDatabase` instead of the real one.

Run your tests and verify that they are all still passing.

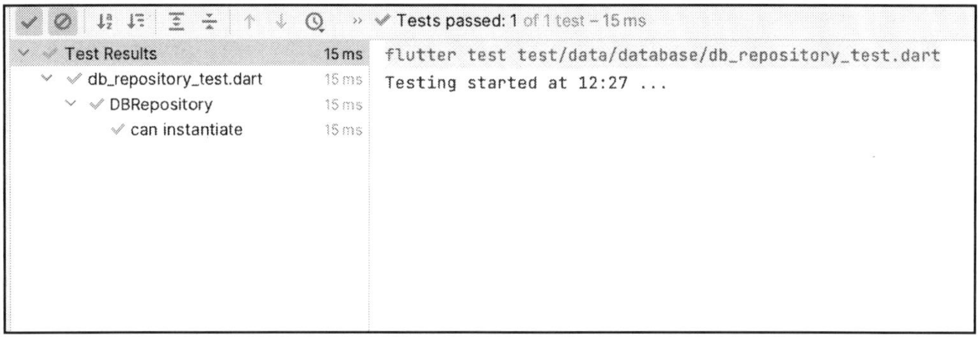

Now, you'll add a new test for `findAllIngredients()` and learn to mock methods.

Start by copying the following test to your group:

```
test('can findAllIngredients', () async {
  // TODO: Arrange
  // TODO: Act
  // TODO: Assert
});
```

Next, you'll work on defining the test's requirements. To call `findAllIngredients()`, you'll need an instance of `DBRepository` with the mocked database version.

Replace `// TODO: Arrange` with the following code:

```
// 1.
final dbRepository = DBRepository(
  recipeDatabase: mockDb,
);
await dbRepository.init();
// 2.
when(mockIngredientDao.findAllIngredients()).thenAnswer(
  (_) async => randomIngredients
      .map((e) => DbIngredientData(
            id: e.id!,
            recipeId: e.recipeId!,
            name: e.name!,
            amount: e.amount!,
          ))
      .toList(),
);
```

1. First, you are initializing a new instance of `DBRepository` using the mocked database `mockDb`.
2. Then, you are mocking the call to `mockIngredientDao.findAllIngredients`. Mocking allows you to mock both variables and methods. This means you can also test behaviors that interact directly with the database and check that the right methods are called.

Next, replace `// TODO: Act` with the code below:

```
final result = await dbRepository.findAllIngredients();
```

Now that the calls to the database are mocked, you can run `findAllIngredients()` and store the result in a variable for later assertions.

Finally, replace `// TODO: Assert` with the code below:

```
// 3.
verify(mockIngredientDao.findAllIngredients()).called(1);
// 4.
expect(result, equals(randomIngredients));
```

3. `verify()` is a special function exported by mockito that allows you to check the behavior of a mock and its variables and functions. With this code, you are ensuring that `mockIngredientDao.findAllIngredients()` is called once when running your repository's code to find ingredients.
4. Like in previous tests, you check that the actual result matches the expected output you used to mock the call to `mockIngredientDao.findAllIngredients()`.

Run your tests again. They should all be passing at this point.

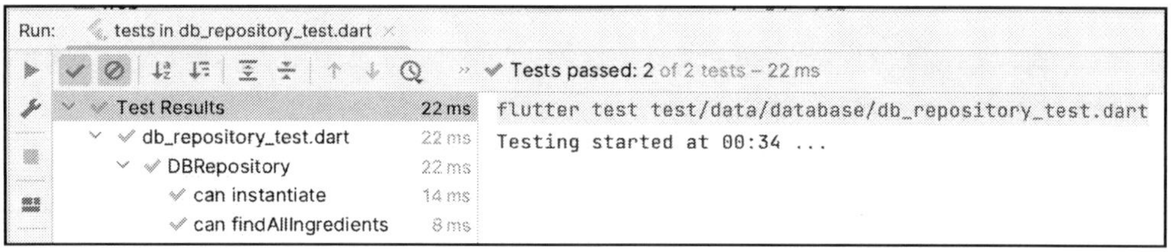

Congrats! You are now mocking parts of the database, to simplify the testing of `DBRepository`. Feel free to go on and add tests for the other methods.

Key Points

- Testing ensures that your Flutter project is of high quality, meets user expectations and is free from defects.
- Testing your code improves confidence when releasing a new version of your app.
- There are multiple types of tests that vary according to different requirements.
- Unit testing is great for building robust and maintainable Flutter apps.
- You can bundle tests together with `group()`.
- To run unit tests, you'll need to use `test()`.
- The complexity of a class matters when you think about testing them.
- Consider mocking when dealing with external dependencies.

Where to Go From Here?

Unit testing is great for building robust and maintainable Flutter apps. In this chapter, you learned the essentials of unit testing a Flutter project, mocking dependencies with mockito, organizing and running tests, handling asynchronous testing and best practices.

By testing your Flutter projects, you can ensure that your apps are well-tested and reliable. Embrace unit testing as an everyday practice, and you'll be on your way to delivering high-quality Flutter applications.

If you want to learn more about testing, check out this video course (https://www.kodeco.com/35357214-testing-in-flutter). It looks more in-depth at the topic of testing Flutter apps and how to make your code easier to test.

If you prefer reading, you can also check this tutorial about unit testing (https://www.kodeco.com/6926998-unit-testing-with-flutter-getting-started), which looks a bit more in-depth at the subject of Unit Testing.

Chapter 18: Widget Testing

Alejandro Ulate

Widget testing is about making your Flutter widgets dance to your tune. It's essential to ensure your UI components not only look good but also work as you intended. In this chapter, you'll:

- Learn the concept of **widget testing**.
- Load **mock data** into the widget tests.
- Ensure that each ingredient displays correctly.
- Understand what **golden tests** are.
- Add golden tests to verify your widget's look and feel.

Learning About Widget Tests

Widget testing plays an important role in ensuring your widgets' reliability and proper functioning. Unlike other testing approaches, widget tests are specifically designed to concentrate on the interaction and underlying logic of the UI elements.

In essence, they act as "unit" tests for your widgets, providing a targeted examination of their behavior, responsiveness and functionality in isolation. This focus helps you identify and address issues early in the development process, contributing to a more robust and error-resistant Flutter application.

Some common scenarios you might want to use widget tests for are:

- **Successful Widget Building**: Widget tests are particularly handy for ensuring your widgets `build` successfully under expected conditions.
- **User Interaction Verification**: These tests enable you to simulate user actions, such as tapping or inputting text, ensuring that your widgets respond as expected.
- **State Changes and UI Updates**: These tests can also help you confirm that state changes within your widgets work as intended and that these changes are reflected in the user interface.
- **Navigation and Routing Logic**: By simulating navigation events, you can verify that your app transitions between screens correctly and that the UI adapts as expected.

Widget tests improve the reliability of your app. They validate critical parts of it, such as building widgets, user interaction, state management, and navigation logic.

It's time you start working on your own widget tests. Start by adding a new test file that matches the following path **test/ui/widgets/ingredient_card_test.dart**. You'll need to create the corresponding directories too.

Then, just so our test suite doesn't fail, add the following code to your test file:

```
void main() {}
```

Use your IDE to run your tests. The result should match the screenshot below:

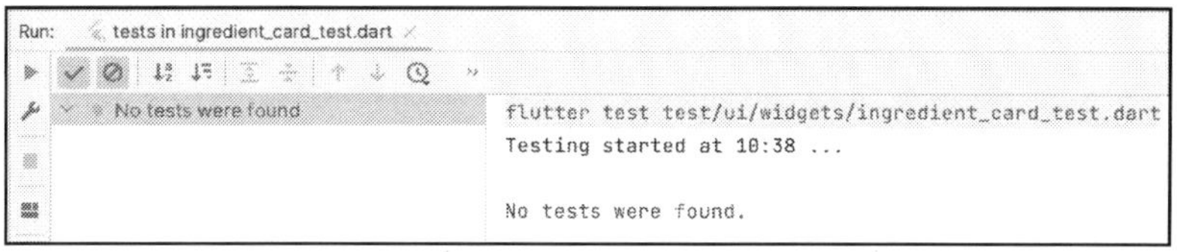

Adding Your First Widget Test

As you recall, a good scenario for you to get your hands on testing is to verify that the widget builds successfully. This way, you can ensure that your widget's structure matches your expectations.

Before creating the test, this is a quick reminder of how the widget you'll test looks:

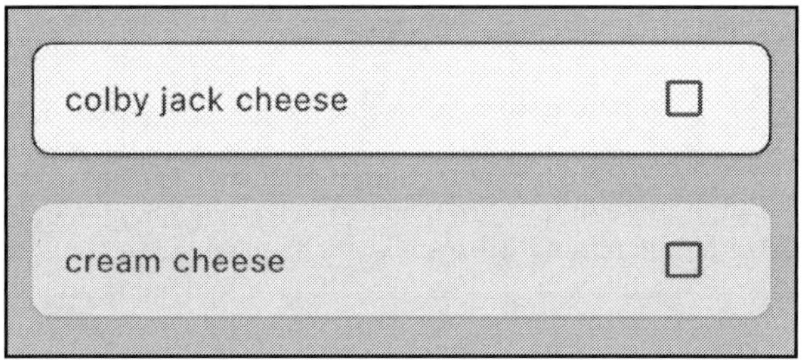

It's important to point out that `IngredientCard` can have multiple variations depending on:

- `evenRow`: changes the **border** and **background color** of the card depending on its value.
- `showCheckbox`: hides or shows the **checkbox** at the right end of the card.
- `initiallyChecked`: marks the checkbox at the right end of the card on the initial `build` of the widget.
- If it's checked, the `name` displays as **striked-through**, otherwise, it's just plain text.

These differences can all produce different results, and they can even combine, ending in more variations. These results are important because they change what you can expect of the widget rendering.

If you've got widgets like `IngredientCard`, it's smart to test them with different situations. Testing with various combinations means you're checking how your widget behaves in different situations.

This helps ensure your widget and all its possible versions work the way they should and stay safe from unexpected changes that might pop up during development.

So, here's the scenario you'll use to verify that `IngredientCard` builds properly:

Given `IngredientCard` is in an `evenRow`, the checkbox is showing as unchecked when the widget builds, then it should be displayed without issues.

Start by adding the following imports at the top of your file:

```
import 'package:flutter/material.dart';
import 'package:flutter_test/flutter_test.dart';
import 'package:recipes/ui/widgets/ingredient_card.dart';
```

This imports Flutter's `material` library along with the testing toolkit. It also imports `IngredientCard`, which you'll be testing.

Then, copy the following code inside `main()`:

```
testWidgets('IngredientCard can build', (WidgetTester tester)
async {
  // TODO: Arrange
  // TODO: Act
  // TODO: Assert
});
```

`testWidgets()` is a special function provided by `flutter_test`. It allows you to build a widget and verify its behaviors. You could build a simple `Text` or a complex widget with a `Scaffold` or even build a complete `MaterialApp`.

You can think of `testWidgets()` as an equivalent for `test()` in unit testing.

`testWidgets()` receives a `WidgetTesterCallback`. This callback gives you access to a `WidgetTester` instance (`tester` in the code above). It allows you to programmatically interact with widgets and the test environment.

Also, you'll be using the same testing technique as you did for unit testing in the previous chapter: **Arrange, Act, Assert**. This gives you an organized way to test behaviors and also a repeatable process for all your tests.

Next, replace `// TODO: Arrange` with this code:

```
// 1.
const mockIngredientName = 'colby jack cheese';
await tester.pumpWidget(
  // 2.
  MaterialApp(
    home: Scaffold(
      body: ListView(
        children: [
          // 3.
          IngredientCard(
            name: mockIngredientName,
            initiallyChecked: false,
            evenRow: true,
            onChecked: (isChecked) {},
          ),
```

```
            ],
          ),
        ),
      ),
    );
```

In detail, here's what the code above is doing:

1. First, pumpWidget() renders the UI from the given widget.
2. You've supplied a MaterialApp and other wrappers around IngredientCard since it has some dependencies around theming and context, which is why this is necessary.
3. Matches the test scenario you were given. showCheckbox is true by default so there's no need to explicitly declare it when building the widget.

Now, for the **Act** part of the test, use the following code and replace // TODO: Act:

```
final cardFinder = find.byType(IngredientCard);
final titleFinder = find.text(mockIngredientName);
```

find() is a helper function that allows you to search through the widget tree for specific elements and returns all the nodes that match the criteria. cardFinder is an example of how to find a certain widget by using the type class. On the other hand, titleFinder looks for a certain text anywhere in the current widget tree.

Finally, replace // TODO: Assert with the following:

```
expect(cardFinder, findsOneWidget);
expect(titleFinder, findsOneWidget);
```

With the code above, you are asserting that both finders can find widgets according to the criteria set. findsOneWidget looks for exactly one widget in the widget tree that matches the criteria.

flutter_test has other assertions already built-in that can help you create finders depending on your case. Here's a quick look at some of them:

- findsNothing, when you want the finder to not find anything.
- findsWidgets, when you want the finder to find one or more widgets.
- findsNWidgets, when you want the finder to find a specific number of widgets.
- findsAtLeastNWidgets, when you want the finder to find at least a specific number of widgets.

Use the IDE to run your tests for `IngredientCard`. They should be passing like in the image below:

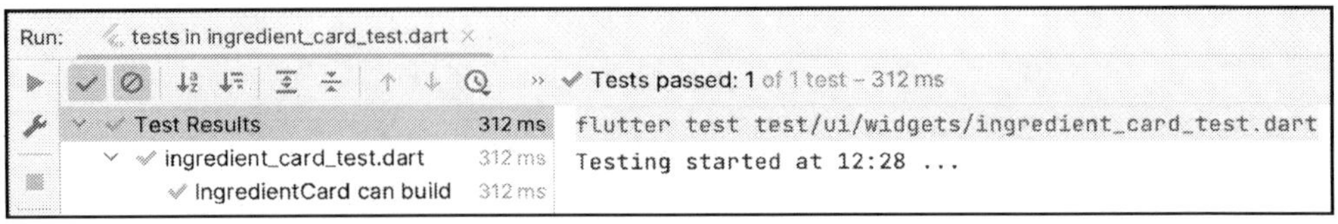

Great job! You've just added your first widget test.

Testing IngredientCard's Behaviors

Widget testing becomes super useful when you want to check how your widgets respond to users. You can use these tests to pretend to be a user, clicking buttons or entering information. This way, you make sure your widgets react the right way and give users a smooth experience.

For example, `IngredientCard` can be checked or unchecked when the user taps it. This is a great scenario to test for since it'll verify how your widget behaves when the user interacts with it.

This is the next test you'll add:

Given `IngredientCard` is in an `evenRow`, unchecked, and the checkbox is showing, when the user taps on it, then `onChecked()` should be called with the new value.

But before diving into the test, you'll reorganize the test file so that you don't repeat yourself in your tests.

Change the contents of **ingredient_card_test.dart** for the following:

```
import 'package:flutter/material.dart';
import 'package:flutter_test/flutter_test.dart';
import 'package:recipes/ui/widgets/ingredient_card.dart';

// 1.
Widget _buildWrappedWidget(Widget child) {
  return MaterialApp(
    home: Scaffold(
      body: ListView(
        children: [
          child,
        ],
      ),
    ),
```

```
  );
}

void main() {
  // 2.
  const mockIngredientName = 'colby jack cheese';
  group('IngredientCard', () {
    testWidgets('can build', (tester) async {
      // 3.
      await tester.pumpWidget(
        _buildWrappedWidget(IngredientCard(
          name: mockIngredientName,
          initiallyChecked: false,
          evenRow: true,
          onChecked: (isChecked) {},
        )),
      );

      final cardFinder = find.byType(IngredientCard);
      final titleFinder = find.text(mockIngredientName);

      expect(cardFinder, findsOneWidget);
      expect(titleFinder, findsOneWidget);
    });
    // 4.
    testWidgets('can be checked when tapped', (tester) async {
      // TODO: Arrange
      // TODO: Act
      // TODO: Assert
    });
  });
}
```

Here's a quick rundown of what you just did:

1. You've added a reusable function to wrap your widgets with a `MaterialApp` parent tree. This is great because you're going to need it in all, if not most, of your tests.
2. Lifted `mockIngredientName` to be available for all your tests. You've also prepared things to `group` tests together.
3. Updated your previous test to use the wrapper `_buildWrappedWidget`.
4. Added the base for your next test.

Run your tests and ensure that they're still passing, like in the image below:

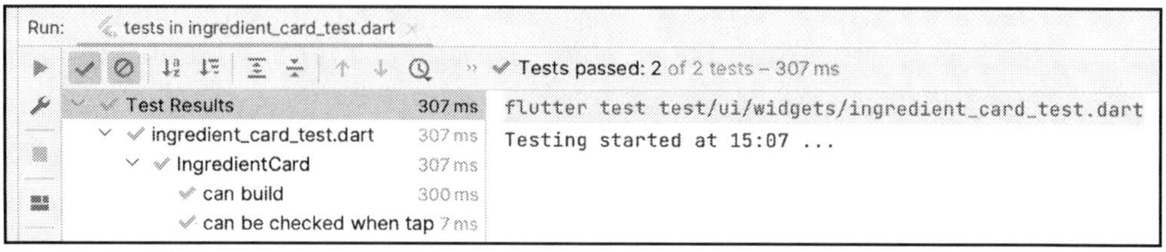

Next, replace `// TODO: Arrange` with this:

```
var isChecked = false;
await tester.pumpWidget(
  _buildWrappedWidget(IngredientCard(
    name: mockIngredientName,
    initiallyChecked: isChecked,
    evenRow: true,
    onChecked: (newValue) {
      isChecked = newValue;
    },
  )),
);
```

You're setting up `isChecked` which'll be useful to verify the behavior when the card is tapped. You've also set `onChecked()` to update `isChecked` when called. That's about it for the **Arrange** step.

Now, use the following code to replace `// TODO: Act` with the code below:

```
final cardFinder = find.byType(IngredientCard);

await tester.tap(cardFinder);
await tester.pumpAndSettle();

final checkboxFinder = find.byType(Checkbox);
```

`tap()` simulates the user tapping the screen of a device. It receives a finder to perform the action on, which in this case is `cardFinder`. Then, `pumpAndSettle()` updates the widget tree frame by frame until it *settles*; hence the name.

Once settled, `checkboxFinder` is also initialized. You'll later use it to verify in the next step.

Finally, replace `// TODO: Assert` with the following:

```
expect(checkboxFinder, findsOneWidget);
expect(isChecked, isTrue);
```

With this code, you are checking two things:

- First, there's one `Checkbox` built and visible inside the widget tree.
- Secondly, that `isChecked` changed correctly to true after calling `tester.tap(cardFinder)`.

Run your tests again. All tests should pass like the image below:

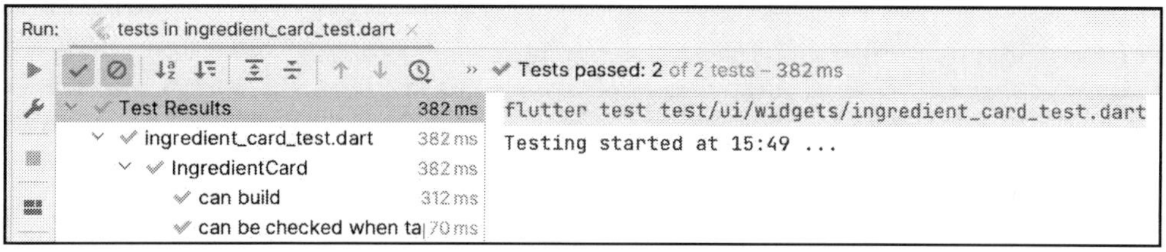

Your tests are working now! Time to try to verify how the widget looks.

Understanding Golden Tests

While widget testing is great for checking how your widgets work, it might not cover everything about how they look. Widget tests focus more on how things function, not so much on the visual details.

In situations where the exact appearance of a widget is crucial, just relying on widget tests might not be enough.

That's where golden tests come in. They specifically look at how your widgets appear. A golden test is a type of test that checks whether the visual output of a widget matches an expected 'golden' image.

The term 'golden' refers to the fact that you have a baseline image (the golden image) that represents the correct appearance of the widget under normal conditions.

If the test suite detects differences between the golden image and the actual widget's UI, then it'll fail the test.

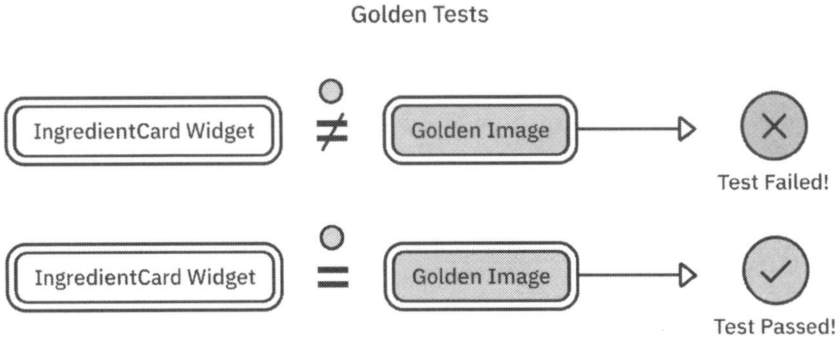

This makes these types of tests particularly useful when working on UI components because they help catch unintended changes in the visual appearance.

If you intentionally change the UI, you might need to update the golden image to reflect the new expected output. This helps prevent unintentional visual regressions.

The `flutter_test` package already has the built-in features to support golden tests. However, using them on your own might require a complex setup that is hard to replicate from project to project.

This is why `golden_toolkit` exists. It contains APIs and utilities that build upon Flutter's Golden test functionality in `flutter_test` to provide powerful UI regression tests in a simpler way.

To add golden tests to your Flutter project, start by adding `golden_toolkit` to your **pubspec.yml** like the following:

```
golden_toolkit: ^0.15.0
```

Remember to run `flutter pub get` afterward to update your dependencies.

Next, create a new file at the root of your project. Name it **dart_test.yaml** and put the following code inside it:

```
tags:
  golden:
```

This indicates that goldens are an expected test tag. All tests that use `testGoldens()` will get this tag automatically. It also allows you to run golden tests from the command-line.

Open a terminal and run the following command:

```
flutter test --update-goldens
```

The output should match something like the following image:

```
Got dependencies!
00:05 +10: All tests passed!
```

Using `--update-goldens` updates all the golden images in your tests. You should use this flag sparingly, as it'll take your tests a little longer to run.

You are now ready to start writing your own golden tests. You'll be working on that in the next section.

Writing a Golden Test

It's time to dive into the process of creating your first golden test. `IngredientCard` supports the light theme very well, and going forward, it's a good idea to test that it always stays that way.

Open **ingredient_card_test.dart** again and add the following code after your first test group:

```
group('Golden Tests - IngredientCard', () {
  testGoldens('can support light theme', (tester) async {
    // TODO: Arrange
    // TODO: Act
    // TODO: Assert
  });
});
```

`testGoldens()` is a special function provided by `golden_toolkit`. It allows you to build a widget and compare it with the golden image. Import `golden_toolkit`.

```
import 'package:golden_toolkit/golden_toolkit.dart';
```

Next, replace `// TODO: Arrange` with the code below:

```
final builder = GoldenBuilder.grid(columns: 2,
widthToHeightRatio: 1)
// TODO: Scenario for Light - Unchecked
// TODO: Other scenarios
```

`GoldenBuilder` builds a column/grid layout for its children. It'll output a PNG file with a grid layout in the test's directory.

This `builder` is needed to compare it to the actual widget you're testing. For now, what's important is that you know that `GoldenBuilder` requires scenarios to build.

A scenario is a specific configuration of your widget that you want to save for later validation. With `IngredientCard`, you'll work on adding four different scenarios:

1. `IngredientCard` in an even row that displays the checkbox as unchecked in a light theme.
2. `IngredientCard` in an even row that displays the checkbox as checked in a light theme.
3. `IngredientCard` in an odd row that displays the checkbox as unchecked in a light theme.
4. `IngredientCard` in an odd row that displays the checkbox as checked in a light theme.

Now it's time to add such scenarios. Replace `// TODO: Scenario for Light - Unchecked` with the following code:

```
// Scenario 1
..addScenario(
  'Light - Unchecked',
  IngredientCard(
    name: mockIngredientName,
    initiallyChecked: false,
    evenRow: true,
    onChecked: (newValue) {},
  ),
)
```

Calling `addScenario()` includes the test scenario into the `builder` that you initialized before.

Next, replace `// TODO: Other scenarios` with the code below:

```
// Scenario 2
..addScenario(
  'Light - Checked',
  IngredientCard(
    name: mockIngredientName,
    initiallyChecked: true,
    evenRow: true,
    onChecked: (newValue) {},
```

```
    ),
  )
  // Scenario 3
  ..addScenario(
    'Light - Odd - Unchecked',
    IngredientCard(
      name: mockIngredientName,
      initiallyChecked: false,
      evenRow: false,
      onChecked: (newValue) {},
    ),
  )
  // Scenario 4
  ..addScenario(
    'Light - Odd - Checked',
    IngredientCard(
      name: mockIngredientName,
      initiallyChecked: true,
      evenRow: false,
      onChecked: (newValue) {},
    ),
  );
```

In the code above, you're also including the other three scenarios discussed before. The main changes are in how you set up the `IngredientCard`. That's pretty much it!

Then, for the next step, replace `// TODO: Act` with the next code:

```
// 1.
await tester.pumpWidgetBuilder(
  // 2.
  builder.build(),
  // 3.
  wrapper: materialAppWrapper(
    theme: ThemeData.light(),
  ),
);
```

Here's an explanation of the code you just added:

1. `pumpWidgetBuilder()` is conveniently included in `golden_toolkit` to simplify building your widget and golden images.

2. `builder.build()` builds the list of scenarios with the layout you set up during the **Arrange** step.

3. `pumpWidgetBuilder()` also allows you to provide a custom wrapper for all your scenarios. This ensures you don't repeat yourself while adding each scenario and also allows you to customize the configuration for your widget.

Finally, replace `// TODO: Assert` with the code below:

```
await screenMatchesGolden(tester, 'light_ingredient_card');
```

`screenMatchesGolden()` wraps the API of `flutter_test` with some extra functionality. This is where `golden_toolkit` simplifies a lot of the setup needed to compare with golden images.

The second parameter of `screenMatchesGolden()` is the name of the golden file that'll be generated. This file will be stored in the current directory of the test in a new folder called `goldens/<name-you-specify>.png`.

Run your tests again with the flag to update your golden images using the CLI command: `flutter test --update-goldens`.

The output should match the following image:

```
→  starter git:(18-widget-testing) ✗ flutter test --update-goldens
00:02 +11: All tests passed!
```

Take a look at your test's directory, too. The test suite generated the golden images used for testing.

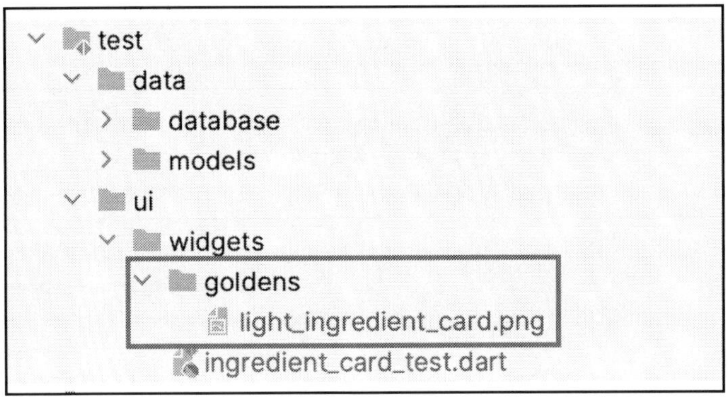

If you open that file, it should look something like the image below:

Just to make sure that your golden tests are working properly, you'll put it to the test. Hypothetically, let's assume a teammate of yours worked on `IngredientCard` and accidentally introduced a bug while coding.

Open **lib/ui/widgets/ingredient_card.dart**. Then, change **line 62** to the following code:

```
value: true,
```

Now, run your tests for `IngredientCard` using your IDE. The result should be like in the image below.

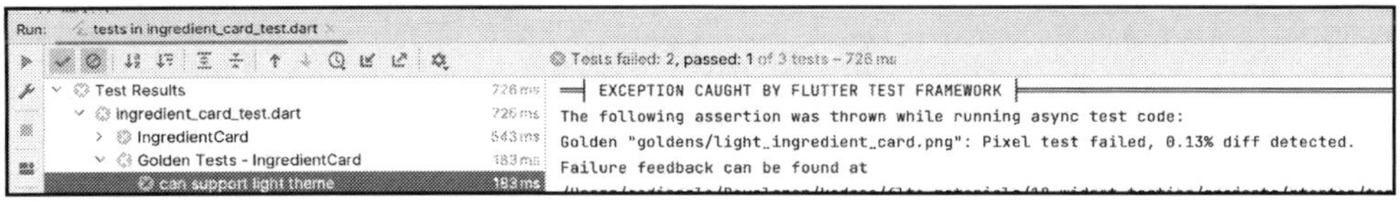

Great! Not only did your widget tests catch the behavior, but your golden test also indicates that the changes break how the widget looks, and you were able to catch it before releasing the app to customers!

Before continuing, return `IngredientCard` to the bug-free version by undoing the change in **line 62**.

Challenges

Challenge 1: Test IngredientCard Can Be Unchecked

You've already added a test to verify the opposite behavior. Use it as an example to test that `IngredientCard` can be unchecked when tapped and if it was initially checked when rendering the widget. Here's a list of the general steps you'll need to complete this challenge:

1. Initialize `isChecked` to `true`.
2. Use `pumpWidget()` to render the UI for your widget.
3. Set `isChecked` to the `newValue` inside `IngredientCard`'s `onChecked()` callback.
4. Find and `tap` the `IngredientCard`.
5. Find `Checkbox`.
6. Perform your assertions.

Challenge 2: Test IngredientCard Supports Dark Theme

Again, you've already tested that `IngredientCard` supports the light theme. Now it's time to check that it also supports the dark theme.

Here's an overview of the steps you'll need to complete this challenge:

1. Use `GoldenBuilder` to build a grid with two columns.
2. Add two scenarios, one for checked and another one for unchecked states.
3. Call `pumpWidgetBuilder()` to render your widget's using `materialAppWrapper` as `wrapper`.
4. Set `materialAppWrapper` theme to `Theme.dark()`.
5. Assert that your screen matches the golden file with `screenMatchesGolden`.
6. Update your golden tests using `--update-goldens` when testing.
7. Run your tests and verify they all pass.

Key Points

- Tools like the `flutter_test` package provide utilities to make testing easier.
- Widget tests are great for verifying behaviors.
- You can verify that a widget builds correctly with a widget test.
- `WidgetTester` allows you to perform multiple interactions with your widgets, like `tap` or even text input.
- Golden tests are bound to a 'golden' image.
- 'Golden' refers to the fact that you have a baseline image that represents the correct appearance of a widget under normal conditions.
- You can catch unexpected changes to your UI with golden tests.

Where to Go From Here?

You could do so much more with widget testing, so be sure to take a look at Testing in Flutter (https://www.kodeco.com/35357214-testing-in-flutter) if you want to learn about testing in much more detail.

There's also a guided tutorial about Widget Testing in Flutter (https://www.kodeco.com/36300023-widget-testing-with-flutter-getting-started) that can also help you dive further into the great world of testing with Flutter.

Take a look at the guide for Integration Testing (https://docs.flutter.dev/cookbook/testing/integration/introduction) that the Flutter team compiled and has published for all Flutter devs.

Section VII: Deployment

Building an app for you own devices is great; sharing your app with the world is even better!

In this section you'll go over the steps and process needed to release your apps to the iOS App Store and Google Play Store. You'll also see how to use platform-specific assets in your apps.

Chapter 19: Platform-Specific App Assets

By Michael Katz & Stef Patterson

So far, you've built Flutter apps using the Dart language and the various Flutter idioms. You then built and deployed those apps to **iOS** and **Android** devices without having to do anything special. You may have even tried running your apps in **Chrome** or as a **desktop** app. It's almost magical.

Sometimes you'll need to add **platform-specific** code and assets to cater to the needs of a particular store or operating system.

For example, you'll need to change how you specify the app **icon**, the **launch assets** and the **splash screen** to suit each platform.

In this chapter, you'll go through the process of setting up some important parts of your app to look great regardless of which platform your users choose.

Open this chapter's **starter** project in your Flutter IDE. Remember to click the **Get dependencies** or execute `flutter pub get` from Terminal.

> **Note**: This chapter is about platform-specific app assets. For your app features to function you'll need to add your **API Key** that you used in the previous section to **lib/network/spoonacular_service.dart**. If you don't plan on using the app features, you can skip this step.

You'll need to use native development tools when working with platform-specific assets, so you'll need to have the latest version of **Xcode** to complete the **iOS** and **macOS** portions in this chapter.

Setting the App Icon

The app icon is one of the most important pieces of any app's branding. It's displayed on the store page and the device home screen, as well as in notifications and settings. It's the avatar for your app, so it must look perfect! To do this, you need to use constraints.

Android and iOS not only use different constraints, but they also specify them differently, which means you need to tweak your icon for each platform.

By default, when you create a new Flutter project it sets the Flutter **F logo** as the project's icon:

Not only is this not branded to your recipe app, but the app stores aren't likely to approve it.

You can have the same icon for **multiple** platforms, or you can set it up for each platform **individually**. For this chapter they're going to look very similar, including when run in Chrome.

Your first task will be to say "_Good-bye, dear Flutter icon!_" by updating your app to have a custom image that looks great on each platform.

Hello, lovely Chef icon!

In addition to adding your app icon, you'll also change the **name** of your app and prepare the **launch screen** for multiple platforms.

Ready to get started? OK then, you'll be starting with iOS.

Setting up iOS Icon and Launch Assets

You'll work on the iOS app icon and name at the same time.

Optimizing the App Icon for iOS

When you create a Flutter project it creates various subfolders for each platform. The Flutter framework generated **ios** and **macos** subfolders that contain the libraries and support files needed to run on iOS and macOS. In those folders there is an Xcode workspace, **Runner.xcworkspace**.

> **Note**: iOS and macOS developers, Flutter apps use **Runner.xcworkspace** instead of the traditional **Runner.xcodeproj.**

There are a couple of ways to open the Xcode project. You can use Finder or your IDE.

In Finder, open the chapter materials files and double-click **starter/ios/Runner.xcworkspace**. If you have Xcode open, you can also navigate to the folder and open it.

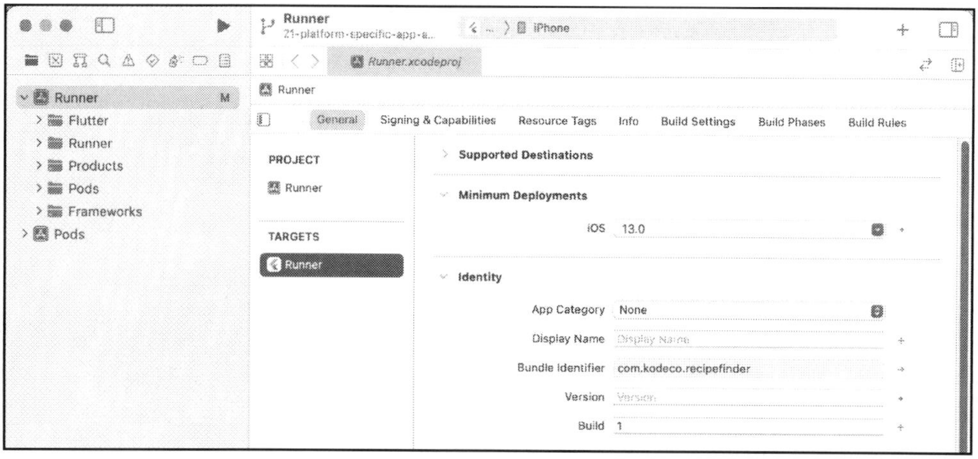

If you're using **Android Studio/IntelliJ** right-click on the **ios** folder, navigate to the **Flutter** item and you'll see **Open iOS Module in Xcode**, like in the picture below.

VSCode is a little different. When you **right-click** on the **ios** folder you'll see **Open in Xcode**.

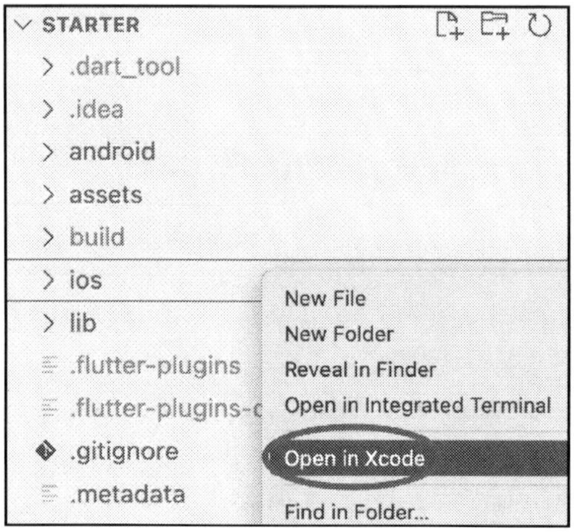

Flutter uses a **workspace** to build the app because, under the hood, it uses **Cocoapods** to manage iOS-specific dependencies required to build and deploy iOS apps. The workspace contains the main **runner** project and the **Cocoapods** project as well as all the supporting files to build and deploy an iOS app.

This project contains a lot of **boilerplate** and helpers to run the app within the iOS app context. Don't worry about building the app from Xcode. Continue to use **Android Studio** or the **command line** to build and deploy to a simulator.

Viewing the App Icon

To see the app icon, open **Runner ▸ Runner ▸ Assets.xcassets**. This is an **asset catalog**, a way of organizing assets in an Xcode project.

Inside, you'll see **AppIcon** and **LaunchImage**.

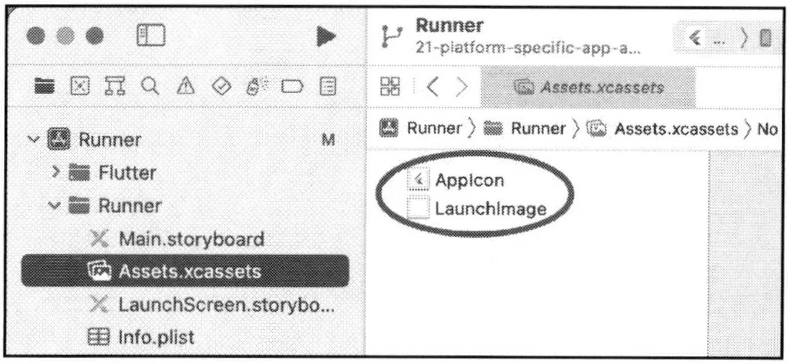

Click **AppIcon** to see all the **devices** and **resolutions** supported by the default Flutter icon.

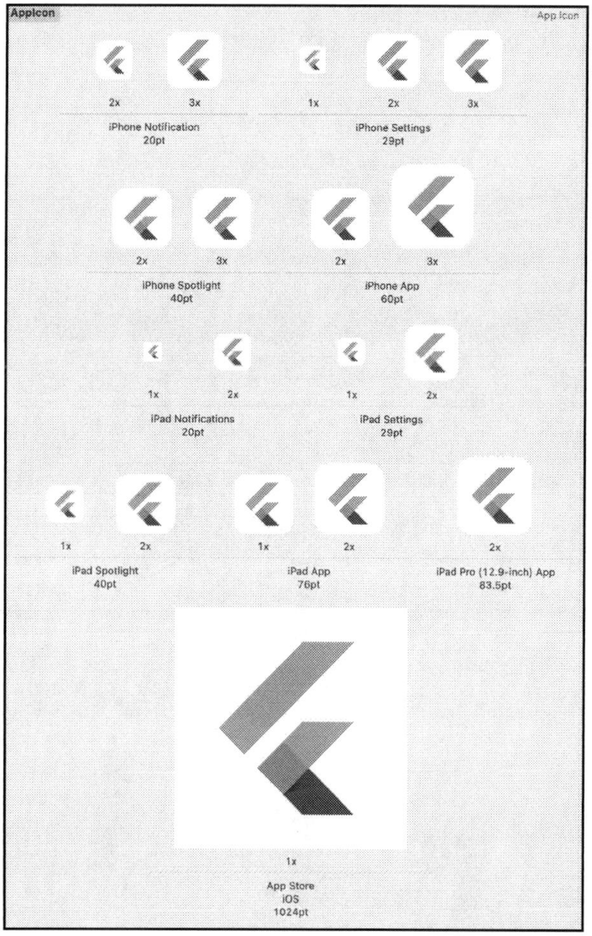

In Finder, open **assets/icons/ios** from the chapter materials. Drag each of the **images** inside into the **asset** catalog, grabbing the right one for each **size**. You can tell which is which by the name.

Don't worry if you grab the wrong one: A yellow warning **triangle** will appear next to any image that isn't the right size.

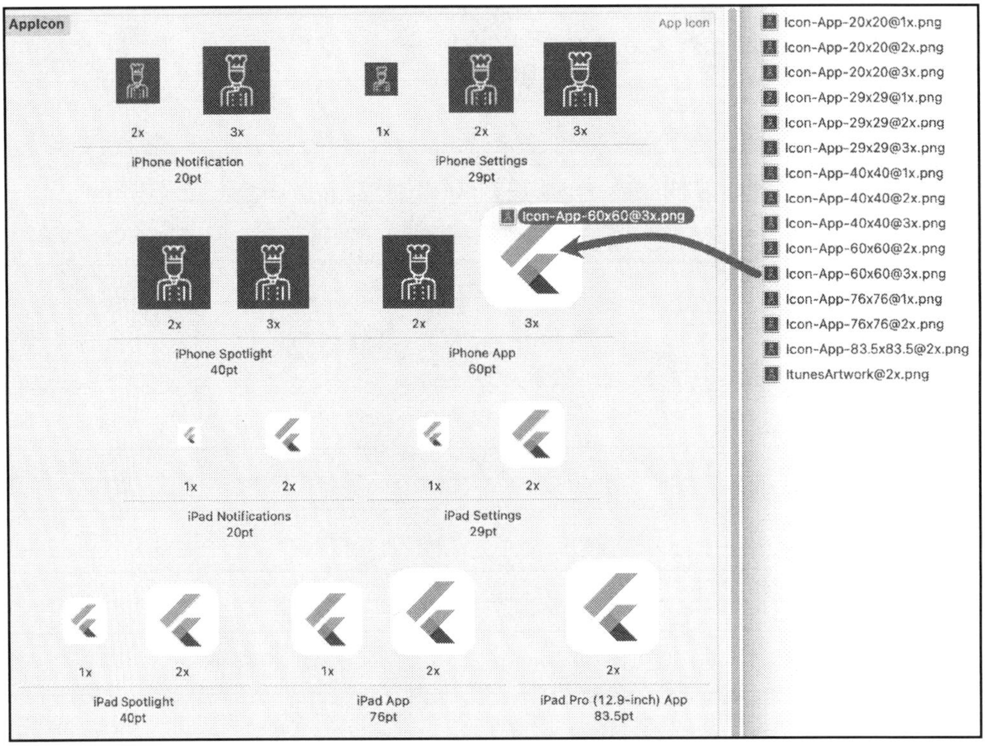

Note: When creating your own app icons, make sure you save them as **PNG** files, without **alpha** channels.

Next, you'll change the **name** of the app, displayed next to the app icon on the device.

Naming Your App

To set your app's name for iOS, open **Runner ▸ Runner ▸ Info.plist**.

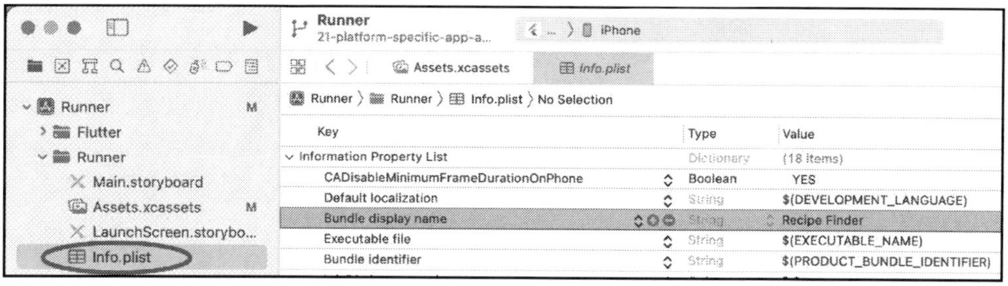

> **Note**: **Info.plist** is similar to the Android **AndroidManifest.xml** in that it contains information about your app for the OS to use.

Under **Information Property List**, change the **Bundle display name** to: `Recipe` .

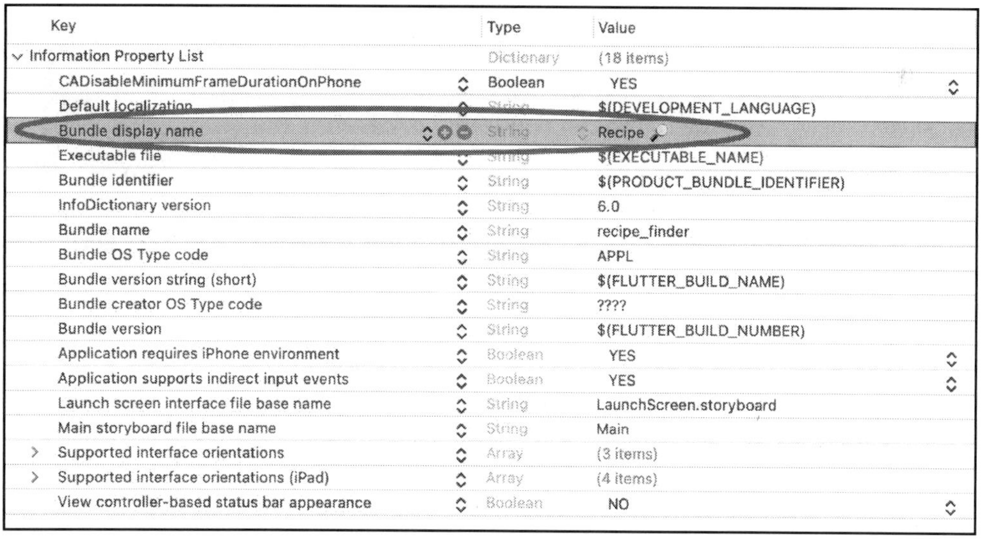

Key	Type	Value
Information Property List	Dictionary	(18 items)
CADisableMinimumFrameDurationOnPhone	Boolean	YES
Default localization	String	$(DEVELOPMENT_LANGUAGE)
Bundle display name	String	Recipe
Executable file	String	$(EXECUTABLE_NAME)
Bundle identifier	String	$(PRODUCT_BUNDLE_IDENTIFIER)
InfoDictionary version	String	6.0
Bundle name	String	recipe_finder
Bundle OS Type code	String	APPL
Bundle version string (short)	String	$(FLUTTER_BUILD_NAME)
Bundle creator OS Type code	String	????
Bundle version	String	$(FLUTTER_BUILD_NUMBER)
Application requires iPhone environment	Boolean	YES
Application supports indirect input events	Boolean	YES
Launch screen interface file base name	String	LaunchScreen.storyboard
Main storyboard file base name	String	Main
Supported interface orientations	Array	(3 items)
Supported interface orientations (iPad)	Array	(4 items)
View controller-based status bar appearance	Boolean	NO

Save these changes, leave Xcode open and return to your Flutter IDE.

Build and run your app for iOS.

That looks better! :]

The last finishing touch is adding a **launch screen**.

Adding an iOS Launch Screen

It takes a few moments for the **Dart VM** to spin up when users launch the app, so you'll give them something to look at instead of a white screen.

In following Apple's Human Interface Guidelines (https://developer.apple.com/design/human-interface-guidelines/) you should have no text included on your launch screen and it should closely resemble your app's landing page. Setting an iOS launch screen is straightforward.

Back in Xcode, select **Assets.xcassets** and this time select **LaunchImage**.

You'll see three boxes to represent the launch image at **1x**, **2x** and **3x** resolution.

In Finder locate **assets/launch image/loading.png** in the chapter materials and drag it onto the **1x** square.

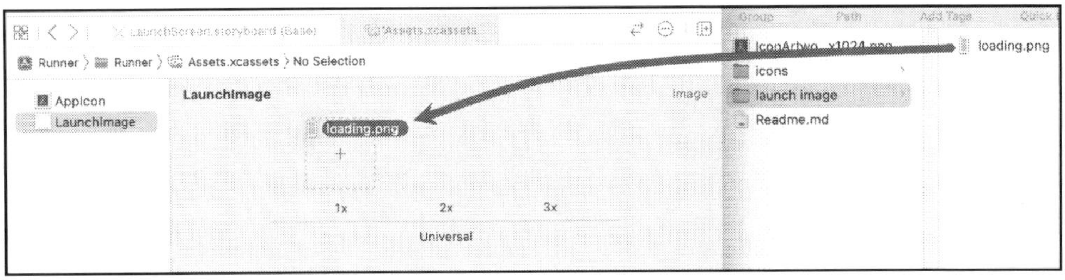

This is a high-resolution image, so you need to tell iOS to scale it for **high-resolution** screens.

In the Inspector pane, change the **Scales** value to **Single Scale**.

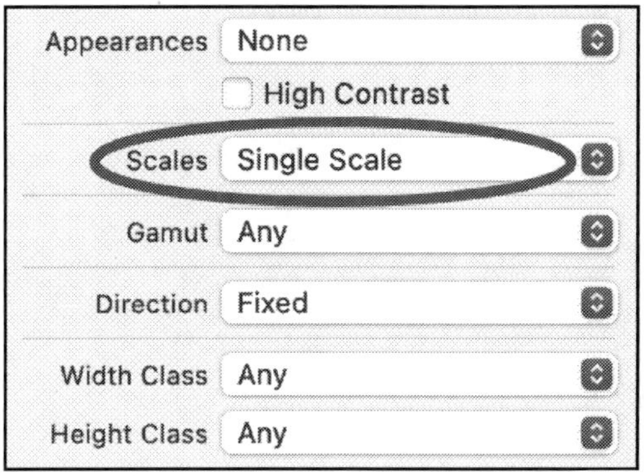

This setting tells the system there's just one version of the image. This is preferred for images like photographs, which have a native high resolution.

You'll see a yellow triangle displayed in the **2x** and **3x** boxes. While pressing **Shift** key, select each of these boxes and press **Delete**.

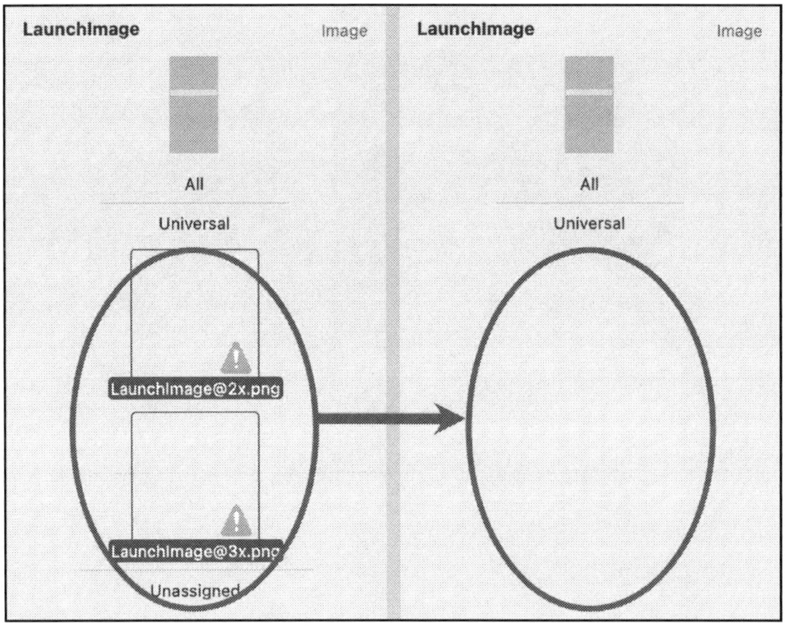

The two boxes are now gone and your new launch screen image is set up.

The user will see this image while the app launches until the **main** screen is ready.

Returning to your Flutter IDE, build and **run** on iOS. Watch closely as the app launch can be fast.

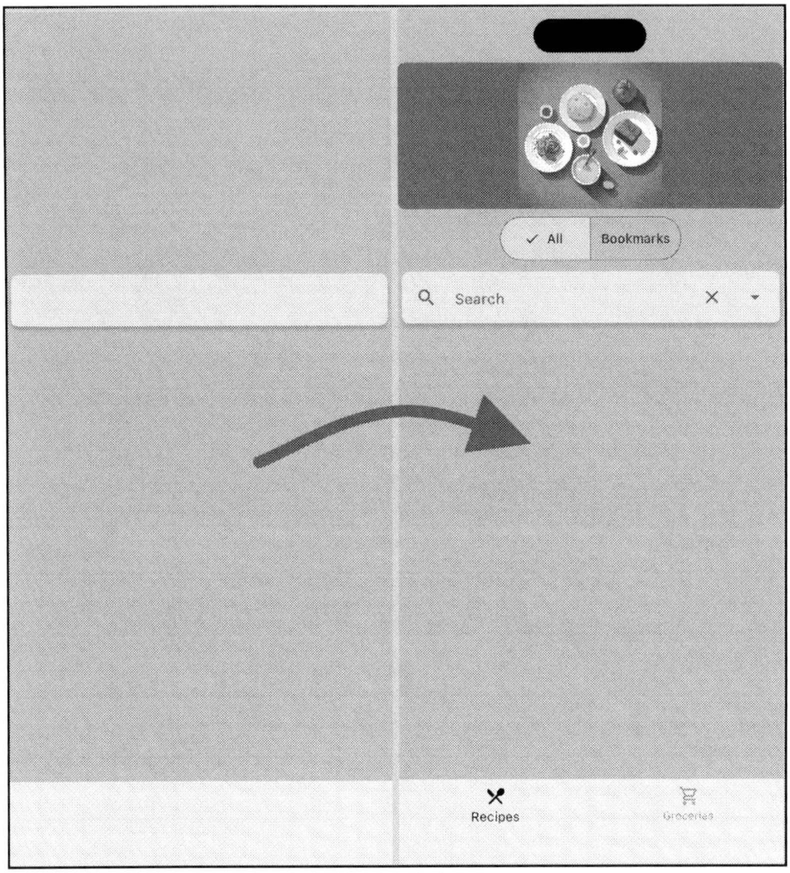

By using the same background as the initial page the result is a **smooth transition** when your app is launched.

Great job! You've set up the iOS side, now you'll set up the macOS version.

Setup macOS Icons

You'll find that setting up the **macOS** icons is very similar to what you did for iOS.

In Finder navigate to **starter/macos/Runner.xcworkspace** and open it with Xcode.

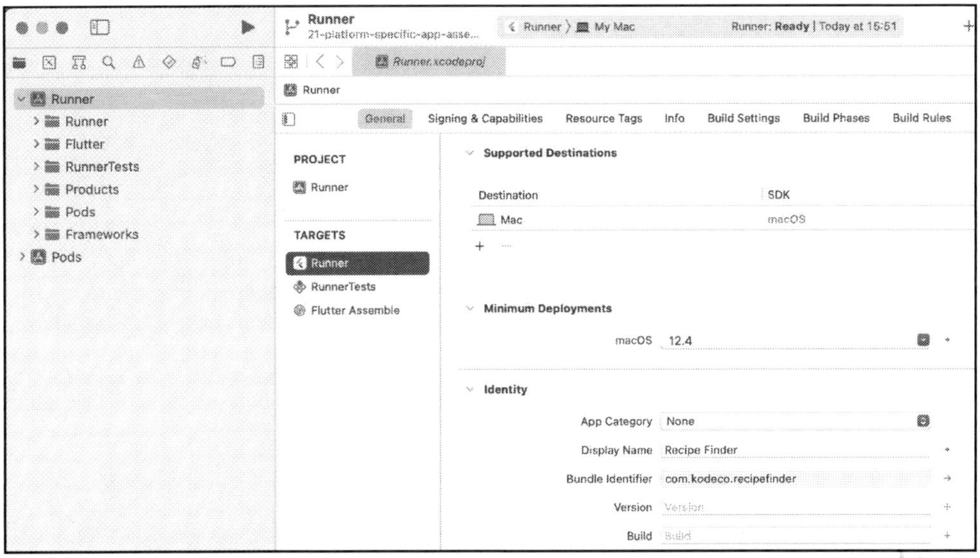

Next, open **Runner ▸ Runner ▸ Resources ▸ Assets.xcassets**. This will look familiar and is similar to the iOS **asset catalog**.

For macOS you'll see only **AppIcon**, no **LaunchImage**.

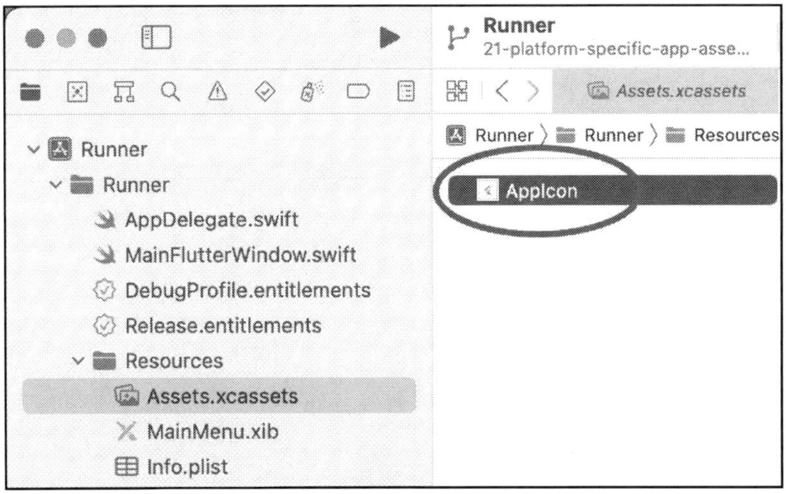

Click **AppIcon** to see the different **sizes** and **resolutions** supported by the default Flutter icon.

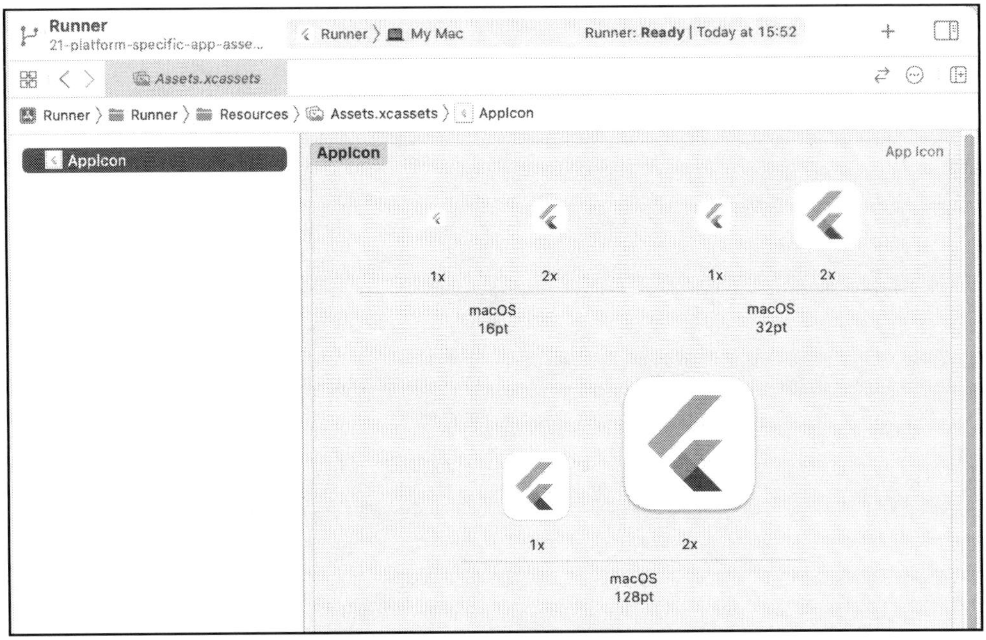

In Finder, open the chapter materials **assets/icons/macos**. Just like you did for iOS icons, drag each of the images onto the **asset** catalog.

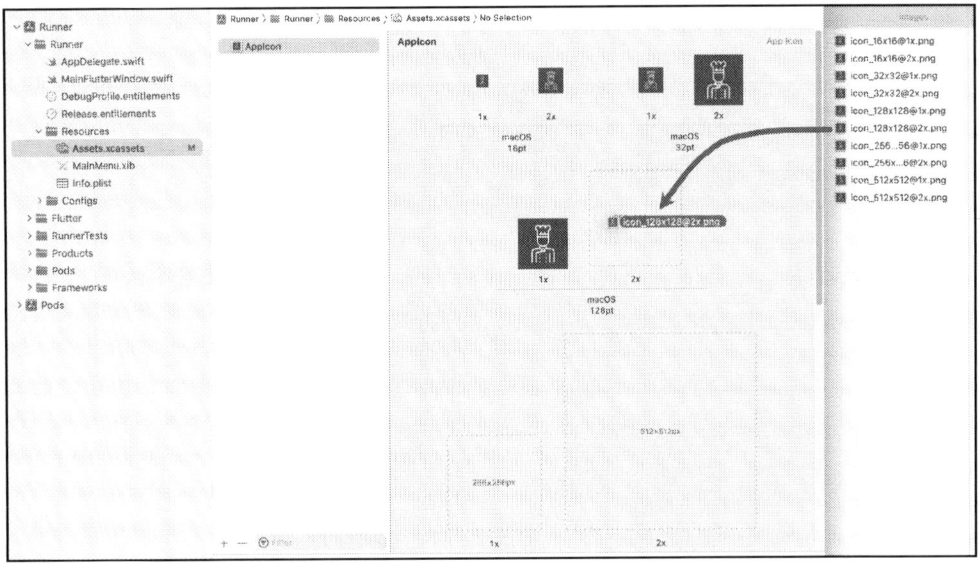

That's it! You've set up the macOS app icon. You won't be renaming the macOS app.

Return to your Flutter IDE, build and **run** on macOS.

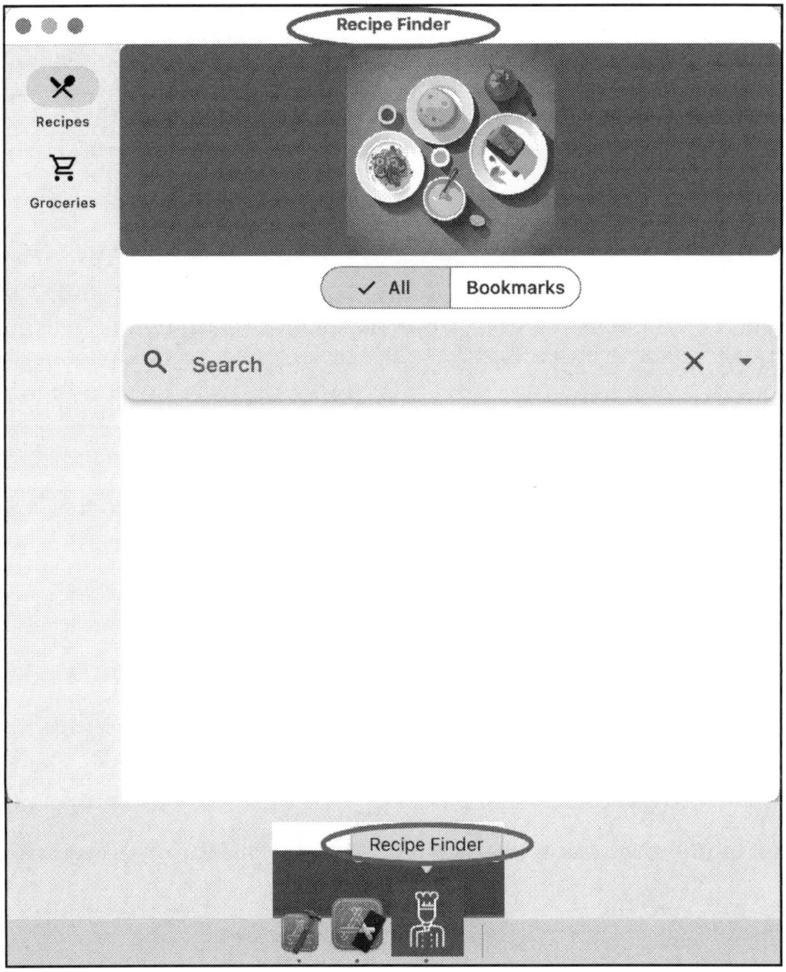

Looks awesome!

> **Note**: You may see warnings from some of the packages, ignore them. The app will still run. If it doesn't run then execute the following from Terminal and then re-run your app.
>
> ```
> flutter clean && flutter pub get
> ```

Now it's time to set up the **Android** icons.

Set Up Android App Icon and Launch Assets

When you work with your own custom artwork and Android apps, there are a few more steps you need to take, beyond just copying and pasting from a folder.

Optimizing the App Icon for Android

In Android Studio open **android/app/src/main/AndroidManifest.xml**. This file defines many of your app's Android properties related to **launching**, **permissions**, **Play Store** and the **Android** system.

One of the properties under `application` defines the launcher screen icon:

The `@mipmap` means that it resolves to a **mipmap-{resolution}** folder to load an asset fit for the device's screen scale. **ic_launcher** is the icon filename.

Under **android/app/src/main/res**, you'll find the various **mipmap-** subfolders.

In Finder, open **assets/icons/android** from the chapter materials. Copy the **res** folder and replace **android/app/src/main/res** in Android Studio.

If you receive a pop-up confirming you want to copy the folders to the specified directories, click **Refactor** or **OK** or **Overwrite for all**, depending on your Android Studio version.

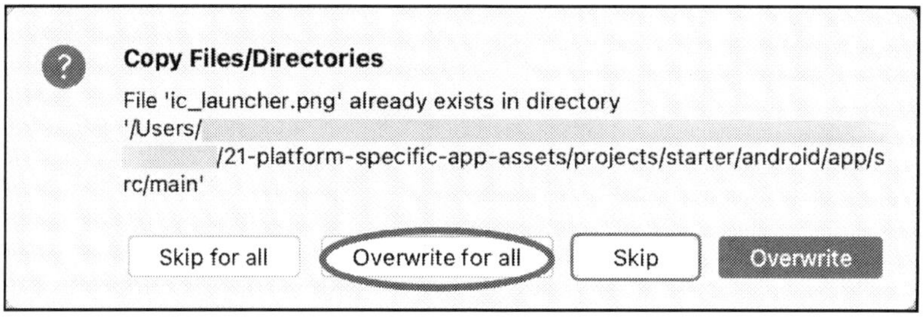

Expand the **android/app/src/main/res** folder and verify you've pasted the **res** folder in the correct place. It should be at the same level as the **java** and **kotlin** folders, not inside the existing **res** folder.

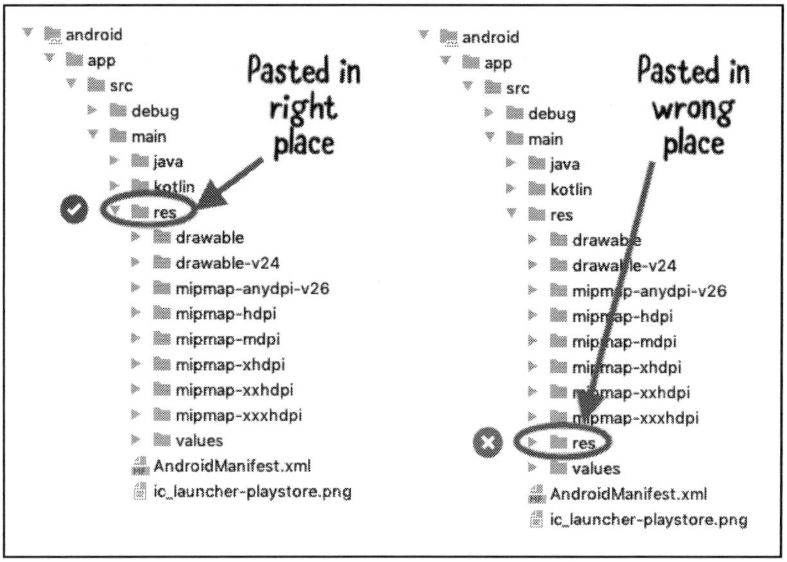

Hot reload and **hot restart** are not enough to see the updated icon.

For these changes to take effect, you need to **stop** the app and **run** it again.

On the home screen, you'll now see the new launcher icon. Run the app on an Android device or emulator to see one of the following:

Great, you've just swapped the default assets for your cool custom ones.

If you need to adjust the icon fill size, or if you're working on your own app later and want to import Android images, you'll need to **import** and **resize** the artwork. That's next!

Personalizing the App Icon for Android

For these next few steps you need to work in the Android portion of your app and not within the Flutter project.

Open the Android folder directly from the **Android Studio** menu, choose **File ▸ Open** and navigate to your project's **android** folder.

Finally, click **Open**.

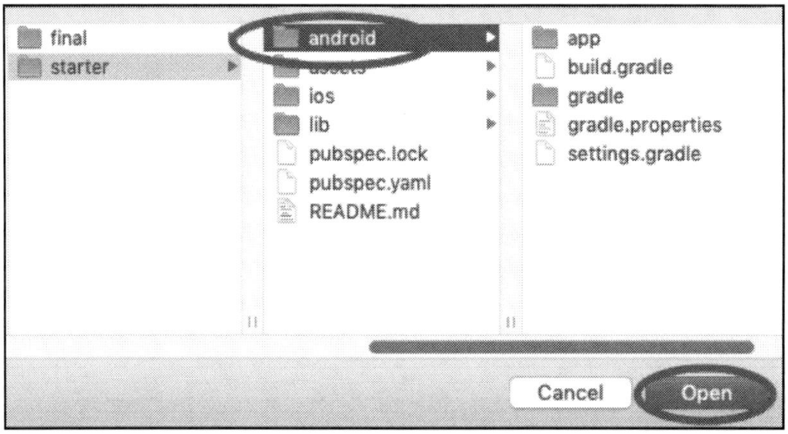

Wait until the **Gradle sync** is complete. The time it takes your project to finish might vary. You'll see messages flashing fast in the bottom right corner of the window until it's done.

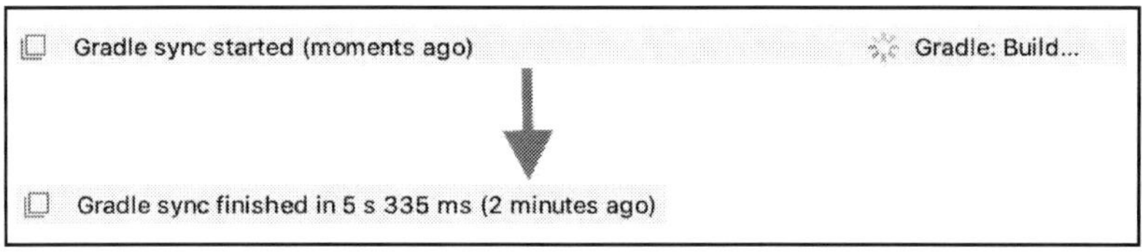

Navigate to the **app** folder, right-click on **res** and choose **New ▸ Image Asset**.

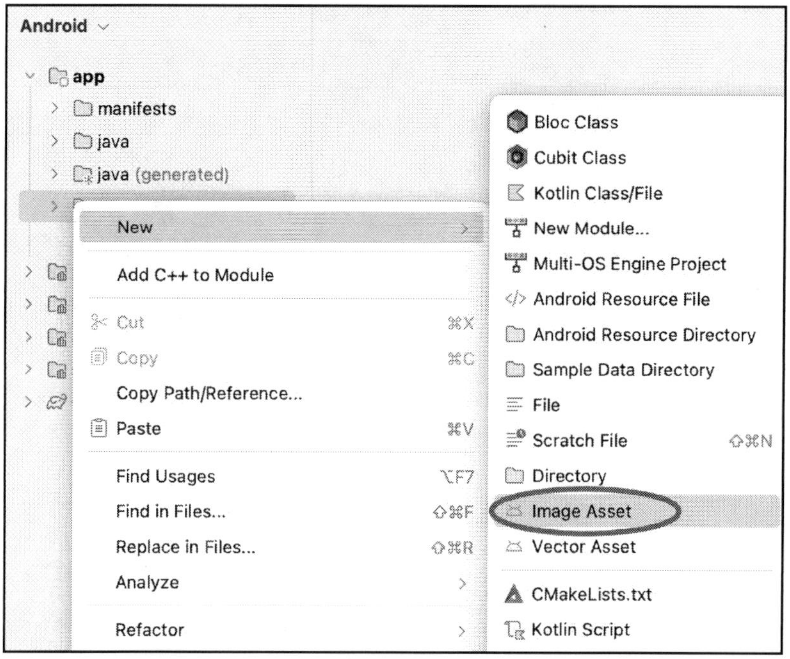

The **Configure Image Asset** pop-up window will display. Click the **folder** icon to open the custom image.

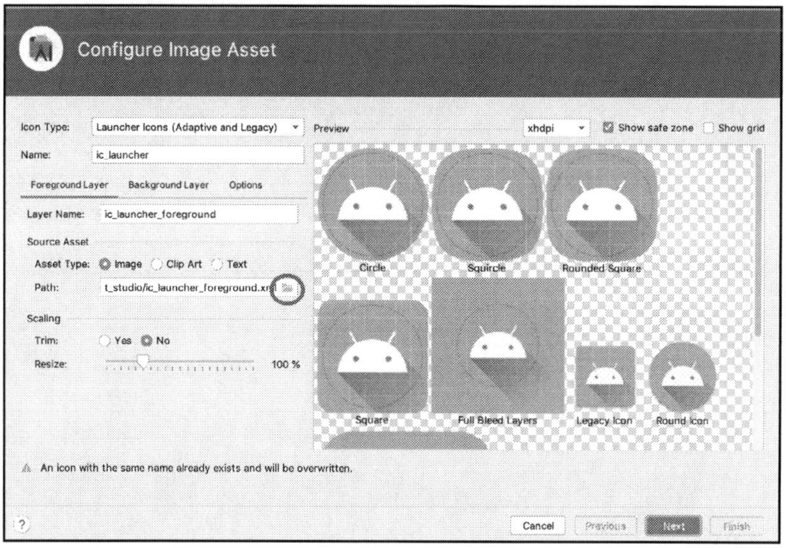

Locate your **master artwork** image. In this case, you'll find it in the project **assets/** folder. Select the **IconArtwork_1024x1024.png** image and click on **Open**.

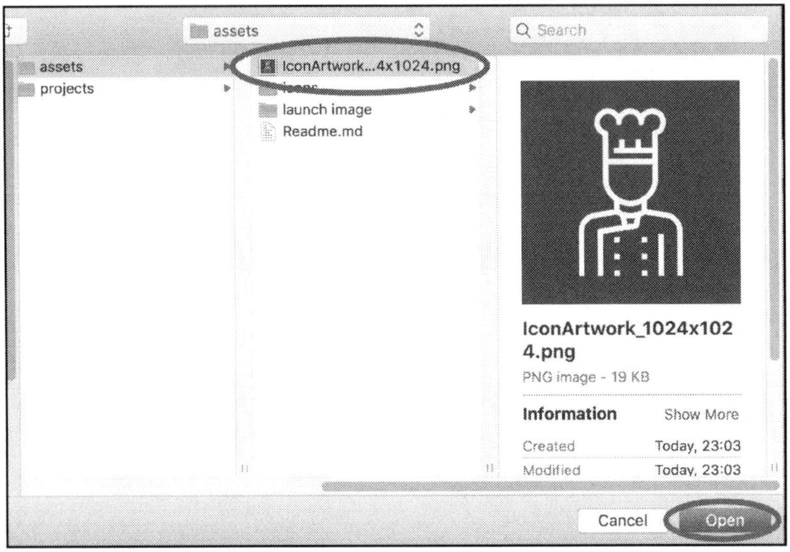

The loaded image will appear like this.

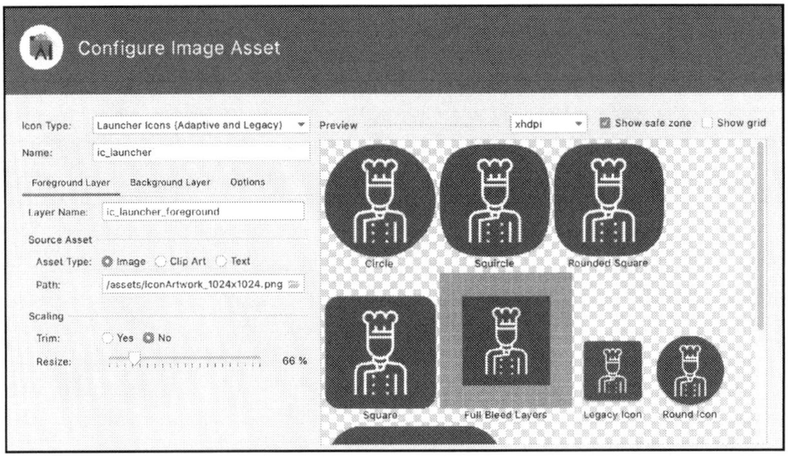

If the cook figure is outside the **safe zone**, use the **Resize** slider to adjust the size. Make sure the cook figure is inside the circle, which is the safe zone, as shown below. When done click **Next**.

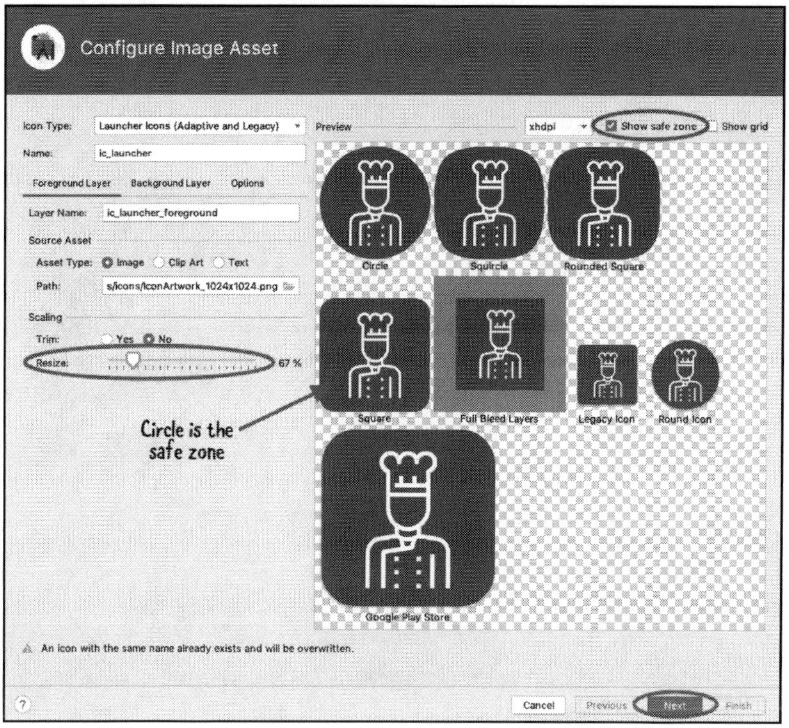

The next screen displays the path where you'll save the assets. Keep in mind this is for the **Android** project, not your Flutter project, so the folder names look different from what you've worked with so far.

Leave the defaults and click **Finish**.

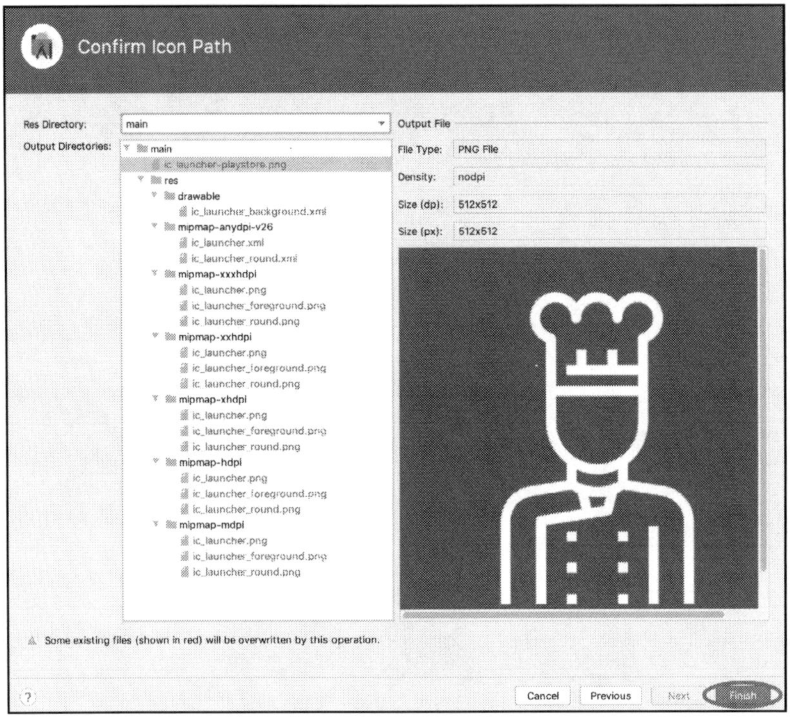

Close this Android project and go back to your **Flutter project**.

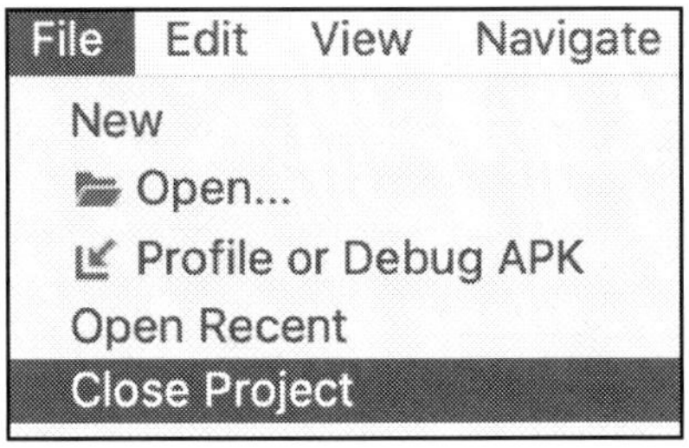

You've now seen how to resize custom artwork for your Android app. What's great is that after you finish these updates, your Flutter app updates automatically!

As before, for these changes to take effect, you need to stop the app and run it again. You'll see the same launcher icon. Run the app on an Android device or emulator to see the following:

Next, you'll change the **app name** which will help address the names with the `...` shown on some devices.

Changing the App's Name for Android

Now that you have a shiny new icon on the device launch screens, you'll notice that the app's name isn't always formatted nicely, which detracts from the experience.

Setting the launcher name is an easy fix, but you also have to do it for each platform.

Return to **android/app/src/main/AndroidManifest.xml**. Find the `android:label` property of the `application` node.

```
    package="com.kodeco.recipe_finder">
    <uses-permission android:name="android.permission.

   <application
       android:label="Recipe Finder"
       android:name="${applicationName}"
       android:icon="@mipmap/ic_launcher">
       <activity
```

Change the text to `Recipe 🔎`.

```
    package="com.kodeco.recipe_finder">
    <uses-permission android:name="android.permission.

   <application
       android:label="Recipe 🔎"
       android:name="${applicationName}"
       android:icon="@mipmap/ic_launcher">
       <activity
```

Build and **run** the app on Android. By choosing a shorter label, the name will fit on more Android devices.

Next, you'll address the Android **splash screen**. Don't worry, it's really easy.

Setting an Android Splash Screen

As of Android 12, there is a default splash screen that animates from the launcher, shows the app icon and then fades into your app's landing page.

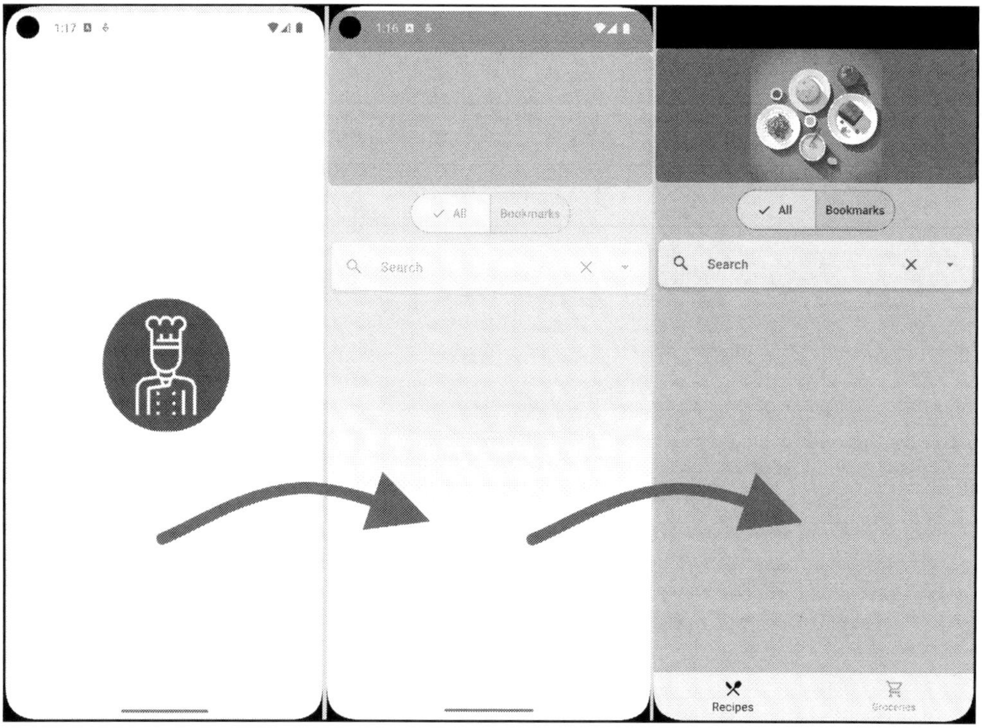

Boom! You get off easy with Android - it's done for you and is a nice developer experience. See, easy, right? ;]

> **Note**: You can customize this animation, but this requires specialized assets and additional skills that are out of scope for this book. For more information, see the Splash Screen Tutorial for Android (https://www.kodeco.com/32555180-splash-screen-tutorial-for-android) or the Android Animations by Tutorials book (https://www.kodeco.com/books/android-animations-by-tutorials/v1.0/chapters/3-xml-animations).

Next, you'll address the web browser tab icon.

Set Up Web App Icon and Title

Have you ever paid attention to the browser tab icon? It's nice to have those when you have a bunch of tabs open on different sites. They can help you quickly identify which site each tab represents.

Plus, it's nice to have a good name for the tab, so you'll also change the title of the tab.

Updating Favicon

The icon displayed on a browser tab is known as the **favicon**. It's a **square** image that represents the website. The favicon is either **16x16** pixels or **32x32** pixels and can be **8-bit** or **24-bit** colors.

In Finder open **assets/icons/web** and drag **favicon.png** into your projects **web** folder in your Flutter IDE. When prompted make sure to overwrite or refactor the file.

Now that you've updated the icon, time to update the title.

Updating Title

There are two ways to set the **title** of the browser tab. You can either set the title in the **HTML** or in the **Dart** code. Each is displayed at different times.

To set the title in the HTML, open **web/index.html** and find the following line:

```
<title>Recipe Finder</title>
```

Replace it so it looks like this:

```
<title>Recipe 🔍</title>
```

When your app is **loading** the title defined in the **HTML** is displayed.

Next, open **lib/main.dart**. In `MaterialApp` Find `// TODO: Update title` and replace the title beneath it with:

```
'Recipe 🔍'
```

The title defined in here is displayed after your app is **fully loaded**.

Build and run on **web/Chrome** and take a look at the tab. Pretty cool, right?

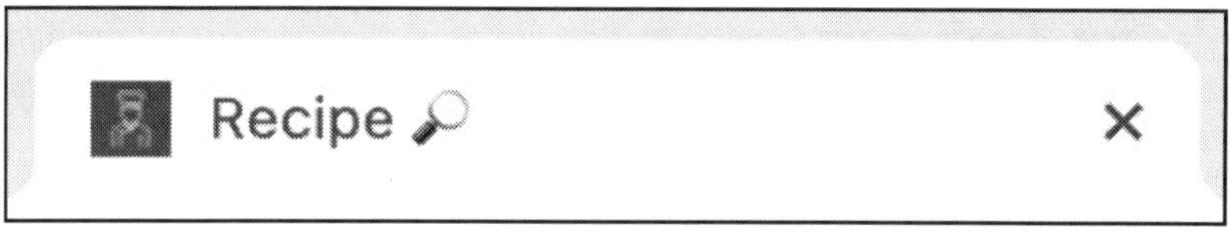

Great job! You've updated your app's **branding** for **iOS**, **Android**, **macOS** and **web**.

The next two chapters will guide you through deploying your app to the **App Store** and **Google Play Store**. Aren't you glad you've branded your app? ;]

Key Points

- Flutter generates **app projects** for iOS, Android, desktop and web, which you can customize with your brand.
- These projects contain resources and code related to **launching the app** and preparing to start the Flutter main view.
- Each platform needs **specific assets** to customize the app launch experience.

Where to Go From Here?

There are some handy packages that can help you generating the icons and spash screen for each platform. For app icons you can use flutter launcher icons (https://pub.dev/packages/flutter_launcher_icons). It will **generate** and **organize** the icons according to the platform.

Similarly, for splash screen you can use flutter native splash (https://pub.dev/packages/flutter_native_splash).

You may have seen other apps with more dynamic or animated splash screens. These are generally created as a whole-screen stateful widget that is displayed while the Flutter VM loads your main screen widget.

Now that you have a new branding for your app, you're ready to **deploy** your app to the **App Store** and **Google Play Store**. That's the topic of the next two chapters.

Chapter 20: Build & Release an Android App

By Michael Katz & Stef Patterson

So you've finished building your app and you're ready to let the world try it out. In this chapter, you'll learn how to prepare your app for distribution through the **Google Play Store**, then release it for internal testing. In the next chapter, you'll do the same for Apple's **App Store**.

The steps you'll follow to launch your app are straightforward:

1. Create a **signed** release build.
2. Prepare the **Play Store** for upload.
3. **Upload** the build.
4. Notify **testers** that the build is ready.

To complete this chapter, you'll need a Google Play **developer account**. If you want to test the download of the release from the Google Play store you'll also need a **physical** Android device.

Set Up for Release

Before you can upload a build for distribution, you need to build it with a **release configuration**. When you create a new Flutter project, you automatically create a **debug** build configuration. This is helpful while in development, but it's not suitable for distribution in the store for several reasons:

- **App bloat**: A debug build is extra large because of the **symbols** and overhead needed for **hot reload/restart** and for source debugging.
- **Resource keys**: It's typical to point your debug app at a **sandbox environment** for services and analytics so you don't pollute **production data** or violate user privacy.
- **Unsigned**: Debug builds aren't signed yet. To upload to the store, you need to **sign** the app to verify you are the one who built it.
- **Google says so**: The Play Store won't allow you to upload a debug build.

The app's configuration spreads across several files. In the next steps, you'll see how to modify some key pieces of your app to prepare your build for submission to the Play Store.

If you're following along with your app from the previous chapter, open it and keep using it with this chapter. If not, just locate the **projects** folder for this chapter, open the **starter** project in **Android Studio** and remember to get dependencies.

> **Note**: If you use the starter app or didn't add it in the last chapter, add your `apiKey` in **lib/network/spoonacular_service.dart** because your app needs to run completely to submit it to the store.

Preparing the Manifest

Debug builds have broad **permissions**, but apps released for distribution need to declare which aspects of the **user's hardware** or systems they need to **access**. The **Android Manifest** file is where you declare permissions.

Open **android/app/src/main/AndroidManifest.xml**. This file describes the app to the **Android OS**.

Confirm the file has the following code, if not add it beneath `package="com.kodeco.recipe_finder">`:

```
<uses-permission android:name="android.permission.INTERNET" />
```

With this line, you tell Android that your app needs access to the internet to run. The Flutter template manifest does not include any permissions, but if you're continuing from a previous chapter, you should have this line.

> **Note**: If your next app requires additional permissions, such as access to the **camera** or **location** information, add them here.

Updating build.gradle

build.gradle is where you describe different **build configurations**. You'll change it next. When you set up the app, you used the default **debug** configuration. Now, you'll add a **release configuration** to produce a **bundle** you can upload to the Play Store.

Open **android/app/build.gradle**.

Under `android {`, you'll see a definition for `defaultConfig`. This describes the **app ID**, **versioning** information and **SDK** version.

When assigning `applicationId`, you usually use **your name** or your **company's name**.

```
applicationId "com.kodeco.recipe_finder"
```

This book uses **com.kodeco.recipe_finder**, which means you need to use a different name when you submit it to the store. To avoid errors because the app already exists in the Play Store, use something unique to you or your business name when you upload your app. Be sure to use **lowercase** letters and don't use spaces or special characters.

Locate `// TODO: Specify your own unique Application ID`. Change `applicationId` beneath it to something unique. For example you could add letters to the end of the text inside the quotes. Be creative :]

Your next step is to create a **signing key** to make your app **secure** enough to be in the Play Store.

Creating a Signing Key

Before you can distribute the app, you need to sign it. This ensures that all future versions come from the same developer.

To sign the app, you first need to make a **signing key** by creating a **keystore**, which is a secure repository of certificates and private keys.

During the next step, you'll see a prompt to enter a password. There are some key things to know:

- Use any **six-character** password you like, but **be sure to remember it**. You'll need it whenever you access the keystore, that is every time you **upload** a new version of the app.
- In addition to a password, you need to provide information about yourself and your organization. This is part of the certificate, so don't enter anything you don't want someone else to see.
- Once you've entered and **confirmed** that information, the tool will create the **.jks** file and save it in the **directory** that ran the command.

Open a Terminal window and navigate to the **root** project directory.

> **Note**: If you started this chapter with the starter project, then the root project directory is the **starter** folder.

On a Mac, run the following command:

```
keytool -genkey -v -keystore recipes.jks -keyalg RSA -keysize
2048 -validity 10000 -alias recipes
```

On Windows, the command is slightly different:

```
keytool -genkey -v -keystore %userprofile%\upload-keystore.jks ^
        -storetype JKS -keyalg RSA -keysize 2048 -validity 10000
^
        -alias upload
```

keytool is a Java command run from **Terminal** that generates a keystore. You save it in the file, **recipes.jks**.

The keystore contains one key with the specified `-alias recipes`. You'll use this key later to sign the bundle that you'll upload to the Play Store.

Note: It's important to keep the **keystore** secure and out of any public repositories. Adding it to **.gitignore** will help protect your file. If someone gets access to the **key**, they can distribute potentially malicious apps on your behalf, causing all sorts of mayhem.

If you wish to add the files to the **.gitignore** file, it is located at the project **root** level. Open the file and add the following at the bottom of the `# Android related` section:

```
**/android/key.properties
./recipes.jks
```

Accessing The Signing Key

Now that you've created a key, you need to supply the build system with the **information** necessary to access it. To do that, you'll create a separate file to store the password information.

Note: It's important to keep this file a **secret** and not to check it into a public repository, just like the **keystore** file. If a malicious actor has this file and your keystore, they can easily impersonate you. To help with this, you added this file to **.gitignore** in the previous step.

In the **android** folder, create a new file: **key.properties**. Set its contents to:

```
storePassword={YOUR PASSWORD}
keyPassword={YOUR PASSWORD}
keyAlias=recipes
storeFile=../../recipes.jks
```

`storePassword` and `keyPassword` should be the same password you supplied in the `keytool` command, without any punctuation or the `{}`.

`keyAlias` is the same as the `-alias` listed at the end of the `keytool` command.

`storeFile` is the path of the keystore you created. It's relative to **android/app**, so be sure to change the path, if necessary.

You need these values to unlock the key in the keystore and sign the app. In the next step, you'll read from the file during the build process.

Referencing The Signing Key

You now have a **key** and its **password**, but signing doesn't happen automatically. During the build, you need to open the keystore and sign the app bundle. To do this, you need to modify the **build**... and when you think about modifying the build process, you should think about **build.gradle**.

Open **android/app/build.gradle**.

Before the `android {` section, locate `// TODO: Add keystore properties here` and add the following:

```
def keystoreProperties = new Properties()
def keystorePropertiesFile = rootProject.file('key.properties')
if (keystorePropertiesFile.exists()) {
    keystoreProperties.load(new
FileInputStream(keystorePropertiesFile))
}
```

Here, you define a new `Properties` that reads **key.properties** and loads the content into `keystoreProperties`. At the top of the file, you'll see something similar that loads the Flutter properties from **local.properties**.

Next, inside the `android` section, locate `// TODO: Add signing release config here` just after the `defaultConfig` block and add:

```
signingConfigs {
   release {
        keyAlias keystoreProperties['keyAlias']
        keyPassword keystoreProperties['keyPassword']
        storeFile keystoreProperties['storeFile'] ?
file(keystoreProperties['storeFile']) : null
        storePassword keystoreProperties['storePassword']
   }
}
```

This defines a **signing** configuration, then directly maps the values loaded from the properties file to the `release` configuration.

Finally, replace the existing `buildTypes` block with:

```
buildTypes {
    release {
        signingConfig signingConfigs.release
    }
}
```

This defines the release `signingConfig`, which is a specific Android build construct, created using the previously declared `release` signing configuration. You'll use this when you create a release build.

Now, you've created a release configuration and set it up. The next step is to build the app for release.

Build an App Bundle

With **build.gradle** in place, you can leave the final steps to create a signed Android App Bundle up to the Flutter build system. The bundle will contain everything you need to upload your app to the Play Store.

Open a terminal window, navigate to the **project directory** and run:

```
flutter build appbundle
```

This will build an **Android App Bundle** (**AAB**) for the project. It may take several minutes to complete. When it's done, the command output will tell you where to find the **.aab** file.

> **Note**: If you receive an error message stating the keystore file was not found, make sure the path you have in **key.properties** for the `storeFile=` line has the correct path to the generated **recipes.jks**.

The bundle is just a **.zip** file containing the **compiled code**, **assets** and **metadata**. You'll send this to Google in the next section.

AAB Versus APK

If you've been working with Android for a while, you might be expecting to create an **APK** file. When you do a debug build from Android Studio, you get an APK file.

You can distribute an Android app as an **APK** or an **AAB**. App bundles are preferred by the Play Store as AAB generates **optimized** APKs during installation and are **tailored** according to users' device configuration, but you can use APKs to distribute in other stores or for sideloading to a device.

> **Note**: Sideloading means installing an app on an Android device without using the official Google Play store. After configuring your device to allow running apps from **unknown** sources, you can install apps that are typically distributed as APK files.

If you want to create an **APK release**, use the following command:

```
flutter build apk --split-per-abi
```

This creates release build APKs. The `--split-per-abi` flag makes separate APKs for each supported target, such as **x86**, **arm64** and so on. This reduces the file size for the output. A "fat" APK, which contains support for all targets, could be substantial in size. To make a fat APK rather than a split APK, just omit that flag.

Uploading to The Google Play Store

Your next step to getting your app out in the wide world is to upload it to the Google Play Store. You'll need a Google Play **Developer account** to do that.

Open https://play.google.com/console/. If you see a prompt to sign up, follow the onscreen instructions to create a developer account. There is a nominal fee to join the Google Developer Program. If you don't want to sign up, you can continue to distribute APK files via **sideloading**.

This book won't cover the specific steps for creating an account, as those instructions change faster than this book. Just follow along with Google's guidance until you are at the **Google Play Console**.

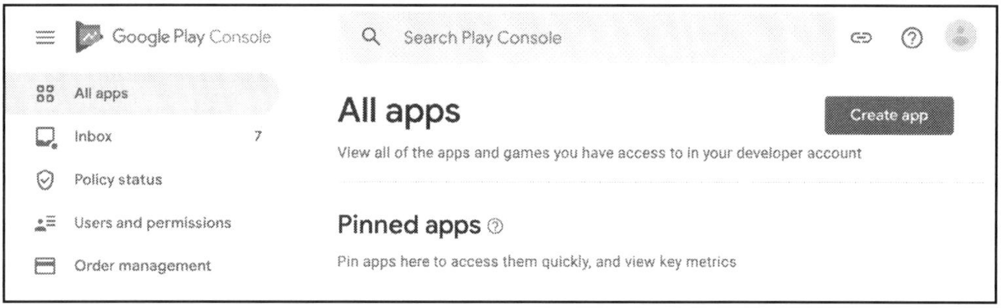

Creating a New App

Once you're in the **Play Console**, the next step is to create an **app**. This gives you a place to upload your build. The big **Create app** button will do the trick — click it to get started. The location of the button depends on whether this is your first app.

Next, you'll see prompts for some basic information about the app. You'll also need to agree to the **Developer Program Policies**.

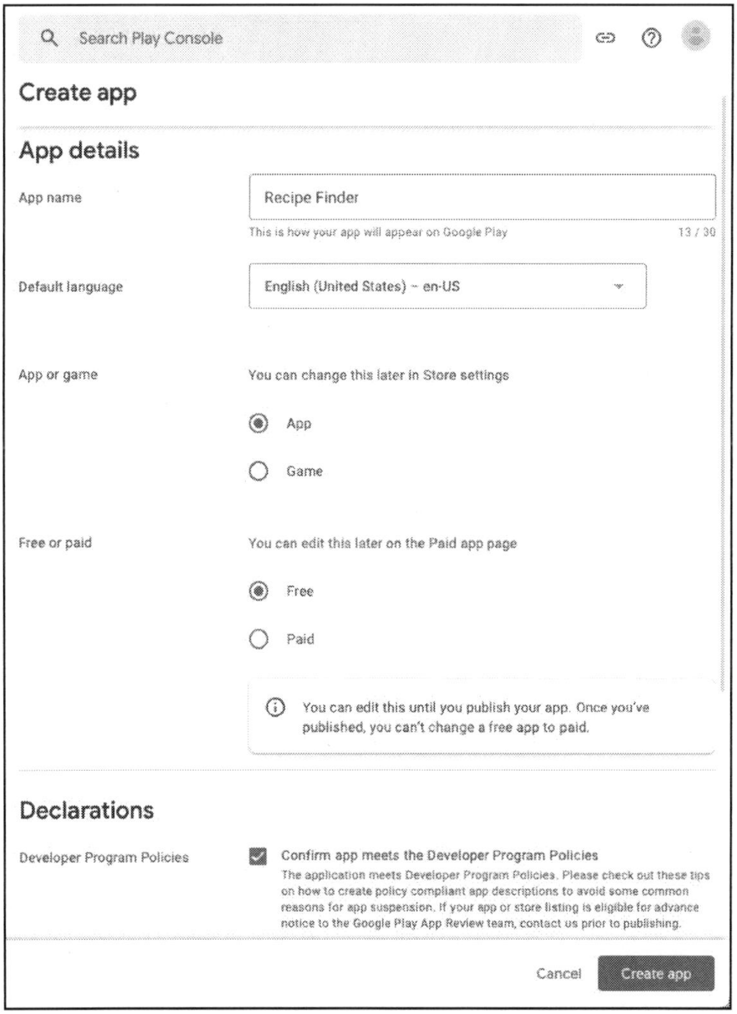

> **Note**: You may have additional questions about the Developer Program Policies. If so, you can find the answers in the Google Play Developer Program Policies (https://play.google.com).

If you're satisfied with accepting the declarations, click **Create app** once again.

Creating an app just creates a record in the Play Store. This lets you deal with **pre-release** activities, uploading builds and filling out store information. It doesn't publish anything to the store or make anything public yet. You have a lot more information to add before you can publish the app.

Providing Assets and a Description

Your next step before publishing is to upload app **assets**, such as **icons** and **screenshots**, and provide a description for the app. You'll do this in the **Main store listing** tab.

On the left, expand **Store presence** under the **Grow** section and select **Main store listing**.

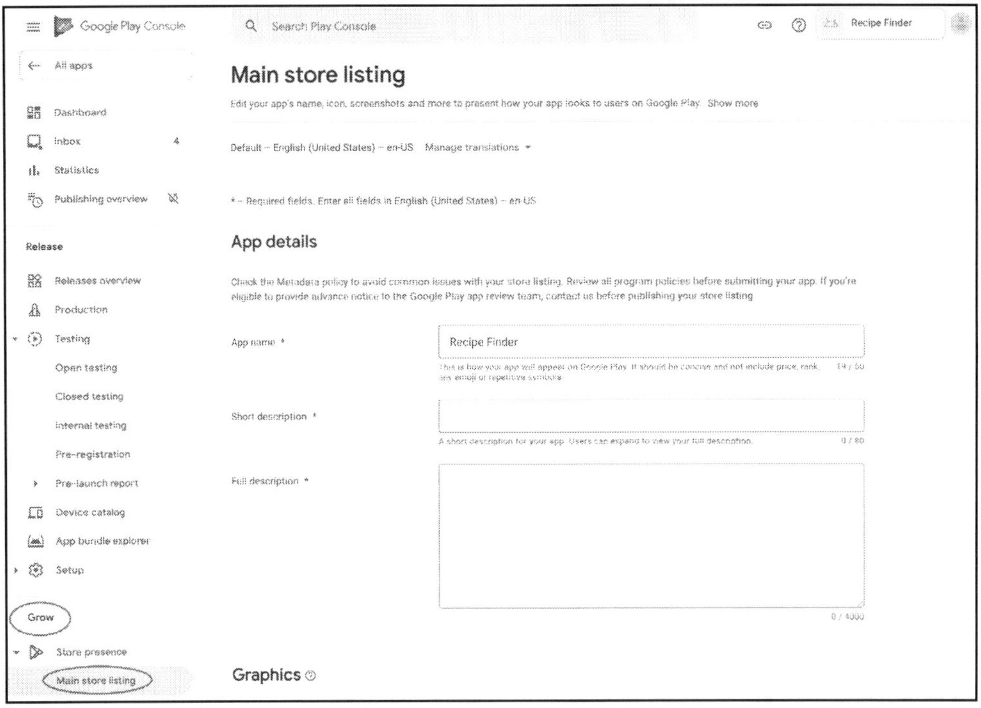

Here, you'll enter the **customer-facing** information about your app, which is required for release. The page has two sections: **App Details** and **Graphics**.

In the **App Details** section, enter a **Short description** and a **Full description**.

For example, a short description for this app might be:

```
This is an app to find recipes on the web.
```

Here's an example for the full description:

```
With Recipe Finder, the world's premier recipe search app,
you'll find all sorts of interesting things to cook. Bookmark
your favorite ones to put together a shopping list.
```

The **Graphics** section lets you upload **special art** and **screenshots**. You'll find sample versions of these in **assets\store graphics** at the top of this chapter's materials.

For the **App icon**, upload **app_icon.png**. This is a large, **512×512px** version of the launcher icon.

The **Feature graphic** is the image you use to **promote** your app in the Play Store. Upload **feature_graphic.png** for this asset. It's a **1024×500px** stylized image that promotes the app branding.

Next, you need to add the screenshots. The store asks for phone, 7-inch tablet and 10-inch tablet image sizes. Fortunately, you don't have to upload screenshots for every possible screen size, just a representative.

For the **Phone screenshots**, upload **phone1.png**, **phone2.png** and **phone3.png**. These all come from screenshots taken on the simulator.

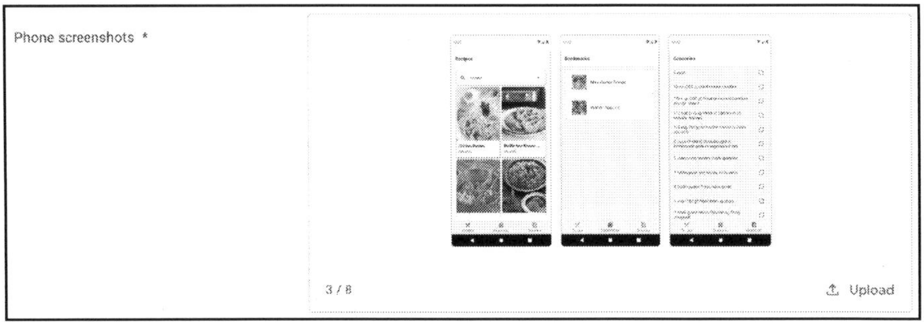

Even though Recipe Finder isn't designed for a tablet, it will run on one. It's good practice to include screenshots for these cases, as well.

For **7-inch tablet screenshots** upload **7in.png**.

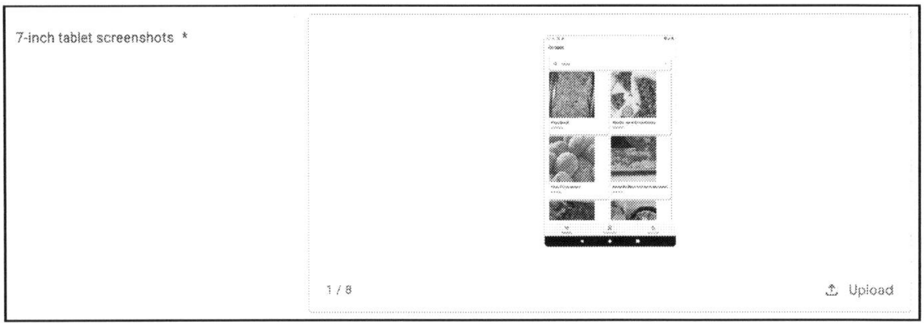

For **10-inch tablet screenshots** upload **10in.png**.

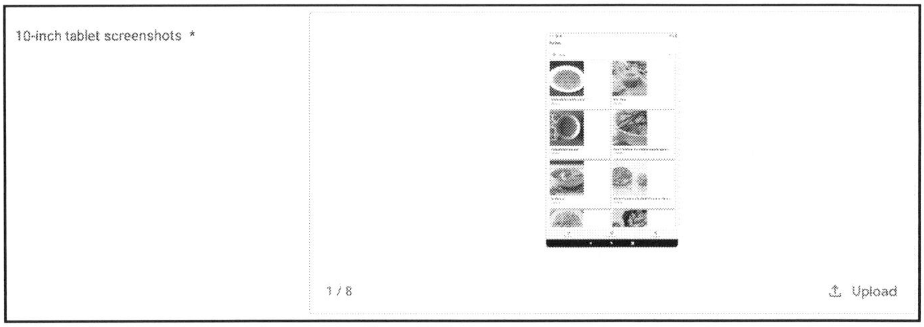

For this chapter, you won't upload a video because that requires setting up a YouTube account. However, a video that shows off your app's features is a good idea for your production apps.

Click **Save** to save the images and details you've entered so far.

Now, you've defined enough of a presence to make an impression.

Entering The Rest of The Information

However, you still haven't added enough information for the Play Store to allow you to distribute your app. Because you can promote an uploaded build for sale in the store, the Play Console wants you to fill out a lot of information first.

Click the **Dashboard** button, which is the top item in the left navigation bar in the console, and find the **Set up your app** section. This shows a checklist of all the items you need to fill out before you can distribute your app.

The steps you performed earlier completed the **Set up your store listing** goal, so it's already checked.

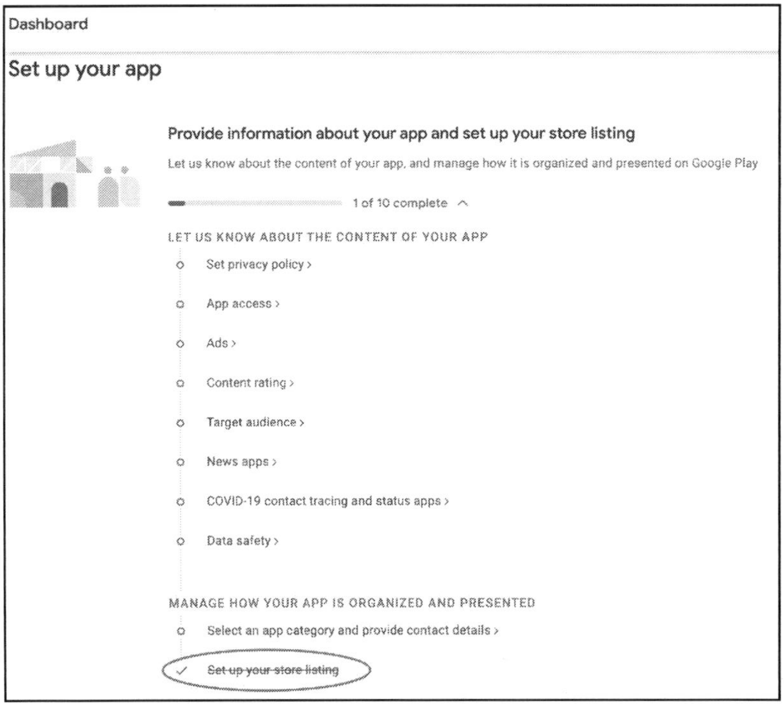

Click each of those items to fill out the required information. If you get lost in the process, go back to the Dashboard and find the **Set up your app** section again.

Because this is a simple recipe app without a lot of controversial content — other than what counts as a "sandwich" — the answers are straightforward. You also have time before your app goes live in the Play Store to modify any of your choices.

The following are sample settings to get you started.

Be sure to click **Save** after updating each page, then navigate back to the **Dashboard** to choose the next step.

Set Privacy Policy

For **privacy policy** you must include a link to where you are hosting your app's privacy policy. This is mandatory for apps targeting children under 13. But it's a good idea for all apps, as customers expect it these days.

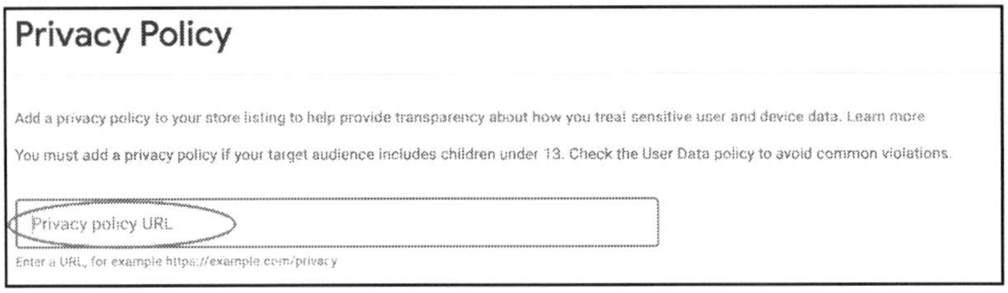

App Access

For **App access**, select that all **functionality** is available since there are no restrictions.

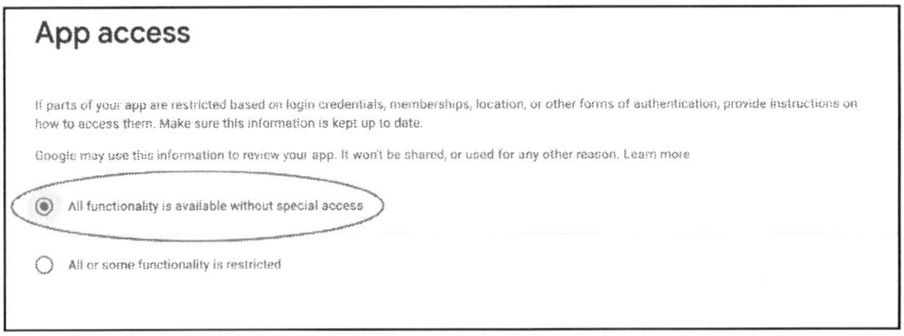

Ads

For **Ads**, indicate that the app doesn't contain ads.

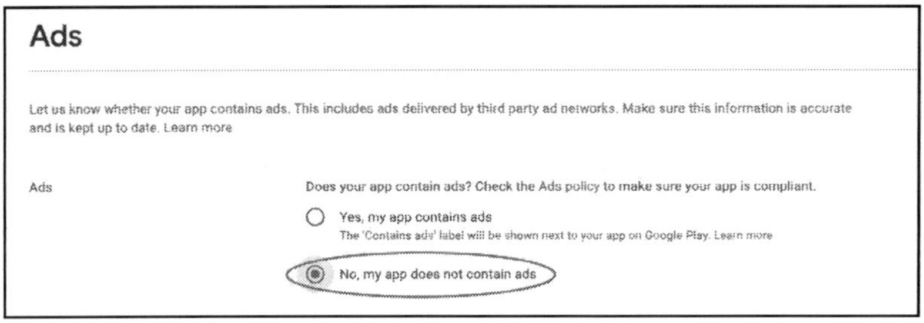

Content Rating

To receive a content rating, you'll have to answer a questionnaire. Click **Start questionnaire**.

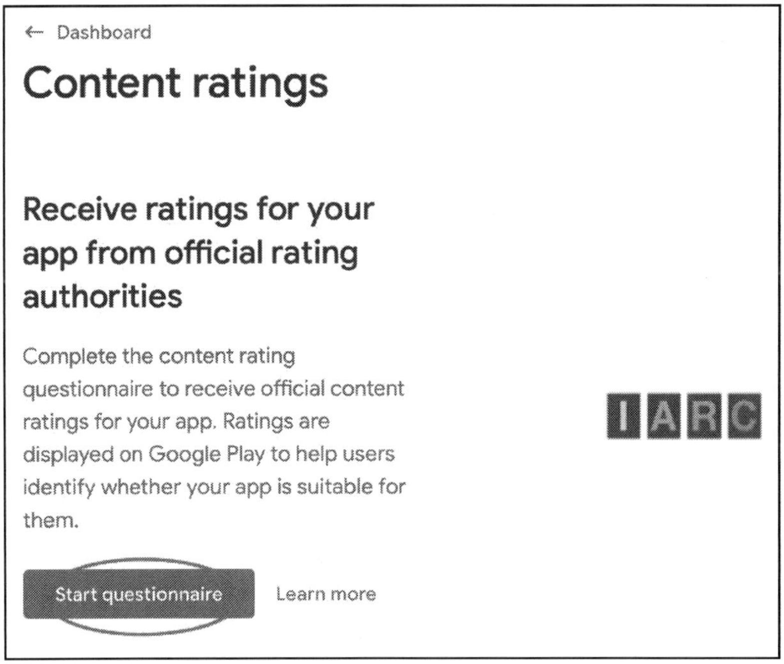

The questionnaire has several steps. The first is specifying the **Category**. Enter your email address, select the **All Other App Types** category and click **Next**.

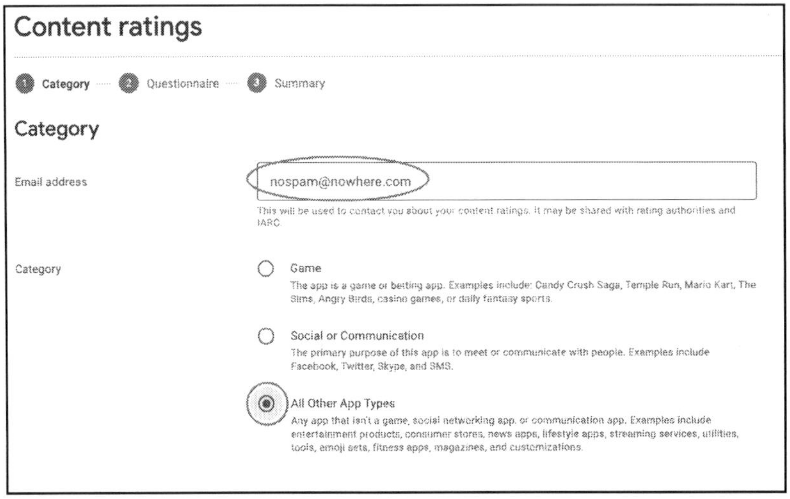

You need to answer several questions regarding your **app's content**. Be sure to read each one before making your selection. Your app just contains recipes without any functionality to even buy ingredients, so you can select **No** for all the content questions, except **Online Content**.

Since your app pulls data from an **API** you need to answer **Yes**. When you're finished answering all the questions, click **Save**.

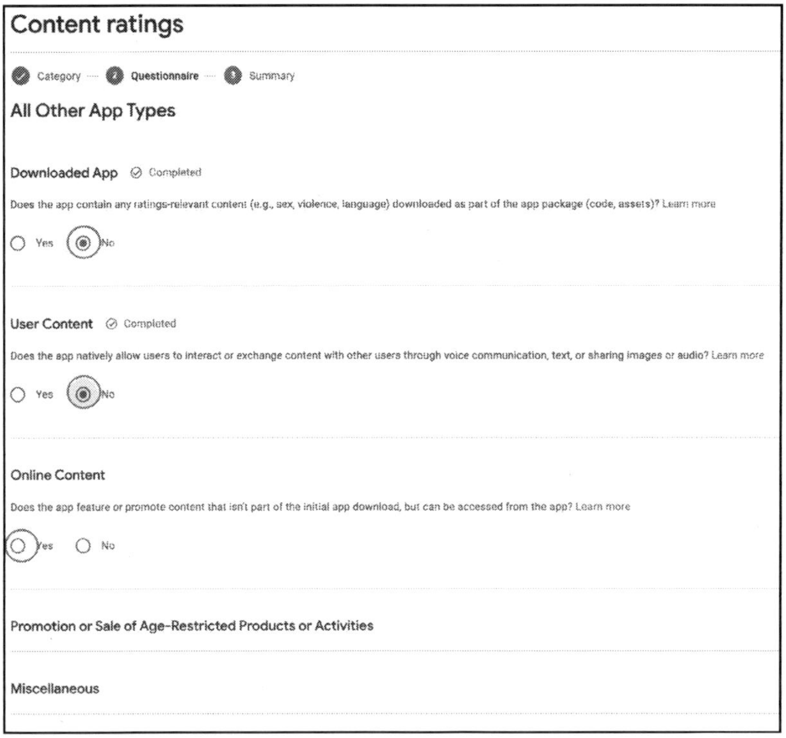

After you've saved your choices, click **Save** and then click **Next** to review the **Summary** page.

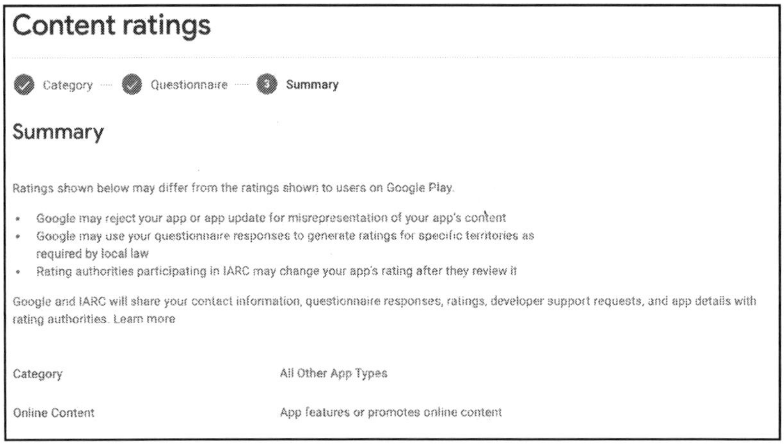

If everything looks good, click **Save**. You'll then see the **Content ratings** page.

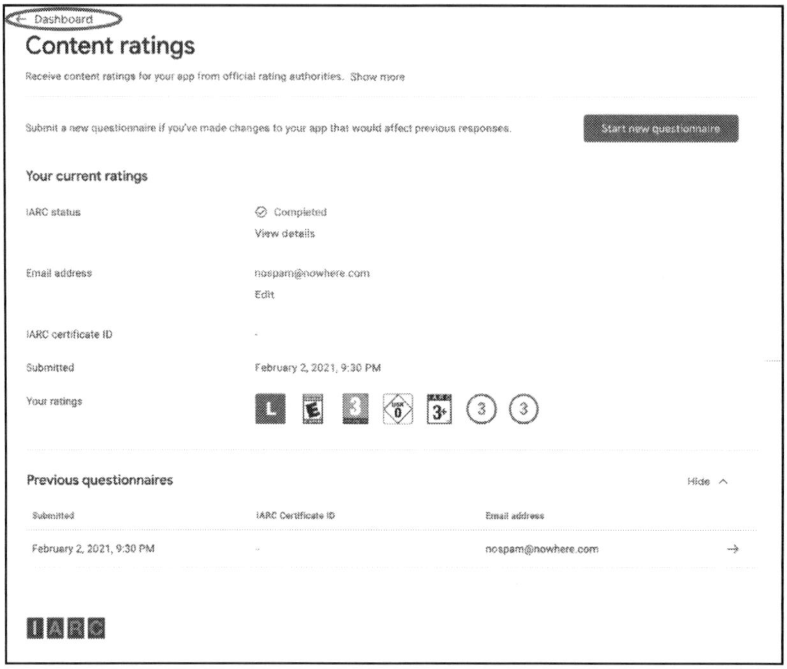

Click the **Back arrow** at the top to return to the **Dashboard** and continue with **Target audience**.

Target Audience

This app is not for children, so simply select **18 and up**. That way, there's no problem if a user looks up a saucy dish, like a **bolognese**.

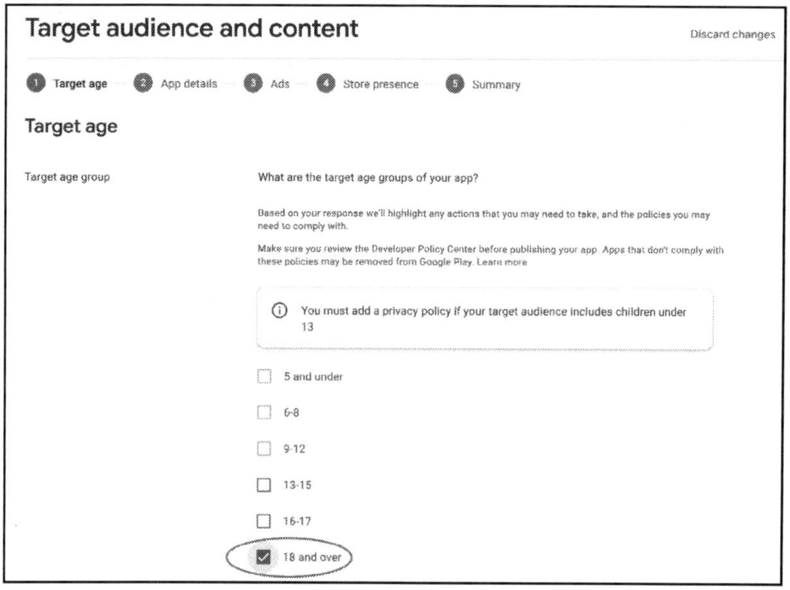

The next question asks about your **Store presence**. Choose your preferred option and click **Next**.

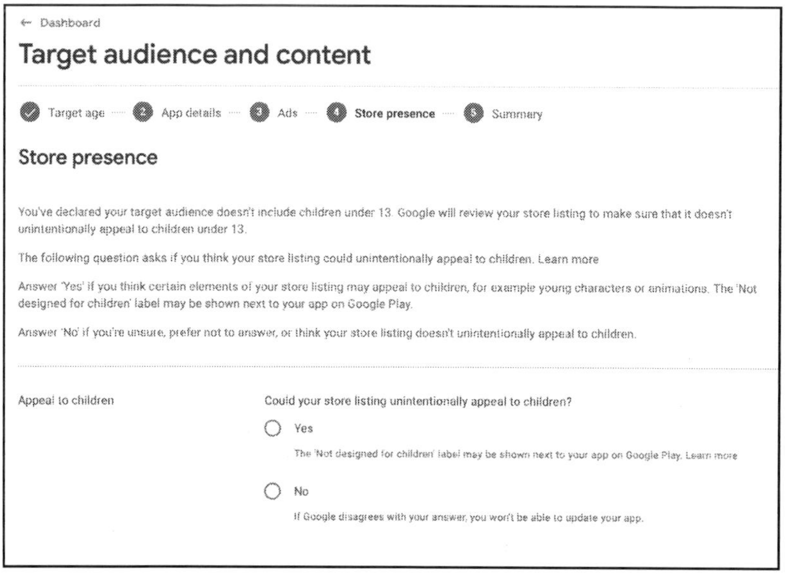

The screen will show you a summary. Note the differences between choosing **Yes** and **No**.

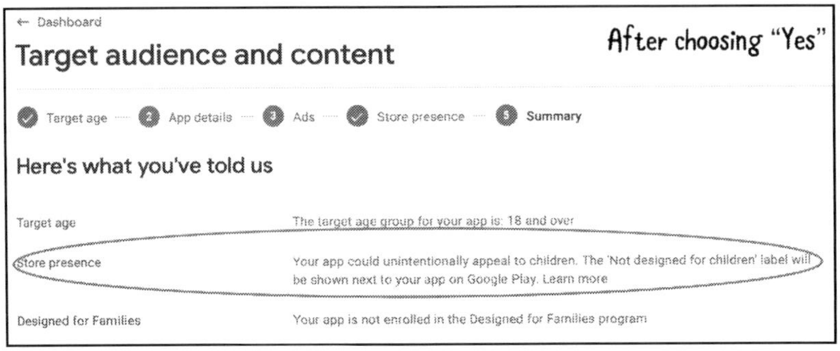

Click **Save** and then the **Back arrow** again to go back to the **Dashboard** and get ready to set details for the **News** section.

News

This is not a news app, so select **No**.

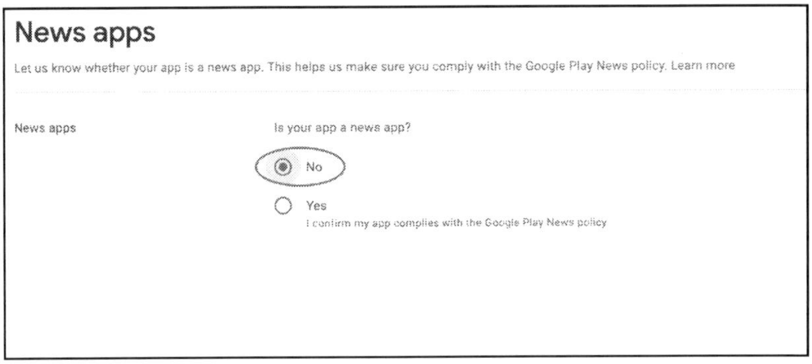

COVID-19 Contact Tracing and Status Apps

This is not a COVID-19 contact tracing or status app.

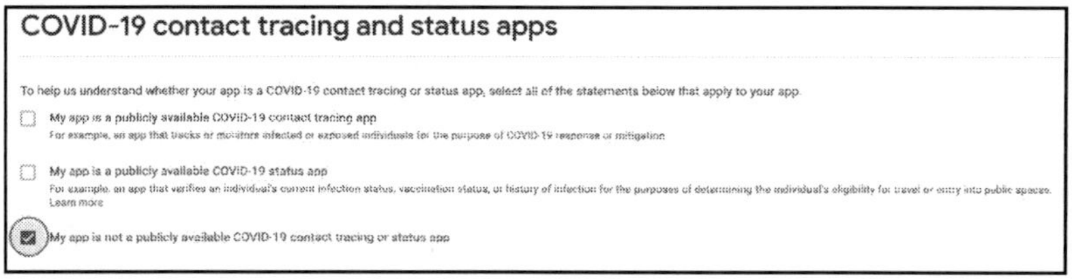

Data Safety

The data safety questionnaire needs information about how the app collects **user data**. Fortunately, this app does not collect any data, so your answers will be simple and easy.

Click **Next** on the **Overview** screen.

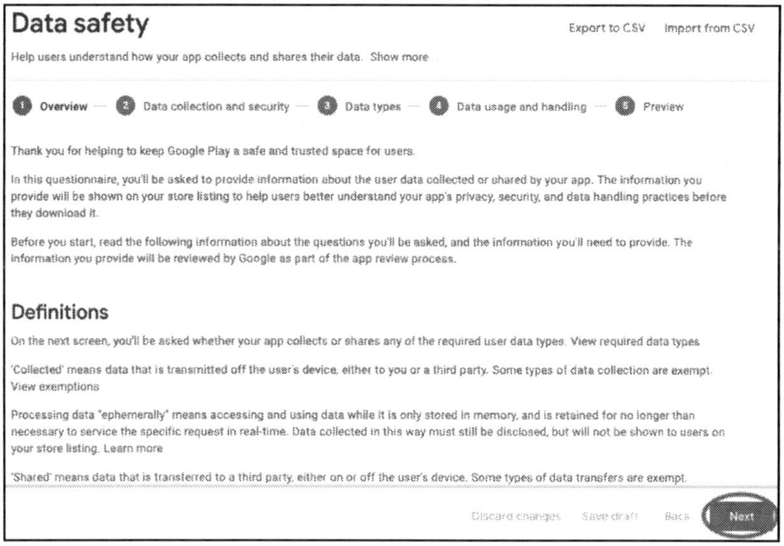

On the **Data collection** form, select **No** and click **Next**.

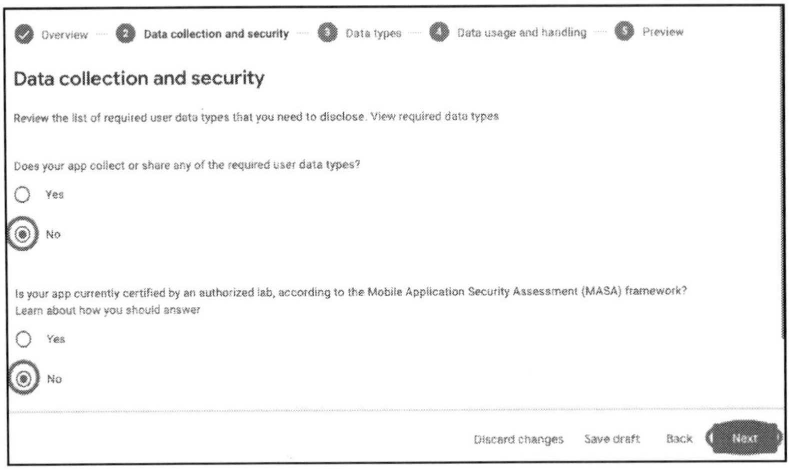

On the **Store listing preview** page, click **Submit** to continue with the app setup process.

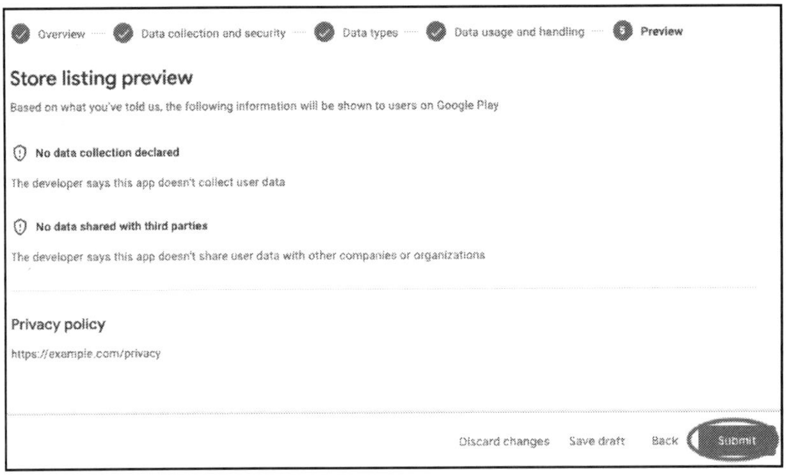

App Category

Return to the Dashboard and click **Select an app category and provide contact details**.

For the app category, select **Books & Reference** because this is a reference app. For the contact details, you need some real business contact info to publish to the store. For testing, however, it's OK to use bogus values.

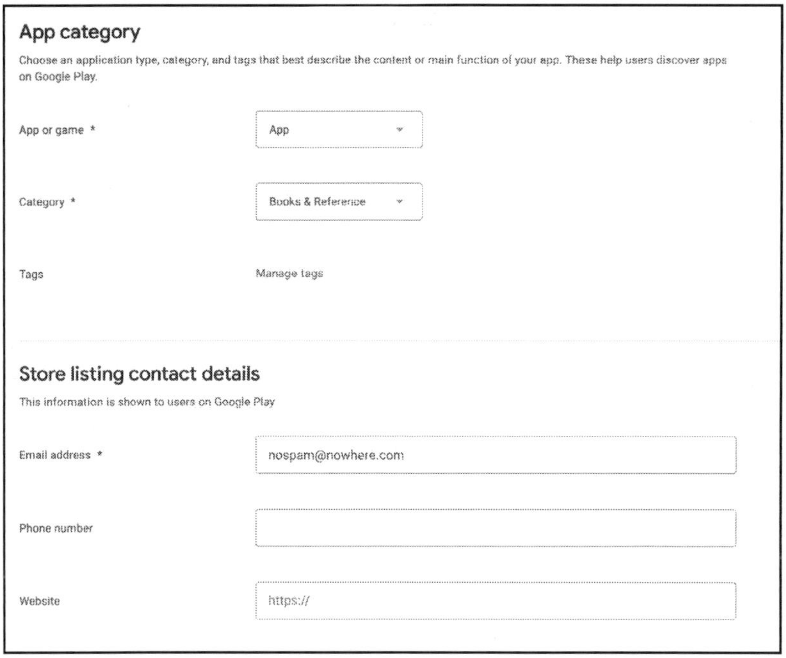

Click **Save** at the bottom right.

App Pricing and Merchant Info

If your Google Play Store account is new and you haven't set up your **financial information** yet, you need to tell Google where to send money. In this case, though, it's not a big deal because this is a free app.

To change the price, find the search field at the top of the Dashboard page, enter **pricing** and click **App Pricing**.

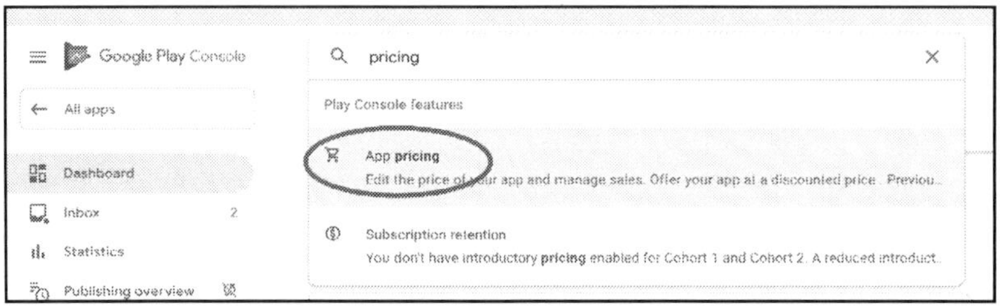

In this case, you'll publish a free app, which is the default value.

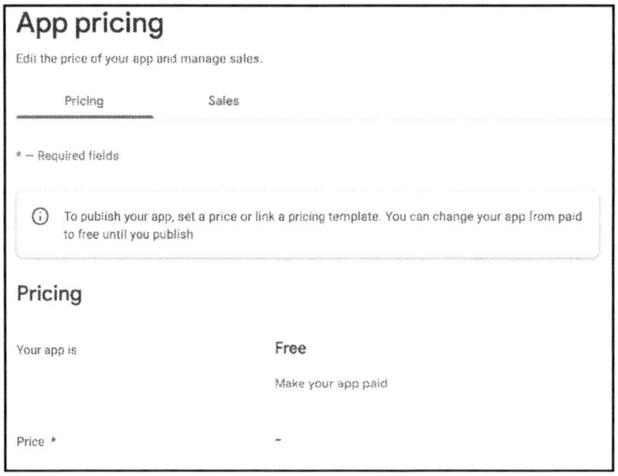

Now, you're finally ready to set up a **release** and upload a build.

Uploading a Build

The next step in your app's journey is to upload a build for testing. The Play Store provides different levels of testing:

- **Internal testing**: Intended for testing within **your organization** or with a small group of friends or customers, limited to **100 people**. You'll generally use this for releases during the **development cycle**.
- **Closed testing**: Allows you to send builds to an **invite-only** list. Use this for **beta** releases or experiments to gather feedback from a wider set of customers.
- **Open testing**: A **public** test that anyone can join. Use this to gather feedback on a **polished release**.

In any of these tracks, the steps to upload a build are similar. This chapter focuses on internal testing.

Go to the **Release** section in the left menu. Expand **Testing ▸ Internal testing** and click **Create new release**.

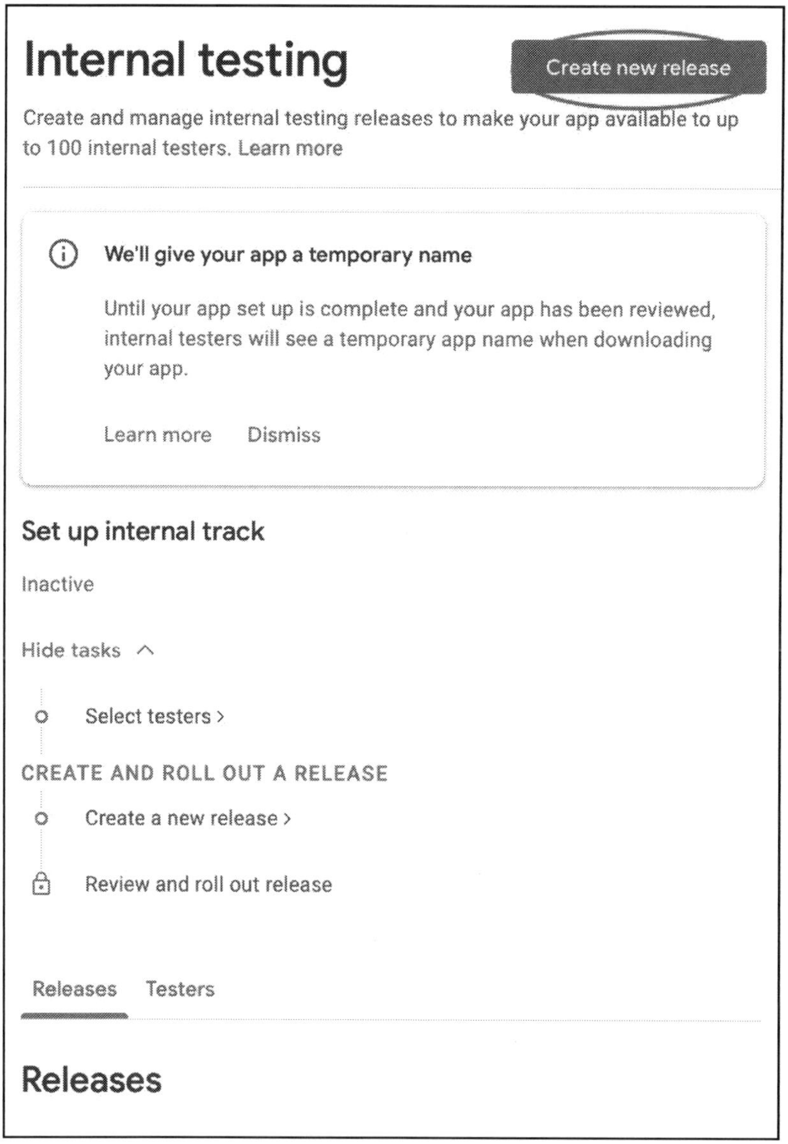

If prompted, read the **Terms and Conditions**. If you don't object to them, accept them.

To use an Android App Bundle, which Google prefers, you must allow Google Play to create your **app signing**. For more information, click **Learn more**. When you're done, scroll down to **App bundles**.

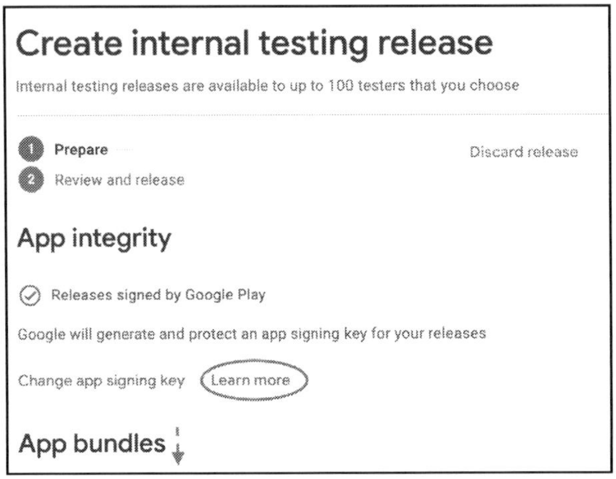

When you ran `flutter build`, it placed **app-release.aab** in your current project's folder hierarchy. The location isn't part of your Flutter project and it isn't visible in your IDE.

By default, the directory is: **build/app/outputs/bundle/release/**. Open Finder or Windows Explorer and navigate to such a folder.

Drag and drop the app bundle file to the **box** in the middle of the **Releases** page.

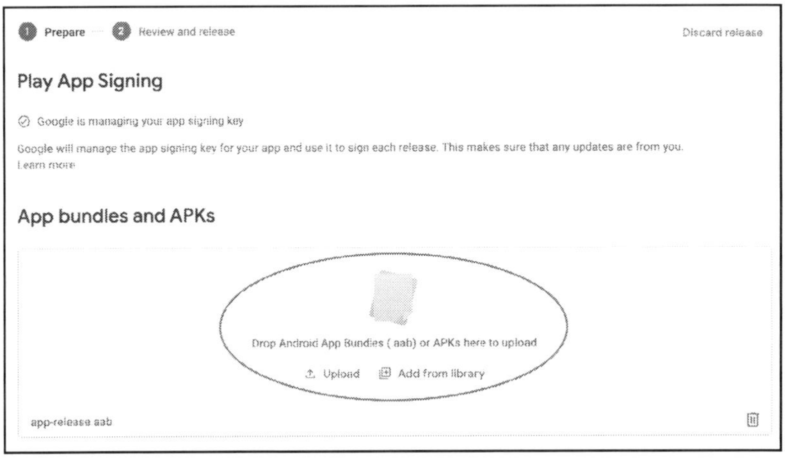

After the upload has completed, all that's left to do is create a **Release name** and **Release notes**.

The release name defaults to the **version number**, but you can rename it to something that you find helpful. For example, **First Testing Release**.

Use the release notes to notify the users about what's changed or if you want them to look for particular issues. You can provide this message in **multiple languages**.

For example:

```
<en-US>
This release is just to demonstrate uploading and sending out a build.
</en-US>
```

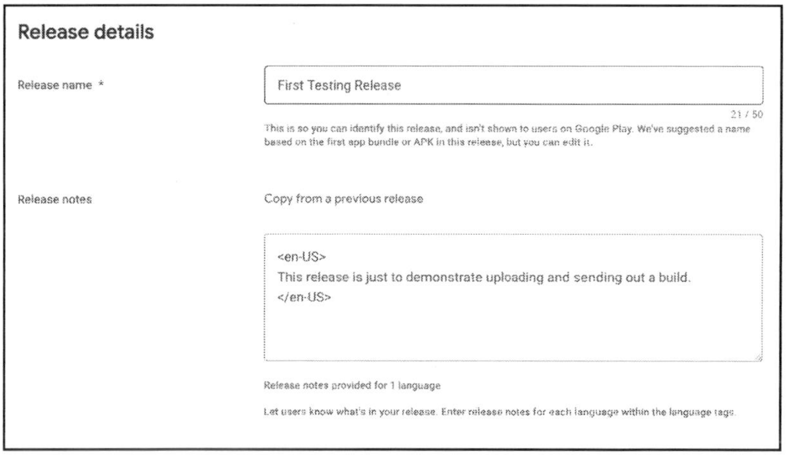

Click **Next** to proceed to the **Create internal testing release** page.

Distribution

On the next screen, if there are any **errors** listed under **Errors, warnings and messages**, you'll have to resolve them before you can proceed. It's OK to roll out with warnings, such as a lack of debug symbols.

Once you've resolved all the issues, click **Save**.

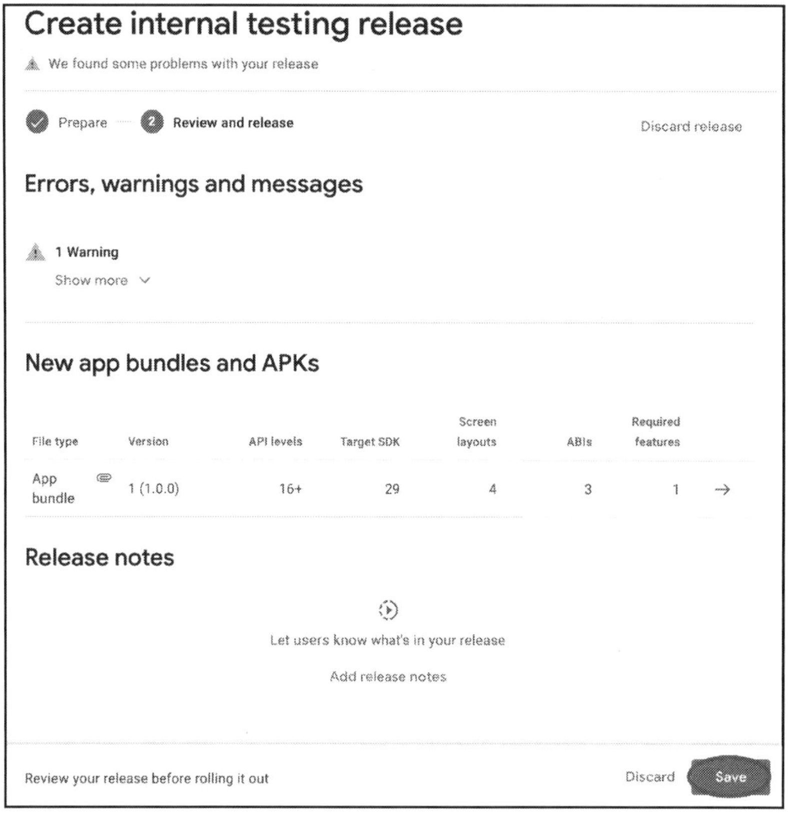

> **Note**: You may see a message similiar to this: **Your temporary app name is com.yourcompanyname.recipe_finder (unreviewed)**.

When the release says **Available to internal testers**, your app is ready for testing. Congratulations!

> **Note**: It will take some time before the app becomes available, from minutes to possibly a few days. Be patient.

Click the **Testers tab**, then **Create email list** to create a new list of testers.

Give the list a **name** and add the Google account email that you use for the Play Store on your phone.

There are a few ways to get the app on your phone. The easiest is to use the web link, which you can find under **How testers join your test**.

Click **Copy link** and send it to yourself on an Android device. Be sure to click **Save**.

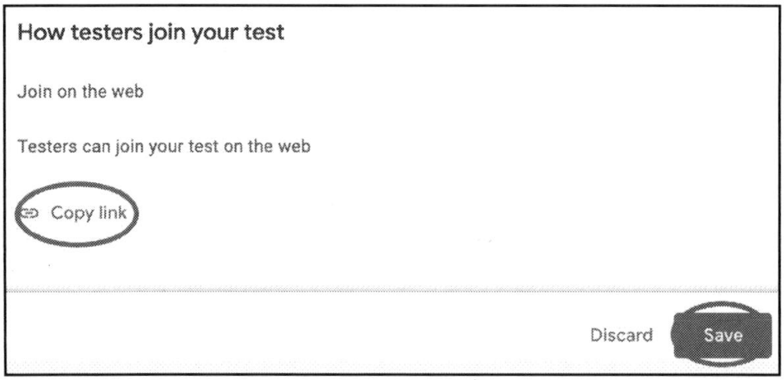

Installing The App

Using the web browser on your Android device, navigate to that link and you'll see the **invitation** to join the test.

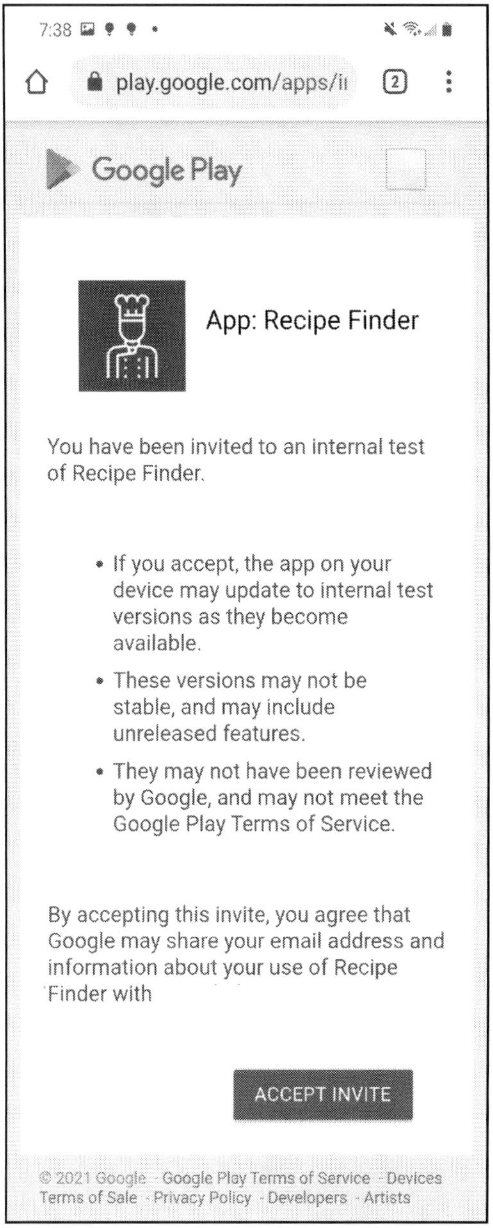

Tapping **ACCEPT INVITE** will give you a link to the Play Store to **download** the app. Once you're in the Play Store, just tap **Install**.

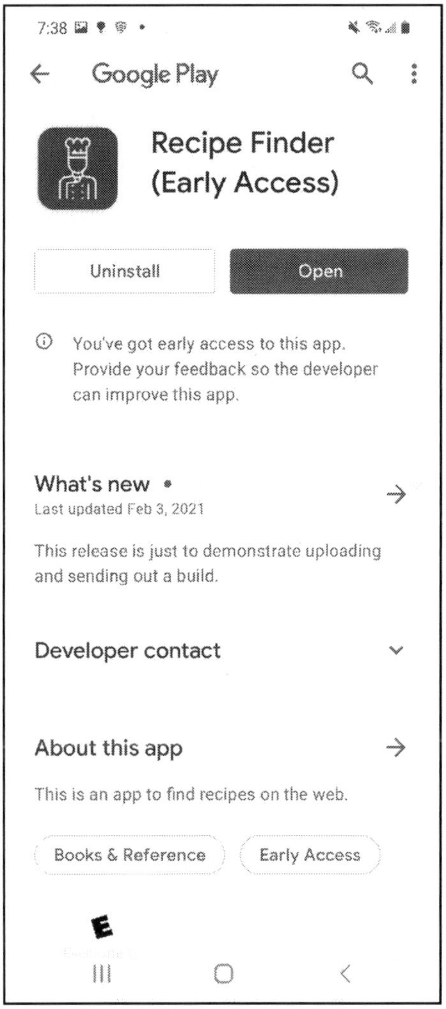

After the app loads, you're ready to go.

Congratulations, you just built a Flutter app on your local machine, uploaded it to Google Play and downloaded it to your device! Take a bow, this is a real accomplishment.

Key Points

- Release builds need a **signed** release configuration.
- To upload to the Google Play Store, you'll need to list all necessary **permissions**.
- To test an app, go to the Google Play Console, create the app with store **metadata**, create a **release**, upload the **build** and **invite testers**.

Where to Go From Here?

For the most part, you don't need the Flutter tools to prepare the app bundle for release. It's all **Android-specific** work. To learn more about how Android Studio can help prepare and sign release builds and how to use the Google Play Console, check out our Android Apprentice book: https://www.kodeco.com/books/android-apprentice. This covers the Google Play Console more in-depth.

In particular, once you've done enough internal testing of your app, you can **promote** the release for **closed testing**. This means that your app goes through **App Review** and is available in the Play Store, but it's unlisted. This lets you share it with even more testers.

After that, you can promote that release for **open testing**, which is a public beta that anyone can join, or send it out as an official **production** release.

In the next chapter you'll release **Recipe Finder** on Apple's App Store. Get ready!

Chapter 21: Build & Release an iOS App

By Michael Katz & Stef Patterson

In this chapter, you'll learn how to use **Xcode** and **TestFlight** to distribute your Flutter app's iOS version.

Unlike with Android, apps can't be **sideloaded** onto iOS devices. To distribute your app to users and testers, you have to go through **App Store Connect**, Apple's developer portal for the App Store. **TestFlight** allows you to send apps to testers and gather feedback from both your internal team and the outside world.

For this chapter, you'll need to use a **Mac** with **Xcode** installed. You'll also need a valid **Apple Developer Program** account to access the App Store.

If you're following along with your app, open it and keep using it with this chapter. If not, locate the **projects** folder for this chapter and open the **starter** folder.

> **Note**: If you use the starter app add your `apiKey` in **lib/network/spoonacular_service.dart** because your app needs to work correctly to **submit** it to the store.

Run `flutter pub get` and then run your app on an iOS simulator to set up the necessary files in the **iOS** folder.

Creating the Signing

It's time to leave Android Studio (or VS Code) and move over to **Xcode**. Open **starter/ios/Runner.xcworkspace**. This workspace includes the main app projects and the **CocoaPods** dependencies you need to build the app. It's the same workspace you used when adding your iOS app icons a couple of chapters ago.

In the Project navigator, check if there's a folder arrow next to **Pods** and has a blue icon next to it as shown below.

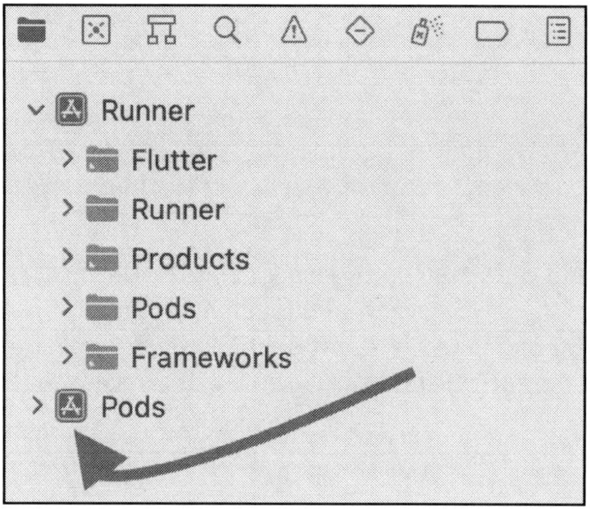

If not, close the Xcode project, return to Android Studio and run your app on an iOS simulator. This will pull all the required files. When you're done, re-open **starter/ios/Runner.xcworkspace**.

Select **Runner** in the Project navigator to open the project editor. Select the **Runner** target and open the **General** tab.

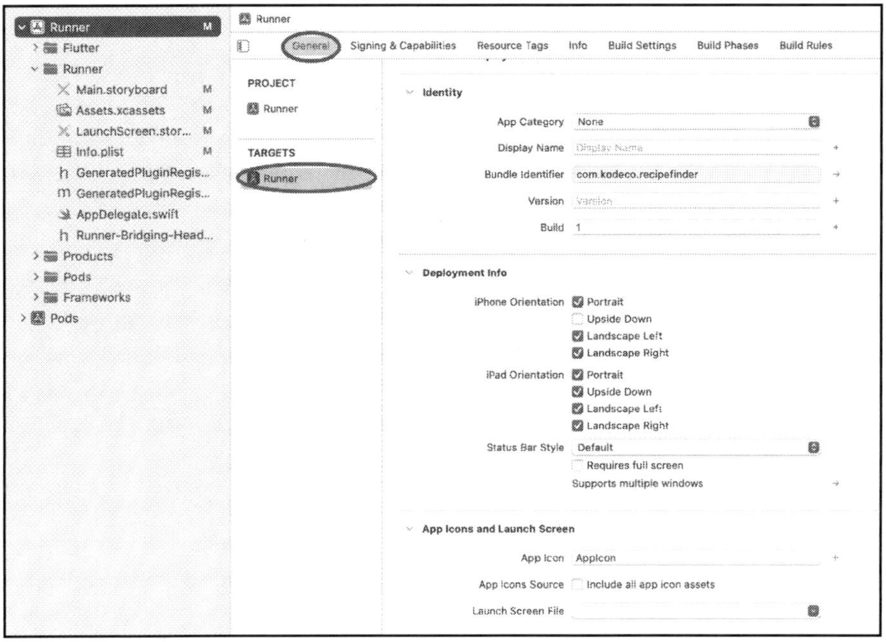

For app submission, it's important to check the **Bundle Identifier**. This has to be **unique** for your app.

If you want to follow along with this tutorial to test out the process — that is, *not submit* — you still have to change the existing value. Try using a random unique string if you are out of ideas.

Next you'll learn about joining the Apple Developer Program. If you already have a valid Apple Developer Program account, move on to the following section: **Creating an App Identifier**.

Creating an Apple Developer Program Account

If you want to enroll in the Apple Developer Program, open https://developer.apple.com/account and sign in with your **Apple ID**. If you see a page prompting you to join the Apple Developer Program, you need to click the link and follow the instructions to enroll.

The instructions are ever-evolving, so this chapter won't explain them. Just follow the prompts, enter all your personal or business information and pay the fee. Once registered, you'll be able to access the **Apple Developer Portal** and the **App Store**.

Creating an App Identifier

In the developer portal, you'll tell Apple about your app.

At https://developer.apple.com/account you'll see the various developer **Program Resources**.

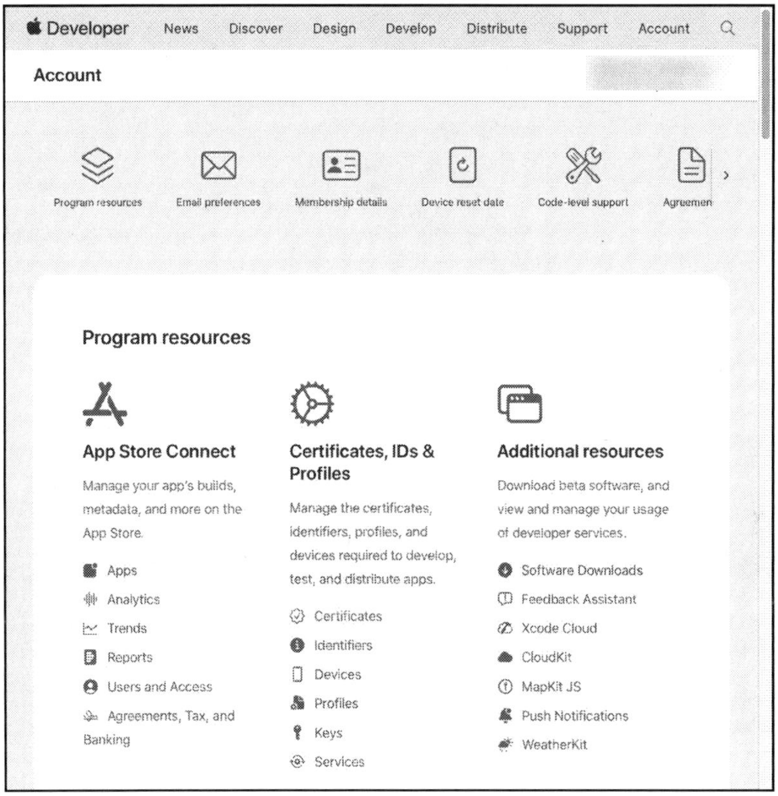

From there, choose **Identifiers** to get to the identifiers list.

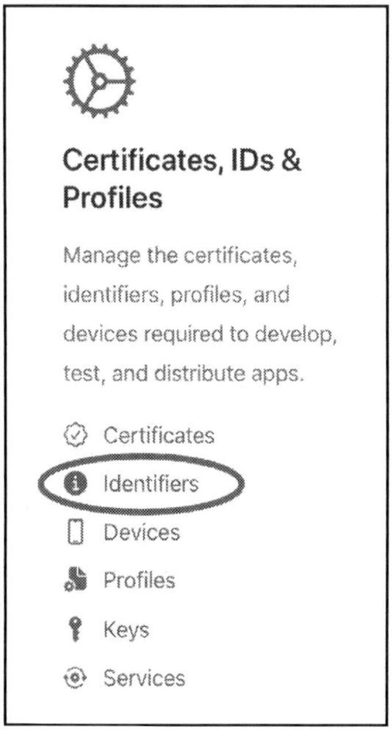

This list displayed contains all the **app identifiers** associated with your developer account. It will include all the **IDs** you create manually or through Xcode.

Click the + button to create a new identifier.

You'll see a long list of identifier types. For this task, select **App IDs** and click **Continue**.

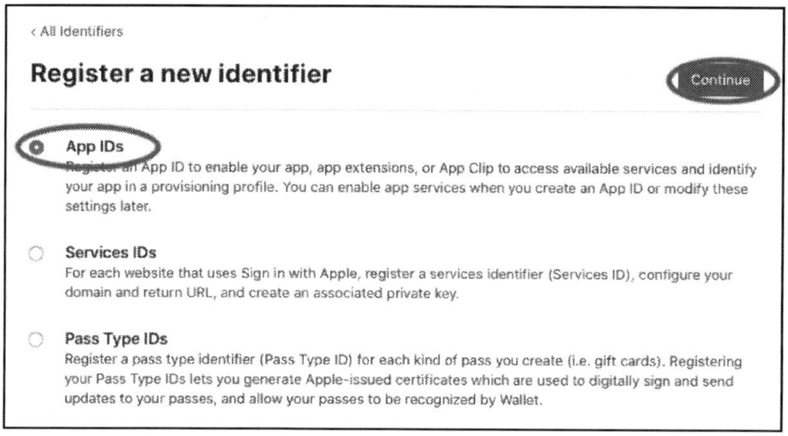

You'll get a chance to choose between an **App** and an **App Clip**. Choose **App** and click **Continue**.

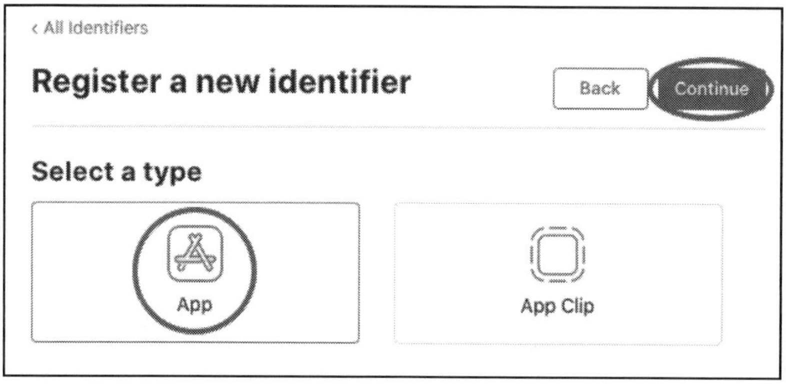

Note: App Clips are **lightweight** versions of your app that users can download quickly and start using. Later, they can download the full app. At the time of writing, these are only experimentally supported with Flutter and are out of the scope of this book. See https://flutter.dev/docs/development/platform-integration/ios-app-clip for more details.

Next, you have the opportunity to set an explicit **App ID**.

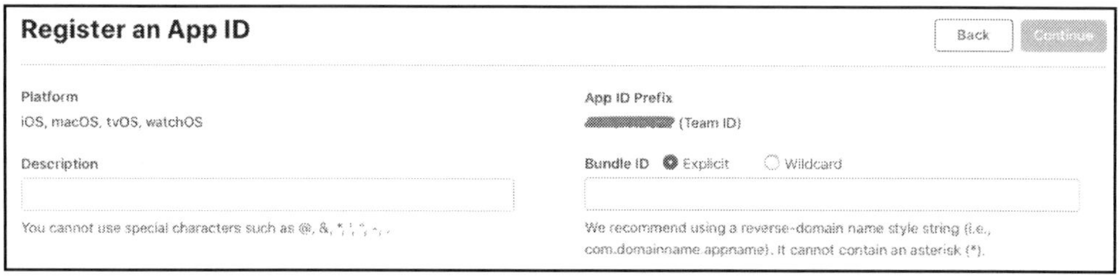

Copy the **Bundle Identifier** you previously chose for your app from Xcode and paste it in the **Bundle ID** field. Remember, this has to be unique so don't use **com.kodeco.recipefinder**.

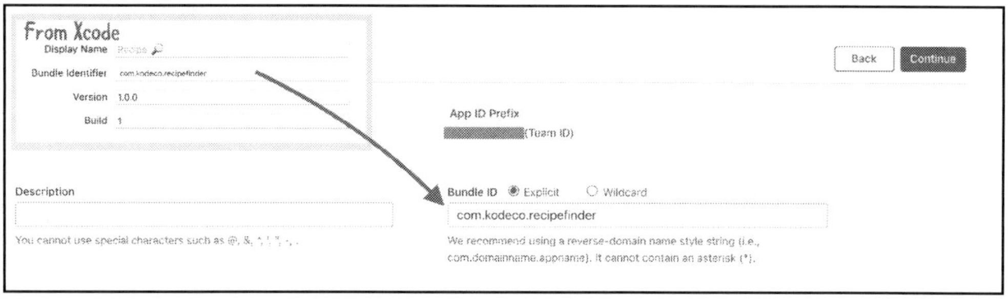

Next, set the description. This is for your use only. It helps you find the app you want from a long list in the console as you make more apps.

There's also a long list of **Capabilities**, which are special entitlements that let your app access parts of the operating system, hardware or Apple's Cloud services. The app for this chapter doesn't require any special capabilities, so you don't need to worry about setting up any of these.

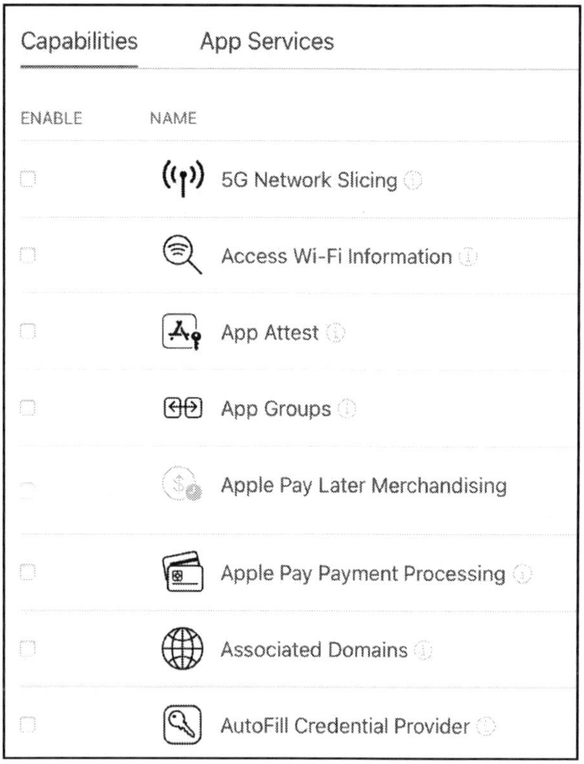

Click **Continue**, then **Register**. After a moment for processing, you'll see the app ID listed in the **Identifiers** list.

Now that Apple knows the identifier, you need to update **Xcode**. You'll bounce back and forth between their website and Xcode a few times.

Setting the Team

In Xcode, click the **Signing & Capabilities** tab. This will allow you to select a team. Select your developer team in the drop-down. If you aren't signed in through Xcode, choose **Add an Account...** to sign in.

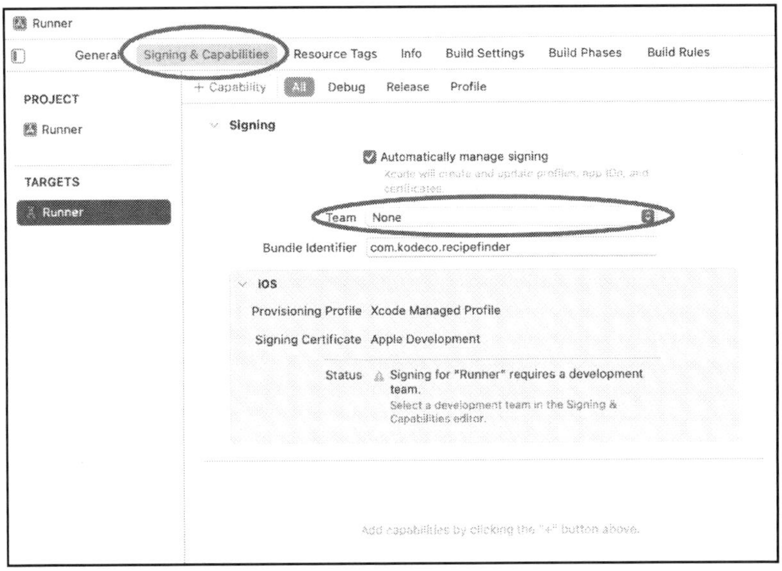

Once you've set the team and fixed any errors, Xcode will create the **signing certificates**.

> **Note**: Instead of letting Xcode manage your app profile, you can deal with those issues manually. You usually do this if you're working in a continuous integration environment. Manual signing is outside the scope of this book, but it's covered in *iOS App Distribution & Best Practices*: https://www.kodeco.com/books/ios-app-distribution-best-practices.

Setting up the App Store

When you submit an Android app, you first have to have a Google Play developer account and then set up the app in the Play Store. For iOS (and macOS) apps, you need to follow the same procedure for Apple.

The first step is to set up a spot for the app in **App Store Connect**. This is Apple's administrative console for developers in the App Store.

Navigate to the App Store Connect website: https://appstoreconnect.apple.com/

> **Note**: You'll need a valid **Apple Developer Program** account to access App Store Connect. If you log in and see an **Enroll** button, then you still have to sign up. Use the instructions above to create an account.

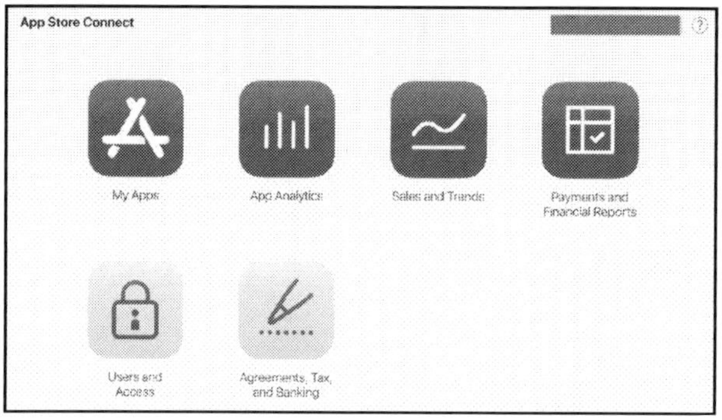

Creating a New App

Before you can upload and distribute a build, you first have to create a record for the app by adding some basic information.

From the main App Store Connect login menu, select **My Apps**. This is where you'll create your app's store listing.

To create a new app record, click the + button and select **New App**.

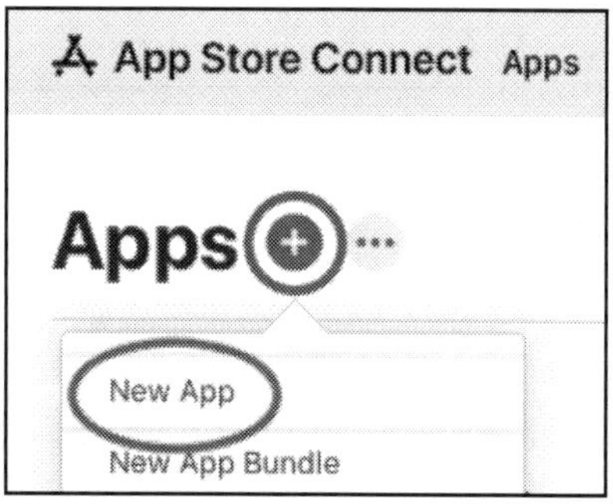

You may have to accept the App Store terms and conditions or enter business or legal info. This might happen now or at any point in the process. The site will let you know when you need to agree and will not let you proceed otherwise. Any time you see that request, resolve the issue and come back.

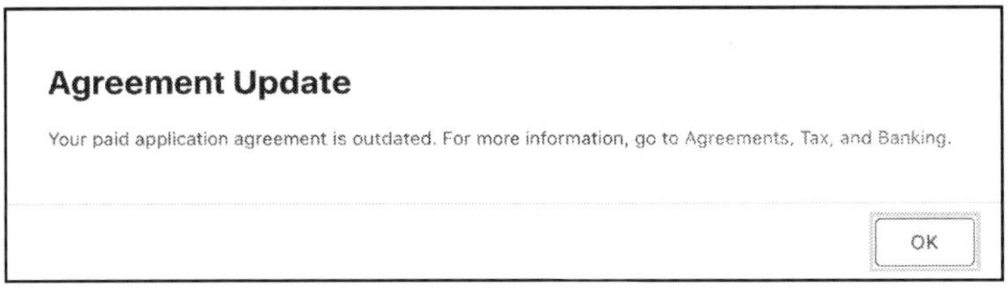

You'll see a window where you can fill in some basic app information:

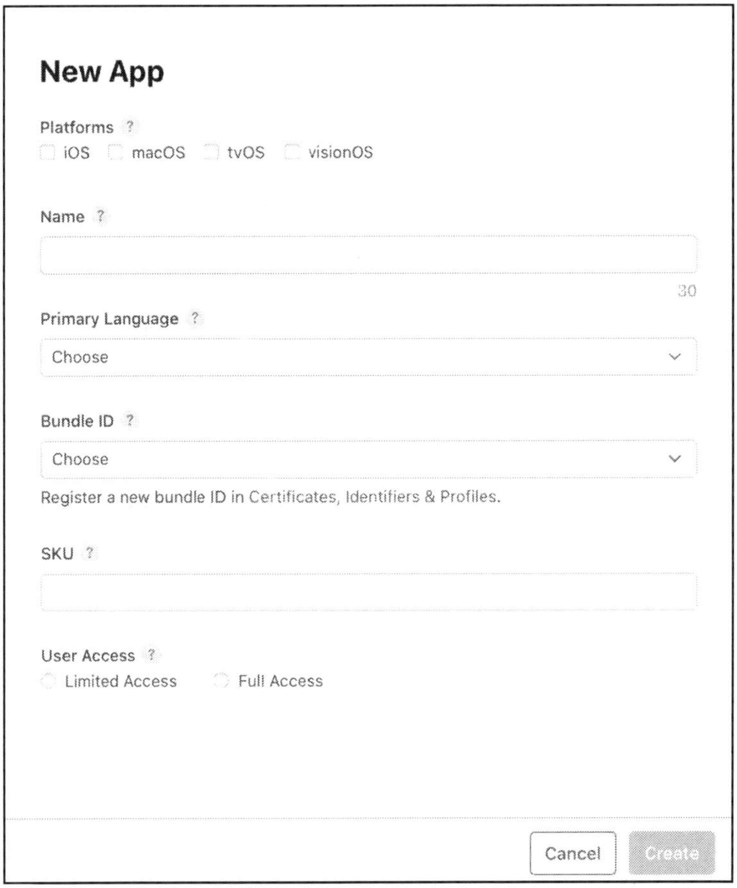

Fill in the following information:

1. Select the **iOS** platform.
2. **Name** is important here because your customers will see it. As with the Android app, you'll need to use something unique. **Recipe Finder** is already taken, and you'll get an **error** message if you pick a name that someone has already used.
3. **Primary Language** is the default language for the app — in this case, US English.
4. For **Bundle ID**, select the identifier you used in the **developer portal** from the drop-down. If it doesn't show up here, go back to the **Identifiers** list and make sure you created an **app ID**.
5. **SKU** is a unique identifier used for **financial reports**. Pick one that you'll recognize when counting the money. :]
6. **User Access** controls access to your team's App Store Connect users. This is important if you have a large team and don't want to show the app to everyone in your organization.

When you're done, your responses should look like this:

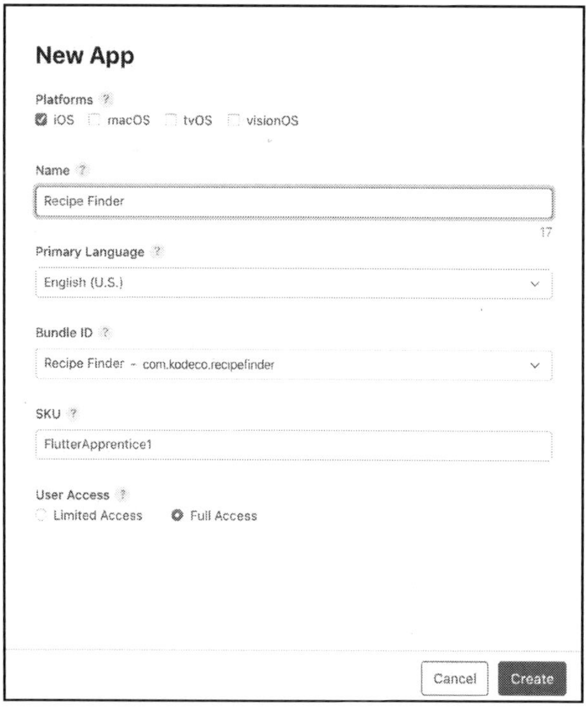

Click **Create** and you'll see a new screen showing your app's App Store Connect entry.

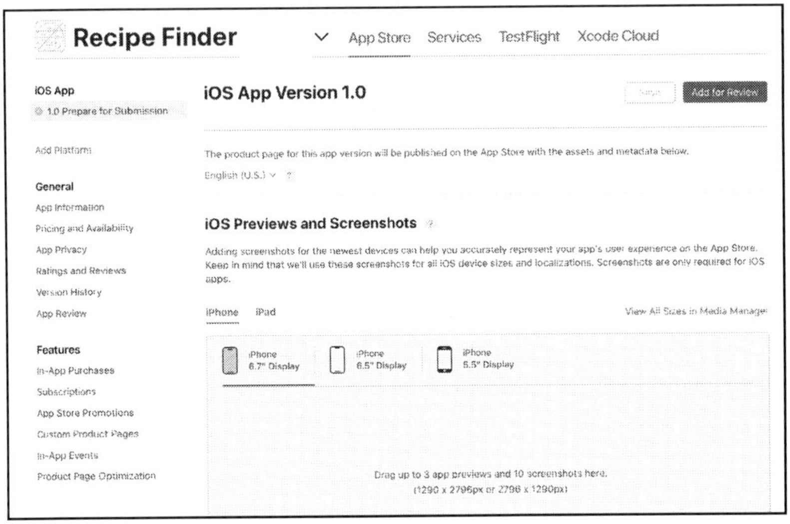

Voilà! Your app is now ready for you to upload.

Uploading to the App Store

On Android, you made an **appbundle** to distribute to the Play Store. iOS has a parallel concept. You'll need to build an **archive** to upload to the App Store. You can do this from either Xcode or the command line. For this chapter, you'll use Xcode.

In Xcode, just above the section where you entered the **Bundle Identifier**, you'll see the tiny app icon with a device.

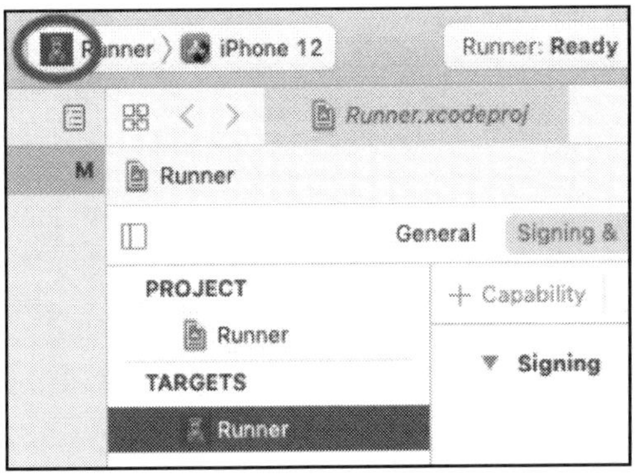

To the right of the tiny app icon, click the device name and set the device to **Any iOS Device** as the build destination. This is important because you can make deployable builds only for actual devices, not the simulator.

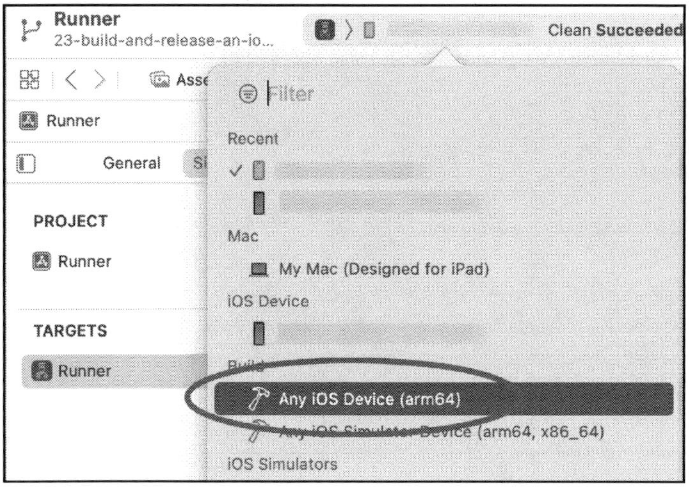

When you upload your app to the App Store, you upload an app **archive**. To create an archive from the menu, go to **Product ▸ Archive**.

Archive builds the app for **distribution** and **packages** it for uploading to the App Store. You'll see a progress bar across the top of your Xcode window.

When it completes, the **Organizer** window will pop up and display the archive.

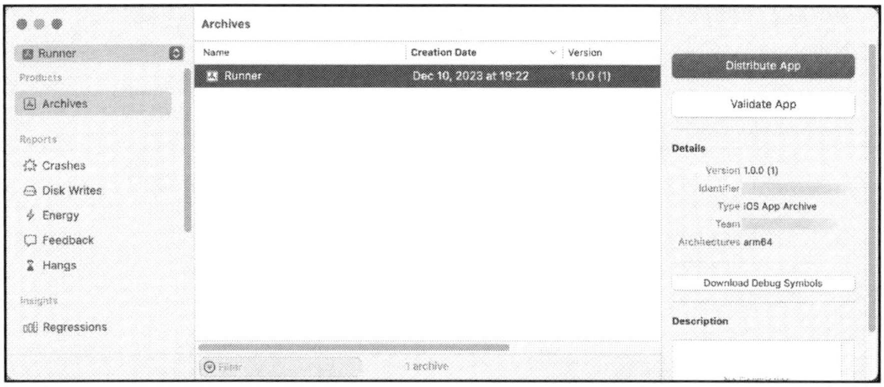

The archive file contains the **app binary** along with **metadata** and **symbols**. The App Store will process this file and get the version that users will finally download on their devices.

Uploading the Build

From the organizer window, click **Distribute App**.

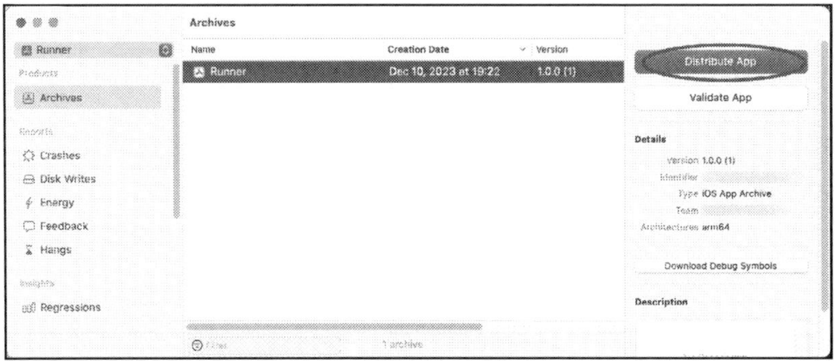

You'll see a list of distribution methods. Choose **App Store Connect** and click **Next**. The other options are for custom distributions typically used in enterprise contexts.

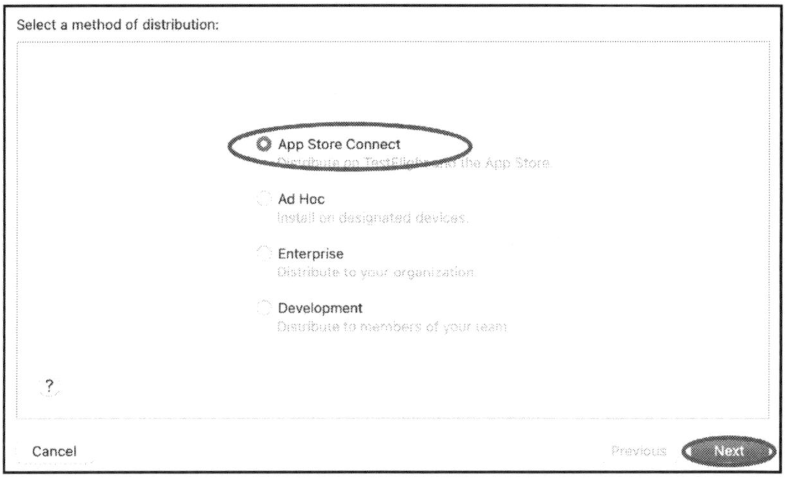

In the next dialog, choose **Upload** to send the build directly to Apple. The **Export** option creates an artifact that you can upload later, through other means. Click **Next**.

The next form covers **distribution** options. You have the option to strip the **Swift** symbols, which reduces app size. The other option is to upload the debug symbols, which makes it possible to symbolicate crash reports that come in from users. Click **Next**.

> **Note**: Starting with **Xcode 14** bitcode apps are no longer accepted. **Flutter 3.7** removed support for bitcode.

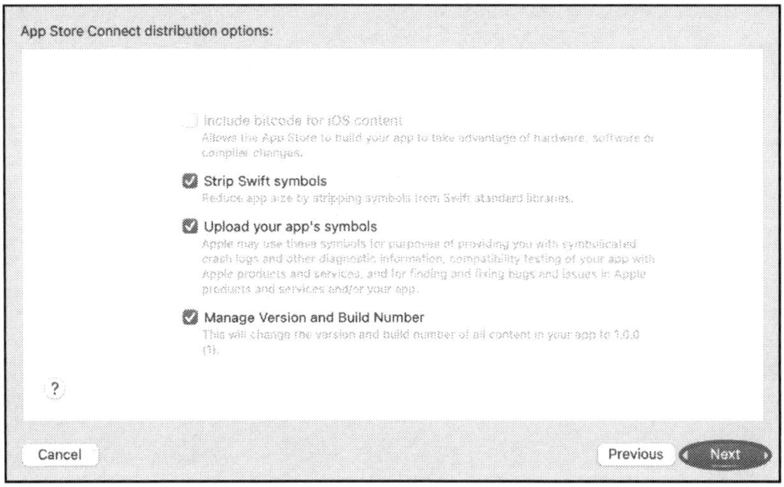

The next form is about app signing. It's easier to let **Xcode** manage your signing, but if you have a CI system doing your builds and uploading to the App Store, you'll have more control with manual signing. For now, click **Automatically manage signing** then click **Next**.

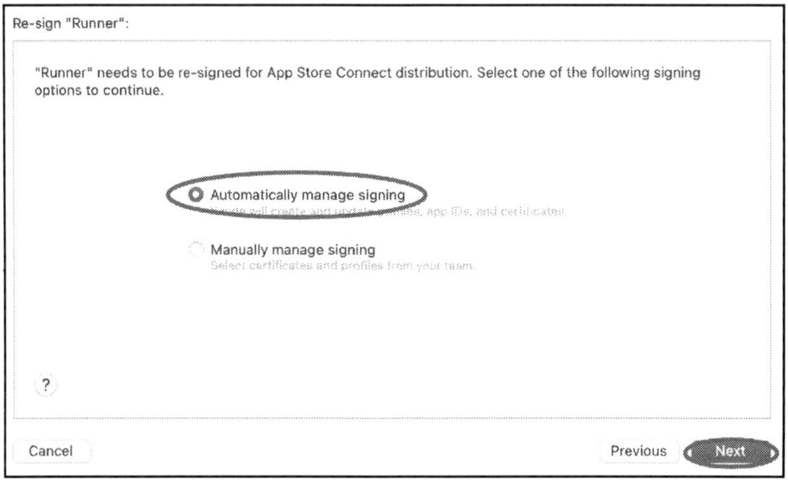

If you have an **Apple Distribution certificate**, skip to the next step. If you don't know what an Apple Distribution certificate is, then you're in the right place.

You need a certificate to sign the app that you'll upload to App Store Connect. Xcode can generate one for you. If your account doesn't have a certificate yet, you'll see the following screen. Select **Generate an Apple Distribution certificate** and click **Next**.

While the certificate generates, you'll see a screen with a spinning wheel. It can flash by or take a little while to generate. When it's done, you'll see the following screen. Be sure to read it.

You'll notice that it warns you that the **private key** is stored locally and cannot be recovered if lost. Apple recommends saving the certificate and key in a safe place.

Click **Export Signing Certificate**, add a password and save it somewhere you can remember. After you've exported the certificate, click **Next**.

Xcode will then sign the app and prepare it for upload.

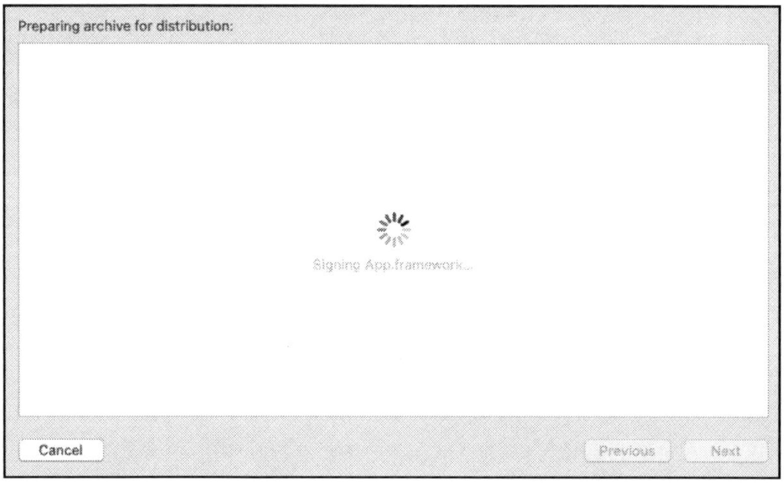

After Xcode creates the archive, the final form will show you the app contents and metadata. This includes any frameworks — such as **Flutter** — and other **dependencies**, as well as all the signing and entitlement information. Click **Upload** to send it to the App Store.

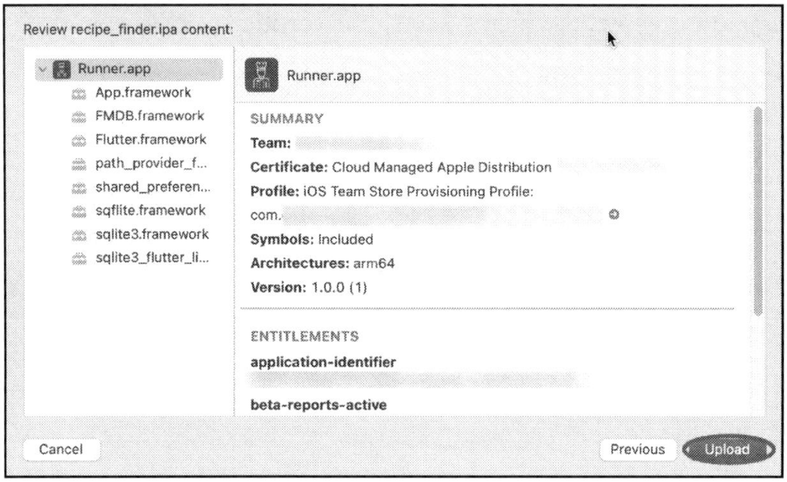

Now, it's important that you've already set up the record in the App Store so there's a place for this information to go. If there are no issues with App Store Connect, like having to accept agreements, then you're done working in Xcode. Otherwise, resolve any errors and try again. Click **Done** when prompted.

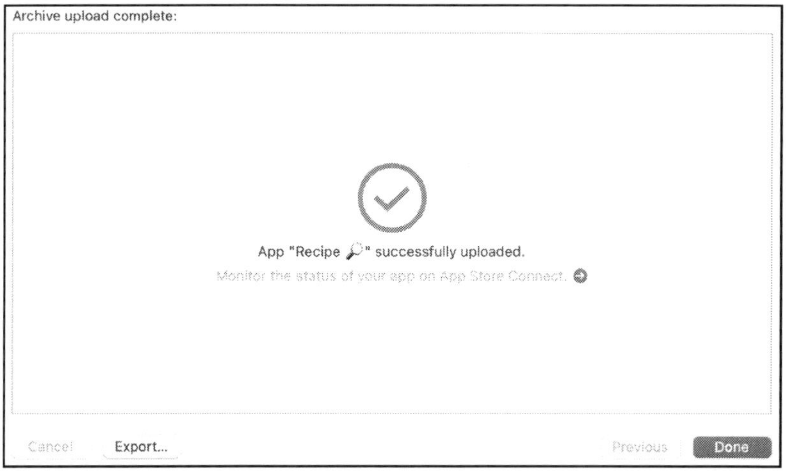

In a few minutes, the app will show up under the iOS builds in App Store Connect. Go to https://appstoreconnect.apple.com/apps, click your app and go to the **TestFlight** tab. Select **Builds ▸ iOS** on the left to see the list of uploaded builds.

You'll see yours is **Processing**.

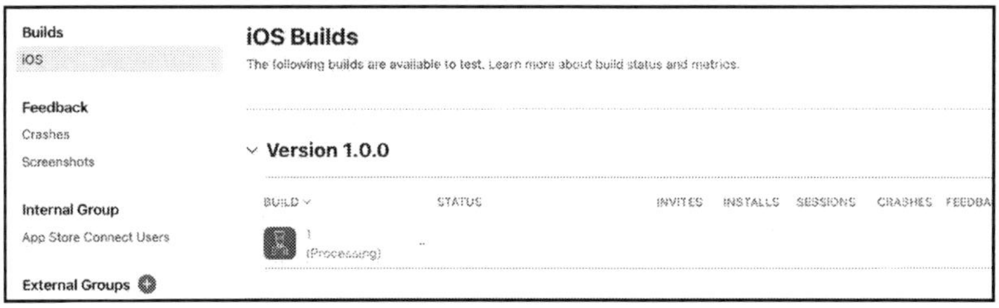

After some time, the status will update to **Ready to Submit**.

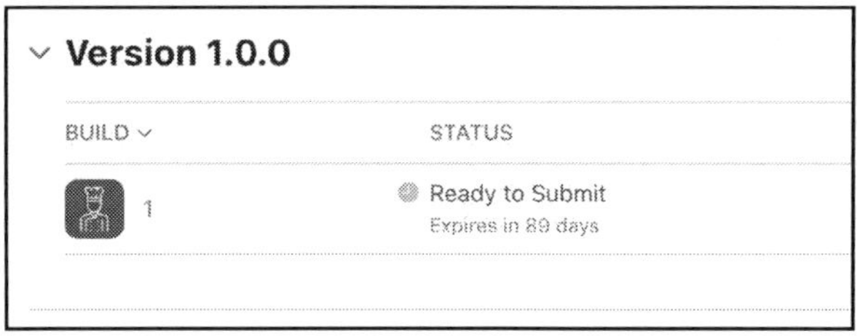

Alternately, you might see an error like **Missing Compliance**:

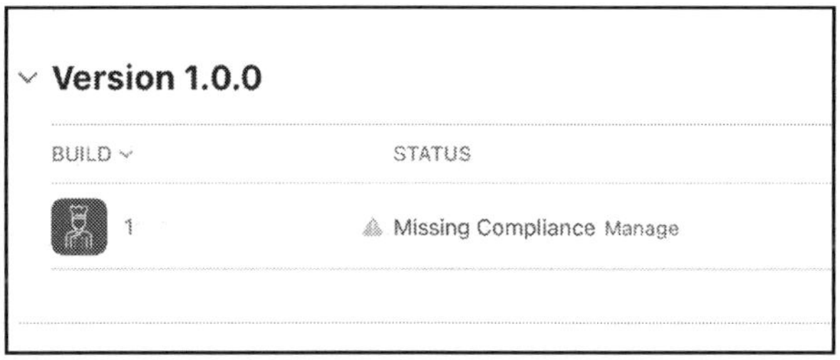

If there's an error, follow the instructions at the link to fix it. If this is the first time you uploaded the build, you'll likely get a compliance issue. Follow your local legal advice on how to answer those questions.

> **Note**: If you receive a message stating **Missing Push Notification Entitlement** and your app does not have push notifications see Flutter GitHub Issue 9984 (https://github.com/flutter/flutter/issues/9984) and Stack Overflow post (https://stackoverflow.com/questions/55167611/flutter-ios-app-submission-issue-warning-missing-push-notification-entitlement) by Kodeco's Jonathan Sande (https://www.kodeco.com/u/suragch).

Once your app is ready to **submit**, you can continue with the **TestFlight** process.

Sharing Builds Through TestFlight

Now, you're ready to test your build. There are two options for test builds: **Internal Testing** and **External Testing**.

Internal testing is for sharing within your **own company** for quality assurance or feedback. Typically, this includes other developers, quality engineers, product managers, designers and marketing specialists. Your mileage may vary.

External testing is for a limited **group** of testers. These can include people within your organization as well as beta test customers, friends, journalists and anyone you want to try your app before you release it.

Select **TestFlight** tab of the App Store Connect console.

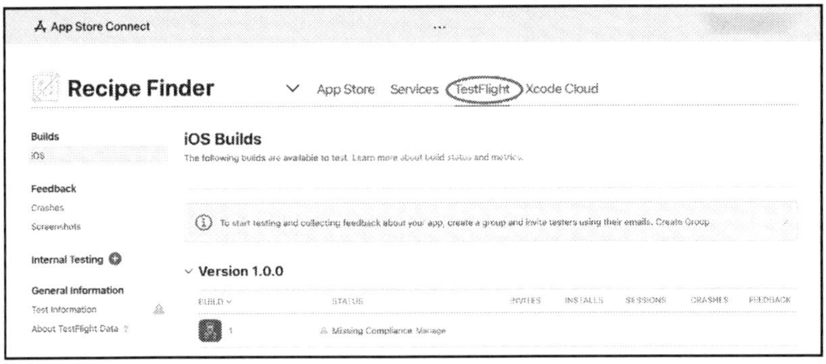

From here you'll see a list of all the builds you've uploaded. You might have messages from App Store Connect and this is also where you'll set up your testing.

Export Compliance

You might see an **Export Compliance** warning. If so, follow the instructions at the link to address it.

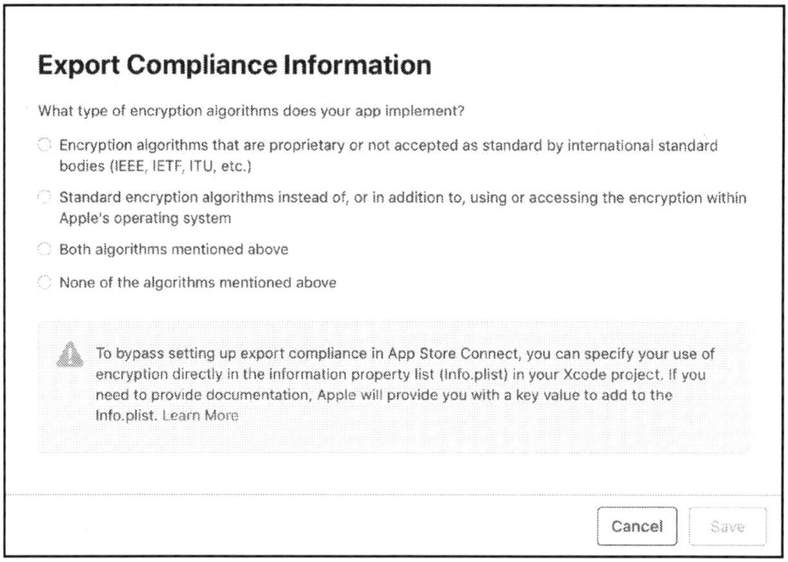

Follow your local legal advice on how to answer those questions.

> **Note**: You may see a message stating that you can bypass setting export compliance in App Store Connect by doing it in your Xcode project. Due to potential local legal issues this is out of scope for this book.

Next, you'll set up your internal testing.

Internal Testing

You can begin internal testing as soon as the app finishes processing and you've addressed any outstanding issues.

Click + next to **Internal Testing**.

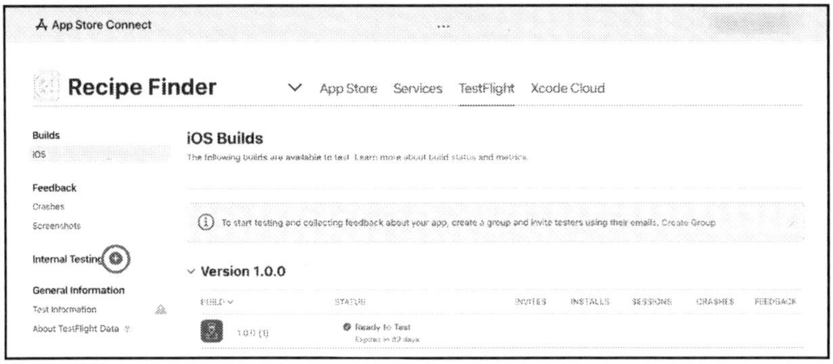

A dialog box will be displayed for you to **name** your internal testing group. This is the name that will show up in the App Store Connect console.

In **Group Name** box, enter **Internal Testers** or something you'd rather name it and click **Create**.

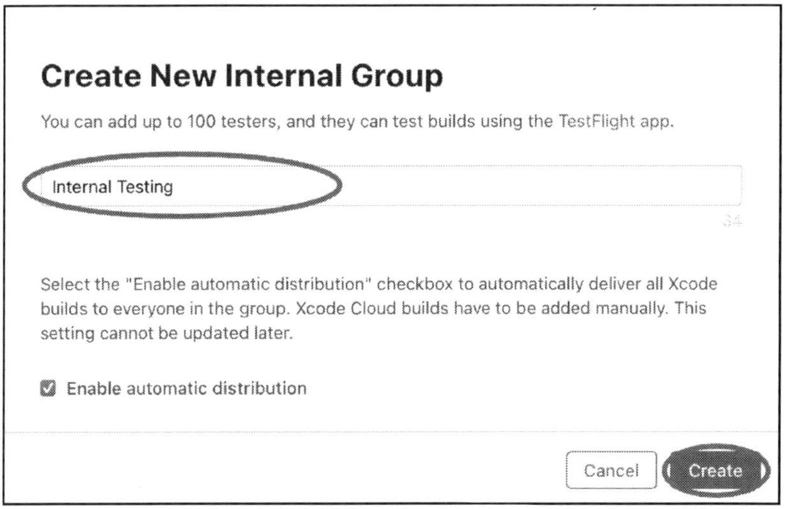

You'll get a **list** of users to add as testers. Internal testing is only open to users who have accounts in your App Store Connect.

At a minimum, you'll be listed as available. To add more people to your account, you'll have to go through the **Users and Access** link from the top navigation bar.

Check the box next to the names you wish to add and click **Add**.

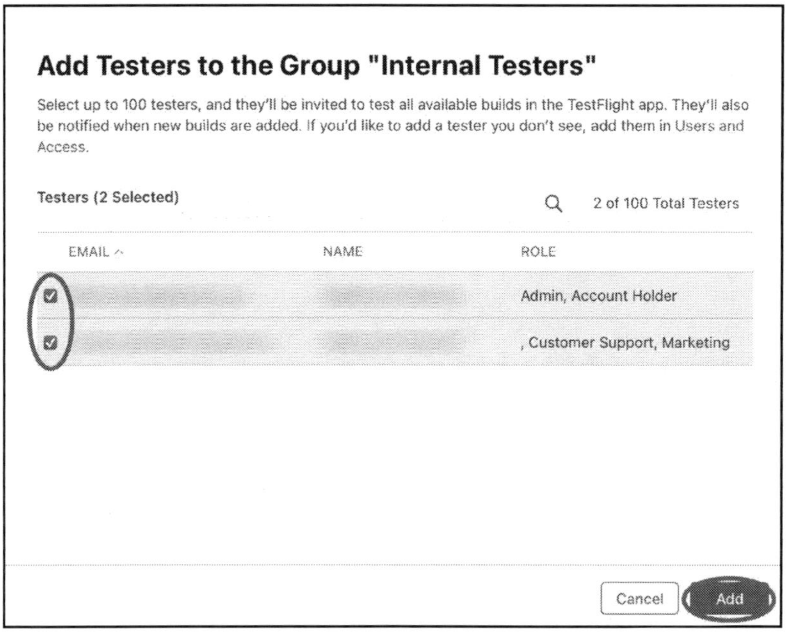

Once you add a tester, they'll appear in the **Testers** list.

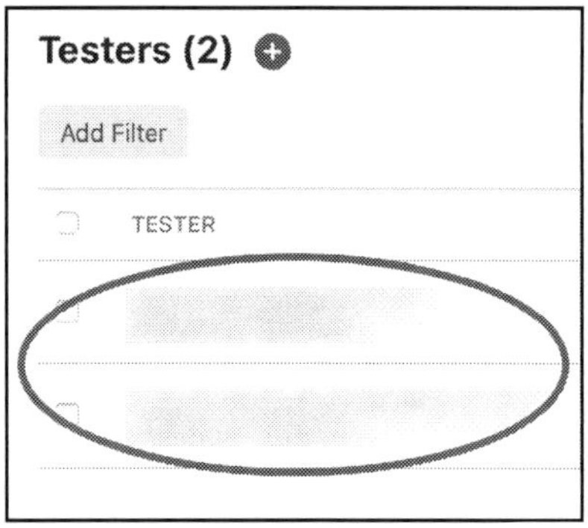

Before testing emails can be sent you need to add a message to your testers explaining what they need to test. Click on the build number, shown here as **1.0.0 (1)**.

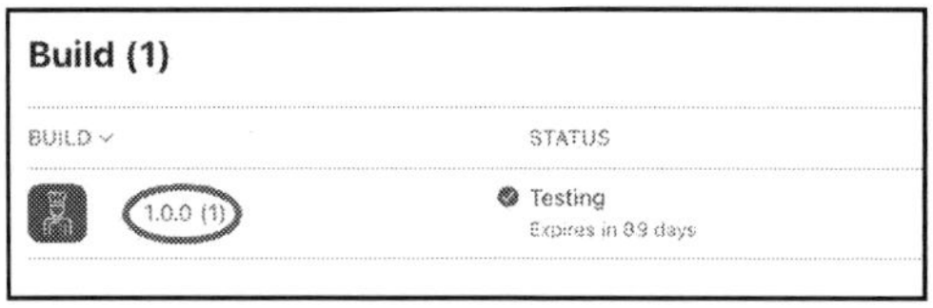

On the **Test Details** page enter a message for your testers and click **Save**. Then click **< iOS Builds** to return to the list of builds.

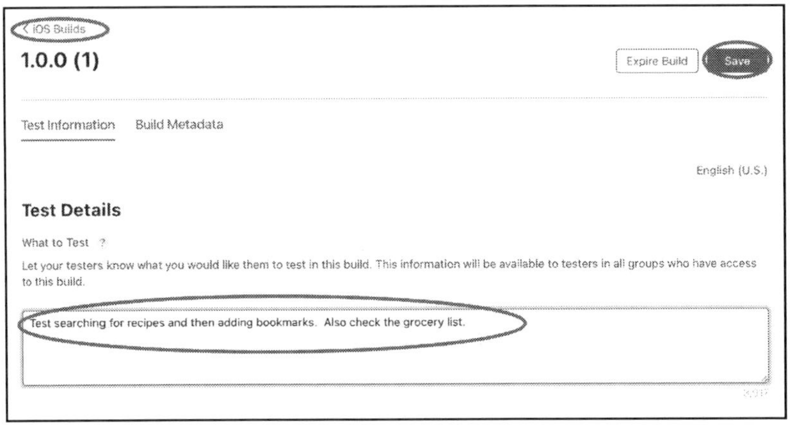

Returning to the **Internal Testing** page, you'll notice that after saving the message, the status is now **Invited**. This means emails have been sent to your testers.

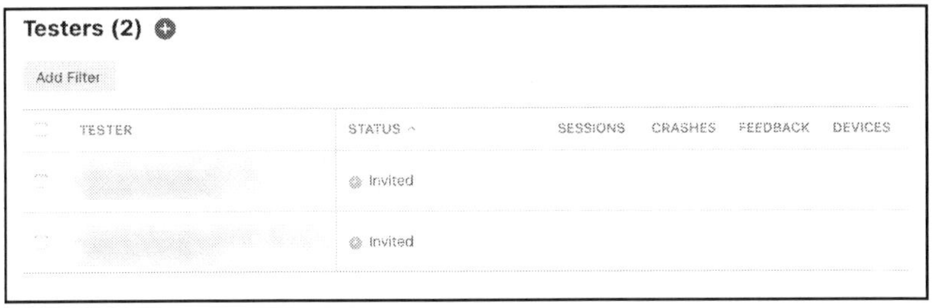

As they test, the columns to the right will show the status of the test. Testers have to accept the email invite before they can install a build.

The invite will provide **instructions** or a button to launch TestFlight. From there, the user will receive a prompt to **install** the app.

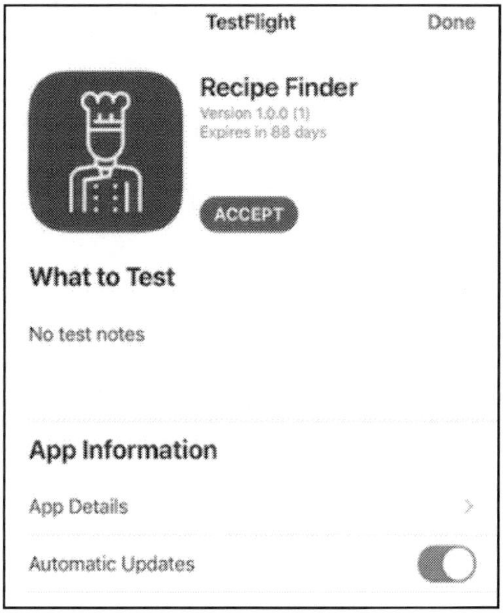

And that's all it takes for the user to get your app on their device! From then on, the App Store will automatically **notify** your testers when a new build is available.

From the same **Testers** list in App Store Connect, you can monitor the app's usage for **crashes** or **feedback** submitted through TestFlight.

External Testing

Internal testing is limited to a few people who are in your store account. Obviously, you don't want to give store access to testers who aren't part of your **organization**.

To get started with external testing, you first have to make a **group**. The App Store lets you separate **testers** into groups, so you don't have to release every build to every tester. For example, you might want a **test team** to get every build, but update customer beta builds only once a week.

Click the **+** next to **External Testing** in the left navigation bar to create a new group.

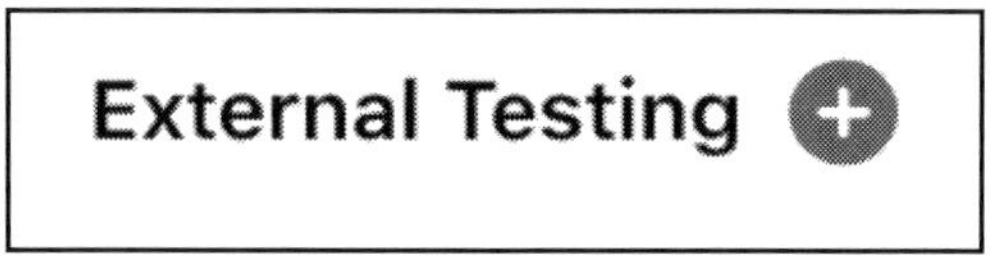

You'll see a window for you to enter the **Group Name**. Enter a name and click **Create**.

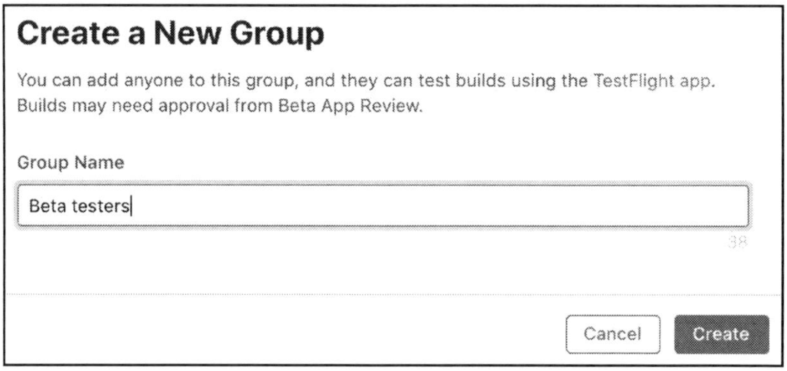

After you create the **group**, you'll see it listed in the **sidebar**.

You can now add testers to your group. One difference from internal testing is that you can **invite** testers right from this panel. You can also create a **web link** to share, letting testers invite themselves to the group.

Before you can create a link or add users, you need to add a build. Click + next to **Builds**.

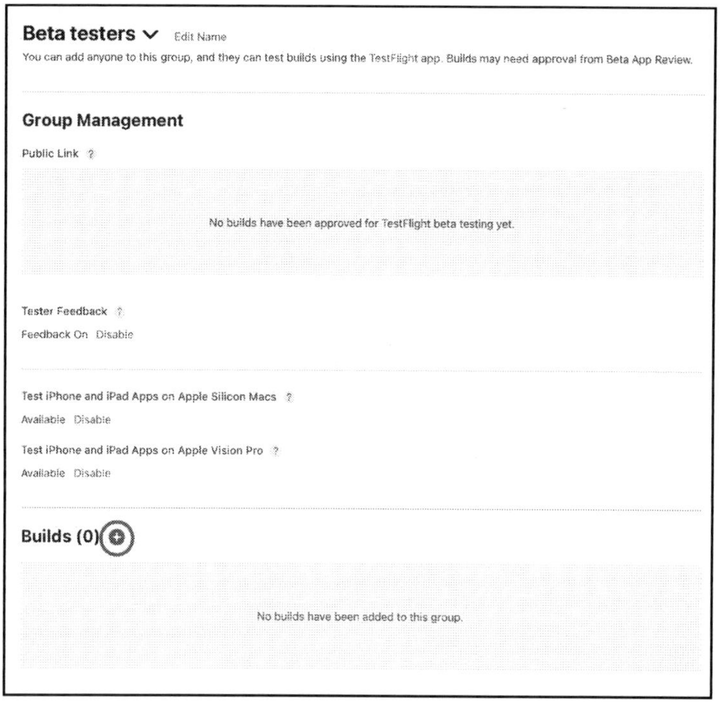

Apple **reviews** apps before it releases them to beta testers. The next window allows you to choose which build you wish to submit to Apple for Beta App Review.

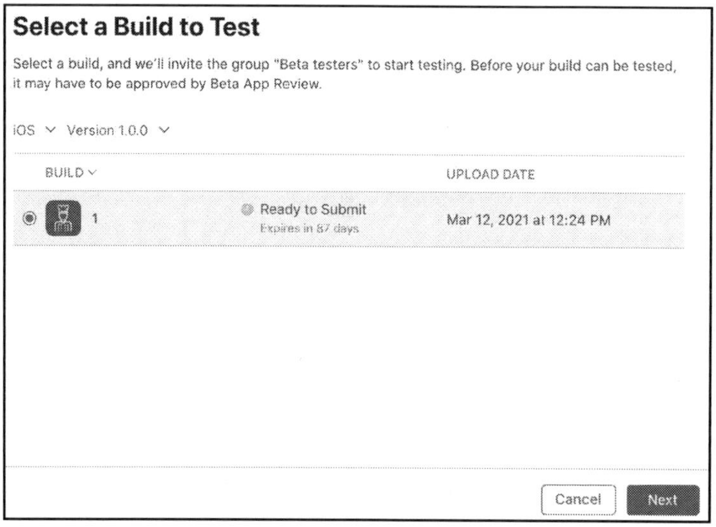

Select the build that you want for Beta App Review to test. Click **Next** to go to the next screen.

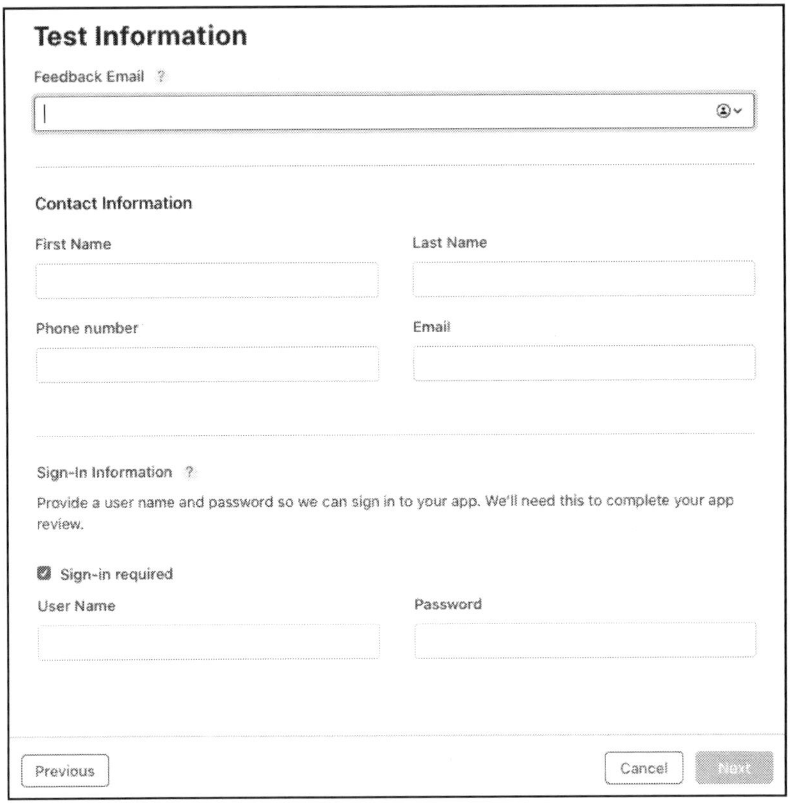

Next, enter your contact information. This lets your readers supply user feedback and lets Beta App Review ask any questions they have. If your app has a login, you have to create an account that app review can use to log in and check out the app. Fortunately, **Recipe Finder** has no login. :]

Enter the information and click **Next** to continue.

Your last step is to enter a little **message** that will be included with the build notification.

This is an opportunity to ask people to check out certain things or to notify them about changes.

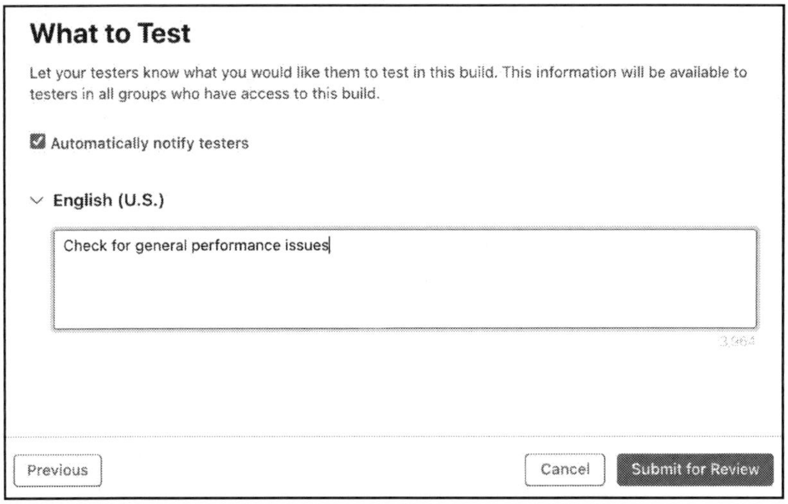

Enter a message and click **Submit for Review**.

This sends your build to Apple for a quick version of an app review. Within a short time — anywhere from a few minutes to a few days — the app will be ready to **test**, assuming there aren't any issues.

Congratulations, now you can distribute the app for testing.

Submitting Your App to the App Store

To submit your app to the App Store for download or purchase, you need to add all the information required under the **App Store** tab, such as **screenshots**, **marketing**, **privacy policy** and **age rating**.

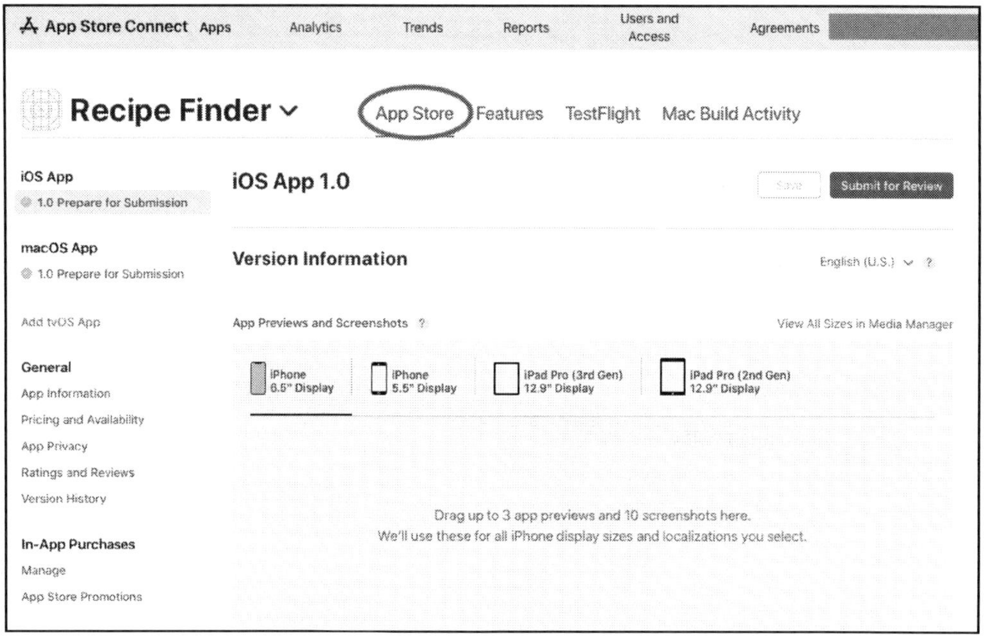

Once that information is complete, you can submit your **TestFlight** build to the full app review. After approval, you can submit your app for release.

And there you have it: simple Flutter app distribution on iOS.

Key Points

- You have to **configure** the Apple Developer Portal and App Store Connect before you can upload a **build**.
- Use Xcode to **archive** the project to easily upload your app to the App Store.
- Use **TestFlight** for **internal** and **external testing** of iOS apps.

Where to Go From Here?

If you want to take this to the next level and learn more about app signing or distributing and selling to customers in the App Store, then iOS App Distribution & Best Practices https://www.kodeco.com/books/ios-app-distribution-best-practices is for you.

Apple's documentation is also helpful if you have questions about terms not covered here: https://developer.apple.com/documentation/xcode/distributing_your_app_for_beta_testing_and_releases.

22 Conclusion

Congratulations! You've completed your introduction to building apps with Flutter. The skills you've honed throughout these chapters will set you up for developing production apps with this exciting toolkit.

If you want to further your understanding of Flutter development with Dart after working through *Flutter Apprentice*, we suggest you read the *Dart Apprentice: Fundamentals*, available here https://www.kodeco.com/books/dart-apprentice-fundamentals.

If you have any questions or comments as you work through this book, please stop by our forums at https://forums.kodeco.com/c/books/flutter-apprentice/ and look for the particular forum category for this book.

Thank you again for purchasing this book. Your continued support is what makes the books, tutorials, videos and other things we do at https://kodeco.com possible. We truly appreciate it!

– The *Flutter Apprentice* team

Made in the USA
Coppell, TX
05 November 2026

11307505R00365